Taking Power

Taking Power analyzes the causes behind some three dozen revolutions in the Third World between 1910 and the present. It advances a new theory that seeks to integrate the political, economic, and cultural factors that brought these revolutions about, and that links structural theorizing with original ideas on culture and agency. It attempts to explain why so few revolutions have succeeded, and so many have failed. The book is divided into chapters that treat particular sets of revolutions: the great social revolutions of Mexico 1910, China 1949, Cuba 1959, Iran 1979, and Nicaragua 1979; the anticolonial revolutions in Algeria, Vietnam, Angola, Mozambique, and Zimbabwe from the 1940s to the 1970s; the reversed revolutions of Iran (1951–53), Guatemala (1944–54), Bolivia (1952–64), Chile (1970–73), Jamaica (1972–80), Grenada (1979–83), and Nicaragua (1979–90); failed revolutionary attempts in El Salvador, Peru, and elsewhere; political revolutions in the Philippines, South Africa, and elsewhere. It closes with speculation about the future of revolutions in an age of globalization, with special attention to Chiapas, the post-September 11 world, and the global justice movement.

JOHN FORAN is Professor of Sociology at the University of California, Santa Barbara, where he is also involved with the programs on Islamic and Near Eastern Studies, Latin American and Iberian Studies, and Women, Culture, and Development. His books include *Fragile Resistence: Social Transformation in Iran from 1500 to the Revolution* (1993), *A Century of Revolution: Social Movements in Iran* (1994), and *Theorizing Revolutions* (1997).

Taking Power

On the Origins of Third World Revolutions

John Foran

CAMBRIDGE
UNIVERSITY PRESS

CAMBRIDGE UNIVERSITY PRESS
Cambridge, New York, Melbourne, Madrid, Cape Town, Singapore, São Paulo

Cambridge University Press
The Edinburgh Building, Cambridge CB2 2RU, UK

Published in the United States of America by Cambridge University Press, New York

www.cambridge.org
Information on this title: www.cambridge.org/9780521629843

First published 2005

Printed in the United Kingdom at the University Press, Cambridge

A catalogue record for this book is available from the British Library

Library of Congress Cataloguing in Publication data
Foran, John.
Taking power: on the origins of Third World revolutions/John Foran.
    p. cm.
Includes bibliographical references and index.
ISBN 0-521-62009-0 (alk. paper) – ISBN 0-521-62984-5 (pb.)
1. Revolutions – Developing countries.   2. Revolutions – Developing countries –
History – 20th century.   3. Insurgency – Developing countries.   4. Social change –
Developing countries.   5. Developing countries – Politics and government – 20th
century.   6. Developing countries – Social conditions – 20th century.   I. Title.
HN979.F67   2005
303.6′4′091724 – dc22   2005045780

ISBN-13 978-0-521-62009-3 hardback
ISBN-10 0-521-62009-0 hardback
ISBN-13 978-0-521-62984-3 paperback
ISBN-10 0-521-62984-5 paperback

No book can ever convey the greatness of a people in revolt.

Enrique Oltuski, *Vida Clandestina:
My Life in the Cuban Revolution*,
translated by Thomas and Carol Christensen
(New York: Wiley, 2002), xxii

Contents

Part Four   Conclusions

Figures

Tables

Acknowledgments

Discounting an essay written in 1975, while a sophomore in college, on the revolutions of early modern Europe (I had a rather elegant – or was it sophomoric? – theory that those on the bottom ended up on the top), this book traces its own origins to 1990, when I began to think about the Iranian revolution – to which I had devoted my research in the 1980s – in comparative perspective. But for a revolution in my own life – the arrival of Cerina in 1996 and then Amal in 1998 – this might have taken only *ten* years. I therefore thank my editors at Cambridge University Press, and especially Sarah Caro, for their patience with me over the years.

Funding for this project came from many sources, including the John Simon Guggenheim Foundation, the Sawyer Seminar of the Advanced Study Center of the International Institute at the University of Michigan, the World Society Foundation in Zurich, the University of California Institute on Global Conflict and Cooperation, the American Sociological Association Fund for the Advancement of the Discipline, and the Wenner-Gren Foundation on Anthropological Research, as well as from two wonderful educational institutions: Smith College, where I worked from 2000 to 2002, and UC Santa Barbara, which has sustained me for the long run, through the generosity of the Institute for Social, Behavioral, and Economic Research, the Academic Senate, and the Interdisciplinary Humanities Center.

First versions of parts of this book have appeared in the journals *Critical Sociology*, *Theory and Society*, *Third World Quarterly*, and *Political Power and Social Theory*, and in my edited books, *Theorizing Revolutions* (Routledge, 1997), and *The Future of Revolutions: Rethinking Radical Change in the Age of Globalization* (Zed Press, 2003). I am grateful to all these outlets for their support of my work and for permission to use this material in various ways, and each is cited in the appropriate place.

I would like to acknowledge the critical feedback of a number of individuals who read and commented on parts of this work, including Richard Appelbaum, Chris Appy, John Booth, Kate Bruhn, Krista Bywater, Rani Bush, Joe Conti, Eve Darien-Smith, Francesca DeGiuli,

James Dunkerley, Terry Elkiss, Mark Elliott, Anthony Francoso, Wally Goldfrank, John Mason Hart, Zeynep Korkman, Josef Liles, Alan Liu, Edwin Lopez, Fernando Lopez-Alves, John Marcum, Chris McAuley, Tim Mechlinski, Becky Overmyer-Velasquez, Marifeli Pérez-Stable, Elizabeth Perry, Charles Ragin, J.-P. Reed, Ramón Eduardo Ruiz, Amandeep Sandhu, Rich Snyder, Alvin So, and Tim Wickham-Crowley. Three special readers and comrades in arms – Jeff Goodwin, Bill Robinson, and Eric Selbin – offered helpful comments and valued encouragement on the whole manuscript. I have still not been able to fully address the many excellent questions all have raised in this work, whose final shape remains my own responsibility, though the product of the labor of many.

I am also indebted to students in a number of classes, and to my research assistants and students Joe Bandy, Keely Burke, Jackie Cabuay, David Espinosa, Tara Farrell, Jennifer Freidman, Noelle Harrison, Jenn Kagawa, Ariana Kalinic, Linda Klouzal, Brianna Krompier, Edwin Lopez, Maria Mark, Markus McMillin, Tim Mechlinksi, Sadie Miller, Camellia Millet-Lau, Veronica Montes, Daniel Olmos, Magdalena Prado, Javad Rassaf, Tamara Simons, Tanya Tabon, Megan Thomas, Veronica Villafan, Becca Wanner, Joan Weston, Richard Widick, Jen Wu, and Vanessa Ziegler for help on the many cases covered in these pages. Their innumerable particular contributions are acknowledged in the appropriate places.

Finally, there are many friends and others to thank on a personal basis for support over the past decade and a half – my parents, Jack and Ramona; my Oakland family – Mary Jane, Bruce, and Alex; my Holyoke family – Bob, Carole, Bobby, Mike, and Betsy; my England family – Nil, Manju, Reena, Ian, Ashoke, Arun, Anil, and Anjuli; my India family – Chetan, Eknath, Anjuli, and Prabhu; and Tom Madden, Nina Sharif, Rich Kaplan, Judy Hamilton (my therapist), and countless others.

This book is wholly dedicated to its inspiration – mi compañera Kum-Kum Bhavnani, who has accompanied me on the journey of life in these revolutionary times, and to the memory of her mother, Raj Bhavnani, who set me an example of how to live, love, and laugh.

Introduction

The twentieth century, as much as any before it, must be judged an age of revolutions. The locus of these revolutions, with the important exceptions of Russia in 1917 and the startling events in Eastern Europe in 1989, has been firmly rooted in the Third World, on the continents of Latin America, Asia, and Africa. The record of these revolutions is highly mixed: almost all have started as popular movements which generated wide hope and optimism both internally and internationally, yet have ended at some later point in time, in economic crisis, political repression, or social failure.

The present study is one not of tragic ends, however, but of hopeful origins. It seeks to extend previous work by myself and others on the causes of successful social revolutions to a consideration of why so few revolutions have earned the label "social" revolutions, while so many have fallen short of the sorts of deep economic, political, and social change that could justify this claim.

This book will survey the causes of a wide variety of Third World revolutions, from cases of successful outcomes (measured in terms of taking and holding state power long enough to engage in a project of social transformation) to their close relations among the anti-colonial social revolutions, comparing and contrasting these with cases that have resulted in short-lived success followed by abrupt reversal, attempted revolutions, political revolutions, and the absence of revolutionary attempts where we might otherwise have expected them to occur.

This work is still unfinished. I have sacrificed some of the depth I initially wanted to bring to it to gain the breadth of scope to test a theory. As Jeff Goodwin noted at the start of his book on comparative revolutions, "There is . . . no 'new' historical data in the pages that follow."[1] Or as Theda Skocpol has put it: "Some books present fresh evidence; other works make arguments that urge the reader to see old problems in a new light. This work is decidedly of the latter sort."[2] I share the aspirations of both of my predecessors in these pages. I imagine that the results will not satisfy many of the historians of the cases touched on here, whose work

1

nevertheless has provided most of the evidence on which I have drawn. Rather, my aim is sociological: to discern distinctive analytic patterns among these revolutionary upsurges, and my hope is to convince readers that there are recurring causal combinations in the historical record. The factors to be tested derive from a multi-faceted theoretical model of the origins of Third World social revolutions that I have been elaborating for the past fifteen (!) years, to which we may now turn.

Part One

Perspectives

1   Theorizing revolutions

... there are real difficulties in grouping revolutions or, for that matter,
any major historical phenomena.

Barrington Moore, Jr.[1]

... successful revolutions always have been, and always will be, unique.

Alberto Flores Galindo[2]

Revolutions powerfully shaped the twentieth-century world we have left,
and promise to continue to do so on into the new millennium. The revolutionary events of the past generation in both the Third World from
Iran and Nicaragua in 1979 to China and Eastern Europe in 1989 and
Chiapas today, pose again old puzzles for social theory even as they her-
ald the new situation of a post-cold war world. Alexis de Tocqueville's
dual observation on the French revolution rings just as true for any of
these more contemporary upheavals: "never was any such event, stem-
ming from factors far back in the past, so inevitable yet so completely
unforeseen."[3] Virtually all of these social movements took analysts by
surprise, and send us back to our theories to detect those distant factors
that, in some sense, caused them.

The present study aims to shed new light on a set of transformational
struggles that may be clustered under the rubric of "Third World revolutions." Part Two looks closely at successes in Mexico between 1910 and
1920, China in the 1940s, Cuba in the late 1950s and Iran and Nicaragua
at the end of the 1970s, as well as their close relations, the thorough-
going anti-colonial revolutions in Algeria in the 1950s, and Vietnam,
Zimbabwe, Mozambique, and Angola, all in the 1970s, and at shorter-
lived revolutions such as Guatemala under Arévalo and Arbenz from 1944
to 1954, Iran's oil nationalization period of the early 1950s, Bolivia's experience from 1952 to the early 1960s, Allende's Chile between 1970 and
1973, Michael Manley's democratic socialism in Jamaica in the 1970s,
and Maurice Bishop's New Jewel Movement in Grenada from 1979 to
1983. By "success," I mean coming to power and holding it long enough
to initiate a process of deep structural transformation; I am not here

5

passing judgment on the long and somewhat disappointing history of such bold experiments in change, important as such a balance sheet would be.

The third part of the book investigates a wide ranging set of contrasting cases, starting with the reversal of the seven short-lived revolutions above, the attempts at revolution between 1975 and the present in Argentina, El Salvador, Guatemala, Peru, the Philippines, China, Algeria, and Chiapas, and moving to a set of political revolutions: China in 1911, Haiti and the Philippines in 1986, and Zaire and South Africa in the 1990s.

The central question we will ask of each is what were the causes of the events? What sets of economic, political, and cultural factors were at work, and in what combinations? What role was played by external factors in each case, what role by internal forces? In the end, we shall seek to discern deep patterns across cases, thereby taking up the challenge posed by Barrington Moore, Jr. and Alberto Flores Galindo, who feel that revolutions are so unique that finding a pattern among them is difficult, if not impossible.

The puzzle at the heart of this book is: Why are social revolutions such rare events? And why have so few succeeded and so many failed? The present chapter will lay the basis for the answers suggested by the subsequent case studies in two ways – by briefly introducing the history of theorizing about social revolutions, and by proposing an original model of the origins of Third World revolutions to use as a guide for comparative-historical investigation.

Defining revolution

The study of revolution is marked by fundamental theoretical and political controversy, beginning with the definition of the term itself.[4] An influential definition of what he calls the "great revolutions" was offered by political scientist Samuel Huntington some four decades ago:

rapid, fundamental, and violent domestic change in the dominant values and myths of a society, in its political institutions, social structure, leadership, and governmental activity and policies. Revolutions are thus to be distinguished from insurrections, rebellions, revolts, coups and wars of independence.[5]

This points to the numerous dimensions of social transformation that revolutions unleash, but substitutes *violence* for the seizure of state power and/or mass participation. A better definition of social revolution has been provided by sociologist Theda Skocpol, who takes up some of Huntington's criteria while moving fruitfully beyond them:

Social revolutions are rapid, basic transformations of a society's state and class structures; and they are accompanied and in part carried through by class-based revolts from below . . .

What is unique to social revolution is that basic changes in social structure and in political structure occur together in a mutually reinforcing fashion. And these changes occur through intense sociopolitical conflicts in which class struggles play a key role.[6]

This definition, which I shall adopt in full as my own, represents an advance in linking political and social changes and in identifying the importance of large-scale participation. In this we find an echo of Trotsky's famous formulation: "The most indubitable feature of a revolution is the direct interference of the masses in historic events . . . The history of a revolution is for us first of all a history of the forcible entrance of the masses into the realm of rulership over their own destiny."[7] The salience of these three factors – political change, structural transformation, and mass participation – allows us to dissociate revolution from violence per se and to explore the revolutionary potential of such strongly reformist democratic movements as those of Juan José Arévalo and Jacobo Arbenz in Guatemala, Michael Manley in Jamaica, and Salvador Allende in Chile, each of whom aimed at serious transformation of their society.

Skocpol's definition has the drawback of not telling us *how much* political and social transformation is required to qualify a case as a social revolution; nor does it define "rapid"; nor, finally, does it stipulate *how long* a revolutionary government must remain in power to constitute a "successful" case. These are judgments for which observers will have different answers. My sustained case studies of "success" include Mexico, where the most radical forces were defeated; Nicaragua, in which power was held only eleven years; and Iran, where socio-economic change may not have been fundamental. Only Cuba and China now seem entirely uncontroversial on this list. I acknowledge these difficulties, and will attempt to defend my decisions at the appropriate points. The definition does have the great merit, however, of throwing into relief what the successful cases have in common with each other, and how they vary from other sets of cases. Anti-colonial revolutions, I will argue, are closest in kind to the five principal cases of success, both in meeting Skocpol's three criteria, and in the patterning of causality. In fact, they differ mainly in that the government overthrown is not an indigenous one but a foreign one. Reversed revolutions are cases where revolutionaries came to power – sometimes by non-violent means – but failed to hold it long enough to fulfill Skocpol's requirement of basic transformation. In my view they represent significant cases of incipient revolutionary transformation;

taking them seriously, as cases of both success and failure, is a novel feature of the present study.

These sets of successful cases by our criteria can be clearly contrasted with such types as attempted social revolutions where revolutionaries never came to power at all, but where the movements were prepared to carry out the deep social transformation in question (obviously, such judgments are based on historical counter-factualizing); and political revolutions, which possess a mass character and alter the outlines of the state, but fail to make deep changes in social structure. In this way one can see Iran as a social revolution, and the Philippines as a political one, or Chile as a social revolution, however short-lived, versus South Africa as an enduring, but only political revolution. I exclude from this analysis movements which lacked mass participation even where significant social transformation arguably occurred, as in the "movement" which toppled Haile Selassie in Ethiopia in 1974, the Afghan revolution of 1978, or the horrific events in Khmer Rouge Cambodia in the 1970s, while including the events in Grenada in 1979 also carried out by a small group, for the society itself was much smaller and embraced the change in power with immediate enthusiasm. These are important distinctions, if difficult judgments, to make, possible only if we take Skocpol's very useful definitional work seriously. This allows us to focus on the conjunction of human agency and structural change, to isolate the causes of those events where people, in large numbers, came together to remake society. I do not pretend to cover the entire universe of relevant cases here, although I have tackled a good part of that universe.[8]

Historical perspectives on revolutions

This study is about the origins of such events. Social science models of the causes of revolutions date back to the 1920s and 1930s.[9] Comparative historians such as L. P. Edwards in *The Natural History of Revolution* (1927), Crane Brinton in *The Anatomy of Revolution* (1938), and G. S. Pettee in *The Process of Revolution* (1938) engaged in a search for common patterns among such major revolutions as the French, American, English, and Russian cases. According to Jack Goldstone, the findings of this first-generation "Natural History of Revolution" school included:

1. Prior to revolutions, intellectuals cease to support the regime.
2. Prior to revolutions, the state undertakes reforms.
3. Outbreaks have more to do with a state crisis than active opposition.
4. After taking power, conflicts arise within the revolutionary coalition.
5. The first group to seize power is moderate reformers.

6. The revolution then radicalizes because moderates fail to go far enough.
7. The radicals then bring about organizational and ideological changes, taking extreme measures to deal with problems and secure power.
8. Radicals impose coercive order ("the terror") to implement their program in the midst of social dislocation.
9. Military leaders such as Cromwell, Washington, Napoleon, and Trotsky often emerge.
10. "Eventually things settle down and pragmatic moderates regain power."[10]

The critique commonly aimed at these pioneers of theory is that they merely *describe* the process of revolution, they do not explain *why* revolutions occur. With respect to more recent Third World social revolutions, it must be noted that many other considerations enter into their causation that were not available to these pre-World War 2 theorists of revolutions among the great world powers, as we shall see. And yet, as description, this list is not at all bad, as some of our case studies – Iran, for example – bear out.

A second generation of somewhat disparate American social scientists in the 1960s tried to explain why and when revolutions arise, using either social psychological or structural-functional approaches to collective behavior, which Rod Aya refers to generically (and dismissively) as the "volcanic model" of revolution.[11] Ted Robert Gurr and James Davies developed theories of political violence based on aggregate psychological states, notably relative deprivation. Davies proposed a "J-curve" – "a period of growing prosperity that raises people's expectations for a better life, followed by a sharp economic downturn that dashes those recently raised expectations" – as a recipe for revolt.[12] Within the then popular modernization paradigm derived from Parsonian structural-functionalism, Neil Smelser and Chalmers Johnson looked for imbalances in the subsystems of a society which disoriented people and made them more prone to embrace radical ideologies.[13] Smelser, in his *Theory of Collective Behavior* (1962) provides a prescient set of factors including structural conduciveness, strain, new beliefs, precipitants, mobilization, and social control. The critique that is generally advanced of all of these approaches hinges on the difficulty of observing and measuring aggregate psychological states and societal disequilibrium, and the corresponding danger of sliding into tautology – a difficulty and danger for all who would theorize revolutions. As Davies himself remarked of Chalmers Johnson: "If one tells an automobile mechanic that the car's engine is dysfunctional, it is just about as clear and true as when one says it about an old society."[14] It is also true that these models have a hard time explaining why revolutions have been so rare (as the types of change initiating the pattern have been widespread), and there is here no mechanism to explain the outcomes of revolution (as the earlier Natural History school did). Goldstone tasks them further with being too "purposive," i.e. seeking to explain revolutions in terms of the rise of oppositional actors in society.[15] However, in my view this emphasis, along with the attendant concern for the values, beliefs, and ideologies of those involved, is a strength of these otherwise not too convincing theories, and in its way compares favorably with the more one-sidedly structural theories that would constitute the third generation.

Beginning in the 1960s and increasingly in the 1970s, a series of structural macro-sociologies of revolution were elaborated, identifying actors and themes ranging from the state, dominant elites, and armies to international pressures and peasant mobilization as the keys to understanding social revolution. An obvious influential precursor was Karl Marx, who stressed the role played by class struggles as structured by the mode of production (unequal social relations based upon a particular labor process) found in societies undergoing economic transition. De Tocqueville, too, in a more *ad hoc* fashion, noted the importance of the state and elites, village autonomy, and ideology in bringing about the French revolution.[16] Structural theories of revolution in contemporary social science were pioneered in 1966 by Barrington Moore Jr.'s path-breaking comparative study, *Social Origins of Dictatorship and Democracy*. Moore identified the vulnerable moment as that of the transition to capitalist agriculture and the changing relations among peasants, the state (usually a monarchy), landlords, and a nascent bourgeoisie in this period. Variations in the relative strength of these social groups produced peasant revolution in China, democracy in France, England, and the United States, and fascism in Japan and Germany. He argued that successful commercialization of agriculture undercuts peasant revolution, that peasants must possess certain solidarity structures to rebel, and that they need allies to make a revolution.[17] Eric Wolf's 1969 survey of six "peasant wars" (by which he really means "revolutions in an agrarian society"[18]) confirms the utility of much of Moore's schema with a look at Third World cases. Though he insists that each revolution has unique historical determinants, patterns do emerge – the commercialization of agriculture threatens peasants' access to land, middle peasants are best placed to rebel, allies must be found among the urban classes, and armed force is necessary to seize the state.[19] Jeffery Paige's 1975 book on Third World peasant movements specifies that revolution occurs only where landed classes depend on the land itself (not capital, machinery, and technology) for their income and peasants are amenable to organization in their capacity as sharecroppers or migrant laborers.[20] Of these three theorists, Paige is the most single-minded in focusing on the peasantry at the expense of urban sectors, the state, and almost all else.

Theda Skocpol's 1979 work, *States and Social Revolutions*, represents a landmark in the sociology of revolutions. For our purposes it clearly illustrates both the undoubted strengths and the distinctive weaknesses of a resolutely structural approach. Skocpol argues for a structural, as opposed to a "voluntarist" or "purposive" perspective:

[Historical revolutions] . . . have been powerfully shaped and limited by existing socioeconomic and international conditions . . . The logic of these conflicts has not been controlled by any one group or class, no matter how seemingly central in the revolutionary process . . . To explain social revolutions, one must find problematic, first, the emergence (not "making") of a revolutionary situation within an old regime. Then, one must be able to identify the objectively conditioned and complex intermeshing of the various actions of the diversely situated groups – an intermeshing that shapes the revolutionary process and gives rise to the new regime.[21]

The particular structures on which she focuses attention are "the nexes of state/state, state/economy, and state/class relationships."[22] Her comparative study of France, Russia, and China yields a common pattern: political crises arose when old-regime states could not meet external challenges because of internal obstacles in agrarian and elite relations. In France, foreign wars led to fiscal crisis which inefficient agriculture exacerbated. Efforts to tax nobles led to elite revolts; peasants took advantage of the crisis and were able to mobilize due to communal solidarity structures. In Russia, collapse in World War 1 led to state crisis; in China the Japanese invasion and World War 2 created an opportunity. Skocpol also provides a theory of outcomes, linking these to pre-revolutionary structural factors and revolutionary crises. The new states are more centralized and stronger vis-à-vis internal elites and lower classes and other states.[23]

Various criticisms can be leveled at this model as it stands (leaving aside for now its potential applicability to Third World cases). On one hand, it is cast at a rather high level of abstraction – an emphasis on relations between states, among classes, and between state and classes covers just about everything. There are also significant variations among even the three cases she analyzes, raising the issue of the degree to which there is a single pattern here at all (not that there must be just one, as we shall see). The limits of a structural approach become apparent too: structures don't change *by themselves*, so change cannot be completely explained in structural terms. As Michael Taylor puts it: "*Social* changes are produced by actions; social *changes* require *new* actions. New actions require changed desires and/or beliefs."[24] In some passages, Skocpol acknowledges the roles played by various actors, but there is a tendency to focus on elites and the state at the expense of dominated classes. The lower classes are by no means absent from the analysis, but the efficacious actors seem to be at the top of the power structure. In terms of mass participation, Skocpol wants to restore the peasantry to center stage to correct what she perceives as an urban bias. She admits that "the different urban industrial and class structures profoundly influenced the revolutionary process and outcomes," but they are treated "as backgrounds against which the (for me) more analytically important agrarian upheavals and political dynamics played themselves out."[25] But why not analyze revolutionary *coalitions* instead of privileging one class's role above all others? Finally, while acknowledging some role for ideologies as "undoubtedly necessary ingredients in the great social revolutions," Skocpol insists that crises have not been made by actors, outcomes have been unintended, and ideologies have been shaped and confounded by structural situations and crises.[26] Again, belief systems, value orientations, and ideologies slip in through the back door in the empirical analyses,[27] but their importance in actually moving people to respond to "structural" crises is systematically ignored or downplayed. These omissions detract from the overall power of what is otherwise *the* central study of revolutions written by a sociologist.

Charles Tilly is another eminent political sociologist who has made important contributions to the study of revolutions, in ways which in part complement and extend Skocpol.[28] Tilly's work has been directed toward understanding broad processes of political conflict or collective action, of which revolutions are one type. His version of what came to be known as resource mobilization theory stresses the importance of studying the organizational and other resources available to contending groups (states, elites, challengers), and sees revolution as a condition of "multiple sovereignty" in which the population shifts its allegiance from the government to a contending group.[29] He also goes beyond Skocpol in his attention to ideological resources and the issue of state legitimacy, as well as the centrality of coalitions (topics addressed below).[30] Like Skocpol, he conceptualizes all of these factors as a return to the *political* level of analysis in response to the psychological emphases of Davies, Gurr, Johnson, and others, but they can be seen in economic and cultural terms as well, suggesting that this self-understanding is too narrow. More recently, this perspective has evolved into political process theory, and its attention to such factors as broad socioeconomic processes, expanded political opportunities, and cognitive liberation frames bears an abstract (if only very general) resemblance to parts of my own model.[31]

This leads us to a set of promising new directions in the sociological study of revolutions that have been increasingly hinted at and developed since the 1980s, and which suggests the outlines of a new, fourth generation of theory. These include the interrelated issues of agency, political culture, and coalitions, and the dimensions of ethnicity (or "race"), class, and gender. The problem of agency is posed by its conceptual absence in the structural approaches of Skocpol and others. Skocpol, in particular, was reacting to theories that relied too much on revolutionaries' conscious control of events, arguing instead that revolutionary crises are not the product of intentional activity and that outcomes were often quite unintended in their consequences. While valid and useful observations in themselves, the claim that "no successful social revolution has ever been 'made' by a mass-mobilizing, avowedly revolutionary movement"[32] errs in the opposite direction, leaving a gap at the center of revolutionary events. Teodor Shanin cautions us against neglecting this moment of subjectivity and agency:

Social scientists often miss a centre-piece of any revolutionary struggle – the fervour and anger that drives revolutionaries and makes them into what they are. Academic training and bourgeois convention deaden its appreciation. The "phenomenon" cannot be easily "operationalised" into factors, tables and figures. Sweeping emotions feel vulgar or untrue to those sophisticated to the point of detachment from real life. Yet, without this factor, any understanding of revolutions falls flat. That is why clerks, bankers, generals, and social scientists so often fail to see revolutionary upswing even when looking at it directly.

At the very centre of revolution lies an emotional upheaval of moral indignation, revulsion and fury with the powers-that-be, such that one cannot demur or remain silent, whatever the cost. Within its glow, for a while, men surpass themselves, breaking the shackles of intuitive self-preservation, convention, day-to-day convenience, and routine.[33]

As Trotsky admonished, "Let us not forget that revolutions are accomplished through people, though they be nameless. Materialism does not ignore the feeling, thinking and acting man, but explains him."[34] Social structure may illuminate both crises and outcomes, but past human actions, however much conditioned they may be, also help explain social structures, as Karl Marx argued in *The Eighteenth Brumaire*, and Michael Taylor has reiterated. Neither individualism nor structuralism is the "ultimate" (only) cause of social change.[35]

Linked to the notion of agency and supplying a complex mediation between structure and action is the role of ideas, values, beliefs, ideologies. The importance of culture generally in social change has been insisted upon over the years by such thinkers as Clifford Geertz, Marshall Sahlins, Raymond Williams, E. P. Thompson, and Michel Foucault. Its salience for the study of revolutions was noted as early as de Tocqueville; more recently, theoretical cases have been made for it by Mostafa Rejai, S. N. Eisenstadt, Ann Swidler, and Forrest Colburn, and concrete applications to revolutionary cases have been offered by Robert Darnton, George Rudé, Christopher Hill, William Sewell, Lynn Hunt, Farideh Farhi, Jack Goldstone, Mark Gould, and Tim McDaniel, among others.[36] Gould, for example, claims in his study of the English revolution that religion provided "a theoretical justification for a challenge to the existing political system . . . [and] the foundation of an organization."[37] Consider also on a more popular level James Scott's work on the moral economy of the peasantry, referring to a norm of reciprocity in relation to the state and landlord, which, if violated, can lead to rebellion.[38] This hints at what I will call "political cultures of opposition" in my own model of social revolution below – the diverse and complex value systems existing among various groups and classes which are drawn upon to make sense of the "structural" changes going on around them. In some cases, revolutionaries tap long-standing cultural traditions (what Tilly calls the "cultural repertoire" of collective action); in others, they innovate these into rather new cultural orientations.[39] This growing preoccupation with culture – now understood as "the cultural turn" in the social sciences – must be built in to any serious theory of revolution today, as Eric Selbin has argued eloquently.[40]

A second problematic relevant to the role played by values revolves around legitimation and its breakdown. Brinton had written of the "desertion of the intellectuals" as a cause of revolution, Lenin noted the incapacity of the upper classes to live in the old way, and Wolf "a crisis of the exercise of power."[41] As Foucault has written on authority more generally:

What makes power hold good, what makes it accepted, is simply the fact that it doesn't only weigh on us as a force that says no, but that it traverses and produces things, it induces pleasure, forms of knowledge, produces discourse. It needs to be considered as a productive network which runs through the whole social body, much more than as a negative instance whose function is repression.[42]

Thus the legitimation claims of the state vis-à-vis civil society bear as much scrutiny as political cultures of opposition, and are in a sense the obverse of these.[43] When the state's raison d'être no longer holds good, when it is effectively combated by competing conceptions, oppositional forces gain a valuable resource for organizing their struggle.

A final new direction in the sociology of revolutions leads back to the age-old question of who, precisely, makes them. Skocpol felt she was restoring the peasantry to center stage in the face of an urban bias in previous historiography on France and Russia.[44] Critics of Skocpol and students of the revolutions in Iran, Nicaragua, and elsewhere then refocused attention on urban actors.[45] The real challenge, however, is to study *coalitions* in revolutions, as a number of scholars have argued.[46] Multiclass alliances, often motivated by diffuse ideals such as nationalism, populism, or religion rather than particularistic ones such as socialism, have made most of the revolutions in world history, and all of the Third World cases that are the subject of this book. Such coalitions, we will see, have dynamics of their own, which most often lead to fragmentation, significantly affecting revolutionary outcomes. In addition to class, it would be well to bear in mind (and until recently most scholars have not) the gender and ethnic composition of revolutionary coalitions as well as regional political economic and cultural variations within particular states.[47]

The search for a single, overarching theory of social revolutions has foundered on the diversity of cases offered by the historical record. As a result, various patterns and typologies have been proposed in the literature. Samuel Huntington distinguished a "Western" type in which a regime simply collapses without much application of force and revolution moves from a moderate to a radical phase while spreading from the city to the countryside, contrasted with an "Eastern" type against colonial regimes or military dictatorships, requiring civil war and spreading from the countryside to the city with radicals assuming the leadership before power is seized. Examples of the Western type include France, Russia, Mexico, Bolivia, and Ethiopia, while the Eastern type is said to have occurred in China, Vietnam, South Yemen, Guinea-Bissau, Mozambique, and Angola.[48] Robert Dix argued for a third type – the "Latin American" pattern – to account for Cuba and Nicaragua, with "semimodern" regimes and more developed societies.[49] Skocpol studies a class of cases she termed "agrarian empires," consisting of France, Russia, and China.

That the Third World needs its own theory is suggested by the different social structures and position in the world-system of these cases from Huntington's Eastern and Western types or Skocpol's agrarian empires. As Skocpol herself notes, Third World revolutions have occurred in smaller, more dependent societies than her cases.[50] Moreover, their social bases have been mixed, not peasant-dominated, reflecting the complexities of Third World class structure and politics. Specifically Third World social revolutions have been theorized by several scholars along lines that bear some resemblance to the present study. Jeff Goodwin has focused attention on the type of regime vulnerable to revolution (exclusionary military dictatorships), although he downplays social structural, world-systemic, and economic factors in favor of a political focus on the state and the revolutionary movement.[51] Ian Roxborough pays more attention to the consequences of economic dependency on social structure and political culture as a factor, while also noting class grievances and the vulnerability of dictatorships.[52] In a study of the Mexican revolution Walter Goldfrank suggests a combination of necessary and sufficient conditions for Third World social revolutions: "1) a tolerant or permissive world context; 2) a severe political crisis paralyzing the administrative and coercive capacities of the state; 3) widespread rural rebellion; and 4) dissident elite political movements."[53] John Walton's framework for the study of "national revolts" (nation-wide violent conflicts that do not always lead to full-fledged social revolutions) also identifies several of the factors I will be studying: uneven development, the role of the state, cultural nationalism, and an economic downturn.[54] This study of three failed insurrections in the Philippines, Colombia, and Kenya proposes a lucid focus on Third World social structure as well as some attention to the cultural orientations of actors, but by arguing that such cases were closer to successful outcomes than is commonly acknowledged, Walton provided no way to discern the reasons for one outcome or the other. Farideh Farhi compares two of our main cases, Iran and Nicaragua, combining Skocpol's emphasis on the state and social structure with a Gramscian analysis of ideology.[55] This approach too resembles my own strategy, although with less attention to dependency and social structure than to the state, and with a tendency to see religion as the major relevant element of ideology, especially in Iran. In a wide-ranging study of Eastern Europe, China, Vietnam, Cuba, Nicaragua, Iran, and South Africa – the last six of which I take up in this book – James DeFronzo identifies a loosely structured model of five factors, including 1) mass frustration, 2) dissident elites, 3) "unifying motivations," 4) a crisis of the state, "which may be caused by a catastrophic defeat in war, a natural disaster, an economic depression, or the withdrawal of critical economic or military support from other nations," and 5) "a permissive or tolerant world context," citing Goldfrank.[56] Like Farhi, this overlaps in some important particulars with my own model, though it is still undertheorized (factor four is really a set of factors, and "unifying motivations" stops short of a strong concept of culture), and misses the significance of dependent development and the vulnerable state. But like Walton and Farhi, it is an insightful starting point for a fuller theory. A more recent synthesis has been offered by Misagh Parsa, who bids us to focus attention on economic factors (particularly the degree of state intervention in the economy), the ideology of state challengers, and the political vulnerabilities of repressive regimes; this work is another positive step toward a more satisfying theory, although it may be criticized for its lack of a well-rounded political economy and class analysis or a sufficiently nuanced conception of culture.[57]

Other theorists – notably Jack Goldstone and Jeff Goodwin – have extended Skocpol's state-centered approach into the early modern past and the contemporary Third World, respectively.[58] These studies have produced compelling, but largely structuralist, explanations of why states break down; they are less useful as guides to how revolutionaries contribute to this process. On the opposite extreme is Eric Selbin, whose study of Bolivia, Cuba, Nicaragua, and Grenada argues that the ability of revolutionaries to make effective ideological appeals to the population largely explains patterns of success or failure in these four cases.[59] Finally, Timothy Wickham-Crowley's analysis of Latin American guerrilla movements is notable on at least two counts: while largely structuralist in inspiration, it begins to break with prior emphases on the state in joining Walton to consider aspects of social structure and the orientations of revolutionaries; and it looks at two successes (Cuba and Nicaragua) in detail, alongside two dozen failed Latin American guerrilla insurrections between the 1950s and 1980s, using the innovative technique of Boolean analysis.[60] The study is limited to Latin American cases, however, and its focus on armed guerrilla movements represents only a subset of the universe of revolutions (leaving out Chile's experiment with democratic socialism under Allende, for example).

These recent studies have all advocated multi-causal approaches to revolutions.[61] They have gradually begun to explore the relationship of culture and agency to social and political structures. They have yet to settle the question of what particular combination of causes is most likely to explain revolutionary success and failure, however. Nor have they studied large enough numbers of cases to fully test any of their models, typically focusing on one geographic region, such as Selbin and Wickham-Crowley, or treating only two or three cases, such as Walton and Farhi. Finally, despite Wickham-Crowley's promising start, as yet no one has made sense of why so few social revolutions succeed, while so many end in such outcomes as failure to come to power, reversal shortly after coming to power, or limited social transformation. Or indeed, why revolutions so rarely occur at all in Third World settings generally, for while most world revolutions have been in the Third World, most Third World countries have not experienced revolutions.

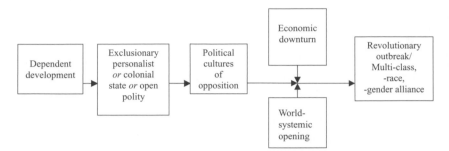

Figure 1.1   A model of Third World social revolutions

A theory of Third World social revolutions

My own work draws on many of the specific insights of this latest generation of scholars, but with its own particular synthesis that insists on balancing attention to such perennial (and all too often reified) dichotomies as structure and agency, political economy and culture, state and social structure, internal and external factors. So many factors have been "brought back in" to the study of revolutions in recent years: states, people, culture. It is now time to find the relation among these and political economy, rather than continue to insist on single overarching principles of explanation. I have in the past been associated with efforts to recenter culture and human agency; I hope that the present effort is not misread as an attempt to privilege any of these factors. It is important now that a *balance* among them be struck, and that this synthesis be clear about how each contributes to the origins of revolutions.

Elsewhere I have argued that five inter-related causal factors must combine in a given conjuncture to produce a successful social revolution: 1) dependent development; 2) a repressive, exclusionary, personalist state; 3) the elaboration of effective and powerful political cultures of resistance; and a revolutionary crisis consisting of 4) an economic downturn; and 5) a world-systemic opening (a let-up of external controls).[62] This model is represented schematically by Figure 1.1, with the addition of repressive colonial and non-repressive, open polities to the type of state that is vulnerable. Let us briefly examine each of these factors in turn.

We begin with a conception of Third World social structure as the complex result of both internal and external developmental dynamics. The world-system, as theorized by Immanuel Wallerstein, generates the external pressures – economic, political, and military – that emanate from the powerful capitalist core nations to the Third World periphery.[63] Here they encounter the pre-existing modes of production of Third World societies, a process which creates over time a new complex of pre-capitalist and capitalist modes of production.[64] I am not here arguing that "The West caused everything," but rather, following F. H. Cardoso and Enzo Faletto, that Third World social structures are the products of the complex inter-meshing of internal and external dynamics. The result, in many Third World countries, is an accumulation process which can be called one of dependent development, essentially one of growth within limits.[65] This refers to the fact that certain Third World economies, at certain moments in their history, do undergo both rapid development – as measured by increases in GNP, foreign trade, and industrial or agricultural output – combined with the negative consequences of this process in the form of such problems as inflation, debt, growing inequality, or overburdened housing and educational infrastructures, among many social ills. This his-torically specific process defines in each case a changing social structure that creates social and economic grievances among diverse sectors of the population, ranging from the urban working, middle, and underclasses, to rural peasants, farmers, and workers, and crossing gender and ethnic lines as well. The argument, then, is that a country's historical insertion into the world economy on dependent terms vis-à-vis core powers sig-nificantly shapes its social structure, a view shared with Wallersteinian world-system analysis. But, in contrast to the earliest dependency theo-rists such as Andre Gunder Frank,[66] theorists of dependent development insist that *some* Third World countries actually do develop in aggregate economic terms. They insist equally that these experiences of growth are generally accompanied by negative repercussions for specific groups and classes.

I wish to further elaborate this argument about Third World social structure by linking such mixed processes to a theory of revolutions, for I hypothesize that it is from this subset of dependent developers that rev-olutions arise. It is important to state that I do *not* believe that all Third World societies experience dependent development. Thus, the objection that I am trying to explain variable outcomes with a constant cannot be sustained. I acknowledge that the concept can be difficult to measure, and the present study will assess the nature of dependency – political, economic, strategic, military, financial – in each of the major cases, as well as the degree to which dependent development can be found in each case.[67] Moreover, since some Third World countries experience depen-dent development without social revolution (Brazil, South Korea), the claim is only that this is a necessary condition for Third World social revolution; my hypothesis is that the process of dependent development is the principle cause of the grievances of the classes and groups that par-ticipate in revolutionary coalitions, as well as the key to a more nuanced understanding of Third World social structure itself. Induction will help us specify further the ways that dependent development contributes to outbreaks of social revolution.

The model further observes that the reproduction of such a social system typically requires a repressive state to guarantee order in a rapidly changing social setting in which much of the population is suffering. The repressive, exclusionary, personalist state which so often (but not always) accompanies dependent development reposes on the combination of repression of lower-class forces and exclusion of both the growing middle classes and the economic elite from political participation.[68] Such states possess an elective affinity for dependent development because they are good at guaranteeing order, at least for a time, but they also tend to exacerbate conflictual relations between state and civil society. Dictators, particularly of the dynastic variety (either by monarchic succession or imposition of new generations) or who succeed themselves indefinitely (whether through patently fraudulent elections or other means), epitomize this personalist type of rule. The shah of Iran and the Somozas in Nicaragua exemplify the first type; Mexico's Porfirio Díaz and Fulgencio Batista in Cuba the second. Such rulers fuel the grievances generated by dependent development, and thereby provide a solid target for social movements from below, often alienating even the upper classes from the state. Because of this, under certain circumstances, they facilitate the formation of a broad, multi-class alliance against the state, because middle and even upper classes may join with lower classes, perhaps feeling less threat of being overturned along with the state. In Chapter Three, we will see that a close cousin – the repressive, exclusionary *colonial* state – is also vulnerable to revolution under certain conditions.

Conversely, *collective* military rule, or rule by the military as an institution, especially when given a veneer of legitimation through regular elections, however fraudulent, tends to elicit more elite support and provide a less vulnerable target for cross-class social movements.[69] Similarly immune to revolution are what William Robinson terms "polyarchies" – elite-controlled, formally democratic polities which effectively exclude radical challengers but are open enough to channel grievances into electoral channels and dissipate them.[70] A much rarer regime type is the truly open democratic polity, where left parties are allowed to organize and elections are not completely controlled by elites. It is a major – and paradoxical – finding of this study that such states, at the opposite end of the political spectrum from dictatorships, are equally vulnerable to revolutionary challenge through the election of revolutionary parties, as happened in Chile in 1970, or more recently, in Hugo Chávez's Venezuela.

Again, however, it must be noted that this provides a necessary, but not sufficient, cause. Many a personalistic ruler is not overthrown (Chiang Kai-shek on Taiwan, Kim Il-Sung and others in North and South Korea), many leave the scene in ways that do not qualify as social revolutions (Duvalier in Haiti, Stroessner in Paraguay, Pinochet in Chile), others exit in political, but not social revolutions (Marcos in the Philippines, Mobutu among others in Africa). These observations should caution us against an overly state-centered approach; the question to investigate becomes under what conditions are governments unable to use force or retain the allegiance of key groups within the population?

For revolutions to occur, an opposition must coalesce. To capture the cultural and ideological dimensions of this intervention of human agents onto the historical stage, I have developed the notion of "political cultures of opposition and resistance" in my previous work.[71] To move toward revolution from the structural determinants of the grievances produced by dependent development and the repressive, exclusionary, personalist and colonial state (or channeled into electoral success in the open polity), broad segments of many groups and classes must be able to articulate the experiences they are living through into effective and flexible analyses capable of mobilizing their own forces and building coalitions with others. Such political cultures of opposition may draw upon diverse sources: formal ideologies, folk traditions, and popular idioms, ranging from ideas and feelings of nationalism (against control by outsiders), to socialism (equality and social justice), democracy (demands for participation and an end to dictatorship), or emancipatory religious appeals (resistance to evil and suffering). The 1985 debate between William Sewell and Skocpol touches on the issue of whether formally articulated ideologies or more deeply embedded cultural idioms inform the actions of revolutionaries.[72] The concept of political cultures of opposition includes elements of both, as Figure 1.2 shows (the dotted lines indicate the more indirect linkages between subjectivity and ideology, or cultural idioms and social forces).[73]

Figure 1.2 suggests that organizational capacity, lived experience, culture, and ideology come together under certain circumstances to produce revolutionary political cultures. Different groups, classes, and actors will construct complex combinations of these, sometimes weaving them into critiques of the regime with great mobilizational potential. How well these multiple political cultures are capable of bringing together diverse sectors into a broad and unified opposition may spell the difference between success and failure. Often a *range* of specific political cultures and ideologies will be activated and elaborated to grasp this process and mobilize opposition in a society. Indeed, this is logical in light of the complexities

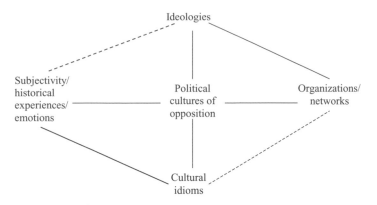

Figure 1.2 The role of culture in the making of revolutions

of Third World social structures and the need for a broad coalition of forces to initiate change. My work on Iran, for example, showed that such cultures are multiple, with variants of secular as well as religious discourses appealing to diverse groups in society, and agreed in this case on two common denominators – the removal of the shah and the lessening of US influence in the country.[74] As a necessary corrective to structural analysts, with this factor I insist on the irreducible role played by human agency and meaning in the making (or not) of revolutions.

Given the structural problems and inequalities entailed by dependent development and repressive states, and the elaboration of one or more powerful political cultures of resistance generated in response to these, a revolutionary situation is likely to occur if a crisis arises that both weakens the state and emboldens the opposition. In this connection, an earlier literature on revolutions spoke of historically contingent "accelerators," "precipitants," and "triggers."[75] But a conjunctural revolutionary crisis, while containing fortuitous elements, is more sociological in origin than these terms imply. Such crises, I hypothesize, are doubly determined. Students of revolution from Alexis de Tocqueville to James Davies have insisted that economic downturns on the eve of revolutions sharpen existing grievances past some breaking point. Recent scholars have disputed this point, both for their general models and in particular cases.[76] I shall argue that such downturns are present in virtually all successful cases. They may be caused by the internal contradictions of dependent development (such as Nicaragua's troubles after the 1972 earthquake), or by external forces and shocks (such as the 1907–08 world-wide recession, the Great Depression, and the 1975 oil-crisis recession). They may even be created by revolutionaries in the course of the struggle, as Castro's

July 26 Movement managed to do by disrupting the 1958 sugar harvest. Logically, such an occurrence would exacerbate existing grievances throughout society, and in particular, it might play the role of final straw in radicalizing the middle class into action with other groups. As Cynthia McClintock has succinctly argued: "Misery matters."[77]

When this factor is combined with a "world-systemic opening" for change, a powerful conjuncture arises for revolutionary movements to succeed. Third World countries enmeshed on unfavorable terms in a world economy typically possess significant economic and political ties with more powerful core economies. A world-systemic opening may occur when, for whatever reason, this "normal" situation is disrupted.[78] This may be the result of distraction in the core economies by world war or depression, rivalries between one or more core powers, mixed messages sent to Third World dictators, or a divided foreign policy when faced with an insurrection. Mexico between 1910 and 1920 exemplifies the first two conditions; Nicaragua and Iran during the Carter administration's human rights-oriented foreign policy the latter two. This *let-up* of external controls adds to the crisis of the state, and creates an opening for the activity of revolutionaries. I consider it world-systemic in that it tends to originate in the relation between core and peripheral states or the impact of war or depression on both.

My primary working hypothesis is *that the combination of all five of these factors is required for a social revolution to succeed.* Any other combination will result in a different outcome. If all of the above conditions are met, then, the model suggests that a revolutionary outbreak has optimal chances of occurring, in which a multi-class, cross-racial, and all-gendered coalition of aggrieved social forces will emerge and coalesce to carry out a revolutionary project. Such broad coalitions will have the best chances for success, in terms of attaining state power. Though the present study will focus on these causes of revolutionary outbreaks and the process by which state power is won through such coalitions, the framework elaborated here also goes some way toward an explanation of the outcomes of social revolutions. Once a measure of power is achieved, broad, heterogeneous coalitions tend to fragment, as their constituent elements begin to struggle among themselves over the shape of the new order (in the case of a protracted revolutionary struggle, as in Mexico from 1910 to 1920, this process begins even earlier). Moreover, as Skocpol has observed, "explanations of the conflicts and outcomes of social revolutions best flow . . . from a prior understanding of the structures and situations of old regimes and from a prior analysis of the causes of social-revolutionary crises."[79] In the case of the Third World, this means that revolutionary states must continue to operate within the limits of dependency and the probability of renewed external pressures and intervention. These forces put further pressure on the coalition to fragment, which can lead to counter-revolutionary coups as in Iran (1953), Guatemala (1954), Chile (1973), and Grenada (1983), or to a strong but undemocratic state (as in post-revolutionary Mexico, Cuba, and Iran to various degrees). The democratic route is the hardest to follow; Sandinista Nicaragua tried this, despite the odds. While not addressing outcomes in as much detail as outbreaks, in Chapter Four I will examine a set of social revolutions in which initial success was reversed, trying to specify the coalitional dynamics and structural contradictions that led to often quite unintended (deviated, distorted, and disappointing) outcomes.

The questions this book will ask of each of its cases include the following: What was the nature and extent of dependent development in each case? What kind of repressive state is vulnerable (and in a few rare cases, how did open polities facilitate the election of revolutionary forces)? What forms did political culture assume, and how was it translated into action? Was there a measurable economic downturn before each outbreak? What role was played by the dominant outside power? To a much lesser degree, this study will sometimes – not always – touch on two further questions which are properly the subject of another study: Who made up the revolutionary alliance, in class, gender, and racial or ethnic terms, with what regional variations, and why did each of these groups participate? Finally, what happened to the revolutionary alliance in the course of the conflict, and how well did it cohere (or how much did it fragment) afterwards? Taken together, the answers to such questions constitute a new understanding of the origins of revolutions in the Third World.

The method of studying revolutions

The logic of the model proposed above is one of complex conjunctural causation, for it argues that a combination of factors may be necessary and sufficient to lead to the outbreak of social revolutions. It also illustrates what Charles Ragin terms *multiple* conjunctural causation since it is based on the possibility that Third World social revolutions may differ somewhat among themselves as well as from the classic agrarian empires studied by Skocpol: "The point is not the number of causal combinations or types but the fact that the same general outcome . . . may result from various combinations of causes."[80]

This logic is also *additive*: that is, while the theory implies that Third World revolutionary outbreaks can be traced back to dependent development, it does not follow that all cases of dependent development lead to revolutions.[81] Most cases of dependent development do seem to require a more or less repressive state (these two, taken together, define a structural situation found in some, but not all, Third World cases). The rest of the factors are in some sense contingent, not inevitable. Thus, *if* political cultures of opposition are elaborated, and *if* a revolutionary crisis occurs, *then* a revolutionary outbreak is likely to succeed. The conditions under which the "if" clauses take place must also be discovered. What we are testing, then, is whether the set of factors identified in the model is indeed necessary and in fact may be the sufficient collective causes of revolutionary outbreak across our numerous cases. Further, we must inquire into each of the elements in the model to specify it in more detail, asking how one relates to the others, and under what conditions the contingent factors (political culture, world-systemic opening, internal economic downswing) are activated.

Causality, of course, is epistemologically difficult to establish; as Carl Hempel and Jon Elster have argued, a theory limited to actual occurrences is not a theory but a description.[82] But can it really be otherwise? And is our theory "limited" to our cases in any simple manner? The two orders of theory and cases are intended to illuminate and extend one another – originally derived from a study of Iran, the factors in the model are here tested against a wider set of cases (indeed the near universe of successful cases to date). What else can it be expected to explain other than actual occurrences (and probable future ones, *when and if* they occur)? A theoretical underpinning has been offered for the links between factors, although these must be worked out even more closely in the case studies. The logic of the present research then consists of that combination of inductive empirical work and deductive theoretical reflection known as abduction – the two procedures are asked to work together to advance both the sociological theory of revolution and to shed light on cases which are not normally considered together.[83] The reader will judge the success and limitations of this operation.

A major issue in this kind of work involves measuring or "operationalizing" the hypothesized causes. This poses special difficulties for the present study. First, qualitative comparative analysis (also known as Boolean analysis) as codified by Ragin,[84] requires the construction of a truth table, in which factors are coded "0" if absent and "1" if present. But factors such as dependent development and political cultures of opposition are complex constructs, and may be present to a greater or lesser degree. I ultimately resolve this matter in an unorthodox fashion with a coding of "1-" to indicate the *partial* presence of a factor; the implications (and limits) of this novel procedure are made clear in the comparative analyses that follow.[85]

Second, the complex, composite nature of some of the factors makes them difficult to measure. Dependent development, as a concrete process, for example, not only manifests itself differently in different periods, but across cases in the same period. Thus – even if reliable data were available across all cases – to specify a certain degree of inflation, trade, GNP, inequality, or other indicators would miss the point. Along with the effectiveness of a political culture of opposition, or the degree of openness of the world-system, this can only be assessed through qualitative arguments. While the presence or absence of a particular type of regime seems less problematic and an economic downturn can be measured in quantitative terms, I have not applied the latter in strictly uniform ways across cases (e.g. a drop of a given percentage in GNP per capita or a certain amount of inflation and unemployment), for two reasons. This is again a composite factor, and, more importantly, its *meaning* may vary from case to case. Herein lies an important point about agency: it is a population's perception of a given economic situation that determines whether it is severe enough to be a factor. But this is even more difficult to know! It can also lead to tautological reasoning: we know a factor was present if the outcome is present, or it may lead us to find only what we are seeking to establish. The only solution to such difficulties which retains the complex and qualitative nature of the factors is to acknowledge them and discuss the evidence for each case as honestly and thoroughly as one can. It goes without saying that contrary evidence must be considered, and that interpretations regarding each factor for any case may be disputed and argued over.

The methodological field in which this study lies is that of comparative-historical sociology. Theda Skocpol's work on France, Russia, and China in *States and Social Revolutions* sets in many ways the standards for such work and is the model for this effort, whatever our theoretical differences. As she notes, with so few and such complex cases, one cannot meaningfully quantify the results.[86] Instead, the canon of such work reposes in the first instance on what John Stuart Mill called the "Method of Agreement": one scrutinizes cases with a similar outcome (here a successful social revolution) for the presence of similar causes. The theory can then be further tested by a "Method of Difference" in which one considers cases where both the outcome and its causes are absent (or less evident, if on a spectrum), but which are in other important ways rather similar to the positive, or successful cases.[87]

But what if there is more than one path to success, and – as must be supposed – many paths to failure? Boolean qualitative comparative analysis is more suitable for this kind of comparative work than either Mill's methods of agreement and difference alone or than quantitative analysis. Both alternatives are ruled out by the number of cases: there are still too few to quantify results yet too many to analyze by simple inspection. Moreover, Boolean analysis permits the possibility of more than one path to the same outcome, which Skocpol's understanding of Millian logic does not; when dealing with multiple types of failure, this assumption more adequately reflects the social world. Finally, unlike quantitative analysis, Boolean analysis treats each case holistically: that is, the causal factors are kept intact as wholes and seen as combinatorial in effect, rather than statistically reduced to proportional contributions to a given outcome.

The pitfalls of comparative-historical work must also be borne in mind. There is the preliminary issue of comparability of cases; one does not usually want to be comparing apples with pears. Here the selection of successful Third World social revolutions defines a response to this problem: our theory is intended in the first instance to apply only to such cases. Could it be modified to consider the revolutions in 1789 France, 1917 Russia, or 1989 Eastern Europe? I believe that it could, and that a broad combinatorial logic would shed new light on these cases, but this is a project which must be left for another place and time (and perhaps scholar!). Related to this is the issue of "world-time": Skocpol, following Wolfram Eberhard, counsels awareness of the impact of changing international structures (e.g., pre- or post-Industrial Revolution) and the influence of one revolutionary experience on another (pre- or post-Russian revolution).[88] The choice of twentieth-century Third World cases minimizes this problem too, although Mexico is a pre-World War 2 outlier, and we will see that the changing geo-political context is quite important in the period 1978–79, and again after 1989, and now, after September 11, 2001. Another logical problem is the overlooking of some important causal factor, to which one's theory renders one blind. Here I think the greater inclusion of culture and agency in my model overcomes a key omission of Skocpol (and in this sense tries to apply a *dialectical* as well as a comparative-historical method),[89] but other theorists may detect key factors missing in both perspectives.

Finally, the comparativist is always open to the charge of superficiality in treating cases outside her/his own "specialty." The in-depth understanding of even a single culture in its historical breadth can be a life's work, and inherently limited. There is no way to avoid this if one wants to search for meaningful causal regularities or interpretive patterns. My own "best case" is that of Iran, the subject of a full-scale previous study; I have for some time now also taught and researched on Latin America and the Third World generally in addition to the Middle East, and it is this long leap that has generated the present ambitious framework in the first place. This work relies on and is in dialogue with that of all the country specialists whose works are cited in these pages, and is open to their considered criticisms and amendments of particular cases. Indeed, I have consulted a number of them in the course of working on each case.

This brings us to the issue of sources. To the degree possible, and depending on the case, a certain amount of primary data have been consulted to fill in a few of the gaps in the existing literature and to enter into some of the disputed points. In particular, I have selectively consulted census data to form a deeper impression of certain aspects of social structure; newspaper accounts both in the United States and in the countries themselves for data on the activities of the protagonists in each revolutionary struggle; interviews with revolutionary participants conducted by my students in their own work; and some archival materials on the role of the United States as the principal foreign power with an important stake in many of the events. To be sure, I have only been able to scratch the surface here, but the effort has been made to go modestly beyond the secondary accounts, while realizing that they are the major sources for this project and trusting them to have consulted a much wider range of the relevant primary data.

The secondary historiography and social science on each case constitutes the bulk of the data. When working on so many major events in the history of twentieth-century social change, it can only be so. Moreover, the amount and quality of the material available is impressive in itself, particularly the historians on Mexico, the oldest case, and the social scientists on Iran and Nicaragua, which have attracted a great deal of attention. The cases of Cuba and China have also inspired vast literatures, though these are of uneven quality and much of it is polemical; these are also the countries which have been most difficult for outsiders to study on the spot (rivaled in this by Iran, but over a much shorter period). The synthesis offered here draws on the best of the available secondary work on each case, systematically seeking data and evidence on the questions and factors that are of interest to us. Indeed, I have needed so many research assistants to help me get a handle on the multiple histories considered in this book that it is correct to say I have often been forced to work with tertiary sources: the notes taken by my research assistants on some of the key secondary historiography! I have endeavored to do all the research for the cases in Chapter Two by myself, and have done my best to fact-check and properly contextualize the data collected on two dozen other cases in this way by my team.

The plan of the book is as follows. Chapter 2 analyzes in chronological turn each of the five major successful Third World social revolutions that history offers us. Each case is systematically approached within the heuristic framework laid out in this chapter. Chapters 3 and 4 then map the variations of success represented by the anti-colonial revolutions of the twentieth century and a set of shorter-lived revolutionary successes that ended in reversal. The task of Chapter 5 is to draw into the discussion a set of key contrasting cases: attempted social revolutions and political revolutions from Latin America to Africa and Asia. The overarching similarities to the successful revolutions, as well as the key differences in terms of the explanatory factors hypothesized above, will be brought out. A concluding chapter assesses the patterns that emerge out of the historical record and speculates on the future of revolutions in a new century. The challenge is to fashion a controlled test of this theory out of the mass of raw data and multitude of conflicting interpretations available to us, and to advance the theoretical field a few steps forward, while simultaneously doing justice to the richness of each of the cases. This book thus seeks to unify several historical fields in a comparative and theoretical social scientific synthesis of the trajectories of a number of seemingly distant or small countries which have had a disproportionate impact on the world we inhabit. It goes part of the way necessary toward understanding the century we have just left and perhaps in a modest way to make the one we have entered recently more hopeful in its inevitable moments of upheaval and transformation.

Part Two

Revolutionary success

2 The great social revolutions

No misunderstanding of Marx is more grotesque than the one which suggests that he expected a revolution exclusively in the advanced industrial countries of the West.

Eric Hobsbawm, "Introduction," to Karl Marx, *Pre-capitalist Economic Formations* (New York: International, 1964), 49.

The list of the undisputed social revolutions of the twentieth century is a short one – Russia in 1917, China in 1949, Cuba in 1959. To this list I propose to add three more: the Mexican revolution of 1910–20, the Iranian of 1979, and the Nicaraguan of the same year. But for the Sandinistas falling from power (through the unprecedented medium of elections in 1990), the last choice would be uncontroversial. The Mexican and Iranian cases, as was noted in Chapter One, have their doubters because, in the absence of a socialist agenda in either case, and given the defeat of the most radical forces in each (Zapata and Villa, the Iranian left), the degree of social transformation that followed fell clearly short of its potential. But each undid a dictatorship and launched (or furthered) substantial projects of economic and social change. If the French revolution was a social revolution, then so were the Mexican and Iranian.

Absent from this list are a few other cases, some of which will be treated later in this book. The revolution that overthrew Haile Selassie in Ethiopia led to significant change, but was made by a handful of military men (and the same can be said of the Afghan Marxists who seized power in 1978, or the brutal regime of Pol Pot in Cambodia in the 1970s, mercifully reversed a decade later in the latter instance and tragically so in the former). The massive anti-colonial movements in Algeria, Vietnam, Mozambique, Angola, and Rhodesia are each closer to the five social revolutions treated here than to any of these others, but they were movements not against internal despots but external usurpers, and will be treated in their own right in the chapter that follows. The reversed revolutions in Guatemala (1944–54), Iran (1951–53), Bolivia (1952–59), Chile (1970–73), Jamaica (1972–80), and Grenada (1979–83) also will prove to have much in common with the great social revolutions, but they too will be treated as a slight variant on the theme, in Chapter Four.

The present chapter aims then to find the common thread among five of the six social revolutions of the twentieth century, excluding only Russia from its purview. That such a thread exists at all across three major geographic zones – Asia, the Middle East, and Latin America (or up to five if one attends to the nuances among Mexico, the Caribbean, and Central America) – is itself prima facie evidence that there is such a thing as the "Third World" and that its revolutions have much in common. In telling this story, however, we shall also see that each case possesses unique features and contributes its own part to our understanding of the general model adopted in this study. That is, we shall learn something of such matters as the workings of dependent development and dictatorship, the varieties of political cultures of opposition, the nature of economic downturns, and the range of ways in which external pressure may be made ineffective. And we shall begin to see the many ways in which large-scale structures shape, yet do not determine, events made by humans, who everywhere have brought creativity, imagination, and courage to the historical table.

Mexico's unfinished revolution, 1910–1920[1]

Our tale begins with a case among the most difficult to analyze, for the Mexican revolution was a complex, multi-sided event, with sharp twists and turns over the course of a decade. I shall argue that the social revolution reached its apogee in late 1914 with the arrival of Villa and Zapata in Mexico City, and that it was subsequently defeated militarily in 1915–16 by Obregón and Carranza, who then laid the groundwork for the carrying out of a less thorough-going social transformation in the 1920s and beyond. The "victory" or "moment" of all-out social revolution in Mexico was thus quite brief. We will nevertheless analyze it as the first great social revolution of the twentieth century, and the last non-Marxist one until Iran and Eastern Europe toward the end of the century.

Nor can the revolution be easily characterized: Was it a bourgeois revolution overthrowing feudalism, or a failed socialist (or proletarian) revolution? The labels "peasant," "popular," "democratic," "nationalist," and "anti-imperialist" have been attached to it, while the outcome has been variously proclaimed a victory, a defeat, or a "permanent," "unfinished," or "interrupted" revolution leading up to the present.[2] All of these terms hint at the somewhat ambiguous, or mixed, outcome of the revolution, an issue we shall return to. Our present task – sorting out the causes of the revolution, is complicated by the long duration of its course, which featured several distinct phases: the 1910–11 uprising against Porfirio Díaz, the 1913–14 Constitutionalist movement against the dictator Huerta, and the bloody infighting of 1915–16 between the victors to that point.

Mexican social (and political) structure on the eve of the revolution has also received various labels – feudal, capitalist, oligarchic, autocratic, neo-colonial.[3] In ethnic terms, creoles (often landowners and clerics of Spanish descent) dominated the top social positions, though they were yielding in some areas to the estimated one-half of the population classified as mixed-race mestizos. At the bottom of the social structure, about one-third of the population were indigenous peoples of diverse cultures, and there were small black and Chinese populations. Alan Knight notes that ethnic categories represented fluid, sociocultural identities, based on "language, dress, income, food, literacy and domicile."[4] In economic terms, rural society was dominated by hacendados (large landlords), urban society by capitalists, merchants, and clerics. Peasants, the landless, and indentured rural workers were found at the bottom, their urban counterparts being workers, artisans, and the unemployed. There were middle-class ranchers in the countryside, and an intelligentsia and professionals in the cities. Women were located across the class structure, though structurally disadvantaged as well. Galeano claims: "In Mexico City, out of every ten young women, two engage(d) in prostitution."[5] Overall, in 1910: "Mexico's labour force was predominantly agricultural, secondarily artisan and only thirdly industrial; for every hundred rural workers, there were perhaps a dozen small farmers and a dozen artisans, four factory operatives (at least one a woman), three miners, one ranchero, and a quarter of one percent of an hacendado."[6] Regional variations are central to Porfirian social structure too: The north was mining-oriented, its land tenure based on ranching; the central valley both more peasant in the countryside, and more proto-industrial in the cities, particularly the capital; the south based on a highly repressive plantation economy.

The dramatic transformation of this social structure during the reign of Porfirio Díaz from 1876 to 1910 constitutes a textbook case of dependent development. A few simple statistics demonstrate the remarkable growth that occurred: Population grew by 1.4 percent a year to 25.2 million, while economic output rose by 2.7 percent annually and exports by 6.1 percent.[7] Foreign trade grew by three- or fourfold between 1888 and 1910, a great boom led by cotton, mining, and other raw materials. Railroads expanded from 666 kilometers of track in 1876 to 24,560 by 1910. Sugar output rose five times, henequen eleven times.[8] Oil production climbed meteorically until Mexico ranked third in the world in 1911, with fourteen million barrels.[9] Mining thrived as well. Gross domestic product grew from 435 million pesos to 1,184 million between 1877 and 1910. In aggregate terms, this meant growth from 513 pesos per capita in 1895 to 768 by 1910.[10]

Alongside these indices of growth, however, could be discerned characteristic limits, external in origin and internal in impact. In all, foreign capital controlled "90 percent of Mexico's eighty largest capitalized business concerns, including nine of the top ten."[11] Mexican capital still accounted for much agricultural and craft production, but textiles were 80 percent French and banking 94 percent foreign.[12] Great Britain had a large stake in the budding oil industry. Towering over the Europeans was the United States, with over $1 billion in investments by 1910, representing 80 percent of foreign investments and more than the entire Mexican bourgeoisie. American companies and individuals controlled about 80 percent of mining, owned over 100 million acres of land, and provided 57 percent of imports, while taking 75.6 percent of exports in 1910. Railroads had a north-south orientation, reflecting American needs. These investments in Mexico came to 45 percent of all US investments abroad.[13]

Internally, the most significant repercussions of dependent development were the crisis in agriculture and deteriorating urban conditions. Peasants were increasingly squeezed from their land and proletarianized as large-scale latifundios encroached on their communal holdings in places like Morelos, where sugar plantations grew rapidly. While no definitive regional figures exist, by one estimate 90 percent of central plateau people were landless on the eve of the revolution, and 67 percent in the provinces of Mexico, Michoacán, and Veracruz. Agricultural production grew at about 0.7 percent a year, less than population, and was shifting to export crops at the expense of subsistence staples like corn, whose output declined from 2.7 million tons in 1877 to 2.1 million two decades later.[14] In the urban economy, artisans lost jobs as foreign imports flooded markets, especially in textiles. By 1900, the railroad building spree was over, industry was contracting, and rural migrants crowded the cities. The cost of staples far outstripped the purchasing power of wages, which in real terms were the same in 1908 as a century before.[15] The squeeze on land and the rise of urban living costs would prove central to the grievances that fed the ensuing struggle; the argument advanced here is that these changes in the political economy and social structure as a whole can be attributed to the process of dependent capitalist development, with its characteristic aggregate growth for the nation and individual hardships for so many of the nation's people.

The authoritarian character of the Porfirian state has been well documented. Its slogan, "Pan y palo" ("Bread and the stick"), suggests the combination of cooptation and repression that undergirded it. Porfirio Díaz came to power in a popular movement in 1876 and ruled continuously till 1911, with the exception of 1880–84. Elections were regularly held but the results cynically manipulated: Civilian politicians were controlled through a vast patronage machine that oversaw appointments from the level of village cacique (political boss) to state governor, some of whom ruled for twenty or more years, enriching themselves in the process. The army could field 14,000 regular troops (there were 30,000 on paper), 2,400 rurales to police the countryside, and several thousand irregulars, in addition to the local police. It was poorly fed and treated at the lower levels and its commanders were rotated at the top to ensure loyalty to Díaz. This force was increasingly called upon to do repressive duty as Díaz aged: 100 strikers were killed at the Cananea mine in 1905 and 200 at the Rio Blanco textile mill a year later. In the provinces, the citizenry was subjected to "arbitrary fines, impressment, deportation, even . . . murder."[16] The anarchist Partido Liberal Mexicano (PLM) was persecuted; its leaders fled. When Francisco Madero mounted a vigorous electoral challenge to Díaz in 1910, he was arrested and the opposition press shut down. The Porfirian state was clearly personalistic (focused on Díaz); exclusionary of all serious challengers, including new elites; and repressive when all else failed.

On the eve of its revolution Mexico was rich in expressions of resistance to Díaz's rule, in the form of vibrant, if nascent, political cultures that included anarchism, agrarian populism, nationalism, and liberalism.[17] Exiled Spanish anarcho-syndicalists brought their ideas to the textile mills of central Mexico. After an initial florescence in the 1870s they were forced underground by Díaz until a new upswing began around 1900, organized in part around the Flores Magón brothers who founded the PLM in 1905, calling for free speech, agrarian reform, and labor legislation. Local revolts in 1906 and 1908 failed and the Flores Magón had to operate outside the country. In the end anarchism was limited to a part of the working class and some intellectuals, and not capable of uniting opposition to Díaz, who repressed it forcefully, but its egalitarian ideals contributed to the anti-authoritarian leveling that appeared after 1910.[18] A deeper and broader rural counterpart took the form of agrarismo – an agrarian populism rooted in the long history of regional and local revolts that continued throughout the nineteenth century as hacienda encroachments touched more and more mestizo and indigenous communities. Indigenous political culture was based on millenarianism, a return of social justice, restoration of lands, and expulsion of intruders. The veneration of saints in Sonora and Morelos added a religious cast to moral outrage as well. In the north and highlands everywhere, ranchers, smallholders, and communal villagers articulated an independent stand against central control – a stance associated with serranos (peoples of the highlands) – that would evolve into the cross-class populism of the various stages of the revolution. There was widespread agreement with the sentiments of Cruz Chavez, "the Tomochic leader of 1892, who told travelers that his people simply wanted that 'no-one should interfere with them, nor bother them for anything, nor meddle in their affairs'."[19] Once events started these feelings would permeate the vigorous, if socially distinct movements of Zapata and Villa. Behind both rural and urban grievances lay a growing nationalism generated in part by the Díaz clique's preference for things foreign, and fueled by the rural encroachments and industrial pay differentials between Mexicans and foreigners in mining, the railways, and elsewhere. The Mexican City newspaper *El Hijo del Ahuizote* had as its banner "Mexico for the Mexicans," giving voice to these concerns.[20]

The first embodiment of these diverse strands was the liberal-democratic ideology of the Madero revolt that touched off the first phase of the revolution. Francisco Madero, from a rich landed family, was educated in Paris and Berkeley in the 1890s and evolved a liberal, "spiritualist" humanism at that time. Government attacks on Liberal clubs in 1902–03 convinced him that the Díaz government would not reform itself, but had to be changed from without. Madero's early views on radical issues were vague and his later rule showed him to be a moderate, but in the period before the revolution he stood for the right to unionize, for improved conditions (yet far short of a real land reform) in the countryside, stopping the onslaught of the large US trusts (though not all foreign capital), and above all, for democracy and fair elections. His 1908 book against the re-election of Díaz and his subsequent campaign for the presidency in 1910 aroused the hope of discontented elements around the country, providing a temporary, if somewhat watered down, fusion of strands of the pro-labor, pro-peasant, nationalistic, and democratic aspirations of a wide segment of the population: "The Maderista programme and philosophy were thus variably conjugated: for some, they implied a progressive, up-to-the-minute polity, well-governed, hard-working and prosperous; for some, a political housecleaning and overdue access to power; for some, a reassertion of old, heroic, liberal values; for some, agrarian restitution and/or village autonomy."[21] This amalgam would prove a political culture of resistance sufficiently inclusive to unify broad forces against Díaz in 1910, when the dual crisis provided an opening.

The internal aspect of this crisis took the form of a series of economic downturns between 1899 and 1911, the most severe between 1907 and 1910. The 1899–1904 financial crises in Europe hit Mexican investments hard, dampening the boom that had begun in the 1880s. In 1905–6 a fall in the price of silver led to less mining output, strikes, and unemployment.[22] The 1907 economic panic and recession in the US brought severe short-term effects to Mexico – declines in economic output, shrinking tax revenues, rising foreign debt, and inflation. This was compounded by a two-year drought that began in 1908. Sugar production fell in Morelos and unemployed workers crowded city streets. Famine in the north and center due to the decline in corn crops necessitated five million pesos of corn imports in 1908, fifteen million in 1909, and twelve million in 1910. Cotton output fell, affecting textiles, where wages declined and unemployment rose. Imports plummeted by 50 percent from 1907–08 to 1908–9, and government income by 26 percent from 1905 to 1908. The state's fiscal conservatism prevented it from spending its way out of the crisis, as debt servicing grew to 25 percent of its budget.[23] Knight argues that aggregate data point to recovery by 1910, but the evidence is fragmentary, and the damage had already been done: The 1907–09 crisis drove many into Madero's camp. Moreover, in early 1911, the economy turned down again and prices soared, especially in the north, just as the rebellion gathered steam. So while Knight rightly notes – "The timetable of middle-class protest was determined not, in some mechanical fashion, by the crises of the business cycle, but by the political chronology of the 1900s – the Creelman interview [in which Díaz had told a North American journalist he would not seek reelection], the impending 1910 elections"[24] – this only highlights the powerful conjunctural effect of economic downturn and political cultures of opposition, both of which were available by 1910–11 where they had not been a decade earlier.

The final link in this chain of processes was the world-systemic opening at the time of Madero's uprising. To some degree, rivalries between Europe and the United States may have stayed American intervention in the 1910–11 crisis, but to a much larger degree the internal policy uncertainties of the Taft administration and the interests of individual American capitalists played a favorable role in Madero's victory. Conflicts arose between the Díaz government and the US over naval maneuvers in Baja in 1907, Mexican refuge for deposed Nicaraguan president Zelaya in 1909, oil contracts with British companies, and land disputes near the border in Texas. Taft personally would have liked to help Díaz but moved rather slowly for various domestic reasons (the Democrats had just gained control of Congress in late 1910 and accused him of connections to Mexican capital).[25] Madero meanwhile activated his extensive ties to wealthy American backers in San Antonio and New York, among them railroad tycoon H. H. Harriman, the bankers James Stillman and George Brackenridge, and the Texas Oil Company.[26] Though Díaz called for Madero's arrest in Texas in late 1910, the US took no action until February 1911, inadvertently aiding Madero. On March 6, 1911, Taft concentrated troops on the border for "routine" maneuvers seemingly aimed at preventing more arms and men from crossing over to the rebels. Ironically, the action was perceived as an insult by Díaz and as a threatening message of dwindling US confidence in him by the Mexican public. Although a number of Americans were accidentally killed at El Paso when Madero's supporters took Ciudad Juarez just across the border in May, the US again took no steps to help Díaz.[27] In the end, while the American government did not intervene for Madero, its studied neutrality hurt Díaz, and important US financial interests backed the rebels.

These developments resulted in a fairly swift victory for the rebels under Madero's banner in the spring of 1911. Several incipient armies responded to Madero's November 1910 call for an uprising to oust Díaz and restore democracy, led by Pascual Orozco and Francisco Villa in the north, Emiliano Zapata south of Mexico City, and numerous local figures elsewhere. By late May there was rebellion throughout Mexico, and the Federal army was stretched to breaking point against up to 70,000 loosely organized insurgents. Díaz, in poor health and with no visible domestic or international support, resigned on May 25, 1911, securing from Madero a compromise that preserved the army and much of the government.[28]

Who made this phase of the Mexican revolution? Victory was the product of a disparate, multi-class alliance of the social groups and classes that had been adversely affected by dependent development and the Porfirian repression.[29] The political center of gravity in 1911 lay in the north, where excluded elites, hard-pressed ranchers, artisans, and miners, dispossessed peasant and indigenous Yaqui and Mayo communities, and urban marginals all played a role. The middle classes everywhere wanted more responsible government; they were perhaps the natural core of Madero's liberal democratic movement. Women engaged in urban bread riots in 1911 and some became revolutionary soldaderas even at this early date. In the center and south, where hacienda encroachments had occurred but enough free villages still remained, as in Morelos, Puebla, and Tlaxcala, peasants engaged in land seizures and joined the rebel armies. These movements included indigenous and mestizo villagers and smallholders. The plantation economy of the south, with its high proportion of peons and few free villages, did not become active to any comparable degree in this phase of the revolution. Throughout Mexico, while leaders tended to come from slightly higher class positions than the rank and file, they were local people in most cases, not outsiders. In two senses, then, the revolution was a multi-class affair: within each region, and across the country as a whole. In Knight's words: "it was a complex, collective experience, to which many groups contributed in different ways and for different reasons."[30] No single social class, geographical area, or economic sector carried the movement by itself.

As is well known, the Mexican revolution did not end in 1911. While space does not permit extensive analysis of its course from 1911 to 1920, the factors used in accounting for its outbreak and initial success exercised continuing force on its subsequent tortuous course and eventual outcome. Madero fell in 1913 after alienating both lower-class rebels and the US. A renewed multi-class coalition ousted the dictator Huerta from power in 1914, then fragmented into complex regional and cross-class movements that engaged in their own civil war, pitting radical forces led by Villa and Zapata against moderate bourgeois leaders Carranza and Obregón. The timing and outcome of these struggles continued to have much to do with such factors as the contending political cultures, internal economic conditions, and the world-systemic conjuncture.

Madero's rule did not resolve the issues that caused the revolution.[31] On October 1, 1911 Madero was elected with 98 percent of the vote in the most honest elections in the country's history. But as Knight notes, he was caught between the demands of the lower classes to solve urgent problems, and of hacendados, army officers, and officials to maintain the status quo, proving himself unable to please either.[32] By the summer of 1911, his failure to address land reform had already alienated Zapata, whose Plan de Ayala called for the return of lost communal lands, expropriation with compensation of one-third of all large holdings, and total expropriation of all large landlords who opposed the plan. Zapata engaged in guerrilla warfare against government troops, whose officer corps Madero had kept intact and whose numbers he had built up from 20,000 under Díaz to 70,000.[33] Another, less clear-cut rebellion was led by Pascual Orozco in the north in 1912 and put down by General Victoriano Huerta, whom Madero had earlier retired for his support of Díaz. To this may be added military revolts, local riots, small-scale peasant uprisings, and wide-spread social banditry.[34] In the process the United States gradually lost faith in Madero as a guarantor of internal order and promoter of US interests in the country, seeing him as far more radical than he in fact was (a perception shared by many members of the elite as well). Ambassador Henry Lane Wilson characterized Madero's government as "inept, capricious, dishonest, tyrannical, intolerant, and hypocritical."[35] The end came in February 1913, when Huerta assumed military command to put down a conservative rebellion in Mexico City led by Felix Díaz, the ex-dictator's nephew. Instead, with the clear support of Wilson, Huerta staged a coup in the midst of the fighting, on February 18, and had Madero killed four days later, with tacit local US approval.[36]

Huerta's counter-revolution was initially backed by the United States, Great Britain, the Catholic Church, the army, and the Porfirian oligarchy.[37] Soon enough, the conditions for his fall came into place, however. Madero's murder, and the subsequent repression of the labor movement and fraudulent elections in October 1913 marked Huerta as a dictator and discredited him with the urban middle and working classes. Resistance to his rule began within days after his coup, as followers of Venustiano Carranza, governor of Coahuila, took up arms, and as revolutionary forces were reactivated by Pancho Villa in the north, Alvaro Obregón from Sonora down the Pacific coast, and Zapata south of the capital. These disparate groups – especially Villa's forces – inflicted numerous defeats on Huerta's undertrained and underpaid army in late 1913 and early 1914. Knight calls them "the old Maderista coalition of 1910–11, the urban civilians and the rural populists; a coalition of awesome power."[38] Economic activity was witnessing "a gradual atrophy" by late 1913, especially in the north, as the revolutionary fighting began to undermine trade, production, investment, incomes, finance, and the currency.[39] The US government, meanwhile, with Woodrow Wilson taking over as president just after the coup, changed its policy from one of cautious support to working for Huerta's removal by the summer and fall of 1913 (Henry Lane Wilson was recalled in July).[40] Wilson sought a capitalist democracy in Mexico, while US oil companies turned vociferously against Huerta when he favored European interests, who were willing to give Mexico a greater share of the profits. This world-systemic opening was effected by the United States letting arms flow to his opponents, now known as the Constitutionalists, and letting the civil war decide matters. The US also intervened militarily against Huerta at Veracruz in April to stop European arms from reaching him. Internally defeated and externally without allies, Huerta finally stepped down on July 15, 1914.

Madero's political revolution now secured, the victors turned to the issue of social revolution in late 1914. In October, all the anti-Huerta forces, already sparring with each other, met in a convention at Aguascalientes, where the chasm was confirmed between the radical followers of Villa and Zapata, on the one hand, known as the Conventionists, and the more moderate supporters of Carranza and Obregón, on the other, known as the Constitutionalists, with both claiming power. While it is hard to definitively distinguish the two sides in class terms, Knight points toward an underlying perception of cultural differences, as the urban, commercial, nationalist, literate, secular, and bureaucratic Constitution-alists viewed their opponents as "parochial, rural, illiterate, Catholic, per-sonalist, and ascriptive,"[41] and Hart notes "the profoundly contrasting goals of the two forces."[42] In November and December, Villa and Zapata occupied Mexico City, meeting for the first time. Neither sought political power, however, and no comprehensive national program was put forward beyond the revolutionary agrarian demands of the Plan de Ayala. Radical as it was in the countryside, the political culture of Zapatismo did not encompass the broad spectrum of the revolution's forces.[43]

In the course of 1915, the most radical forces would be defeated. Carranza and Obregón built a broader alliance than either Villa or Zapata, who were henceforth geographically isolated from each other. Obregón gained crucial working class support by his overtures to Mexico City's progressive labor confederation, the Casa del Obrero Mundial; promised agrarian reform to the peasantry; and was more open than Villa to the participation of women soldaderas in his army.[44] In late 1914 the US had conveniently withdrawn from Veracruz, leaving substantial arms (and access to oil revenues and foreign trade) in the hands of the Constitu-tionalists, who were rightly seen as the less radical alternative.[45] In a series of battles between January and July 1915, Obregón, using World War 1 tactics of trenches and barbed wire, put Villa's more mobile cav-alry on the defensive, securing Mexico City and driving Villa back to Chihuahua with heavy losses, where he no longer posed a threat, though he couldn't be beaten. As Cumberland puts it: "Obregón planned, Villa charged; Obregón thought, Villa felt."[46] Villa's dwindling power was fur-ther attenuated by the inflation touched off by his printing of money and the food shortages caused by the dislocations of the fighting.[47] The Zapatistas took Mexico City one last time in July, then were driven back to Morelos. As Katz puts it: "The Zapata movement tended to be well-nigh invincible at its center, but virtually ineffectual beyond its confines," this due to its lack of arms, transport, and motivation to do more than defend Morelos.[48] By the fall the prickly nationalist Carranza enjoyed grudg-ing US support as the more conservative option, bolstered by a fear of German influence as well as the promise of stability which Obregón's victories portended.[49]

In early 1917 a constitution was drawn up by the winners which reflected their moderate but decidedly revolutionary aims, containing an extremely advanced labor code, asserting state ownership of oil and minerals, and putting an agrarian reform on paper. The drafting of the constitution set the stage for a final struggle between Carranza and the more radical Obregón. Carranza ruled Mexico formally from 1917 to 1920, though supporters of Obregón dominated the 1918 congressional elections. Economic difficulties (unemployment, inflation, debt, and food shortages, compounded by epidemic disease) undermined Carranza's popularity (though minerals and oil kept the state afloat).[50] The US resumed its earlier distaste for Carranza's unremitting nationalism, granting him no loans or significant arms sales in power. Organized urban labor was dealt a blow by the new regime in a series of confrontations, culminating in the unsuccessful general strike of July 31–August 2, 1916 and the establishment in 1918 of the pro-government Confederación Regional de Obreros Mexicanos.[51] Very little land was distributed. Guerrilla movements continued to disrupt the countryside, though the strongest – Zapata's – was worn down by counterinsurgency and the murder of its leader in April 1919. When Carranza tried to keep Obregón out of power in 1920 by naming his own successor, he was killed fleeing the country, leaving Obregón as president from 1920 to 1924. With his nemesis Carranza gone, Villa made peace with the government but he too was assassinated in mysterious circumstances on his hacienda in 1923. By then the revolution was for all intents and purposes over. As Hart puts it: "Obregón Salido functioned as the ultimate compromiser capable of negotiating with Carrancistas, Villistas, workers, Zapatistas, and Americans."[52] Obregón also enjoyed army support and US backing as the final stable force left standing. Obregón himself was killed by a religious extremist in 1928: the revolution devoured its leaders.

What did the revolution accomplish, and how should we evaluate it? In many respects, it is debatable whether it was fully-fledged social revolution, and the most radical workers and peasants (not to mention the women and indigenous fighters in the popular forces) were without doubt defeated.[53] This thesis of defeat is argued most cogently by Ramón Eduardo Ruiz: "Mexico underwent a cataclysmic rebellion but not a social 'Revolution'."[54] Womack concludes: "The difference the so-called Revolution made to the country's modern history was . . . not a radical transformation but simply a reform, accomplished by violent methods but within already established limits."[55] Other eminent historians from Arnaldo Córdova to Jean Meyer and François-Xavier Guerra concur in various ways, with emphases on elites as the main actors and the continuity of post- and pre-revolutionary regimes.[56]

Yet it was something more than a political revolution that removed the Díaz dictatorship. Knight and Hart, in many ways at odds with each other, agree that there was a social revolution, with tremendous mass participation that had consequential impacts on the lives of those who made it.[57] The 1917 constitution, though not anti-capitalist, was "the most progressive law code of its time."[58] A strong and broadly legitimate state arose in the 1920s and 1930s. Though far from democratic, it claimed significant peasant and worker support in its institutions, and forged a single party, eventually and tellingly titled the Partido Revolucionario Institucional (PRI). Two decades after the revolution, Lazaro Cárdenas made good on the promise of oil nationalization in 1938 and distributed significant land back to the communities. It was only after 1940 that this state was definitively turned to the elite project of national capitalist development, resuming the rhythms of dependency that would lead to a new revolutionary movement in 1994 (the story of the latter-day Zapatistas' ongoing attempted revolution is chronicled in Chapter Five).

Adolfo Gilly's brilliant interpretation allows a way through these debates. He sees a definite, yet complexly unfolding social revolution:

> If we use the yardstick of mass intervention and mobilization, weighing up their spatial and temporal extent and the changes in the life, habits and mentality of millions of men and women, then the Mexican Revolution was unquestionably one of the most profound in Latin America and of the greatest anywhere in this century so rich in revolutions . . .
>
> As a result of the explosive social, political and economic contradictions peculiar to capitalist development in Mexico, the Mexican people underwent a hitherto unprecedented experience. They burst onto the historical stage and lived for a time as its main protagonists. Feeling themselves to be the subject, and no longer the mere object of history, they stored up a wealth of experience and consciousness which altered the whole country as it is lived by its inhabitants. It was impossible to ignore or depreciate this change in the decades that followed.[59]

Gilly argues that the outcome was a bourgeois revolution, that the most radical peasant forces aimed at a kind of socialist trajectory, and in so doing, prevented it from stopping short of a bourgeois outcome. It was, therefore, an interrupted revolution, in which "the peasantry . . . shifted the whole logic of the process of capitalist development. [The peasantry] could not block [a bourgeois revolution] completely or substitute a different process, but it interrupted and altered its course and changed the relationship of forces between its political representatives."[60] These tendencies met in the 1917 Constitution as the "centre of gravity for the various participants in the Mexican Revolution."[61] On this interpretation, which I support, the Mexican revolution occupies "a place in world history on the frontier between the last bourgeois revolutions and the first proletarian revolution, the Russian October."[62]

Analytically, we have traced the origins of the Mexican revolution to the confluence of the dependent development and repressive personalist state of Díaz, the elaboration of radical and democratic political cultures of opposition, an economic downturn in 1907–9, and a favorable world-systemic opening when the US proved ambivalent toward Díaz.

Its fortunes after 1911 continued to be affected by these factors, with first Madero falling, caught between the most radical and conservative demands, and losing the goodwill of the US. Huerta then acted as a classical dictatorial foil for the revolutionaries to regroup. Victory eluded the forces of Villa and Zapata in 1914–15 owing to their inability to forge a broad political alliance and cultural consensus, even among themselves.[63] This failure has its urban counterpart: the most militant workers supported Obregón, seeing Villa and Zapata's forces as primitive and unsophisticated, threatening and therefore somehow reactionary.[64] Here we encounter a first principle of explaining revolutionary outcomes: the broad coalitions that overthrew the old regime tend to fragment once this is accomplished. First a radical/moderate split developed, then the moderate victors Carranza and Obregón fell out with each other. Again, economic downturn, US withdrawal of support, and exclusionary political practices helped bring about Carranza's downfall. In the end, though the Mexican revolution just barely qualifies as a social revolution, its causation fits well with our model. This ambiguous outcome of Latin America's first twentieth-century social revolution would set the stage for the last rebellion of the century, in Chiapas, eight decades later.

The longest revolution: China, 1911–1949[65]

With the Chinese revolution of 1949 we come to our first example of a *socialist* revolution in the Third World. John Dunn considers it "probably harder to characterize than any other historical revolution: vast in scope, bemusingly protracted in time, enduringly diffuse in focus, politically still very much unresolved, and formidably occluded and opaque throughout."[66] The case of China was investigated by Theda Skocpol according to the same structural principles as were the French and Russian revolutions: a semi-bureaucratic absolutist monarchy was toppled in 1911, after which a mostly agrarian economy near the limits of its growth combined with Japanese invasion in the 1930s to cause a crisis for the nationalist state of Chiang Kai-shek. This state fell to a communist revolution led by Mao, who provided the missing organizational capacity to the mass peasant base of the revolution.[67] Eric Wolf has challenged this view of a stagnant agrarian economy, noting significant commercialization of agriculture in key regions as the basis of peasant grievances.[68] Rod Aya and Ekkart Zimmermann have joined Skocpol in arguing against a major role for ideas in the events: "the ideological currents did not palpably exist as political reference points when the old regimes [in Mexico and China] were toppled in 1911."[69] But Skocpol's teacher, Barrington

Moore, Jr., provided an early version of what we might term Wolf's "social" interpretation, while also underlining the salience of peasant ideals in the revolutions he studied, in the shape of "a crude notion of equality, stressing justice and necessity of a minimum of land for the performance of essential social tasks."[70] More recently, Alvin So and Stephen Chi have offered a most promising synthetic theory of the revolution:

> The Chinese Revolution is such a complex event that it has to be explained by a combination of the following factors: (a) The degeneration of the GMD's [referring to the Guomindang nationalist movement led by Chiang Kai-shek] Nanjing government laid the foundation for the Communist movement; (b) peasant pauperization and changing agrarian class relations in the 1930s provided the social supports for this movement; (c) Maoism, the Red Army, and peasant mobilization provided the revolutionary ideology, organization, and strategy; and (d) the second Sino-Japanese War provided the timing and the powerful catalyst for revolution.[71]

My own perspective is close to this (nuancing the factors somewhat and adding in only an economic downturn), and builds on elements of these parallel interpretations in an attempt to reconcile their cross purposes by linking internal political economy, external pressures and let-ups, and political cultures of opposition.

From 1644 until the 1911 political revolution, China was ruled by the Manchu, or Ch'ing dynasty – Skocpol's centralized, semi-bureaucratic absolutist monarchy. Its 40,000 officials needed the help of local elites – the landlords and scholars once known as the gentry – to rule the vast countryside. Sharecropping and wage labor were common in a system that was – if not yet capitalist – then certainly not feudal.[72] Eighty percent of the population were peasants with small holdings who either owned their own land (about 50 percent), or rented land (30 percent), or both owned and rented to make ends meet (20 percent).[73] There were very few large estates or common lands to manage, and peasants had to compete with each other for scarce access to land. Nor did peasants possess many independent solidarity organizations of their own; instead, they tended to be politically controlled by local elites, and organized together with them in clans or groups of families. Revolts did sometimes occur in the countryside, but rebellion was dangerous and not likely to succeed.

This state and economy were relatively prosperous for several centuries, relatively stable politically and expanding economically. Population grew from 65–80 million in 1400 to 430 million by the middle of the nineteenth century, when it began to strain the limits of existing agricultural productivity (it would burgeon further to 600 million by 1950).[74] In the nineteenth century, moreover, China came under severe outside pressure from Britain, France, Russia, and Japan, at the same time as it was reaching internal limits to development. Wolf comments that the foreigners sought a Chinese government "weak enough to accept orders and controls from abroad, but strong enough to give orders and exercise control domestically"[75] – which indicates the depth of the contradiction faced by the monarchy, because as Skocpol judges, "China's sheer existence as a sovereign country was profoundly threatened."[76] In 1911 the system broke down, a republic was declared, and the Manchus fell, ending the centuries-old system of monarchy in China (these events are briefly analyzed in Chapter Five, as they constitute one of the first *political* revolutions of the twentieth century).

Let us take up the story at this point. There would be no strong central government after 1911, right up to the revolution in 1949. Power lay in the hands of the provincial armies, each controlled by a local figure known as a warlord. Warlords taxed their populations heavily, and competed with each other in a system Skocpol characterizes as a "balance of weakness."[77] The Confucian-educated elite declined after 1911, but local landlords were left alone, and if anything increased their demands on the peasantry. In the 1920s two new organizations came onto this unstable scene. The Chinese Communist Party (the CCP) was organized in 1921; in Chinese, its name tellingly translated as the "Share Property" Party.[78] One of its founders was a young student leader named Mao Zedong, the son of a wealthy peasant. At about the same time, a nationalist organization, the Guomindang or GMD, became a mass party. It had been founded in 1912 by Sun Yat-sen, on "the Three People's Principles of Chinese nationalism, constitutional democracy (to be realized after a period of tutelage), and 'people's livelihood' (an ill-defined form of socialism in the cities and 'land to the tiller' in the countryside."[79] Sun was replaced after his death in 1925 by a young military leader named Chiang Kai-shek. The two parties united temporarily between 1923 and 1927 at the suggestion of the Soviet Union, the main source of the weapons they used for battles against the warlords. Interestingly, the Soviet Union forced the Chinese communists to subordinate their work to that of the GMD, which they did by working within the labor movement while Chiang's armies scored military victories (Mao, for example, served as deputy director of propaganda for the GMD). Matters came to a head in the spring of 1927 when Nanking was taken by the GMD and made its capital, and Shanghai, an important coastal city, was the scene of a left-wing workers' government (it was Zhou Enlai who organized the workers' uprising that allowed Chiang to take Shanghai without a battle). At this point, differences in degree of radicalism arose between nationalists and communists. As Skocpol puts it, "How much social revolution?"

and "How much anti-imperialism?" became the questions.[80] Though Chiang could be antagonistic to the capitalist class, especially when seeking funds, the right wing of the GMD grew closer to conservative social forces such as landlords, local elites, factory owners, and army officers. In April 1927 Chiang turned his troops against the communist-backed strikers at Shanghai, and killed hundreds of members of the Communist Party.[81] Soviet aid was rejected and the GMD turned to Chinese business interests instead. By 1931, the GMD had fought, bought, and maneuvered its way to nominal control of most of the country, largely defeating the warlords in the 1928–30 Northern Expedition, and confining the communists to one rural region in the south.

But the GMD failed to set up a stable, effective central government. In part, this was due to the underlying economy and social structure of the country. Turn of the century China was perhaps a dubious case of dependent development, but by the 1930s and 1940s, under the spur of the nationalist government and then the Japanese occupation, the still largely agrarian country had begun a process of industrialization that better qualifies for the term. Though there was no heavy industrial base, the working class grew in numbers from 1.5 million in 1919, concentrated in transport and textiles, to some three million unionized workers by 1927. In addition, there were four million students beyond the secondary level in 1915, and 200,000 teachers, with 100,000 Chinese educated abroad between 1872 and 1949, a fertile ground for both GMD and communist nationalism.[82] Industrial growth was significant from 1912 to 1920, spurred by the limits World War 1 imposed on European competition in China, and continued to expand at 6 percent or more annually from 1926 to 1936, accounting for 3.4 percent of net domestic product in 1933. The index of industrial production rose from 100.0 in 1926 to 134.1 in 1931 and 186.1 in 1936 for all of China, and from 100.0 to 378.0 over the same period for Manchuria.[83] Starting with consumer goods, the process deepened into metallurgy, electricity, and other capital and strategic goods.[84] The GMD made infrastructural improvements to air and water transport, as well as communications. Foreign capital, dominated by Great Britain and Japan, controlled 42 percent of China's industrial assets before World War 2: more than 60 percent of coal, 86 percent of iron ore, 88 percent of steel, 76 percent of electricity, 44 to 54 percent of key textile activities, 73 percent of shipping tonnage.[85] Debt payments took a third of government expenditures from 1911 to 1937.[86] The 1929 world crisis revealed the downside of this incipient dependent development: "Silk exports dropped from 136,000 piculs in 1931 to 54,000 in 1934, and 160 of 180 silk factories in central China had to close."[87] Meanwhile, life was difficult for workers, as unemployment reached five million people in

1935; hours were long, pay low, and women were particularly exploited and harassed.[88]

Nor was the GMD popular in the vast countryside, where it left regional landlords in control, and below them, the rural gentry. The situation of the peasantry – up to 85 percent of the population – continued to worsen in the 1930s. In explaining the rise of the communists Wolf emphasized the impact of commercial agriculture in a famous thesis: "The introduction of commercial crops and the commercialization of land affected land prices, tenure conditions, and rent charges. Prices for land doubled and tripled in some areas, and secure tenure was replaced by short-term contracts."[89] Wolf's views fed into a major debate on the conditions of the peasantry. In the early 1930s R. H. Tawney had estimated that 40 to 50 percent of peasant families lacked enough land to provide their food.[90] Contra Tawney and Han-seng Chen, Ramon Myers, and Thomas Rawski argue that the rural sector did well, even registering rising per capita consumption. R. B. Wong notes that this debate is inconclusive, given the difficulties posed by the lack of evidence. So and Chiu agree with Albert Feuerwerker that "there is no doubt that the Chinese peasants experienced a sharp fall in income as a result of the contraction of export markets during the 1930s world depression."[91] Peasant debt grew, they lost titles to land, land inequality rose, and the number of impoverished peasants grew. Jonathan Spence adds arguments that peasant conditions worsened by the 1930s, whether due to foreign imperialism and landlord exactions, or to population growth, antiquated farming techniques, and soil exhaustion. He accepts the thesis of deterioration in their conditions, noting further the 1931 floods that created fourteen million refugees, the dislocations of migrant labor after the Japanese seized Manchuria and attacked Shanghai, the effect of the world-wide depression on cash crop exports, and high GMD-imposed taxes.[92] Spence concludes that "many, perhaps tens of millions – lived in terrible and humiliating poverty, and were too preoccupied with the daily struggle for survival to look far ahead or brood about the national scene."[93]

The GMD state of the period emerged as repressive, exclusionary, and personalist. It was run by a clique around Chiang Kai-shek, who was referred to as the "Generalissimo."[94] Former warlords staffed it, bribery and favoritism ran rampant. The ideological underpinning of Chiang's rule was the "New Life Movement," based on elements of fascism, including contempt for democracy and strong proscriptions on independent personal and social behavior. Chiang stated approvingly in 1933: "The most important point of fascism is absolute trust in a sagely, able leader. Aside from complete trust in one person, there is no other leader or ism. . . . The leader has final decision in all matters."[95] The shallow roots of this hegemonic project were revealed by the May 21, 1936 replies from all over China to novelist Mao Dun's call for people's thoughts on that day:

The respondents mocked the propaganda behind the New Life campaigns for its insincerity, and angrily criticized the disruption to rural life caused by compulsory land requisitions and the forced drafting of labor. They attacked those who collaborated with the Japanese, or presented specious arguments for avoiding conflict . . .

[One] writer, in one of the cleverest and saddest submissions sent to Mao Dun, played on the difference of accents that led Chinese in the north to misinterpret the sentiments of their fellow countrymen in the south. On one street, he observed, hung a sign with this uplifting message:

> Everything prospers, Heaven is protective.
> People are heroes, The place is famous.

But if read with a Cantonese accent, and then reinterpreted according to the sound, the slogan became more depressing:

> Everything disintegrates, Heaven explodes.
> People are extinct, The place is barren.[96]

The GMD ruled through the coercion of execution, assassination, arrest, threat, and censorship. Lloyd Eastman concludes that the hold on power by the GMD "depended almost wholly on the army. It was, in fact, a political and military structure without a social base, inherently one of the least stable of all political systems."[97]

Foreign pressure, in the form of Japanese encroachments on Chinese territory, became severe in the 1930s. When Japan finally invaded in 1937, the GMD did little to mobilize the masses to resist, retreating instead from the rich coastal cities to the far poorer interior, where it was much less suited to thrive. Obsessed with the communist threat, Chiang devoted most of his forces to the struggle against them, rather than the Japanese. In western China, the GMD's revenues fell 63 percent; meanwhile, 41 percent of the budget went to the military between 1928 and 1937.[98] In John Fairbank's telling words, "Instead of learning to live off the countryside as the CCP was doing, the KMT lived off the printing press [referring to the inflation touched off by printing money]."[99] A huge campaign was launched against the communists' southern stronghold, forcing Mao to set out with 80,000 supporters in October 1934 on what would be immortalized as the Long March. In one year they walked 6,000 miles across China from the south and east toward the north and west; at the end they numbered only 8–9,000 people.[100]

But in the process Mao had emerged as the undisputed communist leader and the party had deepened its relationship with the peasants of China and fashioned a strong political culture of opposition out of elements of nationalism and anti-imperialism, popular participation (or at least mass mobilization) in politics, and social and economic justice. Skocpol maintains this successful match of revolutionary leadership and the peasantry had "little to do with revolutionary ideology and everything to do with the 'peculiarities' (as seen from a European perspective) of the Chinese agrarian sociopolitical structure."[101] By this she means that peasants, lacking land and other resources, had no alternative but to respond to the communist overture. Such a view accords little agency to either party, and gives no credit to the skill of the Red Army and CCP in articulating a message of hope that was readily understood and embraced by a considerable part of the rural population. Let us pause then and look at the political cultures of opposition that helped make the revolution a possibility. Political cultures of opposition were just starting to develop by 1911 (and were largely confined to middle-class urban circles), and communist thought did not exist, but by 1949, Mao's army and party had won the battle for ideological hegemony with Chiang's GMD, especially in the countryside, having wrested from them the mantle of nationalist defenders of the country during the world war. In at least two senses, the CCP quite literally *created* its own political culture of opposition, more so than in most revolutions: that is, the Long March itself and the subsequent experience in Yanan (termed the "Yenan Way" by Mark Selden[102]) formed the *content* of a founding legend, and Mao articulated an ideology – Mao Zedong Thought, or more loosely, Maoism – that represented an astute Sinification of classical orthodox Marxism.[103] In both respects, this ideology built on existing idioms, Chinese and Western. An important intellectual precursor was the May 4 Movement, referring to the date in 1919 when 3,000 students protested against the concessions to Japan made by the victors of World War 1 at the Paris Peace Conference. May 4 gave voice to a new generation's strand of nationalism, and the slogan "down with the old, up with the new" became a weapon of criticism of existing political and social arrangements inside China.[104] This critique was sharpened in the 1920s by the brilliant essays and short stories of Lu Xun (1881–1936), whose loose alliance with the CCP was expressed through the founding of the League of Left-Wing Writers:

[Lu] believed in the power of literature to change ideas and was appalled by the callous insensitivity in Chinese social treatment of the poor and handicapped. Throughout his life he was in rebellion against the treatment of individuals by his fellow Chinese. His famous and influential writings got their power from a bitter and sardonic cynicism that expressed his sense of injustice.[105]

From modest personal philosophical beginnings and in light of the experience of urban political checkmate, Mao gradually crystallized a form of *Chinese* Marxism, a flexible reinterpretation of the classic canons of Marx and Lenin that would by the 1940s be codified as Mao Zedong Thought:

for Mao's purposes it could be asserted that the domination of the landlord class ("feudalism") was being modified by the rise of a merchant class centered in towns (a capitalist "bourgeoisie"), backed by "imperialist" exploiters, and the situation might be cured by an establishment of central state authority ("socialism").[106]

The keys to this political cultural project were to blend nationalism and communism, and to prioritize the role of the peasantry.

Revolutionary nationalism grew in the deep roots of resistance to the Japanese occupation after 1932 and especially during World War 2, to the degree that Chalmers Johnson saw it as *the* political culture of the revolution: "the Communist rise to power . . . should be understood as a species of nationalist movement."[107] Certainly it attracted students, workers, and intellectuals to the cause. It built on "the overriding sentiment of Chinese nationalism based on cultural and historical pride, which meant China could not be the tail of someone else's dog."[108] Its bottom-line, irreducible meaning was "China for the Chinese,"[109] a slogan reminiscent of *El Hijo del Ahuizote*'s "Mexico for the Mexicans."

But Mao promised more than this, grafting onto the nationalist current an equally powerful and long-standing message of social justice which appealed to the peasant base of his army and the party.[110] According to Mark Selden, the core of Maoism was based on the values of "equality, mass participation, and self-reliance."[111] Initially rent reduction, and later, during the civil war, substantive land reform, concretized the first of these. This tapped deeply felt experiences of injustice and aroused strong anti-landlord emotions.[112] During World War 2, the Communist Party toned down its land reform message but tried to make life better for the poor through tax and rent policies. Judith Stacey notes that the word for "Soviet" – *soo-wei-ai*, sounded similar to *shih-wo-yai*, meaning "This is mine," a happy coincidence in the countryside. She also detects a gender dimension to this, finding that due to the economic deterioration of the peasantry, the family was in crisis prior to the revolution. The communists in the 1930s tried to improve living conditions in the countryside, thereby restoring the peasant family as the mainstay of the rural economy and resulting in the creation of a more numerous, well-to-do peasant middle class, with families as the basis of the working unit – father, wife, brothers, children all working together.[113]

The second element, mass participation, was enshrined as the "mass line approach":

This means: take the ideas of the masses (scattered and unsystematic ideas) and concentrate them . . . then go to the masses and propagate and explain these ideas until the masses embrace them as their own, hold fast to them and translate them into action, and test the correctness of these ideas in such action. Then once again concentrate ideas from the masses and once again take them to the masses . . . And so on, over and over again in an endless spiral, with the ideas becoming more correct, more vital and richer each time.[114]

As Fairbank notes, "This from-the-masses-to-the-masses concept was indeed a sort of democracy suited to the Chinese tradition."[115] The inevitably military organization of the movement and the fact that the subsequent communist government made increasingly cynical use of the rhetoric of participation should not obscure its initial appeal in the period under question. The third leg of the stool – self-reliance – was embodied in the actual practice of the community Mao established at Yanan after the Long March, a social project that included a training center with its own university, Kangda, the Anti-Japanese Military and Political University, which trained some 100,000 "graduates" who provided a core network for the propagation of the movement's political culture:

From the start Yan'an was never just a base or a border area sanctuary or a bastion, but a utopian community, an expression of intense political desire, a yearning for political change as much engaged in political learning as in conducting war and revolution . . .

Yan'an as a discourse community was a place where language, meaning, and understanding were manipulated objects of conscious action and activity – a design for living out a conceptual inversion.[116]

Taken as a whole, this skillfully crafted political culture attracted a diverse social base to the side of the revolution, comprising poor, middle, and "rich" peasants in the countryside, and students, intellectuals, workers, and soldiers in the cities, including significant numbers of urban and rural women in one capacity or another.[117]

The world system also intervened decisively in the civil war, with three successive moments constituting a powerful world-systemic opening for the Chinese revolution. First, Japan invaded Manchuria in 1931, claiming it as a puppet state, Manchukuo, in 1932. Between 1937 and 1939, Japan occupied the key ports, industrial centers, capital, and most populous and well-to-do parts of the country. The "long" world war then decisively weakened the GMD and ultimately strengthened the CCP. The Japanese overran the GMD strongholds in the cities of east China by 1938, taking the country's industrial areas and the best farmland, and cutting China off from the outside world. Chiang's army "incurred large and irreplaceable losses during the first year of fighting, and thereafter its quality was abysmally low."[118] The GMD and the communists cooperated briefly against the Japanese from 1938 to 1941, but soon fell into their old conflict; Chiang was unable to fight the Japanese head on, saving his best forces for the coming struggle with the communists. The 1944 Ichigo offensive by Japan destroyed some of the GMD's best remaining armies.[119] Using less costly guerrilla tactics, the communists meanwhile were more effective against the Japanese, attracting further support from nationalist students, professionals, and hard-pressed workers and peasants. Their army was up to ten times smaller than Chiang's in 1945, but their morale was higher and their popular support greater.

The second movement in the world-systemic opening came in the form of Soviet actions at the end of World War 2. Following the terms of the Yalta Agreement of February 1945, Stalin declared war on Japan on August 8, 1945, two days after Hiroshima. The Soviet army quickly gained control of Manchuria. The Soviet occupation literally took away much of the industrial base that the GMD could have used to rebuild, for the economic weight of Manchuria was vast:

during 1944–45 it produced 8.5 times more pig iron than had ever been produced in a single year in China proper, 2.5 times more electric power, and 8.5 times more cement. Manchuria in 1944 also harvested 3,549,000 tons of soybeans; if that amount had been available to Nationalist China in the postwar period, it would have generated annually through exports some US $60 million to $90 million in foreign exchange. And Manchuria's 144 lumber mills would largely have eliminated the need for imports of foreign lumber.[120]

This loss meant a balance of exchange problem for the GMD after 1946, fueling inflation and imports which in turn hurt farmers and delayed economic recovery.

The final act in the world-systemic opening was the attenuation of US support for Chiang and the GMD. After 1941 the GMD received substantial aid from the Allies and the United States: during the war, US aid to the GMD government included a $75 million loan in 1940, a $500 million loan in 1942, $25 million annually in aid from 1943 on, and the sale of $900 million in lend-lease military equipment for $175 million at the war's end. Retired American airman Claire Chennault had built the Chinese air force, General Joseph Stilwell led a key military mission against the Japanese, and right after the victory US planes transported half a million GMD troops to occupy key cities. Paradoxically this only made the communists more self-reliant and better guerrilla fighters, whereas a popular tea-house poem ran: "Chiang Kai-shek has a stubborn heart, America is his father and mother."[121] American support for Chiang weakened, however, as World War 2 drew to a close and Truman's envoy, General George Marshall, told Chiang that political reform was essential to continued US aid. By early 1947 Marshall admitted failure in his efforts to mediate the conflict.[122] Thereafter, US policy was confused and divided. Fairbank sees this in terms of a split between the earlier generation of Americans in China – often missionaries – who saw the GMD as the answer, and the late-comers (fewer in number, but including General Joseph Stilwell) who had a sense of the CCP's appeal and power. Since the former dominated policy-making, the policy was "flawed by serious anachronism" and resulted in "mixed counsels in the formation of American policy."[123] The US followed a contradictory policy of demanding "coalition and reform at Nanking and Yenan and yet at the same time . . . suppl[ying] the Nationalists . . . Marshall's mediatory role was thereby given the lie."[124] Stressing US ignorance of the situation at all levels, and almost complete ignorance about the CCP's potential and strength, Fairbank concludes: "Seldom has a national posture been more ineffective and unproductive."[125] The China Aid Act of 1948 provided Chiang with another $400 million, but the seemingly endless flow ended later that year, when Madame Chiang Kai-shek went to Washington asking for $3 billion; not only was this refused, all aid was suspended.[126] In the end, the United States was unwilling and unable to intervene in the civil war, effectively leaving the outcome to the play of internal forces.

These factors combined with an economic downturn caused by the aftermath of war and the ongoing revolutionary conflict to make a difference in the civil war between the nationalists and the communists from 1945 to 1948. Incredible inflation weakened the GMD's efforts in its urban strongholds – prices in Shanghai rose 39 times between September 1945 and February 1947, another 58.6 times by July 1948, and a further 400 times by February 1949, or almost a million times between 1945 and 1949. This was due to GMD corruption, printing of worthless money, scarcity, speculation, and hoarding of goods. The economy was reduced to a barter system by late 1948. Unemployment rose as high as 20 percent in Canton and 30 percent in Nanjing after the war.[127] Confidence in the GMD was shattered, and urban intellectuals, students, workers, and professionals flocked to the communist side.

Of the struggle that followed, Fairbank notes: "for Chiang Kai-shek and the nationalists to lose the civil war was a remarkable achievement."[128] The GMD made both political and military errors, alienating key social forces with its policies and fruitlessly trying to hold the cities with its armies, seriously overextending its supply lines. The CCP, on the other hand, built on a solid peasant base in north China and on what remained of the industrial foundation in Manchuria, emphasizing a more radical land reform after 1946. They fought a smart guerrilla war, and refused to panic even when their rural bases were overrun in 1946–47 (which only meant the return of hated landlords). In the northeast the population responded well to their appeals after the Japanese occupation and the GMD's ineffectiveness. Chiang left some of his best troops in a hopeless position in the major cities, and so their arms and many of their men went over to the CCP.[129]

By May 1948 the GMD armies were being cut off from supplies by the communists' guerrilla tactics, and nationalist troops were deserting in large numbers. In September, Lin Biao took Manchuria once again, a major blow. In November 1948–January 1949, fifty-one GMD divisions and 600,000 men were lost (mostly captured, it seems) in the Huai-hai River campaign.[130] The Red Army, now numbering a million well-armed men, took Beijing without a struggle on January 31, 1949, its troops "riding in [captured] American trucks led by American-made tanks."[131] Chiang resigned as president ten days later, but continued to head the GMD, which ultimately fled the mainland and installed itself in power on the island of Taiwan, where it would rule for half a century. Meanwhile, in China, on October 1, 1949 Mao announced the founding of the People's Republic of China.[132] The first fully-fledged Third World revolution of the twentieth century – and the first socialist experiment in Third World history – had come to power.

The making of a revolution: Cuba, 1953–1959[133]

The Cuban revolution presents the appearance of an almost wholly "willed" revolution: a small band of idealistic young revolutionaries over-turning a military dictatorship through determination, bravery, and luck. And in good measure this is true, but it is not the whole story, even if it is an aspect we must not lose sight of. Much more than in Mexico or China, the Cuban revolution seems a personalized, human-scale conflict, not a structurally-created one. This analysis will argue for the salience of both sorts of factors, and in one respect – the internal economic downswing – we will see the degree to which the Cuban rebels did in fact create their own opportunity.

Cuban social structure presents some broad similarities with other patterns in Latin America, along with its own specific differences. The percentage of the population working in agriculture had dropped from 49 in 1919 to 39 by 1959. Another 39 percent worked in the service sector, with 22 percent in industry (the fourth highest in Latin America at the time).[134] The 1953 census officially estimated the population of

5.8 million to be 73 percent "white," 15 percent "mixed," and 12 percent "black," but some scholars, and many Afro-Cubans, believe the real figure for people of color was as high as one-half or more of the population.[135] At the top of the social structure, Cuba had more millionaires per capita than any other country of Latin America, and "More Cadillacs were sold in Havana than any other city in the world in 1954."[136] Their major economic activities included rural landownership, urban real estate, construction, and tourism, often allied with American capital. This elite, however, played little independent economic or political role, caught between American influence and the dictatorial state. The middle classes included Cuban-, Spanish-, and Chinese-born merchants, and native-born professionals. Another 11 percent – 186,000 in 1950 – were employed by the state. The large overall size of the middle class (22 percent of the employed population) was not matched by economic influence, nor, like the elite, by political representation in the weak party system.[137] Cuba's 400,000 unionized workers averaged $1,600 or more in income a year, though this varied from $400 for a textile worker to $6,000 for an electrical worker. The urban marginal class shaded upwards into the working class, with 250,000 servants, waiters, and "entertainers" in tourism, and downwards into the ranks of the 700,000 unemployed and underemployed.[138] Cubans of African descent, up to at least one-third of the population, were over-represented among the poorest.[139] Working women were likewise disproportionately poor: at 10 to 15 percent of the labor force, the largest category was service workers (38 percent of all women workers), many of them domestics earning $8–25 a month, followed by office workers (20 percent), factory workers (20 percent), professionals (17 percent), and marginal occupations including prostitution.[140] In the rural sector there was a large landless proletariat due to the sugar industry, comprising 500,000 cane cutters and 50,000 mill workers. Small farmers were dependent on the mills to grind the cane and finance the crop. Evictions in the 1940s and 1950s led to the displacement of many squatters into the cities or remote hinterlands such as the Sierra Maestra mountains of Oriente province. This poorest, least healthy, and least educated group on the island engaged in the most land conflicts and would prove most receptive to the July 26 Movement's appeals.[141]

Underlying this social structure and shaping its dynamics was another almost textbook case of the process of dependent development. It is not always recognized that Cuba in the 1950s ranked as "one of the four or five most developed nations in Latin America, and the most developed tropical nation in the entire world."[142] Numerous indices of this development, based largely on sugar monoculture and a half-century of ties with American capital, can be found. Per capita income at $400–500 a year (depending on the estimate) was higher than all but Venezuela and Argentina within Latin America. Seventy pounds of meat were consumed annually per person, twice the level of Peru. Industry, which employed 22 percent of the labor force, had embarked on a proto-import substitution phase after 1927 during the Machado regime, and had grown by 47 percent from 1947 to 1958. Cuba ranked fifth or sixth in Latin America in generation of electricity and production of cement, key items for industrial development. In terms of quality of life indicators, Cuba was second in hospital beds per person to Uruguay, had the lowest death rate in the Western hemisphere, and was fifth in literacy in Latin America.[143] The key to this growth, of course, was sugar: Cuba had been the world's largest producer since the early 1900s, and provided more than half the world market in sugar, amounting to 80 percent of Cuba's exports.[144] The health of the sugar sector determined the pace of development in industry, transport, banking, and trade, and the state of the economy generally.

Among the most developed of Latin American nations in conventional terms by the 1950s, Cuba was at the same time a society marked by enormous disparities of wealth and power, for behind the positive statistics lay the dependent aspects of Cuban development. The United States had $1 billion invested in Cuba in 1958 (up from $657 million in 1952), second only to its investments in the Venezuelan oil industry and representing one-eighth of all US investments in Latin America. American companies employed 160,000 Cubans, owned nine of the ten largest sugar mills (and twelve of the next twenty), produced 40 percent of the sugar, held one-quarter of all bank deposits, ran the telephone system, refined all oil, and (with the mafia) controlled much of the hotel, gambling, and drug businesses. The US Congress determined how much sugar Cuba could export to the US (around 60 percent of Cuban output). The US provided 80 percent of Cuba's imports, at low tariffs. This sweeping control was the legacy of fifty years of expansion following US intervention in the 1895–98 Spanish-Cuban war, control of the party system into the 1920s, and support for Batista's rise in 1934 and 1952.[145] The notorious Platt Amendment in 1900 had given the US the right to intervene in Cuba's politics, external borrowing, and foreign affairs.

The internal impact of this dependent development was likewise dramatic. Estimates of income inequality suggest that the poorest 20 percent got between 2 and 6 percent of income, the richest 20 percent taking 55 percent. In terms of land tenure, the largest 9 percent of landowners had 62 percent of the land, while the bottom two-thirds had only 7 percent. In the countryside, as a consequence of land concentration and proletarianization of the labor force, two-thirds of the population lived in thatched huts, 42 percent were illiterate (versus 12 percent in the cities), 60 percent were undernourished (this was 30 to 40 percent in urban areas). Only 4 percent of farm workers ate meat regularly, 2 percent ate eggs, 11 percent drank milk. During the "dead season" in the countryside, which could stretch to eight or nine months, "families ate roots and bark to stay alive, hunted locusts, lived in woods, in caves."[146] Unemployment affected one-third of the population at some point during each year, reaching much higher in rural areas.

   Holding this political economy together through various means was the state of Fulgencio Batista. The US had blessed and abetted the rise to power of the army sergeant in 1933–34 as an antidote to the progressive measures – abrogation of the Platt Amendment, labor legislation, universal suffrage, and attempts to improve the lives of women, peasants, and children – taken by the government of President Ramón Grau San Martín and revolutionary leader Antonio Guiteras.[147] Batista was forced into "voluntary exile" in Florida when Grau surprisingly won the 1944 elections, returned in 1948, and seized power on March 10, 1952 after lagging in the polls during that year's presidential campaign. If his first administration had been forced into reformist measures and competitive elections by the tenor of the times, in his second he made sure that he remained firmly in control, partly through the vast patronage and corruption networks open to him, and partly through severe repression of opponents. He surrounded himself with a clique known as "the contractors," who plundered the treasury, public works, national lottery, and other patronage niches. He also amassed a fortune estimated at $20 million.[148] The state, it will be recalled, employed one in nine Cubans; Eric Wolf sees it as a kind of multi-class coalition of its own, extending benefits to many social sectors, including labor.[149] This proved an ineffective substitute for political parties, especially as economic problems recurred, elections were perceived as meaningless, and repression mounted. An estimated 20,000 Cubans died between 1952 and 1959 at the hands of the police, army, intelligence service, Bureau to Repress Communist Activities, and hired thugs. The repression lost the government much legitimacy internally, and eventually would be a factor in weakening US support for the regime, as we shall see. The army, however corrupt and low in morale, proved fairly capable of maintaining order in the cities, but even the most indiscriminate repressive practices failed to deter the small guerrilla movement that arose in 1957.[150] Batista's exclusionary, personalized control had weakened his military and alienated civil society, undermining the bases of his rule.

   The deep currents of oppositional culture at work in the Cuban revolution included a long history of rebellions, a tradition of nationalism, and the loose, radical amalgam ultimately fashioned by Fidel Castro's July 26 Movement. The first two fed the third. The Ten Years' War against Spain in 1868–78, the three-sided struggle with Spain and the United States from 1895 to 1898, and the failed 1933 revolution were national-level rebellions that cast long political shadows. The black population remembered with pride uprisings in 1812, 1827, 1843, 1879, and 1912, as well as participation in the other battles. The site of many of these movements was Oriente province, which would play a key role again in the revolution of the 1950s. The nationalist impulse came across in the anthem of the Ten Years' War (now the Cuban National Hymn): "Do not fear a glorious death, for to die for your country is to live. To live in chains is to live overwhelmed by shame and infamy."[151] The growth of US influence and the seeming inability of Cuban politicians to withstand it made both nationalism and democracy appealing to diverse social strata. These perceptions had grown significantly since 1933, and in part this explains the greater success of the 1950s' rebels.

A second major development was the unity ultimately provided by the message of the July 26 Movement. Fidel Castro was influenced early in life by nineteenth-century revolutionary hero José Martí's anti-imperialist nationalism, humanism, and sympathy with the poor, as well as the dramatic political suicide of his idol, Ortodoxo Party leader Eddy Chibás, while on the air at a radio station in 1951.[152] Chibás's death and Batista's coup convinced Castro that more radical forms of struggle were necessary. After the failed attack on the Moncada garrison in 1953, Castro delivered the famous speech, "History Will Absolve Me," declaring at his trial:

What is inconceivable is that there should be men going to bed hungry while an inch of land remains unsown; what is inconceivable is that there should be children who die without medical care; that thirty percent of our campesinos cannot sign their names and ninety-nine percent don't know the history of Cuba; that most families in our countryside should be living in worse conditions than the Indians Columbus found when he discovered the most beautiful land human eyes had ever seen . . .

More than half of the best cultivated production lands are in foreign hands. In Oriente, the largest province, the lands of the United Fruit Company and the West Indian Company extend from the north coast to the south coast . . .

Cuba continues to be a factory producing raw materials. Sugar is exported to import candles; leather exported to import shoes; iron exported to import plows.[153]

While it is true that this text is not socialist in the strict sense, it already indicated clearly enough the blend of elementary social justice and anti-imperialist nationalism that would inform the July 26 Movement founded by Castro while in exile in Mexico in 1955. The Movement proclaimed itself "open to all Cubans who sincerely desire to see political democracy reestablished and social justice introduced in Cuba . . . Young and old, men and women, workers and peasants, students and professionals, can join its fighting groups, its youth cadres, its secret workers' cells, its women's organizations, its economic sections, and its underground distribution apparatus throughout the country."[154]

Though the July 26 Movement's specific positions were often deliberately vague and consciously kept moderate in 1957–58 to attract this diverse social base, it was undoubtedly understood by many Cubans as capable of providing the land reform it openly announced in October 1958, as well as more independence from the United States, and other radical goals.[155] Its ranks contained Marxists and others of more radical inclination than many of the supporting forces in the coalition. Forest Colburn quite rightly notes that the inconclusive debate over whether Castro hid his socialism until 1961 or was a convert after the revolution "obscures how ideas of socialism at the University of Havana and elsewhere in Cuba helped inspire the revolution."[156] There should be little doubt that Castro's radical followers understood his goal as one of relatively deep social transformation well before they came to power. The democratic nationalism and populism of student and middle class organizations, such as Frank País's Acción Nacional Revolucionaria, was of decisive help. Lesser currents that were also present included Catholic social reformism, various tendencies within the labor movement (and more importantly, the general belief among workers that Batista was a dictator), and, late in the rebellion, the transfer of allegiance of a portion of the Afro-Cuban community and its religious symbols from Batista to Castro.[157]

The world-systemic opening that facilitated the success of the Cuban revolution came before the internal economic downturn. Batista, never particularly popular with the US State Department, was still supported well into his reign as the only force that could hold Cuba together, thereby safeguarding US interests there. From 1955 to 1957 the sentiment remained that he should be encouraged to liberalize the system (good advice, in light of our theory). Lower-level State Department criticisms of the regime's brutality were stifled in February 1957 by Secretary of State John Foster Dulles as problematic on the grounds that they "could be interpreted as US intervention [in] internal Cuban affairs."[158] By mid-1957 however a perception was growing that Batista was losing legitimacy in Cuba and might have to be abandoned.

The straw that broke the back of American support for the regime came when oppositional naval officers rose against Batista at Cienfuegos on

September 5, 1957. Batista used substantial US-supplied Military Assistance Program weaponry to crush the rebellion, in violation of American policy that such materiel be used only for external, hemispheric defense against communism. The State Department began to back off from overt support for Batista, worried about "serious criticism from Congress and the United States public."[159] By late 1957 there was deep alarm that Batista might lose control of power, and the US wanted to bring him and the (legal) opposition together to hold fair elections. Batista's failure to do this in February and then June 1958 led to cessation of all arms shipments and a studied neutrality in the civil war under way.[160] In the absence of a third alternative to Batista and Castro, US policy floundered: Some wanted to see free elections under Batista, others (including US ambassador Earl Smith) a renewal of arms to him, while others favored a military junta, and still others felt he could not be supported without losing all credibility in Cuba and the United States. Smith cabled in late March 1958: "At this time it would appear to me that we are in the position of a spectator watching the third act of a Greek tragedy."[161] Meanwhile, the July 26 Movement was well-financed by exiled, local, and American sympathizers, with some help from the Venezuelan interim revolutionary government of 1958, and US diplomats saw no conclusive evidence that it was "Communist-inspired or dominated . . . if we had had conclusive information to this effect, our attitude towards the Cuban situation would have been altered considerably."[162] An eleventh-hour attempt to convene Latin American governments in the Organization of American States in December 1958 met with a lukewarm reception around the continent (with the exception of dictatorships in Nicaragua and the Dominican Republic): Latin American public opinion favored Castro and governments wanted no outside intervention.[163] Though American weapons continued to reach Batista through Nicaragua and the Dominican Republic, loss of support from the country with the greatest stake in Cuba crippled his ability to survive in office, providing a world-systemic opening for the July 26 Movement, whose swift final victory took the United States by surprise. This aspect of events suggests that perceptions of withdrawal of support loom large on all sides (regime, revolutionaries, and the various US actors) and that even slight shifts are significant, because the usual state of affairs is a relatively unproblematic, strong support from the core power (almost always the US).

The internal economic downturn in the causality of the Cuban revolution is of special interest due to its timing. The Cuban economy, so dependent on sugar, was closely tied to the product's price on world markets, output in Cuba, and quotas in the US. World War 2 had brought with it a boom in production and prices for sugar, although hurting other sectors, notably tourism and industry.[164] In the decade leading up to the revolution, 1951 and 1952 were again boom years, in part due to high sugar prices during the Korean War. Both 1953 and 1954 saw downturns in GNP and employment as the war ended; thereafter recovery set in. But, 1956 – the best year for the economy since 1952 – was not a good moment for Castro to launch a rebellion, and most economic indicators were satisfactory in 1957, at least by Cuban standards.[165] However, 1958 started with large losses to tobacco and banana crops due to storms. The progress of the guerrilla war thereafter created its own political-economic dynamic. In the spring of 1958, US losses due to the destruction of the sugar crop by the rebels amounted to $1.5 million. Rail transport began to be interrupted in Oriente province. World conditions now turned unfavorable too, as recession hit the US market and the price of sugar dropped 20 percent. The failure of the April 1958 general strike provided a temporary pick-up through the summer and Havana, in particular, was kept relatively insulated from the turmoil. In the early fall, though, the economy went into an irreversible free fall as the rebels opened new fronts; industry, mining, sales, transport, and tourism all felt the effects of political disruption. By December, economic activity outside Havana had come to a virtual standstill and the coming sugar harvest was in serious jeopardy. Havana itself now was affected by inflation and unemployment, and tourism collapsed. The US embassy reported: "In effect, Castro is creating a general strike in reverse. By playing havoc with the economic life of the country, he is forcing business and industry to shut down and thus shove workers into the streets."[166] The downturn, in the case of Cuba, was unique in that the sugar economy was vulnerable to political unrest. As rebellion spread this meant that the rebels could in some measure *create* the downturn needed to destabilize the government and enlist the population in a struggle for change (this situation was seen to a degree also in China and will be again in Nicaragua and Iran, but in these cases there were prior downturns as well). The theoretical implication is that rebels may start an uprising in the absence of an economic downturn, but popular support and success follow only with its eventual presence.

It remains to chronicle the making of the revolution itself. On the events, which have been well chronicled elsewhere,[167] we may be brief: Castro's forces landed in December 1956 and spent a hard year building strength in Oriente province. In the course of 1958 they achieved growing success against the inefficient army opposing them, and by late in the fall had managed to open other fronts, cutting the island in two. Batista fled precipitously on New Year's Day 1959, leaving the field open to the rebels who secured Havana in early January, bringing his dictatorship to an end.

The more interesting question is: who made the Cuban revolution?[168] Most astute observers acknowledge its urban as well as rural component, making it another variant of our multi-class, populist coalition. Josef Gugler maintains that 60 to 80 percent of the guerrillas were of urban origin, while Wickham-Crowley has it the other way around, guessing that the 600 rebel army members of summer 1958 were 50 to 70 percent peasant, the rest mostly middle class. O. Fernandez Rios puts the social composition of rebel columns at 31–51 percent worker, 31–39 percent peasants, and 39–51 percent "employees."[169] Among the rural population, the squatters of Oriente province provided crucial direct and indirect support, while the sugar proletariat and plains peasants did far less. The July 26 Movement also had a major urban following, especially in Santiago, among workers, the middle classes, and students, organized in the Civic Resistance Movement. The work of Linda Klouzal, Gladys García-Pérez, and Julia Sweig make the diverse, broad nature of the revolutionary forces quite clear.[170] Klouzal notes that "Students worked in student organizations, workers conspired within their factories and unions, peasants assisted rebels within mountain communities, and religious leaders used their influence to get their churches to oppose Batista and to help endangered rebels."[171] Even some large landlords and businessmen were supportive, either out of anti-Batista feelings or as insurance in case of a rebel victory. Women were significant, too, both as fighters (about 5 percent of the rebels) and in urban demonstrations.[172] Afro-Cubans, although held by many to have been pro-Batista, were also found in the rebels' ranks by various observers.[173] The Cuban revolution, then, was made by a substantial multi-class, dual-gender, and to some extent multiracial coalition of aggrieved social forces, and succeeded when internal and external circumstances proved favorable in late 1958. Its legacy – with China's – would be as one of the longest-lived revolutions in world history, and with the deepest degree of social transformation. At the start of the twenty-first century, Cuba remains the one indisputable revolutionary society on the planet. The reasons for this, I suggest, lay partly in the strong presence of the five factors that brought about the revolution in the 1950s, and the successful mitigation of its underlying causes by the revolutionary regime in subsequent decades.[174]

The Sandinista synthesis in Nicaragua, 1977–1979[175]

The third great social revolution in Latin American history has been the Nicaraguan. The best theoretical work done on the subject – by Jeff Goodwin and Farideh Farhi – stresses *political* causation. For Goodwin, the closed nature and international isolation of the Somoza dictatorship, and the broadness of the revolutionary movement, explain the outbreak of revolution better than economic variables or crisis: "The manner in which Central American countries are incorporated into the capitalist world-economy, however one chooses to measure this, does not seem to explain either the incidence or success of revolutionary movements."[176] Farhi does invoke the impact of "combined and uneven development of capitalism on a world scale," but goes on to downplay the economic and social effects of dependent capitalist development since these are found in "almost all peripheral formations," insisting instead that the causes of the revolution be traced to the peculiarities of the dictatorship and the ideologies of all actors involved.[177] I shall be making a case here for the significance of two economic factors – dependent development and a conjunctural downturn – even as I agree with the emphases of Goodwin and Farhi on the state and take note of the special strength of the political cultures tapped by the Sandinistas. Moreover, we must ask why this regime was exclusionary, and what gave rise to political mobilization in the first place?

Nicaragua, with China the poorest and least industrialized of the five countries that experienced a social revolution, has traditionally been primarily an exporter of agricultural products – first coffee, then cotton, cattle, and sugar. The Nicaraguan landed elite was economically divided by region and sector, and politically weakened first by US intervention from the 1910s to the 1930s and then the Somoza dynasty until the revolution. Land concentration in the countryside and the beginnings of industrialization reduced the proportion of the population engaged in agriculture from over 80 percent in 1950 to 60 percent in 1960 and 44 percent in 1977. A heterogeneous middle class arose in the professions, state, and service sector (20 to 30 percent of the economically active), as did a modest-sized working class (16 to 18 percent), with a low level of unionization. Below them was a desperately poor underclass, often unemployed, and in part composed of landless migrants, many of whom returned to the countryside at harvest time. In rural Nicaragua, perhaps 30 percent of the economically active population were self-sufficient producers and owners, another third had some land but needed outside employment, and the rest worked as wage laborers when they could.[178] By 1978, more than "three quarters of the economically active population engaged in agriculture could be classified as landless or poor."[179]

The pattern of dependent development in Nicaragua is arguably less pronounced than in Mexico, Cuba, or Iran, but a strong case can still be made for its heuristic utility as a guide to the transformations accounting for the social structure sketched above. The first point to note concerns the sense in which Nicaragua has been *dependent* on outside forces. The

US has unquestionably loomed large in Nicaraguan history, from outright interventions between 1909 and 1933, including prolonged military occupation, to the backing of the Somoza dynasty thereafter. The US created the National Guard that fought the national liberation revolt of Augusto Cesar Sandino from 1927 to 1933, and handpicked Anastasio Somoza García to lead it; Sandino was murdered in 1934 while in the custody of Somoza's officers. As President Franklin D. Roosevelt is supposed to have said of Somoza in 1939: "He may be a sonofabitch, but he's our sonofabitch."[180] Subsequent US administrations supported his sons Luis and Anastasio Jr., the latter educated at West Point. US control was primarily political, military, and strategic, rather than economic: The proportion of direct American investment was the lowest in Latin America, the economy was locally owned, and trade went as much to Europe, Japan, and Central America as to the US. Still, American multinationals accounted for 76 percent of all foreign enterprises, to which were added in the 1970s a shadier set of investors in hotels, casinos, and tourism.[181]

The second point to be raised is whether the Nicaraguan economy was at any time dynamic enough to be considered a case of *development*, for the country was poor even by Central American standards. This poverty may be traced to the failure of the liberal landowning bourgeoisie to consolidate their hold on society during the reign of José Santos Zelaya from 1893 to 1909. Their project – to commercialize a coffee-based export agriculture – was interrupted and reversed by civil war and US intervention. The period which may sustain the claim to dependent development, however, is from the 1950s to the early 1970s, when agriculture was diversified and commercialized into large-scale cotton exporting as well as cattle, coffee, tobacco, bananas, and sugar. Cotton rose from 5 percent of exports in 1950 to 45 percent by 1965 as the state built the necessary infrastructure (roads, ports, storage) and extended credit for inputs, fertilizer, and machinery. The government did the same to promote tobacco, rice, shrimp, bananas, beef, and other agro-exports, all of which rose dramatically between 1948 and 1979, both in the Nicaraguan context and in comparison with other Central American nations.[182] The Somozas and other investment groups took advantage of the Central American Common Market in the 1960s and 1970s to extend the boom into light industries like food-processing, textiles, tobacco, and cement. Overall growth rates rose from good (5.6 percent annually in the 1950s), to very good (6.7 percent in the 1960s), with an outstanding 10.7 percent a year between 1960 and 1967. Exports rose 11.5 percent a year in the 1960s, tripling in volume.[183] Inflation was kept to 1.7 percent annually in the 1960s. In 1972, a devastating earthquake also touched off a construction boom in 1973–74.[184]

On the other hand, this growth exhibited characteristic limits and negative features as well: Food imports grew to 60 percent of exports in the 1970s, the foreign debt rose from $255 million in 1972 to $1 billion by 1978, and land concentrated in the hands of the top 1.5 percent of landowners who held 41.5 percent of the land, while 78.2 percent of rural families had but 17.4 percent. Per capita income rose from $240 in 1962, to $370 in 1970, and somewhere between $780 and $966 in 1977, but this varies from $5,409 for the top 5 percent to $286 for the bottom 50 percent.[185] Peasants in the interior lost title to ranchers and cotton-growers and worked as a poor, landless proletariat or migrated to the cities to join the ranks of the marginal population there.[186] In the slums of Managua and other cities, really desperate poverty could be found, with disastrous effects in terms of unemployment, health, and housing conditions.

The personalistic, exclusionary nature of the repressive Somozan state hardly needs extensive elaboration. The three Somozas controlled politics from 1933 to 1979, with only brief interludes when they governed behind the scenes, as for two months in 1947 and again in 1963–67. The fraudulent nature of elections is suggested by the returns for 1937, won by a vote of 107,000 to 169! In the process the family enriched itself to the point where the last Somoza was worth over $500 million, controlled 25 percent of agriculture (20,000 square kilometers of land), and as much industrial wealth. If his brother Luis had ruled with a reformist veneer from 1956 to 1967, Anastasio Jr. turned increasingly brutal and corrupt during his tenure. He personified the state in his roles as President, Director of the National Guard, and Supreme Leader of the (Liberal) Party.[187] Repression was the domain of the 7,500-member National Guard, particularly its elite divisions. Although the US trained 4,119 officers between 1946 and 1973, the Guardia never represented a "professional" army, divided into desperately poor conscripts and the corrupt officers and privileged elite units who ran a good portion of the economy, enjoying special schools, hospitals, stores, and residential areas. It lacked training, mobility, and armor as well as morale at the lower levels. In the mid-1970s the Guardia terrorized society, killing at least 3,000 peasants between 1974 and 1977. States of siege and censorship made the task easier. Through all this, the US provided $1.8 million a year in military and $17.3 million in economic aid from 1967 to 1975.[188]

Dictatorship and dependence on the US strongly shaped the emergent political cultures of opposition in Nicaragua. Sandino himself in the 1920s provided the aim – opposition to the oligarchy and US domination and the strategy – guerrilla warfare – later adopted by the revolutionaries. Weber describes the ideals that motivated him as "a form of petty-bourgeois nationalism, tinged with utopian socialist and spiritualist ideology, which grew increasingly radical in the heat of the guerrilla struggle itself."[189] Other elements of his thought drew on freemasonry, theosophy, Zapata's agrarian radicalism, Christian and indigenous millenarian myths, and socialist and anarchist ideas.[190] His army included miners, peasants, workers, and indigenous people. Sandino's ideas and experiences were raised to the status of a national founding myth by the FSLN (the Sandinista Front for National Liberation), created and named for him in 1961. The Sandinismo of the 1960s was also an ideology composed of diverse elements, combining ideas from Sandino's patriotic and nationalist beliefs with liberation theology, Marxism and social justice, and democratic liberalism. For founding member Carlos Fonseca, it was an ideological mixture: "In my own thought, I welcome the substance of different ideologies: Marxism, Liberalism and Christian Socialism."[191] At the popular, political cultural level, for Vilma Espinosa, a rank and file Sandinista, it meant: "the worker learned how to shout, to demand, to fight for his/her things."[192] This sense of empowerment is echoed by union organizer Nestor Pérez, for whom Sandinismo "means people who refuse to live as slaves, people that were against being forced to act against their will, people who raised their heads and believed they had self-confidence and thereby were able and willing to look for their place in the world with dignity and fought to attain it."[193] In recalling the conditions that in his opinion gave rise to the revolution, economist Luis Monjíl makes links between the government, economic problems, and foreign control:

[The Nicaraguan Revolution] came about because in this world there exist social injustices. The Nicaraguan Revolution came about in our country because there were objections. Because this country was tired of a repressive, hateful, racist dictatorship. Because the people were tired of misery, of hunger. That is to say, of foreign forces.[194]

Strategically, the FSLN evolved from a 1960s' emphasis on foquismo to a Vietnamese-style "protracted people's war" in the countryside. Later in the 1970s a faction advocating a mass urban movement arose, while Daniel and Humberto Ortega, among others, favored a third, insurrectional tendency seeking wider alliances and a three-pronged tactic of mass uprising, military offensive, and general strike.

A second stream of oppositional culture flowed out of the liberation theology of the Christian base communities, study groups, and youth clubs that proliferated in the 1970s "to promote spiritual growth and community improvement through social and political action."[195] Both Che and Jesus could symbolize the new human being (and Jesus was "still the most revered example of love and sacrifice among the Christian poor").[196] Paolo Alémán, a working-class activist in the early 1970s, recalls how his participation in Christian movement activities offered a way for him to comprehend Nicaragua's political reality and to encounter the idea of unfair economic distribution as a cause of extreme inequality among classes. The deeper his involvement and understanding, the greater his sense of self-transformation and the more he was impelled to take action. Like other Nicaraguans turned Sandinistas he found a link between his faith and joining the revolutionary struggle in Biblical interpretation. Exposure to radical social and religious literature led to a new self-conception which allowed him to see things differently and motivated him to participate:

because of my [new] formation I assumed a sense of goodness towards humanity . . . [and] because of my religious and revolutionary training I felt more compelled to take action, to do good . . . We used to discuss how in this country there were poor and rich people. This was a new type of conversation for me to the ones I had in my barrio, in my city, about a God that wanted things to remain the same. [In our meetings] it was different because we used to discuss how the rich were rich because the poor were poorer. But how could we then bring about social transformations? [We surmised] that in order to reach power we had to bring down the Somoza dictatorship through armed struggle.[197]

Rural worker José Soto notes: "At the end I managed to understand that the Christian struggle, the struggle of the religious, in other words, the struggle of Christ, meant denouncing the atrocities committed against the public by the government."[198] Nestor Pérez, the working class union organizer quoted earlier, discusses how he was driven to action: "My Christian values 'pushed me' to become a revolutionary, because I was taught to love my fellow man as I would love myself. Seeing my fellow man treated like shit, in poverty, with difficulties, affected me."[199] The political culture of radical Christians led most of them into a strategic alliance with the FSLN, who used the base communities to penetrate the urban barrios, as well as reach peasants and rural wage earners.

To these oppositional cultures may be added the liberal democratic sentiments of a large section of the Nicaraguan bourgeoisie, whether motivated by Somoza's grasping monopoly of economic opportunities or his undemocratic hold on power. The best representative of the latter trend is publisher Pedro Joaquín Chamorro, leader of the Democratic Union for Liberation (UDEL), whose assassination by the regime in January 1978 outraged the population and further alienated the Nicaraguan elite from the regime. The National Patriotic Front organized by the FSLN in February 1979 "united around a twenty-two-point statement of principles with three pillars: national sovereignty, effective democracy, justice and social progress."[200] The desire to restore democracy was shared by all social classes, "propelled by a survival instinct given that the dictatorship was already killing everyone who was young whether or not they were Sandinistas."[201] People simply threw themselves into the struggle "because they were already fed up with the regime."[202]

It was the Sandinistas who came to embody these threads of nationalism, democracy, and social justice, drawing together radical students, religiously-inspired people, and even the liberal-democratic members of the middle and upper classes. As Roberto Hernández, a peasant insurgent, put it:

> I came to understand that Nicaragua wasn't only where I lived, but something bigger; that in all of Nicaragua there were problems . . . We were almost blind . . . We couldn't see the reality around us and then we began to wake up, to see our reality, and we began to struggle. First by means of the church, and then we saw that the best path was the FSLN, which was the only force that identified Nicaragua's real problems.[203]

Nicaragua, in sum, presents probably the clearest case of the strength and efficacy of political cultures of resistance in the making of a multi-class revolutionary opposition, and this speaks to the strength of the Sandinista synthesis.

The beginning of the end for Somoza started with the economic consequences of the December 25, 1972 earthquake, which killed over 10,000 people, displaced 250,000, left 50,000 without work, and destroyed 600 square blocks in Managua. Somoza cordoned off the old downtown, saying Managua would be rebuilt on firmer ground. The new center had "similar seismological properties" in fact, but turned out to be on land owned by Somoza, who made enormous speculative profits, in the process alienating the old small business and service sector: "As one banker put it: 'He's violated the rules of the game that his father and brother had always followed'."[204] The Guardia helped itself to the spoils as well, pocketing with Somoza most of the $300 million in relief funds, and further discrediting its image in the eyes of the people. Though there is some dispute about the precise timing of the economic downturn (Goodwin dates it only to 1978 during the disruption caused by the fighting),[205] there are ample indications that a recession had started to set in by the mid-1970s. The high growth rates of the 1960s and the boom just following the earthquake could not be sustained indefinitely, and seem to have led to a relative decline by the mid-1970s and a sharp downturn produced by the insurrection itself in the latter stages of 1978. Construction boomed in 1973–74 as Managua rebuilt, but slacked off thereafter. Coffee prices rose, but by 1975 a prolonged drought led to a slump that lasted through 1977, compounded by low world prices for cotton, sugar, and meat. After averaging only 1.7 percent a year before 1970, inflation ran at 9.7 percent annually for 1971–76, then hit 11 percent in 1977 and veered out of control during the insurrection by early 1979, when an IMF austerity plan led to a sharp devaluation. And, as in Cuba, by the latter stages of the insurrection, in the first half of 1979 the economy entered into crisis, with capital flight of $315 million, inflation skyrocketing to 75 percent, unemployment reaching 42 percent, exports in decline, and GDP falling by 25 percent for the year.[206] A deep recession then was made through the greed of the regime and the severe disruption brought on by the uprising itself.

The world-systemic opening that facilitated the Sandinista victory was likewise bound up with the timing of the insurrection itself. The US faced conflicting policy imperatives in the wake of its defeat in Vietnam: on one hand there seemed to be a greater need than ever for regional allies to do the frontline work in containing communism; on the other, less trust was placed in authoritarian regimes as viable for that role. Jimmy Carter sought to make human rights abuses in Nicaragua the showcase for his new foreign policy, in part, perhaps, because in 1977 the FSLN still posed no serious threat (Israel, in any case, stepped in to provide up to 98 percent of Nicaragua's arms in the 1970s). Carter thereafter followed a confused policy of rebuke and support, complicated by bureaucratic cross-currents and compromise, as he would in Iran.[207] In January 1978, Somoza arranged the assassination of *La Prensa* editor Pedro Joaquín Chamorro. The US put further restrictions on economic and military aid, and the Nicaraguan elite turned against Somoza: reasoning that no one was safe anymore and resenting his heavy-handed economic competition, they sought a non-revolutionary alternative to the Sandinistas, a desire harbored also by the US government. In August the FSLN staged a widely publicized taking of the National Palace, obtaining $5 million in ransoms for their 500 hostages, and the release of eighty-two prisoners, including founder Tomás Borge. Though US concern to support Somoza now mounted, by November the middle class and elite Broad Opposition Front (FAO) had split up over American interference in its affairs, gradually losing credibility among the public as the FSLN's star rose and Somoza remained intransigent.

As the crisis deepened in early 1979, the US found itself with minimal leverage to intervene, preoccupied with an even more traumatic revolution in Iran and in conflict with key Latin American states like Panama (over the canal) and Mexico and Venezuela (over the oil-induced recession).[208] Much of Latin America opposed any US intervention in Nicaragua, and the Sandinistas received materiel and logistic support from the governments of Costa Rica and Venezuela. On May 14, 1979 the IMF, with US backing, incredibly granted Somoza a $65 million loan; Costa Rica, Panama, and Mexico, however, lobbied against Somoza, with Mexico breaking relations on May 20. On May 28 the five Andean Pact presidents condemned Somoza and on June 16 they recognized the belligerent status of the FSLN. In June and July the final offensive moved to its costly victory (50,000 people – 2 percent of the population – were killed and material damage came to $1.3 billion). The Carter administration's marginal ability to influence the outcome is reflected in the 17–2 vote by the Organization of American States in late June, demanding Somoza's resignation and rejecting a US proposal to send a peace-keeping force to Nicaragua. At the very end, the US called for the expansion of the new governing junta by appointment of a general of the Guardia and a friend of Somoza's. The Sandinistas were now in a position to say no, with strong international backing and no credible alternative for the US to support.[209] The period 1978–79 had proven to be an open world-systemic window of opportunity for their cause.

It remains to ask what social forces, precisely, made the Nicaraguan revolution. The FSLN itself numbered barely 200 members in 1977 but had over 5,000 men and women under arms when they entered Managua on July 19, 1979. Thousands more were active in its various organizations and tens of thousands fought Somoza spontaneously, recognizing Sandinista political authority. The identities of these concentric levels of participation varied somewhat. Roxborough, based on the work of Carlos Vilas, finds that the social composition of "the revolutionaries" (presumably actual FSLN members) was 29 percent students (31 percent in the leadership), 22 percent artisans (17 percent in the leadership), 16 percent workers (18 percent in the leadership), 16 percent white collar (6 percent in the leadership), 7 percent professionals (17 percent in the leadership), 5 percent small traders (8 percent in the leadership), and only 5 percent peasants (13 percent in the leadership).[210] Farhi characterizes the FSLN army as consisting "largely [of] university dropouts."[211] Black maintains that "the core of the insurrection in each town was in the *barrios* of the working class and the migrant rural population."[212] Wickham-Crowley disputes the first part of this, and following Jeffery Paige places emphasis on marginal peasant squatters in the countryside and displaced rural migrants in the towns.[213] Goodwin judiciously notes three social bases: 1) peasants in north-central regions affected by the land enclosures of cattle ranchers, 2) rural workers on the Pacific coast, and 3) "a variety of petty producers and unsalaried workers on the cities – artisans, food vendors, carpenters, shoemakers, and the like."[214] He notes that supporting organizations also included student and labor groups, teachers, left-wing parties, and women's groups, to which we may add in the end the business organizations that joined the May–June general strike. Women made up an estimated 25 to 30 percent of the guerrilla columns' ranks and many important commanders.[215] There were also important spontaneous uprisings by indigenous communities in Monimbó (a suburb of Masaya) and Subtiava (part of León).[216] The Sandinista social base ultimately came to include a wide spectrum of aggrieved social groups and classes, then, spanning small-holding peasants, rural wage earners and squatters, the urban underclass (including recent rural migrants), artisans, students, and radical Christian activists. That they were centered in rural and urban zones where Sandino had been most active and popular in the 1920s and 1930s and where memories of his struggle were kept alive is further evidence of the significance of political cultures of opposition.[217] The Nicaraguan revolution, in sum, reposed on a vast national multi-class coalition of social forces created or adversely impacted by dependent development from the 1950s to the 1970s, unified by Sandinista values and leadership into a broad-based opposition to the Somoza dictatorship.

Iran, 1977–1979: a surprising prototype for the Third World[218]

The mass upheaval that swept Iran in the course of 1978 startled almost all observers, from journalists and diplomats to Iran scholars and theorists of Third World social change: in Charles Kurzman's memorable phrase, it is "the unthinkable revolution."[219] Moreover, the revolution had several notable features: it was the least violent (on the part of the revolutionaries) of the five cases considered in this chapter; it was not made in the name of socialism (nor, however, was it in any straightforward sense "Islamic"); and, with Cuba and China, it has produced a long-lived post-revolutionary state, perhaps the most secure of the three as we make our way into the twenty-first century.

Iran specialists have produced diverse contending explanations stressing: 1) the cultural significance of the revolution,[220] 2) political economy and structural disequilibrium,[221] 3) politics-oriented resource mobilization approaches,[222] and 4) conjunctural, multi-causal analyses, of various emphasis.[223] Among scholars and theorists of revolution, Theda Skocpol found that Iran fitted neither the specific causal pattern she had identified for France, Russia, and China, nor her Third World model, as there was no great elite-state conflict, no mobilized peasantry, and no major shift in world economic or geopolitical conditions to weaken the Iranian state. Instead, she argues for the uniqueness of the Iranian case, advancing various ad hoc mechanisms to explain the revolution (the nature of the rentier state and the existence of a mobilizing ideology and urban network in Shi'a Islam).[224] In this book, I adopt the opposite strategy, taking Iran as prototypical of the causes of Third World revolutions. Let us see how well, then, Iran fits our general model.

The deep structure of the revolution should be sought in the changes experienced in Iranian society between the 1940s and the 1970s, which like Porfirian Mexico presents a textbook case of dependent development. Even after the centralizing modernization project of Reza Shah Pahlavi from 1926 until his forced abdication by the Allies in 1941, the social structure of Iran remained essentially that of earlier in the century, with three-quarters of the population living in the countryside, mostly as crop-sharing peasants, and in the cities, a small emerging capitalist manufacturing sector still outnumbered by a much older craft sector based in the bazaars. Once Reza Shah's son, Muhammad Reza Shah, was secured on his throne after the CIA coup of 1953 he embarked on a policy of land reform and rapid industrialization fueled by oil revenues. A few basic indicators illustrate the "development" side of this: population grew from 14.6 million in 1940 to 33.6 million by 1976, while GNP rose much faster from $3 billion in 1953 ($166 per capita) to $53 billion in 1977 ($1,514 per capita), raising the country from the periphery of the world-economy to a claim on the ranks of the semiperiphery in the language of world-systems theory. Foreign trade skyrocketed from $162 million in 1954 to $42 billion by 1978; gross domestic product grew at 10.8 percent annually between 1963 and 1978, a figure surpassed by only two or three countries in the world.[225]

Given this, we might ask: In what senses was Iran dependent, and what were the negative consequences of this growth? In the shah's much vaunted land reform of the 1960s, over 90 percent of former sharecroppers indeed received some land; however the half of the peasantry that had no sharecropping rights at all received nothing, while the half that did found itself mostly on plots too small to support their families, and up to one-half of all land remained in large landlords' hands. Low incomes, poor health, and limited education remained the lot of those who stayed on the land, with millions migrating to the cities in the late 1960s and 1970s. Inadequate state support and inefficient foreign agribusiness operations slowed growth in the new capitalist agricultural sector to 2–3 percent a year (stagnant given gains in population), while food imports rose to $2.6 billion in 1977. Agriculture was thus a disaster area in itself and contributed heavily to urban discontent through migration as well.[226]

The underside of the showcase sector of modern industry also reveals much about dependent development. Despite impressive growth rates in both the import-substitution and heavy sectors, high tariffs, guaranteed profits, and inflation-driven wage bills meant that very few manufactured goods could be exported. Foreign capital, technology, and management dominated most growth industries, which were either petroleum derivatives or "screwdriver"-type simple assembly of imported parts. Oil and gas had accounted for 77 percent of all exports already in 1963; this rose to 98 percent by 1978, leading to complete dependence on oil revenues to keep the economy functioning, and a corresponding disincentive for the state to tax income effectively. A small but wealthy private sector of capitalists arose, squeezed between the twin leviathans of the state and multinationals, while the working class more than doubled in twenty years to 600–900,000 in factories with over ten workers, a million in construction, 280,000 in transport and communications, 88,000 in oil and mining, and 65,000 in utilities (in all 20–25 percent of the labor force). Pay rose with the oil boom, but work conditions, hours, and urban life generally were still very hard. Another key sector, the educated middle class of professionals, civil servants, and technical workers, also swelled with industrialization and the growth of the state itself. While salaries and opportunities rose, so did inflation and housing costs, with few formal channels open to their political participation.[227]

The petty-commodity urban sector of the bazaar economy contracted somewhat, but persisted in straitened circumstances. Guild artisans were affected by cheap imports and state controls, while the more well-to-do merchants remained important in retail trade but also suffered from the onslaught of chain outlets and modern shopping areas combined with state persecution for their supposed role in causing inflation. The nearly 100,000 members of the ulama (Iran's clergy) lost influence as modern education expanded at their expense, but they continued to draw income from religious taxes and property. Worst off in the cities were the urban marginals who took unskilled work when they could find it (most often in construction), while unemployment, poor diets, and crowded housing made life desperate.[228]

By the late 1970s, significant quantitative and qualitative change had occurred in the hothouse of dependent development. The rural modes of production's share of the workforce declined from 77 percent to as little as 32 percent, the capitalist sector had expanded both in agriculture and urban activities, the tribes had been largely settled, peasants were migrating, the bazaar was hard-pressed. Income inequality was already the worst in Asia in 1970, and deepened as the oil boom skewed it further; inflation rose from under 4 percent annually for 1968–72 to 15.7 percent a year from 1973 to 1977; infant mortality of eighty per 1,000 and life expectancy of fifty-one years had improved but only to the level of India;

undernourishment afflicted 64 percent of city dwellers and 42 percent of the peasantry; illiteracy at 65–70 percent was higher than in India.[229] While the elite enjoyed spectacular luxuries, the middle classes strove to maintain recent gains and the vast majority still suffered widespread hardships in the 1970s at the height of Iran's modernization. As a poor resident of Tabriz said in 1978: "Two kilometers away from our area you can see blocks of luxury flats built for the families of army and air force personnel . . . We do not expect to have those kinds of flats, but we want at least to have water, electricity and work."[230] This was the dark underside of dependent development, and it traces the contours of a social structure with deep, if varying, grievances.

Muhammad Reza Pahlavi emerged as a monarchic dictator by the 1960s, after weathering a democratic challenge in the early 1950s by oil-nationalizing prime minister Muhammad Mussadiq, toppled by a CIA-devised coup in 1953. Oil revenues underpinned the shah's position atop the state and social structure. Revenues jumped almost a thousand times from $22.5 million in 1954 to $20 billion in 1977. This income both paid for state activities and enriched the shah, royal family, and court. By one estimate the Pahlavis controlled one-fifth of the private assets of Iran, with shares in 207 companies involved in agriculture, housing, hotels, autos, textiles, insurance, and publishing companies, among others.[231] Protecting this wealth was the army and the hated intelligence organization, SAVAK. The armed forces grew from 191,000 in 1972 to 413,000 in 1977 (fifth largest in the world), absorbing 25–40 percent of the budget, almost $10 billion in 1978/79. This army was used internally for social control, alongside the police and intelligence services, all trained, armed, or supplied by the United States. SAVAK censored the media, controlled the civil service and government unions, and intimidated political dissidents. Amnesty International estimated there were 25–100,000 political prisoners in 1975, reporting: "No country in the world has a worse record in human rights than Iran . . . The Shah of Iran retains his benevolent image despite the highest rate of death penalties in the world, no valid system of civilian courts and a history of torture which is beyond belief."[232] The majlis (parliament) was made up of two pro-shah parties popularly referred to as the "Yes" and Yes Sir" parties (their formal titles were the Milliyun, or National Party, and Mardom, or People's Party), until 1975 when the shah set up a single ruling party (Rastakhiz, or Resurgence). The shah claimed legitimacy as a progressive, national-minded modernizer; the reality in the popular imagination was as a repressive, US-dominated dictator.[233] The shah and state were autonomous within Iranian society, but dangerously so from the standpoint of their long-term survival.

The United States emerged after the 1953 coup as the undisputed core power in Iran, taking over from Great Britain. In the 1950s and 1960s a "special relationship" was forged between the two countries based solidly on the economic, political, and strategic significance of Iran as a major oil exporter on the Soviet border. Cemented by US aid, oil profits, and investments, this relationship reached a new level in the early 1970s with the Nixon Doctrine of sponsoring strong regional allies to secure a favorable economic and political atmosphere in various parts of the Third World. In a May 1972 secret agreement Nixon committed the United States to supply Iran with any non-nuclear weapons it wanted, an unparalleled degree of cooperation that led to $10 billion in arms sales by 1977 and $40 billion in bilateral trade (mostly arms for oil) projected for 1976–80.[234]

Jimmy Carter would upset this alliance in subtle ways after 1976, providing the world-systemic opening for revolution. As a candidate he criticized American arms policy toward Iran. As president, he announced his intention to base US foreign policy in part on respect for human rights abroad, instructing the State Department to work with human rights organizations to moderate the shah's repression. The shah took all of this quite seriously, reportedly remarking to an aide, "It looks as if we are not going to be around much longer."[235] Despite this, Iran was too important strategically and economically for the special relationship to be abandoned. The flow of arms continued despite some obstruction by Congress. Improbably, Carter developed a strong personal rapport in his meetings with the shah, toasting him in Tehran on December 31, 1977, just one week before serious clashes broke out: "Iran under the great leadership of the Shah is an island of stability in one of the more troubled areas of the world. This is a great tribute to you, Your Majesty, and to your leadership, and to the respect, admiration and love which your people give to you."[236] As late as May 1978 US Ambassador William Sullivan cabled home that Iran was stable and there were no serious outstanding issues between the two countries. In September, Carter himself made a much publicized phone call of support to the shah right after the Bloody Friday massacre of demonstrators. The shah, however, now ill with cancer, continued to doubt that he had full American backing in the crisis.

This mutual ambivalence would continue with even more serious consequences as the revolution unfolded. While Sullivan became increasingly aware of the strength of the revolution in the fall of 1978, Secretary of State Cyrus Vance did not see it, and National Security Advisor Zbigniew Brzezinski advocated the firm hand of repression. Special reporter George Ball advised Carter in December that the shah was finished as an absolute monarch; Brzezinski sent General Robert Huyser to Tehran early in 1979 to hold the military together and help make a coup to save the system if necessary.[237] Carter was ultimately paralyzed by this conflicting advice and his feelings toward the shah, lending "moral" support long past the point of no return (and thus inflaming the opposition), but not enough clear counsel or material support to the shah to deter the revolution.

This non-action of the key world power in the Iranian equation opened the door to the full play of the internal balance of forces, and this helped the revolution from its earliest to its final phases, just as the special relationship of America with the shah from 1953 to 1978 undermined his legitimacy in the first place. The world-system conjuncture, therefore, was favorable to the success of the revolution in the sense that the core world power did not aggressively intervene to prevent it. One may plausibly contend that the revolution would have succeeded regardless, but the cost in human terms would surely have been higher, and unforeseen historical alternatives might have opened up (coup, intervention, different internal coalitions, and so forth).

The other factor at play in the creation of the revolutionary crisis was the downturn that struck the economy after 1976. This had several interlaced contributing causes: the boom and bust cycles of dependent development, internal economic bottlenecks and mismanagement, and the impact of the world-wide recession on Iran. In the euphoria following the fourfold OPEC price rises of 1973–74 the five-year plan for the economy was revised radically upwards and enormous amounts of state expenditures flooded the country. By early 1975, in consequence, "the Iranian economy was almost completely out of control . . . Less and less was being achieved at greater and greater cost."[238] Bottlenecks arose in infrastructure (ports and roads), human capital (skilled and managerial labor), and the technological capacity to absorb so much rapid military and industrial modernization. Then the oil boom burst around 1975, when world demand fell sharply in an international recession in part brought on by the high price of oil itself. Iran's oil exports had fallen 20 percent by the end of the year, leaving a shortfall of $2.7 billion in revenues. The regime fell $3 billion behind in payments on contracts by March 1976; by October the shah was warning: "We have not demanded self-sacrifice from people, rather we have covered them in soft cotton cloth. Things will now change. Everyone should work harder and be prepared for sacrifices in the service of the nation's progress."[239] Two telling indicators at this point were the erosion of business confidence resulting in capital flight of over $100 million a month by 1975–76, and steady increases in consumer prices from 9.9 percent in 1975 to 16.6 percent for 1976 and

25.1 percent by 1977 (rents in Tehran rose astronomically by 200 percent in 1974–75 and 100 percent the next year).

Thus, 1977 would prove to be a hard year. Industrial growth was still positive, but slowed from 14.4 to 9.4 percent. This raises the question of whether the downturn was one of absolute stagnation or merely relative slowing down in the economy; Halliday has argued neatly that "There was no widespread hardship, but the slowing down [of the economy] had political effects."[240] And the effects were real in many sectors: private investment fell 6.8 percent, agricultural production declined 0.8 percent, the state budget was cut by $3.5 billion and borrowing from the West resumed. In January 1977 oil production fell 1.5 million barrels per day as Iran insisted on selling oil for five percent more than Saudi Arabia and the United Arab Emirates, cutting exports and earnings by 30 percent. Unemployment rose as contracts and projects were cancelled or scaled back, affecting urban unskilled labor in particular. The official rate in 1977–78 was 9.1 percent (900,000 out of 9.9 million); rural unemployment ran at around 1–1.5 million people (20–30 percent). Ulama subsidies were cut, adding to grievances among this crucial group. Bazaar shopkeepers continued to be scapegoated and fined for inflation. The new prime minister, Amuzigar, responded to inflation by slowing the economy further, compounding unemployment and other problems of the recession.

These trends underlay the first protests of mid-1977 on, and though moderating somewhat in real terms (if not in the popular imagination) in early 1978, the revolutionary year, political protests would magnify them with strikes, property damage, and growing business disquietude, domestically and internationally. The economic downturn was thus the final structural condition that undermined the shah and touched off the crisis.

A non-violent revolution against a heavily armed dictatorship could not have taken place without remarkable cultures of opposition. Rather than a homogeneous Shi'ism, however, at least five distinct orientations refracted the growing criticisms of various groups in Iranian society. We may label these Khumaini's militant Islam, Shari'ati's radical liberation theology, Bazargan's liberal-democratic Islam, the guerrilla groups' socialism (with Islamic and secular variants), and secular nationalism (both socialist and democratic in form). Taken together, these political orientations inspired and mobilized the various elements composing Iran's multi-class, populist revolutionary coalition.

Ayatullah Ruhullah Musavi Khumaini (1902–89) emerged as the leader of the revolutionary movement in the course of 1978. He had made his reputation as a critic of the government during the agitation over the shah's land and other reforms in 1963, speaking out against "the political and economic exploitation by the West on the one hand . . . and the submission of the regime to colonialism on the other . . . The regime is bent on destroying Islam and its sacred laws. Only Islam and the Ulama can prevent the onslaught of colonialism."[241] From exile in Iraq he issued his 1971 work on Islamic government, an ideological bombshell in that it challenged the legitimacy of monarchy and advocated direct rule by qualified Islamic jurists. Much better known than these ideas were his many criticisms of royal corruption and dictatorship, Western domination, and the economic problems of Iran. Khumaini's militant brand of Islam may also be characterized as populist since it combined progressive and traditional elements and appealed to diverse social strata. With a primary social base among lower-ranking ulama, theology students, and sectors of the bazaar, Khumaini's anti-imperialist bent attracted secular intellectuals, leftists, and workers as well, while his religious idiom appealed to the marginal urban and rural populations whom he extolled as the *mustazafin* (the dispossessed masses). He had the organizational support of a fiercely loyal network of students and ulama in and outside of Iran, including the clerics who were members of the Ruhaniyun-i Mubariz (Organization of Militant Ulama), many of them rising to prominence after the revolution. Together with his uncompromising opposition, personal integrity, and political astuteness, these advantages helped Khumaini emerge as the leader once the movement began.

The chief ideologue of the revolution, along with Khumaini, is generally considered to have been Ali Shari'ati (1933–77). A student of sociology, history, and literature at the Sorbonne from 1960 to 1964, he returned to Iran to teach high school English and then history at the University of Mashhad. After being dismissed for his politics in 1971 he gave enormously popular lectures in Tehran before his arrest, exile, and death in England in June 1977, on the very eve of the revolution. His work was an attempt to fashion a radical, activist Islam fusing politics, social analysis, and religious inspiration. Critical of quietist and status quo ulama, he elaborated a theology of liberation, arguing: "Islam's most basic tradition is martyrdom, and human activity, mixed with a struggle against oppression and establishment of justice and protection of human rights."[242] Recognizing Marxism's utility for analyzing society and history, he felt Islam held the solution, calling ambiguously for an Islamic government that would be a popular, but "directed" democracy. The social base for his ideas lay first among radical university students and intellectuals, but extended also to the more popular urban classes of workers, migrants, and marginals. His writings provided many of the slogans chanted in demonstrations and written on walls in 1978, further proof of his mass appeal, which was second only to Khumaini's.

A third, less influential but still important, trend within Islam was the liberal, democratic version espoused by Mehdi Bazargan (1905–95) and the Liberation (or Freedom) Movement of Iran (Nahzat-i Azadi-yi Iran). A Paris-educated engineer and physicist, Bazargan had been an associate of Mussadiq in the oil nationalization movement. He is regarded as the founder of Islamic modernism in Iran; his works included praise for constitutionalism, democracy, and a mild socialism within a devoutly Islamic framework. He criticized large landownership, called for meeting the needs of the people, and tried to bring progressive ulama and secular forces together, to overcome the weaknesses of the Mussadiq era. Banned in 1963, the Liberation Movement's social base lay in the middle-class strata of merchants, civil servants, students, and professionals.[243]

Similar in social composition were the secular liberal nationalists left over from the National Front, which had been severely repressed after the 1953 coup, reemerged in the 1960–63 anti-shah agitation, and had been driven underground again. Calling for a democratic alternative to autocratic monarchy and an independent foreign policy, its base was limited to a part of the bazaar, white collar workers, and professionals. Resurfacing again in 1977–78, it ultimately subordinated itself to Khumaini's leadership. To its left, the Tudeh (Communist) Party had also suffered a harsh repression after 1953 but managed to carry on in clandestinity and abroad, where it claimed 38,000 members. Its political positions included support for the Soviet Union, calls for a democratic republic, real land reform, rejection of violence, and support for progressive clergy, especially Khumaini. Its social base inside Iran was limited to a portion of the intelligentsia, and in the 1978 strikes it proved to have some supporters in the factories, particularly in the oil industry.[244]

More radical and effective in the anti-shah struggles of the 1970s were the left-wing guerrilla organizations, most notably the Islamic Mujahidin and the Marxist Fada'ian. The Mujahidin grew out of the Liberation Movement in the 1960s, dissatisfied with peaceful methods. Linking Islam and revolutionary activity, they declared their respect for Marxism in 1973 and split over this issue in 1975, with the Islamic wing influenced by Shari'ati retaining the name Mujahidin. Engaging in assassinations and bombings, severely repressed by the regime, the Islamic Mujahidin lost seventy-three members killed after 1975, and the Marxists thirty, including almost all of the original leadership. The Fada'ian was a Marxist-Leninist counterpart that left the Tudeh and like the Mujahidin was based among university students. It too split in 1975–77; it too lost many leaders, and 172 members in all, at the hands of the regime. It was influential in the Iranian Students Association in the United States and had some 5,000 members and many more supporters on the eve of the revolution. Through the Mujahidin and the Fada'ian, many students and intellectuals, and some workers, came to embrace revolutionary and socialist ideas, and provided a small nucleus of armed fighters to staff the final uprising in February 1979.[245]

Out of these several political cultures then, came the ideas and strong emotions[246] that would mobilize millions of Iranians in 1977–79: nationalism, democracy, socialism, Islamic fundamentalism, radicalism, and liberalism all appealed in sometimes complex and overlapping fashion to the various constituencies – young ulama, merchants, students, artisans, intellectuals, workers, and urban marginals – that would loosely coalesce into an urban populist social movement. Without these orientations it is hard to see the shape that a revolutionary movement could have taken; their presence is a significant causal factor in the making of the revolution.

The events moved swiftly. In 1977, on the heels of the shah's mini-liberalization at Carter's insistence and the economic downturn, a series of open letters critical of human rights and constitutional violations were addressed to the government by writers, poets, judges, and lawyers. These were followed by public meetings and university strikes in Iran and anti-shah demonstrations in Washington, DC. A slanderous article against Khumaini on January 7, 1978 in the semi-official newspaper *Ittila'at* led to clashes involving 4–10,000 people (ulama, bazaaris, seminarians) at Qum with between ten and seventy being killed (government and opposition estimates varied widely throughout the year). At the required forty-day mourning interval, on February 18, there were large commemorative processions in twelve cities which turned violent in Tabriz after police shot a young man, provoking demonstrators to attack banks, hotels, liquor and TV stores, pornographic cinemas, fancy cars, and the Rastakhiz offices – all symbols of the regime and Western influence. This event produced the first cries of "Death to the Shah!"; thirteen people died.[247] Between March 28 and 30 demonstrations occurred in some fifty-five places, notably in Yazd where up to a hundred people were killed in a clash that was tape-recorded and distributed throughout the country. Between May 6 and 10 violence broke out again in thirty-four cities, with fourteen to eighty deaths. The shah made public apologies and promised further liberalization and through June and much of July there seemed to occur a lull in protest activity. This was shattered in August during the fasting month of Ramazan. The shah's promise of free elections on the sixth was countered by a march of 50,000 in Isfahan four days later in which one hundred people were killed. Then on August 19 at the oil terminal of Abadan 400 were burned to death in the Rex Cinema under murky circumstances with SAVAK being widely blamed. The rest of the month was marked by more demonstrations and deaths, and the appointment of a new prime minister, Ja'far Sharif-Imami, who promised numerous reforms.[248]

The events of September, which witnessed the massive demonstrations and start of a general strike that sealed the escalation of the conflict, marked the point of no return for the revolutionary process. Ramazan ended on September 4 with a march of 250,000 in Tehran; a half million called for the end of the dynasty three days later. On September 8, known as Bloody Friday, troops fired on crowds around the city; the government claimed eighty-six dead, but bodies in the Tehran morgue had numbers written on them over 3,000. Kurzman argues convincingly that the *total* death toll for all 1978 protests in Tehran was between 700 and 900.[249] From the ninth onward, a series of strikes broke out in the oil industry. These continued into October and spread to the railroads, post offices, newspapers, hospitals, government ministries, and numerous factories. Demands turned increasingly political – for freedoms and the overthrow of the dynasty. Khumaini was forced to leave Iraq on October 6, but landed in Paris where his communications links to Iran and the world were even greater. By late October, oil production had fallen from 5.7 million to 1.5 million barrels a day. November witnessed the closing of universities and the declaration of a martial law government by the shah but under the old and moderate General Azhari rather than a hardliner. Some strikers were forced back to work. The month of December – coinciding with Muharram, the emotionally charged mourning period for Shi'is – proved decisive for the opposition. Millions defied martial law to take to the streets, strikes shut down the economy, American support for the shah finally wavered, the shah himself seemed to lose his remaining resolve.[250]

A period of revolutionary dual power came into effect in January 1979 during the new government of Shapur Bakhtiar, a National Front member who was denounced by that organization for accepting the prime ministership. He was greeted by a continuing general strike and large demonstrations. The shah finally announced on January 11 that he would leave the country on "a vacation," and did so as crowds celebrated wildly on January 16. The next day Khumaini announced the formation of the Council of the Islamic Revolution; on January 19 in Tehran a million people adopted a resolution dethroning the shah and demanding "a free Islamic Republic." Khumaini's return was blocked by the army on January 24 but as more huge demonstrations demanded it, this was allowed on February 1, with three to four million people, perhaps the largest crowd in world history, lining the streets. Khumaini announced a provisional government under Bazargan on February 5, opening a

Table 2.1 *The origins of successful Third World social revolutions*

	Social Structure	State	Political Cultures	Conjunctural Factors	Outcome
Mexico	Dependent development based on rail-roads, oil, commercial agriculture	Díaz's "Bread and Stick" dictatorship	Nationalism, agrarismo, liberalism	US inaction 1910–12 and WW1/Deep recession 1907–08	Broad-based coalition – Complex civil war
China	Beginnings of commercial agriculture and industrialization	Chiang Kaishek/GMD dictatorship	Widespread Communist Party legitimacy	Japanese invasion and Western neglect/Post WW2- hyperinflation	Broad-based coalition – Guerrilla success
Cuba	American-led dependent development of sugar, tourism	Batista's dictatorship	Castro's blend of nationalism, democracy, social justice	US non-support 1958/rebel-made decline 1958	Broad-based coalition – Guerrilla success
Nicaragua	Commercial agricultural boom, 1960s–1970s	Somoza's repression	Sandinista nationalism and social justice/Liberation theology	Carter human rights policy/Post-earthquake crisis, 1972–78	Broad-based coalition – Guerrilla success
Iran	State-led dependent development based on oil	Repressive Shah	Nationalism, democracy, Islamic and secular radicalism	Carter human rights policy/End of oil boom, 1976–78	Broad-based coalition – Unarmed success

Table 2.2 *Causes of Third World social revolutions*

A Boolean Truth Table
(0 = trait absent; 1 = trait present)

			Favorable Conditions			
Cases	(A) Dependent development	(B) Repressive, Exclusionary, Personalist state	(C) Political cultures of opposition	(D) Economic downturn	(E) World-systemic opening	Outcome
Mexico, 1910–20	1	1	1	1	1	1-SR
China, 1949	1	1	1	1	1	1-SR
Cuba, 1953–59	1	1	1	1	1	1-SR
Iran, 1977–79	1	1	1	1	1	1-SR
Nicaragua, 1977–79	1	1	1	1	1	1-SR

complex round of negotiations with the army and its American advisors. A final armed uprising of air force technicians, members of the guerrilla organizations, and ordinary citizens challenged the army between February 9 and 11. The high command then decided to abandon Bakhtiar, who quietly slipped out of the country. At 6 pm on Sunday, February 11, the radio declared: "This is the voice of Tehran, the voice of true Iran, the voice of the revolution. The dictatorship has come to an end."[251] A remarkable revolution had been made by a populist, multi-class alliance of intellectuals, workers, the urban poor, ulama, intellectuals, artisans, and merchants, through a determined general strike and huge demonstrations in which hundreds of thousands of women participated alongside – and in front of – the men.[252]

Conclusion: the route to social revolution

Far from being an anomaly, the Iranian revolution has provided the very prototype of the model I have used in this chapter to understand five great revolutions of the twentieth century. We have spanned eighty years, three geographical regions, and five cases of social revolution – the five strongest cases, in my view. The findings may be summarized in several ways. Table 2.1 shows how the cases "fit" the theory advanced in Chapter One.

Another way to see the pattern among the cases is in Boolean terms, as seen in Table 2.2. This makes clear that it is the presence of all five factors – dependent development, the exclusionary state, widely embraced political cultures of resistance, an economic downturn, and a world-systemic opening – that accounts for the success of these five Third World social revolutions. They may be represented by the equation:

$$\text{Success} = ABCDE,$$

where the capital letters represent the presence of each factor, and this single pattern is found in all the successful cases. It would appear, therefore, that we have found a key to the common causal factors of Third World social revolutions. In the next chapter, we shall extend the scope of our inquiry to cases of anti-colonial social revolutions, looking for further broad similarities with the cases addressed here.

3 The closest cousins: the great anti-colonial revolutions

> The colonial, of whatever society, is a product of revolution; and the revolution takes place in the mind.
>
> V. S. Naipaul[1]

> Revolt is the only way out of the colonial situation, and the colonized realizes it sooner or later . . . The colonial situation, by its own internal inevitability, brings on revolt.
>
> Albert Memmi[2]

The most thoroughgoing of the anti-colonial revolutions which swept the Third World after World War 2 bear striking resemblances to the successful social revolutions just analyzed.[3] The only significant difference between the two types is arguably a relatively minor one: the target in the anti-colonial case was not a local dictator but a foreign, colonial power occupying the country. There is also the fact that the outcomes have not in all cases resulted in such deep social change as to qualify as social revolutions, and therefore this chapter selects those cases which most unambiguously produced social revolutions by our definition's emphasis on substantial social transformation after coming to power. With appropriate modifications that take into account the external locus of political control, we may hypothesize that the same factors are operative as in non-colonial instances.

Thus, for example, a form of dependent development obtained when foreign powers tried to transform colonial economies in certain directions for their own purposes: certainly some urbanization, infrastructural development, and growth in trade and GNP may be expected to occur in such a case (although foreign powers were not as interested in industrialization as an indigenous government would be because they tended to be in the Third World to get access to cheap raw materials such as minerals and foodstuffs, and as new markets for their manufactures).[4] This last qualification explains why these colonial cases do not appear, at first glance, to warrant the term dependent development. I believe, however, that in a certain sense, colonialism – especially settler

88

colonialism – produced a *distinct variant* of dependent development: namely, development for the colonizers, dependency for the colonized. It thus resulted in a segmented society, one part resembling nothing so much as a wealthy, urban, industrialized First World nation, the other nothing more than an impoverished, rural, agricultural Third World one. The two societies coexisting in such close proximity – particularly in the urban shantytowns that arose as pre-colonial social structure was dislocated in the countryside – generated an explosive potential as time passed.

In one remarkable passage in *The Wretched of the Earth*, Frantz Fanon is quite prescient on the colonial variant of dependent development, as well as the repressive nature of the state, and provides us with a few clues to the social psychology of liberation:

The colonial world is a world cut in two . . . In the colonial countries . . . the policeman and the soldier, by their immediate presence and their frequent and direct action maintain contact with the native and advise him by means of rifle butts and napalm not to budge. It is obvious here that the agents of government speak the language of pure force . . .

The zone where the natives live is not complementary to the zone inhabited by the settlers . . . The settler's town is a strongly built town, all made of stone and steel. It is a brightly lit town; the streets are covered with asphalt, and the garbage cans swallow all the leavings, unseen, unknown and hardly thought about . . . the streets of his town are clean and even, with no holes or stones. The settlers' town is a well-fed town . . .

The town belonging to the colonized people, or at least the native town, the Negro village, the medina, the reservation, is a place of ill fame . . . It is a world without spaciousness; men live there on top of each other, and their huts are built one on top of the other. The native town is a hungry town, starved of bread, of meat, of shoes, of coal, of light . . . The look that the native turns on the settlers' town is a look of lust, a look of envy; it expresses his dreams of possession . . . there is no native who does not dream at least once a day of setting himself up in the settler's place.

This world divided into compartments, this world cut in two is inhabited by two different species . . . When you examine at close quarters the colonial context, it is evident that what parcels out the world is to begin with the fact of belonging to or not belonging to a given race, a given species. In the colonies the economic substructure is also a superstructure. The cause is the consequence; you are rich because you are white, you are white because you are rich. This is why Marxist analysis should always be slightly stretched every time we have to do with the colonial problem.[5]

Stretched indeed, but still applied. As Martin Murray notes of colonialism generally, "Indigenous cultures and local customs were thoroughly disrupted, traditional methods of production were undermined, and customary social relations in trade and politics were destroyed. In brief, the entire 'way of life' for enormous populations quickly disintegrated under the impulse of metropolitan military occupation and colonial rule."[6]

The colonial state is also, in some sense, a variant of the repressive, exclusionary state, for although it is not personalist, but collective and bureaucratic in rule, it was often highly repressive and always exclusionary. What Tony Smith has said of Algeria is true in general as well: "A colony won by arms over a people of a totally different culture is maintained by arms until that day when it can assure its predominance by some other means."[7] Because the government is composed of foreigners, the population may be as able (or even more likely) to focus its collective grievances on it as they would on an indigenous dictator. This distinction, too, should not be lost: a collective dictatorship of outsiders is not the same thing as collective dictatorship by an indigenous elite, and, I am arguing, closer to a personalist regime in emotional terms. Strong political cultures of opposition to colonial rule were therefore also likely to arise: ideas of nationalism and independent rule or self-determination were obvious candidates for this role,[8] but so were religion, and, as the twentieth century wore on, socialism, as well as various local myths, legends, and heroic stories of previous struggles against the occupiers. In this sense, Naipaul should be turned on his head: "The colonial . . . *produces* revolution; and the revolution takes place *first* in the mind."

Conjunctural factors likewise turn out to be important. It is interesting to note the cluster of cases that succeeded between 1975 and 1979 – fully seven of our sixteen successful cases (Vietnam, Angola, Mozambique, Zimbabwe, Iran, Nicaragua, and Grenada, with Chile and Jamaica not far off in 1970 and 1972; four of our five anti-colonial social revolutions fall here). This cluster lends weight to the causal significance of both the world-systemic opening and the economic downturn. In this period, Portugal's 1974 revolution is the cause and effect of the Angolan and Mozambican revolutions, and is therefore in part a world-systemic opening that was "made"; the success of Portugal's two colonies then also affects Zimbabwe's prospects. The shifts in US foreign policy that Vietnam opened up helped the class of 1979 succeed (Iran, Grenada, Nicaragua, and [indirectly] Zimbabwe). The economic downturn is also world-wide and in two phases, partly linked to the oil crises of 1970–71 and 1975–77.

Externally, one can find Goldfrank's "permissive world context" at work in various ways: most generally, after World War 2 the growing global sentiment that the era of colonialism was ending, and that Africa and Asia should be – or at least would be – independent (this sentiment

was already "unstoppable" in many colonies by the end of World War 1[9]).
Those countries that resisted this process – France and Portugal foremost
among them, and by default, the US in Vietnam – fell subject to anti-
colonial revolts and international disapproval.

Likewise, internal economic downturns either occurred or, as in Cuba,
the guerrilla struggles themselves helped create these, thus convincing
the colonial power that it was no longer profitable to remain in the country. This confirms our finding that revolutionaries may have begun their
struggles in the absence of such a downturn, but couldn't succeed until
they had disrupted the functioning of the economy enough to produce
the downturn, in some of our cases aided by a world-wide recession, as
noted above.

Finally, in terms of outcomes, the results were sometimes limited precisely because what was being overturned was foreign rule. Thus, once
the colonialists left, an indigenous elite sometimes simply took their place,
though often using revolutionary rhetoric to justify their rule. This limited
type of outcome can be observed in much of the Third World, including, arguably, the new black, majority-ruled nation that has emerged in
South Africa (which will be treated as a political revolution in Chapter 5) –
and I would predict, in the eventual Palestinian state on the West Bank
in Gaza (two outcomes are also determined in part by the collapse of a
socialist model to follow after 1989). A second reason for limited outcomes was, of course, foreign intervention and civil wars, as in Angola
and Mozambique.

Let us briefly survey the five most plausible cases of anti-colonial Third
World social revolutions, as opposed to the many other struggles for decolonization that were not as revolutionary in either goals, strategies, or
degree of mass participation: Algeria 1954–62, Vietnam 1945–75, and
Zimbabwe, Angola, and Mozambique, all in the 1970s. The cases which
concern us, then, cluster in the third quarter of the twentieth century,
presaged by the Chinese revolution and the independence of India from
England in a non-violent struggle at the end of the 1940s.

The Battle of Algeria, 1954–62

The first great anticolonial social revolution of the century was the Algerian struggle against the French.[10] As Joan Gillespie claimed for it in
1960: "The Algerian Revolution stands alone among twentieth-century
revolutions in its complexity."[11] One of the reasons for this is the debates
over why the Algerian FLN (Front de Libération Nationale) won the war:
for conservative critic Edgar O'Ballance, it was not in fact the Algerian

revolutionaries who won, but the French who lost. The former "have been excessively loaded with credit," and won "not by a conventional battle, such as that at Dien Bien Phu, but by political and diplomatic means."[12] The French lacked strong, stable government, made mistakes early, were pressured from all sides (Algerians, French settlers, public opinion in France, and world censure), and "on several occasions came nearer to realisation [of a complete victory] than was apparent."[13] Algerian political economist Mahfoud Bennoune acknowledges that the key to victory was not military prowess, choosing not to emphasize French mistakes but rather the organizational accomplishments of the FLN for its own survival and its popular appeal, combined with the effects of French repression in radicalizing the population.[14] The question that interests us here is the causes of the revolution, and although Eric Wolf included Algeria among his six twentieth-century peasant wars, the revolution has not received much theoretical attention (this is also true of most of the anticolonial revolutions covered in this chapter). Tony Smith is a partial exception among students of the Algerian case, and he offers a useful starting point with a political economic thesis: "the character of the *political* confrontation between the Muslim and French communities in Algeria, begun in its modern form in the 1920's and 1930's, depended in important respects on critical tensions in the country's *economic* development."[15] Let us build on this in the terms of our own model.

Pre-colonial Algeria, a province loosely incorporated within the Ottoman Empire since the sixteenth century, had achieved practical independence by 1719. Its political economy was not feudal, nor tributary, nor commercial, but rather "a military-theocratic pre-capitalist state . . . founded upon a multiplicity of rural tribal or lineage regional subsystems."[16] Many regions were fairly independent of the central authority of the Regency at Algiers, but they were still "loosely linked to the national political and economic organisation of the country through the pre-capitalist marketing networks, religious institutions and pilgrimage."[17] There were rough democratic governing structures in rural tribal society, with "Leaders emanating from the collectivity; freely debated decisions between the heads of different families; a cohesive solidarity of the members of the tribe."[18] Social structure was not classless, but rather broken down into large landowners, peasant farmers, and those with no land who worked for the first two groups. The major urban areas in 1830 were Algiers (60,000 people, down from 100,000 in the eighteenth century), Constantine (35,000), Tlemcen (20,000), Mascara (12,000), Oran (10,000), Miliana (10,000), and Medea (10,000). Primary education and literacy were widespread, perhaps in the order of what they were in rural France at the time, according to French observers of the nineteenth century. Trade with France was already important by the thirteenth century, and France had trading posts ("factories") in Algiers prior to 1830, dealing in wheat, wool, wax, hides, and coral (used to buy slaves from Guinea for the French sugar plantations of the Caribbean). French monopolies came to eliminate Algerian merchants from international trade and explain the decline in the population of Algiers above.

A diplomatic crisis arose as a result of Algerian support for the French Revolution and Napoleon: the Regency had loaned revolutionary France 250,000 francs in 1793, and shipped wheat and horses to Napoleon. When the monarchy was restored after 1815, the government refused to honor the debt or require French merchants to pay their debts. This led to political conflict and military hostilities. At a meeting on April 27, 1827 the French consul Deval claimed that the ruler of Algiers "had struck him with his fan. The French government considered that the honour of France had been insulted, and not only broke diplomatic relations with the Regency but declared a general blockade of the whole sea coast that led to the invasion of Algeria in 1830."[19]

The conquest was marked by violence of a degree "rare in the modern history of colonialism."[20] French troops took Algiers on July 5, 1830, and half of the city's 60,000 inhabitants were killed or driven into exile. In 1846 a military doctor described the city: "Everything one sees here saddens the heart: an indigenous population reduced to the last degree of misery; an innumerable crowd of starving proletarians."[21] Constantine resisted attack in 1836 and cost the French 1,000 men, but it fell in 1837 with thousands of lives lost, both men and women; in 1846, it had 25,000 of its original 35,000 inhabitants, and those that lived there were destitute, as a French official put it: "Constantine is horrible to see; all buildings are falling in ruin, and half of the houses that were there five years ago have been demolished. The indigenous population is in a terrifying state of misery and deprivation."[22] Mascara, capital of the leader of the first resistance, Abd el Kader, was completely destroyed in 1835, with the Duc d'Orléans calling it "the most hideous spectacle I have ever witnessed. I had never imagined what a sacked city, where numerous inhabitants have been massacred, would be like."[23]

The countryside resisted the French vigorously, first under Abd el Kader from 1832 to 1847, then in 1871–72 under a land-holding chief, El Moqrani, who revolted because he was unable to pay off loans he had taken to feed his peasant followers during the famine and epidemic years of 1866–70. His defeat led to further expropriation and punitive tax payments: "The terrible memory of these years when 'justice and truth disappeared,' 'brother was set against brother,' and the [pro-French] chiefs 'grew rich through treason' has remained green in Kabyle chants recorded half a century later."[24] By 1871, the French scorched earth policy inaugurated under General Bugeaud had carried the day: "In 1841, Tocqueville observed with sarcasm that he had to report 'from Africa the afflicting notion that at this moment we are making war in a manner more barbaric than the Arabs themselves'."[25] The peasants who participated up to 1871 were ruined, and 665,591 hectares of their land was taken, to which an indemnity of 68 million gold francs was added. In all, French estimates showed that between 1830 and 1851, 3,336 men were killed in battle, and 92,329 died in hospital, while the total Algerian population is estimated to have declined from 3 million in 1830 to 2,462,000 by 1876.[26] These numbers indicate a massive resistance to colonization, and the descriptions of the conquest and subsequent repression of revolts serve as a precursor to the revolution of the 1950s.

Algeria thereafter became a French colony, one in which a substantial number of French citizens settled, occupying the top administrative positions and acquiring control of the best farm lands, where wine and grains were grown for export to France. Smith considers it "since 1830, the most important colony of France."[27] By the middle of the twentieth century there would be two separate societies in Algeria – an urban, French-educated and French-speaking wealthy settler society, and a rural and urban, Arabic – and Berber-speaking, impoverished Muslim Algerian society (hereafter I will refer to the "French" and "Algerian" populations, respectively). These two societies thus represented the two sides of dependent development, with the benefits of development for the French settlers, and the negative features of dependency for the Algerian population. Bennoune writes of the "coercive restructuring of Algerian society along capitalist lines, resulting in the pauperisation and proletarianisation of the rural population and the development of a colonial agrarian capitalism," adding that "The colonial economy was incapable of satisfying the basic needs of the Algerian population: employment, shelter, medical care, education and transportation."[28] For Markus McMillin, following John Entelis, "The result of colonialism was two completely polarized communities. The Algerians were 'restricted, deprived and humiliated . . .' while the colons, 'possessing advanced technology, efficient organization, and a strong army enjoyed all the advantages of prosperity'."[29] These are but different ways of characterizing the process we have theorized as dependent development.

The key to this project was agricultural expropriation on a massive scale, starting in the 1840s. Tribes were broken up and dispersed. Religious land was expropriated nearly in its entirety. Peasant communities lost their best lands through various means. By 1951, 70 percent of Algerian landowners had less than ten hectares, below the minimum needed for subsistence: "On the whole, the Algerian rural communities, which represented 70 per cent of the total population, received only 18 per cent of the national income. The settlers, who comprised 10 per cent of the total population, acquired 47 per cent of the country's income."[30] The French had over 2.7 million hectares of the best land, and their farms averaged 124 hectares in size, while Algerian farms averaged less than 12.[31] The data on agricultural wages are somewhat contradictory, but generally from the 1930s to the 1950s an Algerian rural worker made about half the daily wages of a French one.[32] This process of French expropriation and Algerian immiseration was accompanied by a new pattern of development based on mechanized agricultural exports of wine, cereals, fruit, and vegetables, with wine accounting for half of the exports and cereals another fifth. As Bennoune puts it: "the function of the colonial economy of Algeria was to export raw materials and manpower to the settlers' metropolis and to import manufactured consumer goods."[33] The total trade of Algeria had grown to $1 billion annually by 1954.[34]

Colonial development was also marked by extensive urbanization without a corresponding degree of industrialization. As total population grew to nine million in the 1950s, of which one million were French, the cities grew apace. Some 1.5 million people were pushed by poverty from the countryside between 1930 and 1954, raising the Algerian proportion of the population to "a decided numerical majority in the towns."[35] Although the French made little effort to industrialize Algeria, industry's share of total investment gradually rose to 36 percent in 1948–54, the growth rate for industry to 4.7 percent from 1931 to 1955, and the value of industrial production from forty-four billion old francs in 1930 to 170 billion by 1955. This growth was led by iron ore, phosphates, and hydrocarbons, with local capital concentrated in food processing, textiles, and construction materials. Industrial development had briefly flourished during World War 2 but failed again as Algeria was reintegrated into global markets thereafter. By 1955, industry still represented just 10 percent of GDP and in 1958, accounted for only 7.8 percent of the labor force. As in agriculture, French wages were roughly double those of Algerians, while 47 percent of the 1.6 million urban Algerians were unemployed in 1954.[36]

The negative effects of this process for the Algerian population were apparent. The 1954 census showed 320,000 school-age children out of 1.9 million (22 percent) attending school, with 85 percent of the population illiterate, including 95 to 98 percent of all Algerian women.[37] With 884,000 inhabitants in 1957, Algiers was technically the second largest city in France; of its 293,470 Algerian inhabitants, at least 86,500 lived in the shantytowns that had sprung up since World War 2, while the rest were crowded into the casbah (the Arab quarter of the city).[38] Income distribution, the tax burden, and (as we have seen) wages were dramatically skewed in favor of the French settlers. The 1955 Maspétiol Study showed the vast majority of Muslims (5,840,000) averaging $45 a year, with about 50,000 at the top earning $502. Another 1,600,000 urban Muslims averaged $121, and 510,000 wage earners, craftspeople, and businessmen averaged $240. On the French side, 440,000 averaged $240 as wage earners, 545,000 $502 as the middle class, and 15,000 $3,181 as the wealthiest group.[39] Smith notes "On one point at least there seems agreement: at the time of the Revolution the Muslim Algerians were a desperately poor people," registering per capita production declines in the key sectors of sheep, wheat, and barley, displacement from the best lands, and demographic growth – at 2.8 percent annually "as high as any in the world."[40] Urban unemployment and rural underemployment were endemic at 900,000 out of 3.5 million in the labor force, and another 400,000 Algerians were working as migrant laborers in France, an important social base for nationalism and revolution.[41]

The state was dominated completely by the French, and while not personalist it was certainly exclusionary of the Algerians. In Bugeaud's 1830s conception, the colonial state was a military state, undergirded by an unself-conscious racism: "[C]ivil colonization . . . will become very military, just as military colonization will become civil . . . I therefore make no differentiation, with regard to the system of government, between the military colony and the civil colony."[42] He spoke of the "necessity to dominate the country in order to colonize it," for "the population is poor, warlike, intrepid, ignorant and [is] in that state of civilization in which man with all his savage independence is more elusive."[43] As we have seen, though there were poor, working-class French settlers[44] and a few Algerians with the income of the French middle class, it was racism that cemented the political pact of domination. Exclusionary, repressive discrimination extended to education, land tenure, wages, and taxes, and soon led to the division of the colony into the two separate, unequal societies that together constituted the colonial pattern of dependent development. Settler racism is well conveyed by the depiction of Jules Roy, who grew up in the country:

One thing I knew because it was told me so often, was that the Arabs belonged to a different race, one inferior to my own. We had come to clear their land and bring them civilization . . .

"They don't live the way we do . . ." The sentence drew a chaste veil over their poverty. What might have seemed the worst misery was merely a refusal to sleep in beds, to eat as well as we did, or to live in solid houses, under roofs. Yes, their happiness was elsewhere, rather, if you please, like the happiness of cattle, and I suppose we always regarded them like the oxen we treated well enough but which could scarcely inspire compassion. "They don't have the same needs we do . . . ," I was always being told. I was glad to believe it, and from that moment on their condition could not disturb me. Who suffers seeing oxen sleep on straw or eating grass?[45]

The legal *Code de l'Indigénat* was enacted in 1881 and lasted into the 1940s. According to Entelis,

an Algerian was forbidden to speak against France and its government; Algerians were prohibited from keeping stray animals for more than 24 hours; natives were not allowed to become school teachers without proper authorization nor were they permitted to travel from one place to another without a visaed permit . . . [other infractions included] delay in paying taxes, giving shelter to strangers without permission, or holding gatherings of more than twenty people.[46]

Napoleon's 1865 decree made Algerians French subjects, but not citizens. To achieve the latter they had to abandon Islam: "This was totally unacceptable. Only a few thousand Algerians ever accepted giving up Islam to have political equality."[47] The French assault on Algerian culture entailed the conversion of many mosques into churches, including ninety-eight of 106 in Algiers.[48]

The political system, while undergoing complex cosmetic changes over the life of the colony, resulted in a disenfranchisement that was "virtually total" for the Algerian population.[49] There were separate European and Muslim electoral colleges, which by 1946 elected the same number of deputies to the French National Assembly, but there were eight times as many Algerians in the population. Only property owners and civil servants among the Algerians could vote. Village assemblies were suppressed and native administrators – referred to as "Ben Oui Oui" (yes men) – were appointed.[50] There was thus from the beginning a small local elite that collaborated with the French, especially to control the rural areas, in exchange for leaving their holdings intact.[51] Muslim nationalists scored "sweeping victories" in the 1947 municipal elections; this would be followed by massive fraud in the elections of 1948 for the Assembly, including "'stuffing' election boxes, threatening voters, and outright arrests of Muslim nationalists," leading many to conclude that elections would never deliver equality.[52] As for repression, the conquest set the tone, followed by the suppression of revolts through 1871, and the horrible massacre at Sétif in 1945 described below.

Political cultures of opposition came to crystallize around ideas of national independence from French control, Islamic identity, and radical ideas about socialist egalitarianism. Alf Heggoy puts it this way:

Algeria's history in the twentieth century reflects a synthesis of Muslim, African, and European characteristics. Algerian nationalism combines Islamic and pan-Arab ideologies taken from the Middle East with political, cultural, social, and revolutionary concepts borrowed from France, particularly from the French Communists, and native egalitarianism as well as other largely Berber attitudes and emotions.[53]

A number of organizations would emerge from the 1920s on to elaborate, give form to, and carry forward the radical nationalist synthesis.

The first of these was the Etoile Nord Africaine (ENA), founded in 1925–26 to uphold "the material, moral, and social interests of North African Muslims."[54] It drew its members from Algerians working in France. Messali Ahmed Ben Hadj became its leader in 1927 and moved it to the left, embracing the "trinity of Islam, nationalism, and social reform," calling for the complete independence of Algeria, Tunisia, and Morocco, and demanding the return of all confiscated land.[55] Banned in 1929, the ENA still managed to establish itself in Algeria by 1933. Its Islamism also made it effective in the countryside, especially in Kabylia, the mountains of northern Constantine, and the Aurès, all later strongholds of the revolution. Meanwhile, the Association of Reformist Ulama had been founded by Sheik Abdelhamid Ben Badis and a group of religious scholars in 1931, pressing for a return to a "pure" Islam, denouncing French-appointed ulama and the worship of saints and shrines. They set up schools in which children were taught the goals of equality and improved economic conditions, beginning each day with the chant: "Islam is my religion, Arabic is my language, Algeria is my country."[56]

In 1937, Messali and the ENA broke from the French Communist Party (PCF) as the latter counseled waiting for the revolution in France, to form the Algerian Popular Party (PPA), in aim and inspiration "only a change of name."[57] After the PPA was banned in 1939 – Messali spent the years 1941 to 1945 in prison – it was reborn once more shortly after World War 2 as the above-ground Mouvement pour la Triomphe des Libertés Démocratiques (MTLD), supported by workers, some students, and intellectuals. The movement was favored to win the Muslim vote in the 1948 elections. After that fraud, some of the militants within its recently formed paramilitary, the Organisation Spéciale (OS), including Ahmed Ben Bella, Hocine Ait Ahmed, Belkacem Krim, Mohammad Boudiaf, and Abdelhafid Boussouf began to "explore the possibilities for revolutionary action."[58] The OS was shattered however in 1950 by the French, and individual activists either fled abroad or into the Aurès mountains. After this, the MTLD split, with its Central Committee opting for a nonviolent path, and Messali objecting to this; he was arrested and

deported to France in 1952.[59] Those who wished to continue the clandestine struggle then formed the Comité Révolutionnaire pour l'Unité et
l'Action (CRUA) from twenty-two former OS members in 1954, most of
them from modest origins and without a university education. It was they
who launched the insurrection on November 1, 1954 and proclaimed the
Front de Libération Nationale.

In terms of building a broad political culture of opposition, the massacre at Sétif in 1945 "decided the revolution of 1954."[60] On May 1,
1945 between eight and ten thousand Muslims gathered to celebrate the
end of the war and to demand equality with Christians, as well as the
release of political prisoners, including Messali Hadj. The police shot a
demonstrator, and the crowd then attacked Europeans, killing several.
As the news spread over the next few days, other French farmers were
attacked and perhaps 100 French citizens were killed in all. The French
killed at least 6,000 (and perhaps as many as 15,000) in quelling the
rebellion.[61] The bloody repression at and after Sétif in 1945 intensified
Algerian nationalism. The poet Kateb Yacine recalls:

My humanitarian feelings were first outraged by the ghastly sights at Sétif in
1945. I was sixteen years old and I have never forgotten the shock of that merciless butchery which took thousands of muslim lives. There at Sétif the iron of
nationalism entered my soul. There have been, it is true, other factors: the economic and political alienation of my people in their own country, for instance.
But it was particularly this betrayal of the values which the French had given us
which opened my eyes.[62]

In the end, by 1956, all the major organizations and almost all sectors of
Algerian society, rural and urban, across the class and gender spectrum,
were in active solidarity with the FLN's nationalist liberation goals. The
Manual of the Algerian Militant, written in 1957 for FLN militants by
Laroussi Khelifa (later Algeria's first ambassador to the United Kingdom)
"clearly points to socialism" in its economic platform, with promises of
doubling the standard of living in five years, placing "all the wealth of the
nation . . . at the service of the people of the country," full employment
for Algerians at home and to attract those abroad to return, the building
of schools and education for all, a comprehensive state health sector, and
"bright, new, attractive housing built in the towns and villages, and each
family provided with a decent home."[63]

In terms of the foundations of oppositional political culture, Kielstra
argues that peasants were motivated by "a general desire to improve
their economic position and to defend the Islamic character of Algerian society, which they shared with their urban proletarian fellow party
activists. Among the urban activists the pauperization of a large part of the

rural population constituted an argument against French colonialism."[64] There was also the emotional current provided by Frantz Fanon's theory of the "cleansing force" of violence, which "frees the native from his inferiority complex and from his despair and inaction; it makes him fearless and restores his self-respect."[65] Finally, the gendered counterpart of this was the role played by radical Muslim women throughout the struggle. Wolf, following Bourdieu (and, we might add, Fanon), notes that the veil came to symbolize the "refusal of reciprocity," and that this lay at the roots of Algerian nationalism.[66] McMillin concludes, very astutely: "Altogether, the most important culture of opposition in Algeria's anticolonialist revolution was the vague and all encompassing term 'nationalism.' It came to unite all the groups and classes who supported Algerian independence, even when violent action was the only means of achieving this goal."[67] From these complex cultural foundations arose the idioms, emotions, and networks of revolt.

Both internal economic downturn and external world-systemic opening came in several phases. The downturn may have started as early as 1930, and lasted for a whole generation. Bennoune puts it this way: "colonial development had engendered a profound general crisis. Indeed, agriculture, which formed the basis of this colonial economy, had been stagnating since the 1920s. In the absence of industrialization, the entire society was being driven into an impasse."[68] The whole period from the Great Depression to the outbreak of the revolution was characterized by "the stagnation of agricultural production and slow industrial growth."[69] French reluctance to industrialize led to economic stagnation. "The logic and exigencies of the colonial system were thus bound to generate a severe socio-economic crisis which accentuated the political antagonism between the colonised and the colonisers."[70] Is this a problem for the thesis of dependent development? I think not. Rather it reflects the peculiarities of the colonial pattern, with its bifurcation into development for the colonizing population and dependency for the colonized. Economic downturn, then, had two rhythms: one a generation long, the consequence of dependent colonial development, for the Algerians, and one more short term, for the French.

In the short term leading up to the revolution, Gillespie notes "salaries in both agriculture and industry did not keep pace with rising cost of living in the five years preceding the rebellion."[71] Wolf adds: "During World War II and after, harvests were poor, wine production was down, and livestock was lost in large numbers."[72] Once the insurrection started, the downturn was sharpened by the dislocation of the events, a pattern we have found in China and Cuba. McMillin sees this as political rather than economic, and caused by French repression, leading in turn to the political strength of the FLN. He therefore simply refers to the "internal crisis," noting "This is a significant finding; unified opposition to the state need not come only from economic frustration."[73] But it is hard to separate the two. He notes that the resettlement campaign caused "economic dislocation" for the Algerian peasantry. Those who migrated to the cities lived in shantytowns. McMillin also notes a downturn *in France* due to the cost of the war. The disruption of everyday life by the FLN in the cities and the growing unrest in the countryside together constituted a kind of economic downturn that made the French question the continued viability of holding onto their colony.

A relatively "long" world-systemic opening also greatly contributed to this sentiment; the events that produced a world-systemic opening in Algeria, as in other colonial cases, were strikingly dramatic. In 1954, France was still recovering from World War 2 and suffering inflation and instability, Tunisia and Morocco were moving toward independence, and the metropole had just been defeated in Vietnam, where the debacle at Dien Bien Phu represented the most "devastating defeat inflicted on a Western regular army by a colonial 'resistance movement.'"[74] The FLN garnered substantial international moral support, from its seating at the Bandung Conference of non-aligned countries in 1955 to the UN's halting recognition of Algeria's right to self-determination. Material aid came from Nasser's Egypt, Syria, and the neighboring French ex-colonies of Tunisia and Morocco, who achieved their own independence without violence in the course of the Algerian war.[75]

The use of torture – "the war without a name" – to suppress the urban attacks of the FLN in Algiers in 1956–57 "tore at French unity." One French officer wrote: "I am more disgusted than ever, Germans were only kids compared with us."[76] The bombing of the Tunisian village of Sakiet on February 8, 1958 shocked international opinion and contributed to the fall of the Fourth Republic. By 1960 there was widespread popular sentiment in France against the war, coming from trade unions, youth, and intellectuals. The "Declaration on the Right of Insubordination in the Algerian War" was signed by 121 intellectuals, including Jean-Paul Sartre, on September 5, 1960. Seventy thousand Algerian workers marched peacefully in Paris in October 1961. The police arrested at least 12,000 and deported 1,000 to Algeria; "no one knows how many were secretly liquidated."[77] This prompted the liberal Christian journal *Esprit* to openly ask its readership "to demonstrate in groups, to oppose racism, to alert civil and spiritual authorities, to form associations, to multiply protests, and incessantly to call for peace in Algeria."[78] By early 1962, more than 500,000 would demonstrate in Paris against the war. Michel Crouzet argues that the intelligentsia as a whole were massively mobilized against the war, making significant analyses of the rise of nationalism and the inevitability of independence, and that the antiwar intellectuals won the "battle of the written word . . . hands down."[79] Philip Dine argues that graphic photos of bodies in *Paris-Match*, which had already distinguished itself in the coverage of Dien Bien Phu, played a role in influencing French public opinion:

> The images of destruction, insecurity, and even military brutality presented by this news magazine may well have had a greater impact on its eight million readers, and thus the metropolitan popular imagination, than all of the previously mentioned displays of intellectual *angst* put together. Indeed, as Jean-François Sirinelli has suggested, the front-page photograph of little Delphine Renard, her face covered with blood following the explosion of an OAS bomb intended for André Malraux, de Gaulle's Minister of Culture, probably did more for the cause of Algerian independence than any petition, manifesto, or committee.[80]

The intransigence of the French settler population, which several times led to insurrections against France in Algeria, and was given expression by the actions of the OAS (the Secret Army Organization), thus contributed its part to the world-systemic opening. Ultimately, events inside France and Algeria, coupled with international opinion, pushed de Gaulle's position from "an Algerian Algeria" (March 5, 1960), to "an Algerian republic" (November 4, 1960), and finally "a sovereign Algerian state" (April 11, 1961).[81] As Wolf puts it: "The government in Paris successfully coped with the threat of instability which emanated from the colony; but it also decided to end that threat in the future by ridding itself of a colony that had become an economic, military, and political liability."[82]

The war itself went through several phases. After the outbreak of urban fighting in 1954, France declared a state of emergency. By April 1956, the French were estimating FLN strength at 8,500 fighters (the ALN) and 21,000 "auxiliaries." The French brought in 250,000 soldiers and conscripted another 200,000. The FLN, limited by this in the countryside, turned to urban actions in late 1956, recruiting 4,000 supporters among the 80,000 residents of the casbah. By October 1957 they had been effectively wiped out by a ferocious counter-insurgency response led by the Tenth Paratroop Division under General Massu, but they had shown the population that it was possible to resist the French state, and the struggle spread again to the countryside, where it was harder for the French to repress it. The FLN turned to building an external army in Tunisia and Morocco, which reached 25,000 men by late 1957, compared with 15,000 inside Algeria. The French were successful in sealing off the two borders. This shifted the struggle back inside the country. In

1960, the movement revived and there were powerful demonstrations in Algiers on December 10 to the slogan of "Vive l'Indépendence."[83]

Meanwhile, on May 13, 1958 there was an attempted insurrection within the French army; the insurgents stated they would hand over power only to de Gaulle, and the National Assembly appointed de Gaulle prime minister on June 1. After voters approved his new constitution and the Fifth Republic, de Gaulle was elected president in December 1958. The following September, de Gaulle proposed self-determination as the solution. General Massu was dismissed on January 18, 1960, one day after making statements to a German newspaper about never giving up Algeria. Settlers took to the streets in Algiers on January 24, setting up barricades, and fourteen policemen and six civilians were killed in the fighting. On January 29 de Gaulle appealed for the loyalty of the army and declared self-determination "the only policy worthy of France." De Gaulle asserted firm control over the army and Algerian policy after this. When he visited Algiers in December 1960 and was met with massive Algerian demonstrations and street violence, he came to see independence as the only solution. A January 8, 1961 referendum showed overwhelming support for self-determination in France, and negotiations started with the FLN. After another failed military-settler revolt in April 1961, the stalemate dragged on one more year before the Evian Agreements were completed on March 18, 1962. On April 8, French voters gave 90 percent support for the Evian Agreements in a referendum; in Algeria, the referendum was passed on July 1 and independence declared on July 3.[84] The costs were high: French estimates place the number of Algerians killed at 141,000, while the FLN puts the figure as high as 1.5 million (plus two million displaced into camps); Schalk judges the figure to have been something over 500,000 Algerian lives lost.[85] Four and a half million Algerians were unemployed at the war's end.

Who had made the revolution? Kielstra has done one of the most carefully reasoned analyses of this question, concluding:

Both logical inference and the available evidence point to the fact that the Algerian Revolution was initiated and led by a political network of people of urban (lower) middle class origin, while it was fought mainly by young, unemployed men from the rural proletariat.[86]

Thus, in his view, the Algerian revolution was not a "peasant war," but drew on the fact that "in the colonial period at least, about half of the population proletarianized," some in the cities (but with links to the countryside), some in the countryside itself. Lyotard notes that the urban strikes and demonstrations involved "on the one hand, all the wage earners (domestics, blue- and white-collar workers in the private and public

sectors, functionaries, teachers, etc.) and, on the other hand, the shop-
keepers and artisans – consequently, the quasi totality of the Muslim population of the cities."[87] The FLN forces included 10,000 women, some
as fighters, some as couriers, most in support roles as nurses, cooks, and
launderers.[88] The first great anti-colonial social revolution of the twentieth century was built on these powerful social bases and it triumphed by
virtue of the same causes as had the great social revolutions.

The Angolan revolution, 1960s–1975: from liberation movement to civil war

The Angolan revolution against Portuguese colonialism, along with its
close relation in Mozambique, heralded the opening of a region-wide process in southern Africa which would continue with Zimbabwe in 1979 and
culminate in the downfall of apartheid in the 1990s.[89] This set of cases
allows us to further refine our understanding of the nature of dependent
colonial development, and the two anti-Portugal movements will illustrate the impact that national struggles can have on the world-system,
for they represent the striking circumstance of a Third World revolution
touching off a First World one in the metropole and thereby contributing
decisively to the world-systemic opening that would facilitate the seizure
of power. Human agency again looms large, acting back on the economic
and political macro-structures that would otherwise contain it.

Angola suffered a harsh dependent colonial development, with roots
in the slave trade and in classical colonialism, refracted through a weak
imperial power, Portugal, which was nevertheless no less tenacious in
holding onto that power than France. Bantu-speaking peoples had established a number of kingdoms and long-distance trading networks in the
region, with the Kongo kingdom at its height from the mid-thirteenth
to the mid-fourteenth centuries. The arrival of the Portuguese fleet at
the mouth of the Congo river in 1482 started a process of contact by
missionaries, traders, and ultimately military expeditions.[90] Luanda was
settled in 1605 as a key port in the slave trade, which lasted until 1836
(slavery itself was abolished only in 1878). By one estimate, more than
four million people were taken into slavery between 1580 and 1836 from
Angola and the Portuguese Congo, bound mainly for Portugal's Latin
American colony, Brazil.[91] A population estimated as high as 16–18 million in 1450 was reduced through slavery, wars, forced labor, and their
attendant social dislocations to 8 million in 1850 and only 4.8 million
in the 1960 census (including 268,903 Europeans).[92] This was divided
among three principal groups whose relations were exacerbated by the
inter-ethnic wars of the slave trade – the Bakongo (whose language is

Kikongo) in the north (some 25 percent of the total population until many were forced into exile after the 1961 uprisings), the Mbundu in north-central Angola, stretching inland from Luanda (whose language is Kimbundu, representing another 25 percent of the population), and the Ovimbundu on the central plateau (whose language is Umbundu, and who constitute about one-third of the population).[93]

Extensive Portuguese control did not exist before 1900, and was limited to the port enclaves of Luanda and Benguela. The far vaster territory of what became known as Angola was only demarcated at the Berlin Conference in 1884, and it took the next several decades to establish an "effective occupation" in the face of Angolan resistance.[94] By the time the Portuguese monarchy fell to revolution in 1910, the main source of profits had shifted from the slave trade to the extraction of rubber, cotton, and coffee through a contract labor system that still encompassed one-tenth of the population in 1954.[95] The nature of the system is well captured by de Andrade and Ollivier:

First, in production, an investment policy directed almost exclusively at developing exports. Second, a self-sustaining budgeting policy aimed at making Angola bear the burden of total current expenditure and public investment. Finally, the fierce exploitation of the indigenous population, forced to work in all sectors of activity at extremely low income levels.[96]

Heimer refers to the mechanisms of "commercial-administrative extraction of African cash crops and cattle, plantations and cattle-raising by individual settlers and share-holder companies, extraction of mineral and non-mineral raw materials."[97] An upsurge in coffee production occurred in the 1950s when the Korean War touched off a commodity boom that led to rising prices for the 50,000 Angolan small farmers who grew a quarter of the crop and the European plantations that controlled the rest.[98] Minerals and agricultural products bound for Europe and North America accounted for the vast majority of exports by 1960: coffee (35 percent), uncut diamonds (14 percent), and sisal (11 percent), with another 25 percent from maize, cotton, sugar, fishing, timber, and iron ore.[99] Oil production started in 1966 and by 1974 comprised 48 percent of a burgeoning export total, leading to a large trade surplus and relegating coffee to 20 percent and diamonds to 8 percent.[100] These agricultural and mineral riches raised Angola above Mozambique, Guinea Bissau, and Cape Verde as "Portugal's African Jewel."[101]

Though Portugal used tariffs and other measures to keep out First World competitors, much of the wealth was captured by other imperial powers, with Portugal taking merely a share of the profits as middleman. British interests operated the Benguela Railway that brought the copper exports of the Belgian Congo and Zambia to the ports; US, British, Belgian, French, and Portuguese capital, headed by South Africa's De Beers, mined Angola's diamonds from the 1920s on in exchange for a 50 percent cut to the colonial government; American oil giants Gulf, Exxon, Texaco, and Occidental were joined by Belgium's Petrofina and France's ELF in an oil boom that took off in the 1960s and 1970s.[102] Though subsistence agriculture stagnated for two decades up to 1973, industry grew as fast as 20 percent annually from 1968 to 1972, and exports boomed, rising from 7.8 billion escudos in 1968 to 19.1 billion in 1973 and 31 billion in 1974. This was led by oil, which grew 1,000 percent between 1967 and 1972, while iron production rose from $1.4 million in 1967 to $45.8 million in the same period.[103] The period from the coffee boom and the first development plan of 1953 to the discovery and production of oil by the early 1970s, then, may be considered one of an increasingly dynamic – if not yet fully mature – dependent colonial development.[104]

The Portuguese economy itself was too weak and undercapitalized to do much more than extract raw materials from its colonies using cheap labor. Forced labor was legal under various guises until 1961, and many were conscripted into it for non-payment of taxes (themselves a source of great wealth in the colonial economy).[105] Moreover, the state could require Angolans to grow commercial crops, and served as the monopoly buyer of the crop.[106] Income estimates from the late 1950s for African farmers range from $33 to $146 a year, depending on the crop and region.[107] The relatively better compensated 26,000 diamond workers made an average annual wage of only $174 in 1961.[108] Such official figures only begin to indicate the degree of hardship for the vast majority of the Angolan population. Boavida estimated that it took a skilled laborer fourteen hours to pay for a kilogram of meat in around 1960, while a report to the Portuguese National Assembly in 1947 found infant mortality to be as high as 60 percent in the colonies, and said of forced labor: "In some ways the situation is worse than under straightforward slavery."[109] In Macqueen's judgment, "Although empirical comparisons are virtually impossible, it is reasonable to suggest that the indigenous populations of Portuguese Africa, at least up to the 1960s, were the most disadvantaged of the European empires."[110]

Meanwhile, Angola also served as an outlet for Portugal's surplus population, attracting poor and wealthy settlers alike to its agricultural settlements and urban jobs. White settlers grew in number from 78,000 to 335,000 between 1950 and 1974, nearly twice the total for Mozambique. As in French Algeria, they were internally stratified, with many of the recent arrivals being displaced peasants who found themselves in urban working-class occupations, and 7,000 unemployed in 1960, with few prospects should they return to Portugal.[111] The existence of an intermediate stratum of mestizos, numbering only 30,000 in 1954, should be noted too; from the late 1800s on, some of its members were mission-educated, but they were blocked from rising far in the colonial bureaucracy.[112] The wealthy segment, on the other hand, owned the more than 2,000 coffee plantations that existed by 1962, pushing thousands of Kikongo farmers into Zaire,[113] while other settlers monopolized the administrative and professional ranks. Thus, while it is true that many urban Portuguese were poor, most lived better in Angola than they had in Portugal.[114] The operation of racism at both popular and official levels meant that "A white immigrant, even if unqualified and without means, could practically always rely upon his being given a chance of not falling below an economic level well beyond the reach of the overwhelming majority of Africans."[115] Prime minister Marcello Caetano stated: "The natives of Africa must be directed and organized by Europeans, but are indispensable as auxiliaries. The blacks must be seen as productive elements in an economy directed by whites."[116]

In the end, despite the inequalities in settler society itself, we can discern the two separate societies noted by Fanon, and Angola evinces the distinctive colonial form of dependent development that we have theorized. For Heimer, it was,

the interest of colonial capitalism in maintaining most of the population, for a transitional period, in separate economies which relied heavily on subsistence agriculture and cattle-raising, in order to reduce the price of labour and to keep down prices for agricultural products and cattle. It would also seem that the logic of Salazar's policy of colonial consolidation required maintaining the majority of the population "outside the boundaries" of a still precarious "modern sector" of the colonial economy, using them without permitting them to leave their separate world, and accepting/demanding their integration only if and when the "modern sector" needed them "inside".[117]

In sum, the Portuguese monopolized both the commanding heights and broad middle sectors of the social and political structure.

The repressive and exclusionary side of the colonial state was developed to hold this unequal social structure in place. When the Portuguese monarchy fell in 1910, the Republic stepped in to administer Angola. The system of harsh exploitation of Angolan labor continued and intensified with the toppling of the Republic in 1926 and the subsequent fascist Novo Estado (New State) of António de Oliveira Salazar which lasted till 1968, and acted in concert with the Franco dictatorship in Spain. In the 1930s, Salazar moved to make taxes payable only in currency, which reinforced the contract labor system, and to require all enterprises to be half-Portuguese in capital after 1948, to increase profits vis-à-vis other First World competitors (this was rescinded in 1965).[118] The new regime's ideology was one of a multiracial Luso-tropical nation.[119] The reality, notes Sadie Miller, was the "need to compensate economic weakness with military brutality."[120] Authoritarianism and semi-feudalism in Portugal added an extra dimension of exploitation to the colonial states in Africa. The hallmarks of the Angolan state were the forced labor system and severe political and military repression of any dissent. Revealingly, the first development plan of 1953–58 had *no* budget for public health or education.[121] The state fits the repressive, exclusionary colonial model, with the further twist of a culture of dictatorship in the metropole.

Political cultures of opposition could build on a long history of resistance to Portuguese rule among the Bakongo, Mbundu, and Ovimbundu peoples marked by uprisings in the nineteenth century and again in 1913–16 to protest Portuguese-imposed kings and the plantation forced labor system.[122] Portugal's entry into the United Nations in the 1950s was accompanied by educational reforms that gradually led to the emergence of a middle stratum of black and mestizo professionals – teachers, intellectuals, doctors, nurses, clerical workers, and others – who came to organize the nationalist resistance.[123] The independence of Ghana in 1957 and the electrifying rise of Lumumba in the Congo in 1960 further inspired this group. Another impetus for change would be the legal and especially educational reforms that followed the 1961 uprising, making all Angolans formally Portuguese citizens and expanding the educational system to the point where up to three-quarters of the children of the Luanda shantytowns had had some schooling by 1970.[124] In this wider context and on this social base would emerge not one but three anti-colonial movements, vastly complicating the struggle for independence and afterwards.

The MPLA (Popular Movement for the Liberation of Angola), founded in 1956 and later led by poet and doctor Agostinho Neto, grew out of both Pan-African cultural and socialist political currents. Its leadership was largely mestizo, its social base urban, and its ethnic base lay in the Mbundu people in the Luanda area.[125] As such it tried to build a nation-wide, non-ethnic political movement. Its 1961 program

proposed equal rights for women, a voting age of eighteen years, the abolition of foreign military bases, the end of the forced labor régime, a minimum wage, and an eight-hour day. Economically, the party required the distribution of estate lands to African farmers, the abolition of the single-crop system, and the transformation of Angola into a modern industrialised country.[126]

Materially, the MPLA received Soviet and Cuban aid after 1964,[127] and in terms of political culture, "Its Marxist roots were . . . arguably stronger than those of any other nationalist movement that led a sub-Saharan colony to political independence."[128] The class aspect of the struggle was clear to MPLA activist Américo Boavida and underscores the existence of the two societies:

> This is a war of an oppressed community against an oppressing majority. A war between slaves and slave-holders, of forced laborers in the countryside against the colonial masters of plantations and farms, of factory workers and apprentices against employers and foremen. It is a war against the oppressive apparatus of a European minority in an African community, with contradictory and irreconcilable economic interests.[129]

The MPLA's insistence on total independence and its emphasis on community welfare and self-help proved attractive to its followers, especially by the struggle's endgame of 1974–76.[130] By 1974, it was split into several factions, the main one led by Neto, who was challenged by eastern military leader Daniel Chipenda and a smaller third group of intellectuals critical of Neto's leadership style, headed by Mário de Andrade.[131]

The FNLA (National Front for the Liberation of Angola) evolved from the Union of the Peoples of Northern Angola, founded in 1958 by Bakongo exiles living in the Congo, and led by the Baptist-educated, non-communist nationalist Holden Roberto. Roberto's personal relationships with Congolese revolutionary Patrice Lumumba, Frantz Fanon, and other leading African revolutionaries produced a classic anti-colonial national liberation declaration in 1960, stressing autonomy, democracy, and non-alignment, although in terms more general than the MPLA's.[132] The organization evolved in a clear anticommunist, pro-Western direction in the 1960s, however, when the increasingly autocratic Roberto married Zairean dictator Joseph Mobutu's sister-in-law and was supported secretly by the CIA.[133] For Ciment, "Whereas the MPLA was cosmopolitan, socialist and integrated, the [FNLA] . . . was provincial, entrepreneurial, anticommunist and ethnically homogeneous."[134] Clashes between the two organizations went beyond political rivalry and turned violent as early as 1961–62.[135]

UNITA (the National Union for the Total Independence of Angola) formed in 1966 two years after Jonas Savimbi left the FNLA's Angolan government in exile over Roberto's politics and their exclusionary ethnic base; Bakongo farmers affiliated with the business-oriented politics of the FLNA, while Ovimbundu people of the central plateau, who worked on European cotton plantations, the trans-Benguela railway, or on northern coffee plantations, joined Savimbi's UNITA.[136] Its 1968 program resembled those of its rivals in its call for women's emancipation, abolition of exploitative labor systems, the end of foreign bases, and, interestingly, a "planned economy to meet all the needs of our population and to construct an industrialised country."[137] Despite its early radical, often Maoist-inspired rhetoric (Savimbi had trained in China and was attracted to that revolution's concepts of rural insurgency and self-reliance), UNITA would come to play a conservative role in the 1975–76 civil war and a decidedly counter-revolutionary one after that.[138]

In 1961 popular uprisings spread across Angola, from cotton and coffee plantations to Luanda. Some of these were spontaneous, fueled by worker and peasant grievances – cotton workers had gone unpaid, coffee cultivators were hurt by falling prices and higher taxes. On February 4, the MPLA sought to free political prisoners in an action reminiscent of the July 26 attack on the Moncada garrison in Cuba. A more serious uprising in March involved coffee workers in the northwest with ties to the FNLA. Paige traces this to "the land expropriations and labor demands of the coffee estates."[139] After several hundred white settlers were killed, Portugal sent 50,000 troops which fought for four months to regain control, in the process indiscriminately killing some 20,000 rural Angolans (up to 50,000 in all may have died due to disease and famine), and turning 350,000 into exiled refugees by 1964, while a quarter of the rural population was ultimately "resettled" in areas controlled by the government.[140] For Neto, "from that moment the People became conscious of the imperative to fight, and the Portuguese had to face an unexpected situation, a prelude to the difficulties in which they would find themselves to maintain their domination."[141]

By the late 1960s a common, widespread sentiment of anti-colonial struggle based on national self-determination, democratic rule, and for the MPLA, socialism, characterized the political culture of resistance to the Portuguese. The length of the struggle into the 1970s and the intransigence of the Salazar regime radicalized these movements beyond the first wave of African liberation movements. In the analysis of the liberation movements, "the Portuguese were exploiting Angola's raw materials to the profit of the metropole and the foreign nations that had increased their financial investments in the colony."[142] All could perhaps agree on this, but the issue of socialist redistribution, overlaid by the different social and ethnic bases of the three movements, signaled the fracture at the heart of the opposition culture that would mark the revolution's dénouement in civil war.

After forty years of rule, in September 1968, Salazar suffered a stroke and was replaced by Marcello Caetano. Caetano found it hard to maneuver between the hard-line Salazar followers who retained power and reformers who sought change both at home and in Africa. The post-Salazar government was simultaneously fighting three colonial wars (in Angola, Mozambique, and Cape Verde/Guinea-Bissau), and coping with an internal revolutionary situation at home (itself the product of those interminable colonial wars). Unlike the French in Vietnam, whose lessons (and mistakes) they studied, the Portuguese state fought an effective counter-insurgency war, based on recruitment of Angolan troops, astute use of intelligence, and flexible tactics. Portugal's problems were more political and economic than strategic: "while Portugal fought an imaginative campaign to retain its colonies in an anticolonial era, no amount of military verve could overcome the political problem of Portugal's legitimacy in Africa."[143] This brings us to the nature of the world-systemic opening that occurred in the mid-1970s.

Western support for Portugal remained strong up to the early 1970s, with the growing importance of oil investments and the hoped-for presence of such strategic minerals as cobalt, uranium, and chrome securing backing for the regime from the US and much of Europe.[144] As an economist put it in 1974: "No one knows how rich the country is going to be. But we know it is going to be very rich indeed. Possibly the richest country on the continent per head of population after South Africa."[145] The Nixon administration extended significant aid to Portugal after 1972 in exchange for the use of an airbase in the Azores.[146] By 1974, however, key allies including the US were urging a negotiated solution to the conflict that would put a pliable non-revolutionary government led by UNITA in power after what increasingly appeared to be the inevitability of independence (starting a policy approach we have seen in the Nicaraguan and Iranian cases). Meanwhile, in Portugal itself, significant portions of the business and governing elite were turning their vision toward integration with Europe rather than colonies abroad: from 1959 to 1972, the share of Portugal's exports to Europe had increased from 40.3 to 61.3 percent, while registering a decline in the colonies from 29.8 to 14.7 percent.[147] When Portugal gained associate status (not full membership) in the European Economic Community in 1970, it was forced to dismantle its protectionist colonial trading system, making the colonies less attractive in terms of profits.[148] Both world opinion and a growing portion of Portuguese society, including the Catholic, Methodist, and Baptist churches inside Angola[149] and disaffected soldiers and officers, began to favor decolonization as well, as the horrors of the 1961 massacre spread to a broader war in all of Portugal's colonies.

The turning point was the Portuguese military revolution of April 25, 1974. That this event was itself in large part the product of the revolutionary struggles in Portugal's colonies is made clear by Van der Waals, who sees its causes in,

the security situation in Guinea and Mozambique [n.b. *not* in Angola] in that year; the socio-political climate in Portugal and the steady drift to the right by an indecisive Caetano; the growth of a young career officers' movement arising out of professional grievances; the prominence of Spinola, a war hero, and his slightly naïve approach to Afro-Portuguese politics as set out in his book *Portugal e o Futuro*; disagreement in the armed forces relating to the future of the African provinces and, lastly, the consolidation of the right and the reaction it provoked from the left.[150]

By then, 10,000 Portuguese troops had died and 20,000 had been wounded in the colonial wars (the struggle in Guinea-Bissau was "particularly intense and enduring" and this, more than the war in Angola, undermined the army's morale), and the army, despite massive evasion of compulsory national service, had swelled from 60,000 in the early 1960s to over 200,000, one of the largest on a per capita basis in the world.[151] The guerrilla movements themselves did not win independence on the battlefield in any direct sense: between 1961 and 1973 on average only 105 Portuguese troops (themselves only 60–70 percent white) died annually in combat in Angola, and in 1973 only fifteen of the eighty-one deaths came in direct engagements.[152] It is also true however that the guerrilla forces were not crushed, and in 1972 the MPLA had control over the eastern border and was active on six fronts. By then, 8–9,000 guerrillas were in the field, supported by 50–70,000 peasants, with further support provided by the up to 400,000 refugees in Zaire and Zambia.[153]

General Antonio de Spínola's *Portugal and the Future* argued that there was no military solution in Africa and called for a greater degree of autonomy in the colonies, though stopping short of independence. It appealed widely both to the discontented officer corps and the disillusioned general population, quickly selling 250,000 copies and sharpening the conflict between right and left in Portugal.[154] When the right forced the dismissals of Spínola and Chief of Staff Francisco da Costa Gomes in March of 1974, 598 officers in Portugal were joined by 120 in Angola, sixty in Mozambique, and fifty in Guinea-Bissau to protest this. At their core was the Armed Forces Movement (MFA), formed in 1973, many of whose members were former students, now conscripted officers, who in one of history's ironies had been exposed to the socialist ideas of Che, Mao, and Amilcar Cabral in military textbooks on guerrilla war at home or in the colonies.[155] As Alvaro Cunhal wrote: "If Portugal wishes to be free, the Portuguese colonies must be free."[156]

Economic downturn made its contribution, too, both in Portugal, where 1974 saw the first trade deficit in decades with inflation reaching 20 percent – higher than anywhere else in Europe[157] – and in Angola itself, where the war finally disrupted the smooth flow of investments and profits as the boom came to an end. Agriculture was ultimately devastated by the exodus of refugees and the resettlement policy: "Coffee exports fell by more than half; diamond production by two-thirds. In the last year of colonialism, industrial production fell by 75 percent and GNP by at least 25 percent."[158] Here we can read the double movement of dependent development and economic downturn, with the 1960s and early 1970s marked by the characteristic macro-economic growth of dependent development, and the eve of the coming to power of the revolution by a downturn, deepened further by the devastation of the civil war that gradually emerged among the opponents of the Portuguese. In its turn the fighting led to the mass exodus of settlers in the summer of 1975, further aggravating the downturn.[159] Rarely have internal downturn and external opening reinforced each other so intensely, in colony and in metropole.

The coup that came to be known as the Revolution of the Carnations (after the flowers given to soldiers by the populace) was made peacefully in Portugal on April 25, bringing the two generals, Spínola and Costa Gomes, and the more radical younger officers of the MFA to power. Despite Spínola's reluctance to move quickly on independence, and the re-appointment of a hard-line former governor-general from the 1960s in Angola, Silvino Silvério Marques, by July the MFA had forced Spínola to promise independence and replace the Salazarist governor-general with a pro-MPLA military administrator.[160] Even after this, Spínola arranged a secret meeting in Cape Verde in September: "Those who attended included Holden Roberto, Jonas Savimbi, Daniel Chipenda (heading the MPLA breakaway faction the 'Eastern Revolt', that was trying to oust the leadership) and the President of Zaire, General Mobutu."[161] This set in motion the Western intervention that would follow in a vain attempt to prevent an MPLA-led revolution. Left-wing members of the MFA forced Spínola to resign later in September, and soon after Costa Gomes assumed the presidency Portugal negotiated truces with the three Angolan liberation movements. An agreement was reached in January 1975 by all four parties at the resort town of Alvor for independence to begin on November 11.

The three-way coalition government of the MPLA, FNLA, and UNITA then fell into a civil war that led to the flight of over 250,000 Portuguese whites and mestizos over the next six months, further damaging the economy as farms were abandoned and enterprises stripped of their assets.[162] Arnold characterizes the deep differences among the three movements as ideological, ethnic, and over the question of power after independence.[163] Portugal largely withdrew its forces, and its internal political turmoil resulted in an unwillingness to guarantee a stable transformation of the police and armed forces, adding fuel to the conflict; in any case, the Portuguese left parties, diverse and shifting as their positions were, pursued a policy of "active neutrality," and did not officially back the MPLA, wherever the left's sympathies lay.[164] The USSR, Eastern Europe, and Cuba supported the MPLA in its fight against the FNLA, backed by the CIA, South Africa, Zaire, and China, aided by the Chipenda faction now expelled from the MPLA, with UNITA sometimes cooperating with the FNLA, sometimes fighting it. The MPLA also enjoyed diplomatic support from the Scandinavian social democracies and the tacit political support of the revolutionary government in Lisbon. It unilaterally declared independence on the appointed day, November 11, 1975, as the People's Republic of Angola, with Neto as president.

A world-systemic opening and the internal realignment of forces would be needed for this declaration to be effective. Cuban troops hampered the South African army's movements in early November, and when the *Washington Post* exposed the South African role on November 22, the international balance shifted in favor of the MPLA, aided by its strategic control of Luanda's port and airport. China abandoned the FNLA in November. A month later, the US Senate voted against continued funding for the anti-communist rebels, leading to a decline in European enthusiasm for an increasingly unpopular intervention, and in early 1976 South Africa withdrew its forces, causing Savimbi's UNITA to retreat into the interior.[165] The post-Vietnam climate made direct US intervention difficult, and the use of South African proxies backfired when it became public knowledge. In January, the Organization of African Unity deadlocked on whether to recognize the MPLA's government or call for further three-way negotiations. The FNLA was pushed out of its northern headquarters at the same time.[166] The world-systemic opening was now complete.

The MPLA and its Cuban allies had control of the country's major cities by February, declaring victory on February 11, 1976; international recognition soon followed. This revolution had been made by a broad coalition (if all three movements are included): in class terms, spanning intellectuals and other middle strata in the leadership, with peasants, rural workers, and urban workers of many kinds in the rank and file; in ethnic terms, by members of multiple ethnic groups; and in terms of gender, by male guerrillas with the significant participation of women in village cooperative work, literacy training, and some guerrilla activity.[167]

The MPLA's superior ability to cross these divisions was a key factor in its victory. The price, however, was high and continued to be paid long after independence came: much economic devastation during the 1974–76 fighting, over 100,000 Angolans killed, tens of thousands in exile, and continued factional divisions and economic stagnation as civil war continued for another twenty-five years.[168]

The patterns of dependent colonial development, colonial rule backed by the Salazar dictatorship, the emergence of strong, if fractured, political cultures of opposition, a world-systemic downturn created in large measure by the independence struggle's impact on the Portuguese revolution, and an economic downturn in Portugal itself, owing much to events in its colonies, had combined to bring about the first of several great anti-colonial social revolutions of the mid-1970s. The imbrication of First and Third World economies, political cultures, and international relations is poignant and striking in this case, as well as that of Mozambique, whose victory predated Angola's by several months.

Mozambique, 1960s–1975: the advantages of relative unity

The Mozambican revolution is intimately tied to the Angolan by virtue of its timing and the colonial power it faced.[169] The differences in the two cases are also instructive, as they reveal much about political culture and the internal specificities of seemingly equivalent colonial situations, which affected the nature of the struggle as well as its clearer outcome in Mozambique. These points of comparison and contrast will become clearer as we analyze the case.

The Portuguese arrived to disrupt the local kingdoms' trade in gold and ivory after 1500, gaining control over mines and establishing early settler plantations through the seventeenth century, only to be driven from the highlands of what is today Zimbabwe in 1692. Portugal was still unable to gain control of the pre-existing trade networks of African and Indian merchants well into the eighteenth century. A new formula for profit was found in the course of the nineteenth century, however, when more than one million Mozambicans were sold into slavery or "bound labor," raising great profits in "export duties" for local elites and the rudimentary Portuguese administration.[170] When the trade was finally banned and ceased, the emphasis shifted to internal exploitation of agriculture and labor. Ports, railways, plantations, mining, and trade were developed largely by British concerns such as the Mozambique, Zambesi, and Nyasa companies, oriented to trade with the British colonies and South Africa; Britain's dominance would shift back to Portugal only after World War 2.[171]

One may question whether Mozambique's development trajectory can be reasonably evaluated as one of dependent development, for as Arnold notes, the colony was "exceptionally poor."[172] The reasons why this is not a case of simple dependency without any significant development are two fold: the colonial pattern does not require as much development as the non-colonial, and it is based on dependency for the colonized population and development for the settler society. Mozambique shows evidence of both. In addition, the country's development in the critical decade and a half leading up to the revolution was increasingly dependent on the capital invested by other First World powers.

As in Angola, Portugal made its Mozambican colony an exporter of primary products (sugar, nuts, and cotton). Tea and sugar experienced a boom during World War 2, with revenues tripling; the trend toward commercial agriculture continued after the war.[173] Another boost to the economy were the wages and taxes of the estimated half million or more miners and plantation workers who migrated to work in South Africa, Northern and Southern Rhodesia, Tanganyika, Zanzibar, and Kenya (perhaps the largest number working outside their own country in all of Africa).[174] By the 1950s, under the Salazar regime's policy of protecting Portugal's colonial markets, the economy had been largely re-oriented to the metropole. In 1961, Portugal provided 29.7 percent of Mozambique's imports, Britain 12.3 percent, South Africa 10.7 percent, and the US 7.1 percent; Portugal took 48 percent of the country's exports.[175]

A qualitatively significant amount of industrialization and infrastructural growth occurred in the 1960s and after, as Portugal was forced once again to relax its control in order to stimulate the growth and self-sufficiency needed to sustain its tenuous hold on empire. In 1961, there were only eighty-one industrial establishments worth more than $150,000 in the country, and the value of all manufactured goods was $14 million.[176] A generation later, Ciment considers that Mozambique had become "one of the most industrialized countries in sub-Saharan Africa," with the eighth-largest industrial output in Africa in 1974.[177] The 1960s saw a major influx of foreign capital, much of it in industry; South Africa led the investors in Portugal's African colonies with one-third of the capital, followed by Great Britain and the US with 15 percent each, West Germany with 11 percent, Spain 6 percent, Belgium 5 percent, Switzerland 3 percent, and France 2 percent.[178] Munslow sees in this "a clear symptom of a dependent economy" in Mozambique.[179]

The period of the late 1960s and early 1970s saw another boost to the economy in the form of a multinational project for the construction of the world's fifth-largest dam, the Cabora Bassa, in Tete province. South Africa, West Germany, France, Britain, and Italy were the leading investors.[180] Arnold points out that "The dam was political from the beginning: the project was designed to mobilize Western finances to create a source of cheap power for South Africa and thereby to draw the West to defend the Portuguese position in Mozambique."[181] This project and the investment it generated were to be the centerpiece for a final round of dependent development, yielding something modestly equivalent to what we have found even in the non-colonial cases of Chapter 2.

The effects on the local population are typical of the negative side of dependent development. From 1899 to 1961, the "chibalo" was imposed on all Mozambican males, requiring them to work for six months a year on state or private projects: "As late as the 1950s the fixed salary for six months of labor was often as little as $3 per month."[182] As they received neither food nor shelter, female relatives often carried food to them, exposing themselves to rape by the overseers. Villages were required to produce quotas of cotton after 1938 or rice after 1942; the cotton produced was sold to textile factories in Portugal at half the world price, and by 1945, cotton was the colony's largest export. Even after reforms and price increases, *yearly* income from cotton producing for families in the north was only $11 in 1957; elsewhere it was as low as $4.[183] A 1959 government report found that "the majority of the population is underfed," and famines and nutritional diseases were rampant.[184] The large number of migrant workers abroad meant women did increasing amounts of agricultural production at home, or migrated to cities, where the only work available was often as nannies or even more commonly, in the sex trade.[185] Few children could be spared from the home economy for school, and at independence as many as 95 percent were illiterate; of six million Mozambicans, there were only 4,500 *assimilados* in 1955 (persons classified as urban and educated – the category was abandoned in 1961).[186] Per capita income at $140 in 1978 was the lowest in southern Africa.[187]

The settler population meanwhile grew slowly from 18,000 in 1928 to 48,000 in 1950 and 220,000 in 1975, responding to promises of land, livestock, and cash bonuses; the vast majority, however, sought to make their lives in the urban areas.[188] In the 1960s, the 3,000 Portuguese farmers and planters held more land than did the 1.5 million African peasants.[189] Isaacman and Isaacman found that in 1962, black and white agricultural laborers' pay differentials were tenfold in the north, while in urban areas Portuguese unskilled workers were paid twenty times more than Africans for the same work; Hanlon notes that a black carpenter's wage was one-thirteenth that of a white carpenter in 1960.[190] Urban areas were divided into the shantytowns of the many and the "city of cement" for the few, separated until the 1960s by passbook laws and racist custom.[191] Sadie Miller sums it up well: "economic benefits reach[ed] only Portuguese settlers in Mozambique, Portuguese investors, and the Lisbon administration."[192] The stark reality of development for the settlers, and dependency for the black population makes indisputably clear that we are again in the presence of dependent colonial development.

Colonial administration was not highly developed until after the fascist takeover of 1926, reflecting the instability of Portugal's own government and the weaknesses of its economy, as well as that of Mozambique. The state relied in part on local elites to collect taxes, for which they received better prices for their crops and the use of forced labor on their plantations.[193] The dictatorships of António Salazar (1932–68) and his successor, Marcello Caetano (1968–74), aimed at reasserting Portuguese control both vis-à-vis foreign powers and the African population. In the process, they sponsored the creation of colonial governments as authoritarian and (by extension) personalist as their own in Portugal, and far more repressive. The right to vote was limited, trade unions banned, political organizing suppressed. In the 1960s, economic coercion and political repression went hand in hand, as a Mozambican peasant explained: "We didn't want to grow cotton, but we had to grow it; we wanted to grow cassava, beans and maize. If we refused to grow cotton, they arrested us, put us in chains, beat us and then sent us away to a place from where one often didn't come back."[194] Migration is a good marker of the repressive nature of the state: of hundreds of thousands who fled the country, many "stressed their attempts to escape the brutality of forced labour: beatings, imprisonment, starvation and sometimes even death."[195]

Already well entrenched in censorship and a system of spies and secret police, military repression reached extreme heights once the guerrilla war started: "Opposition in any form – strikes, protest writing, public rallies – was not tolerated. One prominent Portuguese lawyer estimated that at least 10,000 opponents of the regime were arrested between 1967 and 1973."[196] Torture and murder of prisoners were common. The colonial state in Mozambique thus shows the principal characteristics of the exclusionary, repressive regime that has elsewhere generated revolutionary opposition.

The liberation movement that arose – the Front for the Liberation of Mozambique, or Frelimo – tapped deeply felt nationalist longings and the intense experiences of local exploitation and channeled these in socialist directions. It could also build on memories of relatively recent resistance to Portuguese colonialism, such as the determined movements of the Yao people from the 1890s till their defeat in 1912, the Pan-Zambesian revolt, spanning peasants from seven ethnic groups between 1917 and 1921, the dock strikes between 1918 and 1921 and again in 1933, strikes by women cotton growers in 1947, and boycotts in 1955–58. To these must be added a legendary history of social banditry and ingenious forms of resistance to forced labor and taxes.[197] Minter notes the significance of the timing involved: "the history of wars is hardly more than two generations removed from the present liberation movement, and the memories are alive today."[198]

In the mid-1950s, the Nucleus of African Secondary Students of Mozambique (NESAM) formed, with a base in the small educated elite of blacks and mestizos, including Joaquim Chissano, Mariano Matsinhe, and Eduardo Mondlane.[199] A movement from below began to emerge in the wake of the June 1960 massacre of 500–600 demonstrating sisal workers at Mueda.[200] Several nationalist groups, each with distinct ethnic bases, formed in exile in Tanzania, coming together somewhat tentatively at the insistence of Tanzania's Julius Nyerere and Ghana's Kwame Nkrumah to found Frelimo on June 25, 1962.[201] Eduardo Mondlane, who had earned Mozambique's first PhD in the US in 1960 and then worked as a UN official, served as its president.

The political cultural roots of the revolution were diverse. The initial unifying goal had to be independence, with socialism coming only later. For Mondlane, "The common basis we all had when we formed Frelimo was hatred of colonialism and the belief in the necessity to destroy the colonial structure and to establish a new social structure."[202] Mondlane's successor, Samora Machel, said he started his political education not "from reading Marx and Engels. But from seeing my father forced to grow cotton and going with him to the market where he was to sell it as a low price – much lower than the white Portuguese grower."[203] For the theorist Marcelino dos Santos Marxism came as an intellectual product of discussions and debates with African and European thinkers while he was a student exile abroad; like Agostinho Neto in Angola and Amilcar Cabral in Guinea-Bissau, he studied at the Lisbon Center for African Studies.[204] Iain Christie, who writes of the revolution's "homegrown Marxism," notes that "there was a symbiotic relationship between these three men. With their different backgrounds and temperaments they undoubtedly learned from each other."[205] Early Frelimo leader Jorge Rebelo, looking back twenty years after independence in 1995, recalled: "We all agreed that we were going to gain independence, but this was not the ultimate object; that was in fact the creation of a progressive society which would bring an end to misery in our country. This was not merely a slogan. It was inside of us."[206] A unified nationalism cutting across ethnic and regional lines was forged also in part from the experiences of migrant mineworkers and others in South Africa and elsewhere who had been exposed to diverse progressive currents.[207] Because these workers retained rural ties inside the country such ideas proliferated even more widely.

Eduardo Mondlane was assassinated by a parcel bomb sent by a Portuguese-supported non-socialist Frelimo dissident in Dar es Salaam on February 3, 1969, producing a shock to the organization. Three men – Uria Simango, Samora Machel, and Marcelino dos Santos – led it jointly for a time, plagued by infighting until the business-oriented Simango was expelled and military commander Machel emerged as sole leader in June 1970, with dos Santos as vice president.[208] After this, the movement had the distinct advantage of being a single organization (common to virtually all our cases of success except Angola) and a unified leadership. Frelimo had already taken a socialist direction under Mondlane, who summarized its goals in 1968: "1) Frelimo is a democratic movement, fighting to establish a government in which the majority of the Mozambique population, regardless of color or religion, will choose their leaders freely; 2) socialism will be the economic system followed to determine control of natural and human resources of the country; 3) social welfare of the people as a whole."[209]

A small nucleus of urban workers (urban organizing was dangerous, and the urban population was not large, in any case), a more considerable number of migrant wage earners abroad, a vast number of peasants, and a tiny educated elite and other middle sectors allied in Frelimo. Despite the existence of more than a dozen ethnic groups, ethnicity was ultimately overcome as a major obstacle to the movement's work, which even attracted radical Portuguese supporters. Thus, a strong sense of nationalism based in part on the collective identity of the black population as colonized was a second strand of the revolutionary political culture.[210] Women were massively active in the protracted guerrilla war, in health, education, provisioning and supply roles, and sometimes in combat. Josina Machel noted: "Firstly, it is easier for us to approach other women, and secondly, the men are more easily convinced of the important role of women when confronted with the unusual sight of confident and capable female militants . . . the presence of emancipated women bearing arms often shames them into taking more positive action."[211] For militant Rita Mulumba, "The revolution is transforming our life. Before I was ignorant, while now I speak in front of everyone at meetings."[212] The schools set up in liberated zones empowered young students who worked as adult literacy teachers and served to deconstruct colonial myths, replacing them with new values and identities.[213] In the end, a powerful culture of opposition was forged, supporting a broad revolutionary coalition crossing ethnic, gender, and class lines.

The conjuncture of world-systemic opening and economic downturn came together by the early 1970s, and as in Angola, the revolutionaries contributed powerfully to both. With Mozambique lacking Angola's mineral and agricultural export wealth, until the Cabora Bassa project the stakes were diminished for Western powers other than Portugal in the maintenance of the status quo, and the country did not get as caught up in the cold war as did its counterpart to the west. The complexities of these shifting and contradictory interests among the key external actors bear closer attention.

The UN passed a resolution to ban arms sales to Portugal as early as December 1962.[214] Despite this, Portugal was supplied during the conflict with arms from the US, Britain, France, West Germany, and Italy, ostensibly for use in the context of NATO, but effectively free for deployment in Africa.[215] Britain, France, and the US used their positions on the UN Security Council to mute any significant criticism of Portugal into the early 1970s.[216] Loans came from the US, West Germany, and France, and especially from the Nixon administration through its influence at the Export-Import Bank in 1971, in return for the use of bases in the Azores.[217] South Africa and Rhodesia's white governments also played key roles, the former because of its growing economic interest, the latter because of its concerns over its own guerrilla opposition. For its part, Frelimo enjoyed wide international support from the 1960s on, as it was recognized by the Organization of African Unity, trained by Chinese military instructors, supplied by the Soviet bloc, and financed and supported by Tanzania, Algeria, Egypt, Sweden, Denmark, and such NGOs as the World Council of Churches and the Rowntree Trust in Britain.[218]

Similarly, Portugal's internal downturn formed part of the same economic opening as we saw in Angola. Portugal's first steps into the European Economic Community with associate status in 1970 led to a shift in investment away from the colonies, as Portuguese big business interests moved away from support for Caetano's colonial wars.[219] As Portugal disengaged economically in the colony, however, South Africa stepped in with major investments.[220] The other side of the downturn took place inside Mozambique, where "By the end of 1973 FRELIMO guerrilla forces had mined several trains going from Beira to Southern Rhodesia; raided settler-owned sugar, cotton, and sisal plantations; attacked inland towns; and interdicted traffic going from Beira to Tete and to Cahora [sic] Bassa Dam."[221] After the April 1974 coup in Portugal, the sense of economic crisis in Mozambique intensified, with white settlers leaving, black Mozambicans deserting the colonial army, and the administration disintegrating.[222] Frelimo attacked the railway and increased its raids on white-owned farms. Macqueen sums up the situation in the summer of 1974: "While economic crisis, industrial upheaval, racial tension and military disaffection beset the colony, political division afflicted the metropole."[223]

Economic downturn and world-systemic opening were thus closely linked, and rarely had revolutionaries done so much to bring about both. Frelimo's long-term guerrilla war contributed to the favorable conjuncture of the mid-1970s by undermining the colonial and metropolitan economy and first demoralizing and later radicalizing the young Portuguese army officers who toppled the fascist regime in April 1974. It is clearly part of the same world-systemic opening (and economic downturn) as in Angola, but it contributed its own part and played itself out quite differently due to the internal balance of forces.

The war went better for Frelimo than for the Angolan MPLA: "By 1968 Frelimo had grown from an initial 250 fighters to 10,000 and claimed to control one-fifth of Mozambique and 800,000 people."[224] Portugal in turn claimed to have decimated Frelimo in 1970, and used the same strategy of rural settlements as in Angola, eventually affecting one million peasants, as well as recruiting African troops alongside the Portuguese army, but by the end of 1971 Frelimo again appeared to have the upper hand, disrupting work on the Cabora Bassa dam, and causing significant casualties and damage to the Portuguese army and the transportation system.[225]

By mid-1973, Frelimo held between a quarter and a third of the country, with 1.8 million people in its liberated zones, which boasted schools, adult literacy programs, simple health clinics and systems, agricultural cooperatives that produced subsistence staples, people's shops to supply the peasantry, and, importantly, popularly-chosen local governments.[226] It was active in the Beira Corridor, which ran from the port city to Rhodesia and was the latter's lifeline to the coast. White farms came under attack in 1974, and the South African *Rand Daily Mail* lamented: "Portugal is not winning the war in Mozambique."[227] Its 50–60,000 troops, half of them African, were not adequate to contain the 20,000 guerrillas in the north.[228] News of massacres by government troops further damaged the position of Portugal in European public opinion.[229]

Only two days after the Portuguese revolution, Frelimo stated: "it must be clearly understood that there is no such thing as democratic colonialism."[230] As the Portuguese revolution moved to the left, Frelimo began to operate more openly throughout the country. A cease-fire was agreed on September 7, 1974 and independence was set for June 25, 1975. Conservative settlers of the newly formed FICO ("I am staying") movement immediately attempted an uprising, which the Portuguese army put down in a matter of days. After that, the nine-month transition went reasonably smoothly, and Samora Machel assumed the presidency at Maputo, the port and capital, on June 23, 1975, declaring a socialist course for an independent Mozambique.

The Frelimo rebels, then, like the MPLA, had gone a step further than the Cubans and Algerians in helping to bring about not only an economic downturn but to force a favorable international context for their revolts. Samora Machel was aware of this: "The launching of the struggles and the victories we have won reveal concretely that there is no such thing as fateful destiny: we are capable of transforming society and creating a new life."[231] Unlike the MPLA, Frelimo faced no internal opposition at the time of coming to power, revealing the distinct advantages of relative unity. But the aftermath would also suggest the limits on human agency, for Mozambique would soon face a South African-backed armed movement, RENAMO (the Movement of National Resistance) and become bogged down in a sixteen-year conflict compounded by droughts, costing over a million lives and producing five million refugees.[232] In the end, finally, the victories in Angola and Mozambique would give direct aid to the ZANU guerrillas in Zimbabwe, whose struggle marks the close of the decade of great anti-colonial revolutions in 1980.

Zimbabwe, 1960s–1980: anti-racist revolution

Zimbabwe provides us with a third southern African case contemporaneous with Angola and Mozambique, as well as those further afield in Vietnam, Nicaragua, and Iran, suggesting the extent of the favorable world-wide conjuncture of the late 1970s.[233] The guerrillas' successes in Angola and Mozambique proved materially helpful to Zimbabwe's revolutionaries, who would tap deep cultures of resistance to make their anti-colonial, anti-racist revolution.

The landlocked country now known as Zimbabwe was settled by farming communities 2,000 years ago.[234] In the thirteenth and fourteenth centuries, the important farming and trading city Great Zimbabwe dominated the area (the name means "houses of stone"). In the fifteenth century the city was abandoned, perhaps because local resources had been exhausted by the settlement. A regional empire of the Shona people headed by a king emerged later in the fifteenth century.

This was the civilization that the first European explorers would encounter. The Portuguese landed on the coast in 1498 and moved inland to trade in 1540. Eventually they acquired vast land holdings in the seventeenth century and some of the region's rulers converted to Christianity. From 1684 to 1695, however, the local leader Dombo organized a movement that defeated the Portuguese and expelled them from the interior. The ensuing Rozvi empire lasted until 1830. This success in driving out the better-armed Europeans has few parallels in Third World history and planted the seeds of later resistance. In the 1830s the Ndebele, a Zulu tribe from the south, became rulers over the Shona people, who lived in small-scale communities. The Ndebele retained their language but adopted local religious traditions and crop practices.[235] In 1870 Lobengula became king; he would have to deal with the second wave of Europeans, led by the British.

The British were concerned about the control of the Dutch-descended Boers, who operated gold mines to the south of the area in what is today South Africa. Both the Boers and the British tried to force treaties on Lobengula. In 1888 Lobengula signed a treaty which he later protested he hadn't understood, giving the British a claim to the mineral wealth of the area.[236] This concession was sold to the British South Africa Company, headed by Cecil Rhodes, for $1 million. The Company occupied Zimbabwe with some Shona support over Lobengula's resistance between 1890 and 1893 (the king died in 1894).[237] They set up their capital at Salisbury (today called Harare). Finding little gold, they sold prime land to European farmers. The Africans' livestock was either taken by the Europeans or died of diseases, leaving them only 14,000 of their 200,000 cattle by 1897. A tax on their huts also contributed to this decline by forcing Africans to sell their cattle and go to work for the Europeans.

In 1896 the African population tried another uprising, the Chimurenga, and were at first quite successful in driving out the European settlers. They drew on their religious beliefs, led by their priests and the mediums in contact with the spirits of their ancestors, to unify their forces in the revolt. Women played an important role in this struggle, in some cases as religious leaders. By 1898, British reinforcements had brought the revolt to an end with numerous executions. But the Chimurenga had cost the lives of 10 percent of the European population.[238]

The rebellion involved the British government more directly in the affairs of the colony, now called Rhodesia after Cecil Rhodes. The Africans were pushed onto poor land, and European settlers moved in to take the best farms; there were thus significant numbers of whites – including working- and middle-class people – settling in the country, as in South Africa, a pattern different from most of the rest of colonial Africa, administered by far fewer white bureaucrats, businessmen, and soldiers. In 1922 the settlers voted not to become part of South Africa, but rather to be a self-governing British colony, a sign that the white settler population of Rhodesia would hang onto its privileges fiercely, against both the African population and the British government. Dependent development in Rhodesia thus took the typical colonial form of a wealthy white farmer and business elite and a poor rural African majority, who would later be disadvantaged vis-à-vis the white working class as well.

Tor Skålnes describes the period of self-government from 1923 up to the Unilateral Declaration of Independence (UDI) from Britain in 1965 as "one of very rapid overall growth, fuelled by a heavy reliance on exports, massive government investment particularly in infrastructure, large-scale infusion of foreign capital, and immigration especially after the war."[239] Racist legislation guaranteed foreign investors – mostly British and South African – a cheap black labor pool, and by 1965 multinational capital had control over the mining, primary industry, banking, and insurance services of Rhodesia. An economic boom started after World War 2, with the white population doubling. White workers made deals with the elite to keep African wages low.[240] According to Astrow, white workers earned more in Rhodesia than in South Africa or Britain.[241] The 5 percent of the population that was white took 60 percent of the nation's personal income in the 1950s and 1960s, and only slightly less in the 1970s (this underestimates the gap, since most Africans did not labor for wages in the formal sector).[242]

Southern Rhodesia (which would become Zimbabwe), Nyasaland (later Malawi), and Northern Rhodesia (Zambia) formed the Central African Federation in 1953; the south would use its leverage as coal producers for the north's copper sector to push for "massive fiscal redistribution" that laid the groundwork for its economic and military base.[243] Britain's reluctant shift to support for decolonization and majority rule led to the independence of Malawi and Zambia and the isolation of Rhodesia in the early 1960s. This in turn prompted UDI in 1965.[244]

The threat of international sanctions that followed UDI led to stronger state intervention in directing the economy along lines of protectionism and import-substitution industrialization for greater self-sufficiency. When Britain withheld a payment of £5.1 million owed to Rhodesian investors, Rhodesia defaulted on £8.8 million due to Britain and the UN, netting £3.7 million to balance the national budget.[245] Foreign capital remained dominant, but the regime required it to keep more of its profits inside the country. Indeed, by 1980, foreign capital controlled some two-thirds of the economy.[246]

Even with sanctions, the economy grew at an average of 8 percent annually between 1967 and 1974, led by manufacturing's impressive rate of 12 percent.[247] Foreign trade now made its way through South Africa; both South Africa and Portuguese Mozambique supplied oil.[248] Other nations also violated the UN sanctions, among them France, Italy, Belgium, Greece, Brazil, and Japan.[249] The US used the

Byrd Amendment to import Southern Rhodesia's chrome and minerals in the 1970s, thus circumventing the UN sanctions it formally endorsed.[250]

The main consequence of dependent colonial development was the formation of the two societies we have seen elsewhere. The land acts of 1930 and 1969 prohibited Africans from growing cash crops and relegated them to about half the country in Tribal Trust Lands (TTLs), while the most arable half went to white settlers. In 1969, the average plot size for rural African families was 8.8 acres per capita while for Europeans it was 152.[251] Meanwhile, labor militancy among the black working class in the late 1940s forced the Huggins government to shift its policy from "separate development" to "racial partnership." The not-so-hidden goal was to bring political stability to rural areas and increase productivity in the Tribal Trust Lands by concentrating land in the hands of a few African farmers, ending the chiefs' prerogative to make land allocations. These measures were accompanied by educational reforms that created multi-racial schools:

Huggins may have anticipated stability from his racial partnership strategy, but the Land Husbandry Act failed to guarantee women any land rights with the exception of widows, who could hold only one-third of what the government allotted their counterparts. Migrant laborers had no land rights, and the overcrowding of TTLs left most Africans with smaller plots than promised by the government. Huggins' hope to supply commercial and industrial demands for labor backfired as urban areas were overwhelmed with an influx of landless peasants. The success of the reforms of the Huggins and subsequent Todd governments is exemplified in the 1962 census: 46.6 percent of males and 58.7 percent of females born after 1947 had no schooling and nearly 90 percent of commercial farm workers' children were undernourished.[252]

Meanwhile, black urban and rural income fell significantly short of the Poverty Datum Line:

The 1974 PDL study estimated that a typical black family in Fort Victoria required $914 per annum, in Bulawayo $840, and in Salisbury $882, to meet minimum needs. In that year average earnings in these towns were $528, $562 and $606 respectively. For agricultural workers, Harris and Riddell estimated in 1974 that a childless married couple would need a cash income of over $200 per annum in order to stay above the poverty line: average earnings for black agricultural workers in that year were $160 per annum, and it should be remembered that earnings include not just cash income but also payment in kind.[253]

It can be readily inferred from these data that the pattern of colonial development in Rhodesia produced the inequality and dislocations that we have hypothesized throughout this study as lying at the center of people's grievances.

The colonial settler state of Rhodesia in the 1940s and 1950s resembled the apartheid system in South Africa.[254] Africans were given little opportunity for education; they were paid one-tenth as much as Europeans for the same work; segregation was observed in hotels, restaurants and public transportation. There was no question of voting, except for a few hundred tribal leaders. To vote one had to make over $300 a year, a fortune for an African farmer or worker. The colonial state under Britain and then under Ian Smith's independent Rhodesia was clearly repressive, narrowly based on white rule, and – despite the formal trappings of a (racist) democracy – implicitly personalist under Smith from 1965 to 1980.

The African working and middle classes had been radicalized by the actions of this racist state, engaging in a general strike in 1948 and a coal miners' strike in 1954, both put down by force.[255] The state's anti-subversive legislation allowed detention without trial or formal charges in the 1950s. Troops were used to repress numerous strikes led by rank and file workers in 1972, and when the revolution broke out in earnest about the same time, the state responded with curfews and martial law, "protected villages" (achieved through forced relocation) and the generalized atrocities of counter-insurgency warfare in a fruitless attempt to separate the population from the guerrillas.[256] The Rhodesian state, therefore, fits the profile we have established of the repressive, exclusionary, personalist state, anchored in racism and disregard for international opinion.

The black population began to organize for change in the face of this repression, building on a long tradition of struggle, and on political cultures of resistance going back to the driving out of the Portuguese in the 1690s and the uprising of 1896. The guerrillas would eventually unite the population around the ideals of independence (nationalism), majority rule (the anti-racist struggle for democracy), and, for many, a kind of socialism (understood as land reform and other redistributionist measures).

The nationalist movement took early shape in the 1950s with the Bulawayo-based African National Congress, largely ineffective until joining the more militant Salisbury City Youth League in 1957 to form the Southern Rhodesian African National Congress (SRANC).[257] Moderate trade union leader Joshua Nkomo became its president and SRANC used legal means to resist racial discrimination and fight for democratic rights until banned by the state in 1959. The National Democratic Party (NDP), also led by Nkomo, was then created in 1960; one of its founders was the teacher Robert Mugabe, educated in South Africa and a classmate of Nelson Mandela. When Nkomo agreed to a new constitution in 1961 providing for a legislature composed of fifteen African and fifty whites, popular opposition grew so strong that he was forced to back down.

That same year the Zimbabwe African People's Union – ZAPU – was formed, to carry out sabotage and other acts of armed resistance to white rule. Nkomo was again president, but other members became critical of his conduct and in 1963 formed the Zimbabwe African National Union – ZANU – to struggle for majority rule and land distribution. Its early leader was Ndabaningi Sithole; Mugabe would eventually replace him in the mid-1970s. In addition to their own internal factions, which engaged in complex and sometimes deadly rivalry, the two parties also fought with each other, at times uniting their forces for specific purposes. Mugabe spent a number of years in jail, while Nkomo was often in exile outside the country.

In 1971 Britain's Heath administration offered Smith an agreement guaranteeing majority rule in 100 years. When Smith accepted, Britain sent the Pearce Commission to determine the views of the black population. The African National Congress (ANC) was established in December 1971 to oppose the settlement, with the little known moderate bishop Abel Muzorewa at its head to avoid its being banned. Muzorewa was soon discredited for negotiating with Smith; the Pearce Commission meanwhile found that Africans opposed the agreement by a margin of thirty-six to one.[258]

UDI and the ineffectiveness of UN sanctions among Britain, South Africa, and the United States finally led ZAPU and ZANU to undertake a strategy of guerrilla war for independence and majority rule.[259] They received military aid and training from other African countries – notably the Front-Line States (Zambia, Tanzania, Mozambique, and Botswana), as well as China and the Soviet Union. With aid came pressure, and the politics of exile and factions led to splits within ZANU. The assassination of ZANU's chairman, Herbert Chitepo, in March 1975 brought Mugabe to power in the guerrilla movement, as he condemned Zambia for its role in the murder while Sithole refused to.[260] In 1977, Mugabe moved against the radical leadership of ZIPA, an independent guerrilla group of ZANU and ZAPU fighters seeking victory on the battlefield, rather than through negotiations.[261]

ZANU ultimately emerged as the leading nationalist party, in large measure because of the appeal of its vision of a revolutionary political culture. Its army, ZANLA, recruited more effectively in the rural areas than ZAPU's army ZIPRA, which drew its rank and file from more urban working-class groups and had a more rigid, Soviet-inspired structure and approach.[262] ZANU's forces astutely tapped the historical currents of resistance in Zimbabwe, including the use of Shona spirit mediums and shrines to fashion a cultural nationalism based on an indigenous spirituality.[263]

Cliffe argues that "at its simplest [ZANU's] success . . . depended on their eventual turn to methods that emphasized winning support from the people."[264] In its zones of control, ZANU organized committees to work on problems of agriculture, health, women, and youth. Young people served as messengers between the people's committees and the guerrillas. Women played a major role in the struggle.[265] A survey of high school students in 1970–71 showed that 70 percent of the black students had taken part in nationalist demonstrations.[266] In the countryside, the conditions of life in the protected villages produced a steady stream of support for the guerrillas.

ZANU fused the ideology of pan-Africanism with the demand for majority rule and a pragmatic Marxism, or better put, a loosely-defined socialism. Faced with international pressure and the need for post-independence white support, Mugabe did not promise rapid social transformation, but instead argued "you do not destroy an infrastructure that is in being in order to realize your socialist aims. In fact you can do so by building on the structure that is there."[267] The most radical Marxist-Leninist elements of the guerilla movement had been neutralized during Mugabe's rise to power before the Lancaster Settlement. What remained was a core of nationalism shared by all parties: "since they all accepted that from the beginning Zimbabwe would have to go through a stage of capitalist development – the 'nationalist democratic revolution'– they were led to similar political conclusions."[268] This was the supple formula needed to bring the factions together, however uneasily, under Mugabe's leadership.

The international sanctions and guerrilla war caused economic hardship for the Smith government in the 1970s, providing the internal and external factors conducive to the negotiated settlement that brought independence in 1979 and 1980. While the economy prospered even after UDI until 1974, defense absorbed 40 percent of the national budget by 1972, and its share rose further as the war intensified.[269] Manufacturers and farmers had to pay the costs of the trade diversion across South Africa, and foreign investment began to decline. The war led to white flight, draining production and the military of crucially needed manpower. By 1979, some 2,000 of the 7,000 white settler farms were deserted, especially where the rebels were strongest, in the east.[270] Sanctions hurt agriculture, particularly tobacco (where the country's share of the world market fell from 27 to 10 percent), and the state had to subsidize white farmers.[271] The African population was also hurt by the government's efforts to finance the war, and unemployment fueled the ranks of the guerrillas.[272] The economy could no longer bear up when the two-phase world recession of 1970–71 and 1975–77 was added to the effects of war and sanctions. These hardships weakened the Smith government's control of the situation, and created an atmosphere favoring negotiations.

Smith had famously said: "I don't believe in black majority rule ever in Rhodesia, not in a thousand years."[273] But by the late 1970s he was coming under increasing pressure from the effects of the war, as well as international public opinion, to agree to changes in the system. Sanctions, as we have seen, had an uneven effect as First World powers hypocritically evaded them, but took a cumulative bite over time[274] (in this we can see a world-systemic political factor influencing the economic downturn). A second element of the world-systemic opening was provided by the 1974 coup in Portugal and the subsequent independence of Mozambique, which gave the guerrillas a new source of support (FRELIMO had been supplying them since 1969 in a necessarily more modest way). Here we see the effect of a revolution in one country providing the world-systemic opening used by another.

South Africa and the US began to question Smith's viability as the war progressed, akin to the Carter administration's growing doubts about Somoza and the shah: "the South African government began to consider a black successor to Smith, one not only amenable to all-white interests concerned in Pretoria, Salisbury, London and Washington, but willing to assist in a policy of containing Mozambique."[275] For Nixon and Kissinger, there was the added threat posed by Soviet support for Nkomo, and the fear of more falling dominoes. Kissinger argued that the US had "a stake . . . in not having the whole continent become radical and move in a direction that is incompatible with Western interests."[276] The US and other core nations sought economic stability in the region; as US negotiator Andrew Young put it in the more genteel terms of the Carter administration: "the USA has but one option, and that is neo-colonialism . . . as bad as that has been made to sound, neo-colonialism means that the multinational corporations will continue to have a major influence in the development of the productive capacity of the Third World. And they are, whether we like it or not."[277]

The dénouement followed in several halting steps between 1978 and 1980. Smith first tried some cosmetic changes in 1978, forming a government with several African leaders whom he controlled, most notably Sithole and Bishop Muzorewa, who became prime minister. Both ZANU and ZAPU refused to accept this, and the UN, OAU, and even the newly elected British Conservative Prime Minister Margaret Thatcher did not recognize this government. The Front-Line States of Zambia and Tanzania pressured Nkomo and Mugabe to join in a fragile union as the Patriotic Front (PF). The war was intensified, and under the increasing pressure of guerrilla successes, all sides agreed to free and open elections with international supervision. On September 10, 1979, British Foreign Secretary Lord Carrington invited the PF, Muzorewa, and Smith to Lancaster House in London to negotiate a joint settlement. Davidow notes that Carrington "tenaciously stuck to a well-planned negotiating strategy based on a strong unwillingness to let either of the . . . delegations hijack the conference. He insisted on a step by step approach which forced consideration of the thorny issues one at a time rather than as a complete package which might have proven indigestible."[278] On December 21, 1979, after three months of sessions, all parties signed the Lancaster Agreement.

ZANU and ZAPU agreed to guarantee twenty seats out of 100 for the white parties for seven years, and a very restricted degree of expropriation of white farms, as long as the principle of one person one vote was adhered to, and the majority would control all the institutions of the state, integrating the guerrillas into the army and police.[279] In the February 1980 elections, Mugabe's ZANU won fifty-seven seats, Nkomo's ZAPU won twenty, and the Rhodesian Front of Ian Smith won all twenty seats reserved for whites; Muzorewa took just three seats. Robert Mugabe became the prime minister and promised reconciliation, including both Nkomo and white politicians in his government. On April 18, 1980 the independent nation of Zimbabwe was created. In all, 30,000 Africans had died in the fighting and many more had lived as refugees. Zimbabwe's anti-racist anti-colonial revolution had come to power.

Vietnam, 1945–1975: the three revolutions

Vietnam rivals China as the longest revolution, and it is, with Mexico, an *interrupted* revolution – or perhaps, better, a *series* of revolutions between 1945 and 1975.[280] In Vietnam, we have a revolution carried out in another French colony over a period of thirty years, involving at least three distinct moments: the liberation of the north in 1945 in the wake of World War 2, the expulsion of the French from Vietnam in 1954 following their defeat at Dien Bien Phu, and a revolution in the south between 1959 and 1975 in which the north allied with southern revolutionaries to overthrow a regime massively backed by the United States. It is my contention that there was never a non-colonial phase in the south. While it is artificial to separate these events, the focus here will be on the final stage, the battle for South Vietnam between North Vietnam, the southern People's

Liberation Army/National Liberation Front, South Vietnam, and the US from 1962 to 1975. We will see our five factors powerfully confirmed again, especially the significance of political cultures of opposition and the world-systemic opening.

Before analyzing the last phase in light of our five factors, we should look briefly at the causes of the first two revolutionary moments, 1945 and 1954.[281] Let us begin this story with the August revolution of 1945, which brought about the temporary abdication of the last Vietnamese emperor, Bao Dai, and the declaration of a socialist Democratic Republic of Vietnam (DRV), with Ho Chi Minh as president. The nature of Vietnam's dependent colonial development and repressive, exclusionary state under the French will be discussed in detail below. The 1930s had seen a depression that moved in tandem with the world trend and produced falling prices for rice and rubber, halts in production, and rising unemployment and hunger.[282] World War 2 brought a world-systemic opening in the paradoxical form of Japan's occupation and its weakening of French control, which shattered the racialist myth of Western superiority. The Japanese left the French colonial administration intact until March 9, 1945, when they seized power directly.

The Guomindang government in China initially supported the rebels, as did briefly the US Office of Strategic Services (soon to be known as the CIA).[283] The impact of this opening was compounded by a downturn that started with inflation during the occupation, and then a severe famine in 1945, brought about by the conjuncture of a poor harvest, flooding, Allied bombing, Japanese rice exports and the switch to other export crops, and French and Japanese food storage for their troops; the famine is said to have taken two million lives, one-quarter of the population in the north.[284] As Truong Chinh put it: "Hundreds of thousands of people starved beside granaries full of rice kept by the Japanese and the French."[285] In this one sentence, we can see the coming together of virtually all the factors in our model: dependent development (the shift to rice exports), the repressive state (failing to protect the population from starvation), economic downturn (the famine itself), world-systemic opening (the effects of the uneasy relationship between France and Japan), and political cultures of opposition (the growing perception that the famine was caused by the occupiers).

Such a conjuncture could only aid Ho Chi Minh, Vo Nguyen Giap, Pham Van Dong, and their associates in the Indochinese Communist Party as they fashioned a powerful political culture that appealed to the population's desire for independence; the richness and further development of this culture will also be discussed below. Japan surrendered to the Allies on August 15; the insurrection began three days later, and by August 25 Emperor Bao Dai had resigned and handed over power in the north of the country to the Viet Minh (the shortened name of the communist-led Vietnamese Independence League), who promptly declared the establishment of the Democratic Republic of Vietnam. The French regained control of Saigon with British help and American support in the fall of 1945, and in 1946 were able to take the major cities in the north as well; spurred on by their humiliation during the Japanese occupation, their post-1945 rule would be even harsher as they rejected negotiation with the Viet Minh.

The cold war set the terms of the next phase of the conflict. Newly revolutionary China and the Soviet Union recognized the DRV as the government of Vietnam with its capital at Hanoi, while in 1950 the United States recognized the State of Vietnam with its capital at Saigon under newly restored emperor Bao Dai. The French retained real power under this arrangement, and a French parliamentary commission described their own rule as a "veritable dictatorship . . . without limit and without control."[286] The First Indochina War pitted the DRV's guerrilla forces against a highly repressive French force fighting what was already being called "la sale guerre" (the dirty war), backed with $2.5 billion in aid by the US.[287] China provided crucial weapons, trainers, and food to the north, especially after the armistice in Korea in 1953; thus, just as Vietnam's August revolution must have heartened the Chinese revolutionaries after 1945, Mao's victory in 1949 contributed to the world-systemic opening that helped drive the French out of Vietnam a few years later. The war produced a predictable economic downturn: rice production for 1954–55 was only one-half what it had been in 1938, and this in a population that had doubled in that period.[288] By late 1953, having suffered many of the 22,000 casualties it would incur in the war and facing massive divisions of opinion at home, both public and official, the French were ready to give up their colony and the US was relieved to have extricated itself from the Korean War; in a favorable geo-political conjuncture, the post-Stalin USSR was seeking peace in the region as well.[289] After their defeat at Dien Bien Phu in 1954, the French needed only a face-saving way out (their search for "an honorable settlement" foreshadowing Nixon's "peace with honor");[290] this came with the signing of the Geneva Accords, which divided the country at the seventeenth parallel pending elections to reunify it.

It is said that what the French could not win on the battlefield, they won at the negotiating table. The DRV had controlled 80 percent of the population and 75 percent of the land after Dien Bien Phu,[291] but the promised elections never came. In October 1955, southern prime minister Ngo Dinh Diem deposed Bao Dai and declared himself president of the Republic of South Vietnam. Land reform and forced labor took many lives in the north, while southern communists were tortured and killed by Diem's regime. Many anti-communist and Catholic northerners fled south, damaging the north's economic infrastructure in some cases and providing the Catholic Diem a social base.[292] By the late 1950s there were revolutionary forces operating in the south as the National Liberation Front (the NLF, termed the Viet Cong by the Saigon government). In 1961 John F. Kennedy approved a counter-insurgency plan to support the south and the US sent its first combat troops, touching off the Second Indochina, or Vietnam, War (or, as the northern and southern revolutionaries called it, the American War) – the third phase of the revolution, with fateful consequences for all sides.[293] Let us now consider the causes of the revolution as it unfolded in the 1960s and 1970s, having briefly noted the convergence of both earlier revolutionary triumphs – 1945 and 1954 – with the factors in our model.

The pre-colonial economy was based for centuries on subsistence rice culture, and Vietnam had minimal trade contacts with the commercial powers of India, China, or the Arab world. This remained the state of affairs even after initial trading contacts with the West were established in the sixteenth and seventeenth centuries. This would change relatively quickly in the latter half of the nineteenth century as France entered a struggle with the British for the lucrative China market, which brought them to Vietnam, Laos, and Cambodia, collectively known as Indochina, France's "balcony on the Pacific."[294] The chronological signposts of colonialism include the occupation of Saigon in 1859, the taking of Hanoi after a ten-year war in 1882, and battles against a number of uprisings till at least 1909.

There is some debate over the degree to which colonial Vietnam made a transition toward capitalism, with Martin Murray arguing that it did, as the title of his book, *The Development of Capitalism in Colonial Indochina (1870–1940)*, makes plain.[295] Paul Mus takes a different view, arguing there was no question of an industrial capitalism or proletariat in colonial Vietnam, while acknowledging there were capitalist enclaves in the country.[296] Both may be right. For Murray, "Colonial dependence was maintained not only by state force and violence but also by means of currency and trade controls overlaid by a virtual colonial monopoly over desirable land, labor, and capital in the colonial territories."[297] Dependent development was based on mining and agro-exports, and wrought significant changes in social structure. From the beginning, France aimed to make her colony pay for its own administration, through taxes and labor services imposed on the peasantry, as well as marketing monopolies and customs duties. A further aim was profits in the form of a new export economy based on rice and rubber, as French irrigation systems made the Mekong Delta "one of the world's most productive regions for rice cultivation."[298] Exports grew from 57,000 tons in 1860 to 1,548,000 by 1937, at which time half the country's arable land was under cultivation.[299] The crop was taken from a huge class of small tenant farmers subject to larger landlords in turn beholden to the French state. Rubber was the second largest export, and relied on forced, migrant plantation labor under soul-shattering conditions.[300] Coal, zinc, phosphates, iron ore, tin, sugar cane, and tea were also important colonial exports produced by migrant labor, much of it from the north, whose small villages were hit hard by French taxes. Railroads and textiles fueled the first stages of industrialization, along with such light industries as paper, sugar, food processing, matches, bicycle assembly, and the crucial infrastructure for the export economy in the form of roads, bridges, dikes, and ports.[301] The working class grew to about 200,000 in the 1920s, a small but significant new social force.[302] In the end, the French never pushed for deeper industrialization, preferring to make their profits by control over raw materials, a pattern found in the Portuguese colonies as well, the distinctive stamp of dependent colonial development.

Dependent development is thus a useful way to characterize the colonial situation of Vietnam under both the French, who turned the country into a rice and rubber exporter, and then the US, whose massive aid to South Vietnam kept the economy afloat during the 1960s. We are again in the clear presence of dependent colonial development, measured any number of ways. The highest-ranking Vietnamese official in 1903 earned less than the lowest-ranking French official.[303] In fact, "it is said that the French caretaker of the University of Hanoi earned more than three times the salary of a Vietnamese engineer."[304] Yet there was a Vietnamese elite of merchants, bureaucrats, and some seven thousand large landlords tied to the world powers that benefited from this arrangement, and a new strata of clerks, translators, and village officials who collaborated with the French, whose preference for Chinese merchants and middle-men did not encourage the development of an economically independent middle class (which might have provided a wider political base or fostered a non-communist nationalist alternative).

Meanwhile the average peasant or poor town dweller lived a very difficult life. Some 57 to 70 percent of the peasantry was landless by the 1930s, living by paying large shares of the crop, rent, and/or taxes to the landlords and French, who directly held about 20 percent of the land.[305] The malnourished workers on the Michelin rubber plantation were treated as "prisoners, as wretched ones in tattered clothing whom the assistants overpower through contempt and insults instead of beatings."[306] Twelve thousand out of 45,000 workers at one Michelin plantation died between

1917 and 1944.[307] One index of nutrition is salt consumption; in 1937, it was estimated that the average person consumed only 14.8 of the 22 pounds of salt needed annually to maintain oneself.[308] In the 1920s, only 10 percent of the Vietnamese population was in a school of any kind; by the end of World War 2, this was still less than 20 percent for boys.[309]

Duiker describes the two societies wrought by dependent development in terms we are by now familiar with: "The end result of the French colonization experience was not the creation of a society on the verge of rapid economic development, but a classic example of a dual economy, with a small and predominantly foreign commercial sector in the cities surrounded by a mass of untrained and often poverty-stricken peasants in the villages."[310] For Mus, "In the country the economy continued to be based on little trade and local consumption, while in the cities there developed a modern commercial economy based on worldwide exchange," noting further that "The sharp dichotomy in culture between the cities, where about one-fourth of the Vietnamese live, and the countryside, where about three-fourths live, has been a barrier which these governments have not really been able to overcome."[311] Life on the plantations and in the mining communities was lived in poor housing, with inadequate diets, and few medical or educational facilities.[312] Taxes fell heavily on the Vietnamese to force them into the new economic arrangements, and lightly on the French settlers, to buttress their role in the system.[313]

A generation later, the US solidified this process (and repeated many of France's economic and political mistakes), turning dependent colonial development in a distinctive direction ever closer to the classic dependent development we have seen in the great social revolutions. Industrialization continued with the establishment of industrial zones in Saigon involving such activities as cement and other construction work, apparel, pharmaceuticals, and food processing.[314] Any deepening of the process was blocked by the availability of cheaper Japanese and US goods. In addition, the US was supplying *a million tons* of goods a month to Saigon in 1967, and it must be said that most US investments were war-related – roads, bridges, warehouses, communications systems, airfields, ports.[315] At the military PX in Saigon, US soldiers could purchase "everything from sports clothes, cameras, tape recorders and transistor radios to soap, shampoo, deodorant and, of course, condoms";[316] quantities of these items then found their way into the South Vietnamese economy via the black market. Speculators serviced the elite and middle classes, and gouged the peasants.[317] Prostitution and drugs were rampant, by-products of the war that extended into the highest levels of government, further weakening the regime's legitimacy. Diem spent little on education or health services.[318]

Land reform came belatedly in 1969 when the US and the Thieu regime (1965–75) finally concluded that southern peasants were supporting the communists because of this issue: Duiker judges the "Land to the Tiller" program a success by 1975, yet the war and strategic hamlet campaign had already driven four million peasants – one quarter of the south's population – to urban shantytowns.[319] The ravages of war and urban poverty fed each other and rose in tandem; Stanley Karnow observed the two societies created by dependent development in the 1960s: "For grotesque contrast, no place to my mind matched the *terrasse* of the Continental Palace Hotel, a classic reminder of the French colonial era, where limbless Vietnamese victims of the war would crawl like crabs across the handsome tile floor to accost American soldiers, construction workers, journalists and visitors as they chatted and sipped their drinks under the ceiling fans."[320] As Le Minh Khue, a journalist and novelist from the north said after the reunification of the country: "People in the North always thought the cities in the South must be big and well equipped and luxurious, but when I walked around Danang I soon realized it was merely a consumer city. It lived on goods, so when the products were gone, it was just another impoverished city."[321]

In sum, under the US condominium, the social structure of the south was riven by a new phase of dependent development, no better in its mitigating effects than earlier ones. As Bernard Fall put it early in the 1960s: "without American aid to Vietnam's military and economic machinery, the country would not survive for ten minutes."[322] In LeVan's well-turned phrase, all the US aid succeeded in creating was "an appearance of prosperity in the southern cities."[323] Millions of peasants saw their homes destroyed and their families forced into refugee camps or southern cities: "The war profoundly uprooted Vietnamese society, separating countless people from their ancestral land and their families."[324]

In terms of the colonial state, the governments of the south were generally perceived by the population as under the control of the French and later the Americans, and not truly representative of the will of the people, whereas the north, under its charismatic leader, Ho Chi Minh, who had led the struggle for national independence since the 1940s, seemed to many a more legitimate government. As Jeff Goodwin has said, the movement against the French "triumphed largely because of the racially exclusionary and broadly repressive nature of French colonial politics."[325] As militant Ngo Van put it, "Indochina under the French was a prison, and there was nothing to do but unite against the jailer."[326]

The Bao Dai cabinet was described in 1952 by the US consul in Hanoi as composed of "opportunists, nonentities, extreme reactionaries, assassins, hirelings and, finally, men of faded mental powers."[327] In 1950, Charlton Ogburn of the State Department characterized the emperor himself as "a figure deserving of the ridicule and contempt with which he is generally regarded by the Vietnamese, and any supposition that he could succeed or that a French army in Indochina could possibly be an asset to us could be entertained only by one totally ignorant of Asian realities."[328]

The Diem government was no great improvement on this. Many professionals – teachers, doctors, and lawyers – were alienated by the Diem regime's corruption and penchant for rigged elections, dating to 1955 and 1959. Diem refused to even rule through a party at first; when he finally formed a Leninist-style party he gave it the revealing name of Can Lao (Personalist Labor – the contrived ideology of "personalism," a pastiche of individual freedom and communal needs).[329] This authoritarian, cult of personality approach was favored by US officials over a more democratic polity.[330] Diem promoted members of the Catholic minority, personal favorites, and family members while keeping his senior military officers in the dark about troop deployments.[331] The regime used massive and often indiscriminate repression as well, most obviously against supporters (and suspected supporters) of the Viet Minh, and the government's problems intensified with the army's attacks on Buddhist monks and nuns in 1963. The Kennedy administration soon edged away from Diem, and he was murdered on November 2 in a CIA-backed coup led by the army generals, marking "the start of a series of coups, countercoups, and military regimes in the years to come" – there were seven military rulers in the course of 1964 alone.[332]

General Nguyen Van Thieu became head of state in 1965, and would retain control for the duration of the war by outmaneuvering his main rival, Air Vice Marshall Nguyen Cao Ky in 1967 to become president under a new US-style constitution, though his slate received only 35 percent of the votes.[333] Like other dictators who have fallen to revolutions, he enriched himself in office, making millions of dollars in speculation on the US commercial imports program that was supposed to generate currency for the South Vietnamese government to pay for the war.[334] The regime was thus personalist in the classical sense under both Diem and Thieu, and colonial in the sense of directed and supported by the United States, which financed the latter's 1971 presidential campaign, for example.[335]

The US war itself may be taken as the most cruel and brutal manifestation of the repressive (neo-)colonial state. The extraordinary bombing campaigns that began with "Operation Rolling Thunder" in 1965 and continued off and on until the cease-fire of 1973 saw the US assault North Vietnam, "an area the size of Texas, [with] triple the bomb tonnage dropped on Europe, Asia and Africa during WWII" – at fifteen million tons the equivalent of 400 Hiroshima-sized atomic bombs.[336] CIA counter-insurgency operations such as the notorious Phoenix program "neutralized" over eighty thousand suspected Viet Cong, although the venality of South Vietnamese officers allowed many captured Viet Cong to escape.[337] At least one and a half million Vietnamese were killed in the war; with Mexico, this is by far the greatest cost in lives of any of the revolutions studied in this book. Given these numbers and tactics, and the stated goal of waging a "war of attrition," it is not too far-fetched to consider the US strategy in Vietnam as genocidal, a verdict rendered by the Russell Tribunal chaired by Jean-Paul Sartre in Stockholm in 1967.[338] At the least, we are in the presence of a highly repressive, violent state.

As William Duiker notes, "from a historical perspective, the most striking fact about the Vietnam War is probably not why the United States lost, but why the Communists won."[339] General Vo Nguyen Giap's reply to this suggests the depth and strength of the political cultures of opposition at play on the Vietnamese side:

We sought to break the will of the American government to continue the conflict . . . We were waging a people's war, *à la mannière vietnamienne* – a total war in which every man, every women, every unit, big or small, is sustained by a mobilized population. So America's sophisticated weapons, electronic devices and the rest were to no avail. Despite its military power, America misgauged the limits of its power. In war there are two factors – human beings and weapons. Ultimately, though, human beings are the decisive factor. Human beings! Human beings![340]

The political cultures that animated the revolutionaries in the north and south revolved around long-standing notions of driving out the foreign invaders (in this case, going back to ancient times and the struggle against Chinese encroachment),[341] combined with a populist call for indigenous government and an emerging socialist ideology as the north joined the Soviet bloc in the 1950s. Political cultures of opposition were thus a mixture of "traditional" values of independence and egalitarianism overlaid by modern ideologies of nationalism and socialism. Significant Mandarin-led uprisings had occurred between 1885 and 1909; their failure led a new generation to embrace and adapt new ideas, among them the first expressions of Marxism that began to circulate among teachers, students, professionals, and progressive members of the gentry in the 1920s. Elite and middle-class Vietnamese students who received their education abroad returned to Vietnam only to find they had no scope for serving their country, as it was with their countrymen educated in the new French lycées; a student of the 1930s told the judge who convicted him of agitation that this injustice "turned me into a revolutionary."[342]

John LeVan argues that the "Vietnamese, perhaps out of patriotic zeal, identified their revolutionary strategy, especially the military component, more with the glory of their historical past than either Leninist or Maoist doctrine."[343] Certainly, an intensely felt anti-colonialism animated the struggle: for Ho and his comrades, since the 1940s it had been a question of uniting "patriots of all ages and all types, peasants, workers, merchants and soldiers" to fight the French, then the Japanese, then the French again, and finally the Americans.[344] It is revealing that from 1919 to 1945 Ho had taken the name Nguyen Ai Quoc – "Nguyen who loves his country."[345] To even utter the word "Viet Nam" under the French subjected one to arrest; it became a "rallying cry for revolutionaries."[346] Duiker considers national independence to have been "a sacred issue to virtually all Vietnamese."[347] Giap believes "We won the war because we would rather die than live in slavery."[348] The new upper classes, meanwhile, were too identified with the French and later the Americans to inspire such allegiance, and no non-communist nationalism could take root.[349] Of those that tried, the strongest was the Vietnamese Nationalist Party (VNQDD), which utterly lacked peasant backing, and was crushed ruthlessly by the French after a 1930 uprising.[350] When the Indochina Communist Party faced a similar level of repression, it survived, and indeed, attracted new adherents among workers and peasants.[351]

Over time, however, contra LeVan, a Vietnamese version of Marxist socialism did take deep root as well. It was Ho – who never graduated from the National Academy but was fluent in Vietnamese, French, English, Russian, and Chinese – who brought Lenin's ideas about imperialism to a ready audience, melding Vietnamese nationalism with a Marxist analysis of colonialism; according to Tran Van Giar, "It opened a whole new world to us."[352] Ken Post considers the leadership

a truly remarkable group of people . . . a group to whom Ho passed on his dedication, who together with him turned it into a passion for national liberation and their people's emancipation from exploitation and want which was disciplined, as was his, by their Marxism-Leninism. This proved to be a combination which no French, American or anti-Communist Vietnamese could match, emotionally or intellectually.[353]

Duiker suggests there may have been an elective affinity of sorts between Marxism and Confucianism: "a common emphasis on collective responsibility versus individual rights; the concept of an educated elite with unique access to a single truth as embodied in classical doctrine; and the stress in both ideologies on personal ethics and service to society."[354] For Paul Mus, Confucianism as a political culture contributed to the positive reception of the Viet Minh due to the popular belief that after long periods of stability, revolutionary change comes from a higher power, so that when the French lost their authority to the Japanese, "the Vietnamese peasants . . . sensed a change in the Mandate of Heaven and were awaiting a sign of a new order in the country."[355] This would come with the rise of Ho Chi Minh and his followers. Ho tapped the underlying values of the village community and cast Marxian ideals of equality in this light, using the "symbols and idioms of traditionalist politics"[356] to link the socialist movement to the culture of Vietnam's peasant communities, to the spiritual longing for a stronger communal bond. Thus, the Vietnamese phrase for "socialism," *xa hoi hoa*, can be construed as the village community (*xa*), in union (*hoi*) with *hoa*, "the action in depth through which the 'mandate of heaven,' through the sovereigns who are its bearers, civilize a country and bring into flower all that the social character of man contains."[357] The word for revolution, *cach-mang*, is made up of two words signifying change of fate.[358]

Giap recalls this fusion of nationalism, Marxism, and Confucian ideals:

Marxism promised revolution, an end to oppression, the happiness of mankind . . . Nationalism made me a Marxist, as it did so many Vietnamese . . . [It] also seemed to me to coincide with the ideals of our ancient society, when the emperor and his subjects lived in harmony, when everyone worked and prospered together, when the old and children were cared for. It was a utopian dream.[359]

This desire for social justice could take many forms. For Tran Thi Gung, a woman who grew up twenty-five miles from Saigon, the decision to join the NLF was taken in 1962 when soldiers killed her father while attending a political meeting and told her to go fetch his body. To revenge was joined another set of motives: "the people in my neighborhood suffered from poverty and deprivation and were always brutalized by the police and puppet soldiers. I wanted to do something to liberate my country and help people get enough food and clothing. I believed my mission in life was to continue my father's cause."[360]

The political culture forged by Ho was flexible and resonated well with the population. Post notes that "the really decisive factor [was] . . . the women and men of Viet Nam who responded to the patriotic and emancipatory call . . . Certainly their history and culture prepared them in a most unusual way, and Ho and his Communist followers knew intuitively and intellectually how to use these."[361] For Duiker, as early as the 1940s "The genius of [the Communist Party's] program was that it was able to combine patriotic and economic themes in an artful way to win the allegiance of a broad spectrum of the Vietnamese population," linking "the desire for economic and social justice" with "the restoration of national independence."[362] Duiker, who has made a close study of the Vietnamese side of the war, notes the "aura of legitimacy that the Communist Party acquired among the Vietnamese people by virtue of its generation of struggle against the French."[363] A generation later, in the 1960s, the NLF "won widespread support from the rural and urban poor by its promises of social reform and national self-determination while at the same time allaying the fears of urban moderates and foreign observers alike that it would embark on a program of radical social change after the seizure of power in Saigon."[364]

This suggests the degree to which Vietnamese communism was a vibrant political culture of opposition, tapping idiom and adapting ideology in ways that spoke to people's lived experience, and well-organized and fostered by the cadres and institutions of the NLF. This culture fostered an incredible degree of morale at multiple levels: among the population of the north, the soldiers in the south, and the population which joined or supported them. The appointment of highly dedicated "cadres" to southern combat units contributed to this – unlike South Vietnam's military officers, Viet Cong leaders shared the hardships of the troops and sometimes involved them in the plans they made. A North Vietnamese private undoubtedly spoke for many when he said "we always knew why we were fighting."[365]

The coalition that was brought together was indeed of the broad kind we have seen in all other cases of success. While the majority of the rank and file were peasants, Jeff Goodwin is right to characterize the 1945–54 struggle thus:

The Viet Minh mobilized sharecroppers, to be sure, but also middle and rich peasants (and even some "patriotic landlords"), agricultural estate workers, a number of ethnic minorities in the highlands, and elements from the urban working and middle classes, including many sons and daughters of the traditional Confucian scholar-gentry, who came to hold many important leadership positions within the Communist party.[366]

By the 1960s, this coalition would prove to be multi-class, multi-ethnic, and filled with women at every level as well.

In turning to the conjuncture of economic downturn and world-systemic opening, we see again the effects of war and revolution on both. The revolutionary crisis intensified after American military intervention escalated in the mid-1960s and Viet Cong military activities spread into the south. The country was systematically devastated by the war, epitomized in the famous quote by an American officer: "It became necessary to destroy the town to save it."[367] The war sapped the government's budget, and this, with the black market, led to currency devaluations and skyrocketing debt.[368] Meanwhile, the vast sums poured in by the US distorted the functioning of the economy and led to massive corruption. Both rice and rubber production were in decline by the mid-1960s due to the war.[369] Dependence on US aid to keep the economy functioning turned into economic downturn in the last few years of the war, when both military and economic aid were "drastically reduced"[370] and the economy, "long dependent on massive infusions of US aid, spun out of control, bringing severe inflation and massive urban unemployment."[371]

Without the aggressive US intervention, it is quite possible that the NLF would have come to power in the south by the mid-1960s, either through guerrilla war or by forcing elections, a fact which underscores the significance of the absence or presence of a world-systemic opening. That intervention, in turn, and its successive escalations from Eisenhower through Kennedy to Johnson, reposed on the celebrated "domino theory" of the danger of communism spreading throughout southeast Asia if South Vietnam "fell." Duiker notes that the north consciously adopted the strategy of influencing international public opinion, as it had earlier in the struggle against the French; the "objective was not to win a total victory on the battlefield, but to bring about a psychological triumph over its adversaries, leading to a negotiated settlement under terms favorable to the revolution."[372] As early as 1966, US public opinion wavered, "a trend influenced by the mounting casualties, rising taxes and, especially, the feeling that there was no end in view."[373] Lyndon Johnson's levels of support fell from eight out of ten Americans in 1963 to four out of ten in 1967, and further after the Tet offensive a year later accomplished precisely the goals described by Duiker above.[374] Criticism of Vietnam policy mounted in such prominent places as Senator J. William Fulbright's foreign relation committee hearings, and in such influential media circles as the columns of Walter Lippman, Harrison Salisbury of the *New York Times*, *Time* magazine, and *Life*.[375] In March of 1968, Johnson announced he would not seek re-election. The police riot at the Democratic Convention in August 1968 was another marker of the discontent the war was generating. The massacre at Mylai of as many as 500 unarmed Vietnamese peasants, women, and children by US troops in March 1968 further sickened public opinion in the US when it rose to the surface through courageous testimony and reporting in December 1969, as did such shocking photos as the chief of the national police executing a prisoner in the street in 1968, and of a naked nine-year-old girl running down a rural road, arms outstretched, with napalm wounds in 1972.[376]

The world-systemic opening crystallized with the growth of a peace movement in the United States in the 1960s, the election of Richard Nixon in 1968 with promises to end the American military role, and the attenuation of the US commitment to support the South Vietnamese government at all costs after 1972. When the National Guard killed four anti-war students at Kent State and two at Jackson State University in May 1970, over 400 colleges were shut down and 100,000 marched in Washington.[377] In 1971, polls indicated that Nixon enjoyed the backing of less than half the American public: only 34 percent thought he was handling the war well, versus 58 percent who now thought the war "immoral" and 71 percent who felt the war itself had been a "mistake."[378] In April, 200,000 peace activists marched in Washington; by now, increasing numbers of the returning vets were joining the movement. Low morale in the ranks of the US army also played a role, as units were plagued by drug addiction (with up to one-third of the troops using heroin), "fragging" of officers (grenade attacks on them by enlisted men), and "sandbagging" assigned missions by finding a safe hiding place and calling in with invented reports on their activities.[379] In June, the *New York Times* began to publish the incriminating secret documents leaked to it by Daniel Ellsberg.[380]

Nixon announced the gradual withdrawal of US troops in June 1969. From its peak at 541,000 in that year, the numbers declined to 160,000 by December 1971, and to none by 1974. The US engaged in an erratic pattern of negotiation followed by escalation, as in late 1972 when Le Duc Tho and Nixon were on the verge of agreeing to a cease-fire that was rejected by Thieu as a sellout of the south; when Le Duc Tho then broke off negotiations, Nixon arranged for the massive "Christmas bombing" of the north – 40,000 tons in twelve days, with a pause only on Christmas Day.[381] It was a rearguard action for an elusive "peace with honor." A month later, the Paris peace accords were signed, putting the conflict in temporary abeyance, the revolutionaries still on the ground in the south and the US committed to pulling out of the country, leaving its defense to Thieu's army. With US backing gone, the final outcome was now sealed: a year later, the resignation of Nixon would hasten the war to its finish.

By the 1970s, the Soviet Union and China were getting six thousand tons of aid daily to North Vietnam; the rebels in the south needed only fifteen tons of supplies a day.[382] US bombing did not deter this provisioning, nor did it prevent supplies from getting to the south along the well-maintained Ho Chi Minh trail. Aid levels from the socialist world reached $1 billion for the decade of 1955–65, and $4–5 billion or more for the next decade, as China and the Soviet Union competed to provide the most aid to the north – missiles, artillery, planes, tanks, and ammunition from the latter, and food and support troops from the former.[383] Though small in comparison with the more than $120 billion the US spent between 1965 and 1973 it was enough to offset it.[384] US aid fell from $3.2 billion annually to $700 million in the last three years of the war.[385] Equally importantly, China's support for the north probably deterred US policymakers from a course of total destruction, lest the US

find itself confronting China, or even the USSR.[386] Finally, since South
Vietnam had become completely dependent on US aid to keep going, we
see how the economics of dependent development and the geo-politics
of the world-systemic opening can be conjoined, and turn into the economic downturn that followed the peace accords and the phasing out of
US aid.

As government popularity plunged, the end came quite rapidly, with
communist troops taking Phuoc Long province, fifty miles northwest
of Saigon, in January 1975, then moving on to the Central Highlands
and provinces south of the DMZ (the "demilitarized" zone separating
north and south) in March.[387] Saigon fell on April 30, as the ranking
communist officer on the scene, journalist Colonel Bui Tin, announced
to the people: "You have nothing to fear. Between Vietnamese, there are
no victors and no vanquished. Only the Americans have been beaten. If
you are patriots, consider this a moment of joy. The war for our country is
over."[388] The rebels, using guerrilla tactics, had fought the world's most
powerful army to a bitter standstill, though at great cost: while some
58,000 Americans were killed and half a million suffered post-traumatic
stress, at least two million Vietnamese died (on all sides, but mostly among
the revolutionaries) in the struggle for independence. The reunification
of Vietnam as a single country under socialism had been achieved by a
revolution marked by incredible endurance, tenacity, and verve.

Conclusion: the anti-colonial variant

The major finding of this chapter is that the causal pattern in these anti-
colonial revolutions closely parallels the causal pattern of the five successful Third World social revolutions studied in Chapter 2, with due
allowance for the specific effects of colonial states and political economies.
While development is more dependent than dynamic in these cases, still
it transforms societies enough to generate revolutionary grievances by
creating two societies, one enjoying the fruits of "development," and the
other suffering its effects. And while the colonialist state is not usually
personalist (but cf. Rhodesia and Vietnam), it still represents a concentrated target in the form of an outside force ruling above civil society.
Colonialism also shaped political cultures of opposition in the direction
of intense nationalisms, in each case overlaid with specific socialist, religious, and indigenous currents of resistance. Conjunctural factors are
similar too, with less emphasis perhaps on sudden economic downturns,
and more on world-systemic openings (both, to a greater degree than is
commonly realized, subject to influence by the rebels themselves).

The origins of the five cases are summarized in Table 3.1.

Table 3.2 translates our analyses into Boolean terms.

Table 3.1 *Origins of anti-colonial social revolutions*

	Social structure	State	Political cultures	Conjunctural factors	Outcome
Algeria	Dependent development under the French	French, colonial rule	Nationalism, Islam, socialism	French defeat in Vietnam/Rebel-made downturn	Broad-based coalition – Guerrilla success
Angola	Dependent development under the Portuguese	Salazar dictatorship in Portugal	Nationalism, socialism	Portuguese revolution/ Rebel-made downturn	Broad-based coalition – Guerrilla success
Mozambique	Dependent development under the Portuguese	Salazar dictatorship in Portugal	Nationalism, socialism	Portuguese revolution/ Rebel-made downturn	Broad-based coalition – Guerrilla success
Zimbabwe	Dependent development under the British and UDI	Ian Smith's repressive, apartheid state	Nationalism, socialism, memories of past resistance	International sanctions/ Rebel-made downturn	Broad-based coalition – Guerrilla success
Vietnam	Dependent development under France and US	Colonial under France, client under US	Nationalism, socialism	Effects of anti-war movement in US/ War-caused economic downturn	Broad-based coalition – Guerrilla success

Table 3.2 *Causes of social and anti-colonial Third World revolutions*

A Boolean Truth Table
(0 = trait absent; 1= trait present)

	(A) Dependent development	(B) Repressive, Exclusionary, Personalist or Colonial state	(C) Political cultures of opposition	(D) Economic downturn	(E) World-systemic opening	Outcome
Cases			Favorable Conditions			
Type One: Successful social revolutions						
1. Mexico, 1910–20	1	1	1	1	1	1-SR
2. Cuba, 1953–59	1	1	1	1	1	1-SR
3. Iran, 1977–79	1	1	1	1	1	1-SR
4. Nicaragua, 1977–79	1	1	1	1	1	1-SR
5. China, 1949	1	1	1	1	1	1-SR
Type Two: Anti-colonial (social) revolutions						
6. Algeria, 1954–62	1	1	1	1	1	1-SR
7. Angola, 1970s	1	1	1	1	1	1-SR
8. Mozambique, 1970s	1	1	1	1	1	1-SR
9. Zimbabwe, 1970s	1	1	1	1	1	1-SR
10. Vietnam, 1945–75	1	1	1	1	1	1-SR

It can be readily seen that all five cases conform to the pattern of the social revolutions:

Success = ABCDE

That is, the presence of all five factors led to successful anti-colonial revolutions which resulted in social revolutions of varying depth.

We have now analyzed ten revolutions from across the Third World which bear out to a large degree the model proposed in Chapter 1. One more set of cases of partial (in the sense of temporary) success remains, that of reversed social revolutions, to further test, and nuance, this theory.

Part Three

Revolutionary failure

4 The greatest tragedies: reversed revolutions

> To overthrow the old power is one thing; to take power in one's own hands is another.
>
> Leon Trotsky

With this chapter, we cross the demarcation line of this study from success – always measured by seizing power long enough to undertake a project of deep social transformation – to failure. Here we will consider seven cases – three quite briefly – of *reversed* revolutions, which succeeded in the above sense, only to fail to hold onto power and complete a social revolution. The revolutionary governments range from three years in power – Mussadiq in Iran (1951–53), Chile under Allende (1970–73), or Grenada (1979–83) to just over a decade in the cases of the Bolivian revolution and Sandinista Nicaragua. As events radicalized, internal contradictions and external pressures reversed the revolution, often violently, always fatefully. It is important, then, to look at each revolution at two particular moments: its coming to power, to further test our theory of the origins of social revolutions, and then its subsequent fall from power, as we begin to discern the possible routes to failure, paths which will be pursued in different ways in Chapter 5 as well. Noteworthy also is that we enter, for the only time in this book, the understudied realm of outcomes, for to understand the reasons why an initially successful revolution fails requires us to assess their outcomes. In this sense, we shall follow up on and provide some hints for a theory of outcomes, the subject for another study, perhaps.

These cases thus present further challenges for the larger project. One is the need to reason somewhat counterfactually: how radical *were* these experiments? My argument is that had each of them not been reversed, they could have resulted in structural transformation as deep as in most of the successful cases discussed in Chapters 2 and 3.[1] Another problem for analysis is posed by the fact that in Chile, Iran, Guatemala under Arbenz and Arévalo (1944–54), and Michael Manley's socialist government in Jamaica (1972–80), revolutionaries came to power democratically. Since the governments that were replaced by revolutionaries were not of the exclusionary type, these four cases have fallen largely off the radar screen of students of comparative revolution. Jeff Goodwin, for example, explicitly argues that "neither open, democratic polities nor authoritarian yet inclusionary (for example, 'populist') regimes have generally been challenged by powerful revolutionary movements."[2] In my view this is a mistake, for each meet Skocpol's criteria for social revolution: these governments were engaged in radical projects of political and economic transformation, supported by mass movements from below. That they came to power through elections does not make them less revolutionary than our previous ten cases (or the three others in this chapter): violence is definitely *not* a feature of the definition of social revolution used in this study. To include these cases enriches the sociology of revolution, for they allow us to discern a third type of vulnerable regime; in addition to the exclusionary, repressive, personalist and colonial states of Chapters 2 and 3, we now have four cases of fully democratic polities in which progressive forces had a fair chance to come to power through elections. The emphasis on "fully" democratic polities is important: Goodwin's claim is true of what Robinson calls "polyarchies" – those imperfectly democratic governments that are the norm. The "fully open democracy" is a much rarer type. These cases also suggest the existence of another modality of struggle, for one might even argue that the extremely rapid takeovers of power in Bolivia and Grenada constituted the functional equivalent of an election in the sense that they did not involve the organization and maintenance of an armed struggle, with its inevitably clandestine means and hierarchical command structure (nor, for that matter, did Iran in 1978–79).

A final particularity – and the reason for a separate chapter on these cases – is that they fell from power before having the opportunity to fully consolidate a social revolution. Moreover, they followed three routes to this outcome: internal fragmentation followed by external interventions and sudden coups in Chile, Grenada, Guatemala, and Iran; slower reversals that ended with electoral defeat in Jamaica and Nicaragua (the latter coupled with external intervention and war); and an almost imperceptible backsliding into reaction in Bolivia. We want to see if these diverse forms of reversal have common or different causes.

Before attending to their fall, we must first consider the causes of their rise in light of our model. We will see if the effects of dependent development, the vitality of political cultures, and the same conjunctural factors of internal economic downturn and favorable external situation lie in the background of the events that brought this set of revolutionaries and radical reformers to power. Since the case of Nicaragua has been treated in detail in Chapter 2 (appropriately so, since it was a classic social revolution against a dictator, and lasted over a decade), we will not examine its causes again (see Table 2.1 for a reminder of the argument). The cases of Bolivia, Chile, and Grenada will get full treatment here; for reasons of space, those of Iran, Guatemala, and Jamaica will be treated in far more summary fashion.

Part One: the rise to power of revolutionary movements

At that instant, I physically understood the meaning of the words "take power." I was suddenly filled with an indescribable sensation that was at once revelation, pride, and humble gratitude to life for having granted me that day. When you dream of things like changing the world, there is no power more beautiful than the feeling that you can make it happen, and that day, right there, everything was possible, there was no dream that couldn't be fulfilled.

Gioconda Belli[3]

Bolivia 1952: a sudden rebellion

The Bolivian revolution of 1952 is a case that rarely figures in comparative studies of Latin American revolutions (Ian Roxborough, Alan Knight, and Eric Selbin providing the exemplary exceptions[4]), yet dramatic changes occurred between 1952 and 1960, significant enough to warrant the judgment of social revolution.[5] James Malloy terms it the "uncompleted" revolution;[6] for Eric Selbin, "Because of the failure to consolidate, the revolution offered little protection for the gains achieved under the auspices of the revolutionaries."[7] In the typology used in this study, Bolivia is a classic reversed revolution, a qualifier not that much at odds with Malloy or Selbin. It is possible that the rule of the Movimiento Nacionalista Revolucionario (National Revolutionary Party or MNR) government is not always seen as revolutionary precisely because the gains it achieved in land reform, social programs, labor participation, and other accomplishments were slowly and imperceptibly eroded over these years – the reversal was not sudden, and came well before the coup that formally ended the experiment in 1964. For James Malloy,

There is a tendency to forget that the Bolivian National Revolution of 1952 was once perceived as the second (after Mexico) great progressive social uprising of twentieth century Latin America. The great revolutionary reforms (nationalization of the large tin mines, agrarian reform, enfranchisement of the Indian peasants, etc.) unseated the old oligarchy of tin magnates and landowners (called in Bolivia La Rosca – the screw) and promised an era of economic progress and social justice.[8]

As Jennifer Freidman has put it: "the Bolivian Revolution was a coup-turned-mass movement and put in place a series of truly revolutionary reforms in the MNR's first eighteen months in power, but then the revolution was rolled back more and more through the United States' intervention in the form of economic manipulation and control."[9]

Bolivia's economy in mid-century was the product of a centuries-old semi-feudal agricultural sector, and a more dynamic new economy led by tin mining, infrastructure development, and urban activities. James Malloy sees this in terms of a massive agricultural subsistence economy and a much smaller "national" mining economy oriented to the world market.[10] As we shall see, though this may be debated,[11] the period of the tin boom between 1880 and 1930 roughly but adequately fits the profile of dependent development. Dunkerley confirms this in a theoretical sense, seeing the economy as "structured through combined and uneven development . . . in which a relatively advanced, export-oriented capitalist sector – in this case tin mining – coexisted and inter-related with an archaic, stagnant and predominantly provincial organisation of agriculture."[12]

In the rural heartland, land tenure and wealth were grossly unequal, among the worst in Latin America, with the indigenous majority of impoverished peasants farming small plots either as sharecroppers or in exchange for performing three days of labor a week for the latifundista.[13] Just over 6.3 percent of the country's landowners owned 91.9 percent of the country's cultivable land, and the 615 largest landowners (0.7 percent) controlled fully half the land.[14] Agriculture employed as much as 72 percent of Bolivia's labor force in 1950, but produced only a third of the country's GNP.[15] In the tin enclave, the three companies of the Rosca (which can also be rendered "the small kernel") dominated the mining communities whose workers endured tremendously difficult conditions of life and labor. The mines contributed 25 percent of GDP in 1950 and 95 percent of foreign exchange while employing only 3 percent of the labor force.[16] While small in numbers – a peak of 53,000 workers was reached on the eve of the revolution – capital and labor in this sector enjoyed disproportionate political as well as economic roles in national life, the former as an oligarchic elite, the latter as its most radical opposition. Light manufacturing underwent "an important expansion" in the 1930s and 1940s to 4 percent of the work force and 9 percent of GNP.[17] This was accomplished in the usual manner through import-substitution industrialization, fueled, as elsewhere in Latin America, by the Great Depression and World War 2. The small middle class grew as well, marked by a rise in the number of teachers from 741 in 1900 to 9,322 (including 462 university professors) in 1950.[18]

Dependent development, in the sense of growth within limits, was arguably occurring, if very slowly, in the generation leading up to 1952. Agriculture could not meet the country's needs due to its low levels of productivity and severe inequalities; food accounted for 18.5 percent of all imports.[19] The health of the Bolivian economy was directly tied to the tin sector, itself highly dependent on the world market and on processing in smelters outside the country. The benefits of growth, meanwhile, were spread very unevenly: except for the landowners, rural citizens lived in severe poverty, lacking in health and educational services, and engaged in hard work for inadequate pay and limited nutrition and housing. Miners worked in hot, unsafe conditions, had short life expectancies due to disease, lived with their families in crowded housing, and were paid miserable wages (a 1946 strike demand was for a minimum wage equivalent to thirty-two cents a day).[20] On a per capita basis, GDP was under $120, making Bolivia the second poorest country in the southern hemisphere. In 1950, literacy for Bolivia's 2.7 million people was 31 percent, only 8 percent had a high school education, life expectancy was forty-nine years, and three out of ten children died before the age of one.[21]

Another way to assess the nature of dependent development in such an under-developed society is in line with the anti-colonial type discerned in Chapter 3: the urban and mining sectors experienced something like development, and the countryside did not. Moreover, we have a situation of development for a Spanish-speaking minority, and dependency and underdevelopment for an indigenous majority: in a population of 2.7 million in 1950, one million people spoke only Quechua, and 664,000 only Aymara, an index of the isolation and discrimination that underlay a degree of exploitation characterized by Dunkerley as akin to "a combination of serfdom and apartheid."[22]

Between 1946 and 1952 (a period known as the *sexenio*), a military-backed conservative government ruled the country with strong US support, the latest in a long series of repressive, exclusionary but formally democratic military regimes, most of them short-lived. Behind this state lay the oligarchic power of the tin elite. The new government moved decisively to quell unrest, backing the tin companies' "white massacre" of September 1947 to lower wages and oust the union's leadership, then using tanks and planes to violently suppress a miners' uprising in Catavi in May 1949 in support of exiled labor leader Juan Lechín Oquendo and in August–September of that year an MNR revolt.[23] For Herbert Klein, "What was crucial about this exceedingly violent fighting was . . . the almost total unity of the army against the rebels . . . Never before had the MNR been so completely isolated from the military and never before in the twentieth century had the military stood so firm against so initially successful a revolution."[24] As Dunkerley notes: "However unpopular it might have been, the regime still had the advantage of superior force, full US backing and a formal democratic mandate."[25] The *sexenio* was repressive and exclusionary, even if it wasn't as personalist as other military regimes in Bolivia's past. Arguably this absence of personalism is compensated by the massively repressive nature of the state, and its formal and informal exclusion of the indigenous majority and its middle-class opponents. To this should be added the fraud against the legitimately elected MNR candidate in 1951 in favor of the military and a tin oligarchy concentrated in three families. All this approximates, I would argue, the capricious and exclusionary nature of personalist rule more than might appear at first glance, providing a very solid target for discontent, and arguably giving us the "functional equivalent" that our theory anticipates.

The MNR gradually organized a vibrant social and political movement in the course of the 1940s, after Bolivia's defeat by Paraguay in the 1932–36 Chaco War both delegitimated the military, political, and economic elites and brought peasants, miners, and urban groups into contact through service in the army, the collective suffering and loss of life, and a growing sense of nationalism among what came to be known as the Chaco generation. Dunkerley considers that these events provided "the cultural matrix within which new nationalist and radical political ideas took shape."[26] During the *sexenio*, the MNR gradually purged its fascist-leaning elements, and transformed itself into a more progressive middle-class movement with an increasingly strong working-class following, shifting its amorphous ideology into a set of "'multi-class,' 'reformist,' 'nationalist' and 'democratic' aspirations."[27] By 1952, the party "became a powerful middle and working class movement of socialist reform and the leading opponent of the rule of the traditional elite."[28] The mining sector was led by Juan Lechín and organized in the Bolivian Miners Federation (FSTMB), allied with the MNR, an association which contributed greatly to the radicalization of the party. The Federation's 1946 Thesis of Pulacayo, an avowedly Marxist document, decried the lack of democracy and exclusion of indigenous and working-class people from national political life: "We workers shall not achieve power through the election box, we will achieve power by social revolution."[29] The peasantry was also a significant oppositional force that had long-standing grievances and had engaged in a series of uprisings in the 1930s and 1940s. In sponsoring the First National Indian Congress in 1945, the MNR astutely valorized indigenous Aymara and Quechua issues, declaring on paper the abolition of the *pongueaje* unpaid labor system.[30] The small middle class also contributed its part to this political culture of opposition.

A generation of young people, radicalized by the Chaco debacle, began to show an interest in Marxism.[31] The MNR successfully identified itself with these several class-based cultures of resistance, and built a wide social base, establishing itself as the only national alternative to the status quo. In Dunkerley's view, Bolivia was "economically backward but politically advanced."[32]

The revolutionary "conjuncture" in Bolivia follows its own timeline and is complex in at least three ways: its duration, its entangled compression of economic downturn and world-systemic opening, and the reversal of roles between external power and the state, to some degree. The worldwide depression dealt a heavy blow to the key mining sector, with low international prices compounding problems of rising costs due to declining access to high-quality ore and aging machinery.[33] As tin suffered, the economy stagnated, dragged down further by the archaic nature of the agrarian economy; unemployment, food shortages, and financial crises ensued, and the Chaco War exacerbated these trends and added inflation and government debt to them.[34]

Rapid growth resumed in the 1940s, up to the pre-revolutionary downturn from 1949 on,[35] further evidence for a burst of dependent development. The 1949–52 downturn, meanwhile, is closely linked to the world-systemic opening, which had political economic roots in the vicissitudes of the tin market between World War 2 and the Korean War. Bolivia's cooperation with the Allies during World War 2 created a vast stockpile of tin in the US, keeping prices low. When the Korean War brought new demand at higher prices, Bolivia found itself subject to the US control of the world market.[36] The US and the tin owners could not agree on a price, and by selling tin stocks that it had bought during World War 2 from Bolivia at £200–400 a ton on the world market for £900, "the US was publicly humiliating the Bolivian government."[37] The tin owners protested by stopping work, thereby halting tin exports. The Bolivian-initiated break with the US is not a "traditional" let-up of external controls, reversing the leading role in the split usually taken by the core power. In another reading, the tin oligarchy alienated the US, creating the requisite world-systemic opening.[38]

All of this in its turn exacerbated the internal economic downturn: by March 1952, "No tin had been exported for nine months, mine production was grinding to a halt, foreign exchange was getting scarcer, and inflationary pressures were appearing."[39] The cost of living index more than doubled from 561.3 in 1949 to 1,170.3 in 1952, driving the middle class into the hands of the MNR.[40] In February 1952, La Paz was the scene of a hunger march. In Herbert Klein's view: "As the traditional political system was disintegrating, the social and economic tensions within

Bolivia were increasing. For Bolivia on the eve of the revolution was, para-doxically, both economically stagnant and socially advancing."[41] Thus, economic conflict with the US opened the door for both downturn and world-systemic opening.

In May 1951, the regime bowed to international pressure for elections, and an overconfident elite split its vote between three conservative candidates, while the MNR united behind Víctor Paz Estenssoro and vice-presidential candidate Hernán Siles Suazo on a broad coalitional platform of more effective democracy, nationalization of the tin sector, and land reform. Paz won a large plurality, but the government annulled the results, setting up a junta under General Hugo Ballivián.[42] Popular protests continued into 1952, and on April 9 the MNR called for a civil-military "coup," which turned into a popular civilian insurrection when the military didn't answer the call. Tin miners, factory workers, and middle-class townspeople formed pro-MNR militias that fought the army for three days, through 600 deaths, until the largely leaderless army stood aside.[43] "Whole groups of rank and file soldiers reversed their forage caps – the traditional sign of having changed sides – under the insults, pleading and even angry blows of the *cholas*, working women whose familiar authority frequently overcame the residual fear of the officer class."[44] The MNR came to power on April 11 with wide popular support.

The Chilean path to revolution, 1970

The Chilean path to socialism inaugurated in 1970 by the Popular Unity (Unidad Popular, or UP) coalition of President Salvador Allende departs from the general pattern of successful social revolutions in one significant respect: a long (if not unbroken) history of democratic institutions permitted the emergence of a vibrant socialist challenge within the rules of the democratic game. This is precisely what makes it such an exciting case for scholars of Third World revolutions, and one with ample lessons – not all of them obvious – for the revolutionaries of the future.

Let us start with the nature of the Chilean state, for here we find the crucial anomaly of an inclusionary, relatively non-repressive democratic polity. For a century after independence in 1821, Chile's social and political structures were dominated by a strong central state led by the agricultural and mining elites, who competed for national power through the vehicle of the conservative National Party (Partido Nacional, or PN).[45] Around and after World War 1, however, socialist and communist parties also emerged, vying for the allegiance of the northern miners and the urban working class; the Communist Party of Chile was formally established in 1922, the Socialist Party in 1933, and a precursor social-ist party in 1912. The centrist Radical Party came to play an important buffering role in the 1930s; in the 1960s the Christian Democrats took over this role in the center. The center and right alternated in power after 1938, with reform-minded centrist governments from 1938 to 1952, con-servative rule from 1952 to 1958, and a reformist, centrist state again between 1964 and 1970.

I would argue that this constellation of a liberal political system and strong left oppositional parties paradoxically constitutes in causal terms the "functional equivalent" of a repressive state and effective under-ground political cultures of resistance. That is, a truly democratic polity undergoing the changes wrought by dependent development is open to revolutionary electoral strategies, and constitutes its own variant of the type of regime that is vulnerable to revolution, even though it is the diametric political opposite of a repressive, exclusionary state.

In economic terms, Chile was unarguably one of Latin America's most developed societies by 1970, highly urbanized and moderately industrial-ized, with an economy based on copper and multinational investment.[46] Its economy has historically been based on mining, primarily nitrates in the late nineteenth century, and copper in the twentieth. We have a clear case of dependent development, as social structure was grossly unequal, with peasants in particular living in semi-feudal conditions on the large estates of the central valley. Petras notes perceptively: "The problems of Chile are those of a medium-developed country that has not been able to attain industrial maturity."[47]

In the period leading up to and after World War 1, American com-panies led by the Guggenheim trust invested heavily in Chilean copper, which became the main export of the country. US investments reached $1 billion by 1930, mostly in copper, and the US displaced Britain as the main foreign power in the country. There were a series of political experi-ments in this period as well. A military coup in 1924 opened a period of short-lived civilian and military regimes, notably that of dictator Carlos Ibañez del Campo. The eight years till 1932 interrupted Chile's com-paratively long history of democratic rule, by Latin American standards (or indeed by any standards), while it also led to reforms in education, mining, and the public sector.[48] The effects of the world-wide depression were devastating in Chile, as copper revenues plummeted from $111 mil-lion to $33 million, leading to more coups in 1931 and 1932 (a pattern also seen in Argentina, Brazil, the Caribbean, and Central America). In Chile, however, the prior existence of strong working-class parties meant that military rule was discredited rather than legitimated, and there fol-lowed four decades of uninterrupted civilian democratic rule. Between

1938 and 1952, the Popular Front, a coalition of mostly centrist parties (in particular the middle-class Radical Party) with left-wing support,
presided over a vigorous period of import-substitution industrialization
(ISI) and infrastructural improvement led by the populist state.[49] Their
social base lay in the growth of the Chilean middle class, which supported
the Radical or National parties, and the working class, which provided
support for what were by then Latin America's most numerous and well-
organized Socialist and Communist parties. The Popular Front turned
rightward after suppressing the Communist Party in 1948 in exchange
for US favors.[50] By the 1950s, ISI was exhausted as a development strategy and the Chilean industrial bourgeoisie had proven itself a risk-averse
group producing for a limited, protected internal market with the aid of
state subsidies.[51]

Beginning in 1958, Chileans elected three successive one-term governments, each with a very different development strategy. In 1958, the
conservative National Party under Jorge Alessandri came to power by nar-
rowly defeating the left's Salvador Allende. Alessandri followed a classic
free market style of capitalist development, reducing the government's
role in the economy and inviting foreign companies to invest in Chile.[52]
By 1958, 80 percent of foreign capital in Chile was US-owned.[53] Inflation was contained by keeping wages low. This strategy ran into problems, however – there were few productive investments made by the
private sector and eventually inflation broke out again when the government devalued the currency. A new party, the Christian Democrats
(Partido Democrata Cristiano, or PDC), made gains in local elections in
1963. The Christian Democrats' support came from the middle classes –
white-collar workers, skilled workers, professionals, and managers. It also
got votes from women and slum dwellers and had some support in the
countryside because it promised a land reform. The electorate, significantly, expanded from 1.25 million (16 percent of the population) in
1960 to 2.84 million (28.3 percent) in 1971.[54]

In order to prevent a victory by Allende and the left in the 1964 presidential elections, Chilean businessmen and the United States threw their
support behind the Christian Democrats. The CIA poured $3 million into
the campaign in favor of the Christian Democrats (who received as much
as $20 million from all outside sources, some above board),[55] and their
candidate, Eduardo Frei, won the election with 56 percent of the vote to
Allende's 39 percent. Frei's development strategy had a progressive social
content. It was based on a vision called "communitarianism" in which
the state promoted social welfare, ostensibly without getting involved in
class struggles: "We do not propose for the country either a socialist road
or a capitalist road, but one that emerges from our national reality and

our national being, in which the state predominates as the administrator of the common good."[56] The Christian Democrats called for land reform (but never implemented it) and for the state to own 51 percent of the copper sector – a policy known as the "Chileanization" of copper – which did not effectively dispossess the American companies, who continued to make large profits in Chile. US influence remained preponderant, in the form of loans, continued control of Chile's spectacularly lucrative copper industry (the third largest in the world after Zambia and Canada), and the near monopoly on telecommunications of the International Telephone and Telegraph company (IT&T), which also owned land and hotel chains worth $150 million in all.[57] The foreign-owned sector had the largest and fastest-growing industrial firms, in paper, chemicals, rubber, electrical, metal, and transportation products, and controlled 50 percent of wholesale commerce.[58] Total foreign investment between 1954 and 1970 reached $1.67 billion.[59] By 1970, twenty-four of the top thirty US multinationals had investments in Chile.[60] Chile's foreign debt was the second highest in per capita terms in the world, rising from $598 million in 1960 to $2.36 billion in 1970.[61] Importantly, the state was also active in the economy, with ownership of steelworks, railroads, airlines, and the oil sector, controlling some 40 percent of GDP in 1970.[62] A final index of dependent development is the growth rate of 7 percent annually for industry in the first part of the 1960s and 4.3 percent a year over the long period 1915–64, compared with average overall growth in GNP of 1.6 percent annually over the same period.[63] But the social results were typically skewed: in 1965, 0.3 percent of landholders held 55 percent of the land, while the bottom 50 percent had 0.7 percent; in 1960, the top 5 percent of the population garnered 25 percent of total income and the bottom 50 percent only 16 percent, while the middle 45 percent had 59 percent.[64]

   In political cultural terms, class struggle and class consciousness were quite pronounced. David Collier hypothesizes that foreign control of the copper enclave led in part to the Marxist and anti-foreign capital nature of the labor movement.[65] In Chile, the labor movement, socialist and communist parties, and newer, further left groups, vied with Christian Democrats of all stripes for public support. Under Frei, landowners and the business elite became alarmed at the prospect of land reform, while unions were angered by the decline in living standards and repression of strikes. The Christian Democrats themselves divided into left and right wings. Communitarianism had united the party's centripetal forces, but compelled to choose between inflation and recession the party chose to implement policies that lost it working-class support without regaining the confidence of the elite. In May 1969 the party split, with the left wing forming the Unitary Popular Action Movement (MAPU), and seeking an alliance with parties on the left.

The Communist and Allende's (minority) wing of the Socialist Party favored a gradualist approach to deep social transformation. On the other hand, Sater and Collier consider the radical militants in the MIR (Movimiento de la Izquierda Revolucionaria, or Movement of the Revolutionary Left), MAPU, and that part of the Socialist Party whom they term the "ultras" as "the heirs of the heady radicalization of the 1960s . . . Their revolutionary aims were utopian and far-reaching."[66] Sometimes this meant a doctrinaire Marxism, sometimes a more libertarian one. The UP itself represented a brilliant but fragile center-point between these views, irreconcilable in theory but capable of mobilizing an enthusiastic electoral base of workers, students, and parts of the middle classes and peasantry behind the unifying political culture of the "Chilean path toward socialism." It exerted a powerful attraction in the Chilean context precisely because it advocated neither an orthodox vanguardist party approach nor a "Third World"-style armed struggle guerilla strategy. The political cultures of Chile's left and centrist social forces – perhaps two-thirds of the population – therefore presented a vibrant, varied panorama of social justice-oriented, class conscious, and articulate reformers and democratic revolutionaries, inspired by the radical currents of the 1960s, the tradition of Chilean democratic reformism, and a strong sense of economic nationalism.

By the election of 1970, the conjuncture was likewise favorable for Allende's accession to power: the centrist-reformist Christian Democratic government of Eduardo Frei had presided over an economic recession, while the United States underestimated the threat Allende posed and did not interfere decisively in the election, as they had in 1964. For Frei's first two years the economy had done rather well, but GNP went flat in 1967 after increasing by 6 percent in 1965 and 9 percent in 1966. Inflation had declined from 46.0 percent in 1964 to 22.9 percent in 1966 but rose again to 32.5 percent in 1970, stopping the upward trend in wages and salaries.[67] Unemployment followed a similar curve; the rate for industrial workers in greater Santiago fluctuated from 5.4 percent in 1964 to 4.6 percent in 1966 and rose to 6.3 percent in 1970. The number of recorded strikes grew in number from 245 in 1960 to 1,073 in 1966 (the number of strikes remained high at 977 in 1969 and the workers involved had risen from 195,345 to 275,406 in the three years).[68] Stallings, who has written perhaps the best political economy of the period, refers specifically to the "economic downturn" after 1967.[69] For Valenzuela, "there was a mild recession in 1967," by comparison with the mid-1950s, which were "far worse in every respect from an economic point of view."[70]

This may be, but it underscores two points I wish to make in this study: that the downturn assumes relevance only in the context of ongoing dependent development (the booms and busts of Chilean history and also the general consolidation of dependent development by the 1960s), and that it attains causal significance only in combination with other elements.

The elections for president were a three-way contest between the conservative National Party, which ran former president Jorge Alessandri; the left Popular Unity coalition of communists, socialists, the Radical Party, MAPU, and two smaller parties, with Salvador Allende of the Socialist Party as their candidate; and the Christian Democrats, who ran Radomiro Tomic from the remaining left wing of the party. The United States, meanwhile, underestimated the threat Allende posed and did not interfere decisively in the election, as they had in 1964, putting less money into the campaign, assuming Alessandri would win.[71] Alessandri's expected victory did not materialize, however, as the results were:

Allende (UP)	1,075,616	36.6 percent
Alessandri (PN)	1,036,278	35.3 percent
Tomic (PDC)	824,849	28.1 percent[72]

After the election, the US mobilized covert operations to prevent the ratification of Allende by the Chilean Congress. This eventuated in the assassination of pro-constitutional general René Schneider, but the move backfired, rallying the Christian Democratic legislators to Allende's side and forcing the US to retreat from support for a coup. US contacts told former Brigadier General Roberto Viaux, their potential coup leader, that "if he moved prematurely and lost, his defeat would be tantamount to a 'Bay of Pigs in Chile'."[73] For Robinson Rojas Sandford, "The lack of coordination among the Pentagon, President Nixon, and the CIA was to create a fragmentation in the team of conspirators."[74] The world-systemic opening, therefore, while narrow, was indeed sufficient to allow Allende to come to power. Allende's victory with a slim plurality of the vote then launched his Popular Unity coalition on the "Chilean path to socialism." Thus it was that the Third World's first freely elected socialist president came to power in Chile.

Grenada's swift success, 1979

The rise of the New Jewel Movement under Maurice Bishop in Grenada in 1979 completes this set of cases. It experienced a rapid and unexpected success in this phase, leaving a longer story to tell about its demise four years later.[75]

Economically, the country presents a variant of the colonial, plantation model, with the rhythm of development, after Britain acquired the island from France in the 1763 Treaty of Paris. After the exhaustion of coffee and sugar, a small, white oligarchy and later a lighter-skinned black Creole plantocracy enriched itself from the diversified export of crops like nutmeg, mace, cocoa, and bananas, while a bare minimum of infrastructure and almost no industry was put in place. The rural work force moved between wage labor on plantations, subsistence farming its own small plots, and other forms of wage labor outside the home in order to survive. The degree of dependent development in the generation leading up to the revolution may be questioned, but our argument is that we have a case intermediate between colonial and classic dependent development in Grenada. Colonial in the sense that under British and Commonwealth rule two separate societies were created – the planter elite and the popular classes. Classic, too, within the limits set by the small scale of an island economy, as in the 1960s and 1970s there was a boom of sorts based on tourism, construction, commercial expansion, real estate, and the first phase of manufacturing: in the context of a society of no more than 110,000 people, this should be seen as at least proto-dependent development. The downside of dependent development was quite clear: income inequality, inflation, debt, poor housing and health care, and limited educational opportunities marked the lives of the majority.[76]

Eric Matthew Gairy ruled as an increasingly idiosyncratic autocrat under a parliamentary, or Westminster system for more than a quarter of a century. With origins as a popular and outspoken labor leader, he was first elected prime minister for the new Grenada People's Party in 1951. Gairy would win five of the seven general elections over the next twenty-five years as leader of the Grenada United Labour Party (GULP), and he headed the government continuously from 1967 on, taking the country to independence on February 7, 1974.[77] The achievement of independence for Grenada had the paradoxical effect of intensifying Gairy's authoritarian side, and turning him from a popular leader into a dictator. It was in this period that he engaged in extensive self-enrichment and came to rely more and more on his notorious "Mongoose Gang (or Men)" and the "Night Ambush Squad" (also known as the "Green Beasts") to repress the rising opposition of the New Jewel Movement through beatings, arrests, disappearances, and outright murders, including that of NJM leader Maurice Bishop's father, Rupert, during a 1974 strike (the Mongoose, ironically, were led by Willis Bishop, Maurice's cousin).[78] Gordon Lewis, the most eminent historian of Grenada, refers to Gairy's rule as one of "destructive personalism";[79] he treated the country as his "private estate" and involved himself in the most minute details

of the government.[80] Gairy used his original base in the Grenada Manual
and Metal Workers Union to weaken the labor movement; strikes were
restricted under the 1978 Essential Services Amendment Act.[81] The government controlled radio and newspapers, either by law or high licensing
fees, forcing dissent underground.[82] Like Somoza in Nicaragua, Gairy
alienated the economic elite by his greed for land and other business
opportunities, misuse of public funds, and disregard for the legislature.[83]
Though Britain did not like Gairy's repression, they viewed him as prefer-
able to the NJM in power; meanwhile, Pinochet's Chile provided military aid and a model for the repression.[84] Gairy won elections through
fraud, and when the fledgling New Jewel Movement allied with the traditional opposition party, Herbert Blaize's Grenada National Party, in the
People's Alliance to win 48 percent of the vote in 1976 and six of the
fifteen seats in parliament, their frustrating experience close to the center
of power showed them how Gairy, in fact, had no intention of giving up
his monopoly on power.[85]

It was in this context that a tentative opposition took shape, based
on a radical if pragmatically populist alternative, and influenced by the
black power movement in nearby Trinidad, a growing sense of Grenadian
national identity, Caribbean-wide economic integration and sovereignty,
and a budding independent labor movement. Maurice Bishop started
his career by helping found a discussion group called FORUM in St.
Georges, composed of young, radical professionals.[86] This grew into the
Movement for the Advancement of Community Effort (MACE). He
merged MACE with Kendrick Radix's Committee of Concerned Citizens to form the Movement for the Assemblies of the People (MAP) in
1972 in St. Georges. That same year, Unison Whiteman founded the
Joint Endeavour for Welfare, Education, and Liberation of the People
(JEWEL) in St. David's parish in the countryside, with an emphasis
on agricultural cooperatives and pride in Grenada's tradition of community action that "almost unconsciously, advocated forms of primitive
socialism."[87] Young people, men and women, workers and students, grav-
itated to these alternatives to Gairy's increasingly repressive populism. A
number of academics took leadership positions, many exposed to socialist
theory in Britain, North America, or the University of the West Indies.[88]
The two organizations merged in a historic union on March 11, 1973 as
the New Jewel Movement (NJM). Its goals called for farm cooperatives,
price controls, and the improvement of "housing, apparel, education,
public health, food and recreation for the people."[89] The state brought
intense repression on the group, most viciously the November 18, 1973
Mongoose Gang attacks on Bishop, Whiteman, Radix, Hudson Austin,
Selwyn Strachan, and Simon Daniel, known as "Bloody Sunday," which

backfired against Gairy in the eyes of the horrified population.[90] The NJM joined with groups in the business community, union movement, churches, and other civic organizations in the Committee of 22 to demand Gairy's ouster in a three-month strike at the beginning of 1974.[91]

Black Power, as articulated by Walter Rodney and the anti-colonial movements of the Eastern Caribbean, was an important cultural idiom for the New Jewel, blended as it was with Marxian socialism into a strong race- and class-based critique of power.[92] For Bishop, "the Black masses of the Caribbean had long been the victims of colonialist oppression . . . historically, White colonialist societies had exploited the wealth of Black societies like Grenada, and no longer could this be tolerated."[93] Tanzania's ujamaa model of vesting power in local communities was another explicit point of reference.[94] For George Louison, who would later be an NJM minister, the aims of the movement included "to build popular democracy, to raise political and academic consciousness, identify with the progressive forces such as the Non-Aligned Movement, socialist countries and liberation movements, practice good neighbourliness, plan the economy with balanced development and build Grenada with the clear assurance of the involvement and agreement of the masses."[95] In November 1974, the NJM issued a People's Indictment calling for "power to the people," and charging that "The Gairy Government was BORN IN BLOOD, BAPTIZED IN FIRE, CHRISTENED WITH BULLETS, IS MARRIED TO FOREIGNERS AND IS RESULTING IN DEATH TO THE PEOPLE."[96] Bernard Coard, an academic based at the University of the West Indies in Trinidad, also returned to the island to support the NJM after 1976; his Organization for Research, Education and Liberation pushed the party in a more explicit socialist direction, becoming "a party within the party."[97] Maurice Bishop was the Castro-like figure who both articulated and embodied this political culture, with a charismatic appeal across social classes and the political spectrum.[98] After the 1976 elections his place as the leader of the society-wide opposition to Gairy and the antidote to Gairy's own cult of personality was secure, as was the New Jewel's brand of radical politics as the political culture most suited to galvanizing a broad-based opposition to Gairy's dictatorship, explicitly calling for a coalition of the working class and middle classes, young people, women, and farmers.[99]

The economy, always precarious, suffered a serious recession in 1974; by 1978 export earnings were restored, but unemployment of up to 50 percent, inflation, the government deficit, foreign reserves, and balance of payments problems remained acute.[100] The unemployment rate for women in 1979 was 69 percent, and for young people under twenty-five as high as 80 percent.[101] This was compounded by a decline in

development loans and the end of the British grant made at independence. In real terms, per capita income was lower in 1979 than in 1970,
falling 3 percent a year in the five years leading up to the revolution.[102]
Gairy's monopoly of economic opportunities contributed to this "marked
economic decline," and the elite dissatisfaction that grew with it in the late
1970s.[103]

The world-systemic conjuncture and the revolution itself opened up
suddenly in 1979. On March 13, the New Jewel, believing that Gairy
was about to arrest its leadership, moved to thwart him, leading a brief
uprising under the command of Hudson Austin that toppled Gairy,
who was out of the country, before the United States or Britain could
react. The fact that it took only forty-six men (of whom only eighteen
were armed) to overcome the armed forces, should not obscure the
popular aspect of the uprising: when Bishop announced the new government over the radio, enormous, enthusiastic crowds acclaimed it.[104]
Gairy appealed to the United States for military support to reverse this
"Communist" takeover, but Michael Manley of Jamaica and Guyana's
Forbes Burnham, in addition to the governments of Trinidad and Barbados, quickly recognized the People's Revolutionary Government (PRG)
and successfully urged non-intervention on Britain and the Commonwealth nations.[105] The United States for its part was preoccupied with
the unintended consequences of Jimmy Carter's human rights foreign
policy orientation in Iran and Nicaragua; it deferred to Britain, and recognized the PRG shortly afterwards.[106] When Gairy officially resigned a
week later, a crowd of 20,000 – one-fifth of the population – came out to
celebrate.[107] We have, therefore, all the requisites of a social revolution – a
mass movement taking power with the aim of transforming both state and
society.

*Iran 1951, Guatemala 1944, and Jamaica 1972: two elections
and an uprising*

This analysis could be further deepened by increasing the universe of
reversed revolutions to include three other cases: the rise and fall of
the nationalist democratic government of Muhammad Mussadiq in Iran
between 1951 and 1953, the radically reformist democratic regimes of
Arévalo and Arbenz in Guatemala from 1944 to 1954, and the democratic socialist experiment under Michael Manley in Jamaica that lasted
from 1972 to 1980. While each of these cases deserves a full-length treatment, they are presented here and later in this chapter in the briefest
of sketches primarily for reasons of practicality, and secondarily because
they are arguably somewhat less clearly social revolutionary cases than

Bolivia, Chile, Nicaragua, and Grenada. Let us take a brief look, then, at the rise of each to power, in light of our model.

Between 1944 and 1954 Guatemala lived through a period of increasingly radical social change.[108] If we focus on the circumstances under which a progressive, elected government led by Juan Jose Arévalo took power from the dictator Jorge Ubico in the course of 1944, we find a process of dependent development led since the turn of the century by foreign corporations such as the United Fruit Company. These companies commercialized and concentrated Guatemalan agriculture to produce coffee and bananas at the expense of the small and medium producers, mestizo and indigenous. The depression brought renewed state repression and dictatorship to control labor; World War 2 brought further recession as GDP fell. Ubico's fascist sympathies alienated US policy-makers, and internal opposition arose based on emerging sentiments in favor of democratic rule, national economic autonomy, and to a lesser degree, indigenous demands. In June 1944 urban demonstrations and a general strike compounded deteriorating economic conditions to force Ubico's resignation.[109] In the fall, against a backdrop of indigenous mobilizations, elections brought the reformer Juan José Arévalo to power. He would be followed in 1951 by the more radical Jacobo Arbenz, setting the country on a path of deeper social transformation based on land reform.

In Iran, the British were the dominant Western power, presiding over that country's development and substantially setting its terms, as they controlled Iran's oil, paying eighteen cents a barrel, meaning that Iran received only 10 to 20 percent of the value of its oil.[110] Though a succession of autocratic dynasties had ruled for hundreds of years, a democratic window opened up under the untried and relatively weak shah Muhammad Reza Pahlavi after World War 2 that led to the election of nationalist icon Muhammad Mussadiq as prime minister in 1951 at the head of a coalition of religious and secular parties known as the National Front, reposing on a political culture of nationalism, further democratic gains, and social reforms. An economic recession also contributed to this electoral result, combined with British underestimation of Mussadiq and the gradual emergence after World War 2 of a climate of national liberation across the Third World. Mussadiq was extremely popular in Iran, enjoying broad support from the lower and middle classes, including the working class (although the communist Tudeh Party was not part of the National Front), and engaged in a series of reforms in his brief tenure as prime minister. The most dramatic and consequential of these was the May 1, 1951 nationalization of Iran's oil, setting up a monumental conflict with the British over the next two years.

Jamaica in the 1970s followed a combination of the paths of Guatemala and Chile before it.[111] Dependent development was nourished with American and British corporate capital focused on the bauxite and agro-export sectors, clearly transforming the economy and social structure in the period after World War 2 in the manner we have characterized as aggregate economic growth and widespread social deprivation. As in Chile, a formally democratic system facilitated the eventual rise of a left-leaning electoral option in the form of Michael Manley's People's National Party (PNP). Another political culture that contributed to electoral victory in 1972 was Rastafarianism, a utopian political-religious-cultural movement that helped mobilize the black population.[112] The internal conjuncture of 1972 was one of recession and unemployment, while an international climate that permitted reasonably free and fair elections contributed to Manley's victory and the inauguration of a leftward trajectory that would culminate in the declaration of democratic socialism in the fall of 1974, giving the world in effect its second democratically elected socialist president, following hard on the heels of Allende's victory.

Part Two: falling from power

As in the classic Greek tragedies, everybody knows what will happen, everybody says they do not want it to happen, and everybody does exactly what is necessary to bring about the disaster . . .
                    Radomiro Tomic to General Carlos Prats (August 1973)[113]

We are now at a momentous turning point in this book. We have examined some seventeen cases of Third World revolutions that came to power (something approximating the universe of such cases, though there are a few others that can be argued for and about). We can now turn – in the middle of this chapter – to the second part of this book, a study of failures of multiple sorts: social revolutions, such as these six, plus Nicaragua, that failed to hold onto power once attained; and in the next chapter, to attempted social revolutions that never came to power, and political revolutions that succeeded in overthrowing dictators and monarchies but failed to bring about deep social transformation. This universe of failure is much larger than that of success, and entails more variation, as we shall see. Let us return to our seven cases of reversed revolutions, with the accent now on their reversal.

Thinking about falls from power of revolutionary governments may be expected to require its own theory, differing from the fall of ancien régimes. This is not the place to fully work out such a theory.[114] Still, we may identify some preliminary commonalities and particularities of these cases in light of the factors we are working with in the present study. In terms of social structure, dependent development, once set in motion, cannot be done away with overnight: each government ran into the constraints this posed even as reforms brought about some gains. In this sense, the daunting resilience of dependency acts as a break on the revolutionary impetus to development. Six of the seven governments ruled democratically, and the seventh, Bishop's in Grenada, was widely popular and likely would have won elections in the period of its rule. Progressive political cultures thrived everywhere, but at the same time, internal right-wing oppositions grew in the space opened up by democracy and societies polarized politically. Conjunctural factors also worked against the new regimes: all experienced economic difficulties as the programs they put in place dislocated previous production and distribution systems, while the unleashed demand for consumption and the need for productive investment worked at cross purposes.[115] In the end, all faced serious overt or covert intervention from the United States, designed to create counter-revolutionary governments. This was the outcome in all seven cases, through violent CIA-sponsored coups in Iran, Guatemala, and Chile, direct and indirect military intervention in Bolivia, Nicaragua, and Grenada, and the election of Edward Seaga's Labour Party in Jamaica. In some sense, then, the persistence of the same factors that brought revolutionaries to power worked in reverse to unseat them, a process whose causes we now set out to investigate.

Bolivia after 1952[116]

With the sudden collapse of the army to an MNR-led civilian uprising on April 11, 1951 "began Latin America's most dynamic social revolution since the Mexican holocaust of 1910."[117] The accomplishments of the first eighteen months indisputably rank it in the class of social revolutions: nationalization of tin, deep land reform, universal suffrage, and significant political power for workers and rights for Bolivia's indigenous population.

Within a week, the Bolivian Workers Confederation (the COB) had been formed to represent all of labor, headed by Juan Lechín, who became minister of labor, and directed by left-wing members of the MNR (including Trotskyists) and of the new Bolivian Communist Party (PCB).[118] The COB immediately pressed for nationalizations and land reform. The military was not completely abolished, but reduced greatly in number and temporarily turned into a public works force, while armed power lay in the hands of the militias formed during the uprising, both in town and countryside.[119] Universal suffrage, decreed in July, expanded the electorate from 200,000 to about a million, though the peasantry's vote was still the object of much manipulation. The result was a far more open polity than Bolivia had ever experienced.[120]

Caught between the demands of the population and pressure from the US, Paz appointed a commission to study the issue of nationalizing the tin mines. The legislation was passed on October 31, 1952, setting up the Bolivian Mining Corporation (COMIBOL) to replace the Patiño, Hochschild, and Armayo families of the Rosca and their foreign partners, who were compensated between $18 and $27 million, with assurances to the United States that the MNR "was not anti-private property, anti-United States, or pro-Soviet."[121] This left COMIBOL in charge of 75 to 80 percent of the country's tin production.[122] A year later, workers' control over management was decreed; by then, the government was the largest economic entity in the country in terms of both output and employment.[123] Meanwhile, over the opposition of the right wing of the party, peasant mobilization in the Cochabamba valley and elsewhere led to spontaneous land seizures in the countryside, and a period of acute conflict put pressure on the government to legitimize in August 1953 the de facto agrarian reform that had already occurred.[124] The reforms broke up the large estates, abolished the pongueaje "voluntary" labor system for good, and promised state assistance for peasants on their new plots.[125] Rural education, health care, and other services were also embarked upon.[126] Though only eight million of thirty-six million hectares of arable land changed hands by 1968, and just 28 percent of rural families had received land by 1960, the reform was genuinely popular and tied much of the peasantry to the MNR for a generation.[127]

With universal suffrage, nationalization of tin, temporary neutralization of the army, and land reform in place, the Bolivian revolution's status as a social revolution is secure. But the revolution itself was not secure. My argument is that a severe economic crisis in 1952–54 brought about a world-systemic closure, marked by the government's turn to the US for loans and other forms of assistance after 1953. The effects of the terms imposed by the US – a kind of structural adjustment program before such things had names – then weakened the supple political culture of the broad-based coalition of workers, peasants, and the urban middle class that was backing the MNR, led to splits and conflicts within the party which the conservatives won, and ultimately to a weakened democratic polity verging on an "outright dictatorship"[128] by 1964 that resulted in the formal downfall of the MNR to a military coup that year. The key events, as we shall see, took place between 1953 and 1956.[129]

The first step in the chain of events was a severe economic downturn in the first two years of the revolution. This had multiple causes and dimensions, amounting to a serious crisis for the new revolutionary government. Agriculture was naturally disrupted by the unplanned land seizures, and as peasants actually came to control more land as small subsistence plots, they kept what they produced off the markets in order to raise their own standards of living.[130] Mining was also dislocated by the nationalization, as COMIBOL operated at a deficit due to sliding world prices (due in no small measure to the US's surplus stocks) and an exodus of skilled technicians and managers.[131] To this must be added the negative effects on foreign reserves of the indemnification of the Rosca and foreign investors, which turned a balance of payments surplus of $9.7 million in 1951 into a deficit of $10.3 million in 1954.[132] Under these circumstances, inflation soared out of control at 100 percent annually in 1952–54 (with the highest rate in the world between 1952 and 1956), a blow to all social classes, including the middle classes and the elite.[133] In the first five years of the revolution, per capita GDP fell from $122 to $96, a decline of more than 20 percent.[134] In Jennifer Friedman's apt judgment, "The economic crisis brought social change in the country to a halt."[135]

Phase two of the reversal of the revolution came when the MNR concluded that it had to seek aid from the United States to weather the economic crisis. As Klein puts it: "The Bolivian government astutely obtained massive assistance, despite the existence of a hard-line anti-communist government in Washington, but they had to pay a heavy price for it."[136] This reliance on the US closed the world-systemic opening of the early 1950s. The first $9 million in aid came in late 1953, and by 1958 the US had provided $78 million and accounted for as much as one-third of the government's budget, with Bolivia the largest per capita recipient of US aid in Latin America between 1952 and 1964.[137] With unusual foresight, the US saw this aid as the best mechanism to reverse the revolution, challenged as it had been by the Guatemalan revolution in the early 1950s and the Cuban to come at the end the decade. Conservative scholar Robert Alexander noted "that more could be gained by going along with the Bolivian regime, and trying to convince it of the necessity of modifying policies considered extreme in Washington, than by opposing it."[138]

While US assistance prevented economic collapse, the conditions placed on the aid had serious consequences of their own that would prove fatal for the revolution. Among these were keeping the economy open for trade, privatization of the oil sector, dependence on food aid, retreats from welfare provision, conservative fiscal and monetary policies, and training for the reconstituted army. The US-imposed Economic

Stabilization Plan of 1956, a precursor of the structural adjustment programs that would plague the Third World a generation later, required that in exchange for another $25 million in aid the government cut workers' wages, lay off mine workers, deregulate foreign investment and its own currency, slow land reform, and slash its development projects to balance its budget.[139] The MNR was compelled to accept its terms to get the continued aid it needed to sustain itself financially; George Jackson Eder, the plan's architect, wrote of it: "It is true that I was 'invited' to Bolivia by President Paz, but it was an invitation extended virtually under duress, and with repeated hints of curtailment of US aid'."[140] Ten years later he noted with satisfaction that it "meant the repudiation, at least tacitly, of virtually everything the Revolutionary Government had done."[141] This was followed in 1961 by a $37.5 million package known as the Triangular Plan for its joint US, German, and Inter-American Development Bank funders, as part of Kennedy's Alliance for Progress blueprint for development as an antidote to revolution.[142] Two of our cases define the varieties of US policy in the region in the 1950s, as Knight observes: "To Latin America as a whole – the USA sought to show – Bolivia offered an example, Guatemala a warning."[143]

In effect, 1956 was the turning point for the revolution, as the economic impact and unpopularity of these steps sharpened political polarization within the broad revolutionary coalition and its underlying political cultures of opposition. Opposition to the MNR arose in the mining sector and labor movement, and the party itself split into two factions, with the conservative forces around newly elected president Siles turning toward the US, the army, and the MNR's peasant base to retain power, against Lechín and the MNR radicals within the COB. Paz, the ostensibly neutral balance between the camps, tilted decisively toward Siles and the US, and came to approximate a personalistic, exclusionary, repressive autocrat after he came to the presidency again in 1960, now directing "both government and party in a closed, bureaucratic fashion with the assistance of a small group known as the '*maquinita*' (little machine)."[144] Although the FSTMB had forced government concessions in 1959 with a two-week strike that cost the state $2.8 million in export earnings, this led to a counterattack by the government, which, having abolished workers' control, now turned the mining areas into military zones of occupation.[145] The most radical peasants were likewise estranged from the government by the course of events, and the strength of their armed militias and unions made them a target for government force as well; moreover, as Dunkerley notes, the perceived benefits of land reform allowed Paz to "turn to the peasantry over the following years as a dependable ally in the struggle against the militant miners."[146] The MNR was the site of deep conflict within its ranks, as vice president Lechín battled president Paz and former president Siles, who controlled the party bureaucracy.[147] The victory of the latter in this struggle weakened the crumbling social base of the revolution even further.

The end came when Paz brought the army back to full strength to maintain order in the early 1960s. This included training by the US in the Canal Zone and $90 million in military assistance. Whitehead observes: "It seems probable that American pressure encouraged the build-up of the army after 1960, influenced the political views taught to trainee officers, encouraged the use of the army to settle the internal power struggle, and possibly offered limited encouragement to the plans for a coup."[148] In 1963, Paz broke with the COB, pushed Lechín out of the party into the opposition, and named General Hugo Barrientos as his vice-presidential running mate. Even with arrests, exilings, censorship, and police action, the MNR could no longer control the increasing strikes and demonstrations against its unpopular rule throughout the country. On November 2–4, 1964, following the recent example of Brazil, the army staged its coup, installing Barrientos in what became a five-year dictatorship that ended only with his death in a helicopter crash.[149] Some of the social gains, notably land reform, survived, but the social revolution itself was now definitively reversed.[150]

Chile 1973

The period of rule by the UP in Chile between 1970 and 1973 witnessed an attempt to construct a "Chilean path toward socialism" with great creativity and popular enthusiasm. It also encountered serious opposition from vested interests in society, the army, and the United States government. Chile provides us with a textbook case of the complex interaction between politics and economics, and of internal and external forces in the reversal of revolutions.

The development strategy of the UP alliance was clearly expressed in the opening sentence of its economic program: "The central objective of the united popular forces is to replace the current economic structure, ending the power of national and foreign monopoly capitalists and large landowners, in order to initiate the construction of socialism."[151] Such a transition to socialism would require major structural changes, notably the nationalization of much of the industrial sector (to be called the Area of Social Production), reorienting the economy to basic consumer goods, and the implementation of an effective agrarian reform. Other goals included providing better health, housing, and social security, and ending discrimination against women.

The core of the policy was to raise wages at the expense of profits, thereby squeezing the private sector, much of which was to be taken over by the state and run at a lower rate of profit. By the end of 1971, 150 industrial plants were under state control, including twelve of the twenty largest firms; by October 1972, another sixty-one firms had been nationalized, as well as two-thirds of all credit institutions, including three of the four large foreign banks.[152] Altogether, the state increased its share of national production from about 40 percent to 60 percent by 1973.[153] As the economy expanded – GNP grew 8.3 percent in 1971, the highest rate in many decades – industrial unemployment in the Santiago area declined from 6.3 percent in 1970 to 3.5 percent in 1972 and 2.9 percent in 1973, inflation was brought down from 32.5 percent in 1970 to 20.1 percent a year later as prices were partially frozen, and workers' real incomes rose by about 25 percent, a huge increase.[154]

In July 1971 the US-owned copper mines were nationalized, and after a calculation of the companies' "excess profits" from 1955 to 1970, it was determined that Chile owed the two big American companies Anaconda and Kennecott Copper nothing for the mines. It was calculated that 12 percent was the world-wide profit rate for the copper industry, and that the two American multinationals had made $774 million above this in Chile from 1955 to 1970; after deducting the book value of the companies and taking amortization and depreciation into account, it was determined that Anaconda owed Chile $78 million and Kennecott owed $310 million![155] Land reform was equally decisive: by 1973, 50 percent of agricultural land had been expropriated, either legally by the state (all farms over 175 acres), or directly by farm workers, in the case of medium-sized farms below this threshold, resulting in "a fundamental alteration of the rural power structure."[156]

Nationalization, however, caused an escalation of ongoing US plans to destabilize the Chilean economy, which were coordinated for the Nixon administration by Henry Kissinger, who opined, with no sense of irony, "I don't see why we have to let a country go Marxist just because its people are irresponsible."[157] In other words, the US would decide what was best for Chile, and if that meant replacing a democratically-elected Marxist with a military government, that was perfectly acceptable to Kissinger and Nixon (not to mention the copper companies and IT&T, which had also been expropriated in Chile). The US cut off loans to Chile and blocked World Bank and other sources of money: US ambassador Edward Korry remarked: "Not a nut or a bolt will reach Chile . . . We will do all in our power to condemn Chileans to utmost poverty."[158] This is consonant with CIA director Richard Helms's notes from a meeting with Nixon and Kissinger at the White House on September 15, 1970:

One in 10 chance perhaps, but save Chile!
worth spending/not concerned risks involved
no involvement of Embassy
$10,000,000 available, more if necessary
full time job – best men we have
game plan
make the economy scream
48 hours for plan of action.[159]

The real motives behind US counter-revolution in Chile may be those expressed in a CIA study conducted in 1970 before Allende won the elections:

The US has no vital national interests with Chile . . . The world military balance of power would not be significantly altered by an Allende government . . . An Allende victory would represent a definite psychological set-back to the US and a definite psychological advantage for the Marxist idea.[160]

Henry Kissinger put it this way: "I don't think we should delude ourselves that an Allende takeover in Chile would not present massive problems for us, and for democratic forces and for pro-US forces in Latin America, and indeed to the whole Western Hemisphere."[161] In the course of the Allende years, the CIA spent $8 million (worth $40 million on the black market) on the opposition parties, press, and strikers to overthrow him.[162] It is hard to disagree with Lois Oppenheim that Kissinger "saw Allende as more dangerous than Fidel Castro, precisely because of the international appeal of Allende's strategy of nonviolent social transformation."[163]

The dislocation of the economy from 1972 on had both internal and external causes. As a result of the drop in aid and economic sanctions, Chilean industry ran into problems getting raw materials, spare parts, technology (and technicians), and new machinery. Private banks and other international lenders were naturally reluctant to loan Chile money, making foreign debt service impossible. The balance of payments deficit increased as copper prices fell and food imports grew to 56 percent of Chile's export earnings.[164] Meanwhile inflation returned because workers and peasants now had more money to spend, driving up prices, while shortages led to a thriving black market and more inflation. Agriculture declined as the land reform disrupted production, and landowners took land out of production. The reform also pitted sharecroppers (legally entitled to the land) against casual laborers (the two-thirds of the work force left outside the terms of the reform), and the divisions in and outside the UP about how to improve the lives of the latter were exploited by the PDC's insistence on the rights of the former, whose unions they tended to dominate.[165] Politically, Allende did not control the entire state machinery – he did not have a majority in Congress, the support of the judiciary, the loyalty of the entire civil service, nor that of much of the army high command, which had been trained in the United States. The upper classes owned most of the mass media, and used it against him (the CIA also gave money to conservative newspapers and radios to do a vicious smear campaign playing on fears of communism).

Faced with these difficulties the UP convened a high-level strategy conference at Lo Curro in June 1972 to try to elaborate a strategy capable of maintaining the momentum of the revolutionary process.[166] At this meeting, a significant difference of opinion emerged, underscoring the weight of political cultures for the success – or failure – of revolutions. The Communist Party, Allende's wing of the Socialist Party, and the Radical Party wanted to slow things down and try to rebuild an alliance with the progressive wing of the Christian Democrats, thereby regaining the support of the middle classes, a strategy known as the "consolidation line." This group wanted to dampen the pace of nationalizations, especially the spontaneous ones that were going on in some factories, in order to rebuild trust with the private sector; maintain payments on the foreign debt to appease the United States; and call for a "battle of production" appealing to workers to hold down wage increases in order to reduce inflation and shortages. Politically, this meant rebuilding an alliance with the progressive wing of the Christian Democrats, to bring the middle classes back into support for the process of change, and to win a stronger electoral plurality, or even a majority. Once this political base was consolidated, it was argued, the transformation of Chilean society could proceed on a more solid footing.

Against this view, much of the Socialist Party, the MAPU, and the MIR called for more activism and mobilization of the working class (since the MIR was not formally part of the UP coalition, it was not directly represented at Lo Curro). This "mobilization line" wanted to enlarge the Area of Social Production both legally and by encouraging worker and peasant seizures of factories and land; to suspend payments on the foreign debt to retaliate against the blockade; and to implement rationing of basic goods to fight speculation and combat the shortages. Politically, this meant mobilizing the working class and peasantry for even more radical (but still largely constitutional and legal) changes. By building a deeper base among the working classes of Chile, both electoral gains and the political will for radical changes could be preserved.

One other option also hung over the deliberations – the MIR's proposal for sharp class confrontation and eventual armed struggle against the right and the repressive forces of the army and police. According to this logic, the whole process was in grave danger because the right-wing opposition would not play by the rules of the constitutional game. Therefore, the left should prepare for a direct seizure of power, and above all, take away the army's ability to end the revolution with a coup.

Although the formal outcome of the meeting at Lo Curro was the adoption of Allende's "consolidation line," in practice, both strategies were carried forward at the same time – the government tried to build bridges to the Christian Democrats and the middle classes, while grassroots activists carried out land seizures and factory occupations. For Jack Spence,

The dilemma of the consolidation line lay in the implication that its implementation would require repressing mobilizations. The opposite line, however, faced the task of rapidly broadening the minority of workers and peasants who had mobilized and unifying them to face the political conflict that would follow.[167]

As each group tried to carry out its own program for social transformation, class conflict grew throughout 1972.[168] In October and November, truck drivers, retail merchants, and professionals went on a so-called "bosses' strike" against the government. The government responded by having trade unions and neighborhood groups take over the distribution of goods. The strike ended in a stalemate, with more factory occupations and worker support for the government, but more shortages of goods and a loss of middle class support. Allende had to bring military figures into his cabinet to shore up the authority of the government.[169]

The poignancy of Allende's own politics rings nowhere more clearly than in his August 1972 meeting with residents of the Santiago shantytown named "Assault on the Moncada," where he went after a confrontation with the police that left one dead officially, and four according to the community. After expressing his sorrow at what had happened, he accepted nine of their thirteen demands outright, explaining that

Chile is not living through a full-blown revolution, but rather a revolutionary process which is being deepened all the time. Chile is not the Soviet Union, or Cuba, or China. We are living with the contradictions of a capitalist regime. We cannot close Congress, as you wish, because we are committed to walk the path of a revolutionary process in pluralism, democracy, and freedom . . . The fact that you have to get up at dawn to get to work, while I ride in a car, that when you turn on the faucet cold water comes out, while hot water comes out of mine – I know all this and it is painful, comrades. I am crying in despair, but we can't solve this overnight. How could I not believe that you deserve adequate housing, and that this is only fair?[170]

In 1973 class polarization deepened, leading to fragmentation and weakening of the populist alliance. The de facto UP split in 1972 had the complex result of gaining a large working-class majority despite a high level of commitment to a broader coalition, while the economic realities of inflation and shortages alienated middle-class strata and their Christian Democratic representatives even further from the UP coalition. The middle classes were led out of the coalition by the newly conservatized PDC,[171] while some parts, whose size is neither to be overemphasized or dismissed, of the urban marginal and working classes (and probably of the peasantry as well) were alienated by the excesses of the MIR and the radical Socialists. Marc Cooper describes an indoor rally held on July 26, 1973 to commemorate the Cuban Revolution, attended by 10,000 members of all sectors of the left that self-imploded as the Communist speaker, minister of labor Luis Figueroa, denounced "adventurous attitudes that could lead to civil war," and was in turn drowned out by MIR and Socialist Party militants as fights began to break out in the crowd. MIR shouts of "Political Consciousness! And Rifles!" were countered by CP shouts of "Ultra-leftism Betrays Socialism!" The SP and most in the crowd shouted "Allende! Allende! El pueblo te defiende!" The Communists' supporters marched out of the building, and momentum collapsed. Cooper sees this as a turning point, at least symbolically. His friend, Socialist Orlando Jofre, said later that night to him: "You know, we are so close – or rather we *were* so close. So close, but we aren't going to make it. It's all over, brother. It's all over."[172]

Despite inflation and rightwing sabotage of the economy, the UP increased its share of the vote in the March 1973 congressional elections from 36 percent to 44 percent (analysis of the vote shows increased blue-collar support, and decreased white-collar and middle-class voters for the UP).[173] This outcome meant that the UP's enemies could not get the two-thirds vote needed to impeach Allende and remove him legally. The rightwing opposition therefore hardened its tactics. In May the copper miners – at least those organized by the Christian Democrats and the white collar sector of the work force – went on strike against the government, a somewhat incongruous situation of workers opposing an elected socialist government. On June 29, 1973 there was an attempted military coup with assistance from the fascist, or extreme rightwing civilians of Patria y Libertad, which failed when part of the army remained loyal to the government (again, showing perhaps the residual strength of a hard-won democratic political culture, even within the army). On July 29 came the second truckers' strike, combined with much rightwing terrorism against people and trucks, buses, gas stations, pipelines, and trains. Chile's inflation rate for the period from October 1972 to October 1973 peaked at over 500 percent.[174] Amidst an intense economic downturn, Chile's population was bombarded by anti-communist messages in much of the media, perfectly free to say whatever it wanted.

As events built to a climax, one discerns an eerie parallelism between the views of the left and the right. Orlando Sáenz, president of the National Industrial Society (SOFOFA) and widely believed to be part of the fascist Patria y Libertad grouping, stated: "An imminent change is due that will determine the course of our future. In a few more months, Chile will have been subsumed in a Marxist dictatorship or will have emerged in the full light of liberty,"[175] echoing an editorial in the leading journal of the left, *Punto Final*, "For Chile, the cards are on the table. It will either be socialism or fascism – nothing in between."[176] Graffiti saying "DJAKARTA" or "Jakarta is coming now" could be seen on the walls in the wealthy sections of Santiago as early as January 1972.[177] The slogan of the Communist Party, "No – to the civil war,"[178] went unheeded as the center collapsed, both in its own terms and within the left and the right. Last-ditch efforts to achieve a minimum compromise between the Christian Democrats and the UP were made at La Moneda on July 30–31, 1973, but ended without plans for the resumption of talks.[179] The center and the left had lost confidence in each other, and in themselves as capable of unity. The Christian Democrats, in particular, had abdicated their role as defenders of democratic legality, declaring on August 14 that the UP government was illegal.[180] That some elements on the left did the same only hastened the collapse of the system, and with it the revolution. The PN, for its part, considered Allende and his government to be "illegitimate."[181]

Finally, on September 11, 1973 came the brutal military coup that overthrew the government. The army was the main maker of the coup, and certainly the US gave ample encouragement, material aid, logistical support, and swift diplomatic recognition to the junta. Inside Chile there was support from fascist and anti-communist groups, large landowners, industrialists, and owners of the mass media. But all of these groups together would not have had much of a social base despite their material resources. A key social force behind the coup, then, was Chile's middle classes, economically hard hit by inflation and shortages, and politically close to the Christian Democratic Party, the centrist party that ultimately chose the extra-legal right over the parliamentary left. Groups like professionals, small shop owners, truck drivers, and others, who all had their own associations much like workers have labor unions, provided an atmosphere of public support for the military coup. For Stallings, the Chilean bourgeoisie were "the prime movers in the propaganda campaigns, the owners' strikes, the hoarding and sabotage, the arrangements with the military. The United States certainly provided aid and assistance wherever and whenever possible."[182]

The workers, unarmed and unprepared for a civil war, could not resist the coup which brought General Augusto Pinochet to power. Allende died fighting in the presidential palace. His final words, broadcast to the nation, were:

> Probably Radio Magallanes will be silenced and the calm metal of my voice will not reach you. It does not matter . . . I have faith in Chile and in her destiny. Others will surmount this gray, bitter moment in which treason seeks to impose itself. You must go on, knowing that sooner rather than later the grand avenues will open along which free people will pass to build a better society.[183]

The junta – the new military leadership – killed some 3,000 supporters of the UP in its first few months in power, most of them arrested, tortured, and then disappeared.[184] Chileans would restore their fragile democracy only fifteen years later, after numerous demonstrations and incalculable suffering, through a decisive repudiation of Pinochet at the polls, but the Allende years represent a lost option for a transformation of society that still awaits its moment.

Grenada 1983

Scholars and activists alike have attributed the reversal of the Grenadian revolution to such diverse factors as ideological and cultural divisions within the NJM (and the People's Revolutionary Army) over the proper blend of socialism and democratic participation, strategic differences over the pace of change, the hostility and eventual military intervention of the United States, a deteriorating economy, and the troubled nature of the personal relationship between Bernard Coard and Maurice Bishop.[185] Our task is to assess these factors and others on their own terms and in light of our model and the other cases in this chapter. It will be my argument that the fall of the New Jewel Movement shows the causal role of political culture – and human agency – in determining outcomes as well as any other case in this chapter. For while other factors were at work, including external ones, it was the internal breakdown of the leadership that carries the bulk of the explanatory weight here.

Grenada's significance as perhaps the first – with Jamaica – socialist revolution in an English-speaking country and as an important experiment in socialist transformation in a small, dependent country is noteworthy, and its accomplishments deserve our acknowledgment. Serious efforts were made to diversify the economy, reduce inequality and alleviate suffering, and to involve the population in new forms of participation. With help from Paolo Freire, the Centre for Popular Education made inroads on adult illiteracy; in terms of material well-being, loans for repair of housing were soon made available, as well as free medical and dental care, free milk and school lunches, and free secondary education.[186] Volunteers of all ages worked on housing, roads, public art, and other community projects. Women were mobilized with equal pay, maternity leave, and scholarships to study abroad and for training as carpenters, fisherfolk, plumbers, and in agricultural cooperative work; many took leadership positions.[187] Given charge of economic policy, deputy prime minister and finance minister Bernard Coard had considerable success in translating this vision into economic gains. Unemployment fell from 50 percent to 12 percent in the four years of NJM rule.[188] GNP grew a healthy 6 percent in 1982, and 14 percent overall for the years 1979–82. Real wages rose 10 percent as inflation declined from 21.1 percent in 1980 to 6.1 percent in 1983; the NJM claimed that per capita income rose from $450 in 1978 to $870 in 1983, and at the very least income tax was abolished for the poorest 30 percent while prices on essentials were controlled.[189] Foreign investment increased over tenfold from $3.5 million in 1979 to $42.3 million in 1982, while remittances from abroad rose from $6.2 million in 1978 to $16.2 million in 1980 and stayed high afterwards.[190] The budget moved from a deficit of $3.2 million in Gairy's last year to a surplus of $1 million in the NJM's first year.[191] The state made investments in tourism and agriculture, and set up a program of loans to farmers and small businessmen.[192] Infrastructure and services received substantial government funds, and in the summer of 1983 the World Bank and IMF issued favorable judgments on the direction of economic policy, with the IMF even opposing US desires to cut off its loans.[193]

   Politically, the NJM followed what we might call a "mixed democracy" model – a middle road between Cuban party centralism and Nicaraguan pluralist democracy. The People's Revolutionary Government (PRG), while not democratic in the formal sense, was a far cry from the Gairy dictatorship. Its misgivings about the Westminster system of governing were translated into extensive consultations with the people of Grenada about their needs and desires. There was a commitment to socialism as an alternative in the long run, and in the context of the people having the opportunity to control their own destiny. Many popular assemblies and forums were held, local parish- and zonal-level councils were formed with authority to discuss and debate government decisions, and diverse groups were brought into the government, including business leaders and professionals. As one forty-year-old mason put it:

Democracy is where one knows and can give a good picture of *where* your government is going, *why* they are going there and what you would enjoy and benefit on reaching there . . . Then if I suggest things – like I came up with the idea of workers' education on the job, then I discuss it with my union and they take it up with the party, and the next thing we know we get two blackboards and it begins![194]

Detention and censorship – both of which existed to some degree – were kept to a minimum.[195] The NJM itself kept a firm hold on power (it had only forty-five full party members in 1979 and seventy-two by 1983),[196] and Bishop exercised a charismatic appeal, but at the time of the NJM's demise there were debates within the party about a transition to elections and representative government going on in the context of first drafting a new constitution.[197] In Ferguson's judgment, "The sense of political involvement felt by most Grenadians stood in stark contrast to the autocratic political system of 'parliamentary democracy' as practised by the previous regime."[198] It is doubtful, then, that the government was perceived by the majority of the population as repressive, personalistic, or exclusionary, and in this sense, Grenada fits the pattern already established in revolutionary Chile and Nicaragua, and to a lesser degree, in Bolivia. Arguably, of course, this openness was a factor in its fall. I would suggest, though, that had free and open elections been organized early on, the virtually certain victory of the NJM could have averted or made more difficult some of the external hostility to the revolution, and might well have strengthened the hand of Bishop over the Coard faction.[199]

In addressing the reversal of the revolution, let us start with economic considerations. Dependent development, of course, remained in place. Despite the impressive activation of the economy documented above, Grenada remained dependent in terms of its position as a small agricultural society inserted into the world economy on highly disadvantageous terms, and this did set limits on the government's ability to consolidate the revolution through more dynamic economic improvement. Falling prices for cocoa and nutmeg led to a trade deficit that burgeoned from $61 million in 1979 to $91 million in 1980.[200] Payne and his colleagues make the case that the economy was deteriorating "sharply," as the airport project diverted other development funds, and mounting problems with roads, electricity, and water service damaged the morale of the population.[201] But can it be argued that the revolution failed due to economic downturn or crisis? Becca Wanner, who has explicitly tried to apply my theory to this case, concludes that "though economics may have had some influence on the revolution's disintegration . . . I do not think any possible economic downturn constituted a major factor in the outcome."[202] After a thorough survey of government and external data, Gordon Lewis similarly concludes that "prognostications about the economic collapse of the revolution seem unbelievable when compared with the available statistical evidence for the economic record of 1982–83."[203] A different argument that the economic situation played a role can perhaps be made in that the Coard faction's case against Bishop included this charge; in that sense, we have an instance of the perception counting as much as the reality, which we have seen is sometimes true for the operation of world-systemic openings, particularly with respect to Carter's foreign policy, as well. In the context of our model, however, the real effects of dependency and the perception of an economic downturn can at best be seen as minor factors in the reversal of the revolution.

What of the world-systemic conjuncture, then? A review of the evidence must also place this factor on the list of secondary causes. Grenada enjoyed the non-intervention of Britain right up to the end. Support came from Mexico, France, Canada, Nicaragua, Nigeria, the Scandinavian nations, the European Economic Community, and other countries in the form of loans and development aid. The Soviet Union, East Germany, Libya, and North Korea provided various sorts of military assistance.[204] The NJM, for its part, issued principled condemnations of such regimes as Pinochet's, Duvalier's, and South Africa, and declared its support for the FDR in El Salvador and SWAPO in Namibia.[205] Economically, the material and human aid of Cuba was enormously positive, especially in the areas of health, education, housing, agriculture, and tourism, including the construction of a proper international airport at Port Salines, with a $40 million commitment for labor, building materials, oil, and machinery that had increased to $60 million by 1983 as other sources of funding dried up.[206]

Relations with its other neighbors in the Eastern Caribbean shifted over time, as most countries, doubtless with US encouragement, expressed criticisms of the failure to hold early elections. Right-wing governments were confirmed in power in the December 1979 elections in St. Vincent and the 1980 elections in Antigua, handily defeating the NJM-style parties that were in formation. The earlier pledges of support from reformist Dominica and St. Lucia dried up due to corruption in the first and electoral defeat in the second; relations with Trinidad never blossomed. Grenada and Guyana fell out in June 1980 when the NJM called Burnham's government to account for complicity in the murder of scholar-activist Walter Rodney.[207] Most significantly, the pro-NJM Manley government lost the 1980 elections in Jamaica, and the new prime minister, cold warrior Edward Seaga, became a severe critic of the NJM.[208] Seaga and other Caribbean leaders would call on the US to intervene (at the Reagan administration's request, it seems) in the October 1983 crisis.

The extensive solidarity shown Grenada by Cuba, moreover, proved a mixed blessing. Frank Ortiz, US ambassador to Barbados and the Eastern Caribbean, sent the NJM a note three weeks after it came to power informing Grenada that the US "would view with displeasure any tendency on the part of Grenada to develop closer ties to Cuba," or to turn to Cuba to forestall a counter-coup. Bishop replied: "No country has the right to tell us what to do or how to run our country, or who to be friendly with . . . We are not in anybody's backyard, and we are definitely not for sale."[209] The US refused to recognize Grenada's new ambassador, Dessima Williams, on the grounds that she was too young, nor would it allow its own outgoing ambassador, Sally Shelton, to accept Bishop's invitation for talks to restore a dialogue between the two nations.[210] As Jimmy Carter reversed course under the impact of the three revolutions of 1979, he defined Grenada, Nicaragua, and Jamaica as threats to US interests in the Caribbean.[211] US foreign policy tilted further toward an aggressive interventionism when Ronald Reagan came to power in 1981. While the US intervened in the Central American cases with great military weight in the 1980s and to great effect, the war in Grenada was at first more one of words and rhetoric, and of only marginal consequence in the reversal of the revolution until the crisis of the very last phase, which was not of US making.[212] Vice president George Bush stated at a Miami conference on business in Latin America that Grenada was "repressive," "economically weak," and "dependent" on Cuba and the Soviet Union.[213] US Rear Admiral R. P. McKenzie referred to Nicaragua, Cuba, and Grenada as "practically one country" and to the problem as a "political-military" one.[214] Bishop remarked in spirited fashion to a group of Caribbean journalists in April 1982: "Like an overgrown child at his bathtime, President Reagan is about to drop into what he believes is his bathtub, his fleet of toy battleships and aircraft carriers filled to the brim with plastic planes and clockwork marines."[215]

Led by US ambassador to the United Nations Jeane Kirkpatrick and others, the US engaged in propaganda attacks on Bishop in the local and world media, and the NJM was only too aware of the impact of similar campaigns against Allende and Michael Manley.[216] In June of 1981, the United States International Communication Agency organized a conference for Caribbean newspaper editors, offering them assistance if they would help isolate Grenada through hostile reportage; by September, CIA-funded networks of publishers were printing identical front-page editorials vilifying Grenada without the knowledge even of their own staff.[217] Ironically, NJM closures of slanderous press opponents added fuel to the critics of its censorship.[218] US-trained labor leaders who had broken strikes for Gairy now engaged in protests against the NJM, often against the wishes of their rank-and-file.[219] In August 1981, the US organized war games in the Eastern Caribbean against a "hypothetical" target called "Amber" and the "Amberdines," in which a US invasion was staged to rescue US hostages.[220] The US also used its influence at the World Bank and IMF to block loans, as it had done so successfully in Chile.[221] This posture of threat and rhetoric would take more concrete form in the dénouement of the revolution, but only after the problems of political culture led to an internal implosion.

The principal cause of the reversal of the revolution lies in the specific complexities of the political culture inside the New Jewel Movement itself. This is more than a story of personality differences between the two principals, finance minister Bernard Coard and prime minister Maurice Bishop, although personality played its role and was magnified by the small scale and face-to-face politics of island life.[222] Size worked to the advantage of the NJM when it came to mobilizing the population, and the political culture it established and built with the overwhelming majority of its supporters seems to have been both strong and vibrant, if still under construction. The genuine love felt for Bishop also cemented the approval of the revolution in the eyes of the people; Gordon Lewis speaks of "the almost spiritual transformation of popular mood."[223] But both scale and personal appeal worked against the revolution within the party itself, and a faction eventually developed around Coard that expressed ideological and personal reservations about the direction of events under Bishop. It is also the case that perceived economic problems, and real US pressure, exacerbated and contributed to the internal conflict. The tragedy of Grenada is that the great majority of the population was for the revolution, but the fragmentation of the revolutionary coalition occurred in the leadership of the revolution.

Coard, though an intellectual, was not a gifted speaker, but excelled as a party theoretician and is generally held to have been more Leninist in outlook than Bishop. Though an astute revolutionary, Bishop was less interested in or knowledgeable about matters of Marxist ideology, and more comfortable with a supple synthesis of Marxism, Black Power, and other revolutionary idioms, including radical democracy. His strength lay in his overwhelming popularity among the people, while Coard built stronger ties with the leadership of the 1,000-man People's Revolutionary Army (PRA) than with the popular assemblies.[224] Gordon Lewis sees Coard as arrogant, difficult, not willing to accept criticism, and "ambitious to become undisputed leader of the revolution," pushed in this direction also by his wife.[225] Bishop is described by Gordon as honest, patient, pragmatic, looking for consensus, and open in character. He had a tremendous popular touch, playing cards and laughing easily with people in their shops.[226] He was the undisputed star of the revolution, and this posed problems for some of the other leaders. From the point of view of Coard and others, Bishop was guilty of "onemanism," and personified what was lacking in the revolution: tighter organization, proper knowledge and application of Marxist-Leninist principles, and rule by committee.[227] The sheer volume of work for the small size of the party also strained the nerves of all concerned. Perhaps the best way to reconcile arguments stressing ideology versus personality is to accept that there were elements of both at work – as the concept of political cultures of opposition would have it – and that the two men represented not so much different goals but differences over the pace of change and the means, with Coard wedded to more central control legitimated by active popular bodies, and Bishop willing to explore the re-writing of the constitution to enable elections as early as 1985.[228]

These differences among former friends, emergent only four months into the revolution in 1979 according to Gosine and Millette,[229] sundered the party in the course of 1983. Coard's faction, having lost the popular contest to Bishop, went on the attack behind closed doors. Coard sought formal leadership of the party, though not necessarily of the government. At a general meeting convening full members of the party on September 25, Coard's supporters attacked Bishop and proposed joint leadership, with Coard to take over "party organization, tactics and strategy and Bishop concentrating on direct work with the masses, organization of the popular democratic institutions, regional and international work, and chairmanship of the weekly meetings of the Political Bureau."[230] Bishop, for his part, apparently exhausted by travel and the internal strife, vacillated, asking for time to consider the proposal. His willingness to accept criticism and personal modesty also served him less than well in a ruthless power struggle of the kind that was unfolding. Surprisingly, he left the country on yet another trip abroad, to Hungary and Czechoslovakia, while the crisis intensified. According to Bishop supporter Vincent Noel, party members were operating in a state of anxiety and paranoia as October began, threatening each other with guns, and afraid to sleep in their homes.

Bishop returned on October 8. On Wednesday, October 12, the Central Committee of the party put him under house arrest, cutting off his phone and disarming him. The next day, an all-party meeting voted to expel him, on charges of circulating a rumor that the Coard faction was planning his assassination (Payne et al.'s account notes the Coard faction's fear that Bishop or his supporters were plotting to murder *them*).[231] Bishop spoke for forty-five minutes at this meeting. In the next week the Coard group moved to gain control of the army and to disarm the popular militias. Gordon Lewis gives details of some of the "negotiations" in the

October 12–18 period, but as he himself admits they don't seem to have been very genuinely engaged on either side, and in any case, the accounts of this period are contradictory and difficult to sort out, given the evidence. Bishop is said to have told Michael Als, a visiting Trinidadian union activist: "dem men tough as hell and I just as tough. We go see. They have their model and I have mine."[232] On October 17, events finally spilled openly into the public realm, as the party decisions were announced over the radio. The next day, a general strike began and crowds began to assemble in support of Bishop. Meanwhile, the five government ministers who supported Bishop resigned: foreign minister Unison Whiteman, Lyden Ramdhanny (a non-NJM businessman), Norris Bain, George Louison, and minister of education Jacqueline Creft. Soon graffiti appeared proclaiming, "No Bishop, no revo."[233] On October 19, a crowd estimated at 3–4,000 people rescued Bishop; another 7–8,000 "party members, young people, civil servants, businessmen, housewives, even young schoolchildren" awaited him in the market square.[234] Bishop was found tied up and very weak; he could only say "the masses, the masses."[235] In a fateful decision, he was taken to the communications building at Fort Rupert, where he was revived enough to give orders to establish phone contact with supporters and the outside world. According to press secretary Dan Rojas, his message was that no outside intervention was necessary, that Cubans were *not* involved, and that Grenadians abroad should give their support.[236] Three army personnel carriers arrived at the fort, shelling it and opening fire on the crowd. Bishop's forces there surrendered to stop the shooting. Contradictory accounts exist about what happened next. Gordon Lewis finds most credible the report of "near" (not direct) eye-witnesses that shortly afterward, Bishop, Unison Whiteman, Jacqueline Creft, and Norris Bain were all executed in cold blood. Bishop's body was later destroyed by the RMC, suggesting a cover-up of its deeds.

That afternoon, the victors dissolved the PRG and dismissed the cabinet, declaring power in the hands of a sixteen-person Revolutionary Military Council (RMC), ostensibly led by PRA General Hudson Austin on behalf of the Coard faction; five of its members came from the NJM's Central Committee.[237] The Revolutionary Military Council promptly declared a four-day curfew, and requested assistance from Cuba, which rejected any aid to the murderers of Bishop, stating

No doctrine, no principle, no opinion calling itself revolutionary, and no internal split can justify such atrocious acts as the physical elimination of Bishop and the prominent group of honest and dignified leaders who died yesterday. The death of Bishop and his comrades must be explained and if they were executed in cold blood those responsible must be punished as an example.[238]

The RMC response charged that "the deep personal friendship between Fidel and Maurice . . . has caused the Cuban leadership to take a personal and not a class approach to the developments," and that this now opened the door to intervention.[239]

The available evidence of popular reaction to the death of Bishop is overwhelmingly of revulsion and anger.[240] The RMC was therefore forced to backtrack frantically on its military agenda, instead promising a "broad-based" civilian government within two weeks that would include businessmen.[241] They hastened to tell the US that "The RMC has no desire to rule the country . . . [The promised civilian government] will pursue a mixed economy and will encourage . . . foreign investment . . . The RMC of Grenada takes this opportunity to reassure the honourable . . . USA of its . . . highest regards."[242] A hostile world press, meanwhile, epitomized by the British tabloid *Daily Express*, described the events as a "Russian and Cuban-backed coup" against Bishop, who had stood in the way of turning Grenada into a Soviet base; this seems a better reflection of the US than the British government's attitude.[243]

On October 25, the US invaded Grenada, at the formal request of the Organization of Eastern Caribbean States,[244] and ostensibly out of concern for the safety of American medical students on the island, sealing the reversal of the revolution. That the United States could act so quickly and decisively when the opportunity fell into its lap is evidence that US pressure on Grenada was indeed substantial, as well as the seriousness of the Operation Amber military exercise of 1981; it cannot, however, be considered the main cause of the reversal of this revolution, for it is unthinkable without the prior disintegration of the revolution from within.

The case of Grenada is arguably unique in the intimate scale of both the rise and fall of the New Jewel Movement, but it also stands as irrefutable evidence of the importance of human agency in revolutionary causes and outcomes, and of the daunting political cultural complexities of maintaining coalitions in power. Gordon Lewis notes that to frame an explanation of the outcome in terms of personality versus ideology is "almost meaningless . . . Person and ideology do not exist separate from each other."[245] In another astute observation, Lewis likens Bishop, Coard, and the other leaders to actors locked into a tragedy of Shakespearean dimensions, who embodied (or perhaps had unleashed?) "impersonal social forces which ultimately they could not control."[246] The tragedy is that the hope and alternative offered by the NJM was cut short by the reversal of its revolution. This underscores, perhaps, the wisdom of bringing together the roles played by subjectivity, experience, and emotion in our concept of political cultures of opposition and resistance.

Nicaragua in the 1980s

The Nicaraguan case makes a good comparison with the Chilean, as like Allende and the UP, the FSLN operated under conditions of democratic pluralism and a mixed economy.[247] The manner of their fall from power, however, took the form not of a coup, but of an electoral defeat. Let us see what causes – common or particular – may have produced this reversal by other means.

The Sandinistas came to power in July 1979 after a devastatingly costly armed uprising, amidst a situation of economic bankruptcy and crisis. But they had certain assets too – most notably a broad base of popular support among the lower classes, workers, middle classes, students, women, peasants, and even some of the business sector. They worked hard to preserve this alliance, trying to bring about reforms to benefit the poor majority of the population at the same time as they tried to retain the support of industrialists and large farmers to keep the economy going. Their basic economic strategy was to reactivate the economy through the satisfaction of basic needs by investing in health and education, bringing about a land reform, and providing credit to small farmers, small private producers, coops, and the new state sector.

Economically, this model of a "mixed economy" sought a middle path between the market-dominated system of capitalism and the state-controlled system of communism. The state sector accounted for roughly 40 percent of GNP, and encompassed 50 percent of all large farms and 25 percent of all industry: exports and banking were nationalized, some 180 industrial and commercial enterprises were expropriated by the state, and about one-fifth of the country's arable land was taken over. Even as the state's share of GDP rose from 11 percent under Somoza in 1977 to 39 percent under the Sandinistas in 1982, the private sector retained the majority of economic activity, accounting for 60 percent of GNP and 80 percent of agriculture.[248] Thus, unlike in Chile, the Sandinistas were able to create a state sector without expropriating either foreign capital or the national bourgeoisie, instead simply taking over Somoza's share of the economy.

This model worked rather well between 1979 and 1983. Despite a recession throughout Latin America, the Nicaraguan economy grew a total of 22.5 percent over this period. By 1983, food consumption was up 40 percent, rents had been cut by 50 percent, medical care was free, and infant mortality had declined by 28 percent. A literacy campaign in 1980 reduced illiteracy from 50 to 12 percent. Land reform was a complex process, aimed first at creating cooperative and state farms out of Somoza's landholdings, but by 1987 it had brought five million acres of land to 100,000 families, more than in all of Central America combined.[249]

All of these accomplishments made the Sandinistas rather popular inside the country, and in the 1984 elections, the Sandinistas received 67 percent of the votes in what most observers termed a fair and free election. The media was free from censorship, and opposition parties were free to organize and criticize the government. This transition to a democratic polity was the second major accomplishment of the revolution. The state also restructured the military, replacing Somoza's hated and repressive National Guard with a new army formed around a core of FSLN guerrilla veterans and Sandinista-led popular militias recruited during the insurrection. They thus had control of the military and police, a further advantage not enjoyed by Allende.

Storm clouds were already appearing on the horizon, however. Sandinista political culture was a powerful synthesis of nationalist, socialist, and democratic strands, but even with the supporting culture of liberation theology, it was unable to hold together a coalition as broad as that which brought the FSLN to power in 1979. Despite the guarantees for private property made from the start and eventually enshrined in the 1987 Constitution, the industrial and agricultural elites never gave much support to the revolutionary project, withdrawing their representatives from the Governing Junta in 1980 in favor of increasingly organized electoral and military opposition, and attacking the Sandinistas as totalitarian and undemocratic in the press they controlled. The leadership of the Catholic Church joined this opposition even as many priests and lay Catholics were ardent supporters of the revolution; Pope John Paul II backed the hierarchy's attack on liberation theology and echoed the bourgeoisie's accusations of totalitarianism on the part of the Sandinistas.[250] The fact that the initial approach to land reform did not give peasants individual plots, and the tone-deafness of the Sandinistas to the issues of the partly English-speaking indigenous population of the Atlantic coast provided some popular supporters for these elite opponents of the regime, who would coalesce with US support into the basis of the armed contra opposition.[251]

The world-systemic opening that had appeared in 1978–79 with the Carter administration's human rights-oriented foreign policy quickly closed when Ronald Reagan assumed the presidency in 1981. The Reagan administration proved extremely hostile to the revolution, fundamentally out of fear at the height of the cold war that this model of a mixed economy, democratic polity, and independent foreign policy would be attractive throughout Latin America and the Third World, reducing the ability of the United States to exercise its political and economic influence. In 1982 the United States virtually created the contras out of former members of Somoza's National Guard, who were trained, supplied, and funded by the CIA and US military, and commanded by leading figures of the bourgeois opposition. The United States also secretly mined Nicaragua's harbors. All of these activities were found illegal by the World Court in 1986, a decision the Reagan administration ignored. The reasoning behind US pressure was that the Sandinistas probably could not be overthrown in this way, but by embroiling them in the mire of what is euphemistically called a "low-intensity conflict," the Nicaraguan model could be weakened and made less attractive for other countries. This was indeed the case, on a number of dimensions – politically, militarily, and economically.

The Sandinistas eventually defeated the contras in the field, but they had to impose a draft to expand the army from 13–18,000 in 1980 to 40,000 by 1984, aided by 60–100,000 citizens in armed local militias.[252] Rural dissatisfaction was partly assuaged by shifting the emphasis of the land reform away from state farms and cooperatives to individual grants of land.[253] Even with US aid, contra troop levels peaked at about 15,000 in 1985–86, and they were never able to hold even a small town for more than a few hours; they certainly never managed to incite a generalized anti-Sandinista revolt.[254] On the other hand, contra attacks continued right through the 1990 elections that unseated the Sandinistas, even after a cease-fire was agreed to in March 1988 as part of the Central America-wide peace accords brokered by Costa Rican president Oscar Arias, and the US continued to supply the contras with "humanitarian" aid even after Congress banned direct military aid in February 1988 in the wake of the Iran-contra scandal.[255] Thirty thousand Nicaraguans were killed and tens of thousands wounded as a result of the contra war.

The war and external pressures may also have influenced the Sandinistas' decision to establish a representative democracy sooner rather than later. In late 1983, the US had leaked a fraudulent document, codenamed "Operation Pegasus," that detailed plans for an imminent US invasion of Nicaragua.[256] Rather than provoking the expected restriction of civil liberties, however, the Sandinistas moved the date of the first elections ahead to 1984:

The decision to hold elections, announced in December of 1983, two months after the United States invasion of Grenada, clearly came in response to growing fears that Nicaragua would be next. If elections were going to establish enough international legitimacy to stymie the United States, the FSLN realized, Nicaragua's opposition parties would have to take part.[257]

This caught the US and internal opposition off balance. The right-wing pro-US candidate, Arturo Cruz, withdrew from the election, maintaining that free elections could not be held; a senior White House official cynically noted later that "The [Reagan] administration never contemplated letting Cruz stay in the race because then the Sandinistas could justifiably claim that the elections were legitimate."[258] Predictably denounced by the Reagan administration as a "Soviet-style sham," the elections were judged generally free and fair by observer delegations from the British and Irish parliaments, the Dutch government, the Socialist International (representing a number of the governments of Europe), and the US-based Latin American Studies Association. Six opposition parties won one-third of the vote and thirty-five of ninety-six seats in the National Assembly.[259]

The consequences of dependent development, impossible to shake even under revolutionary circumstances, combined with US pressure and the inevitable mistakes and contradictions of Sandinista economic policy to produce a severe economic downturn in the late 1980s. Economically, even in the period of early successes, there had been problems of inflation, shortages of certain goods (although not basic commodities), and a great amount of foreign indebtedness. The contra war exacted a heavy toll on the economy and society of Nicaragua; the northern provinces in particular, which produced most of the country's basic foodstuffs, were adversely affected. The costs of the war have been calculated as equal to three years of GDP, meaning years lost to economic development. By 1987, the military budget ate up 60 percent of government spending (nearly one-third of GDP).[260] US aid was cut off and the US blocked loans to Nicaragua at the World Bank and the IMF. The World Bank ceased its operations in Nicaragua, despite an internal report concluding that its programs there had been "extraordinarily successful."[261] In January 1985 the US vetoed a $59.8 million loan from the Inter-American Development Bank for a large-scale agricultural project, even though the bank declared the project "viable technically, institutionally, financially, economically, and legally."[262] The following veiled threat was delivered by US Secretary of State George Schultz to the bank's president, Antonio Ortiz Mena: "our joint long-term goal of strengthening the Inter-American Development Bank and expanding its resource base would be undercut by Board approval of this proposed loan."[263] The same year, the US declared a total trade embargo on Nicaragua, cutting off commercial relations with the country.

It has been suggested that "Whatever the level of FSLN mismanagement and corruption, the combined effects of the war, the financial blockade, the embargo, and destabilization by the internal bourgeoisie guaranteed that no FSLN policy, regardless of how well conceived, could be successful."[264] Nonetheless, while the economic crisis in Nicaragua was undoubtedly caused in large measure by US military and economic aggression, it was unintentionally aggravated by Sandinista economic policies that were aimed, ironically, at shoring up the Front's political base among the lower classes. The agrarian reform, for example, led to severe labor shortages in the agro-export sector because it "provided alternative sources of employment to the rural poor, thereby alleviating the extreme need that had driven them to work in the agroexport harvests in the past."[265] This, in turn, worsened a severe foreign exchange shortage that resulted in, among other things, a shortage of spare parts, compounded by the US trade embargo. Hyperinflation was caused in part by the combination of the regime's redistributive policies, which pushed up demand, and lagging supply due to the shrinkage of imports and production. Declining labor productivity also stemmed from the dearth of skilled administrators, economists, and accountants in the country. The commitment to retain redundant workers in state enterprises, and to provide social services to the population also strained the state's budget.[266]

But the external determinants of the Sandinistas' plight cannot be downplayed in any causal analysis. In addition to the contra war and the trade embargo, there was Nicaragua's legacy of economic dependency, which the US took full advantage of. The economic crisis was further aggravated by falling world-market prices for Nicaragua's principal exports (coffee, cotton, sugar, and cattle), which contributed to the growth of foreign debt, and by high interest rates on that debt. External aid to the Sandinistas, especially from the Soviet Union and Eastern Europe, dropped substantially after 1985, prompting one observer to conclude that "the reduction in socialist bloc assistance may be the most important dimension underlying the crises of 1987 and 1988."[267]

By 1985–87, these developments had reversed the earlier successes of the economy. In 1985 alone, GDP fell by 30 percent and inflation hit 300 percent. By 1986, purchasing power was down 60 percent from the levels of 1979, although the "social wage" made up for some of this, as free education, access to health care, and other services meant that people could do much more with the same income as before. In 1988 and 1989 the situation continued to worsen. The impact of the inflation – which reached 33,000 percent in 1988 – is clear enough: the standard of living deteriorated, with reports of increasing hunger in the countryside, the return of certain diseases because universal immunization could no longer be afforded, and a growth in illiteracy rates as children had to earn money rather than go to school. Both agricultural and urban workers were forced into the informal economy: reportedly, "By 1985 a street vendor selling three cases of soft drinks each day could earn much more than a cabinet minister."[268] More than a third of the population was unemployed or underemployed by the end of the decade.

In response to this economic crisis, the Sandinistas implemented "shock" austerity measures in 1988 and 1989, including massive and repeated devaluations of the currency, the lifting of price controls, cuts in government spending, and increases in credit to the private sector. Critics complained that these "reforms" did not differ from those traditionally prescribed by the International Monetary Fund, and, in fact, it proved impossible "to maintain workers' standard of living while attempting to provide incentives for agro-export capitalists, given external restrictions."[269] Carlos Vilas reports that "Real wages fell from an index of 29.2 in February 1988 (1980 = 100) to 6.5 in June 1989 and to 1 by December . . . Tuberculosis and malaria spread widely, and during the first trimester of 1989 infant mortality due to diarrhea was double that of a year earlier."[270]

The military pressure of the US-sponsored contras, the deep economic crisis, a changing world political atmosphere – all produced considerable dissatisfaction with Sandinista policies by 1990. In February of that year they lost elections to a coalition of fourteen parties, most of them on the right, in the National Opposition Union (UNO) headed by Violeta de Chamorro, the wife of the assassinated publisher. Most observers explained the opposition's win by the weariness of the Nicaraguan people from the war, which they must have felt the US would continue as long as the Sandinistas were in power, combined with the hope that US economic aid would follow a UNO victory.

The outcome of the elections was conditioned in its most fundamental aspects by a decade of counterrevolutionary war that left thousands dead, wounded and crippled, the economic and social infrastructure in ruins, hundreds of thousands of people displaced – drafted into military service, relocated to refugee camps, forced to flee to the cities to escape attack – and basic goods in desperately short supply. The people voted against that.[271]

Not surprisingly, polling during the 1990 electoral campaign indicated that the economy (52 percent), the war (37 percent), or both (8 percent) were viewed as the decisive issues in the election. And while a majority of those polled (52 percent) blamed Nicaragua's economic problems on the contra war or the US economic embargo – more than twice the 24 percent who cited government mismanagement – 61 percent felt that UNO would be able to "reconcile" Nicaragua with the United States, while only 50 percent felt that the FSLN could do so, and fully 36 percent were convinced that the FSLN could not do so.[272] The anti-Sandinista vote, in other words, apparently "reflected a decision by a significant number of Nicaraguans to believe that the United States would *not* accept a Sandinista victory and [was] a rational choice, under those premises, to bring an end to the war, the embargo, and the destruction of the economy."[273]

The Sandinistas lasted the longest in power of our seven cases, but proved as vulnerable in the end as the others. Their adherence to radical democracy in the midst of an externally-induced economic crisis, like Allende in Chile, opened the door to their defeat. That this defeat was electoral, and not the result of a coup, meant that their revolutionary legacy would be their success in turning Nicaragua away from dictatorship toward democracy. Over a decade later, as little remains of the social gains of the revolution, this outcome looks more like the *political* revolutions in the Philippines, South Africa, and Zaire that will be touched on in Chapter 5. From another point of view, the promise of the first four years of Sandinista rule, it is also a key reversed social revolution, made the more bitter for a people that had "learned how to shout."

Iran 1953, Guatemala 1954, and Jamaica 1980: two coups and an election

When Iran proved that it could produce oil without British help in 1951–52, the British organized a boycott of the country's oil, and got most of the Western world, including the United States, to support them in this.[274] Mussadiq, however, ran the economy fairly well even without the oil revenues. The British then turned to other tactics, and began to plot a coup by the Iranian army against Mussadiq. When the Eisenhower administration came into office in January 1953, the US agreed to take over the plan for the overthrow of Mussadiq with the help of pro-shah forces in Iran. This was justified on the grounds that the communist Tudeh Party was poised to take over from Mussadiq, making no distinction between Mussadiq, who was a nationalist, and the Tudeh Party. Thus was set in motion the first use of covert CIA action by the United States to overthrow a foreign government. The CIA worked with the shah, military officers, and other conservative forces in Iran, indirectly aided by those who had left the National Front, including some of the ulama, and ironically, by the Tudeh, which did not fully support Mussadiq.

Events came to a climax in August 1953. When Mussadiq asked for a national referendum to dissolve the majlis, which had made it difficult for him to rule, the measure passed by a landslide. The shah then tried to dismiss Mussadiq, but failed and fled the country on August 16 to widespread demonstrations of rejoicing. On August 17 and 18, crowds attacked the police and US information centers; some of the rioters had been hired by the CIA to create an impression that the government of

Mussadiq was not in control. The US ambassador called on Mussadiq to use his police to disperse the crowds, which he did, thereby taking his own supporters off the streets. On August 19, three days after the shah had fled, the military launched a successful coup against Mussadiq, led by a general who had been in hiding with the CIA. Other CIA agents and royalists paid crowds of the urban poor to demonstrate for the shah, who returned in triumph. Three hundred people died in the coup. National Front leaders, including Mussadiq, received jail sentences. Tudeh Party leaders were executed. The shah now owed his position to the United States, which had organized and funded the military coup that brought him back, and embarked on a twenty-five year reign that finally came to an end with his own deposal by the social revolution in 1978–79.

In Guatemala, the land reform alienated the US because it threatened the paramount position of the United Fruit Company in the dependent economy of the country. Ironically, the architect of the reform, President Arbenz, a socialist in orientation, misunderstood the nature of land tenure in the indigenous Mayan countryside, and efforts to give small individual plots to peasants led to acute conflicts among plantation workers who tended to accept the parcels and indigenous communities who sought a collective approach to the land in keeping with their own political cultures. Class and race therefore combined rather tragically to fragment the popular coalition.[275] It is unclear how great a factor the economy was in the coup that came in 1954,[276] but the international conjuncture of intense US pressure upon Guatemala and direct support for the military plotters opened the door to the reversal of the revolution, to whose aid the splintered masses did not rally.

In Jamaica, Michael Manley and the PNP's process of broad social transformation under the rubric of "democratic socialism" eventually fell afoul of dependency and recession even as he had some success in raising living standards in his first term and gained re-election in 1976.[277] When Jamaica nationalized its bauxite at the expense of North American aluminum companies, US economic maneuvers forced Manley to turn to the IMF and World Bank, who in turn required fiscal and other policies that undercut the forward momentum of democratic socialism. Living standards declined by one-quarter in a single year.[278] The US also covertly accelerated the acute political polarization and climate of violence that brought about Manley's fall in the 1980 elections to Edward Seaga, whom we have seen already as a cold war protagonist doing Ronald Reagan's bidding in the events that would bring down the New Jewel in Grenada.[279] Jamaica's promising start on the path of radical reforms foundered on the difficulties of maintaining a broad

Table 4.1 *Coming to power*

	A.	B.	C.	D./E.	
	Social structure	State	Political cultures	Conjunctural factors	Outcome
Guatemala 1944	Dependent development under United Fruit Co.	Ubico dictatorship/1944 election	Nascent democratic, nationalist radical currents	Anti-fascism/Downturn and general strike	Urban-based coalition ousts Ubico non-violently and elects Arévalo
Iran 1951	Dependent development under British in the 19th/20th c.	Pahlavi monarchy's post-WW2 democratic opening	Nationalism, social reforms of National Front	British under-estimate Mussadiq, post-WW2 national liberation climate/Recession	Urban-based coalition elects National Front and Mussadiq
Bolivia 1952	Mining enclave, limited dependent development	Repressive, exclusionary nature of the *sexenio*, fraud in 1951	Socialism populism, nationalism	US inattention/Recession	MNR and civilian militias oust military
Chile 1970	Mining/industrial dependent development	Genuinely democratic polity	Vibrant democratic socialist challenge	US under-estimates threat/Recession in 1969–70	Allende elected with narrow plurality
Nicaragua 1979	Commercial agricultural boom, 1960–70s: dependent development	Somoza's repression	Sandinista nationalism and social justice/ Liberation theology	Carter human rights policy/ Post-earthquake crisis, 1972–78	Broad-based coalition – Guerrilla success
Grenada 1979	Dependent development, mostly under British	Gairy's repressive, exclusionary rule	New Jewel populism/democratic aspirations	Britain and US passive/Recession	Sudden uprising brings NJM to power
Jamaica 1972	Adversely impacted and diversified by dependent development	Genuinely democratic polity	Social(ist) democratic challenge/ Rastafarianism	Democratic elections/ Recession, unemployment	Clear-cut electoral victory for Manley

Table 4.2 *The rise and reversal of revolutions*

A Boolean Truth Table
(0 = trait absent; 1 = trait present)

	A.	B.	C.	D.	E.
	Dependent development	Vulnerable state: repressive or open*	Political cultures of opposition	Economic downturn	World-systemic opening
Coming to power					
1. Guatemala 1944	1	1/1*	1	1—	1
2. Iran 1951	1	1*	1	1	1
3. Bolivia 1952	1	1—	1	1	1
4. Chile 1970	1	1*	1	1	1
5. Jamaica 1972	1	1*	1	1	1
6. Nicaragua 1979	1	1	1	1	1
7. Grenada 1979	1	1	1	1	1
Reversal of revolutions					
1. Iran 1953	1	1*	1—	1	0
2. Guatemala 1954	1	1*	1—	1—	0
3. Bolivia 1964	1	1*	1—	1	0
4. Chile 1973	1	1*	1—	1	0
5. Jamaica 1980	1	1*	1—	1	0
6. Grenada 1983	1	1*—	0	0	0
7. Nicaragua 1990	1	1*	1—	1	0

enough coalition of forces to win elections in conditions of economic hardship and acute external pressures.

Conclusions: success and failure in one act

Let us sum up the arguments of this chapter with the aid of three tables on the rise and later fall of these seven governments.

Table 4.1 shows us the conditions for the coming to power of revolutionary governments, and Table 4.2 represents the factors for both success and reversal in the form of a truth table amenable to Boolean analysis.

In Boolean terms, we may express the causal combinations that underlay the coming to power of our cases in the following way, drawing on Tables 4.1 and 4.2 (recall that "A" signifies the presence of factor A, "a" its absence).

Coming to Power

Guatemala	ABCDE
Iran	ABCDE
Bolivia	ABCDE
Chile	ABCDE
Jamaica	ABCDE
Nicaragua	ABCDE
Grenada	ABCDE

As argued in the text, all five factors are found across these cases, further confirming our theory of the causes of Third World revolutions. The only questions of possible non-fits of data to theory are the degree to which there was an economic downturn on the eve of Ubico's ouster in Guatemala in June 1944, and the nature of the state in Bolivia, where the government was clearly repressive and exclusionary, but not personalistic. Thus I have coded these two entries as "1 –" in Table 4.2; for the purposes of theory, we will give them the benefit of the doubt in the absence of clear evidence or argumentation to the contrary.

The most important new finding here has to do with the nature of some of the regimes that proved vulnerable to social revolution. In particular, Chile is joined by the cases of Iran and Jamaica to offer us a new type of vulnerable state – the open democratic polity. Thus two sub-types exist among this set of cases: the usual model for success in the cases of Guatemala, Bolivia, Nicaragua, and Grenada, and a second type: and the presence of an open democratic polity in Iran, Chile, and Jamaica (in fact, Guatemala is a case of both sub-types, as first the Ubico dictatorship [type 1] was overthrown in June, and then Arévalo was elected in December [type 2]). These findings both powerfully confirm the general model we have been evaluating in this book by showing it to be broadly applicable to another seven cases (making seventeen in all), and expanding it significantly in terms of the second factor – the vulnerability of a certain type of state – by identifying a third sub-type of state that is vulnerable to revolution, the genuinely open democratic polity. Recall that the first vulnerable sub-type – the repressive, exclusionary, personalist state – was found in the five classical Third World social revolutions of Chapter 2, and the second vulnerable sub-type – the repressive, exclusionary, colonial state – was found in the five great anti-colonial revolutions of Chapter 3. Note also that our third sub-type is as rare as the first in Third World history, since the majority of Third World states for most of the twentieth century have been ruled either by collective military governments or the very limited formal democratic states that Robinson calls "polyarchies."

In turning now to the conditions under which these revolutions were reversed, we can start with the summary provided in Table 4.3. Note

Table 4.3 *Falling from power*

	A. Social structure	B. State	C. Political cultures	D./E. Conjunctural factors	Outcome
Iran 1953	Continued dependency amidst gains	Increasingly democratic under Mussadiq	Splits in National Front, religious forces move right	US-British coup plans/ Economic difficulties of oil-less economy	CIA-devised coup restores Pahlavi monarchic dictatorship
Guatemala 1954	Continued dependency amidst gains	Democratic under Arbenz	Revolutionaries ignore Maya, growing right-wing opposition	US & UFCO plotting/ Economy stable	CIA-devised coup restores dictatorship
Bolivia 1964	Continued dependency amidst gains	Democratic under MNR	Splits inside and outside the MNR	US military aid/ Economic hardships	MNR moves to right, then coup in 1964
Chile 1973	Continued dependency amidst gains	Democratic under Allende	Intense left/right polarization, UP fragments	US blockade and intervention/ Hyperinflation, crisis	CIA-supported coup establishes dictatorship
Nicaragua 1990	Continued dependency amidst gains	Democratic under the FSLN	Increasing left/right polarization	US-*contra* war/ Severe economic downturn	Electoral defeat of FSLN
Grenada 1983	Continued dependency amidst gains	Revolutionary popular under Bishop	Fatal splits in New Jewel Movement	US intervention/ Economy stable	Fall of New Jewel Movement
Jamaica 1980	Continued dependency amidst gains	Democratic under Manley	Increasing left/right polarization and violence	US economic and political maneuvers/ Economic hardships	Conservative Seaga government elected

that in this table, we introduce for the first time in this study codings of "1 –." The meanings of such codings is that the factor in question had some significant limitations (as with the political cultures of opposition in most of our cases after taking power), or represents a situation more or less mid-way between presence and absence (as in the case of the degree to which the NJM in Grenada was democratic – given the absence of formal elections the coding would be "1 –" but assessed by the other measures discussed in the case it can be considered a "1*–"). Note too, that the meaning of the vulnerable state in part B of Table 4.2 is "democratic": in other words, the question to code here is: "Was the state democratic?" The logic of the analysis reposes on the argument that democratic revolutionary polities are in fact vulnerable to counter-revolution (see the discussion of this below).

If we return to Table 4.2 to present these cases in their distinctive combinations of factors, a slightly more complex variety of factors can be seen at work in the failures of these governments to hold onto their hard-won power. Here, I am translating the "1 –" codings into *absences* of the factor in question; that is, if there was some problem with the full effectivity of the factor, it is coded as absent for the purpose of assessing the reversals of these revolutions. This conservative interpretation of the binary is warranted since we are trying to distinguish the problems that these governments faced as they struggled to stay in power. Since Grenada's degree of political openness proved a vulnerability, its 1*– is coded as present.

	Falling from Power
Iran	ABcDe
Guatemala	ABcde
Bolivia	ABcDe
Chile	ABcDe
Jamaica	ABcDe
Nicaragua	ABcDe
Grenada	ABcde

Two distinct combinations of factors are found among the seven cases: Iran, Bolivia, Jamaica, Chile, and Nicaragua form one cluster (ABcDe), and Guatemala and Grenada a second (ABcde). These patterns can be easily "reduced" in Boolean terms to a single pattern that accounts for or covers all seven cases: ABce (the reason for this is that any two patterns that are similar in all but one factor can be logically simplified to a pattern of the factors which they have in common, since they produce the outcome in question both when the dropped factor is present and when it is absent).[280] The pattern can be interpreted as follows: revolutions have been reversed when they continue to be subject to the effects of dependent development (which is impossible to undo in a short period of time, if ever), when they have open, democratic institutions (see the discussion below on the reasons for and implications of this), when the revolutionary political cultures that brought them about are attenuated due to internal differences of opinion or the difficulties of continuing to effectively engage their broad coalitions (compounded by the fragmenting effects of the opponents of the new government, internal and external), and when the world-systemic window that opened to permit their coming to power closes, as can happen in a variety of ways detailed below. These four factors, in conjunction, are found in all seven cases, and the revolutions were reversed regardless of the presence or not of an economic downturn (in fact, such a downturn was found in five and perhaps six of the cases, so it lent its weight as well).

This finding suggests a possible theory for reversals of revolution: revolutionaries fall from power when political fragmentation and polarization, economic difficulties, and outside intervention occur together in a mutually reinforcing fashion.

Our comparison also suggests that there has been a pattern for the reversal of democratic revolutionaries by the United States – a coordinated program of counter-revolutionary destabilization that combines the following factors to bring about either electoral defeat or military coup: 1) a closing of the world-systemic opening that facilitated the revolutions, by a) attacking the political legitimacy of the revolutionary states making full use of their democratic natures in utilizing covert and overt propaganda to undermine the regime in the eyes of the population, and b) giving substantial material aid and assistance to opposition parties, military officers, and/or counter-revolutionary armies, combined with 2) an assault on the economic success of the revolution, playing on both the legacy of dependent development and the potential for economic downturns through a wide variety of actions, including economic blockades, cutting off sources of external funding and trade, and working with internal forces to disrupt production and distribution. The combination of these measures goes a long way toward weakening the political cultures that sustain a revolution, leading to internal splits, disaffection of the social bases of the revolution, and the acute political polarization necessary to sustain a coup or defeat a revolutionary government through elections.

This raises a final crucial issue for discussion. Why have democratic revolutionary regimes been historically vulnerable to reversal, as in these seven cases, whereas the one-party post-revolutionary regimes that arose in the classical and anti-colonial cases of Mexico, Cuba, China, Iran, Algeria, Vietnam, Angola, Mozambique, and Zimbabwe did not fall from power? I would like to suggest here that democratic regimes are vulnerable not because they are imperfect or undesirable revolutionary instruments, but rather because they can be destabilized by external intervention in ways that less democratic regimes cannot. There is a seeming paradox in this, because even semi-democratic regimes prove difficult for revolutionaries to overthrow, while "undemocratic" revolutionary states prove difficult for their opponents to overthrow (but not impossible, as the Eastern European revolutions of 1989 prove). This does not mean that revolutionaries – past or future – are advised by the lessons of history to establish non-democratic one-party states. It must be observed that in the context of the cold war, the period into which sixteen of our seventeen cases – all but Mexico after 1920 – fall, democratic revolutionaries have been vulnerable to overthrow because their radical nationalism could be targeted as "communism" in US policy-making circles to justify intervention. This would set in motion the counter-revolutionary measures undertaken by the US and their internal allies in each country. The problem was not, therefore, the "unsuitability" of democracy as a form of revolutionary governance, but its vulnerability in the context of the cold war. I would suggest that since this condition no longer obtains in the early twenty-first century, we should not draw hasty conclusions that democratic revolutionaries will fail as they ostensibly have in the past, an argument to which I will return in the conclusion to this book. Nor am I convinced that the reversal of these revolutions was in some sense an inevitable result of this single factor, and this for several reasons. First, the logic of the model is that no single factor can produce a revolution or (now) its reversal; both theory and Boolean method suggest that it is particular conjunctures of the presence and absence of factors that "cause" outcomes. The empirical analysis in this chapter confirms this insight. Second, and in part following from this, I believe that there is room for alternative outcomes in history; to assume otherwise is to read history teleologically. *Could* Allende have found a way out of his dilemma at the Lo Curro conference in June 1972? This is a profound question, which I have asked of my students repeatedly over the years in a classroom exercise where we vigorously debate his options.[281] My students – and all the more so, the members of the UP itself – have been capable of generating plausible alternative courses of action that would have set other logics in motion. Certainly some of these would not have led to the coup. Flexibility and imagination should temper both historical and comparative analysis, and political action itself.

5 The great contrasts: attempts, political revolutions, and non-attempts

> Revolution is the only form of "war" in which ultimate victory can only be prepared by a series of "defeats."
>
> Rosa Luxemburg[1]

This chapter will take up three further types of "failure," in the sense that social revolutions did not occur in conditions where we might otherwise expect them to. These include attempted social revolutions, political revolutions, and non-attempts. If we return to Theda Skocpol's touchstone definition of social revolutions as "rapid, basic transformations of a society's state and class structures . . . accompanied and in part carried through by class-based revolts from below,"[2] we can derive useful definitions of the sorts of cases we would want to contrast these with to strengthen our empirical tests of the theory of their origins. Attempted social revolutions are the clearest example of this, for the goal of the revolutionaries was the same as in the successful cases – political and socio-economic transformation through class-based revolts from below. Note that this requires a conceptual counterfactual, for in the absence of success, how would we know that what was attempted was a social revolution? Here, we must rely on our readings of the intentions of the revolutionaries and nature of their movements, and I believe that most close observers of the eight struggles discussed below would agree that social revolutions were indeed on the agenda of the actors involved.

Political revolutions are another important variant on our theme since they are revolutions made by mass-mobilizing movements and resulting in significant political change, but where the social and economic transformations that we associate with social revolutions do not accompany these changes. We will therefore study five such cases to further test the range of our model, for they should bear some resemblance in origin to social revolutions, yet have some crucial difference(s) in causal terms (or else they would have resulted in social revolutions, logically speaking); that is, if we can find a political revolution in full possession of all five factors, that would be a problem for our claim that we have a theory of the origins of *social* revolutions.

We can also test our model against cases of non-revolution. Since that is a rather large universe – most countries at most moments in history did not experience even a revolutionary attempt – we will single out cases where some of the factors leading to one or another kind of revolution (social, political, or attempted) are present, as the most useful test of our theory, for here we are trying to establish that it is the absence of our set of factors that might account for the lack of an attempt at revolution. We will see how closely we can approximate the ideal test, wherein four of our five factors were present, and no attempt was made (note that if such a pattern were found in the case of an attempted revolution or a political revolution, that too would be a confirmation of the necessity of all five factors coming together to produce a social revolution).

A final variant on this theme would be to study revolutions from above, that is, cases where political and social transformation occurred (two of Skocpol's definitional criteria), and where this is accomplished not by a class-based revolt from below but instead by a small group of state officials or by a group or individual who has come to power through a coup. The most well-known cases would include Turkey under Atatürk in the 1920s and 1930s, Nasser's Egypt in the 1950s, the progressive military regime in Peru between 1968 and 1975, and perhaps the Derg in Ethiopia in 1974–75 and the communists who seized control of Afghanistan in 1978. These cases are beyond the scope of this study, and some of them have been well analyzed by Ellen Kay Trimberger.[3] It would be interesting to revisit her analysis in light of our model, a task I must leave for another day (or another scholar!).

Attempted revolutions

The guiding principle of my analysis of these cases – Argentina in the mid-1970s, El Salvador in the 1980s, Guatemala between the 1960s and 1980s, the Philippines in the mid- to late 1980s, China in 1989, Peru from the early 1980s to 1992, Algeria in the 1990s, and Chiapas since 1994 – was that they should exhibit substantial similarities to the successful cases already studied (to explain the seriousness of the attempt), but also equally significant *differences* in some of the factors at work (to account for their failure). Argentina, Guatemala, and the Philippines will be treated only in passing, and at the end of this section.

El Salvador's near revolution

From 1979 to 1992 El Salvador underwent perhaps the most intense revolutionary experience in human history that has failed to come to power.[4] Dependent development, a repressive state, vigorous oppositional cultures, and economic difficulties helped produce a very serious popular armed challenge by 1979. Yet throughout the 1980s, the army and the rebels fought to a standstill, eventually concluding a peace settlement in 1992 that brought an end to the civil war with the promise of significant political reforms but not social revolution.

The key to Salvadoran political economy and social structure, from independence in 1821 to the present day, has consistently been the social arrangements and tensions generated by the concentration of agricultural land in the hands of a well-entrenched oligarchy of large landowners traditionally known as the "fourteen families" (in reality, some fifty to sixty families constituted this elite). In the late nineteenth century this oligarchy successfully expropriated much Indian-held village land to cultivate coffee for export, dominating politics as well until 1930. When markets crashed at the onset of the Great Depression in 1930–31 the army overthrew a liberal government and crushed a general uprising by massacring some 30,000 people. This traumatic event ushered in a new system of military rule in favor of the coffee oligarchy, first under the personalistic Martínez dictatorship from 1931 to 1944, then in a more bureaucratic, institutional guise under such military-dominated parties as the National Conciliation Party (the PCN) from the 1950s to the late 1970s.

A model of dependent capitalist development was consolidated in the 1960s under the impetus of the Alliance for Progress, a US-inspired development strategy designed to avert further Cuban-type revolutions by sponsoring land reform and modernization, with military aid to counter opposition. President Kennedy singled out El Salvador in this regard: "Governments of the civil-military type of El Salvador are the most effective in containing communist penetration in Latin America."[5] The Salvadoran elite and military retained control of this process, benefiting greatly from import-substitution industrialization and participation in the new Central American Common Market, but initiating no land reforms. Para-military groups were organized to co-opt some peasants and intimidate the rest in an effort to sustain this phase of dependent development. Small but increasingly vocal urban middle and working classes came into existence, and their political aspirations were channeled into the reform-minded Christian Democratic opposition party. Unlike in Nicaragua, then, an internally more cohesive upper class and a marginally more open political system made broad cross-class resistance difficult, while strong military rule was staunchly supported by an elite unified against pressures from below.[6]

The 1972 elections marked a decisive turning point in the eventual elaboration of revolutionary political cultures of opposition in El Salvador. In stealing the victory from Christian Democrat José Napoleon

Duarte, the army and oligarchy made it plain they would not give up power through elections, though, significantly, they still did not resort to dictatorship, but held regular elections at five-year intervals. Economic hardship, blatant electoral fraud, and military repression stimulated the appearance in the 1970s of four major guerrilla organizations. These groups recruited among students, professionals, peasants, agricultural wage laborers, trade unionists, and shantytown dwellers, as well as religiously-inspired activists.[7] While liberation theology played a major role in El Salvador as in Nicaragua in the 1970s, and there were reformist, trade unionist, and other broadly-based oppositional currents, the political culture of the emerging left-wing revolutionary coalition was Marxist, anti-imperialist, and class-oriented, a stance not calculated to mobilize the broadest coalition of social forces. The Christian Democrats siphoned off support among peasants, workers, and the middle classes, while the business sector was solidly on the side of the military. A difference with the Nicaraguan case, then, throughout the 1970s, was the lesser breadth of this incipient coalition in class terms, its more radical socialist orientation, and its separation into various oppositional organizations.

These differences in state power and political cultures of opposition were further compounded by the domestic and international conjunctures of the late 1970s. The economic conditions engendered by dependent development were indeed deplorable: extreme inequality in landholding, high unemployment and underemployment, the lowest per capita income in Central America, shockingly high rates of illiteracy, malnutrition, and infant mortality.[8] These crisis-like conditions, however, were painfully "normal" throughout the 1970s; a partial difference with successful social revolutions then was the stable nature of crisis in the domestic economy.[9] Conditions, already terrible, may not have perceptibly worsened, although this would provide little consolation to the victims of dependent development.

By the 1970s the ideological center of gravity of the revolution was an uncompromising Marxist-Leninist standpoint embodied in the FMLN (Farabundo Martí National Liberation Front).[10] This is not to deny the significance of liberation theology in El Salvador in this period, for it too shaped the outlook of many of the young people who joined and led the revolution. But as the hoped-for swift uprising of 1979–80 devolved into the stalemated revolutionary civil war of the 1980s, the armed wing of the revolution represented by the FMLN defined the political cultural terms of the struggle as resolutely anti-imperialist and class-based. They failed to secure any broad support from middle-class sectors, or even some of the peasantry and urban lower classes for whom they fought. Instead, the centrist Christian-Democratic Party of José Napoleon Duarte dominated the electoral opening of the mid-1980s, coming to power in 1982–84, then ceding a thin hegemony to the right-wing ARENA Party in 1989, whose president Alfredo Cristiani finally negotiated a peace settlement with the rebels in 1992. To this argument may be added the neglect by the FMLN of the emerging feminist revolutionary culture within its own ranks.[11]

Note that I am not arguing that only culture explains the defeat of the Salvadoran revolution (and labeling the outcome itself presents a paradox, for the revolutionaries were not defeated in the field and the FMLN is playing a crucial political role in the new El Salvador). Other factors clearly contributed their effect as well: the collective nature of military rule in El Salvador created a broad base of elite support for the regime, and the expansion of political participation in the course of the civil war to include the centrist Christian Democrats in the electoral game siphoned off some middle-class and even rural worker support from the rebels as well. This polarization into two camps, with a wavering middle in between them, was then solidified by the limitations of the political culture of the FMLN rebels, with its largely Marxist-Leninist discourse of acute class war. Instead of a relatively swift victory for the revolutionary forces, the outcome in El Salvador was a decade of wrenching civil war.

Finally, the world-systemic opening that facilitated revolutionary successes in Iran and neighboring Nicaragua in 1979 began to close even in the last year of the Carter presidency (1980) as US Democrats balked at allowing another Third World revolution: "Only if the alternative to a tyrant was politically acceptable to the United States would Washington risk withdrawing its support from a trusted ally."[12] The opening closed entirely in the Reagan years, during which the US intervened massively to prop up the regime in El Salvador with $6 billion in military and economic aid between 1979 and 1992.[13] These unfavorable factors produced a costly, brutal civil war that could end only with a negotiated settlement. Outside intervention, coupled with the internal cohesion of the Salvadoran elite and the difficulties of constructing a broad multi-class alliance under these conditions thus slowed and ultimately prevented a revolution from succeeding in conditions where we would otherwise not have been surprised to see another successful case.

The Sendero Luminoso in Peru

Another extremely strong Latin American insurgency occurred in Peru starting in 1980, where the sui generis quasi-Maoist Marxists of Sendero Luminoso (the Shining Path) threatened to seize power for a decade or more from the civilian governments of center-right populist Fernando Belaúnde Terry (1980–85), center-left APRA (American Popular

Revolutionary Alliance) leader Alán García Pérez (1985–90), and free market populist conservative Alberto Fujimori (1990–2000).[14] Gathering strength in the Andean provincial capital of Ayacucho after 1980 under the shadowy leadership of a charismatic intellectual named Abimael Guzmán (known as Comrade Gonzalo), the movement represented an alliance – however problematic – between radical intellectuals and the indigenous population of the underdeveloped Andean highlands, proclaiming itself in pursuit of a whole new world. At its height in the late 1980s, Sendero succeeded in establishing further bases of support in the shanty-towns of Lima, the lowland capital, more clearly the site of dependent development and its contradictions in the Peruvian setting. Economic downturns occurred with some frequency in the late 1980s as Peru struggled with a huge foreign debt and as successive development strategies failed to control inflation and unemployment.[15] By 1992, 30,000 people had died in the conflict, 4,000 had disappeared, and 200,000 had been displaced.[16]

Sendero's political culture was an idiosyncratic blend of Maoism, the French revolution, Pol Pot, Peruvian revolutionary theorist José Carlos Maríategui, and its own interpretation of indigenous cultures of opposition, with a strong accent on revolutionary chiliasm, a cult of leadership, and the purifying effects of violence as strategy and goal: "The organization seemed able to channel intense feelings of frustration toward the larger goal of revolution."[17] Far more than the Marxism-Leninism of the revolutionaries in El Salvador in the same period, this ideology was not calculated to appeal to broad segments of the population, and never achieved a hegemonic claim even on the left. Even at its height around 1989, therefore, the movement failed to attract sufficient cross-class support to build a broad populist coalition for revolutionary, extra-constitutional social transformation in Peru. Indeed, it never sought such an alliance, a fatal flaw in its vision. Instead, explicitly targeting the traditional left, represented in the person of President Alán García (and to his left the optimistically named Izquierda Unida, as well as Peru's other armed revolutionary current, the Tupac Amaru Revolutionary Movement – the MRTA), Sendero had alienated its natural allies on the political spectrum by the mid-1980s. The savagery of the guerrillas' assault on civil society, ideologically and with intense physical violence, produced both fervent adherents and, as in El Salvador and Guatemala, few middle- and upper-class supporters. It also came to alienate significant portions of the rural population as well, as it fought not just the army but all civilian opponents and many neutral communities.[18] In a sense, Sendero's failure to articulate a coalitional political strategy stemmed from its neglect of the effects of dependent development on Peru's class structure, and its analysis that Peru's was a feudal society. Its distaste for the Soviet Union, China, and Cuba also did little to create a favorable world-systemic conjuncture.

Nor was the regime vulnerable in the classic sense: Peru maintained a functioning democracy in the 1980s under the left-oriented government of Alán García, and while Alberto Fujimori later dissolved Congress, he was careful to obtain military and a surprising amount of popular support. Despite intense military repression and the autogolpe (self-coup) of April 5, 1992 by Fujimori that concentrated unusual (but not unlimited) discretionary powers in his hands, the political institutions of Peru never approximated an exclusionary, personalistic dictatorship.[19] And while dependent development continued unabated, along with economic suffering for much of the population, Fujimori's neoliberal shock treatment brought down inflation after 1991 and reinstituted the rhythms of international capital (aid, trade, and investment). The international community (the United States followed by Europe), initially hostile to Alán García's plans to limit debt repayment as well as the excesses of the counterinsurgency under Fujimori, had also swung behind Fujimori's political economic project by 1993–94, preventing any world-systemic opening from developing. Thus, the fortuitous discovery and capture of Guzmán in September 1992 set back Sendero's project indefinitely and put the movement clearly on the defensive. Now split into two factions, one following Guzman's tactical call from prison to negotiate peace, and the other, known as the Red Path, still committed to armed actions, its future prospects look bleaker than ever, even as its capacity to disrupt daily life continues to some degree.[20] The same holds true for the MRTA, a far smaller guerrilla opposition which remains even further from power than Sendero Luminoso after its late 1996 hostage-taking of diplomats ended in a government rescue operation that killed all the participating guerrillas.

In Peru we have another case of an attempt that failed despite a very strong insurgency, due to some deep problems with the movement's political culture, the government's skillful political course avoiding either dictatorship or too open a polity, its reversal of a severe economic downturn, and the world-systemic conjuncture. A host of factors thus militated against a revolutionary success for the Shining Path.

China, 1989

China's revolution of 1949 wrought an enormous transformation in living standards, much of it highly positive, at the same time as it entailed dramatically devastating social and personal dislocations owing to its authoritarian twists and turns – the Cultural Revolution of the 1960s, Mao's death in 1976, and the opening to the world market and private investment in the 1980s. The state's encouragement of private enterprise, foreign investment, and market relationships led by 1988 to various social problems – inflation, housing shortages, unemployment, growing income inequality, and a perception (undoubtedly true) of rampant corruption in the government and ruling Communist Party.[21] There was thus a feeling among students, intellectuals, and many others that what China needed was political reforms granting more democratic participation to mitigate the contradictions of a socialist form of dependent development and to solve the problems economic liberalization was causing.[22]

This would culminate in a vast new social movement between April and June of 1989, initiated by students but soon joined by many workers and ordinary citizens, centered in Beijing but also present in many other cities.[23] The students engaged in nonviolent forms of protest – demonstrations, occupying the huge central square of the capital, and hunger strikes. When the number of protestors reached one million people, the government declared martial law. But for two weeks, the demonstrators, now increasingly consisting of working people, prevented the army from entering the center of the city. The government could tolerate student demonstrators; what terrified it was the organization of the working class into independent unions, and the possibility that the army might not be relied upon to repress the movement. There was a great fear on the part of the entrenched ruling bureaucracy, led by octogenarian Deng Xiaoping, that the scenario that later transpired in Rumania, where the army and populace together violently overthrew the dictator Ceausescu, would occur in China. In the end, the movement was crushed by the army with substantial loss of life, not just of students in Tiananmen Square but of ordinary citizens trying to prevent the army from reaching the square.[24] In order to quash this emerging cross-class solidarity and to wipe out the opposition for a generation, great violence was resorted to. In the terms of our model, we find (socialist) dependent development and economic downturn in full force, but a state that, however repressive, was only partially exclusionary and not personalist (although it was perhaps construed as both by the political cultures of opposition that emerged). This political culture in formation reposed on a vibrant impulse for democratic participation and redress of emergent social inequalities, but had little time or opportunity to attract a wide social base. And the world-systemic opening was hard to achieve in a context where the state has the luxury of presiding over an economy that is almost a world unto itself.

The question of whether China today is on the verge of a second social revolution, and the Chinese people will succeed in a new round of protests for democracy can also be thought through in terms of the model. The post-1989 conjuncture seems decidedly less favorable: the same structural conditions of dependent development and a repressive, semi-exclusionary regime obtain, to be sure, but the opposition was dealt a severe blow from which it has not recovered, the economy barrels along at high rates of growth, and the West stands more solidly behind the regime, which it views as a major economic player in the new century. The future will be the judge of whether "Market-Leninism" – the attempt to liberalize the economy without democratizing the state – can succeed. Unless the opposition finds ways to regroup, coupled with the inevitable downturns ahead in the new economic cycle, and tensions over human rights or other violations (vis-à-vis Taiwan or Hong Kong, for example, or international economic rivalry), the moment of revolution in China may have passed with the massacre of 1989.[25]

Algeria in the 1990s

In 1992, world-system and political culture worked together to prevent what had looked at the time a most likely site for the world's next revolution in Algeria.[26] As we saw in Chapter 2, the Front de Libération Nationale (FLN) succeeded in waging one of the great historical anti-colonial revolutions against France, ultimately taking power and proclaiming independence in 1962. The revolution, however, quickly turned authoritarian and conservative, with the military gaining control of the ruling party and running the economy in the name of "African socialism," and using Islam as the state religion to push women out of paid work into their old roles.[27] For a while, in the 1970s, Algeria relied on oil revenues to keep the economy afloat through a process constituting an oil-led form of dependent development, but by the early 1990s the FLN had arrived at an impasse, no longer considered legitimate by the majority of the population. After riots and demonstrations for democracy in 1990, the government announced elections in the fall of 1991, which produced an overwhelming landslide for the opposition Islamic Salvation Front (the FIS). The prospect of turning power over to Islamists[28] split the ruling party, and a thinly disguised military coup occurred just before the final round of the elections scheduled for January 1992, with Western banks and governments promptly granting a $1.45 billion credit to ease pressure on the new military regime.

The world will thus never know if the Islamist party could have governed democratically or solved some of Algeria's massive economic problems because the old regime, backed by the West, showed it will not give up power through democratic means. The FIS was driven underground, its leadership arrested, and some groups within it turned to guerrilla tactics. Over 20,000 Algerians have died in the violence since 1992, including government officials and FIS activists, but also other public figures opposed to Islamic rule. From time to time, the military government promised to negotiate open elections, and these were duly held at the end of 1995, confirming the FLN in power under retired general and new president Liamine Zeroual. The FIS – like the government – split over the issue, with a moderate wing taking part in 1995 and an intransigent opposition literally sticking to its guns. The FIS was excluded from the June 1997 elections, whose conduct was criticized by United Nations observers, and its military wing continued to engage in armed actions.[29]

An analytic assessment of Algeria's trajectory in light of the model shows the presence of dependent development and economic downturn. The political culture of militant Islamism propounded by the FIS found significant but not quite clear-cut majority support in 1991–92 (it is interesting that elections require less popular support for a regime change than the great social revolutions – witness Chile in 1970–73). When the government forced the issue by abrogating a FIS electoral victory, it approximated the exclusionary, near personalist type of regime that is most vulnerable to overthrow. But its repeated promises to negotiate created a small opening for it, and the natural response of the FIS to go underground and initiate a violent civil war undermined the latter's chances of building a broad coalition (already somewhat problematic on the electoral plane, as much of the anti-FLN population remained and remains fearful of an Islamist government as well). Finally, the international conjuncture has been most inhospitable to the FIS as even an electoral alternative to the FLN: in the anti-Islamic and anti-Muslim atmosphere stirred up by the 1991 Gulf War; the continuing isolation of Iran, Iraq (till 2003), Libya, and the Sudan by the West, led by the United States; and the strong economic and moral support tendered by successive socialist and conservative regimes in France to the FLN, it is hard to imagine anything like a world-systemic opening in operation since 1990 in Algeria. The future here thus seems clouded by a political stalemate: splintered government and opposition circles that make political dialogue and economic reconstruction difficult for a tragically traumatized civil society.

Guatemala since the 1960s, Argentina in the 1970s, and the Philippines after 1986

Beginning in the 1960s, Guatemala witnessed a vigorous guerrilla struggle for almost thirty years as the opposition regrouped from the 1954 defeat.[30] At no time did all five factors come into a favorable conjuncture for success: as in El Salvador, the military found institutional rather than dictatorial means to control the political game, and increasingly opened it in the 1980s to the center, while the rebels for much of the period embraced uncompromising Marxist-Leninist stands in opposition, with a conspicuous lack of success in mobilizing a broad, multi-class coalition, as it was for a long time tone-deaf to the Mayan majority's issues. The United States provided significant training and support to the army and government (especially before 1975 and again in the 1980s), or was alternately defied by the regime when it could tap other international sources of arms and support in places like Argentina and Israel. The economy through this period, while evincing the skewed and unequal results of dependent development, passed through an arguably "stable" process of crisis, rather than a sudden or discernible worsening of the already bad conditions. The result was a three-decade long civil war of varying intensity, successfully contained by the repressive arm of the governments that have ruled Guatemala. In the early 1990s, the Central American peace accords brought an end to the civil war and the inauguration of genuine elections, which have not to date yielded as promising results for the former guerrillas as in El Salvador, as the left has failed to mobilize the countryside, a trend with roots deep into the Arbenz period.

Argentina, long an economic powerhouse in Latin America, experienced another round of dependent development led by import-substitution industrialization during Juan Perón's populist experiment from 1946 to 1955. The charismatic leader returned from exile in 1973, and when he died in July 1974, and his wife Isabel assumed the presidency, the regime began to approximate a repressive and personalist one (Isabel was considered by some to be a tool of her Rasputin-like minister of welfare, José López Rega). Economic downturn struck at the same time, caused by oil prices and the hyperinflation endemic to the Argentine economy. Judging conditions to be conducive, two clandestine urban guerrilla groups formed by radical students after 1970, the Peronist Montoneros and the Guevarist ERP (Revolutionary Army of the Poor), attempted an uprising (the parallel case of the Tupamaro urban guerrillas in neighboring Uruguay is also worthy of study). In fact, the Argentine population did not rally to this violent vision of revolution, and in the absence of world censure of the repressive tactics of the government, the urban guerrillas were swiftly quelled by brutal counter-insurgency warfare by the army, which afterwards instituted a reign of terror known as the dirty war, in which 30,000 Argentines, the vast majority of them not guerrillas, were kidnapped, tortured, and disappeared. In Argentina, we have a strong case for the weight of political culture and world-system in preventing a social revolution, even with three other factors present.[31]

The Philippines is unique in constituting a case of, first, a successful political revolution (the fall of dictator Ferdinand Marcos to the People's Power movement in 1986, discussed later in this chapter), and then, or concurrently, the failure of a more radical project for social change led by the leftwing labor and communist movement against the democratically elected governments of Corazón Aquino and her successors. In this sense, we must approach it as we did China earlier, in two phases, although in the Philippines, the two are telescoped chronologically and the social revolutionary project did not succeed. We will look at the preliminary, political revolution in more detail below; here, the following brief indicators may suggest the reasons for the failure of social transformation. The reasoning is broadly similar to the cases of El Salvador, Guatemala, and Peru: Aquino represented the most democratic, and hence unassailable, government of all four cases, an image enhanced by the contrast with the Marcos dictatorship that had just been overthrown. The radicals, meanwhile, while enormously energetic in organizing many sectors of society in both town and village, and across gender lines, still suffered from the ability of their critics to label their political culture communist, thereby reducing its cross-class appeal. Finally, US support for Aquino was very strong, again, as in El Salvador, given the threat from the left. The result has been a difficult economic conjuncture but a relatively stable political consolidation without social transformation.[32]

A comparative analysis of attempts

We have now surveyed seven attempted revolutions, with Chiapas to follow later in this chapter as an ongoing case that points toward a possible future for revolutions under conditions of globalization. Other important ongoing cases that I am not able to treat here include the Maoist rebellion against the Kingdom of Nepal, and the tragic situation unfolding in Palestine and Israel, both quite likely to result eventually in some kind of political revolution. Table 5.1 shows our eight cases in terms of the model.

Table 5.2 represents a "truth table" showing all the cases of this chapter and relevant features of each.

Boolean analysis allows us to sort these cases for the salient patterns among them. This involves representation of each case in terms of the presence, absence, or partial effectiveness of the five factors ("1" and its variants such as "1−" are recoded as a capital letter denoting factor A, B, C, etc., and "0" is denoted by a, b, c, and so forth). Thus, for example, the pattern for Argentina in the first row can be represented as ABCDe, meaning that Argentina in 1975–76 possessed four of the five factors, lacking only a world-systemic opening. Here we are coding generously:

Table 5.1 *Attempted social revolutions*

	Social structure	State	Political cultures	Conjunctural factors	Outcome
Argentina, 1975–76	Dependent development	Repressive Peronist government in crisis	Urban guerrilla movement without much support	Strong US support/ Economic downturn	Montoneros crushed and indiscriminate repression by military
El Salvador 1980–92	Adversely impacted and diversified by dependent development	Collective military rule with broad elite support	Marxism-Leninism, liberation theology, but polarized	Carter-Reagan intervention/"Stable" eco- nomic crisis	Prolonged civil war – Negotiated settlement
Guatemala 1960s–92	Adversely impacted and diversified by dependent development	Collective military rule with broad elite support	Mostly Marxist-Leninist	US supports government/"Stable" economic crisis	Prolonged guerrilla war/Negotiated settlement
Peru 1980–92	Modest dependent development	Democratic in 1980s/ Fujimori auto-golpe	Sendero Luminoso's extreme Maoism	US support/ Downturn reversed in 1990s	Prolonged guerrilla war/Rebels greatly weakened
Philippines after 1986	Stagnant dependent development	Democratic under Aquino	Mostly Marxist	US support/"Stable" economic crisis	Guerrilla struggles without success
China 1989	Socialist dependent development	Semi-personalist repressive, exclusionary state	Students' democratic egalitarian political culture	No outside pressures/ Economic downturn	Student movement crushed by CCP and army
Algeria in the early 1990s	Socialist dependent development	Semi-open FLN state allows elections	Radical-democratic Islamists of the FIS	French and Western support for coup/Economic difficulties	State and army prevent FIS electoral victory
Chiapas since 1994	Dependent development and NAFTA	Semi-open, repressive PRI state	Radical currents of neo-Zapatismo	Solid US support for PRI/ Economic downturn	Zapatista gains in Chiapas/fall of PRI

Table 5.2 *Paths to failure*

A Boolean Truth Table
(0 = trait absent; 1 = trait present)

Cases	(A) Dependent development	(B) Repressive, exclusionary, personalist state or open polity*	(C) Political cultures of opposition	(D) Economic downturn	(E) World-systemic opening	Outcome
Attempted social revolutions						
Argentina, 1975–76	1	1(−)	1−	1	0	0-Coup
El Salvador, 1979–92	1	1−	1−	1−	0	0-Negotiations
Guatemala, 1960s–92	1	1−	1−	1−	0	0-Negotiations
Peru, 1980s–92	1	1*−	1−	1/0	0	0-Repression
Philippines, 1986–90s	1	1*−	1−	1−	0	0-Repression
China, 1989	1	1−	1−	1	0	0-Repression
Algeria, 1991–92	1	1−	1−	1	0	0-Coup
Chiapas, 1994–	1	1−/1*	1?	1	0	?-Ongoing
Political revolutions						
China, 1911	1−	1	1−	1−	1/0	Political Rev
Philippines, 1986	1−	1	1−	1−	1/0	Political Rev
Haiti, 1986	0	1	1−	1−	1/0	Political Rev
South Africa, 1994	1	1	1/1−	1−	1/0	Political Rev
Zaire, 1996	0	1	1−	1	1/0	Political Rev
No attempt at revolution						
Iran, 1979–	1	1*−	1−	0	1−	0-stability
Egypt, 1981–	1	1*−	1−	1−	0	0-stability
Argentina, 1983–	1	1*−	0	1	0	0-stability
Turkey, 1983–	1	1*−	0	1/0	0	0-stability
Brazil, 1987–2000	1	1*−	1−	1−	0	0-stability
South Korea, 1988–	1+	1*−	1−	0/1	0	0-stability
Taiwan, 1989–	1+	1*−	0	0	0	0-stability
Cuba, 1991–	1(+)	1−	0	1	1−	0-stability
Iraq, 1991–2003	1	1	0	1	1−	0-stability

Favorable Conditions

Thus "1 –" for political cultures of opposition is considered the presence, or at least partial effectiveness, of that factor; alternatively, and for other purposes (see below), a "1 –" may be considered the absence of the factor in question.

Thus, in attempting to chart the patterns presented by these cases of attempted social revolution in Boolean terms, some strategic decisions must be made about interpreting the coding "1 –" that occurs and recurs in the table. Boolean truth tables require yes or no answers to generate their 1's and 0's for presence or absence of relevant factors. However, in these cases, many of the factors are present, but only up to a point. This complex reality requires a new Boolean technique: interpreting the "1 –'s" as present to explain why there was an attempt at revolution, and as absent (or more accurately, only partially present and therefore in some sense limited or unfavorable to revolution) to explain their lack of success. The occasional codings involving a backslash – such as "1/0" for economic downturn in Peru – represent the presence of the factor at one moment in the period covered (in this case 1989 in Peru), and not in others. Note too that two kinds of regime are here considered vulnerable to revolutions: the classic repressive, exclusionary, personalist dictatorship, and the genuinely open polity; if the latter is present, as in Mexico after the 2000 elections, the coding is "1*"; for the Philippines after 1986 and Peru in the 1980s, a coding of "1* –" is required to capture the situation of an elite-controlled democracy not truly open to the left, what Bill Robinson refers to as a "polyarchy." In fact, a truly open regime should not be considered a favorable factor at all if the revolutionaries are not pursuing an electoral route to power, and in this case a "1*" effectively means a non-vulnerable state.

If we code all cases of "1 –" as instances of presence, however partial or qualified, of the factors in question, we may have a plausible explanation of how and why social revolutions were attempted at all in these places at these points in time. The individual cases look like this:

Argentina, 1975–76	ABCDe
El Salvador, 1979–92	ABCDe
Guatemala, 1960s–92	ABCDe
Peru, 1980s–90s	AbCDe
Philippines, 1986–90s	AbCDe
China, 1989	ABCDe
Algeria, 1991–92	ABCDe
Chiapas, 1994–	ABCDe

Two patterns can be discerned: in Argentina, El Salvador, Guatemala, China, Algeria, and Chiapas, four of the five factors that produce a social revolution were at least partially present, and in each case, it was the same four: dependent development, a repressive, exclusionary state, a reasonably popular political culture of opposition, and an economic downturn. All that was unfavorable was the world-systemic opening, which is not found in any of these cases. Peru and the Philippines resemble this pattern on four of the five factors, differing only in that the type of state the revolutionaries faced was not vulnerable (in both cases, it was a reasonably, if not fully democratic, state). Using Boolean minimization procedures, the type of state therefore drops out of the pattern common to all, since both vulnerable and non-vulnerable regimes possessed otherwise similar features in all the other factors. Thus the pattern ACDe covers all eight attempts: the dislocations of dependent development, elaboration of oppositional cultures, and economic downturns touched off attempts at social revolution, regardless of the type of state and in the absence of a favorable world-systemic opportunity. This confirms our theory insofar as all five factors were not found present in any of these cases, even in the most generous interpretation of partial presence.

Now taking the opposite tack and emphasizing the partial, flawed effectivity of the factors coded "1−" and considering them absent (along with our ambiguous coding of Zapatista political culture in Chiapas), we have the following patterns:

Argentina, 1975–76	AbcDe
El Salvador, 1979–92	Abcde
Guatemala, 1960s–92	Abcde
Peru, 1980s–90s	Abcde
Philippines, 1986–90s	Abcde
China, 1989	AbcDe
Algeria, 1991–92	AbcDe
Chiapas, 1994–	AbcDe

Again there are two distinct patterns, this time with each of the four cases: Argentina, China, Algeria, and Chiapas all possessed only dependent development and an economic downturn as fully favorable to revolutionary success; all lacked vulnerable regimes, effective political cultures of opposition, or a permissive world context. El Salvador, Guatemala, Peru, and the Philippines, on the other hand, were similar to the first four in all respects except that they lacked an economic downturn as well (recall that Peru in 1989 fitted the first pattern as well). These two variations can be reduced similarly with respect to the role played by such downturns, which drops out of the reduced expression of the pattern to yield the formula Abce as the common pattern in the movements' failures: meaning that despite the presence of dependent development, rebels could not succeed when the states they faced were not repressive, exclusionary dictatorships (or genuine democracies), their political cultures did not facilitate broad cross-class alliances, and outside powers supported rather than abandoned incumbent regimes. These factors cluster together logically as well, for regimes that allow some political participation make it difficult for cross-class alliances to coalesce and can often attract outside military and economic support, which is even more likely to be forthcoming from the United States when the oppositional culture is, or can be labeled, Marxist-Leninist.

This set of cases, then, considered in both aspects, broadly confirms the theory of success insofar as revolutionary attempts possess almost all of the characteristics of successful cases, and also give us a working theory of failure, in that these same characteristics are crucially limited in scope or depth.

A look at political revolutions

Political revolutions are another important variant on our theme in that these are revolutions made by mass-mobilizing movements and resulting in significant political change, but where the social and economic transformations that we associate with social revolutions do not follow the transfer of power. They thus meet only two of Skocpol's three criteria for a social revolution. The theoretical issue at stake is whether our model can point to relevant factors both enabling such revolutions to occur and yet preventing them from becoming full-fledged social revolutions. A definitional problem exists here, too: how much "social transformation" is required to qualify a process as a social revolution? The cases chosen for study here seem clear enough to avoid this problem: the fall of the Manchu dynasty in 1911 only led to social revolution thirty-eight years later; the People's Power movement that toppled Marcos in the Philippines in 1986 led to little economic change; the same can be said of the fall of the Duvalier dictatorship in Haiti as well as that of Mobutu in Zaire a decade later. Perhaps the most disappointing case of all is the outcome of the long and valiant struggle to rid South Africa of apartheid led by Nelson Mandela's African National Congress (ANC), which has to date done far too little – or simply been unable – to meet the urgent demand for social change by that country's newly empowered black majority. We will take the cases in chronological order this time, starting with three brief sketches and ending with two somewhat longer treatments.

The fall of the Manchus in China, People's Power in the Philippines, and the ouster of "Baby Doc" in Haiti

The fall of the Manchu dynasty in China in 1911 ushered in a whirlwind of social change that ended only with the social revolution led by Mao a generation later. Chapter 2 traced the progress of a proto-dependent development and the autocratic nature of the late Manchu state. The political culture that launched the revolution reposed on nascent sentiments of nationalism and democracy aimed at foreign control and imperial arrogance respectively. The economic downturn at the end of the first decade of the twentieth century was gradual rather than precipitous, the product of a conjuncture of population pressures on agriculture, the deterioration of state-administered water works, and the ill effects of regional elites usurping the central state's taxing power, compounded by the reparations that the Manchus had to pay Western powers after the Boxer Rebellion.[33] The world-systemic opening took the form of multiple Western and Japanese imperial pressures on the Chinese rulers, who found themselves caught between the incompatible demands of their would-be foreign masters and the growing dissatisfaction of their subjects. The civil-military uprising that began at Wuhan in October 1911 led to a swift collapse of the monarchy when urban actors across many provinces joined in.[34]

It is instructive to compare the situation in 1911 with that in 1949. We can mark clear differences in terms of the degree of dependent development and the evolution of effective political cultures of opposition, with a less well-defined economic crisis in 1911 compared with the precipitous downturn after World War 2. This case suggests that the process of dependent development must be advanced to the point where the social structure is dislocated enough to crystallize a broad cross-class coalition for change, one which moreover is cemented by a vigorous and flexible oppositional political culture.

Haiti toward the end of the twentieth century, so different in size, and distant in time and space, offers a broadly similar pattern of political but not social revolutionary change.[35] In development terms, the island is more a case of sheer dependency and underdevelopment than dependent development, as it has ranked at the very bottom of all countries in the Americas on most indices of development and social welfare. On the other hand, the state under the Duvaliers, père et fils, was a quintessentially repressive, exclusionary, and personalistic police state, its stability guaranteed by the feared paramilitary known as the *tontons macoutes*. Under these conditions, the opposition had little chance to organize more than a very rudimentary resistance culture, drawing on relatively weak liberal democratic and liberation theology currents. Crisis economic conditions brought out largely unorganized street demonstrations against Jean-Claude Duvalier between 1984 and 1986, and the regime's crackdown led the United States to withhold further aid and to encourage conspirators in the army to stage the February 6, 1986 coup that ended the Duvalier dynasty. The outcome, however, was a new elite-military alliance that stymied further attempts at reforms, radical or otherwise, marked by the political turmoil of the 1990s and the 2004 US-backed removal of democratically-elected president Jean-Bertrand Aristide. As in China, the limits to social revolution seem to lie in the combination of a less differentiated class structure than that of a mature dependent development and the formidable difficulties of organizing a political culture capable of social revolution in a highly repressive polity (while this was accomplished in other places, such as Nicaragua, the effects of dependent development facilitated the presence of the types of social actors necessary to bring this off).

The Philippines produced a dramatic political revolution between 1983 and 1986 that toppled the dictatorship of Ferdinand Marcos and brought Corazón Aquino, a democratic reformer, to power.[36] The case parallels turn-of-the-century China and 1980s Haiti in the presence of a repressive, personalist, and quite exclusionary dictatorship and a series of economic difficulties (including unemployment and dropping incomes, low growth, and debt) that grew after the assassination of opposition figure Benigno Aquino in 1983. At the crucial moment, when reform-minded officers within the armed forces rebelled in February 1986, and found thousands of moderate and left-wing supporters among the urban population, the United States played a positive role in easing Marcos from power as Reagan offered Marcos asylum, and Senator Paul Laxalt advised Marcos to "Cut and cut cleanly. The time has come."[37] The opposition forces that underpinned this event ranged from the 1,500 officers of the Reform the Armed Forces Now Movement (RAM), the liberal middle-class opposition symbolized by eventual president Cory Aquino, and the radical nationalist and socialist forces in the National Democratic Front (NDF), the political wing of the revolutionary New People's Army. While the latter would prove too exclusive a basis to mobilize a cross-class coalition for social revolution in 1986 and after – as we have seen – all these forces came together to contribute to the ouster of the Marcos dictatorship. That dependent development went so much further in the Philippines than it had in turn-of-the-century China or then contemporary Haiti, and the stronger democratic political cultures that accompanied this process in the Philippines may explain why the political revolution there produced a more stable democratic outcome than in the other two cases.

The uprooting of apartheid

One of the most inspiring – and lengthy – struggles for revolutionary change in the twentieth century came in the movement that overturned apartheid in South Africa in 1994, forging a genuine democracy in that country in its place.[38] There is no space here to cover the historical details of the original African communities there, the arrival of Dutch traders – the Boers – around 1650, their wars of expansion against the African population and move into the interior, the rise of British power in the region in the nineteenth century, the discovery of gold, and the Anglo-Boer war in 1899 won by Britain. In the first part of the twentieth century the restrictive segregation laws known as apartheid were put into place, depriving blacks of the vote, of most of their land, and of the right to live in the cities and to move freely around the country.

South Africa became an independent state, under very conservative white control by the Boers, in 1934. This process was opposed by the African National Congress (ANC), a multi-racial, black-led organization, whose leadership included Nelson Mandela. After demonstrations in 1960 were repressed violently and Mandela was imprisoned in 1963, the ANC waged a guerrilla struggle that proved unable to take power from the well-armed government. In 1976 another rebellion occurred in Soweto, the black township outside Johannesburg, inspired by the Black Consciousness movement, whose leader Steve Biko was arrested and beaten to death while in prison.

Domestic and international developments put increasing pressure on the white government after this, however. The anti-colonial revolutionary victories in the nearby states of Mozambique, Angola, and Zimbabwe gave the ANC important logistical and political support in their struggle. Black migration to urban areas built up a young, educated, politically aware population. Progressive movements against apartheid in the West also forced governments and corporations, including the United States and various multinationals, to suspend economic relations with South Africa, although many corporations retained a profile there, attracted by the country's mineral and industrial wealth (South Africa is the world's largest exporter of platinum and gold, second in diamonds, and third in uranium). The impact of international sanctions, growing debt, and the contradictions of a racist political economy produced difficult economic conditions in black areas, and the downturn was felt even in white communities by the late 1980s.

In that decade, the long-ruling National Party under Pieter Botha began to make small changes in the superficial aspects of apartheid under growing international economic and domestic black pressure. After suffering a stroke in early 1989 he was succeeded by the more liberal Frederik de Klerk, who stated his seriousness about abandoning white rule altogether. Continued black strikes and demonstrations, along with some support from liberal whites, prompted de Klerk to free Nelson Mandela after twenty-seven years in prison, in February 1990. After this, the ANC and de Klerk engaged in delicate negotiations over the form of a transition to a true democracy. The process culminated in elections in 1994, which Mandela and the ANC won easily, completing a remarkable political revolution. In analytic terms, the conditions favorable for a social revolution were dependent development and a repressive, exclusionary state (both of the colonial type), powerful political cultures of resistance articulated through and around the ANC with democratic and social justice strands, a relatively biting economic downturn, and eventually a world-systemic opening brought about largely by political pressure on Western governments to withdraw support from the regime.

Why, then, the *political* outcome? In part, this followed from an international conjuncture after the collapse of the East Bloc that rendered the ANC's socialist economic alternative decidedly unfashionable by the time it took power. Related to this was the shift in the nature of the white minority state from exclusionary and repressive to genuinely open to the election of its opposition, the ANC. This required the ANC's transformation from guerrilla movement to political party, and had a dampening effect on its program once in power, as did the end of the socialist model after 1991 and the internal guarantees of white privilege tied up in quasi-colonial dependent development. South Africa today faces significant issues of development, notably how to deliver a better standard of living to its black majority, with many people living in truly appalling conditions. We arrive at a painful apparent trade-off: anti-colonial revolutions can come to power through violence, as in Algeria and Vietnam, but then deprive people of political freedoms, or they can force democratic changes, as in South Africa, but with little immediate prospect of economic betterment. Yet the uprooting of apartheid and the creation of a genuinely open democracy were huge political and human accomplishments, and the future may hold further surprises as globalization is challenged world-wide from below.

From the Congo to Zaire, and back

A final case to consider is the state which emerged out of the ill-fated independence struggle touched off in 1960 by Patrice Lumumba in the Belgian Congo.[39] His overthrow and execution, at which Belgium, the US, and even the U.N. connived, resulted in the rise of the dictatorship of Joseph Mobutu (who then took the name Mobutu Sese Seko) over the country he re-named Zaire. Mobutu presided for two decades over a process of growing deterioration and poverty.[40] Development in Zaire was never of the magnitude that the term "dependent development" requires, as there has been limited industrialization, negative economic growth, and little foreign investment outside the mineral enclave.[41] While increasingly unpopular in the Western circles which sponsored his rise and rule (Belgium, Britain, France, the United States), Mobutu hung onto power into 1997 despite ever more widespread human rights abuses of the population generally and the opposition in particular.

When I first drafted an essay touching on the future of Zaire in 1996, I noted that an exclusionary state and economic downturns, particularly in the preceding three years, seemed to favor Mobutu's ouster. I argued that while this could indeed come at any time, it was not likely to be the result of a social revolution, given the limits of economic development and disunity of the opposition, predicting

this does not preclude the emergence of an effective civil opposition to the dictatorship; rather it highlights the importance of it for success. Unless such a formula is found and such an opposition articulates a political culture capable of galvanizing the population and gaining international support or at least neutrality, the future would seem to hold further repression under Mobutu or the limited change that a military coup would bring.[42]

Shortly after I wrote these words, a major political change did come to Zaire in the form of the overthrow of Mobutu by an armed insurgency led by Laurent Kabila's Alliance of Democratic Forces for the Liberation of Zaire-Congo (ADFL).[43] Arising out of relative obscurity in October 1996, the rebels made short work of Mobutu's disintegrating national army in a long march to the capital, Kinshasa, where they took power in May 1997.

What had changed in the socio-political equation to facilitate this successful political revolution? Two of the "missing" factors fell into place: Kabila's relatively successful mobilization of an opposition to Mobutu, and a world-systemic opening occasioned by the West's acknowledgment that the ailing dictator could no longer be sustained. The political culture that Kabila tapped succeeded on the widely popular minimal platform of ousting the dictatorship. The international conjuncture finally favored the opposition's success as well: the end of the cold war rationale for Western support of Mobutu; the spillover of a complex refugee situation in Rwanda; significant unrest in a number of the countries bordering Zaire; Angolan, Kenyan, and especially South African efforts to broker a peaceful end to the regime; and the rapid spread of the movement, which took Mobutu's long-standing supporters in France, Belgium, and the United States by surprise. Led by the US, these outside forces finally switched their strategy to trying to influence the new regime. The result was not quite the ouster I anticipated in 1996, but it was a political revolution. There has been no revolutionary transformation of Zaire (now again named Congo) as the opposition was neither unified nor agreed on this, the social structural dislocations of dependent development do not exist in the country to fuel it, and the international community did not favor such an outcome.

A comparative analysis of political revolutions

See Table 5.3 for a summary of our discussion of these five cases.

In searching for the paths to political revolution, we should repeat the procedure used in understanding attempted social revolutions. Thus, judging factors coded "1−" in 5.2 as present, we find two patterns: in China, the Philippines, and South Africa, the pattern ABCDE, and in Haiti and Zaire the degree of sheer underdevelopment gives the variant path aBCDE. We interpret this as an account of why a revolution of any type occurred, as this is quite close to the model for social revolution.

In emphasizing the limits to these factors by interpreting all cases of "1−" as absent, and further noting that the world-systemic openings were not deep enough to permit social revolutions (the "0" in the "1/0" couplet), we find the following patterns to account for the political, rather than social, outcomes of these events:

China in 1911	aBcde
Haiti in 1986	aBcde
Philippines in 1986	ABcde
South Africa in 1994	ABcde
Zaire in 1996	aBcDe

China and Haiti present the same pattern, with vulnerable states, but only limited degrees of all the other variables. The Philippines and South Africa follow a path similar to China and Haiti except for their more vigorous dependent development, while Zaire resembles China and Haiti, except for a more pronounced economic downturn.

These three routes to political revolution can then be compared and reduced to two with Boolean minimization, as follows: since aBcde in China and Haiti differs from South Africa and the Philippines' ABcde only with respect to dependent development, that factor becomes irrelevant in their causal logic, yielding Bcde. Zaire's aBcDe differs from China and Haiti only with respect to the degree of economic downturn, yielding aBce. The two reduced expressions that cover all five cases can be factored to the Boolean equation Bce (a + d), suggesting that social revolutions did not occur in these cases due to the limits of their political cultures of opposition and *lack* of a world-systemic opening conducive to far-reaching change, combined in the cases of Zaire, China, and Haiti with very limited development, and in the Philippines and South Africa with

Table 5.3 *Political revolutions*

	Social structure	State	Political cultures	Conjunctural factors	Outcome
China 1911	Limited proto-dependent development	Manchu dynasty's repressive, exclusionary state	Nascent democratic and nationalist political cultures	Colonial pressures/Gradual economic downturn	Political revolution abolishes monarchy/Warlords rule
Philippines 1986	Dependent development	Marcos dictatorship's repressive exclusionary state	Democratic nationalist, socialist currents	US lets Marcos fall/Moderate economic downturn	People's Power brings Corazón Aquino to power
Haiti 1986	Severe under-development	Duvalier dictatorship's repressive exclusionary state	Nascent oppositional currents	US withdraws support for Duvalier/Chronic economic downturn	Duvalier falls to mass movement, but military stays in control
South Africa 1994	Dependent development	The repressive, exclusionary, apartheid state	ANC's socialist democratic anti-racism	First World withdraws support/Relative economic downturn	Political revolution – ANC wins 1994 elections
Zaire 1996	Very limited dependent development	Mobutu dictatorship's repressive exclusionary state	Divided and limited but militarily effective opposition	France, Belgium, USA stand aside/A lengthy economic downturn	Mobutu overthrown by Kabila's rebel army

relatively less severe economic downturns. Political culture and world-systemic opening thus act as powerful deflectors of revolutionary movements and brakes on social transformation after they take power.

It is also interesting that the Philippines and South Africa experienced democratic outcomes, suggesting that the social structure produced by dependent development and the more articulated political cultures of opposition in each country (perhaps in turn related to this social structure), differentiate this outcome from that of the emergence of military rulers after the overthrow of dictatorship or monarchy in China, Haiti, and Zaire. This set of cases further nuances and supports the theory of successful social revolutions by showing how the partial existence of some of the key factors produces instead a political transformation alone.

No attempt: the reasons why

Let us complete this survey of the revolutionary past with a brief look at the present, including a number of situations where countries possess both a history of political agitation or instability and a number of the factors identified by the model as contributing to revolutionary outbreaks. I should note at the outset that I have decidedly mixed feelings about theorizing revolutions in a way that encourages prediction. This stems from a profound belief and background assumption in my scholarship that social change is directed in substantial part by the activities of people, and that no structuralist explanation can do justice to this irreducible element. This means that any model or theory of how people behave can be falsified by people themselves, in part because knowledge of such a theory alters the circumstances in which people act, and in part because people's actions cannot be controlled and predicted by our theories about them.[44] As for predicting revolutions, on the one hand I feel that if the model I am developing is capable of explaining past instances, it is likely to be able to say something about the present and future too, but only with the caveats just noted. That is, the epistemological status of the following pages as prediction is dubious; it is better to think of it as a discussion understood in terms of trends, of possible futures, or as educated guesses about potentials for change. I believe that "scientific" prediction is a pernicious chimera in the social sciences, and appearances to the contrary, this study should not be read as an example of it, again for the reasons noted, as well as others.[45]

That said, I have chosen the nine cases that form this type in Table 5.2 on the basis of their special significance, either as major Third World economic powers (Argentina, Brazil, Turkey, South Korea, Taiwan), as post-revolutionary societies (Iran and Cuba), or as key geo-strategic sites in the world-system (Egypt and Iraq). This set of contrasting cases will further highlight the importance of factors which may be lacking or incompletely developed in each case, as well as suggest the conditions which would have to obtain for revolutions to occur in the future. A glance at Table 5.2 immediately reveals the special salience of political cultures of opposition and the international conjuncture.

Iraq: where political culture prevented revolution?

Iraq under Saddam Hussein until 2003 presented an exclusionary personalist regime of the first order. Indeed, we also find the presence of a marked degree of dependent development, since Iraq stands out as one of the most educated, urbanized, industrialized, and dynamic societies and economies of the Middle East over the whole period since the political revolution that overthrew the monarchy in 1958.[46] The rise of Saddam Hussein in 1979 eventually crystallized what had been a collective exclusionary state into a personalist one.[47] Saddam Hussein, it is true, legitimated his rule through institutional arrangements that included elections. And Fidel Castro in Cuba does the same, apparently. Hussein, however, was closer to the pure type of dictator that has proven vulnerable to revolution, in the mold of Porfirio Díaz, Batista, the shah of Iran, or Somoza, whereas the Cuban revolution has deep roots in Cuban society, and the current Iranian regime, though less solidly legitimated, can claim something similar. And let us not underestimate the degree to which Saddam had a following inside Iraq, and could draw on his asserted nationalist credentials of standing up to Iran and the United States.

In the 1980s, diverse political cultures of opposition sought to define themselves in Iraq, including the long-standing Kurdish nationalist insurgency of the north and west, the militant Shi'ism of segments of the south around Basra and the shrine town of Karbala, and a struggling, mostly exiled liberal reformist strand that sought a return to democracy. But even during the intense international and internal crises provoked by Iraq's invasion of Kuwait and the US-led restoration of the Kuwaiti monarchy the regime stood firm. The weaknesses of the opposition showed most clearly after most of the Iraqi army was crushed in the retreat from Kuwait in March 1991, when the rebellions in the south and in Kurdistan, however vigorous and determined, were unable to unite the center of the country or coordinate their plans and visions for a post-Hussein Iraq (indeed the Kurdish vision was more for a division of Iraq into autonomous regions, and the Shi'i vision for an Islamist state). Saddam's elite Republican Guard, held back in the war over Kuwait, ruthlessly crushed the Shi'i rebels in the south while the United States stood by (closing the world-systemic opening it had itself created), then isolated and eventually contained the Kurdish threat after that. Policy makers in the US apparently favored a military putsch against the dictatorship rather than the popular uprising that President Bush had initially called for. A White House official said on March 18, 1991:

We had been assuming all along that Saddam would survive the war and that he would survive the current fighting in Iraq. The feeling was that after the dust settled, and Iraq found itself still saddled with sanctions and war reparations payments, they would start looking for scapegoats and Saddam would eventually fall.[48]

Despite the long-standing international blockade and a fairly severe internal economic downturn, Saddam Hussein remained in power until the massive US attack on his country in March 2003, in large measure because the opposition was utterly unable to find a basis for unity and effective organization of a nation-wide resistance against a still somewhat popular leader (and the post-war resistance inside Iraq to the US occupation reflects this residual popularity). We have a case of political stability for over a decade despite the presence of four factors favoring revolution, thereby pointing toward the causal significance of political cultures of opposition in deterring revolutions.

Iran and Egypt: the counter-revolutionary power of repressive tolerance

Even more remote from successful revolutionary challenge would seem to be the other Middle Eastern dependent developers of Iran and Egypt. In the Islamic Republic of Iran, itself the product of a revolution against the shah (see the analogy with revolutionary Cuba below), the political economy remains as definite an instance of dependent development as it was under the shah since the early 1960s: the country has been and remains a regional economic giant with heels of clay.[49] Urbanization, rising GNP, and oil-fueled growth continue to produce only hardship for much of the urban and most of the rural population. The regime, however, has created a set of sturdy political institutions that have successfully outlived the charismatic Ayatullah Khumaini, who even as supreme religious authority from 1979 to his death in 1989 could not qualify as an exclusionary personalist ruler. The political system opened further in the 1990s, permitting the election of liberal-minded Islamic reformer Muhammad Khatami as president in 1997. The rules of the political game restrict wider ideological competition, at the same time involving enough of the population in the process to make widespread extra-legal opposition difficult. Meanwhile, the steady pressure emanating from the United States is largely mitigated by the willingness of Europe, Japan, China, and other countries to invest in and trade with Iran. By disqualifying en masse the reformist candidates in the 2004 elections, however, the hard-line authoritarian clerics and economic elites around supreme religious and political leader Ali Hussein Khamenei have increased their vulnerability to a strong counter-thrust from the reformist majority of the population. Much depends on the ability of the opposition to find a formula capable of maneuvering in this more threatening atmosphere, internally and externally. If the economy turns down, and the complex international conjuncture opens up, their chances will be enhanced.

Egypt under Hosni Mubarak is a less solid but nonetheless equally instructive case of the interplay of a government clever enough to legitimate itself without loosening its grip on power and an opposition that, however vigorous, seems to date incapable of finding a way to build a broad coalition of forces to oppose it.[50] Since the revolution from above that brought Gamal Abdal Nasser to power after 1952, Egypt has embarked on a precarious path of dependent development, first with Soviet aid, and then, after the transition to Anwar Sadat in 1970, in partnership with the United States. During this period the country has seen vast transformation and attendant upheaval of both the rural and urban social structures. Hosni Mubarak succeeded Sadat after the latter's assassination at the hands of militant Islamists in the army in October 1981, and has firmly controlled the political system since, using elections astutely to maintain his hold on power through the vehicle of the National Democratic Party, and to avoid the outright characterization of his regime as personalist. Economic downturns have been common enough in the last quarter century; what is lacking in the Egyptian equation for revolution (as it was in Iraq, Iran, and Zaire) is the sort of united and broad-based opposition that would be required, as well as any world-systemic opening, given the close relations and enormous amounts of aid that have been forthcoming from the United States for over three decades. In terms of political cultures of opposition, the government allows moderate Islamist opposition parties to operate, while repressing more radical Islamic groups. The appeal of Islam grows, in part because both secular alternatives have been discredited: socialism under Nasser and capitalism under Sadat have been tried, and "failed," or at least found wanting.

What does the future hold? The severity of the underlying economic problems is a large question mark hanging over Egypt's future, fueling Islamic activism in the shantytowns of Cairo and the Delta and the villages of the south.[51] One scenario – which we might term the "Eastern European model" – would be the government democratizing sufficiently so that the radical Islamists turn their backs on violent strategies for change, but this seems rather remote. Perhaps new social movements, involving students, intellectuals, women in various settings, the urban poor, and others hold out a possibility for progressive change in the longer-term future. The most likely future is one of further economic deterioration offset by US aid and support, with oppositional unity defused by the secular-religious divide and successfully "managed" by the ruling party. Egypt, like Iraq, would need a different set of relations among the secular left, the liberal democratic currents, and the variants of Islamist opposition to tilt the balance toward a revolutionary outcome. And like Iran, its polyarchic, semi-open, restricted polity is just inclusive enough to defuse opposition.

Cuba: the advantages of culture

If Iran and Egypt look reasonably stable, Cuba from the early 1990s to 2004 has been an even more unlikely site of revolution. Dependent development, though of a uniquely socialist type as in China, has been in place on the island since the 1959 revolution (an extension and redirection of capitalist dependent development before that). Its impressive gains in quality of living indicators set Cuba apart from the rest of Latin America and most of the Third World, for a time making it a candidate for genuine development (thus the tentative "1(+)" coding of Table 5.2), yet the problems of an aging sugar monoculture, incomplete industrialization (which was designed to be complementary to the now defunct socialist bloc), and the inescapable poverty of the resource base of Cuban socialism make for the mixture of positive and negative indices we have termed dependent development. There is also the (now historical) issue of Cuba's "dependence" on the Soviet Union. Until 1991, 80 percent of trade was with the Soviet Union, which also provided a yearly subsidy of $3–5 billion. The problem was not any exploitation of Cuba in the way we usually mean when we speak of dependency, but the literal dependence of Cuba on the Soviet subsidy, a windfall which evaporated after the Soviet Union's collapse. The cut-off of the subsidy and other trade advantages in the early 1990s unleashed a severe economic downturn, with GNP dropping by as much as 40 percent from 1989 to 1992, trade shrinking drastically, oil imports plummeting, shortages in agricultural, industrial, and infrastructural inputs, and attendant hardships for the population. US pressure, meanwhile, remained constant and substantial.

Yet Castro – a personalist ruler if there ever was one – remained securely in place despite the presence of these several features of the model. The explanation would seem to rest very heavily on the resilience of the political culture of the Cuban revolution as a substantial legitimating vehicle for the regime and the gains of the revolution. Unlike in Iran, Cuba's broad populist coalition did not fragment (aided in this by the migration of oppositional upper and skilled middle classes in the early 1960s), but instead deepened even as the revolution radicalized into a project of deep social transformation. And it was held together, in no small part, by the enthusiasm of the population for the new socialist political culture. The longevity of the Cuban revolution suggests that the process of elaborating effective political cultures requires complex negotiations between such "universals" as Marxism-Leninism and, in Cuba's case, the much longer-standing notions of a specifically Cuban nationalism, democracy, and ideals of social, racial, and economic justice.[52] It was these inflections that gave the Cuban revolution its particular imprint as a powerful force for socialist change within Cuba and indeed, as a model for further rearticulation with other local traditions elsewhere (interestingly, never as successfully as in Cuba).

The question today, and the one on which the future of the Cuban revolution would seem to hinge, is how much remains of this effervescent support for Castro and Cuban socialism inside the country, and how well it will outlive his inevitable passing from the scene and the inexorable spread of capitalist globalization from above? Somehow, Castro retained a basic level of public support through the crisis of the 1990s, though how much is difficult to say. As one grocer put it: "To put up with things is a national custom."[53] Economic change has come in the form of increased tourism, biotechnology, joint ventures with foreign companies, and the ebb and flow of small private enterprises, but the very intensity of the US animosity toward Castro institutionalized in the successive tightenings of the embargo undertaken by US politicians Robert Torricelli, Dan Burton, Jesse Helms, Bill Clinton, and George W. Bush has been turned thus far by the regime to political capital, as it taps the wellsprings of Cuban nationalism and pride in their revolution. To date, Cuba showcases the advantages of political culture for sustaining revolutions (and thereby preventing counter-revolution), even in a globalizing world.

South Korea and Taiwan: the advantages of real development

South Korea and Taiwan since the 1970s represent the undisputed economic powerhouses of the Third World.[54] They have industrialized and thrived in a competitive world economy to the point where "dependent development" barely covers their experience of growth (hence, their clear "1+" codings in Table 5.2). Their states, while exclusionary and repressive under the military in South Korea and Chiang Kai-Shek's KMT in

Taiwan, progressively opened themselves to greater participation in the late 1980s. In terms of political cultures, a vigorous student and labor movement in South Korea forced the state to democratize in 1987–88 (and could be analyzed as a political revolution), but it was not calculated to go beyond this to enlist the growing middle class in a revolutionary project. In Taiwan, a similar process unfolded with less conflict a year later. Nor has the conjuncture been conducive to revolution in either case at any point in the last twenty years: too dynamic economically, both have enjoyed extensive superpower support from both the United States and Japan. Thus, sustained economic growth has created more prosperous middle and working classes who have succeeded in wresting democratic reforms from the state rather than engaging in revolution. Even the dramatic economic crash of 1997 did little to alter their achievement.[55] This case quite plausibly suggests, that indirectly, real development, above and beyond dependent development, is an antidote to revolution, especially when paired with a democratic polity.

Argentina, Brazil, and Turkey: dependent development and democracy

The Latin American counterparts of East Asia's dragon economies are Argentina and Brazil (plus Mexico, whose Zapatista rebellion is treated in the next section of this chapter). Both experienced a pronounced form of dependent development after the 1960s, with Argentina lagging somewhat behind. Both (especially Argentina) experienced serious economic downturns, sometimes repeatedly, at various points in the 1990s and early years of the twenty-first century. The factors conducive for revolution end there, however. One is hard pressed to find a world-systemic opening in these cases: both have enjoyed close relations with the United States since the return of democracy. Indeed, Argentina's transition to democracy after the debacle of the Malvinas/Falklands war in 1983 did away with military rule, and its newly open political system managed well enough to allow the alternation in power of the Radical and Peronist parties. This stability, and the weathering of the severe political crisis produced by the economic collapse of 2002, was further enhanced by the absence of any strong radical challengers, a legacy of the failure of both Peronist populism and the post-1983 Radical Party of Raul Alfonsín to capture the popular imagination. New forms of struggle, worthy of study, have arisen out of the 2002–3 political crisis.[56] The transition to democracy in Brazil had a similar dampening effect on national-level protest, which was channeled into the electoral fortunes of the Workers Party (PT), and its charismatic leader, Ignacio "Lula" da Silva, who on his

Table 5.4 *No attempt at revolution*

	Social structure	State	Political cultures	Conjunctural factors	Outcome
Iran after 1979	Oil-led dependent development	Semi-popular authoritarian Islamic polyarchy	Little internal opposition till rise of reformists under Khatami	Limited US pressure, but Euro-Japanese support/No downturn	Electoral challenge by reformers, little change
Argentina since 1983	Dependent development	Democratic governments since 1983	No strong radical challengers	Strong US support/Economic collapse in 2003	Stable democratic rule, even in 2003 crisis
Egypt since 1981	A precarious dependent development	Authoritarian polyarchic democracy under Mubarak	Strong Islamist challenge, but limited middle and upper-class support	Strong US support for Mubarak/Economic hardships	Continued rule of Mubarak
Turkey since 1983	Standard dependent development	Democratic government since 1983	Islamist opposition in and out of power	Strong US support/No major downturn	Stable democratic rule after 1980 coup
Brazil since 1987	Standard dependent development	Democratic government since 1989	No strong left party until 2003 elections	Strong US support/No major downturn	Stable democratic rule since 1989
South Korea since 1988	Dynamic dependent development	Democratic government since 1988	Strong student and union movements	Strong US and Japanese support/Economic crisis in 1997	Stable transition to democracy in 1988
Taiwan since 1989	Dynamic dependent development	Democratic government since 1989	Limited internal opposition	Chinese pressures countered by strong US support/No downturn	Stable transition to democracy in 1989
Cuba since 1991	Dependent development without inequality	Personalist, non-exclusionary regime under Castro	Very limited internal opposition; extremist opposition in Miami	Strong but self-limiting US pressure/Subsidized hardships	Continued rule of Castro, but for how long?
Iraq until 2003	Oil-led dependent development	Hussein's repressive, exclusionary dictatorship	Divided among Kurds, Islamists, and weak secular liberals	US pressure on Hussein/Economic hardships	Rule of Saddam Hussein until 2003

third try achieved the presidency in 2003, an event which may be open to analysis as an attempted social revolution.

If we turn to the Middle East, a similar pattern can be observed in Turkey, the region's third economic giant with Iran and Egypt. Turkey has historically exhibited vigorous enough growth to warrant the label of dependent development and economic downturns have occurred at various times, but after coups in 1971 and 1980, the military returned power to civilians for good in 1983. Since then, secular and religious parties all along the political spectrum have vied relatively peacefully for hegemony through elections and coalition-building. As a close American ally, the government has not suffered international pressure or neglect. The result is another case of a democratic polity undercutting the emergence of radical political cultures of opposition.

Comparing non-attempts

The patterns underlying this cursory survey of select Third World non-revolutionary situations can be approached in various ways. Table 5.4 summarizes our discussion of the cases.

If we return to our Boolean truth table, Table 5.2, and code "1+," "1*," "1*−," "1−," and "1/0" (indicating the factor was present at some times in the period under question, but absent at others) as instances of the presence of the factor, we get the following, most generous expressions of their closeness to revolution:

Iran, 1979 to the present	ABCdE
Egypt, 1981 to the present	ABCDe
Argentina, 1983 to the present	ABcDe
Turkey, 1983 to the present	ABcDe
Brazil, 1987 to 2000	ABCDe
South Korea, 1988 to the present	ABCDe
Taiwan, 1989 to the present	ABcde
Cuba, 1991 to the present	ABcDE
Iraq, 1991 to 2003	ABcDE

It is obvious that no case possesses all five factors posited by the theory. This by itself is evidence for their collective necessity and sufficiency in bringing about social revolutions. In an ideal test of the theory, we would find cases where four of the five were present, and one absent; this would imply the necessity of that factor as part of a theory of revolution. Three of the factors in the model actually turn up in this fashion: the absence of only an economic downturn in Iran, a world-systemic opening in Egypt, Brazil, and South Korea, and an oppositional political culture in Cuba and Iraq. This should greatly increase our confidence in each of these factors as a cause of social revolution. Two other patterns are found here: in Argentina and Turkey, the absence of a revolutionary political culture or a world-systemic opening; and in Taiwan, the lack of any favorable factor except dependent development and vulnerable regime.

If we take the most restrictive interpretation of the cases by coding "1+," "1−," "1*−," and "1/0" as *absences* of the factors in question, the cases look like this:

Iran, 1979 to the present	Abcde
Egypt, 1981 to the present	Abcde
Argentina, 1983 to the present	ABcDe
Turkey, 1983 to the present	ABcde
Brazil, 1987 to 2000	ABcde
South Korea, 1988 to the present	abcde
Taiwan, 1989 to the present	abcde
Cuba, 1991 to the present	abcDe
Iraq, 1991 to 2003	ABcDe

These patterns reveal far more absences of the relevant factors: South Korea and Taiwan lack all five; Iran and Egypt lack all but dependent development; Cuba lacks all but economic downturn; Turkey and Brazil each lack three factors. The only cases possessing more than two favorable factors are Iraq under Saddam Hussein and Argentina but even here both political culture and world-systemic opening were not conducive to revolution (Iraq, of course, produced a short-lived political insurrection in March 1991 and Argentina strong protests in 2002–3). There are thus in this sample of the large universe of non-attempts, three patterns explaining this outcome: bcde + abce + ABce, which can be factored to ce (bd + ab + AB). While suggestive only, this result points to the special salience of the limits to political culture and the lack of a world-systemic opening (especially in the context of a non-exclusionary state in every case but for Iraq) as deterrents to a revolutionary attempt, and this is quite plausible, since without a political culture of opposition to the regime, it is hard to see how a revolution could break out, and since a regime that is not weakened within the world-system or vulnerable on its own terms is even less subject to challenge.

Chiapas: the first revolution of the new millennium

Our final case for discussion is the one which may suggest the outlines of the most likely – and most hopeful – face of revolution as the world faces the new century. It is fitting to end this survey of contrasts with the great social revolutions by taking a closer look at the ongoing Zapatista rebellion. We started this comparative history of a century of revolutions with Mexico in 1910. Indeed, Mexico ranks with China (1911, 1949, 1989) and Iran (1905–11, 1951–53, 1978–79) as a member of that rarest set of cases – countries which have experienced multiple revolutions in the past century. Let us not forget the courageous student-worker movement for democracy in 1968, to which the aptly named Díaz Ordaz government replied with a massacre of hundreds of peaceful demonstrators at the Plaza of the Three Cultures in Mexico City on October 2, 1968.[57] The repression of this movement would set in motion a train of events leading eventually to the public appearance of the Zapatistas on New Year's Day, 1994.

The long boom of the 1940s through 1980 brought on a classic process of dependent development in Mexico, with many parallels to the first boom of 1890–1910 under Porfirio Díaz. Remarkable industrialization, expansion of trade, and per capita GNP growth took place under the aegis of the unintentionally ironically named Partido Revolucionario Institucional (Party of the Institutional Revolution). But this was characteristically accompanied by rampant inequalities (despite the revolution's land reform, 1 percent of farms possessed 5 percent of usable land by 1961) and foreign control: "By the mid-seventies, 70 percent of earnings from the capital goods industry went to foreign capital."[58] Mexican development was also drained by the second largest foreign debt in the Third World (after Brazil), nearly $25 billion in 1976, and the "Third World debt crisis" was born when Mexico nationalized all domestic private banks in September 1982. The incoming government of Harvard-trained economist Miguel de la Madrid turned to the IMF, and the 1980s was a decade of economic disasters, with the peso plummeting, the debt surpassing $100 billion in 1986, and the definitive end of the long boom that had been brought about by a nationalist and populist economic development strategy.

In the elections of July 1988 a new political force arose to challenge what Peruvian novelist Mario Vargas Llosa once termed the PRI's "perfect dictatorship" and Karen Kampwirth an "inclusive dictatorship."[59] Workers, peasants, and professionals supported the left coalition known as the National Democratic Front, whose candidate was Cuauhtémoc Cárdenas, son of the popular former president Lazaro Cárdenas. The younger Cárdenas had left the PRI to participate in a coalition with socialists and other progressives around a platform of land reform, income distribution, and a moratorium on foreign debt payments. This was enormously popular, and many – indeed most – observers believe that he actually won the election. But the government announced computer failures when it was counting the vote, and several days later declared its candidate, another Harvard-trained economist, Carlos Salinas de Gortari, the winner.[60]

From 1988 to 1994, Salinas de Gortari presided over a situation of political and economic crisis. Politically, the PRI made implicit deals with the conservative opposition, the pro-business PAN (Party of National Action), in order to counter the challenge from the Democratic Revolutionary Party (PRD) on its left, as Cárdenas's organization restyled itself to contest the legacy of the Mexican revolution. The PAN was allowed to win the 1989 elections for governor in Baja California, while the Democratic Revolutionary Party's candidates were deprived of their victories in Michoacán and Guerrero. In addition, serious violations of human rights continued on a daily basis, aimed at intimidating and in over 250 cases eliminating dissident voices among intellectuals, labor leaders, peasants, and other oppositional figures.[61]

To deal with the economic crisis, the government accepted the US-IMF-World bank prescriptions of neoliberal structural adjustment, selling off state-owned industry (including 70 percent of the petroleum sector), supporting the re-privatization of small communal land holdings into large agribusiness projects, and banking on a closer relationship with the United States symbolized by the 1993 negotiations for the North American Free Trade Agreement (NAFTA). Salinas de Gortari staked his future on the pact in hopes of a third great wave of growth, even if this meant becoming more of an appendage of the United States. The PRI issued new textbooks on Mexican history containing revealing changes from previous editions. Whereas the old fourth grade texts had said that Porfirio Díaz "was very bad for the life of Mexico, because the people were not given the chance to elect their leaders," the new version taught that the Porfiriato was a period of stability and peace, in which industrial growth occurred by attracting foreign investment. On the other hand, the revolutionary land reform program of Zapata was not mentioned, nor the name of Cuauhtémoc Cárdenas uttered in the account of the 1988 election. The subtext was that economic modernization came first, democracy second, in the priorities of the Salinas administration.[62]

But there would be political consequences to the rewriting of history for the analogy of the Porfiriato to the PRI of the 1990s begged the question: was the Mexican revolution finished, or not? The startling events of January 1, 1994 in the southern state of Chiapas underscored the question.[63] On the very day that NAFTA went into effect as a treaty among Canada, the US, and Mexico, some 2,000 guerrillas under indigenous and often female command of a previously unknown guerrilla group calling itself the Zapatista Army of National Liberation (EZLN) seized a number of towns, labeling NAFTA and its free-market reforms "a death sentence for the indigenous people of Mexico."[64] While some of the rebels, almost all indigenous people of Mayan origin, have said their goal is "for socialism, like the Cubans have, but better,"[65] their demands were for such things as land, health care, education, and democratic elections. The most well-known of its leaders, long known only as Subcomandante Marcos,[66] issued poetic communiqués and used the international media including the internet to make the call for radical reform.

The roots of this rebellion run deep: in the 1910 revolution and after, Chiapas was largely by-passed, as an elite of cattle ranchers and coffee growers allied to the PRI ran the state. About 60 percent of the workers of the state made less than the $3.33 minimum daily wage in 1990; 30 percent were illiterate; one-third had no electricity and over 40 percent no running water in their homes.[67] The government first reacted to the rebellion with massive army repression that resulted in 100 "official" deaths (but as many as 500 in reality), numerous cases of torture, and other abuses. It followed this with a series of promises and reforms: dismissal of the state's governor, pledges of food and scholarship aid, and an agreement with the two national opposition parties to reform the electoral process (caps on campaign spending, equal access to the media, and so forth, but stopping short of allowing independent observers at the polls). The rebels issued a set of four basic demands: "'economic demands' related to the poverty of Indians in Chiapas, 'social demands' stemming from racism and other problems, a call for democratic liberties throughout Mexico, and issues related to the formal cessation of hostilities."[68] When the government offered an amnesty, one of the leaders asked in a letter printed in the Mexico City newspapers: "What do we have to ask pardon for? . . . For not dying of hunger? For not shutting up about our misery? For having shown the rest of the country and the entire world that human dignity survives and is in their most impoverished people?"[69] And indeed, the world's attention focused on the situation in Mexico, so in that respect, the rebels quickly won a large measure of success. As one graffiti in Mexico City put it: "Chiapas is Mexico."[70]

Meanwhile, later in 1994, elections were held once again. The PRI's candidate, Luis Donaldo Colosio, was assassinated on March 23, 1994 in Tijuana, in a desperate and violent power struggle between reformist and conservative wings of the PRI. His replacement as PRI candidate, the third consecutive US-trained economist to govern Mexico, Ernesto Zedillo, was elected in August. In December of 1994 interest payments on the debt of $160 billion could not be met, causing the value of the peso to crash and leading to another bail-out by the banks (itself a sign of international – especially US – support for the regime) and a new round of economic belt-tightening for most of the population, in the form of a drop in wages accompanied by rising inflation and unemployment.[71] In the meantime, ex-president Salinas de Gortari had to flee the country, leaving his brother Raúl in prison on charges of fraud, drug laundering, and involvement in another political assassination (that of PRI Secretary General José Francisco Ruiz Massieu). The Zapatistas boycotted the 2000 elections which brought an end to the perfect dictatorship when the PAN's leader Vicente Fox captured the presidency, but the result was unthinkable without the Zapatistas' role in the delegitimation of the PRI.

The rebellion in Chiapas poses some difficult and important questions for students of revolution to ponder: what is the future of revolutions in a globalizing world? Can Third World revolutionaries on the doorstep of the United States, having faced down a cagy "institutionalized dictatorship," find new formulas to create the type of cross-class (and in Mexico, multiracial) populist alliance of men and women that the historical record of social revolution suggests is required for success? And in the post-cold war era, what would "success" look like, in any case? A few thoughts on this will be offered in the concluding chapter of this book.

I do believe that Chiapas offers a new and hopeful model of revolutionary change for us to study, one which may go further than the classic cases of the past along the lines of a creating a truly participatory, more democratic, less racist and sexist society. And this in spite of the collapse of socialism and the proclamation of a new US-led world order on Mexico's front doorstep, and carried through by means among the more peaceful in the historical record of attempted revolutionary transformations. For now, we will have to wait and see how the rebellion goes; this may be a long wait unless some fairly substantial concessions are made by the government, for the rebels have said they are prepared to fight for twenty or thirty years if necessary. One future scenario would involve unacceptable levels of military repression, further governmental scandal and corruption, and economic mismanagement of a kind that might make the regime appear less open to reform and change as well as alienate the US to the degree that all five factors would then be fully present (the classic path to social revolution). An alternative (and very different) scenario would be the successful transformation of the EZLN into part of a new social movement and an electoral force capable of defeating the PRI and the PAN in open and fair elections, to then initiate a process of real change (the Chilean path in a new world context). Either way, Chiapas, writ large upon Mexico and beyond, could indeed transform what we mean by "revolutionary success," if it prospers – a large "if."

Concluding thoughts on the failure of revolutions

The results of this survey of attempted revolutions, political revolutions, and non-attempts were summed up in Table 5.2. We have already analyzed each of these types comparatively, using Boolean techniques of qualitative comparison.

The patterns that have failed to bring about a revolution can be arrayed by type:

Attempted revolution = Abce

Political Revolution = Bcde + aBce

Stable/no attempt = bcde + abce + ABce

Focusing first on the eight attempted revolutions and five political revolutions (closer contrasts to social revolutions than non-attempts), we have three patterns for failure:

Failure = Abce + Bcde + aBce

These can be simplified with Boolean algebra to the expression:

Failure = ce (Ab + Bd + aB)

That is, attempted revolutions and political revolutions failed to become full-fledged social revolutions as their political cultures were limited in some way and the world-systemic opportunity was not present, *and* one further factor – a vulnerable state, economic downturn, or dependent development – was absent. We may note the similarity with societies in which revolutions were not attempted, even with some of the factors present, as long as powerful political cultures were not sufficiently articulated and no world-systemic opening was present:

Stable/no attempt = ce (bd + ab + AB),

If we wish to compare all twenty-two cases at once, we can make use of the common factoring in all three types to observe the following patterns:

Failure = ce (Ab + Bd + aB + bd + ab + AB)

Since we can logically reduce pairs such as "Ab" and "ab" to "b," "Bd" and "bd" to "d," "Ab" and "AB" to "A," and "aB" and "ab" to "a," the patterns can be further simplified to

Failure = ce (b + d + a + A).

If we now discard the case of Iraq (the "A" in the expression) as an outlier since it occurs in a single case and there is no compelling reason to suppose that the presence of dependent development, a repressive dictatorship, and an economic downturn were the causes of the stability of the regime, we arrive at a final, most simplified set of routes accounting for the other twenty-one cases of failure:

$$\text{Failure} = ce\ (b + d + a).$$

We might interpret this result as suggesting that the causes of failure were the combination of problematic political cultures, an unfavorable international conjuncture, and any one of the other factors in the model. Among the conclusions to be drawn from this exercise is a further demonstration that all five factors are needed for a social revolution to occur and succeed, and that the absence of any of the five factors is sufficient to block a social revolution from succeeding. Most notably, two of the five factors – political cultures of opposition and world-systemic opportunity – may be the single most salient reasons for failure, underlining the sheer weight of the world system, and the wisdom of our return to the subjective realm of culture.

Part Four

Conclusions

6   The past and future of revolutions

The duty we owe history is to rewrite it.

Oscar Wilde

The twentieth century we have so recently departed has surely been one of the great ages of revolutions, in Skocpol's sense of "rapid, basic trans-formations of a society's state and class structures . . . accompanied and in part carried through by class-based revolts from below."[1] From the events of 1917 in Russia that so profoundly shook the world, to the great Third World social revolutions in China, Cuba, and Nicaragua (and the lesser ones – in transformational terms – in Mexico and Iran) and the anti-colonial revolutions in Algeria, Vietnam and southern Africa; from the shorter-lived but no less remarkable democratic revolutions in May 1968 in France, Chile under Allende, and Manley's Jamaica, and the more enduring "velvet" revolutions of 1989 in Eastern Europe, to the current struggle in Chiapas, the historical record is rich in dramatic experiences of ordinary people undertaking extraordinary collective acts.

   This book has surveyed this epoch of revolutions, and it is time to draw up a balance sheet and look ahead to the future of revolutions in a new age of globalization. This chapter, then, provides an overview of the findings of our study, a look at the unsettled present, a glimpse into the revolutionary future, and ends with some thoughts on what scholars and activists might want to take with them to the social transformations that surely lie ahead.

What have we learned about the origins of revolutions?

Table 6.1 presents a concise summary of the data on the thirty-nine cases that have been presented in this study, evaluating each in terms of the presence or absence of each of the causal factors in the model for the origins of successful Third World social revolutions.[2] The reader may also wish to refer to Tables 2.1, 3.1, 4.1, 4.3, 5.1, 5.3, and 5.4 for text on each of the cases.

Table 6.1 *The causes of Third World revolutions*

A Boolean Truth Table

(0 = trait absent; 1 = trait present)

Cases	(A) Dependent development	(B) Repressive, exclusionary, personalist or colonial state or open polity*	(C) Political cultures of opposition	(D) Economic downturn	(E) World-systemic opening	Outcome
Type one: Successful social revolutions						
1. Mexico, 1910–20	1	1	1	1	1	1-Social revolution
2. Cuba, 1953–59	1	1	1	1	1	1-Social revolution
3. Iran, 1977–79	1	1	1	1	1	1-Social revolution
4. Nicaragua, 1977–79	1	1	1	1	1	1-Social revolution
5. China, 1949	1	1	1	1	1	1-Social revolution
Type two: Anti-colonial (social) revolutions						
6. Algeria, 1954–62	1	1	1	1	1	1-Anti-colonial SR
7. Vietnam, 1945–75	1	1	1	1	1	1-Anti-colonial SR
8. Angola, 1970s	1	1	1	1	1	1-Anti-colonial SR
9. Mozambique, 1970s	1	1	1	1	1	1-Anti-colonial SR
10. Zimbabwe, 1970s	1	1	1	1	1	1-Anti-colonial SR
Type three: Short-lived social revolutions: coming to power						
11. Iran, 1951	1	1*	1	1	1	1-Social rev/Elections
12. Guatemala, 1944	1	1/1*	1	–	1	1-Social rev/Elections
13. Bolivia, 1952	1	1–	1	1	1	1-Social revolution
14. Chile, 1970	1	1*	1	1	1	1-Social rev/Elections
15. Jamaica, 1972	1	1*	1	1	1	1-Social rev/Elections
16. Nicaragua, 1979	1	1	1	1	1	1-Social revolution
17. Grenada, 1979	1	1	1	1	1	1-Social revolution

Favorable Conditions

Type four: Reversed social revolutions: falling from power

11a. Iran, 1953	1*	1–	1	0	0-Coup
12a. Guatemala, 1954	1*	1–	1–	0	0-Coup
13a. Bolivia, 1964	1*	1–	1	0	0-Coup
14a. Chile, 1973	1*	1–	1	0	0-Coup
15a. Jamaica, 1980	1*	1–	1	0	0-Electoral defeat
16a. Nicaragua, 1990	1*	1–	1	0	0-Electoral defeat
17a. Grenada, 1983	1*–	0	0	0	0-Coup

Type five: Attempted social revolutions

18. Argentina, 1975–76	1(–)	1–	1	0	0-Coup
19. El Salvador, 1979–92	1–	1–	1–	0	0-Negotiations
20. Guatemala, 1960s–92	1–	1–	1–	0	0-Negotiations
21. Peru, 1980s–92	1*–	1–	1/0	0	0-Repression
22. Philippines, 1986–90s	1*–	1–	1–	0	0-Repression
23. China, 1989	1–	1–	1	0	0-Repression
24. Algeria, 1991–92	1–	1–	1	0	0-Coup
25. Chiapas, 1994–	1–/1*	1?	1	0	?-Ongoing

Type six: Political revolutions

26. China, 1911	1–	1–	1–	1/0	Political revolution
27. Philippines, 1986	1	1–	1–	1/0	Political revolution
28. Haiti, 1986	0	1–	1–	1/0	Political revolution
29. South Africa, 1994	1	1/1–	1–	1/0	Political revolution
30. Zaire, 1996	0	1	1	1/0	Political revolution

Type seven: No attempt at revolution

31. Iran, 1979–	1*–	1–	0	1–	0-stability
32. Egypt, 1981–	1*–	1–	1–	0	0-stability
33. Argentina, 1983–	1*–	0	1	0	0-stability
34. Turkey, 1983–	1	0	1/0	0	0-stability
35. Brazil, 1987–2000	1*–	1–	1–	0	0-stability
36. South Korea, 1988–	1+	1*–	0/1	0	0-stability
37. Taiwan, 1989–	1+	1–	0	0	0-stability
38. Cuba, 1991–	1(+)	1–	0	1–	0-stability
39. Iraq, 1991–2003	1	1–	0	1–	0-stability

Let's review each of the major types in turn, moving through the various pathways to success and failure around which this study has been organized.

Type one: successful Third World social revolutions

Chapter 2 represented the heart of this book insofar as it offered a theoretically-organized narrative about each of the five "great" Third World social revolutions of the twentieth century: Mexico, China, Cuba, Iran, and Nicaragua. I argued that the presence of all five factors – dependent development, the exclusionary state, widely-embraced political cultures of resistance, an economic downturn, and a world-systemic opening – accounts for the success of these revolutions in coming to power. This may be represented by the equation:

$$\text{Success} = \text{ABCDE},$$

where the capital letters represent the presence of each factor. As this single pattern is found in all the successful cases, it appears that we have uncovered a single route to social revolution in the Third World, one that requires the coming together of our five causal factors in time and space. When this happens, the broad coalition of forces needed to successfully carry out a social revolution takes the stage.

Type two: anti-colonial revolutions

Chapter 3 took up the origins of the anti-colonial revolutions which swept the Third World after World War 2 as a further test of the model. We chose the five cases that have generally been acknowledged as social revolutions: Algeria, Vietnam, Angola, Mozambique, and Zimbabwe. Important modifications of the model were made to take into account the specific effects of colonial states and political economies. While development is more dependent than dynamic in these cases, still it transforms societies enough to generate revolutionary grievances; in fact, we identified a variant of dependent development we called "dependent colonial development": namely, development for the colonizers, dependency for the colonized. Though the colonial state was by definition not personalist, it did represent a concentrated target in the form of an outside force ruling above civil society. It was often extremely repressive, and by its very nature it excluded the majority of the population from political representation as effectively as any dictatorship has. Colonialism also shaped political cultures of opposition in the direction of intense nationalisms, in each case overlaid with specific socialist, religious, or indigenous currents of resistance. The conjunctural factors were similar too, with less emphasis perhaps on sudden economic downturns, and more on world-systemic openings, and both, to some degree, subject to influence by the rebels themselves. Just as the revolutionaries contributed to the making of economic downturns in Cuba and China, this common consequence of protracted guerrilla warfare is even more apparent in drawn-out, violent anti-colonial struggles, and obtained in all five of our cases. In addition, the revolutionaries contributed to the world-systemic opening in complex ways as well, especially in the impetus that the Angolan MPLA and Mozambique's Frelimo gave to Portugal's 1974 revolution, and that their success gave to the revolutionaries in Zimbabwe. These findings from Chapters 2 and 3 underscore the ways in which agency and structure are mutually constitutive, as well as showing the double dialectic of relations in the world system, where the Third World is not merely a passive victim of First World power but can act back, challenging that power and shaping the course of events. And we found striking resemblances to the successful social revolutions analyzed in Chapter 1, for in Boolean terms, all five cases conform to the pattern of the great social revolutions:

$$\text{Success} = \text{ABCDE};$$

that is, the presence of all five factors once again led to successful social revolutions.

Type three: short-lived social revolutions

A final important set of (temporarily) successful cases consists of countries which experienced a relatively brief period of revolutionary rule that was ultimately reversed: Iran, Guatemala, and Bolivia in the 1950s, Chile and Jamaica in the 1970s, and Nicaragua and Grenada in the 1980s. These seven cases also fit the general outline of the model advanced in this book, if due allowance is made for the existence of open and democratic, rather than dictatorial, state systems in Iran, Guatemala, Chile, and Jamaica. This permitted us to identify a third type of vulnerable state – the genuinely democratic polity in which revolutionary parties have a chance to come to power because competition is significant across the political spectrum and electoral results are respected. The effects of dependent development, vitality of political cultures, and the same conjunctural factors of internal economic downturn and favorable external situation lie in the background of the events that brought revolutionaries or radical reformers to power in these countries as well. In Boolean language, the pattern ABCDE is found once again, adding seven new cases of successful social revolution to our list, for a total of seventeen cases of revolutions coming to power that fit our model quite closely.

Type four: the reversal of revolutions

In Chapter 4, we also started the second part of the book, with a dual aim: to begin to explain the multiple reasons that revolutions have failed, and in the context of the short-lived revolutions of Chapter 4, to begin theorizing the outcomes of revolutions. We made a start on the latter by following the trajectories of the same seven revolutionary governments after taking power. In Boolean terms, two distinct combinations of factors are found among the seven cases: Iran, Bolivia, Jamaica, Chile, and Nicaragua form one cluster (ABcDe), and Guatemala and Grenada a second (ABcde). These patterns can be interpreted as follows: revolutions have been reversed when they continue to be subject to the effects of dependent development (which is impossible to undo in a short period of time, if ever); when they have open, democratic institutions, which are subject to conflict and subversion; when the revolutionary political cultures that brought them about are attenuated due to internal differences of opinion or the difficulties of continuing to effectively engage their broad coalitions (compounded by the fragmenting actions of the opponents of the new government, internal and external); and when the world-systemic window that opened to permit their coming to power closes. This pattern suggests a possible theory for reversals of revolution: revolutionaries fall from power when political fragmentation and polarization, economic problems (often, though not always, including economic downturns), and outside intervention occur together. The apparently negative causal role that was played in the reversal of revolutions by fashioning or maintaining democratic institutions was a troubling finding that opened up a discussion of the relationships between democracy and revolution that will be resumed later in this conclusion.

Type five: attempted social revolutions

Chapter 5 took up three further types of "failure," in the sense that social revolutions did not occur in conditions where we might otherwise have expected them to. These include attempted social revolutions, political revolutions, and non-attempts. Of these, attempted social revolutions are the clearest example of a contrasting case for our model of success, for the goal of the revolutionaries was the same as in the successful cases. The guiding principle of my analysis of these cases – Argentina in 1975–76, El Salvador in the 1980s, Guatemala between the 1960s and 1992, the

Philippines in the mid- to late 1980s, China in 1989, Peru in the 1980s and early 1990s, Algeria in the early 1990s, and Chiapas since 1994 – was that they should exhibit substantial similarities to the successful cases already studied (to explain why there was an attempt), but also equally significant differences in some of the factors at work (to account for their failure). We found that six of the eight cases possessed to some degree all of the factors except a favorable world-system, and the other two – Peru and the Philippines – lacked this and also faced a regime that was not as vulnerable as the others. There were thus substantial reasons for these attempts, yet none possessed all the factors necessary for success.

This theoretical assumption involved a new Boolean technique: coding the "1–'s" as present to explain why there was an attempt at revolution, and as absent (or more accurately, only partially present and therefore in some sense limited or unfavorable to revolution) to explain their lack of success. The use of Boolean techniques to simplify the patterns yielded the formula Abce as the common pattern in the movements' failures, meaning that despite the presence of dependent development, rebels could not succeed when the states they faced were not repressive, exclusionary dictatorships (or genuine democracies, if the movements were mainly non-violent in nature and/or pursuing an electoral route to power, as in China, Algeria, and Chiapas), their political cultures did not facilitate broad cross-class alliances, and outside powers supported rather than abandoned incumbent regimes.

This set of cases, then, confirmed the theory of success insofar as revolutionary attempts possess almost all of the characteristics of successful cases, yet one or another factor's absence or partial presence gave us a working theory of failure, in that when these same characteristics are crucially limited in scope or depth, revolutions do not succeed. To be sure, the outcome of reversal in the case of Nicaragua's social revolution in 1990 and the current electoral strength of the "failed" FMLN-led revolution in El Salvador problematize the meanings of success and failure in interesting ways that point toward the future of revolutions.

Type six: political revolutions

Chapter 5 also looked at political revolutions as another important variant on our theme in that these are revolutions made by mass-mobilizing movements and result in significant political change, but the social and economic transformations that we associate with social revolutions do not come about. In searching for the paths to political revolution, we repeated the procedure used in understanding attempted social revolutions. Thus, coding factors judged "1–" in Table 6.1 as present, we found two patterns: ABCDE in China, the Philippines, and South Africa, and the variant path aBCDE in Haiti and Zaire, with their more marked degree of sheer underdevelopment. We interpreted this as an account of why a revolution of any type occurred, as this is quite close to, and in many cases, the same as, the model for social revolution. In emphasizing the limits to these factors by coding all cases of "1−" as absent, we then identified three distinct patterns to account for the political, rather than social, outcomes of these events, and after Boolean minimization, two patterns remained: Bce (a + d). We concluded that social revolutions did not occur in these cases due to the limits of their political cultures of opposition and lack of a world-systemic opening conducive to far-reaching change, combined in the cases of Zaire, China, and Haiti with very limited (if any) dependent development, and in the Philippines and South Africa with relatively less severe economic downturns. The theoretical import of this was that political culture and world-systemic opening act as powerful deflectors of revolutionary movements that put brakes on social transformation after they take power. These cases thus nuance further the theory of successful social revolutions by showing how the partial existence of some of the key factors produced instead a mass-made political transformation alone, stopping short of deeper social transformation.

Type seven: no attempt at revolution

Chapter 5 also offered a very brief consideration of a sampling of the large number of cases where no revolution has been attempted in the Third World – the true universe of failure being quite large. The patterns underlying this cursory survey of select Third World non-revolutionary situations can be discerned in various ways. Since no case possessed all five factors posited by the theory, this constituted further evidence that it takes all five to bring about a social revolution. We also found cases that lacked a single factor: the absence of only an economic downturn in Iran, a world-systemic opening in Egypt, and an oppositional political culture in Cuba and Iraq, which logically enhances the plausibility of each of these factors as a cause of social revolution.

When we made the most restrictive interpretation of the cases, coding "1+," "1*−," "1−," and "1/0" as absences of the factors in question, we ended up with three patterns explaining the nine failures: bcde + abce + ABce, which factored further to ce (bd + ab + AB). This result pointed to the limits to political culture and the lack of a world-systemic opening (especially in the context of a non-exclusionary state in eight of the nine cases) as deterrents to a revolutionary attempt, and we found this quite plausible as in the absence of a strong revolutionary opposition, it is hard to see how a revolution could break out, even less so in regimes that are not weakened within the world-system or vulnerable on their own terms.

A summary of results

We have now completed our long, comparative tour of Third World revolutions. This book has constituted an extended test of a model of the origins of Third World social revolutions, and a reflection on the question of "Why do so few revolutions succeed, while most fail (or do not even break out in most places at most times)?" The procedures of Boolean analysis have yielded the following sets of patterns, based on Table 6.1:

Type one: Successful Third World social revolutions (cases 1–5, covered in Chapter 2)

$$\text{Success} = ABCDE$$

Type two: Anti-colonial (social) revolutions (cases 6–10, covered in Chapter 3)

$$\text{Success} = ABCDE$$

Type three: Short-lived social revolutions (cases 11–17, covered in Chapter 4)

$$\text{Coming to power} = ABCDE$$

Type four: reversed social revolutions (cases 11a–17a, covered in Chapter 4)

$$\text{Falling from power} = ABce$$

Type five: attempted social revolutions (cases 18–25, covered in Chapter 5)

$$\text{Factors favoring attempt} = ACD$$
$$\text{Reasons for failure} = Abce$$

Type six: political revolutions (cases 26–30, covered in Chapter 5)

$$\text{Factors favoring revolution} = ABCDE$$
$$\text{Factors explaining lack of a social revolution} = Bcde + aBce$$
$$= Bce\,(a + d)$$

Type seven: no attempt (cases 31–39, covered in Chapter 5)

$$\text{Stable/no attempt} = bcde + abce + ABce$$
$$= ce\,(bd + ab + AB)$$

If we attempt to summarize the model of success, we can look at the first seventeen cases, and find that there were two routes to power: the presence of all five original factors in the five classic cases of success (Mexico, China, Cuba, Nicaragua, and Iran), the five anti-colonial revolutions (Algeria, Vietnam, Angola, Mozambique, and Zimbabwe), and in three of the short-lived social revolutions (the overthrow of Ubico in Guatemala in June 1944, Bolivia, and Grenada). In three cases – Iran, Chile, and Jamaica (and to some degree, in Guatemala's December 1944 election of Arévalo) – social revolutionaries did not face an exclusionary, personalist regime, but rather a genuinely democratic polity, and came to power through elections. The answer to the question of why all these cases succeeded lies in the combination of dependent development, vulnerable state, oppositional political cultures, economic downturn, and world-systemic opportunity posited by the model.

To the question, why do most attempts fail, or not result in social revolutions, and why do most countries not experience revolutions at all, we have found several answers. The reversed social revolutions in Iran, Guatemala, Bolivia, Chile, Jamaica, Grenada, and Nicaragua suggested that the continued effects of dependent development and an economic downturn, coupled with schisms in the unity of the revolutionaries (at least in part due to political cultures), the vulnerability of relatively democratic revolutionary regimes, and external pressures have combined to overturn revolutions in progress. This is a contribution to a theory of revolutionary outcomes, for it identifies at least some of the factors which have undermined revolutionaries even where they have achieved a firm hold on power.

The pattern of attempted revolutions in Argentina, El Salvador, Peru, Guatemala, the Philippines, China, Algeria, and Chiapas provides a further answer to the question of why many revolutions fail: in these cases, revolutionaries took advantage of the effects of dependent development and economic downturns and elaborated political cultures to rally the opposition. Revolutionary struggles broke out in unfavorable international contexts, however, and regardless of the type of state faced. The causes of failure included the strength of the relatively inclusive and non-personalist repressive regimes the rebels fought, the limits of the political cultures they elaborated, the relative stability and horrible "normality" of economic difficulties, and substantial outside aid to the governments.

Political revolutions resulted in China, the Philippines, Haiti, South Africa, and Zaire when all five factors posited by the model came into play up to a degree. But up to a degree only: three patterns forced these movements to stop short of social transformation. In China and Haiti, relative economic and political cultural underdevelopment, lack of economic crisis, and outside pressures moderated the outcome despite the presence of a repressive state; the Philippines and South Africa followed a similar path except for their more vigorous dependent development, while Zaire resembled China and Haiti as well, except for a more pronounced economic downturn. The analysis of these five cases may suggest – but by no means fully demonstrates – a future theory of the causes of political revolutions.

Finally, we have looked at a number of cases which possess some of the factors tending toward revolutionary mobilization but in which no revolution in fact was even attempted. We have traced this to the absence or limits of the key factors, in several combinations.

If we look at all the combinations which did not produce successful social revolutions, we find six distinctive routes to failure in cases 11a through 39:

$$\text{Failure} = \text{ABce} + \text{Abce} + \text{Bcde} + \text{aBce} + \text{bcde} + \text{abce}$$

These can be reduced further to Ace + Bce + bce + cde + ace, and ultimately reduced to:

$$\text{Failure} = \text{ce} + \text{cde}$$

This means that in every single instance of failure – whether reversal of a social revolution, failure of an attempt, the limited outcome of a political revolution, or no attempt at all where one might be expected – the political cultures of opposition at work were in some way not effective enough, and the international conjuncture was unfavorable. Moreover, in virtually every case, at least one of the other three factors was missing as well. This suggests that the majority of the actual historical cases at our disposal lacked at least three of the factors necessary to produce a social revolution. The larger equation also points to the causal power of every factor in the model, in one pattern or another.

In the end, we are left with a fairly comprehensive test of the model across most of the universe of successful cases. It is my hope that readers will appreciate the strength of these findings, just as I readily acknowledge the study's inevitable limitations of empirical depth, theoretical insight, and methodological rigor. I will leave it to others to do further work on these and other cases, and I look forward to the theoretical innovations, methodological improvements, and empirical knowledge that such work will surely generate.

Finally, one wonders what modifications would need to be introduced to take on that much smaller set of non-Third World social revolutions offered by history in the case of the seventeenth-century English civil war, the French and Russian revolutions of 1789 and 1917, and the events of

1989 in Eastern Europe. I hope that in the process of advancing our understanding of the comparative-historical sociology of Third World revolutions, the present study has suggested ways to do this, for I believe that the Third World contains lessons – once again – for the First (and Second): namely, the continued importance of economic contradictions, the significance of political cultures, and the need to simultaneously consider internal and international levels of analysis and the subtle interplay of structure and agency.

A concern with the future of revolutions

As we now enter headlong the era of globalization, the future of revolutions is beginning to receive sustained scholarly attention.[3] This is, to be sure, an intrinsically creative and speculative sort of work, attempting to answer such questions as:

Is the age of revolutions over?

If so, why?

If not, what might the revolutions of the future look like?

The discourse and tactics of revolution may be moving away from armed struggle (though we have seen that this was never the sole option for revolutionaries); the international loci and foci may be moving (with the demise of the Soviet Union and the tentative consolidation of democracies in Latin America); the actors may be changing (with more women and ethnic minorities active, though both have long histories of revolutionary activism). But it appears to me that revolutions are going to be with us to the end of history, and – pace Francis Fukuyama – that is not in sight.

Still, the question posed by the current craze for "globalization" in the social sciences and popular imagination is: has it become *harder* for revolutions to occur in a world of global corporations and commodity chains, global cultural forms, instantaneous communication and swift travel, the collapse of Soviet-style socialism, and a no longer bipolar political arrangement? This question is compounded by the events of September 11, 2001, and the subsequent overt US quest for global military dominance in the service of economic empire.

The conservative position is that the age of revolutions is – of course – over.[4] And even as they refused to accept the celebratory end of history thesis, by the mid-1990s many activists and citizens in both First and Third Worlds implicitly seemed resigned to the view summed up by the dispirited acronym TINA – "There is no alternative" – originally uttered by a jubilant Margaret Thatcher.[5] In a vein more sympathetic to those who would still like to transform the world, Jeff Goodwin and Eric Selbin have debated this proposition, with somewhat different (though not diametrically opposed) conclusions. Focusing on the type of state that historically has been vulnerable to revolution, Jeff Goodwin sees a diminished stage in the future for sharp revolutionary conflict – though not other progressive social movements – with the passing of colonialism and indiscriminately repressive dictatorships.[6] Eric Selbin, well known for his advocacy of agency-centered explanations of revolutions, has countered, a bit surprisingly, with an economic argument: "as global gaps between the haves and have-nots increase and neoliberalism fails to deliver on its promise, revolution will be more likely."[7] To this he has added his characteristic emphasis on cultures of resistance, noting that revolutions have always promised new beginnings, tapped into timeless myths and inspired magical possibilities; thus he wagers confidently that people will continue to articulate compelling stories about change to enable social change.

My own views coincide with Selbin in this far from settled debate, feeling as I do that North-South inequality will only continue to deepen on many levels with the "triumph" of neoliberalism, and that the Third World left has not suffered a fatal or permanent blow to its political creativity with the collapse of what has until now passed for socialism. Moreover, both Goodwin and Selbin, as well as Mark Katz, who has commented on this discussion,[8] have not taken seriously enough the possibility that revolutionaries may take non-violent and/or democratic routes to power, and in fact, have done so, in Guatemala in the 1950s, the French May of 1968, Allende's Chile, Jamaica under Michael Manley, Iran (both in the Mussadiq era and in 1978), Eastern Europe and China in 1989, and Chiapas, to name the most notable cases (it is of course true that none of these found lasting success, with the ironic exception of the restoration of capitalism in the socialist bloc).

The issues that would need to be deeply engaged in order to take this debate a step further include: what is the impact of globalization, for good or bad, on the prospects of revolution? Should we reconsider the forms revolutions may take in changing circumstances? How are political cultures – especially notions about radically democratic revolutions – evolving, and what role will the new technologies, particularly those associated with cyberculture, play in them? What is the import of the world-shattering events of September 11, 2001 for world-systemic openings and closures? Finally, what relationship – if any – exists or might come to exist between the emergent global justice movement and national revolutionary actors? Addressing these matters necessarily raises the question of how we might think about and analyze the future, to which I will turn first.

How to study the future

In *The Future of Revolutions* volume on which I shall now draw, I gathered a group of scholars to debate these questions, and it was surprising to see how resistant the group initially was to speculate boldly beyond the present. It is of course true that we cannot know the future. Social scientists have in fact nevertheless spent much time and effort making predictions of all kinds.[9] As Carlos Vilas notes, it is risky to assess the probability of a revolution in any given situation, and the question can only be settled when and if the anticipated revolution occurs.[10] Vilas quotes Eric Hobsbawm to the effect that revolutionary situations are "about possibilities, and their analysis is not predictive."[11] *Thinking about* the future, I submit, is different from predicting it, and seems both less presumptuous and potentially more liberating in freeing the thinker from the problems of prediction and in opening up insights that might provide clues as to how to achieve a better future. It is in this spirit that I should like to proceed.

Let me suggest three ideas about the methods that might be useful in speculating beyond the present. One is to base one's analysis on the past. This means talking about past revolutions and trying to "filter" what might be different about the present through them in order to make some conjectures about what the future might look like. This seems a soundly social scientific way to proceed as it is grounded in comparison and historical case study. A second, not unrelated approach, is to look at the future in terms of theories. The variety of theories about the causes, processes, and outcomes of revolutions are of course generated mainly through comparison of past cases. Thus, we might take the elements of those theories and again filter through them what we take to be the characteristics of how the present may be changing, measuring these against the factors identified by our theories and projecting them into the future.[12] A third, rather wide open angle, is achieved by simply applying our imaginations, sociological and otherwise, to the future and speculating with playful seriousness about what might come. Each of us will bring to this different measures of theory, casework, and imagination, into which, as Carlos Vilas notes, also enter our personal ideological biases, hunches, fears or wishes.[13] The best approach is probably to attempt all three.

Globalization: the highest stage of capitalism?

In his classic 1916 account of imperialism, Lenin conceived it as the highest stage of capitalism, and dated its rise in words that echo eerily almost a century later: "the beginning of the twentieth century marks the turning point from the old capitalism to the new, from the domination of capital in general to the domination of finance capital."[14] Just as the years around 1800 gave us the dawn of industrial capitalism, and those around 1900 the dawn of imperialism (and eventually neo-colonialism), in the early years of the new millennium the dawn of globalization seems to be breaking. As imperialism represented for Lenin a special stage in capitalism, globalization may well represent a special stage in imperialism and neo-colonialism. It is, less controversially perhaps, the latest stage in the development of capitalism.

But what *is* globalization? This conclusion is hardly the place to enter into a long discussion of the vast and growing literature on this multi-sided phenomenon. It would be hard to do better than the list of features identified by David Harvey in *Spaces of Hope* (here paraphrased and somewhat extended by myself). These are:

1. the breakdown since the 1970s of the US-controlled Bretton Woods trade system, and its transformation into today's more decentralized and financially volatile system with other poles in Japan and Europe, coordinated through a set of transnational institutions;

2. a "galloping" wave of technological innovation, akin to past advances but accelerated by the intermeshing of applied science and the international arms trade;

3. the new forms of media and communication that are changing workplaces and allowing financial transactions to take place instantaneously, as well as generating entirely new needs and wants;

4. the reduced costs of moving commodities and people;

5. the development of transnational corporate export processing zones (EPZs), new forms of flexible production, and elaborate global commodity chains;

6. a constantly growing wage labor force, more exploited, diverse, and divided than in the past, further shaped by hyper-urbanization and migrations that have changed the face of the working class;

7. the loss by many states over control of fiscal policy to the international lending institutions and rule-making bodies such as the World Trade Organization;

8. the rise of such pressing ecological threats as global warming, the imminent advent of "peak oil" production, and the adverse consequences of the biogenetic revolutions in food and medicines; and

9. culture coming to the forefront in unpredictable ways as processes of both homogenization and resistance speed up.[15]

To this admirable working list let us add an equally momentous political development: the collapse of socialism in the USSR, Eastern Europe, and elsewhere in the 1990s, bringing with it the end of the bipolar antagonisms of the cold war and the opening of a new period of US military hegemony in the service of an ever more elusive quest for economic paramountcy.

Two themes in the globalization literature deserve special mention since they bear on the future of revolutions quite directly: the debate on the extent of world poverty, and the thesis on the declining significance of the nation-state. The first hinges on the degree to which globalization has reduced or exacerbated inequality and poverty world-wide in the last decade or so. It seems clear enough that North-South relations remain highly hierarchical and unequal: economic disparities are on the rise virtually everywhere in the world, with the assets of the three richest people in the world in 1998 exceeding the combined GNP of the twenty-five least developed countries, with a population of over 500 million, while the assets of the 200 richest people in the world in the same year exceeded the combined income of 41 percent of the world's people.[16] World Bank studies suggest, at least by one estimate, that "*world* income inequality in the 1980s and early 1990s grew much more rapidly than domestic income inequality in the US and the UK . . . global inequality has grown [in the past twenty years] as much as it did in the 200 years [previous]."[17] The gap in per capita income levels between the First and Third Worlds tripled between 1960 and 1993;[18] it can only have widened further since. And poverty has grown in absolute as well as relative terms: 200 million more people entered absolute poverty between 1995 and 1999.[19] As Robin Hahnel puts it:

As best as I can tell, for every NIC (Newly Industrializing Country) there were 10 FEBs (countries Falling Ever-more Behind) during the neoliberal "boom". And for every wealthy beneficiary of rising stock process, rising profit shares, and rising high-end salaries, there were 10 victims of declining real wages, decreased job security, and lost benefits. The recent experiment in deregulation and globalization was indeed both "the best of times and the worst of times". But unfortunately it was the best of times for only a few, and the worst of times for most. At least that is what had been happening *before* the bubble burst in July 1997.[20]

The general trend seems established: Chossudovsky discusses the complexity of the data and confirms this, opening his survey thus: "The late 20th century will go down in world history as a period of global impoverishment."[21] It is true that the link between poverty and inequality and globalization is complex and indeed disputed,[22] but if we consider the devastating consequences of Third World debt and structural adjustment for development, the impact of globalization seems clear enough, and suggests that dependent development will remain an all-too-relevant concept for assessing the prospects for revolution in the near and medium-term future.

There is also a widespread assumption in the literature that globalization has weakened the power of nation-states. Though this is a complex issue as well and even further from being settled, here I am more skeptical, and for reasons that bear on the future of revolutions. The world economy is changing, to be sure, as transnational companies develop ever greater capacities to escape the regulation of states, control the distribution of profits along commodity chains, and depress the wages of workers. This debate can be addressed on several levels, of which at least two are salient for our purposes: whether state power is in fact waning irreversibly, and whether state power is therefore no longer a viable or desirable goal for revolutionaries.

The declining significance of the state is most often attributed to the loss by Third World states over control of fiscal policy to IMF structural adjustment programs, the vulnerability of all states to the volatility of huge unregulated financial markets, and the passing of sovereignty in trade matters to transnational bodies like the WTO that favor multinational corporations in economic disputes with nation-states. These new facts are indisputable, but some see in this situation of crisis a *renewed* role for states to play in trying to buffer their citizens against such forces, making the state a key potential locus of resistance to globalization – defending jobs, ethnic and cultural identities, the environment, welfare benefits, and much more.[23] As Farideh Farhi puts it:

The state may no longer be perceived as the body to be "taken over" and turned into an instrument of drastic social change. But the way it inserts itself into social, economic and cultural life and the way its institutional arrangements inhibit "meaningful" as opposed to superficial or procedural democratic participation have become more and more crystallized as the focal point of political struggle in countries as varied as Iran, Indonesia, Peru, Mexico and so on.[24]

George and Jane Collier present the interesting thesis that there has been a shift from economic weakening of states through structural adjustment and trade agreements to strengthening a formally democratic law and order state with military and legal guarantees for foreign investors. This shift – or perhaps better put, the addition of a second emphasis – in globalization strategies appears to be a response to the unrest unleashed by the imposition of structural adjustment programs (i.e. dependent development).[25]

We should perhaps therefore not rush too quickly to conclude that the classic revolutionary goal of seizing state power is no longer relevant or viable. For Jeff Goodwin, "Rather than uniformly diminishing states, in fact, globalization has been just as likely to spur attempts to employ and, if necessary, expand state power for the purposes of enhancing global competitiveness . . . There is no reason to believe, in any event, that in the future people will accept the depredations of authoritarian states and shun revolutionaries on the grounds that state power 'ain't what it used to be'."[26] At the same time, new revolutionary movements like the Zapatistas *have* questioned this goal, reflecting their subtle understandings of the workings of political power in conditions of globalization: that creating democratic spaces for the free discussion of political, economic, and cultural alternatives to globalization is a more suitable goal for revolutionaries than direct seizure of state power, and that linking the national liberation struggle to both local needs and global concerns might be the most effective – if an even more daunting – coalition-building project for deep social transformation. The global diffusion of democratic polities since the 1980s means that at least some Third World states will be genuinely open to the rise of the left through elections.

This leads to consideration of our third factor: political cultures of opposition. Farideh Farhi, Jeffery Paige, Abdollah Dashti, and Chris McAuley have all advanced visions of a more participatory culture based on their readings of the past.[27] For Val Moghadam, this culture is becoming more feminist in the current conjuncture.[28] John Walton puts it thus: "The broader lesson is the emergence of a new global political consciousness . . . which attempts to define a coherent code of global justice embracing indigenous people, peasants, the urban poor, labor, democrats and dolphins."[29] Eric Selbin is perhaps the most focused contributor to this debate:

There is a global or transnational role played by the ideas, myths and conceptions which people share with one another . . . Thus memories of oppression, sagas of occupation and struggle, tales of opposition, myths of once and future glory, words of mystery and symbolism are appropriated from the pantheon of history of resistance and rebellion common to almost every culture and borrowed from others and fashioned into some sort of usable past which confronts the present and reaches out to the future.[30]

Among these symbols are to be found Zapata's white horse, Che's beret, Sandino's hat, Ho's pith helmet, bamboo walking stick and wispy beard, Cabral's knit cap. Selbin asks of the future: "Will they wear Che t-shirts in Algiers as they did in Teheran in 1979? 'See' Zapata's horse in Havana as some did in Nicaragua? Sing the 'Internationale' or perhaps even air the 'Marseillaise' in Jakarta?"[31] The answers to such questions will suggest the ways in which the old and new might jointly make the revolutionary cultures of the future.

Noting that the new technologies of web and e-mail are a contested terrain, Doug Kellner urges radical democratic activists to look to its possibilities for resistance and the advancement of political education, action and organization, while engaging in struggles over the digital divide . . . If forces struggling for democratization and social justice want to become players in the cultural and political battles of the future, they must devise ways to use new technologies to advance a radical democratic and ecological agenda and the interests of the oppressed.[32]

Cyberculture, then, also presents itself as one of the tools of the revolutionary political cultures of the future, at once a form of organization and a venue for exercising agency and subjectivity. Moreover, as Noel Parker notes, there is an important connection between the trend toward global inequality and its mediation by new technologies: "there is plenty of evidence that inequalities of wealth and of power become both more marked and, through the effects of global communication, more *visible* under conditions of globalization."[33]

In my own view, the most revolutionary cultures of the future will repose on a magical mixture of realism and utopianism, guaranteed by radically democratic forms of decision making; I will say more about this in the last section of this conclusion.

An aside on September 11: the crisis every/no one was waiting for . . .

The world-system has changed dramatically as well: we now live in an era doubly marked by the processes of globalization and the events of September 11, 2001.[34] The world presently faces one of its most acute crises in the memory of anyone now living. This is hardly a controversial statement, but it is a surprising state of affairs from the point of view of September 10, 2001, or November 1, 2000. The coming to power of the Bush administration through a highly questionable electoral victory set the tone for what can now be seen as one of the most dangerous moments for the people of Iraq, Afghanistan, Syria, Iran, Saudi Arabia, Colombia, Cuba, El Salvador, Brazil, Haiti, Venezuela, North and South Korea, or Israel/Palestine – among many others – and the planet's population as a whole, not to mention the people of the United States itself. The attack on the World Trade Center and the Pentagon on September 11, 2001 permitted the imposition of an extremist, aggressive foreign policy (even by the standards we have seen in this book), aimed at making and unmaking governments in the Middle East and potentially far beyond. The policy is not only dangerous for the world's citizens but it is also risky for US and other elites, the project of neoliberal globalization that enlightened transnational capitalists are engaged in, and, as is becoming increasingly apparent, for the Bush administration itself. This is *in addition to* the existing and increasingly acute evils of world poverty and hunger, ecological suicide, social and state violence against women and populations of color, the erosion of welfare states and democratic rights, and other pressing problems of the age of US-led corporate globalization. The central questions of our time may well be: *How* did this state of affairs come to pass? *Where* is it heading? And, most importantly, what can be *done* about it?

The Bush administration early on determined that the militaristic model of such right-wing ideologues as those in the neo-conservative Project for a New American Century was the best way to assert hegemony over the world. The terrorist attacks of September 11 – like Saddam Hussain's invasion of Kuwait a decade earlier – provided the administration with an opportunity to project its new but unstated foreign policy agenda onto the crisis. Plans to attack Iraq predated September 11, and came out into public view within hours of the attack.[35] September 11 also conveniently dealt with the end of the cold war: new enemies would be constantly found or created in the Muslim world and elsewhere; these are wars that can be won (if only on the battlefield); and this justifies an ever more massive military budget. This vicious cycle is calculated to block any move toward a less militarized society or what activists a decade ago termed a peace dividend: cutting defense spending because the cold war is over, and using the savings for reactivation of the economy and solving pressing social problems at home, and perhaps even more significantly – if we are truly concerned about eliminating the economic causes at the root of terrorism – abroad. In fact, it has allowed the large steps toward an authoritarian police state taken by US Attorney General John Ashcroft and the so-called Patriot Act, suggesting that war is also an extension of *domestic* politics.[36] Nor let us forget Tariq Ali's apt aphorism: "Economics, after all, is only a concentrated form of politics, and war a continuation of both by other means."[37] If the 1991 Gulf War, then, was based on a project of international hegemony through roll-back of the defeat suffered by US foreign policy with the Iranian revolution of 1979, the March 2003 Gulf War followed the same lines in a more extreme direction: a project of imperial hegemony through unilateral pre-emptive war abroad and manipulation of public opinion coupled with a climate designed to demonize dissent at home.

What was the Bush administration's real goal domestically? Let us speculate: militarization of society and economy, the erosion of democracy at home and abroad, an ideological and frontal assault on the global justice movement, all in the name of a chimerical pursuit of global economic, political, and moral paramountcy. The contradictions in this are

numerous and leap readily to mind: alienation of the transnational corporations and governments all over the world; further loss of global economic advantage as the US runs the risk of economic collapse under
the burden of debt and the specter of deflation; the possibility of US
and world recession becoming a global depression. In sum, the policy
increases the risk of a rather acute crisis of global capitalism.

But hegemony – even the thinly concealed (and hotly denied) imperial
version of Bush and his team – requires a measure of consent. This is
perhaps the major contradiction at the heart of the Bush administration's
goals. In Iraq itself, many parties and groups have called for a broad-based
conference to elect a transitional government, only to be rebuffed by the
first US administrator Paul Bremer, who formed instead a pliant advisory
council in late July 2003 to provide the thinnest veneer of legitimacy for
US occupation and rule.[38] One of the leaders of the Shi'ite community,
Abdul Karim al-Enzi, commented succinctly within weeks of the war's
end: "Democracy means choosing what people want, not what the West
wants."[39]

Denied the fruits of democracy, the armed guerrilla resistance to the US
occupation of Iraq only grew in 2003–4. A long-term occupation by US
military forces faces enormous difficulties, raising the question of whether
a fully-fledged counter-insurgency war will be sustainable given world
and US public opinion. Democracy comes not by replacing an internal
tyranny with an external power, but by internal and external pressure for
self-rule by all who have a stake in the country. In El Salvador, where a
bitter civil war (1980–92) was prolonged to a position of stalemate by the
US, democracy has been steadily built in the aftermath as the left agreed
to participate in an electoral struggle in exchange for democratic, social,
and civil guarantees by the elite and the military, proving that building
a democracy after a war happens when the people affected by the war
are the ones doing the building, and not those who inflicted it from the
centers of power in the first place. Related to this is the issue of democracy at home in the US, where the Bush administration's Patriot Act
has eroded civil liberties almost to breaking point, in the process equat-
ing dissent with treason: historian Eric Foner aptly asks, "If we surrender
freedom of speech in the hope that this will bring swifter victory on current
and future battlefields, who then will have won the war?"[40] The implications of all this for world-systemic openings may not be entirely clear,
but the argument will be made below that under certain circumstances,
such openings are likely to continue to occur in the future, and this
despite the election of George W. Bush to a second term on November 2,
2004.

How might the revolutions of the future have better end(ing)s?

In view of these changing realities, and given our study of the past, let us take up a final question: how might the revolutions of the future – whatever form they take – have better outcomes?[41] That is, what have we learned from the revolutionary record to date that might be of use to revolutionaries in the near to middle-run future (say, the next half century)?

Our theoretical and empirical study of the origins of Third World social revolutions suggests some of the lessons that lie hidden in the revolutionary record. Let me try stating a few in propositional terms:
- revolutions have usually been driven by economic and social inequalities caused by both the short-term and the medium-run consequences of "dependent development" – a process of aggregate growth by which a handful of the privileged have prospered, leaving the majority of the population to suffer multiple hardships
- they have typically been directed against two types of states at opposite ends of the democratic spectrum: exclusionary, personalist dictators or colonial regimes, and – more paradoxically – truly open societies where a democratic left had a fair chance in elections
- they have had a significant cultural component in the sense that no revolution has been made and sustained without a vibrant set of political cultures of resistance and opposition that found significant common ground, at least for a time
- they have occurred when the moment was favorable on the world scene – that is, when powers that would oppose revolution have been distracted, confused, or ineffective in preventing them – and when economic downturns internally have driven a critical mass within society to seek an alternative
- finally, they have always involved broad, cross-class alliances of subaltern groups, middle classes, and elites; to an increasing extent women as well as men; and to a lesser degree racial or ethnic minorities as well as majorities.

Once in power, a series of related difficulties have typically arisen, which result from the continued significance of the patterns above for revolutionary transformation:
- dependent development has deep historical roots that are recalcitrant to sustained reversal, however much the material situation of the majority can be improved in the short and medium run
- truly democratic structures have been difficult to construct following revolutions against dictators, while those revolutionaries who have

constructed democracies have been vulnerable to non-democratic opponents, internal and external
- the challenge of forging a revolutionary political culture to build a new society has generally foundered rapidly on the diversity of subcurrents that contributed to the initial victory, compounded by the structural obstacles all revolutions have faced
- few revolutions have been able to withstand the renewed counter-revolutionary attention of dominant outside powers and their regional allies
- given the above, the broad coalitions that have been so effective in making revolutions are notoriously difficult to keep together, due to divergent visions of how to remake society and unequal capacities to make their vision prevail; meanwhile women and ethnic minorities have consistently seen at best limited reversal of patriarchy and racism after revolutions.

In addition to these linked causal and outcome issues, there seem to be recurrent trade-offs or contradictions in the revolutionary record as well. For example, the participation of massive numbers runs up against the leadership's need to take decisive measures to deal with all kinds of problems once in power; this in part explains the often bloody narrowing of substantively democratic spaces even as so many previously disenfranchised members of society are gaining new rights and opportunities. When movements have been radically democratic, as in Chile and Jamaica in the early 1970s, they have had troubles articulating a program acceptable to all parties at the debates, and withstanding illegal subversion from the right. Similarly, there are a series of economic trade-offs associated with many revolutions, particularly in the Third World: impressive gains in employment, wages, health, housing, and education have after short periods been eroded by internal economic contradictions (demand-driven inflation, limited human and material resources, labor imbalances) and powerful international counter-thrusts (boycotts and embargoes on trade, equipment, loans). As if these political and economic contradictions are not daunting enough, massive external violence has often also been applied, whether covert or openly military in nature, further undermining prospects for democracy and development.

These patterned realities have produced disappointing outcomes, including authoritarian, relatively poor socialisms in Russia, China, Cuba, and Vietnam (the only revolutions to last much longer than a generation, except for Iran, where the degree of economic change has been limited); violent overthrows of revolutionaries in Guatemala, Chile, and Grenada; slow strangling of change leading to political reversals in Mexico (by 1940), Bolivia (by 1960), Manley's Jamaica and Sandinista

Nicaragua; and blocking the path to power altogether in El Salvador in the 1980s, China in 1989, and Iraq in 1991, among many other places. This is not to mention the containment of social revolution in the form of far more limited political revolutions in places like the Philippines in 1986, Zaire in 1996, and, in a different and complex way, in the Eastern European reformist capitalist revolutions and the spectacular overthrow of apartheid in South Africa. No revolutionary movement of the twentieth century has come close to delivering on the common dreams of so many of its makers: a more inclusive, participatory form of political rule; a more egalitarian, humane economic system; and a cultural atmosphere where individuals and local communities may not only reach full self-creative expression but thereby contribute unanticipated solutions to the dilemmas faced by society. Yet the past may hold other messages for the future, if we know how to read them.

What, then, *is* to be done? In the post-1989 conjuncture, it is a truism that there exists a crisis of the left. At the same time, as Forrest Colburn has argued sensibly and hopefully, it is only *after* 1989 that "A new revolutionary political culture may emerge, one that may prove more capable of fulfilling its promises."[42] The Zapatistas in particular, together with the emerging global justice movement, have offered some radically new ways of doing politics to the revolutionaries of the future. Certainly many First (and Third) World academics romanticize these cases, but the richness of Zapatista discourse, the élan of their projects and actions on the Mexican political scene, their direct and indirect impact on the emerging global justice movement, and the gender and ethnic composition of their ranks suggest the potential significance of this experiment for future attempts at change.

Javier Eloriaga, a member of the National Coordinating Commission of the FZLN (the unarmed, civil society political wing of the Zapatista movement), notes that "they say we are dreamers or fanatics. The institutional left continues to regard politics as the art of the possible. And Zapatismo doesn't. We have to do politics in a new way. You can't accept only what is possible because it will bring you into the hands of the system. This is a very difficult struggle. It is very, very difficult."[43]

Sergio Rodriguez, founding member of the FZLN (and before that, a leader in the Trotskyist Partido Revolucionario de Trabajadores), raises the issue of whether this new form of political action can be harnessed and organized, even as he speaks eloquently of its transformative power:

When the Zapatistas came to Mexico City [at the time of the National Consultation of 1999] and traveled all over the country, I remember being in the Zócalo [the central plaza] where people were saying goodbye to the Zapatistas.

There were these mothers with young people and children who accompanied the Zapatistas to the vans. I realize that there, in that moment, something was being created. I don't know what to call it. I don't know how you could organize it. I don't know how it would be expressed politically. But this relationship is more than thousands of speeches and discourse and propaganda. This is a life relationship. They lived together. They talked and spent time together. Two different communities lived together. There was a chemistry there that is impossible to break down. I think that someone would have to be totally blind or have a lot of bitterness not to see this. Luis Hernandez once said that Zapatismo is a state of being. In the beginning of the century, when the socialists and the anarchists organized clubs and strikes they said that socialism was a way of life. Zapatismo is like that too. It is a way of expressing yourself. It isn't just economic or social or political or cultural. It is that and more. Organizing it is very difficult, maybe impossible. I say that it is there. It is an underground relationship between communities. And it creates a very powerful force . . . In very few countries, there is a force that is so strong. It isn't what we dreamed of in the sixties. It isn't pure and orthodox. But I think that it is better the way that it is.[44]

Core Zapatista principles include: "mandar obedeciendo" ("to rule, obeying" – the insistence that leaders serve at the pleasure of the community and its struggle, not vice versa); "para todos todo, nada para nosotros" (for everyone, everything, nothing for ourselves); "walking at a slower pace" (i.e. the recognition that change is a long and slow process, not secured with the mere seizure of power or electoral victories); and indeed, "not aspiring to take political power."

This last raises an intriguing question for us to ponder. As the second declaration of the Lacandón jungle put it in 1994: "this revolution will not end in a new class, faction of a class, or group in power. It will end in a free and democratic space for political struggle."[45] But what does *this* mean and how is it to be done? For Subcomandante Marcos, "This democratic space will have three fundamental premises that are already historically inseparable: the democratic right of determining the dominant social project, the freedom to subscribe to one project or another, and the requirement that all projects must point the way to justice."[46] The dethroning of the ruling PRI, Mexico's seventy-year-old "perfect dictatorship," in the July 2000 elections contains many lessons, no doubt, of which one is the success of the Zapatistas in altering the political landscape of Mexico. Though too many observers see their role in this historic event as minimal, it would be hard to imagine the collapse of authoritarianism without the insurgency in Chiapas undermining the government's legitimacy. The new government of Vicente Fox immediately offered to resume negotiations, which the Zapatistas equally quickly accepted; talks soon broke down again as Mexico's two dominant conservative parties, the PRI and Fox's PAN, proved recalcitrant. The rebels thus face new challenges, but seem to me all the more well-positioned to meet them in a more democratic, or at least more fluid, political climate.

One innovative Zapatista practice is embodied in the phrase "dar su palabra" (literally, to have one's say). This refers to a dialogue in which everyone present participates, in which the value of the unique vantage point of each member of a community and the insights this affords is appreciated. It usually means taking far longer to arrive at a collective decision, but it also ensures that decisions arrived at have maximum input from the community they will affect, and (hopefully) a stronger consensus (or at least a more open sense of disagreements) behind them. As the Zapatistas put it, "In the world we want, many worlds fit."[47] Meanwhile, Mexican artist and scholar Manuel De Landa may have provided the beginnings of an answer to the daunting organizational question, again from observing Zapatista practices: he uses the term "meshworks" for self-organizing, non-hierarchical, and heterogeneous networks.[48] This is a lead worth pursuing, and it has taken shape in the United States around the anti-WTO and G-8 demonstrations in Seattle and Washington, DC, in November–December 1999 and April 2000, respectively, soon followed in the fall of 2000 in Prague and Melbourne and the summer of 2001 in Genoa – a list which has grown to include Cancún and Miami in 2003, where the World Trade Organization and the Free Trade Area of the Americas were dealt severe blows by the global justice movement. The combination of "having one's say" and organizing meshworks has an important US antecedent, the direct action movements of the 1980s that fought nuclear weapons, US intervention in Central America, and the prison industrial complex, among other issues. Their tactics of nonviolence, consensus decision-making and fluid leadership, so effective at the local level in the initial phases of radical mobilization, ran into complex difficulties when it came time to build a national-level movement encompassing diverse groups, and led to tensions at the local level within groups between old and new activists, producing leadership burnout and membership dropout.[49]

These limitations must be confronted in the future, if revolutions are to succeed. Revolutionaries may be well positioned to negotiate the problem of *levels* of struggle, as they straddle the boundary between grassroots and global conflict. This raises the question of the supposedly declining significance of the nation-state in the new global conjuncture: while its powers and competencies have certainly come under strong pressure from global financial institutions and the transnationals, it yet remains one of the most likely sites for revolutionary activity, as the terrain on which political democracy, economic development, and oppositional alliances meet and play themselves out. The new communications technologies are another contested arena linking levels, strikingly evidenced by the Zapatistas' use of both fax and the internet. The anti-globalization protests in Washington, DC in April 2001 were in part organized by a website maintained by the group A16 (April 16), for several months prior to the mobilization.[50] Whatever their potential for enhancing the repressive powers of states and corporations, such technologies also represent tools for the education of and communication among social forces from below to foster meshworks of what we might call "netizens." Deep and clear thinking about all these matters is required work for would-be revolutionaries.

Finally, under the heading of magical cultures, we arrive at the frontier of emotions to ask what do we know about the social psychology of liberation? Here, four US women, cultural producers and activists, have insights that recognize the power of this dimension of social change better than most theorists, and I am proud that the concept of political cultures of opposition includes it.[51] In *The Feminist Memoir Project*, photographer Paula Allen and playwright Eve Ensler celebrate the strength that can be drawn from this source: "Being an activist means being aware of what's happening around you as well as being in touch with your feelings about it – your rage, your sadness, your excitement, your curiosity, your feeling of helplessness, and your refusal to surrender. Being an activist means owning your desire."[52] Alice Walker writes in *Anything We Love Can Be Saved: A Writer's Activism*:

There is always a moment in any kind of struggle when one feels in full bloom. Vivid. Alive. One might be blown to bits in such a moment and still be at peace. Martin Luther King, Jr., at the mountaintop. Gandhi dying with the name of God on his lips. Sojourner Truth baring her breasts at a women's rights convention in 1851 . . . To be such a person or to witness anyone at this moment of transcendent presence is to know that what is human is linked, by a daring compassion, to what is divine. During my years of being close to people engaged in changing the world I have seen fear turn into courage. Sorrow into joy. Funerals into celebrations. Because whatever the consequences, people, standing side by side, have expressed who they really are, and that ultimately they believe in the love of the world and each other enough *to be that* – which is the foundation of activism.[53]

Poet Adrienne Rich cautions that this power, arising in individuals, must become a social, interpersonal force to realize its potential to shake the world:

When we do and think and feel certain things privately and in secret, even when thousands of people are doing, thinking, whispering these things privately and in secret, there is still no general, collective understanding from which to move. Each takes her or his own risks in isolation. We may think of ourselves as individual rebels, and individual rebels can be easily shot down. The relationship among

274   Part Four: Conclusions

so many feelings remains unclear. But these thoughts and feelings, suppressed and stored-up and whispered, have an incendiary component. You cannot tell where or how they will connect, spreading underground from rootlet to rootlet till every grass blade is afire from every other. This is that "spontaneity" that party "leaders," secret governments, and closed systems dread.[54]

The revolutionaries of the past and present have been enormously creative and expressive at critical junctures, as celebrated in the May 1968 student slogan "Power to the imagination!" While we are thankfully far from there being some new hegemonic reigning oppositional culture, the revolutionaries of the future will likely forge multiple liberatory cultures out of old and new ideas, ideals, and ideologies in the best sense.

I have suggested elsewhere that love and dreams need to be woven into the fabric of such globalized political cultures of resistance.[55] Love is arguably the emotion that most strongly underlies the vital force that impels many ordinary people into extraordinary acts, across time and place. Expressing hope and optimism, it provides a constructive counterpoint to those other powerful animating emotions, hatred and anger. Love of life, love of people, love of justice all play a role across revolutionary political cultures. This is something that the revolutionaries of the future will need to learn to nurture and build upon.

Dreams, too, can feed revolutions. In Patricio Guzmán's remarkable, powerful film, *Chile: Obstinate Memory*, the former director of public relations for Salvador Allende's Popular Unity government, ex-professor Ernesto Malbran, says:

The UP was a ship of dreamers propelled by a collective dream, which ran aground. The dream was to carry along and unite the entire country. It was a dream of justice: the right to an education, good health, and shelter. Dreams that don't come true confirm the saying: "Don't believe in dreams as they are not nourishing." That's wrong. It was a noble dream. The failure of a dream is hard to take. Especially knowing you can't progress without dreams. Because dreaming is part of the way we apprehend life.[56]

Or as "Old Antonio," the mythical Chiapan character invoked in many of Subcomandante Marcos's communiqués, sees it:

Antonio dreams that the land he works belongs to him. He dreams that his sweat earns him justice and truth; he dreams of schools that cure ignorance and medicines that frighten death. He dreams that his house has light and his table is full; he dreams that the land is free, and that his people govern themselves reasonably. He dreams that he is at peace with himself and with the world . . .

A wind comes up and everything stirs. Antonio rises, and walks to meet the others. He has heard that his desire is the desire of many, and he goes to look for them . . .

In this country everyone dreams. Now it is time to wake up.[57]

Nowhere has this power of dreams and myths been better expressed than in the marvelously poetic stories and strikingly beautiful symbolic acts of the Zapatistas.

Indeed, articulating a revolutionary economic alternative to corporate capitalism and globalization from above no longer seems such a fool's quest. Tapping the magical possibilities of a political culture of liberation might help us make further progress on this. One principle for such a political economy might be called, simply, the economics of "social justice." Recalling the principle of "para todos todo, nada para nosotros," a woman who is active in the FZLN notes:

> in the Zapatista movement, people are working for something much broader than themselves . . . for a change that will benefit everyone. I mean the Zapatistas don't have anything to hand out to people. There is no housing or powerful political positions to obtain. This isn't for your own benefit. It is a benefit for the whole country. It is for all the people who have been fucked over like the indigenous people.[58]

Social justice has been the foundation of the economic side of revolutionary political cultures the world over, assuming many local expressions – "Land and Liberty" in Mexico in the 1910s; "Bread, Land and Peace" in 1917 Russia; "Equality," from 1789 France to 1990s' South Africa; "Socialism with a Human Face" in 1968 Czechoslovakia; "a preferential option for the poor" in the 1970s' language of liberation theology in Central America; "Dignity" in Chiapas, and "Fair Trade" and "Democracy" in Seattle. Thus, defining what it means must be specific to particular times and places, but inventorying these and assessing what common meanings social justice has had across cases is a project of some urgency for activists and scholars of revolution, an important task some of us might want to pursue.

A second need is that of protecting revolutions in a hostile world-system. The impact of the new global conjuncture is difficult to fully grasp, but it is far from uniformly dampening. The end of the cold war may in fact have opened up opportunities for revolutionaries to operate if the other four factors are in place, precisely because the countries in question can no longer be treated as pawns in a larger geo-political struggle between the United States and the Soviet Union. Democratic revolutionaries and non-violent movements in particular may find new spaces in which to maneuver. The post-September 11 US invasion of Iraq, its massive military budget, its pursuit of an obscenely expensive and chimerical space missile "defense" system, its 2004 intervention in Haiti, and much more suggest that the imperial grand intent remains intact, but at the same time it alienates allies as well as would-be adversaries, and may indicate a greater willingness for easy symbolic expressions of global power than any real ability to effectively halt local rebellions as they arise (neither the Taliban nor Saddam Hussain fit the requirements of being democratic, non-violent, *or* revolutionary challenges to global capitalism). The disarray of all leading First World nations in the face of imaginative anti-globalization protests since 1999 may also portend the limits of US power. The danger, of course, is that in the new counter-revolutionary discourse of US power, the term "terrorist" has become a proxy for "communist" in a new post-cold war world, now to be aimed at the real targets – national and global revolutionaries. Susan George warns of the "faulty but sometimes effective logic" of "You're antiglobalization, therefore you're anti-American, therefore you're on the side of the terrorists."[59] On all of this much more might be said, and I may well be wrong to discern openings here; my point is that the actions of the revolutionaries of the near-term future will surely influence the degree and type of interventions they face.

One obvious way forward would be to build on the lessons of the radically democratic revolutions of the past. In counterpoint to Jeff Goodwin's insight that "The ballot box is the coffin of revolutionaries,"[60] democracy in its many forms may become one of the best weapons of the revolutionaries of the future. Though May 68, Allende, Tienanmen, Mussadiq, Arbenz, and Manley all experienced defeat, they gave us a form that the radical reformers and revolutionaries of today in Chiapas, Iran, Uruguay, South Africa, El Salvador, Brazil, Venezuela, and beyond are already imaginatively appropriating and trying to deepen. Among these movements are to be found new goals, tactics, and coalitional possibilities as well as anti-hierarchical and creative political cultures, a sort of message to the future. All such democratic revolutionary movements can yield valuable lessons in fighting a *structure*, harder as this is than overthrowing a dictator. Out of the ashes of past failures may yet grow the seeds of future breakthroughs to a new world.

By way of concluding thoughts

"Magical realism" then is a poetic way of referring to and relying on the immense creative potential of people the world over to fashion what Perry Anderson once called a "concrete utopianism," or what David Harvey has named a "dialectical utopianism" and Daniel Singer a "realistic utopianism."[61] That this must be more socially inclusive than it ever has been in the past seems crucial, as FMLN representative and former guerrilla Lorena Peña puts it in the Salvadoran context: "A proposal of the left that doesn't integrate the elements of class, gender and race, is not viable or objective, and it doesn't go to the root of our problems."[62] That it must somehow also prove capable of forging strong and imaginative consensus agreements around complex, cross-cutting issues makes the task even more formidable. The proper response to the pessimists of the dispirited acronym TINA – "There is no alternative" – is, of course, TATA: "There are thousands of alternatives!"[63] It appears to me that only a radically deepened process of democratic participation can realize this promise, informing magical political cultures, making visible an economics of social justice, and (just maybe) disarming the US and other global interventionist forces.

We end, then, with a new set of paradoxes and challenges:
• to find a language capable of uniting diverse forces and allowing their not necessarily mutually compatible desires full expression
• to find organizational forms capable of nurturing this expression and debate as well as enabling decisive action when needed, both locally and across borders
• to articulate an economic alternative to neoliberalism and capitalism that can sustain itself against the systemic weight of the past and the pervasive and hostile reach of the present global economic system
• and to make all this happen, in many places and at different levels (local, national, "global") over time, working with both the deep strengths and frailties of the experiences and emotions of human liberation.

In negotiating the contradictory currents of the future, we must somehow be magical as well as realistic, finding a path marked by pleasures as well as perils.

The new conditions of globalization call forth new versions of the broad alliances that have made revolutions in the past. The neo-conservative dream of the US becoming the world's sole power in the post-cold war is increasingly being countered by the growing strength of "the other superpower" – the global justice movement for peace, economic justice, and real equality bubbling up from below, so extraordinarily impressive world-wide and in the US. It showed that it has support all over the world on February 15, 2003 when millions of people came together in public. It struck another strong blow at the WTO's Ministerial Meetings in Cancun that September, and again at the FTAA deliberations in Miami in December. It celebrated its diversity and growing numbers at the 2004 World Social Forum in Bombay, India. As Kevin Danaher and Roger Burbach suggest:

If we look closely we can see the pieces of the first global revolution being put together. Every revolution up until now has been a national revolution, aimed at seizing control of a national government. But the blatant corporate bias of global rule-making institutions such as the IMF, World Bank and WTO have forced the grassroots democracy movement to start planning a global revolution. It is a revolution in values as well as institutions. It seeks to replace the money values of the current system with the life values of a truly democratic system.[64]

The end of the cold war has an upside for progressive movements that activists and scholars are increasingly aware of. Another world *is* possible, as the global justice movement likes to say. Let us accept the invitation of Joe Feagin and Hernán Vera to practice what they call "liberation sociology," or of Michael Burawoy, to do a more "public sociology" aimed at multiple potential publics, from "media audiences to policy makers, from think tanks to NGOs, from silenced minorities to social movements."[65] As Carlos Vilas put it, "Political success, for both insurgencies and governments, is a contingency, and contingency, as Commander Ruiz's *magia*, has to be tirelessly worked out. Then it may, or may not, show up."[66]

If we cannot know the future, it becomes all the more incumbent to speculate as fully as we can about its possibilities. For, as Eduardo Galeano has concluded: "If we can't guess what's coming, at least we have the right to imagine the future we want."[67] Where we are today, and where we may be going, is not the same place. At least, it need not be, and will not be, if enough people refuse to accept it.

The jury on the potential of democratic revolutions is still out, since the final verdict of history cannot be rendered until the end of history, a vanishing horizon. I prefer to wager on a belief in the openness of historical processes, past, present, and future: *que viva la revolución!*

Notes

INTRODUCTION

1. Jeff Goodwin, *No Other Way Out: States and Revolutionary Movements, 1945–1991* (Cambridge University Press, 1999), from the preface.
2. Theda Skocpol, *States and Social Revolutions: A Comparative Analysis of France, Russia, and China* (Cambridge University Press, 1979), xi.

CHAPTER 1

1. Barrington Moore, Jr., *Social Origins of Dictatorship and Democracy: Lord and Peasant in the Making of the Modern World* (Boston: Beacon Press, 1966), 427.
2. Alberto Flores Galindo, "Peru: a self-critical farewell," pp. 8–10 in *NACLA Report on the Americas*, volume xxiv, number 5 (February 1991), 9.
3. Alexis de Tocqueville, *The Old Regime and the French Revolution*, translated by Stuart Gilbert (Garden City, New York: Doubleday & Company, Inc., 1955 [1856]), 1.
4. For a discussion of the term's history and a number of definitions, see Ekkart Zimmermann, *Political Violence, Crises, and Revolutions: Theories and Research* (Boston: G. K. Hall & Co., 1983), 294–8.
5. Samuel P. Huntington, *Political Order in Changing Societies* (New Haven: Yale University Press, 1968), 264; see also idem, "Civil violence and the process of development," pp. 1–15 in *Adelphi Papers*, volume 83 (1971), 5.
6. Skocpol, *States and Social Revolutions*, 4–5.
7. Leon Trotsky, *The Russian Revolution: The Overthrow of Tzarism and the Triumph of the Soviets*, selected and edited by F. W. Dupree (Garden City: Doubleday & Company, Inc., 1959 [1930]), ix–x.
8. Not considered here, mainly for reasons of time, are social revolutions in Eritrea and Cape Verde/Guinea Bissau, a reversed revolution in Patrice Lumumba's Congo in 1960–61, the enduring struggle for Palestinian statehood, or the Maoist insurgency in Nepal.
9. I am largely following Jack Goldstone's classifications in "Theories of revolution: the third generation," pp. 425–53 in *World Politics*, volume xxxii, number 3 (April 1980), and "The comparative and historical study of revolutions," pp. 187–207 in *Annual Review of Sociology*, volume 8 (1982). Except where they impinge on or otherwise inform social science theories, I here omit discussion of the ideas of revolutionaries themselves, although Marx, Lenin, and Trotsky among others anticipated much in the theories discussed, as did

the non-revolutionary observer de Tocqueville. A blueprint of how to make a revolution is not the same thing as a theory of how revolutions actually occur, despite significant overlap and borrowing, and despite the importance of revolutionary ideas among the causes of social change.

10. On these points see Goldstone, "The comparative and historical study," 189–92. On the degree to which Edwards noted much of the above, see Zimmermann, *Political Violence*, 357. That de Tocqueville was an influential precursor, consider his object – "to bring together some of those aspects of the old regime . . . and to show how the Revolution was their *natural*, indeed inevitable, outcome": *The Old Regime*, 203, emphasis added.

11. See Rod Aya, "Theories of revolution reconsidered: contrasting models of collective violence," pp. 39–99 in *Theory and Society*, volume 8, number 1 (July 1979), 49.

12. Goldstone, "The comparative and historical study," 192–3, summarizing James C. Davies, "Toward a theory of revolution," pp. 5–19 in *American Sociological Review*, volume 27 (1962). Ted Robert Gurr's main relevant work is *Why Men Rebel* (Princeton University Press, 1970). Here again de Tocqueville is a precursor with a theory of rising prosperity and frustrated expectations as a root cause of the French Revolution: *The Old Regime*, 171–7.

13. This model has been taken up by James Rinehart in *Revolution and the Millennium: China, Mexico, Iran* (Westport: Praeger, 1997). At a certain level of abstraction it is not so distant from my own perspective.

14. James C. Davies, "The circumstances and causes of revolution: a review," pp. 247–57 in *Journal of Conflict Resolution*, volume 11, number 2 (June 1967), 253. For other critiques, see Aya, "Theories of revolution reconsidered," and Goldstone, "Theories of revolution," 431–4.

15. Goldstone, "The comparative and historical study," 193. This is Skocpol's objection to them as well in *States and Social Revolutions*.

16. See de Tocqueville, *The Old Regime*, 8–9, 13, 26–32, 204–8.

17. Moore, *Social Origins of Dictatorship and Democracy*, 459, 468, 479.

18. Ian Roxborough, *Theories of Underdevelopment* (London: Macmillan, 1979), 95.

19. Eric R. Wolf, *Peasant Wars of the Twentieth Century* (New York: Harper Colophon Books, 1969), 279–301.

20. Jeffery M. Paige, *Agrarian Revolution: Social Movements and Export Agriculture in the Underdeveloped World* (New York: Free Press, 1975). For critiques, see Arne Disch, "Peasants and revolts," pp. 243–52 in *Theory and Society*, volume 7 (January–May 1979), and Margaret R. Somers and Walter L. Goldfrank, "The limits of agronomic determinism: a critique of Paige's agrarian revolution," pp. 443–58 in *Comparative Studies in Society and History*, volume 21, number 3 (July 1979).

21. Skocpol, *States and Social Revolutions*, 17–18.

22. Ibid., 292. Interestingly, Trotsky foreshadows these concerns: "In the historic conditions which formed Russia, her economy, her classes, her State, in the action upon her of other states, we ought to be able to find the premises both of the February revolution and of the October revolution which replaced it": *The Russian Revolution*, xii.

23. Skocpol, *States and Social Revolutions*, 162–3.
24. Michael Taylor, "Structure, culture and action in the explanation of social change," pp. 115–62 in *Politics and Society*, volume 17, number 2 (June 1989), 121.
25. Skocpol, *States and Social Revolutions*, 235. See also 112–13, 172.
26. Ibid., 170.
27. See ibid., 78, 163, 187.
28. Skocpol acknowledges Tilly, along with Marx, as the most important of her models: *States and Social Revolutions*, 13–14.
29. Charles Tilly, *From Mobilization to Revolution* (Reading: Addison-Wesley, 1978).
30. Charles Tilly, "Does modernization breed revolt?" pp. 425–47 in *Comparative Politics*, volume 5 (1973), 447.
31. For influential statements, see Doug McAdam, John D. McCarthy, and Mayer Zald, editors, *Comparative Perspectives on Social Movements* (Cambridge University Press, 1996); and Doug McAdam, Sidney Tarrow, and Charles Tilly, "To map contentious politics," pp. 17–34 in *Mobilization*, volume 1, number 1 (1996). For incisive critiques, see Jeff Goodwin and James M. Jasper, "Caught in a winding, snarling vine: the structural bias of political process theory," pp. 27–54 in *Sociological Forum*, volume 14, number 1 (1999), and Jeff Goodwin and James M. Jasper, editors, *Rethinking Social Movements: Structure, Meaning, and Emotion* (Lanham: Rowman and Littlefield, 2003).
32. Skocpol, *States and Social Revolutions*, 17. She argues further, polemically, that "Revolutions are not made; they come": ibid. But why not both? In fact she hints at this in a footnote: "the idea of *conjuncture* – implying the coming together of separately determined and not consciously coordinated (or deliberately revolutionary) processes and group efforts – seems a more useful perspective on the causes of social revolution than does the idea of intergroup coalition": ibid., 298 note 44.
33. Teodor Shanin, *The Roots of Otherness: Russia's Turn of the Century*, volume II: *Russia, 1905–07: Revolution as a Moment of Truth* (New Haven: Yale University Press, 1986), 30–1.
34. Trotsky, *The Russian Revolution*, 249. Trotsky seems to consider agency and structure as coequally important: "The dynamic of revolutionary events is directly determined by swift, intense and passionate changes in the psychology of classes which have already formed themselves before the revolution," yet on the other hand, "Entirely exceptional circumstances, independent of the will of persons or parties, are necessary in order to tear off from discontent the fetters of conservatism, and bring the masses to insurrection": ibid., x. In an apposite metaphor on the relationship between spontaneity and organization, leaders and masses, he writes: "Without a guiding organization the energy of the masses would dissipate like steam not enclosed in a piston-box. But nevertheless what moves things is not the piston or the box, but the steam": ibid., xi.
35. Taylor, "Structure, culture and action," 117.
36. See, for example Mustafa Rejai, *The Strategy of Political Revolution* (New York: Doubleday, 1973), 33–4; S. N. Eisenstadt, *Revolution and the Transformation*

of Societies: A Comparative Study of Civilizations (New York: Free Press, 1978);
Ann Swidler, "Culture in action: symbols and strategies," pp. 273–86 in
American Sociological Review, volume 51, number 2 (April 1986); Robert
Darnton, "What was revolutionary about the French revolution?" pp. 3–
10 in *The New York Review of Books* (January 19, 1989), and his other
works; George Rudé, *Revolutionary Europe 1783–1815* (London: Fontana,
1973 [1964]), 74; Christopher Hill, *Intellectual Origins of the English Revolution* (Oxford: The Clarendon Press, 1965); William H. Sewell, Jr., "Ideologies
and social revolutions: reflections on the French case," pp. 57–85 in *Journal
of Modern History*, volume 57, number 1 (March 1985), along with Theda
Skocpol's rejoinder, which follows this article; Lynn Hunt, *Politics, Culture,
and Class in the French Revolution* (Berkeley: University of California Press,
1984); Farideh Farhi, *States and Urban-Based Revolutions: Iran and Nicaragua*
(Urbana: University of Illinois Press, 1990); Jack A. Goldstone, *Revolution
and Rebellion in the Early Modern World* (Berkeley: University of California
Press, 1991); Tim McDaniel, *Autocracy, Modernization, and Revolution in
Russia and Iran* (Princeton University Press, 1991); Forrest Colburn, *The
Vogue of Revolutions in Poor Countries* (Princeton University Press, 1994); and
Mark Gould, *Revolution in the Development of Capitalism: The Coming of the
English Revolution* (Berkeley: University of California Press, 1987).

37. Gould, *Revolution in the Development of Capitalism*, 285, following Lawrence
Stone, *The Causes of the English Revolution 1529–1642* (New York: Harper &
Row Publishers, 1972), 100ff.

38. James C. Scott, *The Moral Economy of the Peasant: Rebellion and Subsistence in
Southeast Asia* (New Haven: Yale University Press, 1976).

39. Tilly, *From Mobilization to Revolution*, 151–9, 224–5. See also Craig Jackson
Calhoun, "The radicalism of tradition: community strength or venerable disguise and borrowed language?" pp. 886–914 *in American Journal of Sociology*,
volume 88, number 5 (March 1983).

40. Eric Selbin, "Revolution in the real world: bringing agency back in," pp. 123–
36 in John Foran, editor, *Theorizing Revolutions* (London: Routledge, 1997).

41. Crane Brinton, *The Anatomy of Revolution* (New York: Prentice-Hall, Inc.,
1952 [1938]), 42–53; Wolf, *Peasant Wars*, 282–3.

42. Michel Foucault, *Power/Knowledge* (New York: Pantheon, 1980), 119.

43. For a sense of the new ways of looking at the state and politics through a
cultural lens, see Gilbert M. Joseph and Daniel Nugent, editors, *Everyday
Forms of State Formation: Revolution and the Negotiation of Rule in Modern
Mexico* (Durham: Duke University Press, 1994), and James C. Scott, *Seeing
Like a State: How Certain Schemes to Improve the Human Condition Have Failed*
(New Haven: Yale University Press, 1999).

44. Skocpol, *States and Social Revolutions*, 112–13.

45. See hints in Goldstone, "The comparative and historical study," 200, and the
more developed arguments in Robert H. Dix, "Why revolutions succeed and
fail," pp. 423–46 in *Polity*, volume 16, number 3 (Summer 1984), as well as a
descriptive overview in Josef Gugler, "The urban character of contemporary
revolutions," pp. 399–412 in Josef Gugler, editor, *The Urbanization of the
Third World* (Oxford University Press, 1988).

46. On coalitions, see Gould, *Revolution in the Development of Capitalism*, 364; Wolf, *Peasant Wars*, 289, 294; and John Foran, "The strengths and weaknesses of Iran's populist alliance: a class analysis of the constitutional revolution of 1905–1911," pp. 795–823 in *Theory and Society*, volume 20, number 6 (1991).
47. See John Foran, "Studying revolutions through the prism of gender, race, and class: notes toward a framework," pp. 117–41 in *Race, Gender & Class*, volume VIII, number 2 (2001), and the sources cited therein. Regional aspects of particular revolutions have been noted by, among others, Walter L. Goldfrank, "Theories of revolution and revolution without theory: the case of Mexico," pp. 135–65 in *Theory and Society*, volume 7 (1979); William Brustein, "Regional social orders in France and the French revolution," pp. 145–61 in *Comparative Social Research*, volume 9 (Greenwich: JAI Press, 1986); and Timothy P. Wickham-Crowley, *Guerrillas and Revolution in Latin America: A Comparative Study of Insurgents and Regimes Since 1956* (Princeton University Press, 1992).
48. Huntington, *Political Order in Changing Societies*, 266–7, with the list of cases extended beyond the 1960s by Matthew Soberg Shugart, "Patterns of revolution," pp. 249–71 in *Theory and Society*, volume 18, number 2 (March 1989), 252. See also the comments of Zimmermann, *Political Violence*, 320, 558 note 113.
49. Robert H. Dix, "The varieties of revolution," pp. 281–94 in *Comparative Politics*, volume 15, number 3 (April 1983).
50. Theda Skocpol, "Analyzing causal configurations in history: a rejoinder to Nichols," pp. 187–94, *Comparative Social Research*, volume IX (Greenwich: JAI Press, 1986), 191.
51. Goodwin, *No Other Way Out*.
52. Ian Roxborough, "Theories of revolution: the evidence from Latin America," pp. 99–121 in *LSE (London School of Economics) Quarterly*, volume 3, number 2 (Summer 1989), and "Exogenous factors in the genesis of revolutions in Latin America," paper delivered at the annual meeting of the Latin American Studies Association, Miami (December 1989).
53. Goldfrank, "Theories of revolution," 148.
54. John Walton, *Reluctant Rebels: Comparative Studies of Revolution and Underdevelopment* (New York: Columbia University Press, 1984).
55. Farideh Farhi, "State disintegration and urban-based revolutionary crisis: a comparative analysis of Iran and Nicaragua," pp. 231–56 *in Comparative Political Studies*, volume 21, number 2 (July 1988), and *States and Urban-Based Revolutions*.
56. James DeFronzo, *Revolutions and Revolutionary Movements* (Boulder, CO: Westview Press, 1991), 10.
57. Misagh Parsa, *States, Ideologies, and Social Revolutions: A Comparative Analysis of Iran, Nicaragua and the Philippines* (Cambridge University Press, 2000).
58. Goldstone, *Revolution and Rebellion in the Early Modern World*, and Goodwin, *No Other Way Out*. See also Jeff Goodwin and Theda Skocpol, "Explaining revolutions in the contemporary Third World," pp. 489–509 in *Politics & Society*, volume 17, number 4 (December 1989), and Jack A. Goldstone, Ted

Robert Gurr, and Farrokh Moshiri, editors, *Revolutions of the Late Twentieth Century* (Boulder, CO: Westview Press, 1991).

59. Eric Selbin, *Modern Latin American Social Revolutions*, second edition (Boulder, CO: Westview Press, 1999).

60. Wickham-Crowley, *Guerrillas and Revolution in Latin America.*

61. For further critical evaluation of much of this work, see John Foran, "Theories of revolution revisited: toward a Fourth Generation?" pp. 1–20 in *Sociological Theory*, volume 11, number 1 (March 1993) and "Revolutionizing theory/revising revolution: state, culture, and society in recent works on revolution," pp. 65–88 in *Contention: Debates in Society, Culture and Science*, volume 2, number 2 (Winter 1993), as well as Jeff Goodwin, "Toward a new sociology of revolution," pp. 731–66 in *Theory and Society*, volume 23, number 6 (1994), and Jack A. Goldstone, "Toward a fourth generation of revolutionary theory," pp. 139–87 in *Annual Review of Political Science*, volume 4 (2001).

62. This model was first elaborated in my case study of Iran, *Fragile Resistance: Social Transformation in Iran from 1500 to the Revolution* (Boulder, CO: Westview Press, 1993), and subsequently developed in several of the comparative essays that the present book builds on: "A theory of Third World social revolutions: Iran, Nicaragua, and El Salvador compared," pp. 3–27 in *Critical Sociology*, volume 19, number 2 (1992); "The causes of Latin American social revolutions: searching for patterns in Mexico, Cuba, and Nicaragua," pp. 209–44 in Peter Lengyel and Volker Bornschier, editors, *World Society Studies*, volume III: *Conflicts and New Departures in World Society* (New Brunswick: Transaction Publishers, 1994); "The future of revolutions at the fin-de-siècle," pp. 791–820 in *Third World Quarterly*, volume 18, number 5 (1997); and "The comparative-historical sociology of Third World social revolutions: why a few succeed, why most fail," pp. 227–67 in John Foran, editor, *Theorizing Revolutions* (London and New York: Routledge, 1997).

63. His major works are Immanuel Wallerstein, *The Modern World-System I: Capitalist Agriculture and the Origins of the European World-Economy in the Sixteenth Century* (New York: Academic Press, 1974); *The Capitalist World Economy: Selected Essays* (Cambridge University Press, 1979); *The Modern World-System II: Mercantilism and the Consolidation of the European World-Economy, 1600–1750* (New York: Academic Press, 1980); and *The Modern World-System III: The Second Era of Great Expansion of the Capitalist World-Economy: 1730–1840s* (New York: Academic Press, 1989).

64. On modes of production in development studies, see Aidan Foster-Carter, "The modes of production controversy," pp. 47–77 in *New Left Review*, number 107 (January–February 1978), and John G. Taylor, *From Modernization to Modes of Production: A Critique of the Sociologies of Development and Underdevelopment* (London: Macmillan, 1979).

65. On dependent development, see Fernando Henrique Cardoso and Enzo Faletto, *Dependency and Development in Latin America* (Berkeley, CA: University of California Press, 1979), and Peter Evans, *Dependent Development: The Alliance of Multinational, State, and Local Capital in Brazil* (Princeton University Press, 1979).

66. Andre Gunder Frank, *Latin America: Underdevelopment or Revolution* (New York: Monthly Review Press, 1969).
67. The notion of types or dimensions of dependency is found in Roxborough, "Theories of revolution," 111, and "Exogenous factors," 4.
68. The vulnerabilities of this type of state are now widely agreed upon in the literature on revolutions; all that varies is the terminology used to characterize it. Thus, in Wickham-Crowley's colorful language, it is a "mafiacracy," for Farhi, a "personalist authoritarian" regime, for Goldstone, a "neopatrimonial" state, for Shugart, a "sultanistic regime." Robert Dix probably first identified the weaknesses of this type of state. See Wickham-Crowley, *Guerrillas and Revolution in Latin America*, 9; Farhi, *States and Urban-Based Revolutions*; Jack A. Goldstone, "Revolutions and superpowers," pp. 35–48 in J. R. Adelman, editor, *Superpowers and Revolutions* (New York: Praeger, 1986); Shugart, "Patterns of revolution;" and Dix, "Why revolutions succeed and fail."
69. El Salvador in the 1980s is a good example of the durability of such a regime: see Timothy P. Wickham-Crowley, "Understanding failed revolution in El Salvador: a comparative analysis of regime types and social structures," pp. 511–37 in *Politics & Society*, volume 17, number 4 (December 1989), and Manus I. Midlarsky and Kenneth Roberts, "Class, state, and revolution in Central America: Nicaragua and El Salvador compared," pp. 163–93 in *Journal of Conflict Resolution*, volume 29, number 2 (June 1985), for an early typology along similar lines.
70. William I. Robinson, *Promoting Polyarchy: Globalization, US Intervention, and Hegemony* (Cambridge University Press, 1996).
71. Foran, *Fragile Resistance*, and "Discourses and social forces: the role of culture and cultural studies in understanding revolutions," pp. 203–26 in John Foran, editor, *Theorizing Revolutions* (London: Routledge, 1997). This concept draws on the work of A. Sivanandan, James Scott, Farideh Farhi, Stuart Hall, Ann Swidler, Raymond Williams, Clifford Geertz, E. P. Thompson, and Antonio Gramsci, among many others. See Farhi, *States and Urban-Based Revolutions*; Clifford Geertz, *The Interpretation of Culture* (New York: Basic Books, 1973); Antonio Gramsci, *Selections from the Prison Notebooks* (New York: International, 1971); Stuart Hall, "Politics and ideology: Gramsci," pp. 45–76 in Stuart Hall, Bob Lumley, and Gregor McLennan, editors, *On Ideology* (London: Hutchinson, 1978), "Marxism and culture," pp. 5–14 in *Radical History Review*, volume 18 (1978), and "The problem of ideology: Marxism without guarantees," pp. 28–44 in *Journal of Communication Inquiry*, volume 10, number 2 (1986); James C. Scott, *Domination and the Arts of Resistance: Hidden Transcripts* (New Haven: Yale University Press, 1990); A. Sivanandan, "Imperialism in the silicon age," pp. 24–42 in *Monthly Review*, volume 32, number 3 (July–August 1980), first published in *Race and Class* (Autumn 1979); Swidler, "Culture in action"; E. P. Thompson, *The Making of the English Working Class* (New York: Vintage Books, 1966 [1963]); and Raymond Williams, *Culture and Society, 1780–1950* (New York: Columbia University Press, 1960). I first coined the term in my master's thesis: John Foran, "Dependency and social change

in Iran, 1501–1925," Department of Sociology, University of California, Santa Barbara (1981).

72. See Sewell, "Ideologies and social revolutions," and Theda Skocpol, "Cultural idioms and political ideologies in the revolutionary reconstruction of state power: a rejoinder to Sewell," pp. 86–96 in *Journal of Modern History*, volume 57, number 1.

73. This diagram was first presented in Foran, "Discourses and social forces," 219, and the concept is developed further in Jean-Pierre Reed and John Foran, "Political cultures of opposition: exploring idioms, ideologies, and revolutionary agency in the case of Nicaragua," pp. 335–70 in *Critical Sociology*, volume 28, number 3 (October 2002).

74. Foran, *Fragile Resistance*.

75. Zimmermann, *Political Violence*, referring to Chalmers Johnson, *Revolutionary Change* (Boston: Little, Brown, 1966), 112, and Mark N. Hagopian, *The Phenomenon of Revolution* (New York: Dodd, Mead, 1974), 166. See also the careful work of Jean-Pierre Reed in Chapter Two of his PhD dissertation, "Revolutionary subjectivity: the cultural logic of the Nicaraguan revolution," Department of Sociology, University of California, Santa Barbara (2000).

76. On Iran, for example, see Mansoor Moaddel, *Class, Politics, and Ideology in the Iranian Revolution* (New York: Columbia University Press, 1993). The proponents of the downturn as a factor are de Tocqueville, *The Old Regime*, and Davies, "Toward a theory of revolution."

77. Cynthia McClintock, *Revolutionary Movements in Latin America: El Salvador's FMLN and Peru's Shining Path* (Washington: United States Institute of Peace Press, 1998), 29. Thanks to Eric Selbin for pointing out this quote.

78. This idea was pioneered by Goldfrank, "Theories of revolution and revolution without theory," who refers to it as a "permissive world context." It loosely parallels or turns somewhat on its head Skocpol's argument that international *pressures* were the cause of revolution in the case of the powerful agrarian empires she studied, since it can take the form of pressure by a core power on a Third World state.

79. Skocpol, *States and Social Revolutions*, 280.

80. Charles C. Ragin, *The Comparative Method: Moving Beyond Qualitative and Quantitative Strategies* (Berkeley: University of California Press, 1987), 25.

81. Cf. what Gould, following Smelser, calls a "value-added" model: Gould, *Revolution in the Development of Capitalism*, 69; Neil Smelser, *Theory of Collective Behavior* (New York: The Free Press, 1962).

82. Jon Elster, *Logic and Society: Contradictions and Possible Worlds* (New York: Wiley, 1978), cited by Adam Przeworski, "Some problems in the study of the transition to democracy," pp. 47–63 in Guillermo O'Donnell, Philippe C. Schmitter, and Laurence Whitehead, editors, *Transitions from Authoritarian Rule: Comparative Perspectives* (Baltimore: The Johns Hopkins University Press, 1986), 49.

83. This procedure bears some similarity to what Dietrich Rueschemeyer refers to as "analytic induction" – "a theoretical framework guides a case-by-case analysis in which explanatory propositions are developed, tested, extended, and modified": Dietrich Rueschemeyer, "Review of Michael W. Doyle,

Empires (Ithaca: Cornell University Press, 1986)," pp. 306–7 in *Contemporary Sociology*, volume 17, number 3 (May 1988), 306. See also Skocpol's comments on comparative-historical analysis in *States and Social Revolutions*, 39–40, or Glaser and Strauss's notion of "grounded theory": Barney G. Glaser and Anselm L. Strauss, *Discovery of Grounded Theory: Strategies for Qualitative Research* (Chicago: Aldine Publishing Company, 1967).

84. Ragin, *The Comparative Method*.

85. Ragin has more recently advocated a different approach to this problem in *Fuzzy-Set Social Science* (University of Chicago Press, 2000).

86. Skocpol, *States and Social Revolutions*, 5, 36. Cf. Zimmermann: "In many respects revolutions appear to be a subject too complex to be handled in plain quantitative analysis": *Political Violence*, 405.

87. Skocpol, *States and Social Revolutions*, 36. See the critical discussions of Skocpol's method in Elizabeth Nichols, "Skocpol on revolutions: comparative analysis vs. historical conjuncture," pp. 163–86 in *Comparative Social Research*, edited by Richard F. Thomasson (Greenwich: JAI Press, 1986), Michael Burawoy, "Two methods in search of science: Skocpol versus Trotsky," pp. 759–805 in *Theory and Society*, volume 18, number 6 (November 1989), and William H. Sewell, Jr., "Three temporalities: toward an eventful sociology," pp. 245–80 in Terrence J. McDonald, editor, *The Historic Turn in the Human Sciences* (Ann Arbor: University of Michigan Press, 1996), as well as Skocpol's rather acerbic rejoinders: "Analyzing causal configurations in history: a rejoinder to Nichols," pp. 187–94 *Comparative Social Research*, edited by Richard F. Thomasson (Greenwich, CT: JAI Press, 1986), and "Reflections on recent scholarship about social revolutions and how to study them," pp. 302–44 of Theda Skocpol, *Social Revolutions in the Modern World* (Cambridge University Press, 1994).

88. Skocpol, *States and Social Revolutions*, 23–4, citing Wolfram Eberhard, "Problems of historical sociology," in Reinhard Bendix et al., editors, *State and Society: A Reader* (Berkeley: University of California Press, 1973), 25–8. See Burawoy's trenchant critique of the way Skocpol "freezes history" in his "Two methods in search of science."

89. For a brief discussion of what I mean by a dialectical method, see *Fragile Resistance*, 416. My model is Jean-Paul Sartre, *Search for a Method* (New York: Vintage, 1963).

CHAPTER 2

1. An earlier version of the first part of this analysis is found in my essay, "The causes of Latin American social revolutions." I have been helped in my work on Mexico by research assistants David Espinosa, Magdalena Prado, Veronica Villafan, and Joan Weston.

2. For a sampler of the variety of views on the revolution, see Walter Goldfrank, "World system, state structure, and the onset of the Mexican revolution," pp. 417–39 in *Politics and Society*, volume 5, number 4 (Fall 1975), 417. The interruption thesis is argued forcefully by Adolfo Gilly, *The Mexican Revolution*, translated by Patrick Camiller (London: New Left Books, 1983);

288 Notes to pages 35–36

see especially 337, from which Goldfrank takes his cue. This is an expanded and revised version of *La revolución interrumpida* (Mexico City: El Caballito, 1971).

3. Goldfrank, "World system, state structure," 417–18. I do more extensive analysis of Mexico's social structure on the eve of the revolution in John Foran, "Race, class, and gender in the making of the Mexican revolution," pp. 139–56 in *International Review of Sociology – Revue Internationale de Sociologie*, volume 6, number 1 (1996), and John Foran, Linda Klouzal, and Jean-Pierre Rivera (now Reed), "Who makes revolutions? Class, gender, and race in the Mexican, Cuban, and Nicaraguan revolutions," pp. 1–60 in *Research in Social Movements, Conflicts and Change*, volume xx (1997).

4. Alan Knight, *The Mexican Revolution*, volume i, *Porfirians, Liberals and Peasants* (Cambridge University Press, 1986), 3. See also Charles C. Cumberland, *Mexican Revolution: Genesis under Madero* (Austin: University of Texas Press, 1952) (hereafter referred to as *Mexican Revolution*, I), 4–6.

5. Eduardo Galeano, *Memories of Fire*, volume iii, *Century of the Wind* (New York: Pantheon Books, 1988), 23.

6. Knight, *The Mexican Revolution*, i, 79, citing *Mexican Year Book* (Los Angeles, 1922), 340–4.

7. Knight, *The Mexican Revolution*, i, 23.

8. John Mason Hart, *Revolutionary Mexico: The Coming and Process of the Mexican Revolution* (Berkeley: University of California Press, 1987), 131–4, 161.

9. Friedrich Katz, *The Secret War in Mexico: Europe, the United States and the Mexican Revolution* (University of Chicago Press, 1981), 27.

10. John Womack, "Economy during the revolution, 1910–1920: historiography & analysis," pp. 80–123 in *Marxist Perspectives*, volume 1, number 4 (December 1978), 94 table 1.

11. Hart, *Revolutionary Mexico*, 92.

12. Goldfrank, "World system, state structure," 431.

13. On US interests in Mexico, see Anita Brenner, *The Wind that Swept Mexico: The History of the Mexican Revolution 1910–1942* (Austin: University of Texas Press [1943], 1971), 17; Charles C. Cumberland, *Mexican Revolution: The Constitutionalist Years* (Austin: University of Texas Press, 1972), 244 (hereafter cited as *Mexican Revolution*, ii); Hart, *Revolutionary Mexico*, 47–50, 133; and Goldfrank, "World system, state structure," 421 note 9.

14. Knight, *The Mexican Revolution*, i, 93–7. The classic study of these processes in Morelos is John Womack, Jr., *Zapata and the Mexican Revolution* (New York: Alfred A. Knopf, 1969). On rural development in the Porfiriato, see also Friedrich Katz, "Labor conditions on haciendas in Porfirian Mexico: some trends and tendencies," pp. 1–47 in *Hispanic American Historical Review*, volume 54, number 1 (February 1974). A revisionist view of the hacienda, which stresses its dynamism (and is not therefore inconsistent with the logic of dependent development), is found in Simon Miller, "Mexican junkers and capitalist haciendas, 1810–1910: the arable estate and the transition to capitalism between the insurgency and the revolution," pp. 229–63 in *Journal of Latin American Studies*, volume 22, part 2 (May 1990). John Sheahan observes that Mexico in 1910 had the most concentrated landownership

and the most foreign investment in *Patterns of Development in Latin America: Poverty, Repression, and Economic Strategy* (Princeton University Press, 1987), 296.

15. Cumberland, *Mexican Revolution*, II, 15; Hart, *Revolutionary Mexico*, 55.

16. Knight, *The Mexican Revolution*, I, 30. On the Porfirian state, see ibid., 15ff.; Cumberland, *Mexican Revolution*, I, 7–8; Goldfrank, "World system, state structure," 427–48; Hart, *Revolutionary Mexico*, 176; and John Womack, Jr., "The Mexican revolution, 1910–1920," pp. 79–153 in Leslie Bethell, editor, *The Cambridge History of Latin America*, volume V, *c. 1870 to 1930* (Cambridge University Press, 1986), 83.

17. This contra Ekkart Zimmermann, who claims, citing Rod Aya: "The futility of drawing on revolutionary ideologies and revolutionary intentions for explaining the incidence and the outcome of revolutions is demonstrated by AYA: 'In two key cases, Mexico and China, the ideological currents did not palpably exist as political reference points when old regimes were toppled in 1911'": Zimmerman, *Political Violence, Crises, and Revolutions*, 540 note 9, quoting Aya, "Theories of revolution reconsidered," 64. Aya and Zimmerman overlook our distinction between ideology and political culture (see Chapter One).

18. The classic studies of Mexican anarchism are John M. Hart, *Anarchism & the Mexican Working Class, 1860–1931* (Austin: University of Texas Press, 1978), and James D. Cockcroft, *Intellectual Precursors of the Mexican Revolution, 1900–1913* (Austin: University of Texas Press, 1968). I have drawn here on Hart, *Revolutionary Mexico*, 56–62, 91–4; Knight, *The Mexican Revolution*, I, 45–7; and Goldfrank, "World system, state structure," 432.

19. Knight, *The Mexican Revolution*, I, 122. See also ibid., 113–27, 155–63, and Hart, *Revolutionary Mexico*, 28, 45.

20. Hart, *Revolutionary Mexico*, 48. See also Rodney D. Anderson, "Mexican workers and the politics of revolution, 1906–1911," pp. 94–113 in *The Hispanic American Historical Review*, volume 54, number 1 (February 1974).

21. Knight, *The Mexican Revolution*, I, 413. On Madero's ideas, see ibid., 55–6; Cumberland, *Mexican Revolution*, I, 30–46; and Katz, *The Secret War*, 41–2.

22. On these crises, see Hart, *Revolutionary Mexico*, 140, 145.

23. Data on the 1907–10 downturn is drawn from ibid., 163–8, 172–4; Cumberland, *Mexican Revolution*, I, 12–14; Goldfrank, "World system, state structure," 434; Knight, *The Mexican Revolution*, I, 93–4, 134–5; François-Xavier Guerra, "La révolution mexicaine: D'abord une révolution minière?," pp. 785–814 in *Annales: E. S. C.*, volume XXXVI, number 5 (Septembre-Octobre 1981), 805–7; Gilly, *The Mexican Revolution*, 333; and "High Prices in Mexico," *New York Times* (January 15, 1910), 4.

24. Knight, *The Mexican Revolution*, I, 65. See also ibid., 130, 182, 206, 211.

25. On the US and Díaz, see Goldfrank, "World system, state structure," 433, 435; Hart, *Revolutionary Mexico*, 247–9; and John Womack, Jr., "The Mexican Revolution," 84.

26. Hart, *Revolutionary Mexico*, 240–7; Katz, *The Secret War*, 39.

27. Cumberland, *Mexican Revolution*, I, 127–41. For a dissenting view arguing the insignificance of the US in the events, see Knight, *The Mexican*

Revolution, I, 184–6. But precisely such non-action is an important kind of world-systemic opening, when one has the power to do more to support an ally under siege.

28. The events are chronicled by Cumberland, *Mexican Revolution*, I, 119–50.

29. I discuss this in more depth in Foran, Klouzal, and Rivera, "Who makes revolutions?" and John Foran, "Reinventing the Mexican revolution: the competing paradigms of Alan Knight and John Mason Hart," pp. 115–31 in *Latin American Perspectives*, volume 23, number 4, issue 91 (Fall 1996).

30. Knight, *The Mexican Revolution*, I, 335. To construct a picture of the social bases of 1911, I have drawn on ibid., 30, 60–3, 132–3, 175–8, 192–7, 223–7, 352, 426; and Hart, *Revolutionary Mexico*, 49.

31. Sources for my discussion of the 1911–14 period include Cumberland, *Mexican Revolution*, I; Hart, *Revolutionary Mexico*; Katz, *The Secret War*; Knight, *The Mexican Revolution*, I, 239ff; and Arnaldo Córdova, *La ideología de la revolución mexicana: la formación del nuevo régimen* (Mexico City: Ediciones Era, 1973), 103–7.

32. Knight, *The Mexican Revolution*, I, 246.

33. Ibid., 456, 466.

34. Ibid., 382–3.

35. From a Wilson dispatch of February 4, 1913, quoted in Cumberland, *Mexican Revolution*, I, 231 note 9. Knight feels the Taft administration followed a consistent policy of neutrality in 1912, thereby favoring Madero: *The Mexican Revolution*, I, 321. Womack presents a more irregular policy: "The Mexican Revolution," 89–91. Hart documents attacks on US-owned properties: *Revolutionary Mexico*, 365.

36. A careful reading of the diplomatic correspondence in the US National Archives, which I undertook in 1993–94, bears this out. Despite prudent reservations in Washington, Wilson in Mexico City acted independently and aggressively against Madero, rejoicing in a dispatch of February 20 that "A wicked despotism has fallen": United States National Archives 812.00/6277, Wilson, Mexico City to State Department (hereafter I will cite these archives as USNA). On February 26, after Madero's murder, he alleged: "the Government of Madero during its entire existence was anti-American and that neither appeals nor veiled threats affected it in its incomprehensible attitude; that during the last three and perhaps six months of its existence it presented the aspect of a despotism infinitely worse than that which existed under General Diaz": USNA 812.00/6394, Wilson, Mexico City to Secretary of State. See also Katz, *The Secret War*, 98–112, and Knight, *The Mexican Revolution*, I, 485.

37. Hart, *Revolutionary Mexico*, 263, 284, 365; Alan Knight, *The Mexican Revolution*, II, *Counter-revolution and Reconstruction* (Cambridge University Press, 1986), 1, 102–3. Goldfrank, "Theories of Revolution," 165 note 76, following Michael C. Meyer, *Huerta: A Political Biography* (Lincoln: University of Nebraska Press, 1972), and Womack, "The Mexican Revolution," 95, sees Huerta's regime as continuous with Madero in its policies, overlooking its entirely undemocratic nature.

38. Knight, *The Mexican Revolution*, II, 18.
39. Ibid., 47–8, 129–34; Womack, "The Mexican Revolution," 94, 96; Cumberland, *Mexican Revolution*, I, 64.
40. Brenner, *The Wind That Swept Mexico*, 39–41; Cumberland, *Mexican Revolution*, I, 96, 109; Katz, *The Secret War*, 150–2, 157–202; Knight, *The Mexican Revolution*, II, 30–1, 68–75; Womack, "The Mexican Revolution," 99–100; Hart, *Revolutionary Mexico*, 284, 288–9.
41. Knight, *The Mexican Revolution*, II, 231.
42. Hart, *Revolutionary Mexico*, 269; cf. 276.
43. Some scholars, most notably Arturo Warman, have pointed to Zapata's efforts to construct a non-agrarian program, but this side of Zapatismo was never articulated or communicated well enough: Arturo Warman, "The political project of Zapatismo," pp. 321–37 in Friedrich Katz, editor, *Riot, Rebellion and Revolution: Rural Social Conflict in Mexico* (Princeton University Press, 1988), 322.
44. On this last point, see Elizabeth Salas, *Soldaderas in the Mexican Military: Myth and History* (Austin: University of Texas Press, 1990), 46–7.
45. Hart, *Revolutionary Mexico*, 280, 291–9, 311.
46. Cumberland, *Mexican Revolution*, II, 201.
47. Katz, *The Secret War*, 285–6; Knight, *The Mexican Revolution*, I, 409; Gilly, *The Mexican Revolution*, 332.
48. Katz, *The Secret War*, 125.
49. On the USA in this period, see Cumberland, *Mexican Revolution*, II, 312–19; Hart, *Revolutionary Mexico*, 153; and Katz, *The Secret War*, 298–315. Hart makes the strongest case for a pro-Constitutionalist, anti-Villa US policy, noting that Villa's strength was finally destroyed in November 1915 when the US allowed Carranza to send troops across its territory to rout Villa and capture his heavy artillery at Agua Prieta: *Revolutionary Mexico*, 320; see also 285–99.
50. Katz, *The Secret War*, 293, 319–21; Knight, *The Mexican Revolution*, I, 448; II, 413–29, 439; Cumberland, *Mexican Revolution*, II, 398, 400.
51. John M. Hart, "The urban working class and the Mexican revolution: the case of the Casa del Obrero Mundial," pp. 1–20 in *Hispanic American Historical Review*, volume 58, number 1 (February 1978), 20; Cumberland, *Mexican Revolution*, II, 386–9.
52. Hart, *Revolutionary Mexico*, 336.
53. For discussions of numerous competing views of the revolution, see David C. Bailey, "Revisionism and the recent historiography of the Mexican revolution," pp. 62–79 in *Hispanic American Historical Review*, volume 58, number 1 (1978); Richard Tardanico, "Perspectives on revolutionary Mexico: the regimes of Obregón and Calles," pp. 69–88 in Richard Robinson, editor, *Dynamics of World Development* (Beverly Hills: Sage Publications, 1981); Paul J. Vanderwood, "Resurveying the Mexican revolution: three provocative new syntheses and their shortfalls," pp. 145–63 in *Mexican Studies/Estudios Mexicanos*, volume 5, number 1 (Winter 1989); and Alan Knight, "Revisionism and revolution: Mexico compared to England and France," pp. 159–99 in *Past and Present*, number 134 (February 1992).

54. Ramón Eduardo Ruiz, *The Great Rebellion: Mexico, 1905–1924* (New York: W. W. Norton and Company, 1980), ix; see chapter 1, "On the meaning of revolution," and part IV, "The ubiquitous barriers."
55. Womack, "Economy during the revolution," 97; cf. Womack, "The Mexican revolution," 81.
56. Córdova, *La ideología*, 33; François-Xavier Guerra, *Le Mexique: De l'Ancien Régime à la Révolution*, two volumes (Paris: Editions L'Harmattan, 1985); Jean Meyer, "Mexico: revolution and reconstruction in the 1920s," pp. 155–94 in Leslie Bethell, editor, *The Cambridge Modern History of Latin America*, volume V: *c. 1870 to 1930* (Cambridge University Press, 1986).
57. Knight, *The Mexican Revolution*, II, 527; Hart, *Revolutionary Mexico*. See Foran, "Reinventing the Mexican Revolution."
58. Benjamin Keen and Keith Haynes *A History of Latin America* (Boston: Houghton-Mifflin, 2000), 286.
59. Gilly, *The Mexican Revolution*, 325, 335.
60. Ibid., 340.
61. Ibid., 327.
62. Ibid., 359.
63. John Tutino, "Social bases of insurrection and revolution: conclusion," pp. 353–71 in John Tutino, *From Insurrection to Revolution in Mexico: Social Bases of Agrarian Violence, 1750–1940* (Princeton University Press, 1986), 361–2.
64. Hart, *Revolutionary Mexico*, 305; Hart, "The urban working class," 12–13.
65. I thank my research assistant, Tanya Tabon, for undertaking a preliminary assessment of this case in a paper, "China's social revolution of 1949," Department of Sociology, University of California, Santa Barbara (1995), on which I have drawn.
66. John Dunn, "Conclusion," pp. 388–99 in Tony Saich and Hans van de Ven, editors, *New Perspectives on the Chinese Communist Revolution* (Armonk: M. E. Sharpe, 1995), 389. He goes on to note: "It is also, palpably, of immense political and historical importance – very possibly, now that the cold war has ended without unleashing full-scale thermonuclear war, the single most important historical event of the twentieth century:" ibid.
67. Skocpol, *States and Social Revolutions*, passim.
68. Wolf, *Peasant Wars*, 130–1.
69. Zimmermann, *Political Violence, Crises, and Revolutions*, 64, 540 note 9, quoting Aya, "Theories of revolution reconsidered."
70. Moore, *Social Origins of Dictatorship and Democracy*, 497; see also 202, 214, 220. Interestingly, for the case of China Moore doesn't lay great stress on the Communist Party's ideology or culture: ibid., 223. Reading Moore on China clearly raises a number of puzzles.
71. Alvin Y. So and Stephen W. K. Chi, *East Asia and the World Economy* (Thousand Oaks: Sage, 1995), 125.
72. Moore, *Social Origins of Dictatorship and Democracy*, 166.
73. Skocpol, *States and Social Revolutions*, 68.
74. Ibid., 74; Wolf, *Peasant Wars*, 103.
75. Wolf, *Peasant Wars*, 117.

76. Skocpol, *States and Social Revolutions*, 73.
77. Ibid., 238.
78. Wolf, *Peasant Wars*, 141, has this as "Share production," but the proper translation is "Share property." I thank Alan Liu on this point.
79. Timothy J. Lomperis, *From People's War to People's Rule: Insurgency, Intervention, and the Lessons of Vietnam* (Chapel Hill: University of North Carolina Press, 1996), 135.
80. Skocpol, *States and Social Revolutions*, 244. I have drawn on Skocpol throughout this paragraph.
81. Lomperis, *From People's War to People's Rule*, 136; Wolf gives the number killed as 5,000: *Peasant Wars*, 144–5.
82. Data on the working class and students comes from Wolf, *Peasant Wars*, 137–8. Moore is again ambivalent on the precise significance and impact of industrialization on social structure: *Social Origins of Dictatorship and Democracy*, 177, 187, 197.
83. Jonathan Spence, *The Search for Modern China* (New York: W. W. Norton & Company, 1990), 425 table, based on J. K. Chang, *Industrial Development in Pre-Communist China* (Edinburgh University Press, 1969), 103 table 28.
84. James E. Sheridan, *China in Disintegration: The Republican Era in Chinese History, 1912–1949* (New York: The Free Press, 1975), 224.
85. Carl Riskin, *China's Political Economy: The Quest for Development since 1949* (Oxford University Press, 1987), 19–20; Spence, *The Search for Modern China*, 383.
86. Sheridan, *China in Disintegration*, 222.
87. So and Chi, *East Asia and the World Economy*, 126.
88. Spence, *The Search for Modern China*, 426–7.
89. Wolf, *Peasant Wars*, 130. Skocpol dismisses this external thesis as the reason for peasants' problems: *States and Social Revolutions*, 153, 327–8 note 126. Wolf admits: "We must not imagine that these novel processes advanced everywhere at the same rate and with the same intensity": *Peasant Wars*, 131.
90. R. H. Tawney, *Land and Labour in China* (London: George Allen and Unwin, 1932), 71, cited by Wolf, *Peasant Wars*, 134.
91. So and Chi, *East Asia and the World Economy*, 128 (see also 129), who cite Han-seng Chen, *Landlord and Peasant in China: A Study of the Agrarian Crisis in South China* (New York: International Publishers, 1936); Albert Feuerwerker, *Economic Trends in the Republic of China, 1912–1949*, number 31 (Ann Arbor: Michigan Papers in Chinese Studies, 1977); Ramon H. Myers, "How did the modern Chinese economy develop?," pp. 604–28 in *Journal of Asian Studies*, volume 50 (1991); Thomas. G. Rawski, *Economic Growth in Prewar China* (Berkeley: University of California Press, 1989); and R. B. Wong, "Chinese economic history and development: a note on the Myers-Huang exchange," pp. 600–11 in *Journal of Asian Studies*, volume 51 (1992).
92. Spence, *The Search for Modern China*, 434.
93. Ibid., 425.
94. This paragraph draws on Skocpol, *States and Social Revolutions*, 250–1.

95. Sheridan, *China in Disintegration*, 217–18, quoting Chiang from Lloyd East-man, "Fascism in Kuomintang China: the Blue Shirts," pp. 1–31 in *China Quarterly*, number 49 (January–March 1972), 5–6. Cf. Chiang's statement: "Wherever I go there is the Government, the Cabinet, and the center of resistance [to the Japanese]": Lloyd E. Eastman, *Seeds of Destruction: Nationalist China in War and Revolution 1937–1949* (Stanford University Press, 1984), 217, quoting Edgar Snow, "The Generalissimo," pp. 646–8 in *Asia* (December, 1940), 646.

96. Spence, *The Search for Modern China*, 417–18, quoting Sherman Cochran and Hsieh Cheng-kuang, with Janis Cochran, translators and editors, *One Day in China, May 21, 1936* (New Haven: Yale University Press, 1983), 210ff, 245. I have corrected Spence's quote slightly.

97. Eastman, *Seeds of Destruction*, 2.

98. Ibid., 219; Sheridan, *China in Disintegration*, 222.

99. John King Fairbank, *The Great Chinese Revolution: 1800–1985* (New York: Harper & Row, Publishers, 1986), 243.

100. Spence, *The Search for Modern China*, 404–9. The numbers offered for the start and finish of the march vary, but the losses were clearly devastating: see Lomperis, *From People's War to People's Rule*, 138, and Fairbank, *The Great Chinese Revolution*, 233–4.

101. Skocpol, *States and Social Revolutions*, 154.

102. Mark Selden, *The Yenan Way in Revolutionary China* (Cambridge: Harvard University Press, 1971).

103. More properly, the ideology was referred to as Mao Zedong Thought rather than the grander term "Maoism," and it was officially adopted at the Seventh Party Congress in April–June 1945: Fairbank, *The Great Chinese Revolution*, 257–8.

104. Lomperis, *From People's War to People's Rule*, 134; Benjamin L. Schwartz, "Themes in intellectual history: May Fourth and after," pp. 406–50 in John K. Fairbank, editor, *The Cambridge History of China*, volume XII: *Republican China 1912–1949*, part 1 (Cambridge University Press, 1983), 407.

105. Fairbank, *The Great Chinese Revolution*, 254; see also 253 and Schwartz, "Themes in intellectual history," 449.

106. Fairbank, *The Great Chinese Revolution*, 251. See also Tony Saich, "Writing or rewriting history? The construction of the Maoist resolution on party history," pp. 299–338 in Tony Saich and Hans van de Ven, editors, *New Perspectives on the Chinese Communist Revolution* (Armonk: M. E. Sharpe, 1995), 302.

107. Chalmers A. Johnson, *Peasant Nationalism and Communist Power: The Emergence of Revolutionary China 1937–1945* (Stanford University Press, 1962), ix.

108. Fairbank, *The Great Chinese Revolution*, 251.

109. Lomperis, *From People's War to People's Rule*, 142.

110. Lucien Bianco, "Peasant responses to CCP mobilization policies, 1937–1945," pp. 175–87 in Tony Saich and Hans van de Ven, editors, *New Perspectives on the Chinese Communist Revolution* (Armonk: M. E. Sharpe, 1995), 176, also citing Chen Yung-fa, *Making Revolution: The Communist*

Movement in Eastern and Central China, 1937–1945 (Berkeley: University of California Press, 1986), 99.

111. So and Chi, *East Asia and the World Economy*, 131–2, citing Mark Selden, from the introduction to his edited volume *The People's Republic of China* (New York: Monthly Review Press, 1970), 12–20.

112. Bianco, "Peasant responses to CCP mobilization policies," 179–80, and Chen, *Making Revolution*, 187.

113. Judith Stacey, "Peasant families and people's war in the Chinese revolution," pp. 182–95 in Jack A. Goldstone, editor, *Revolutions: Theoretical, Comparative and Historical Studies* (New York: Harcourt Brace Jovanovich, 1986), 187.

114. Mao, quoted in Stuart R. Schram, *The Political Thought of Mao Tse-tung* (New York: Praeger, 1969), 316–17.

115. Fairbank, *The Great Chinese Revolution*, 247; see also 231.

116. David E. Apter, "Discourse as power: Yan'an and the Chinese revolution," pp. 193–234 in Tony Saich and Hans van de Ven, editors, *New Perspectives on the Chinese Communist Revolution* (Armonk: M. E. Sharpe, 1995), 200, 210.

117. Ibid., 207; Bianco, "Peasant responses to CCP mobilization Policies," 181; and Joseph K. S. Yick, *Making Urban Revolution in China: The CCP–GMD Struggle for Beiping–Tianjin 1945–1949* (Armonk: M. E. Sharpe, 1995), 186–91.

118. Eastman, *Seeds of Destruction*, 8.

119. Fairbank, *The Great Chinese Revolution*, 258.

120. Eastman, *Seeds of Destruction*, 224. The argument of this paragraph draws heavily on Eastman.

121. Lomperis, *From People's War to People's Rule*, 145.

122. Spence, *The Search for Modern China*, 490.

123. Fairbank, *The Great Chinese Revolution*, 259.

124. Ibid., 262.

125. Ibid., 268.

126. Lomperis, *From People's War to People's Rule*, 145–6.

127. Spence, *The Search for Modern China*, 498–501. See also Eastman, *Seeds of Destruction*, 221.

128. Fairbank, *The Great Chinese Revolution*, 263.

129. Ibid. 264–6.

130. Lomperis, *From People's War to People's Rule*, 139.

131. Fairbank, *The Great Chinese Revolution*, 267.

132. This paragraph draws on Spence, *The Search for Modern China*, 505–12.

133. This section draws extensively on my essay, "The causes of Latin American social revolutions." I have also been helped by the research of my student, Vanessa M. Ziegler, "The rise and fall of Fulgencio Batista in Cuban politics," MA thesis, Latin American and Iberian Studies, University of California, Santa Barbara (2000).

134. These data are drawn variously from Susan Eckstein, "Restratification after revolution: the Cuban experience," pp. 217–40 in Richard Tardanico, editor, *Crises in the Caribbean Basin*, volume IX of the *Political Economy of the*

World-System Annuals (Beverly Hills: Sage, 1987), 228 table 9.2; Carmelo Mesa-Lago, "Revolutionary economic policies in Cuba," pp. 63–83 in Philip Brenner, William M. LeoGrande, Donna Rich, and Daniel Siegel, editors, *The Cuba Reader: The Making of a Revolutionary Society* (New York: Grove Press, 1989), 64–5; and USNA, 737.00/7–1758, State Department, "Cuba" (June 1958), 1. W. MacGaffey and C. R. Barnett analyze the 1953 census in *Cuba: Its People, Its Society, Its Culture* (New Haven: HRAF Press, 1962). A comprehensive recent study of Cuban social structure is Jorge Ibarra, *Prologue to Revolution: Cuba, 1898–1958*, translated by Marjorie Moore (Boulder: Lynne Rienner, 1998).

135. See Foran, Klouzal, and Rivera, "Who makes revolutions?," 23–4, citing Carlos Moore, *Castro, the Blacks, and Africa* (Los Angeles: Center for Afro-American Studies, UCLA, 1988), 358–9, and Chris McAuley, "Race and the process of the American revolutions," pp. 168–202 in John Foran, editor, *Theorizing Revolutions* (London: Routledge, 1997). Andres Oppenheimer notes that Moore calculated the nonwhite population at 45 percent in 1959 and 58 percent in 1990, and that the 1981 census put the figure at 34 percent, "but government officials admit that the figure is unreliable: the Census Bureau had asked Cubans whether they were black, white, or mulatto, and an overwhelming majority of mulattos – living in a country with a history of endemic racial discrimination – had classified themselves as white": *Castro's Final Hour: The Secret Story Behind the Coming Downfall of Communist Cuba* (New York: Simon and Schuster, 1992), 442 note.

136. Medea Benjamin, Joseph Collins, and Michael Scott, *No Free Lunch: Food & Revolution in Cuba Today* (New York: Food First and Grove Press, 1986), 5. On the elite see also Wolf, *Peasant Wars*, 260.

137. Wolf, *Peasant Wars*, 261; Wickham-Crowley, *Guerrillas and Revolution*, 161–2.

138. Wolf, *Peasant Wars*, 261–2; Benjamin et al., *No Free Lunch*, 4–5.

139. Frank J. Taylor, "Revolution, race, and some aspects of foreign relations in Cuba since 1959," pp. 19–41 in *Cuban Studies*, volume XVIII (1988), 22; Wolf, *Peasants Wars*, 252–4; Terence Cannon, *Revolutionary Cuba* (New York: Thomas Y. Crowell, 1981), 113; Foran, Klouzal, and Rivera, "Who makes revolutions?," 24.

140. Benjamin et al., *No Free Lunch*, 4; Johnetta B. Cole, "Women in Cuba: the revolution within the revolution," pp. 307–17 in Jack Goldstone, editor, *Revolutions: Theoretical, Comparative, and Historical Studies* (San Diego: Harcourt, Brace, Jovanovich, 1986), 308–9; Republica de Cuba, Consejo Nacional de Economia, "Empleo y Desempleo en la fuerza trabajadora Agosto 1958," Informe Tecnico, number 8 (Havana, 1958), 2 table 2.

141. Wolf, *Peasant Wars*, 256–7; Wickham-Crowley, *Guerrillas and Revolution*, 97, 132, 141.

142. Wickham-Crowley, *Guerrillas and Revolution*, 166.

143. Many of these data can be found in Benjamin et al., *No Free Lunch*, 1. See also Edward Gonzalez, *Cuba Under Castro: The Limits of Charisma* (Boston: Houghton Mifflin Company, 1974), 18; Mesa-Lago, "Revolutionary

economic policies," 66; USNA, 837.00/2–2158, Foreign Service Despatch 673, Price, Havana, to State Department (February 21, 1958); and 837.00/3–2058, Foreign Service Despatch 749, Gilmore, Havana, to State Department (March 20, 1958).

144. Benjamin et al., *No Free Lunch*, 9.
145. On US interests in Cuba, see ibid., 10–11; *Foreign Relations of the United States, 1955–1957*, volume VI, *American Republics: Multilateral; Mexico; Caribbean* (Washington, DC: United States Government Printing Office, 1987), 870; Gonzalez, *Cuba Under Castro*, 18, 31; Marifeli Pérez-Stable, *The Cuban Revolution: Origins, Course, and Legacy* (New York: Oxford University Press, 1993), 15; and Wolf, *Peasant Wars*, 256.
146. Cannon, *Revolutionary Cuba*, 41. Data in this paragraph are also drawn from Benjamin et al., *No Free Lunch*, 2–6, 12; USNA, 837.00/2–1056, Foreign Service Despatch 560, Boonstra, Havana, to State Department (February 10, 1956); and 837.00/7–1356, Foreign Service Despatch 28, Price, Havana, to State Department (July 13, 1956). See also Hugh Thomas, *Cuba: The Pursuit of Freedom* (New York: Harper & Row, 1971), 746, and Pérez-Stable, *The Cuban Revolution*, 20.
147. Keen and Haynes, *A History of Latin America*, 437; Ziegler, "The rise and fall of Fulgencio Batista," 21–2. Ramón Eduardo Ruiz has cautioned me (personal communication, May 17, 1999) that the Grau regime was more "well-intentioned" than "radical," but here, as elsewhere in the external origins of revolutions, perception counts as much as reality.
148. Thomas, *Cuba*, 736.
149. Wolf, *Peasant Wars*, 265. On the evolution and corruption of the state, see Cannon, *Revolutionary Cuba*, 43–58; USNA, 737.00/2–1058, Foreign Service Despatch 615, Daniel Braddock, Havana, to State Department (February 10, 1958); 737.00/8–758, Memorandum of Conversation, Leonhardy, with Dr. Joaquin Meyer, State American Republics Department (August 7, 1958); and Keen and Haynes, *A History of Latin America*, 438–9.
150. On the repressive forces, see Cannon, *Revolutionary Cuba*, 109; Wickham-Crowley, *Guerrillas and Revolution*, 171–3; and USNA, 737.00/5–1958, Foreign Service Despatch 97, Paul Wollam, Santiago de Cuba, to State Department (May 19, 1958).
151. Quoted in Cannon, *Revolutionary Cuba*, 23. This paragraph also draws on Timothy P. Wickham-Crowley, "Winners, losers, and also-rans: toward a comparative sociology of Latin American guerrilla movements," pp. 132–81 in Susan Eckstein, editor, *Power and Popular Protest* (Berkeley: University of California Press, 1989), 154; idem, *Guerrillas and Revolution*, 132; Roxborough, "exogenous factors," 9; and Noelle Harrison, "Cuba: making sense of a revolution," unpublished paper, Department of Sociology, University of California, Santa Barbara (Fall 1990), 16–18.
152. Robert E. Quirk, *Fidel Castro* (New York: W. W. Norton & Company, 1993), 33, who notes that it's not sure Chibás intended to kill himself with the gunshot to his abdomen, and that ironically, he didn't realize his show was over time and off the air. He died eleven days later.

153. Fidel Castro, *La revolución cubana, 1953–1962* (Mexico City: ERA, 1972), quoted by Galeano, *Memory of Fire*, 148–9. Castro's remarks at his trial were later issued in a revised version as a pamphlet.

154. Quoted in Cannon, *Revolutionary Cuba*, 67.

155. On Castro's views and the July 26 Movement's positions, see ibid., 54–7, 97; USNA, 737.00/8–458, Foreign Service Despatch 5, Park Wollam, Santiago de Cuba, to State Department (August 4, 1958), 11; "Ideario Economico del Veinte y Seis de Julio," found in USNA, 837.00/3–959, Foreign Service Despatch 982, Gilmore, Havana, to State Department (March 9, 1959); and Wickham-Crowley, *Guerrillas and Revolution*, 176–8. For comprehensive treatments, see Sheldon B. Liss, *Fidel! Castro's Political and Social Thought* (Boulder: Westview Press, 1994), and Quirk, *Fidel Castro*.

156. Colburn, *The Vogue of Revolution*, 28.

157. Wickham-Crowley, "Winners, losers, and also-rans," 164; idem, *Guerrillas and Revolution*, 38; USNA, 837.06/12–3055, Foreign Service Despatch 466, J. de Zangotita, Havana, to State Department (December 30, 1955); and 837.06/10–1457, Foreign Service Despatch 309, John F. Correll, Havana, to State Department.

158. Dulles is quoted in *Foreign Relations of the United States*, 841 note 3. See also ibid., 797–8, 799.

159. Ibid., 854. See also 845–6, 865 note 1, 869.

160. Countless State Department documents on Cuba make reference to the US policy of non-intervention in the affairs of other countries. On the other hand, dozens of documents from 1957 and 1958 have been removed from the files.

161. USNA, 737.00/3–3058, Telegram 613, from Smith, Havana, to Secretary of State (March 30, 1958). For support of elections, see USNA, 737.00/9–2658, Foreign Service Despatch 320, Braddock, Havana, to State Department (September 26, 1958); for arms renewal, 737.00/7–1658, Telegram 79, Smith, Havana, to Secretary of State (July 16, 1958), and 737.00/10–2158, Telegram 386, Smith, Havana, to Secretary of State (October 21, 1958); for guarded intimations of support for a military coup, 737.00/8–758, William G. Bowdler, Political Officer, Havana, Memorandum of Conversation with Sr. Vasco T. L. Da Cunha, Brazilian ambassador to Cuba (Confidential) (August 7, 1958); and for State Department doubts about continued support, 737.00/7–2458, Office Memorandum from C. A. Stewart to Mr. Snow (Secret) (July 24, 1958).

162. USNA, 737.00/10–3158, Memorandum of conversation between Mr. Rubottom and US businessmen, State Department (October 31, 1958). On aid to the rebels, see Wickham-Crowley, *Guerrillas and Revolution*, 87.

163. See State Department correspondence in USNA for December 1958.

164. Thomas, *Cuba*, 732–5; Louis A. Pérez, *Cuba: Between Reform and Revolution* (Oxford University Press, 1988), 282–5.

165. The details in this paragraph are based on a reading of numerous State Department economic reports found in the National Archives.

166. USNA, 837.06/12–458, Foreign Service Despatch 591, J. F. Correll, Havana, to State Department (December 4, 1958).

167. The best guides to the events are Ramón L. Bonachea and Marta San Martín, *The Cuban Insurrection, 1952–1959* (New Brunswick: Transaction, 1974); Thomas, *Cuba*; and Gladys Marel García-Pérez, *Insurrection and Revolution: Armed Struggle in Cuba, 1952–1959*, translated by Juan Ortega (Boulder: Lynn Rienner, 1998). Other important accounts of the revolution include Ramón Eduardo Ruiz, *Cuba: The Making of a Revolution* (New York: W. W. Norton & Company, 1968), and Pérez-Stable, *The Cuban Revolution*.

168. This question is taken up at more length in Foran, Klouzal, and Rivera, "Who makes revolutions?," 24–34. Scattered data on the participation of the main social sectors is found in the US National Archives.

169. Josef Gugler, "The urban character of contemporary revolutions," pp. 399–412 in Josef Gugler, editor, *The Urbanization of the Third World* (Oxford University Press, 1988); Wickham-Crowley, *Guerrillas and Revolution*, 26; O. Fernandez Rios, "El Ejercito Rebelde y la dictadura democratico-revolucionaria de las masas populares," in *Revista Cubana de Ciencias Sociales* (1985), cited by Roxborough, "Theories of revolution," 107 table 1.

170. Linda Klouzal, "Revolution firsthand: Women's accounts of the experience, meanings, and impact of participating in the Cuban insurrection," dissertation in progress, Department of Sociology, University of California, Santa Barbara; Gladys Marel García-Pérez, *Insurrection and Revolution: Armed Struggle in Cuba, 1952–1959* (Boulder: Lynne Rienner Publishers, 1998); and Julia E. Sweig, *Inside the Cuban Revolution* (Cambridge: Harvard University Press, 2002). Klouzal's work is brilliant at showing the texture of the movement, and the role of women in particular, within it.

171. Klouzal, draft of "Revolution firsthand," in chapter 5, "The grassroots nature of resistance," 15.

172. Julia Shayne discusses the activism of women in detail in *The Revolution Question: Feminisms in El Salvador, Chile, and Cuba* (New Brunswick: Rutgers University Press, 2004). See also Foran, Klouzal, and Rivera, "Who makes revolutions?," 32–3, and Klouzal, "Revolution firsthand."

173. On the debates, see Foran, Klouzal, and Rivera, "Who makes revolutions?," 29–32 and the sources cited therein.

174. For this argument on its longevity and the possible futures of the revolution, see Foran, "The future of revolutions," 798–9.

175. This section is an expansion of my essay, "The causes of Latin American social revolutions." I thank Jean-Pierre Reed for permission to quote from several interviews he conducted for his master's thesis and dissertation in Nicaragua, and my research assistant Joe Bandy for locating World Bank economic data.

176. Jeff Goodwin, "Revolutionary movements in Central America: a comparative analysis," Center for Research on Politics and Social Organization, Working Paper Series, Department of Sociology, Harvard University (1985), 67. Though this is an early work, Goodwin does not seem to have changed his mind on this point by *No Other Way Out* (2000).

177. Farhi, "State disintegration," 231, 234.

178. This sketch of social structure draws on Edelberto Torres Rivas, "El Estado contra la sociedad: Las raíces de la revolución nicaragüense," pp. 113–43 in his *Crisis del Poder en Centroamérica* (San José, Costa Rica: Editorial Universitaria Centroamericana, 1981), 115–16; Henri Weber, *Nicaragua: The Sandinist Revolution*, translated by Patrick Camiller (London: Verso, 1981), 28–9, 28 table 3; George Black, *Triumph of the People: The Sandinista Revolution in Nicaragua* (London: Zed Press, 1981), 70; Farhi, "State disintegration," 235, 240; and idem, *States and Urban-Based Revolutions*, 73–4. Other fine overviews of the whole period include James Dunkerley, *Power in the Isthmus: A Political History of Modern Central America* (London: Verso, 1988), and Thomas W. Walker, *Nicaragua: The Land of Sandino* (Boulder: Westview, 1986).

179. T. David Mason, "Women's participation in Central American revolutions: a theoretical perspective," pp. 63–89 in *Comparative Political Studies*, volume 25, number 1 (1992), 68.

180. See the fascinating discussion of this alleged remark in Selbin, *Modern Latin American Revolutions*, 196 note 124. See also Keen and Haynes, *A History of Latin America*, 469ff., and Torres Rivas, "El Estado," 142 note 5.

181. Weber, *Nicaragua*, 34, 34 note 11; Black, *Triumph of the People*, 37, 39, 41.

182. Paige presents dramatic data that clinch the case for dependent development in my view: Jeffery M. Paige, *Coffee and Power: Revolution and the Rise of Democracy in Central America* (Cambridge: Harvard University Press, 1997), 91 table 11; see also Farhi, *States and Urban-Based Revolutions*, 39.

183. The World Bank, *World Data* (CD-Rom, 1994), reports the following on Nicaragua's exports:

Year	Manufactured exports ($ millions)	Food Exports ($ millions)
1965	7.7	55.1
1970	28.1	96.9
1975	63.2	185.3
1977	105.1	347.3
1978	142.0	468.8
1979	71.9	382.3

184. Economic data in this paragraph is drawn from Farhi, *States and Urban-Based Revolutions*, 39; Weber, *Nicaragua*, 17, 24, 38; and Black, *Triumph of the People*, 62.

185. Data on income is drawn from World Bank, *World Data*. The higher figure for 1977 comes from data compiled by ECLA (the Economic Commission for Latin America), cited in Weber, *Nicaragua*, 27 table 2.

186. Weber, *Nicaragua*, 27; Wickham-Crowley, *Guerrillas and Revolution*, 241–2.

187. Torres Rivas, "El Estado," 127 (for the 1937 election results), 139–40; Keen and Haynes, *A History of Latin America*, 472–5; Weber, *Nicaragua*, 17; Black, *Triumph of the People*, 43; Farhi, "State disintegration," 235, 235 note 3.

188. Weber, *Nicaragua*, 32; Farhi, *States and Social Revolutions*, 58–9 note 22, 33–4, 46; Wickham-Crowley, *Guerrillas and Revolution*, 268–9; Black,

Triumph of the People, 52; John A. Booth, *The End and the Beginning: The Nicaraguan Revolution* (Boulder: Westview, 1985), 94–5; Goodwin, "Revolutionary movements in Central America," 21.

189. Weber, *Nicaragua*, 12. Sandino's ideas are treated most fully in Donald C. Hodges, *Intellectual Foundations of the Nicaraguan Revolution* (Austin: University of Texas Press, 1986).

190. John Beverley and Marc Zimmerman, *Literature and Politics in the Central American Revolutions* (Austin: University of Texas Press, 1990), 13, drawing on Hodges's seminal work.

191. Carlos Fonseca, *Desde la cárcel yo acuso a la dictadura* (Managua: Cárcel de la Aviación, July 8, 1964), quoted by Black, *Triumph of the People*, 90. Hodges gives the publisher as Secretaría Nacional de Propaganda y Educación Política del FSLN, with no date.

192. From a 1997 interview conducted by Jean-Pierre Reed, with whom I have written on the political cultures that made the revolution in depth in Reed and Foran, "Political cultures of opposition." All names in these interviews have been changed.

193. From a 1997 interview conducted by Jean-Pierre Reed.

194. From a 1990 interview conducted by Jean-Pierre Reed.

195. Farhi, "State disintegration," 247.

196. Farhi, *States and Urban-Based Revolutions*, 100. See further ibid., 81 note 43, and Roger N. Lancaster, *Thanks to God and the Revolution: Popular Religion and Class Consciousness in the New Nicaragua* (New York: Columbia University Press, 1988).

197. From a 1997 interview conducted by Jean-Pierre Reed.

198. From a 1997 interview conducted by Jean-Pierre Reed.

199. From a 1997 interview conducted by Jean-Pierre Reed.

200. Black, *Triumph of the People*, 140.

201. Quote from a thirty-year-old worker, in Instituto de Estudio del Sandinismo, *Y se armo la runga! Testimonios de la insurreción popular sandinista en Masaya* (Managua: Editorial Nueva Nicaragua, 1982), 158. This quote has been translated by Jean-Pierre Reed.

202. Israel Ramirez Guevara, a worker in the Sandinista land reform institute, twenty-five years old, in *Y se armo la runga!*, 128, translated by Jean-Pierre Reed.

203. Quoted in Lynn Horton, *Peasants in Arms: War and Peace in the Mountains of Nicaragua, 1979–1994* (Athens: Center for International Studies, Ohio University, 1998), 67.

204. Dix, "Why revolutions succeed and fail," 437 note 28, quoting Stephen Kinzer, "Nicaragua: universal revolt," in *The Atlantic Monthly* (February 1979), 12. See also Walton, *Reluctant Rebels*, 168 (on seismological properties); Farhi, *States and Urban-Based Revolutions*, 41; Roxborough, "Exogenous factors," 10; and Black, *Triumph of the People*, 66.

205. Caution should perhaps be exercised about the economic situation in the 1974–77 period, as Central Bank data indicate a relatively healthy picture: see Banco Central de Nicaragua, *Indicadores Económicos* (Managua: BCN, 1979). I owe this insight to an anonymous manuscript I reviewed in 1995.

206. Goodwin, "Revolutionary movements," 11; Weber, *Nicaragua*, 38–42, 49; Black, *Triumph of the People*, 67. On the upward trend for coffee prices, see Forrest D. Colburn, *Post-Revolutionary Nicaragua: State, Class, and the Dilemmas of Agrarian Policy* (Berkeley: University of California Press, 1986), 78 table 11.

207. On US policy see Farhi, "State disintegration," 241–4, 254 note 9, and idem, *States and Urban-Based Revolutions*, 48–9. On Israel, Black, *Triumph of the People*, 56.

208. See Selbin, *Modern Latin American Revolutions*, 201 note 62 on US actions against the FSLN. Bill Robinson insists on this point as well, arguing that US policy was clear: to replace Somoza with a non-revolutionary alternative (personal communication, September 2004).

209. Weber, *Nicaragua*, 36–7, 47–8.

210. Roxborough, "Theories of revolution," 109 table 2, based on Carlos Vilas, *Perfiles de la Revolución Sandinista* (Havana: Casa de las Américas, 1984), 176–8.

211. Farhi, "State disintegration," 254 note 10.

212. Black, *Triumph of the People*, 134.

213. Wickham-Crowley, *Guerrillas and Revolution*, 209–10, 232–5, 275. Wickham-Crowley presents data on the significance of guerrilla support in areas where peasant squatters were numerous: "Winners, losers, and also-rans," 148–9, and *Guerrillas and Revolution*, 233–4. Paige's major work on the revolution is *Coffee and Power*.

214. Goodwin, "Revolutionary movements," 26. See also ibid., 30.

215. Weber, *Nicaragua*, 51; Wickham-Crowley, *Guerrillas and Revolution*, 215. On all questions of women in the revolution, the major source is now Karen Kampwirth, *Women and Guerrilla Movements: Nicaragua, El Salvador, Chiapas, Cuba* (University Park: The Pennsylvania State University Press, 2002).

216. Wickham-Crowley, *Guerrillas and Revolution*, 214.

217. Wickham-Crowley, "Winners, losers, and also-rans," 154–5, citing Booth, *The End and the Beginning* (1982 edition), 41–6, 116–21; Wickham-Crowley, *Guerrillas and Revolution*, 246–7.

218. This section is condensed from my essay, "The Iranian revolution of 1977–79: a challenge for social theory," pp. 160–88 in John Foran, editor, *A Century of Revolution: Social Movements in Iran* (Minneapolis: University of Minnesota Press, 1994). I would like to thank my research assistant Javad Rassaf for his study of the Iranian press.

219. Charles Kurzman, *The Unthinkable Revolution in Iran* (Cambridge: Harvard University Press, 2004).

220. Said Amir Arjomand, "The causes and significance of the Iranian revolution," pp. 41–66 in *State, Culture and Society*, volume I, number 3 (1985), 56–8, 60; and Said Amir Arjomand, *The Turban for the Crown: The Islamic Revolution in Iran* (New York: Oxford University Press, 1988), 189–91, 196, 205. See also Hamid Algar, "Preface" to Ali Shari'ati, *Marxism and Other Western Fallacies. An Islamic Critique*, translated from the Persian by R. Campbell (Berkeley: Mizan Press, 1980), 12, and 'Ali Davani, *Nahzat-i Ruhaniyun-i Iran* [Movement of the Clergy of Iran], volume VIII (Tehran:

Bunyad-i Farhangi-yi Imam Reza, 1981). Those who stress the cultural significance of the revolution, starting with some of the actors themselves – notably Ayatullah Khumaini, essentially argue that the shah was overthrown for failing to adhere to Islam, since, as Khumaini put it: "I cannot believe and I do not accept that any prudent individual can believe that the purpose of all these sacrifices was to have less expensive melons . . . [The people who were killed by the thousands died] For Islam. The people fought for Islam": this is a composite quote from Khumaini, in Radio Tehran, September 8, 1979, text in *Foreign Broadcast Information Service* (September 10, 1979), n.p., and in Oriana Fallaci, "An interview with Khumaini," pp. 29–31 in *The New York Times Magazine* (October 7, 1979), 30.

221. See Thomas Walton [M. H. Pesaran], "Economic development and revolutionary upheavals in Iran," pp. 271–92 in *Cambridge Journal of Economics*, volume 4, number 3 (September 1980), 271, 288; Nikki Keddie, *Roots of Revolution: An Interpretive History of Modern Iran* (New Haven: Yale University Press, 1981), especially 177; Ervand Abrahamian, "Structural causes of the Iranian revolution," pp. 21–6 in *MERIP (Middle East Research and Information Project) Reports*, number 87 (May 1980); Ervand Abrahamian, *Iran Between Two Revolutions* (Princeton University Press, 1982); Amin Saikal, *The Rise and Fall of the Shah* (Princeton University Press, 1980); Jerrold D. Green, *Revolution in Iran: The Politics of Countermobilization* (New York: Praeger, 1982); and Mehran Kamrava, *Revolution in Iran: The Roots of Turmoil* (London: Routledge, 1990).

222. For different emphases on the political, see Misagh Parsa, *The Social Origins of the Iranian Revolution* (New Brunswick: Rutgers University Press, 1989); Valentine M. Moghadam, "Populist revolution and the Islamic state in Iran," pp. 147–63 in Terry Boswell, editor, *Revolution in the World System* (Greenwich: Greenwood Press, 1989); and Homa Katouzian, "Toward a general theory of Iranian revolutions," pp. 145–62 in *Journal of Iranian Research and Analysis*, volume 15, number 2 (November 1999).

223. See Fred Halliday, "The Iranian revolution: uneven development and religious populism," pp. 187–207 in *Journal of International Affairs*, volume 36, number 2 (Fall/Winter 1982–83), and Farhi, *States and Urban-Based Revolutions*, and "State disintegration and urban-based revolutionary crisis."

224. Theda Skocpol, "Rentier state and Shi'a Islam in the Iranian revolution," pp. 265–84 in *Theory & Society*, volume 11, number 3 (1982); and "What makes peasants revolutionary?," pp. 157–79 in Scott Guggenheim and Robert Weller, editors, *Power and Protest in the Countryside* (Durham: Duke University Press, 1982). See also her remarks in "Reflections on recent scholarship about social revolutions and how to study them," pp. 301–44 in Theda Skocpol, *Social Revolutions in the Modern World* (Cambridge University Press, 1994), 314, 337 note 3, where she explicitly acknowledges our disagreement.

225. On population, see Fred Halliday, *Iran: Dictatorship and Development* (New York: Penguin Books, 1979). 10; on GNP and income, Abrahamian, "Structural causes," 22; Pesaran, "The system of dependent capitalism," 504; and Homa Katouzian, *The Political Economy of Modern Iran: Despotism*

and Pseudo-Modernism, 1926–1979 (New York University Press, 1981), 325 table 16.2.

226. On rural Iran, see Eric J. Hooglund, *Land and Revolution Iran, 1960–1980* (Austin: University of Texas Press, 1982); Grace Goodell, *The Elementary Structures of Political Life: Rural Development in Pahlavi Iran* (New York: Oxford University Press, 1986); and Afsaneh Najmabadi, *Land Reform and Social Change in Iran* (Salt Lake City: University of Utah Press, 1988).

227. On the industrialization process, see the works of Katouzian, Abrahamian, Halliday, and Keddie, as well as M. S. Ivanov, *Tarikh-i Nuvin-i Iran* [Modern History of Iran], translated from the Russian by Hushang Tizabi and Hasan Qa'im Panah (Stockholm: Tudeh Publishing Centre, 1356/1977); Wilfrid Korby, *Probleme der industriellen Entwicklung und Konzentration in Iran* (Wiesbaden: Dr. Ludwig Reichert Verlag, 1977); and Massoud Karshenas, *Oil, State and Industrialization in Iran* (Cambridge University Press, 1990).

228. For data on all these classes see Foran, *Fragile Resistance*, chapter eight, and the references therein.

229. See Pesaran, "Economic development," 33; Kamran M. Dadkhah, "The inflationary process of the Iranian economy: a rejoinder," pp. 388–91 in *International Journal of Middle East Studies*, volume 19, number 3 (August 1987), 389 table 1; Abrahamian, *Iran Between Two Revolutions*, 431, 446–7; Katouzian, *Political Economy*, 271–2; Ivanov, *Tarikh-i Nuvin*, 254, 297; and Halliday, *Iran*, 13, 164.

230. Quoted in Kurzman, *The Unthinkable Revolution*, 82–3.

231. See Robert Graham, *Iran: The Illusion of Power* (New York: St. Martin's Press, 1979), 152–63; Dilip Hiro, *Iran Under the Ayatollahs* (London: Routledge and Kegan Paul, 1985), 253; Abrahamian, *Iran Between Two Revolutions*, 437–8; and interviews with Sir Peter Ramsbotham, 'Ali Amini, and Ahmad Ghoreishi,' Iranian Oral History Collection, Harvard University.

232. Amnesty International, *Annual Report 1974–75* (London: AI Publications, 1975), 8. On the repressive apparatus, see, among many others, Graham, *Iran*, 140–9, 163, 168–83; Halliday, *Iran*, 87–8, 90–6; and Reza Baraheni, *The Crowned Cannibals: Writings on Repression in Iran* (New York: Vintage Books, 1977), 131–218.

233. Farhi, *States and Urban-Based Revolutions*, 87–8; Katouzian, *The Political Economy of Modern Iran*, 192–3, 197, 234–5, 241–2; Graham, *Iran*, 133–8; Abrahamian, *Iran Between Two Revolutions*, 419–21, 438, 440–1; Saikal, *The Rise and Fall*, 63, 90–1, 190.

234. On the United States and Iran, see Halliday, *Iran*, 83, 91–5, 153 table 2, 248, 254–6, 339 note 1; Saikal, *The Rise and Fall*, 51, 56–8, 205–7; and the overviews by James A. Bill, *The Eagle and the Lion: The Tragedy of American-Iranian Relations* (New Haven: Yale University Press, 1988); Richard Cottam, *Iran and the United States: A Cold-War Case Study* (University of Pittsburgh Press, 1988); and Mark J. Gasiorowski, *US Foreign Policy and the Shah: Building a Client State in Iran* (Ithaca: Cornell University Press, 1991).

235. Quoted in Ahmad Ashraf and Ali Banuazizi, "The state, classes and modes of mobilization in the Iranian revolution," pp. 3–40 in *State, Culture and Society*, volume I, number 3 (1985), 4. This paragraph and the next draw

heavily on Bill, *The Eagle and the Lion*, and on State Department documents held by the National Security Archive in Washington, DC, especially
a January 29, 1980 White Paper on Iran.

236. Quoted in Bill, *The Eagle and the Lion*, 233. Some observers say this
made the shah overconfident of US support, emboldening him to take the
offensive with the slanderous letter against Khumaini that touched off the
first protests in Qum: see Dariush Humayun, *Diruz va Farda: Seh Guftar
darbareh-yi Iran-i Inqilabi* [Yesterday and tomorrow: three talks on revolutionary Iran] (USA: n.p., 1981), 62.

237. Kurzman, *The Unthinkable Revolution*, 157–8, 234 note 79.

238. Graham, Iran, 86–7. Data in this paragraph is drawn from ibid., 98–103;
"Iran: the new crisis of American hegemony," pp. 1–24 in *Monthly Review*,
volume 30, number 9 (February 1979); Dadkhah, "The inflationary process," 389 table 1; and Halliday, *Iran*, 165–6.

239. The shah in *Kayhan International* (October 26, 1976), quoted by Graham,
Iran, 103. In August 1974 he had promised: "We do not expect Iranians to
tighten their belts, eat less and labour away for the promised heaven which
is put off by a year every day. We try to offer the nation the welfare and care
we have promised – today:" in *Kayhan International* (August 2–3, 1974),
quoted by Graham, *Iran*, 103.

240. Halliday, "The Iranian revolution," 194. Data and analyses on 1977 are
found in idem, *Iran*, 145; idem, "The genesis of the Iranian revolution,"
pp. 1–16 in *Third World Quarterly*, volume 1, number 4 (October 1979), 9;
Pesaran, "Economic development," 286; Saikal, *The Rise and Fall*, 183, 191;
Katouzian, *The Political Economy*, 259–60; Nikki Keddie, "Iranian revolutions," pp. 579–98 in *American Historical Review*, volume 88 (1983), 588;
Kurzman, *The Unthinkable Revolution*, 96ff.; and National Security Archive
document 1745, telegram from the American Embassy, Tehran, to Secretary of State (November 16, 1978), 1–5.

241. Khumaini, from a collection of speeches and letters published in 1973,
quoted in Hossein Bashiriyeh, *The State and Revolution in Iran, 1962–1982*
(New York: St. Martin's, 1984), 60 1. On Khumaini's ideas and social
base, see Keddie, *Roots of Revolution*, 207, 242; Imam Khomeini, *Islam and
Revolution: Writings and Declarations of the Imam Khomeini*, translated and
annotated by Hamid Algar (Berkeley: Mizan Press, 1980); Abrahamian,
Iran Between Two Revolutions, 445, 475, 477–9, 532–3; idem, "Khomeini:
fundamentalist or populist?", pp. 102–19 in *New Left Review*, number
186 (March–April 1991); and Kurzman, *The Unthinkable Revolution*, 142,
151. An important study of many aspects of the emergent political culture is Hamid Dabashi, *Theology of Discontent: The Ideological Foundation
of the Islamic Republic in Iran* (New York: New York University Press,
1993).

242. Ali Shari'ati, *From Where Shall We Begin? & The Machine in the Captivity of
Machinism*, translated from the Persian by Fatollah Marjani (Houston: Free
Islamic Literatures, Inc., 1980), 30. See also Shari'ati, *Marxism and Other
Western Fallacies* (significantly the title is not his); Abrahamian, *Iran Between
Two Revolutions*, 464–70; Keddie, *Roots of Revolution*, 215–19, 221, 224;

and Brad Hanson, "The 'westoxication' of Iran: depictions and reactions of Behrangi, Al-e Ahmad, and Shari'ati," pp. 1–23 in *International Journal of Middle East Studies*, volume 15, number 1 (February 1983).

243. On Bazargan and the Liberation Movement of Iran, see Shahrough Akhavi, *Religion and Politics in Contemporary Iran: Clergy-State Relations in the Pahlavi Period* (Albany: State University of New York Press, 1980), 112–15; Keddie, *Roots of Revolution*, 210–15; Abrahamian, *Iran Between Two Revolutions*, 458–9; and H. E. Chehabi, *Iranian Politics and Religious Modernism: The Liberation Movement of Iran under the Shah and Khomeini* (Ithaca: Cornell University Press, 1990).

244. On the National Front, see Sussan Siavoshi, *Liberal Nationalism in Iran: The Failure of a Movement* (Boulder: Westview Press, 1988), and Parsa, *Social Origins*, 169–77. On the Tudeh, Halliday, *Iran*, 231, 233–7, 262, 289, 297; and Abrahamian, *Iran Between Two Revolutions*, 451–7.

245. On the Mujahidin, see Abrahamian, *Iran Between Two Revolutions*, 480–1, 489–95; Halliday, *Iran*, 240, 242; Keddie, *Roots of Revolution*, 238–9; Bashiriyeh, *The State and Revolution*, 74; and Ervand Abrahamian, *The Iranian Mojehedin* (New Haven: Yale University Press, 1989). On the Fada'ian, Halliday, *Iran*, 241–2, 246–7; Keddie, *Roots of Revolution*, 237, 239; and Abrahamian, *Iran Between Two Revolutions*, 480–5.

246. Kurzman, *The Unthinkable Revolution*, 116, 125, 142.

247. Ibid., 46.

248. Good sources for blow-by-blow accounts of 1978 include Parsa, *Social Origins*; Paul Balta and Claudine Rulleau, *L'Iran insurgé* (Paris: Sindbad, 1979); Abrahamian, *Iran Between Two Revolutions*; Keddie, *Roots of Revolution*; and Michael M. J. Fischer, *Iran: From Religious Dispute to Revolution* (Cambridge: Harvard University Press, 1980). I have also drawn on *Kayhan* (January–May 1978); Ashraf and Banuazizi, "The State," 9–10; Iranian Students Association in the US, *Shah's Inferno: Abadan August 19,1978* (Berkeley: ISAUS, 1978), 2ff; and Kurzman, *The Unthinkable Revolution*, 33ff.

249. Kurzman, *The Unthinkable Revolution*, 177.

250. In addition to works cited in the last footnote, I have drawn on *The Manchester Guardian* (September 5 and 6, 1978); *Le Monde* (September 6, 1978); Davani, *Nahzat-i Ruhaniyun-i Iran*; Mohammed Amjad, *Iran: From Royal Dictatorship to Theocracy* (New York: Greenwood Press, 1989), 126; Terisa Turner, "Iranian oilworkers in the 1978–79 revolution," pp. 279–92 in Petter Nore and Terisa Turner, editors, *Oil and Class Struggle* (London: Zed, 1981); "How we organized strike that paralyzed Shah's regime. Firsthand account by Iranian Oil Worker," pp. 292–301 in ibid.; and William H. Sullivan, "Dateline Iran: the road not taken," pp. 175–86 in *Foreign Policy*, number 40 (Fall 1980), 180. For evidence on the shah's shaky state of mind, see Hussain Fardust, *Zuhur va Suqut-i Saltanat-i Pahlavi: Khatarat-i Artishbud-i Sabiq Hussain Fardust* [The rise and fall of the Pahlavi dynasty: memoirs of former Field Marshal Hussain Fardust], two volumes (Tehran: Ittila'at Publications, 1991), and Marvin Zonis, *Majestic Failure: The Fall of the Shah* (University of Chicago Press, 1991).

251. This is a composite quote based on Abrahamian, *Iran Between Two Revolutions*, 529, and Graham, *Iran*, 237. In addition to the sources already cited, on these events see A. B. Reznikov, editor, "The downfall of the Iranian monarchy (January–February 1979)," pp. 254–312 in R. Ulyanovsky, *The Revolutionary Process in the East: Past and Present* (Moscow: Progress Publishers, 1985).
252. I discuss this coalition in more detail in "The Iranian revolution of 1977–79," 178–81.

CHAPTER 3

1. V. S. Naipaul, *The Overcrowded Barracoon and Other Articles* (London: Deutsch, 1972), 37, quoted by Jürgen Osterhammel, *Colonialism: A Theoretical Overview*, translated by Shelley L. Frisch (Princeton: Markus Wiener Publishers, 1997), 95.
2. Albert Memmi, *The Colonizer and the Colonized* (New York: Orion Books, 1965), 127–8.
3. The recent definition of colonialism by Jürgen Osterhammel is useful in setting up my argument: "*Colonialism* is a relationship of domination between an indigenous (or forcibly imported) majority and a minority of foreign invaders. The fundamental decisions affecting the lives of the colonized people are made and implemented by the colonial rulers in pursuit of interests that are often defined in a distant metropolis. Rejecting cultural compromises with the colonized population, the colonizers are convinced of their own superiority and of their ordained mandate to rule": *Colonialism*, 16–17. Osterhammel also points out the repressive, exclusionary rule of the colonial state (ibid., 57, 59) and provides hints about both dependent development and political cultures, explored elsewhere in this chapter.
4. Indeed, Jan Nederveen Pieterse notes that "the beginnings of the application of development to the South . . . started with colonial economics": "After post-development," pp. 175–91 in *Third World Quarterly*, vol. 21, no. 2 (2000), 183.
5. Frantz Fanon, *The Wretched of the Earth* (New York: Grove Press, 1963), 38–40.
6. Martin J. Murray, *The Development of Capitalism in Colonial Indochina (1870–1940)* (Berkeley: University of California Press, 1980), 38.
7. Tony Smith, "Muslim impoverishment in colonial Algeria," pp. 139–62 in *Revue de l'Occident Musulman et de la Méditerranée*, no. 17 (1974), 146.
8. Aijaz Ahmad points out perceptively that colonialism itself was rooted in particular *European* nationalisms: "Woman, nation, denomination," talk at the University of California, Santa Barbara (April 12, 2000).
9. Osterhammel, *Colonialism*, 97.
10. I would like to thank my student, Markus McMillin, for his early application of the model to the case of Algeria, an extraordinary theoretical and empirical undertaking from which I have learned a great deal: "The dynamics of an anti-colonialist social revolution: a study of French Algeria," BA

Honors Thesis, Department of Political Science, University of California, Santa Barbara (1991).
11. Joan Gillespie, *Algeria: Rebellion and Revolution* (New York: Frederick A. Praeger, Publishers, 1960), 3.
12. Edgar O'Ballance, *The Algerian Insurrection, 1954–62* (Hamden: Archon Books, 1967), 11.
13. Ibid.
14. Mahfoud Bennoune, *The Making of Contemporary Algeria, 1830–1987: Colonial Upheavals and Post-Independence Development* (Cambridge University Press, 1988), 85. This magisterial political economy draws in turn on Abdellatif Benachenhou, *Formation du sous-développement en Algérie: essai sur les limites du développement du capitalisme en Algérie 1830–1962* (Algiers: Entreprise Nationale "Imprimerie Comerciale," 1978).
15. Smith, "Muslim impoverishment in colonial Algeria," 140.
16. Bennoune, *The Making of Contemporary Algeria*, 17; see also 3, 31. This whole discussion of pre-colonial Algeria and the conquest is based upon Bennoune's work.
17. Ibid., 18.
18. Ibid., 22, quoting Lucette Valensi, *Le Maghreb avant la prise d'Alger, 1770–1830* (Paris: Flammarion, 1969), 34.
19. Bennoune, *The Making of Contemporary Algeria*, 31.
20. Ibid., 36.
21. Quoted in ibid., from Mostefa Lacherof, *L'Algérie: Nation et société* (Paris: Maspero, 1965), 159.
22. Quoted in Bennoune, *The Making of Contemporary Algeria*, 38, from Lacherof, *L'Algérie*, 170–1.
23. The Duc d'Orléans, *Récits de Campagne* (Paris: Calmann Levy, 1892), 139–40, quoted in Bennoune, *The Making of Contemporary Algeria*, 38.
24. Wolf, *Peasant Wars*, 220–1.
25. Bennoune, *The Making of Contemporary Algeria*, 41, quoting Tocqueville in Charles A. Julien, *L'histoire de l'Algérie contemporaine* (Paris: PUF, 1964), 316.
26. Bennoune, *The Making of Contemporary Algeria*, 58, 42, 42 table 2.1.
27. Smith, "Muslim impoverishment in colonial Algeria," 139.
28. Bennoune, *The Making of Contemporary Algeria*, 3, 76.
29. McMillin, "The dynamics of an anti-colonialist social revolution," 90–1, quoting John P. Entelis, *Algeria: The Revolution Institutionalized* (Boulder: Westview, 1986), 34. McMillin also provides a remarkable diagram of the social formation in 1954, grouped into various classes and modes of production: 78, Figure 3.1.
30. Bennoune, *The Making of Contemporary Algeria*, 63; see also 43–55, 60, 62 table 4.2, and Smith, "Muslim impoverishment in colonial Algeria," 162, appendix II.
31. Bennoune, *The Making of Contemporary Algeria*, 61–2, Gillespie, *Algeria*, 33–4; Nico Kielstra, "Was the Algerian revolution a peasant war?," pp. 172–86 in *Peasant Studies*, volume 7, number 3 (Summer 1978), 173, citing M. A. E. Calvelli, "Etat de la propriété en Algérie," Thèse de l'Université d'Alger, Faculté de Droit (1935), 96.

32. Bennoune, *The Making of Contemporary Algeria*, 65, 65 table 4.5.

33. Ibid., 73.

34. McMillin, "The dynamics of an anti-colonialist social revolution," 74.

35. Smith, "Muslim impoverishment in colonial Algeria," 159; see also Gillespie, *Algeria*, 29, and Bennoune, *The Making of Contemporary Algeria*, 69.

36. The data on industry in this paragraph are drawn from Bennoune, *The Making of Contemporary Algeria*, 71–5, and McMillin, "The dynamics of an anti-colonialist social revolution," 39–40.

37. Bennoune, *The Making of Contemporary Algeria*, 68; Gillespie, *Algeria*, 36.

38. Bennoune, *The Making of Contemporary Algeria*, 74; Rita Maran, *Torture: The Role of Ideology in the French-Algerian War* (New York: Praeger, 1989), 92.

39. Gillespie, *Algeria*, 34, table, citing France, Government-General of Algeria, *Rapport du Groupe d'Etude des Relations Financières entre la Metropole et l'Algérie* (June 1955), 79, 80; see also Smith, "Muslim impoverishment in colonial Algeria," 149.

40. Smith, "Muslim impoverishment in colonial Algeria," 140. On declining per capita production of most foodstuffs, see Bennoune, *The Making of Contemporary Algeria*, 59.

41. Bennoune, *The Making of Contemporary Algeria*, 77; Gillespie, *Algeria*, 32. Bennoune puts unemployment as high as 1,438,000 in 1954: 69.

42. Maran, *Torture*, 93, quoting Thomas-Robert Bugeaud, *L'Algérie: des moyens de conserver et d'utiliser cette conquête* (Paris: Dentu, 1842), 32, 34.

43. Maran, *Torture*, 95, citing first Bugeaud, *L'Algérie*, 5, and then General Théophile Duvivier, *Algérie: Quatorze observations sur le dernier mémoire du Général Bugeaud* (Paris: Librarire Garnier, 1842), 65.

44. "71% of the pieds-noirs earned half or less the Franch [sic] national average": Smith, "Muslim impoverishment in colonial Algeria," 153 note 42.

45. Jules Roy, *The War in Algeria* (New York: Grove Press, 1961), 17.

46. Entelis, *Algeria*, 32.

47. McMillin, "The dynamics of an anti-colonialist social revolution," 88, citing Entelis, *Algeria*, 30 and Tanya Matthews, *War in Algeria: Background for Crisis* (New York: Fordham University Press, 1961), 15.

48. McMillin, "The dynamics of an anti-colonialist social revolution," 86, citing Edmund Stevens, *North African Powder Keg* (New York: Coward-McCann, Inc., 1955), 181.

49. Smith, "Muslim impoverishment in colonial Algeria," 154–5.

50. McMillin, "The dynamics of an anti-colonialist social revolution," 24–5.

51. Wolf, *Peasant Wars*, 221.

52. McMillin, "The dynamics of an anti-colonialist social revolution," 90.

53. Alf Andrew Heggoy, *Insurgency and Counterinsurgency in Algeria* (Bloomington: Indiana University Press, 1972), 3.

54. Gillespie, *Algeria*, 40.

55. McMillin, "The dynamics of an anti-colonialist social revolution," 96, quoting Richard Brace and Joan Brace, *Ordeal in Algeria* (New York: D. Van Nostrand Company, Inc., 1960), 32. On the ENA, see also Entelis, *Algeria*, 46; Bennoune, *The Making of Contemporary Algeria*, 79; and Kielstra, "Was the Algerian revolution a peasant war?," 175.

56. McMillin, "The dynamics of an anti-colonialist social revolution," 100, quoting Gillespie, *Algeria*, 46. See also Kielstra, "Was the Algerian revolution a peasant war?," 175–6.

57. Bennoune, *The Making of Contemporary Algeria*, 80; see also McMillin, "The dynamics of an anti-colonialist social revolution," 97, 106.

58. John Ruedy, *Modern Algeria: The Origins and Development of a Nation* (Bloomington: Indiana University Press, 1992), 153; see also Kielstra, "Was the Algerian revolution a peasant war?," 176–7.

59. On the MTLD, see Bennoune, *The Making of Contemporary Algeria*, 81, and McMillin, "The dynamics of an anti-colonialist social revolution," 106–8.

60. Wolf, *Peasant Wars*, 236, citing Swiss journalist Charles-Henri Favrod, *La F. L. N. et l'Algérie* (Paris: Plon, 1962).

61. Wolf, *Peasant Wars*, 236, puts the number at 15,000; Alistair Horne offers a detailed discussion of the events: *A Savage War of Peace: Algeria 1954–1962* (London: Macmillan, 1977), 25–7.

62. Quoted in Arslan Humbaraci, *Algeria: A Revolution That Failed: A Political History Since 1954* (New York: Frederick A. Praeger, 1968), 45.

63. Robert B. Revere, "Revolutionary ideology in Algeria," pp. 477–88 in *Polity*, volume v, number 4 (Summer 1973), 485, 484, quoting Laroussi Khelifa, *Manuel du Militant Algerien*, volume I (Lausanne: La Cité Editeur, 1962), 162–4.

64. Kielstra, "Was the Algerian revolution a peasant war?," 175.

65. Wolf, *Peasant Wars*, 244, quoting Frantz Fanon, *The Damned* (Paris: Présence Africaine, 1963), 73.

66. Wolf, *Peasant Wars*, 226, citing Pierre Bourdieu, "Guerre et mutation sociale en Algérie," pp. 25–7 in *Etudes Méditerranéenes*, number 7 (1960), 27; see also Fanon's chapter on "Algeria unveiled," pp. 35–68 in *Studies in a Dying Colonialism*, translated from the French *L'An Cinq de la Révolution Algérienne* by Haakon Chevalier (New York: Monthly Review Press, 1965).

67. McMillin, "The dynamics of an anti-colonialist social revolution," 109–10. See also McMillin's excellent diagram of the origins of the Algerian "all-class alliance": ibid., 124 Figure 6.1.

68. Bennoune, *The Making of Contemporary Algeria*, 70.

69. Ibid., 4.

70. Ibid.

71. Gillespie, *Algeria*, 35.

72. Wolf, *Peasant Wars*, 235.

73. McMillin, "The dynamics of an anti-colonialist social revolution," 155; see also 119, 120, 127, 132, 150.

74. McMillin, "The dynamics of an anti-colonialist social revolution," 114, quoting Alistair Horne, *A Savage War of Peace*, 68.

75. McMillin, "The dynamics of an anti-colonialist social revolution," 128–31; Martin Evans, *The Memory of Resistance: French Opposition to the Algerian War (1954–1962)* (Oxford: Berg, 1997), xiv, xvi; Guy Arnold, *Wars in the Third World since 1945* (London: Cassell, 1991), 8, 10.

76. McMillin, "The dynamics of an anti-colonialist social revolution," 117, who finds the quote in Jabhat al-Tahrir al Qawmi, *Genocide in Algeria* (Cairo: The Front of National Liberation, 1957), 11.

77. David L. Schalk, *War and the Ivory Tower: Algeria and Vietnam* (New York: Oxford University Press, 1991), 93; see also McMillin, "The dynamics of an anti-colonialist social revolution," 133–4.

78. Schalk, *War and the Ivory Tower*, 93.

79. Ibid., 110, quoting Michel Crouzet, "La bataille des intellectuels français," *La Nef*, numbers 12–13 (October 1962–January 1963), 47. On Sartre and other French intellectuals, see Annie Cohen-Solal, "Camus, Sartre and the Algerian War," pp. 43–50 in *Journal of European Studies*, volume 27 (1998).

80. Philip Dine, "French culture and the Algerian war: mobilizing icons," pp. 51–68 in *Journal of European Studies*, volume 27 (1998), citing Jean-François Sirinelli, "Les intellectuels dans la mêlée," pp. 116–30 in Jean-Pierre Rioux and Jean-François Sirinelli, editors, *La Guerre d'Algérie et les intellectuels français* (Brussels: Editions Complexe, 1991).

81. Jean-François Lyotard, *Political Writings*, translated by Bill Readings and Kevin Paul Geiman (Minneapolis: University of Minnesota Press, 1993), 277.

82. Wolf, *Peasant Wars*, 242.

83. Wolf, *Peasant Wars*, 238–41; McMillin, "The dynamics of an anti-colonialist social revolution," 120.

84. This paragraph draws primarily on McMillin, "The dynamics of an anti-colonialist social revolution," 137–46.

85. Schalk, *War and the Ivory Tower*, 93–4, citing the "most careful and convincing examination of these estimates" (209 note 107) by Guy Pervillé, "Bilan de la guerre d'Algérie," in *Etudes sur la France de 1939 à nos jours* (special issue of *L'Histoire*) (Paris: Editions du Seuil, 1985), 297–301. Around 17,250 French soldiers were killed and 51,800 wounded, plus several thousand French civilians; the war cost 50 billion new francs.

86. Kielstra, "Was the Algerian revolution a peasant war?," 181.

87. Lyotard, *Political Writings*, 189.

88. On this point, see Val Moghadam, "Gender and revolutions," pp. 137–67 in John Foran, editor, *Theorizing Revolutions* (London: Routledge, 1997), 146–8, drawing on Peter Knauss, *The Persistence of Patriarchy: Class, Gender and Ideology in Twentieth Century Algeria* (Boulder: Westview, 1987).

89. This whole section on Angola is greatly indebted to the work of my research assistant, Sadie Miller, at Smith College in 2001, and a report she wrote on the case: Sadie Miller, "The Angolan anti-colonial revolution," unpublished paper, Smith College (2001), from which I have learned much and drawn extensively, as I have on her reading notes and the materials she gathered. I have also benefited from feedback by John Marcum, and research assistance by Daniel Olmos at UC Santa Barbara in 2004.

90. "Angola," pp. 75–8 in *The World Guide 2001/2002* (Oxford: New Internationalist Publications, Ltd., 2001), 75.

91. Américo Boavida, *Angola: Five Centuries of Portuguese Exploitation* (Richmond: LSM Information Center, 1972), 47.

92. The 1450 figures – likely far too high – are from Boavida, *Angola*, 47; the 1850 one is from *The World Guide*, 75; the 1960 ones are found in Mario de Andrade and Mark Ollivier, *The War in Angola: A Socio-economic Study* (Dar es Salaam: Tanzania Publishing House, 1975), 15. Population recovered to 5.67 million according to the 1970 census: Phyllis M. Martin, *Historical Dictionary of Angola* (Metuchen: The Scarecrow Press, 1980), 21 table 3.

93. Ernest Harsch and Tony Thomas, *Angola: The Hidden History of Washington's War* (New York: Pathfinder Press, 1976), 25–6.

94. F. W. Heimer, *The Decolonization Conflict in Angola 1974–76: An Essay in Political Sociology* (Geneva: Institut Universitaire des Etudes Internationales, 1979), 5–6.

95. Boavida, *Angola*, 50.

96. de Andrade and Ollivier, *The War in Angola*, 33.

97. Heimer, *The Decolonization Conflict in Angola*, 7.

98. Paige, *Agrarian Revolution*, 226, 230.

99. de Andrade and Ollivier, *The War in Angola*, 20, citing data from the Banco de Angola.

100. Catherine V. Scott and Gus B. Cochran, "Revolution in the periphery: Angola, Cuba, Mozambique, and Nicaragua," p. 43–58 in Terry Boswell, editor, *Revolution in the World-System* (New York: Greenwood Press, 1989), 44 table 4.1.

101. Michael Wolfers and Jane Bergerol, *Angola in the Frontline* (London: Zed Press, 1983), 1.

102. de Andrade and Ollivier, *The War in Angola*, 42, 50; Harsch and Thomas, *Angola*, 19; Lawrence W. Henderson, *Angola: Five Centuries of Conflict* (Ithaca: Cornell University Press, 1979), 210. Heimer notes, interestingly, "the extent to which, during given periods, the Angolan colonial economy was a function of other economies, has not yet produced conclusive results": Heimer, *The Decolonization Conflict in Angola*, 7 note 27. In other words, the dependent colonial development of Angola nested inside Portugal's own dependent development vis-à-vis core First World powers.

103. Martin, *Historical Dictionary of Angola*, 23 table 5, 24 table 6; Henderson, *Angola*, 211–12.

104. Heimer concurs in this judgment of considerable transformation: *The Decolonization Conflict in Angola*, 12–13, as does James Ciment, *Angola and Mozambique: Postcolonial Wars in Southern Africa* (New York: Facts on File, Inc., 1997), 34.

105. On the practice and extent of forced labor, see Paige, *Agrarian Revolution*, 242–52.

106. Ciment, *Angola and Mozambique*, 34.

107. de Andrade and Ollivier, *The War in Angola*, 43.

108. Ibid., 42.

109. Boavida, *Angola*, 54; de Andrade and Ollivier, *The War in Angola*, 46, quoting from the January 22, 1947 report of Captain Henrique Galvão.

110. Norrie Macqueen, *The Decolonization of Portuguese Africa: Metropolitan Revolution and the Dissolution of Empire* (New York: Longman, 1997), 12.

111. Harsch and Thomas, *Angola*, 53; Macqueen, *The Decolonization of Portuguese Africa*, 12. Heimer puts the number of whites in 1974 no higher than 320,000, or 5 percent of the population: *The Decolonization Conflict in Angola*, 8 note 28.

112. Ciment, *Angola and Mozambique*, 30.

113. de Andrade and Ollivier, *The War in Angola*, 18.

114. Arnold, *Wars in the Third World*, 10.

115. Heimer, *The Decolonization Conflict in Angola*, 12.

116. Ciment, *Angola and Mozambique*, 35, quoting People's Press Angola Book Project, *With Freedom in Their Eyes: A Photo-Essay of Angola* (San Francisco: People's Press, 1976), 12.

117. Heimer, *The Decolonization Conflict in Angola*, 10.

118. Gillian Gunn, "The Angolan economy: a history of contradiction," pp. 181–97 in Edmond J. Keller and Donald Rothschild, editors, *Afro-Marxist Regimes: Ideology and Public Policy* (Boulder: Lynne Rienner, 1987), 182–4.

119. Ciment, *Angola and Mozambique*, 31.

120. Miller, "The Angolan anti-colonial revolution," 4.

121. de Andrade and Ollivier, *The War in Angola*, 35.

122. Harsch and Thomas, *Angola*, 27. A key source on all the movements is John A. Marcum, *The Angolan Revolution*, volume II, *Exile Politics and Guerilla Warfare (1962–1976)* (Cambridge: MIT Press, 1978).

123. Heimer, *The Decolonization Conflict in* Angola, 14; de Andrade and Ollivier, *The War in Angola*, 54.

124. Heimer, *The Decolonization Conflict in Angola*, 13, 13 notes 63 and 64.

125. Norrie Macqueen, "An ill wind? Rethinking the Angolan crisis and the Portuguese revolution, 1974–1976," pp. 24–44 in *Itinerarie*, volume 26, number 2 (2002).

126. James Duffy, *Portugal in Africa* (Cambridge: Harvard University Press, 1962), 219–20, quoted in Harsch and Thomas, *Angola*, 27.

127. Macqueen, *The Decolonization of Portuguese Africa*, 194.

128. John A. Marcum, "The People's Republic of Angola: a radical vision frustrated," pp. 67–83 in Edmond J. Keller and Donald Rothchild, editors, *Afro-Marxist Regimes: Ideology and Public Policy* (Boulder: Lynne Rienner, 1987), 69.

129. Boavida, *Angola*, 36–7.

130. Wolfers and Bergerol, *Angola in the Frontline*, 3.

131. Macqueen, *The Decolonization of Portuguese Africa*, 171; Henderson, *Angola*, 229.

132. Harsch and Thomas, *Angola*, 28–9; Henderson, *Angola*, 192; Marcum, *The Angolan Revolution*, II, 32.

133. Harsch and Thomas, *Angola*, 28; Ciment, *Angola and Mozambique*, 40; Macqueen, *The Decolonization of Portuguese Africa*, 30; Marcum, *The Angolan Revolution*, II, 15, 17, 102ff.

134. Ciment, *Angola and Mozambique*, 39.

135. Macqueen, *The Decolonization of Portuguese Africa*, 29.

136. Ciment, *Angola and Mozambique*, 33; Henderson, *Angola*, 194. On Savimbi and UNITA, see Marcum, *The Angolan Revolution*, II, 134ff, 161ff.

137. From the 1968 UNITA pamphlet, *Angola – Seventh Year*, quoted by Harsch and Thomas, *Angola*, 47.
138. Harsch and Thomas, *Angola*, 67.
139. Paige, *Agrarian Revolution*, 270.
140. Henderson, *Angola*, 178, 185; Ciment, *Angola and Mozambique*, 39; de Andrade and Ollivier, *The War in Angola*, 59; Macqueen, *The Decolonization of Portuguese Africa*, 37.
141. Quoted in Henderson, *Angola*, 175.
142. This is Henderson's characterization: *Angola*, 211.
143. John P. Cann, *Counterinsurgency in Africa: The Portuguese Way of War, 1961–1974* (Westport: Greenwood, 1997), 194. See also 187–9, 193; Wolfers and Bergerol, *Angola in the Frontline*, 1; and Macqueen, *The Decolonization of Portuguese Africa*, 158.
144. Henderson, *Angola*, 210.
145. Arnold, *Wars in the Third World*, 14, quoting the *Sunday Times* (October 20, 1974).
146. Henderson, *Angola*, 236.
147. Ibid., 213.
148. Ciment, *Angola and Mozambique*, 36, 44. Malyn Newitt, *A History of Mozambique* (Bloomington: Indiana University Press, 1995), 533.
149. Henderson, *Angola*, 222.
150. W. S. Van der Waals, *Portugal's War in Angola, 1961–1974* (Rivonia, South Africa: Ashanti Publishers, 1993), 237.
151. The quote is from Macqueen, "An ill wind?" 23. See also Van der Waals, *Portugal's War in Angola*, 244, and Macqueen, *The Decolonization of Portuguese Africa*, 76.
152. Macqueen, *The Decolonization of Portuguese Africa*, 37, 158.
153. Arnold, *Wars in the Third World*, 12–13.
154. Macqueen, *The Decolonization of Portuguese Africa*, 73–4; Van der Waals, *Portugal's War in Angola*, 247.
155. Henderson, *Angola*, 225; Van der Waals, *Portugal's War in Angola*, 246.
156. Cunhal's *Rume à Vitória* is quoted by Miguel Urbano Rodrigues in his 1966 preface to Boavida, *Angola*, 17.
157. Van der Waals, *Portugal's War in Angola*, 244.
158. Gunn, "The Angolan economy," 184.
159. Macqueen, "An ill wind?" 36.
160. Macqueen, *The Decolonization of Portuguese Africa*, 163–4.
161. Wolfers and Bergerol, *Angola in the Frontline*, 6.
162. Macqueen, *The Decolonization of Portuguese Africa*, 177, 186; Ciment, *Angola and Mozambique*, 49; Gunn, "The Angolan Economy," 187. See also Harsch and Thomas, *Angola*, 64–5, 87; Henderson, *Angola*, 255; and Ciment, *Angola and Mozambique*, 47, on the civil war.
163. Arnold, *Wars in the Third World*, 13.
164. Macqueen quotes socialist-leaning minister for inter-territorial co-ordination António de Almeida Santos as saying "I . . . sympathise with the MPLA, . . . I love Angola, feel for the MPLA and its cause, but I love above all the peace:" "An ill wind?" 29–30.

165. Ciment, *Angola and Mozambique*, 52–3. Henderson and Macqueen cover the 1975–76 developments well in *Angola*, 247–58 and *The Decolonization of Portuguese Africa*, 177ff, respectively.
166. Henderson, *Angola*, 256.
167. Catherine V. Scott, "'Men in our country behave like chiefs': women and the Angolan revolution," pp. 89–108 in Mary Ann Tétreault, editor, *Women and Revolution in Africa, Asia, and the New World* (Columbia: University of South Carolina Press, 1994).
168. Ciment, *Angola and Mozambique*, 53–4.
169. This section on Mozambique is also greatly indebted to the work of my research assistant, Sadie Miller, at Smith College in 2001, and a report she wrote on the case: Sadie Miller, "The Mozambican revolution," unpublished paper, Smith College (2001), as well as reading notes and the materials she gathered.
170. Allen Isaacman and Barbara Isaacman, *Mozambique: From Colonialism to Revolution, 1900–1982* (Boulder: Westview, 1983), 14–8; James Hanlon, *Mozambique: The Revolution Under Fire* (London: Zed, 1984), 16.
171. Hanlon, *Mozambique*, 17.
172. Arnold, *Wars in the Third World*, 41.
173. Ciment, *Angola and Mozambique*, 34.
174. Barry Munslow, *Mozambique: The Revolution and Its Origins* (London: Longman, 1983), 89. In "Mozambique," pp. 388–90 in *The World Guide 2001/2002* (Oxford: New Internationalist Publications, Ltd., 2001), 388, the figure working abroad is put at one million, while the Committee of Returned Volunteers, New York Chapter, Africa Committee, *Mozambique Will Be Free* (New York: Committee of Returned Volunteers, 1969), 12, makes the estimate of 300,000.
175. Isaacman and Isaacman, *Mozambique*, 47 table 3.6, 48 table 3.7.
176. Ibid., *Mozambique*, 46.
177. Ciment, *Angola and Mozambique*, 11, 34.
178. Munslow, *Mozambique*, 48.
179. Ibid., 11.
180. Macqueen, *The Decolonization of Portuguese Africa*, 46.
181. Arnold, *Wars in the Third World*, 42; Newitt, *A History of Mozambique*, 528–9.
182. Isaacman and Isaacman, *Mozambique*, 42.
183. Ibid., 45–6.
184. Quoted in ibid., 55.
185. Ibid., 57, 58–9.
186. Hanlon, *Mozambique*, 21; Isaacman and Isaacman, *Mozambique*, 3.
187. Isaacman and Isaacman, *Mozambique*, 8. While it is true that this could reflect the initial disruptions of the post-independence economy, it is also indicative of the poverty that the colonial system bequeathed the nation in 1975. Per capita income would reach only $210 as late as 1998, with life expectancy at forty-four years, this due largely to the ravages of the AIDS epidemic: *The World Guide*, 390.
188. Newitt, *A History of Mozambique*, 467, 477; the 1975 figure is found in Arnold, *Wars in the Third World*, 45.

189. Isaacman and Isaacman, *Mozambique*, 43.
190. Ibid., 56, 58; Hanlon, *Mozambique*, 20.
191. Isaacman and Isaacman, *Mozambique*, 57–8.
192. Miller, "The Mozambican revolution," 7.
193. Isaacman and Isaacman, *Mozambique*, 31.
194. The quote is found in Ciment, *Angola and Mozambique*, 34, who cites Eduardo Mondlane, *The Struggle for Mozambique* (New York: Penguin, 1969), 85–6.
195. Hanlon, *Mozambique*, 23.
196. Isaacman and Isaacman, *Mozambique*, 103.
197. Miller, "The Mozambican revolution," 7–8 summarizes these; see also Isaacman and Isaacman, *Mozambique*, 22, 62–7.
198. William Minter, *Portuguese Africa and the West* (New York: Monthly Review Press, 1973), n.p., is quoted by John S. Saul, editor, *A Difficult Road: The Transition to Socialism in Mozambique* (New York: Monthly Review Press, 1985), 49.
199. Isaacman and Isaacman, *Mozambique*, 78.
200. Hanlon, *Mozambique*, 24; Ciment, *Angola and Mozambique*, 42; Arnold, *Wars in the Third World*, 41. An eyewitness account is found in the Committee of Returned Volunteers, *Mozambique Will Be Free*, 10.
201. Isaacman and Isaacman, *Mozambique*, 81; Macqueen, *The Decolonization of Portuguese Africa*, 21; Munslow, *Mozambique*, 81.
202. Quoted in Iain Christie, *Samora Machel: A Biography* (London: Zed, 1989), 124.
203. Quoted in Isaacman and Isaacman, *Mozambique*, 46. A version of this story also appears in Christie, *Samora Machel*, 123.
204. Christie, *Samora Machel*, 125; Macqueen, *The Decolonization of Portuguese Africa*, 18.
205. Christie, *Samora Machel*, 125.
206. From a 1995 interview quoted in John S. Saul, "Inside from the outside? The roots and resolution of Mozambique's un/civil war," pp. 122–66 in Taisier M. Ali and Robert O. Matthews, editors, *Civil Wars in Africa: Roots and Resolution* (Montreal: McGill-Queen's University Press, 1999), 127.
207. Ciment, *Angola and Mozambique*, 33; Newitt, *A History of Mozambique*, 521. Hanlon also notes that ethnic lines were crossed and that Portuguese was the common language required of the revolutionaries: *Mozambique*, 29.
208. Arnold, *Wars in the Third World*, 41; Macqueen, *The Decolonization of Portuguese Africa*, 45, stresses the disunity in the organization after the assassination.
209. The quote is from a February 1968 article in *Motive* magazine, found in Committee of Returned Volunteers, *Mozambique Will Be Free*, 3.
210. Compare Munslow: "the movement was not fighting whites, but a system that employed Portuguese peasants and workers in a conscripted army to defend the interests of its wealthy rulers" (*Mozambique*, 109), and Macqueen, who wrote of Angola, Mozambique, and Guinea-Bissau: "despite the class analysis which the three Marxist movements put at the centre of their programmes, their support was to a great extent ethnically determined" (*The Decolonization of Portuguese Africa*, 58).

211. LSM Information Center, *The Mozambican Woman in the Revolution* (Oakland: LSM Press, 1977), 7. See also Miller, "The Mozambican revolution," 13–14. Machel's views on the organizing abilities of women are consonant with Julia Shayne's concept of "gendered revolutionary bridges": Julia D. Shayne, "'The revolution question': feminism in Cuba, Chile, and El Salvador compared (1952–1999)', PhD dissertation, Department of Sociology, University of California, Santa Barbara (2000). For an overview of the activities of women before, during, and after the revolution, see Kathleen Sheldon, "Women and revolution in Mozambique: a luta continua," pp. 33–61 in Mary Ann Tétreault, editor, *Women and Revolution in Africa, Asia, and the New World* (Columbia: University of South Carolina Press, 1994).
212. Quoted in Isaacman and Isaacman, *Mozambique*, 92; see also 211, note 33.
213. Ibid., 94.
214. Arnold, *Wars in the Third World*, 41.
215. Ibid., 43.
216. Macqueen, *The Decolonization of Portuguese Africa*, 56.
217. Isaacman and Isaacman, *Mozambique*, 104–5.
218. Arnold, *Wars in the Third World*, 41, 43.
219. Newitt, *A History of Mozambique*, 533, 537–8.
220. Ibid., 537.
221. Isaacman and Isaacman, *Mozambique*, 105.
222. Macqueen, *The Decolonization of Portuguese Africa*, 130.
223. Ibid.
224. Arnold, *Wars in the Third World*, 41.
225. Ibid., 42.
226. Isaacman and Isaacman, *Mozambique*, 93–6; Arnold, *Wars in the Third World*, 43.
227. Arnold, *Wars in the Third World*, 43.
228. Quoted in ibid., 43.
229. Newitt, *A History of Mozambique*, 535.
230. From a statement of the Executive Committee of Frelimo, quoted in Macqueen, *The Decolonization of Portuguese Africa*, 126. This paragraph draws on Arnold, *Wars in the Third World*, 44–5, and Macqueen, *The Decolonization of Portuguese Africa*, 124ff.
231. Samora Machel, *Samora Machel: An African Revolutionary: Selected Speeches and Writings*, edited by Barry Munslow and translated by Michael Wolfers (London: Zed, 1985), xxi.
232. *The World Guide*, 390.
233. I am indebted once again to the work done by my research assistant, Sadie Miller, on this case, including the preparation of a report titled "The revolution of Zimbabwe," Smith College (2001).
234. This history to 1900 draws on Gay Seidman, David Martin, and Phyllis Johnson, *Zimbabwe: A New History* (Harare: Zimbabwe Publishing House, n.d.), and on Christine Sylvester, *Zimbabwe: The Terrain of Contradictory Development* (Boulder: Westview, 1991), 14 and passim.
235. Sylvester, *Zimbabwe*, 14.
236. Ibid., 10.

237. Sadie Miller notes: "Thus there is a varying sense of oppression and identification between the two main ethnic groups in Zimbabwe. As in many African states, the settlers divided and isolated groups based on internal ethnic differences to more easily colonize Zimbabwe. The Shona-settler alliance was used to create the myth that settlers freed the oppressed Shona nation from the Ndebele aggressors": "The revolution of Zimbabwe," 2–3, citing also Sylvester, *Zimbabwe*, 13–14.

238. James R. Scarritt, "Zimbabwe: revolutionary violence resulting in reform," pp. 235–71 in Jack A. Goldstone, Ted Robert Gurr, and Farrokh Moshiri, editors, *Revolutions of the Late Twentieth Century* (Boulder: Westview, 1991), 237.

239. Tor Skålnes, *The Politics of Economic Reform in Zimbabwe: Continuity and Change in Development* (New York: St. Martin's Press, 1995), 40.

240. Colin Stoneman and Lionel Cliffe, *Zimbabwe: Politics, Economics and Society* (London and New York: Pinter, 1989), 17; Scarritt, "Zimbabwe," 240–2.

241. André Astrow, *Zimbabwe: A Revolution That Lost Its Way?* (Zed Press: London, 1983), 7.

242. Scarritt, "Zimbabwe," 239.

243. Anthony Verrier, *The Road to Zimbabwe: 1890–1980* (London: Jonathan Cape, 1986), 136; see also 135.

244. Scarritt, "Zimbabwe," 235–9.

245. Astrow, *Zimbabwe*, 14; Sylvester, *Zimbabwe*, 46.

246. Colin Stoneman and Rob Davies, "The economy: an overview," pp. 95–126 in Colin Stoneman, editor, *Zimbabwe's Inheritance* (St. Martin's Press: New York, 1981), 117–19; Scarritt, "Zimbabwe," 242.

247. Astrow, *Zimbabwe*, 14.

248. Scarritt, "Zimbabwe," 243.

249. Sylvester, *Zimbabwe*, 46.

250. Jeffrey Davidow, *Dealing with International Crises: Lessons from Zimbabwe* (Muscatine: The Stanley Foundation, 1983), 5.

251. Scarritt, "Zimbabwe," 240.

252. Miller, "The revolution of Zimbabwe," 9, citing Astrow, *Zimbabwe*, 11 and Sylvester, *Zimbabwe*, 40, 42.

253. Stoneman and Davies, "The economy," 103, citing R. Riddel and P. S. Harris, *The Poverty Datum Line as a Wage Fixing Standard*, Mambo Occasional Papers, Socio-Economic Series, number 4 (Gwelo: Mambo Press, 1975), 67.

254. Sylvester, *Zimbabwe*, 22, 31, 35.

255. Astrow, *Zimbabwe*, 11.

256. Ibid., 26, 64; Scarritt, "Zimbabwe," 244, 252.

257. Astrow, Zimbabwe, 31–2; Scarritt, "Zimbabwe," 246.

258. Astrow, *Zimbabwe*, 44.

259. Ibid., 36.

260. Lionel Cliffe, "Zimbabwe's political inheritance," pp. 8–35 in Colin Stoneman, *Zimbabwe's Inheritance* (New York: St. Martin's Press, 1981), 26; Astrow, *Zimbabwe*, 88.

261. Astrow, *Zimbabwe*, 105–6.

262. Cliffe, "Zimbabwe's political inheritance," 27; Terence Ranger and Mark Ncube, "Religion in the guerrilla war: the case of Southern Matabeleland," pp. 35–57 in Ngwabi Bhebe and Terence Ranger, editors, *Society in Zimbabwe's Liberation War* (Oxford: James Currey, 1996), 35, who note the "remarkable study" by David Lan, *Guns and Rain: Guerrillas and Spirit Mediums in Zimbabwe* (London: James Curry, 1985).

263. Miller notes: "Sources vary tremendously on the importance of Shona spirit mediums and indigenous spirituality in creating a cultural nationalism (Astrow, *Zimbabwe*, for example, barely mentions their importance, while Ranger and Ncube emphasize spirituality in guerilla's connections in rural communities)": "The revolution of Zimbabwe," 23–4, citing Ranger and Ncube, "Religion in the guerrilla war," 57; see also Cliffe, "Zimbabwe's political inheritance," 27.

264. Cliffe, "Zimbabwe's political inheritance," 29; this paragraph also draws on Stoneman and Cliffe, *Zimbabwe*, 27.

265. On women, see Sita Ranchod-Nilsson, "'This, too, is a way of fighting': rural women's participation in Zimbabwe's liberation war," pp. 62–88 in Mary Ann Tétreault, editor, *Women and Revolution in Africa, Asia, and the New World* (Columbia: University of South Carolina Press, 1994).

266. Scarritt, "Zimbabwe," 245.

267. Quoted in Astrow, *Zimbabwe*, 144.

268. Astrow, *Zimbabwe*, 136.

269. Scarritt, "Zimbabwe," 245.

270. Astrow, *Zimbabwe*, 63.

271. Skålnes, *The Politics of Economic Reform*, 66; Astrow, *Zimbabwe*, 59.

272. Astrow, *Zimbabwe*, 64, 66; Davidow, *Dealing with International Crises*, 4.

273. Quoted in Seidman, Martin, and Johnson, *Zimbabwe*, 123.

274. Davidow, *Dealing with International Crises*, 4; Sylvester, *Zimbabwe*, 46.

275. Verrier, *The Road to Zimbabwe*, 147.

276. Quoted in Stoneman and Cliffe, *Zimbabwe*, 29.

277. Quoted in ibid, *Zimbabwe*, 29–30.

278. Davidow, *Dealing with International Crises*, 10; see also Sylvester, *Zimbabwe*, 55.

279. Davidow, *Dealing with International Crises*, 10–11; Scarritt, "Zimbabwe," 257–8; Stoneman and Cliffe, *Zimbabwe*, 33.

280. A huge thanks to my research assistants, beginning with Jennifer Kagawa, who did an enormous amount of reading and analysis on this case in 1998–99, culminating in a research report, "The Vietnamese case," Department of Sociology, UC Santa Barbara (1999), and ending with Linda Klouzal and Richard Widick, who did more work in 2002–3. Thanks also to Chris Appy, who provided missing information, and much else, as well as Jeff Goodwin, for comments on this section.
  I think I found the idea of Vietnam as interrupted somewhere in Ken Post's epic: *Revolution, Socialism, and Nationalism in Vietnam*, five volumes (England: Dartmouth Publishing Company, 1989–94). I regret having limited time to learn from this work.

281. I take much of the factual information in this paragraph from H. John LeVan's chronology: "Vietnam: revolution of postcolonial consolidation," pp. 52–87 in Jack A. Goldstone, Ted Robert Gurr, and Farrokh Moshiri, editors, *Revolutions of the Late Twentieth Century* (Boulder: Westview Press, 1991), 85–6.
282. Kagawa, "The Vietnamese case," 8; Stanley Karnow, *Vietnam: A History* (New York: Penguin, 1997), 136; Wolf, *Peasant Wars*, 167.
283. DeFronzo, *Revolutions and Revolutionary Movements*, 123.
284. On the inflation, see Wolf, *Peasant Wars*, 167; on the famine, see Goodwin, *No Other Way Out*, 92; DeFronzo, *Revolutions*, 124; and Stein Tonnesson, *The Vietnamese Revolution of 1945: Roosevelt, Ho Chi Minh and de Gaulle in a World at War* (London: Sage Publications, 1991), 293–4. Another key work is David Marr, *Vietnam 1945: The Quest for Power* (Berkeley: University of California Press, 1995).
285. Truong Chinh, *Primer for Revolt* (New York: Praeger, 1963), 26, quoted by LeVan, "Vietnam," 65.
286. Quoted in Goodwin, *No Other Way Out*, 110.
287. Karnow, *Vietnam*, 148.
288. LeVan, "Vietnam," 61–2.
289. Karnow, *Vietnam*, 207. Non-French military deaths came to another 50,000, while the Vietnamese lost 500,000 dead and a million wounded: Goodwin, *No Other Way Out*, 112 note 3.
290. French prime minister Laniel referred to "an honorable settlement" in November 1953: Karnow, *Vietnam*, 207.
291. Goodwin, *No Other Way Out*, 114 note 4.
292. Karnow, *Vietnam*, 238–42.
293. For a brilliant account of how the US "fell into" this involvement in a country about which most Americans – including policy makers – knew little or nothing, see David Halberstam, *The Best and the Brightest* (Greenwich: Fawcett Crest, [1969] 1972).
294. William J. Duiker, *Vietnam: Revolution in Transition* (Boulder: Westview Press, 1995), 26–8.
295. Martin J. Murray, *The Development of Capitalism in Colonial Indochina (1870–1940)* (Berkeley: University of California Press, 1980).
296. John T. McAlister, Jr. and Paul Mus, *The Vietnamese and Their Revolution* (New York: Harper & Row, 1970), 121, 129.
297. Murray, *The Development of Capitalism*, x.
298. Osterhammel, *Colonialism*, 73.
299. Wolf, *Peasant Wars*, 165–6. Duiker however notes exports of 300,000 "metric tons" in the 1930s: *Vietnam*, 35.
300. Wolf, *Peasant Wars*, 168–9. Murray considers the conditions on the rubber plantations akin to slavery or indentured servitude: *The Development of Capitalism*, 253.
301. Duiker, *Vietnam*, 34.
302. Ibid., 42.
303. Karnow, *Vietnam*, 125.
304. Le Chau, *Le Viet Nam socialiste: une économie de transition* (Paris: Maspero, 1966), 43, cited by Wolf, *Peasant Wars*, 178.

305. Wolf, *Peasant Wars*, 166, 175, 177; Karnow, *Vietnam*, 129; DeFronzo, *Revolutions*, 108.
306. From a French report of 1937, quoted in Murray, *The Development of Capitalism*, 310.
307. Karnow, *Vietnam*, 129.
308. Wolf, *Peasant Wars*, 171.
309. Duiker, *Vietnam*, 33; Karnow, *Vietnam*, 126.
310. Duiker, *Vietnam*, 133.
311. McAlister and Mus, *The Vietnamese*, 40, 156–7.
312. Murray, *The Development of Capitalism*, 372.
313. Ibid., 91.
314. Duiker, *Vietnam*, 134.
315. Karnow, *Vietnam*, 451.
316. Ibid., 453.
317. Ibid., 456.
318. Ibid., 249.
319. Compare Duiker, *Vietnam*, 134 (see also 69), with Karnow, *Vietnam*, 454.
320. Karnow, *Vietnam*, 454.
321. From an interview in Christian G. Appy, *Patriots: The Vietnam War Remembered from All Sides* (New York: Viking, 2003), 511.
322. Bernard B. Fall, *The Two Viet-Nams* (New York: Praeger, 1963), 289–90, cited by LeVan, "Vietnam," 61.
323. Le Van, "Vietnam," 55.
324. Appy, *Patriots*, 102.
325. Goodwin, *No Other Way Out*, 80–1. He adds a second key factor immediately after this clause: "Japan's decision not to sponsor a popular non-Communist nationalist leadership" during World War 2: 81; see also 123–5.
326. Quoted in Goodwin, *No Other Way Out*, 106.
327. Quoted in Karnow, *Vietnam*, 195.
328. Quoted in ibid., 192.
329. Duiker, *Vietnam*, 92–3.
330. Interview with CIA and USAID operative Rufus Phillips, in Appy, *Patriots*, 53–4.
331. Karnow, *Vietnam*, 246, 252.
332. LeVan, "Vietnam," 85; see also Karnow, *Vietnam*, 294–302; Duiker, *Vietnam*, 65–6; and DeFronzo, *Revolutions*, 137.
333. Karnow, *Vietnam*, 466.
334. Ibid., 456.
335. Ibid., 650.
336. Ibid., 431. The calculation of 400 atomic bombs is found in William J. Duiker, *Sacred War, Nationalism and Revolution in a Divided Vietnam* (New York: McGraw-Hill, 1995, 2).
337. Appy, *Patriots*, reports the claim that 80,000 were "neutralized," of whom more than 26,000 were killed; Karnow, *Vietnam*, 616–17, says over 6,000 were killed in 1969 alone.
338. See Jean-Paul Sartre, *On Genocide* (Boston: Beacon, 1968).
339. Duiker, *Sacred War*, 2.
340. Quoted in Karnow, *Vietnam*, 20–1.

341. Cf. heroine Trieu Au's impassioned cry from a struggle she led against China, dating to 248 AD: "I want to rail against the wind and the tide, kill the whales in the sea, sweep the whole country to save the people from slavery, and I refuse to be abused": quoted in Karnow, *Vietnam*, 112. For McAlister and Mus, the national identity was formed by centuries of "conquest, resistance, conspiracy, rebellion, and dissension": *The Vietnamese*, 51.
342. Quoted in Karnow, *Vietnam*, 127; see also Wolf, *Peasant Wars*, 179.
343. LeVan, "Vietnam," 74.
344. Ho is quoted by Karnow, *Vietnam*, 138.
345. DeFronzo, *Revolutions*, 118.
346. McAlister and Mus, *The Vietnamese*, 7.
347. Duiker, *Sacred War*, xvii.
348. From an interview in Appy, *Patriots*, 42.
349. McAlister and Mus, *The Vietnamese*, 165, referring to colonial times. For Jeff Goodwin, the lack of a credible alternative to the communists is a crucial key to their success: *No Other Way Out*. See also Tonnesson, *The Vietnamese Revolution of 1945*, 96–7.
350. DeFronzo, *Revolutions*, 114.
351. Ibid., 116.
352. Quoted in Karnow, *Vietnam*, 134.
353. Ken Post, *Revolution, Socialism and Nationalism in Vietnam*, volume v: *Winning the War and Losing the Peace* (Aldershot: Dartmouth, 1994), 349.
354. Duiker, *Sacred War*, 256; see also Duiker, *Vietnam*, 88–9.
355. McAlister and Mus, *The Vietnamese*, 17–18; see also 21, 60–4, 114–21.
356. Ibid., 114–15; see also 138, 160–1.
357. Paul Mus, *Viet-Nam: Sociologie d'une guerre* (Paris: Editions du Seuil, 1952), 253, 261, quoted by Wolf, *Peasant Wars*, 189.
358. LeVan, "Vietnam," 64.
359. Quoted in Karnow, *Vietnam*, 155.
360. From an interview in Appy, *Patriots*, 16.
361. Post, *Revolution, Socialism and Nationalism in Vietnam*, volume v, 350.
362. Duiker, *Sacred War*, 252.
363. Ibid.
364. Ibid.
365. Quoted in Karnow, *Vietnam*, 476.
366. Goodwin, *No Other Way Out*, 84.
367. This now classic quote comes from an American major in February 1968, referring to Ben Tre, a provincial capital of 35,000 people in the Mekong Delta, as reported for the Associated Press by Peter Arnett: Peter Braestrup, *Big Story: How the American Press and Television Reported and Interpreted the Crisis of Tet 1968 in Vietnam and Washington*, abridged version (New Haven: Yale University Press, 1977), 193.
368. Dennis J. Duncanson, *Government and Revolution in Vietnam* (London: Oxford University Press, 1968), 371–2.
369. Duiker, *Vietnam*, 134–5, notes that by 1965 Vietnam was no longer a net rice exporter, and that rubber production declined from 78,000 tons to 20,000 tons between 1961 and 1972.
370. LeVan, "Vietnam," 78.

371. Appy, *Patriots*, 494.
372. Duiker, *Sacred War*, 253.
373. Karnow, *Vietnam*, 558. See also Fredrik Logevall, *Choosing War: The Lost Chance for Peace and the Escalation of War in Vietnam* (Berkeley: University of California Press, 1999) for detailed evidence of opposition to "Americanization" of the war in 1964–65 in the US press and Congress.
374. Gareth Porter, "Coercive diplomacy in Vietnam: The Tonkin Gulf crisis reconsidered," pp. 9–22 in Jayne Werner and David Hunt, editors, *The American War in Vietnam* (Ithaca: Cornell Southeast Asia Program, 1993), 3; Karnow, *Vietnam*, 559.
375. Karnow, *Vietnam*, 500, 501, 503, 504, 559.
376. For remarkable accounts of My Lai, see Appy, *Patriots*, 343–53. The photo of the execution is on the cover of Jeff Goodwin's *No Other Way Out*, where it epitomizes his thesis about the effects of the indiscriminate use of state violence in producing revolutions. The story of Kim Phuc, who now lives in Toronto, is told in Denise Chong, *The Girl in the Picture: The Story of Kim Phuc, the Photograph, and the Vietnam War* (New York: Vintage, 2000).
377. Karnow, *Vietnam*, 626.
378. Appy, *Patriots*, 393; see also Karnow, *Vietnam*, 647.
379. Appy, *Patriots*, 394–5, who notes 126 reported fraggings in 1969, 271 in 1970, and 333 in 1971.
380. Karnow, *Vietnam*, 647–8.
381. Ibid., 666–71.
382. Ibid., 469.
383. Duiker, *Vietnam*, 139; Karnow, *Vietnam*, 471; Appy, *Patriots*, 80.
384. Karnow, *Vietnam*, 31.
385. Appy, *Patriots*, 494.
386. Duiker, *Sacred War*, 257–8; Duiker, *Vietnam*, 77.
387. Appy, *Patriots*, 494.
388. Quoted in Karnow, *Vietnam*, 683–4.

CHAPTER 4

1. Of course, one might reply that if the elected revolutionaries had undertaken deeper structural transformation, then the revolution might not have been reversed, as Bill Robinson has pointed out to me. This has the makings of a fine debate, best addressed in a discussion of revolutionary outcomes, beyond our scope here.
2. Jeff Goodwin, "State-centered approaches to social revolutions: strengths and limitations of a theoretical tradition," pp. 11–37 in John Foran, editor, *Theorizing Revolutions* (New York: Routledge, 1997), 18.
3. Gioconda Belli, *The Country under My Skin: A Memoir of Love and War*, translated by Kristina Cordero with the author (New York: Alfred A. Knopf, 2002), 250.
4. Roxborough, "Theories of revolution," 101; Selbin, *Modern Latin American Revolutions*; Alan Knight, "Social revolution: a Latin American perspective," pp. 175–202 in *Bulletin of Latin American Studies*, volume 9, number 2 (1990).

5. I wish to thank Jennifer Freidman of Smith College for her extensive research into the Bolivian case, her careful reading notes, and her paper, "Bolivia 1952–1964: a reversed social revolution," Smith College (2001), which I have drawn on extensively here.

6. James M. Malloy, *Bolivia: The Uncompleted Revolution* (University of Pittsburgh Press, 1970).

7. Selbin, *Modern Latin American Revolutions*, 30.

8. James M. Malloy, *Bolivia: The Sad and Corrupt End of the Revolution*, UFSI Reports, Number 3 (Hanover: University Field Staff International, 1982), 3.

9. Friedman, "Bolivia 1952–1964," 2.

10. Malloy, *Bolivia: The Uncompleted Revolution*, 25–6.

11. Cf. James Malloy, whose work I greatly respect: "In Bolivia, modernization was never generalized, and no self-sustaining basis of development was ever achieved. As a result, historical immobilism occurred within which the country was fractured and was neither wholly modern nor wholly traditional. But neither was it transitional: for after a certain point, it was in transit to nowhere. It was immobilized, crystallized, and contracting", Malloy, *Bolivia: The Uncompleted Revolution*, 32. How, exactly, are we to square this assessment with our own categories of dependent development and economic downturn?

12. James Dunkerley, *Rebellion in the Veins: Political Struggle in Bolivia, 1952–1982* (London: Verso, 1984), 6.

13. Jonathan Kelley and Herbert S. Klein, *Revolution and the Rebirth of Inequality: A Theory Applied to the National Revolution in Bolivia* (Berkeley: University of California Press, 1981), 89–90.

14. Herbert S. Klein, *Parties and Political Change in Bolivia 1880–1952* (Cambridge University Press, 1969), 394–5.

15. Ibid., 394.

16. Richard S. Thorn, "The economic transformation," pp. 157–216 in James Malloy and Richard S. Thorn, editors, *Beyond the Revolution: Bolivia Since 1952* (University of Pittsburgh Press, 1971), 158.

17. Klein, *Parties and Political Change*, 396; see also Susan Eckstein, *The Impact of Revolution: A Comparative Analysis of Mexico and Bolivia* (London: Sage, 1976), 12.

18. Klein, *Parties and Political Change*, 393.

19. Ibid., 396.

20. Dunkerley, *Rebellion in the Veins*, 14.

21. Ibid., 5; Klein, *Parties and Political Change*, 391–3.

22. Dunkerley, *Rebellion in the Veins*, 19; see also 23 for statistics on indigenous language-speakers.

23. Ibid., 35.

24. Klein, *Parties and Political Change*, 390–1.

25. Dunkerley, *Rebellion in the Veins*, 36.

26. Ibid., 28.

27. Ibid., 36.

28. Kelley and Klein, *Revolution and the Rebirth of Inequality*, 94.

29. Quoted in Klein, *Parties and Political Change*, 386.
30. Ibid., 379–80.
31. Malloy, *Bolivia: The Uncompleted Revolution*, 64ff.
32. Dunkerley, *Rebellion in the Veins*, 251.
33. Klein, *Parties and Political Change*, 396.
34. Malloy, *Bolivia: The Uncompleted Revolution*, 31, 69–70.
35. Ibid., 30 table.
36. Dunkerley, *Rebellion in the Veins*, 11–12.
37. Laurence Whitehead, *The United States and Bolivia: A Case of Neo-Colonialism* (Watlington: Haslemere Group, 1969), 7.
38. This is suggested by Dunkerley, *Rebellion in the Veins*.
39. Whitehead, *The United States and Bolivia*, 7.
40. Klein, *Parties and Political Change*, 398.
41. Ibid., 391.
42. Dunkerley, *Rebellion in the Veins*, 37; Klein, *Parties and Political Change*, 399–400.
43. Dunkerley, *Rebellion in the Veins*, 38–40; Klein, *Parties and Political Change*, 401.
44. Dunkerley, *Rebellion in the Veins*, 38–9.
45. Ian Roxborough, Philip O'Brien, and Jackie Roddick, assisted by Michael Gonzalez, *Chile: The State and Revolution* (New York: Macmillan, 1977), 5–6.
46. This section makes use of my text, "Allende's Chile, 1972," case study, Department of Sociology, University of California, Santa Barbara, available at http://www.soc.ucsb.edu/projects/casemethod/
47. James Petras, *Politics and Social Forces in Chilean Development* (Berkeley: University of California Press, 1969), 26.
48. For important qualifications on the democratic tradition of the armed forces, see the discussion in Valenzuela, who yet concludes that "in the early 1960s Chile may have ranked first in democratic stability in Latin America," Arturo Valenzuela, *The Breakdown of Democratic Regimes: Chile* (Baltimore: Johns Hopkins, 1979), 25, and 20–1 on the military.
49. Petras, *Politics and Social Forces*, 10.
50. Ibid., 130.
51. Ibid., 66.
52. Barbara Stallings, *Class Conflict and Economic Development in Chile, 1958–1973* (Stanford University Press, 1978), chapter 4.
53. Philip O'Brien, "Was the United States responsible for the Chilean coup?," pp. 217–43 in Philip J. O'Brien, editor, *Allende's Chile* (New York: Praeger, 1976), 219.
54. Valenzuela, *The Breakdown*, 27.
55. Ibid., 35–6.
56. From Frei's annual message to Congress, May 21, 1968, quoted in Stallings, *Class Conflict and Economic Development*, 65.
57. Armando Uribe, *The Black Book of American Intervention in Chile*, translated from the Spanish by Jonathan Casart (Boston: Beacon Press, 1975), 20–1, citing Anthony Sampson, *The Sovereign State of ITT* (New York: Stein and

Day, 1973). Sarah Wilkinson's essay, "Watching a country go Communist: United States influence in events leading up to the Chilean coup, 1973," unpublished paper, Department of Latin American Studies, Smith College (2002), alerted me to Uribe's work.

58. Stallings, *Class Conflict and Economic Development*, 42–6.
59. Keen and Haynes, *A History of Latin America*, 345.
60. The number of top US corporations operating in Chile in 1970 is given in the film, "Controlling interest: the world of the multinational corporation" (California Newsreel, 1978).
61. Stallings, *Class Conflict and Economic Development*, 45.
62. Collier and Sater peg the state's share of GNP at 40 percent: Simon Collier and William F. Sater, *A History of Chile, 1808–1994* (Cambridge University Press, 1996), 341; Stallings has it rising from 40 percent of GDP in the late 1960s to 47 percent by 1970, and 40.6 percent of employment: *Class Conflict and Economic Development*, 46, 47 table 2.3; Valenzuela has the state's share of GNP at just 14 percent, though he estimates state control of credit and public investment at over 50 percent, and considers the state's role in the economy as greater than any in Latin America save Cuba – all this *before* Allende's election: *The Breakdown*, 13.
63. Valenzuela, *The Breakdown*, 18.
64. Stallings, *Class Conflict and Economic Development*, 35, 49–50. Valenzuela notes similar inequality in the 1960s but a somewhat different distribution, with "60 percent of the population commanding 28 percent of the national income and 14 percent commanding 42 percent": *The Breakdown*, 18.
65. David Collier, editor, *The New Authoritarianism in Latin America* (Princeton University Press, 1979), 202 note 49.
66. Collier and Sater, *A History of Chile*, 332.
67. Data presented here on the downturn are drawn from John Sheahan, *Patterns of Development in Latin America* (Princeton University Press, 1987), 208, 223 tables 9.1 and 9.2, and Stallings, *Class Conflict and Economic Development*, 247 table A.6 and 252 table A.11.
68. Valenzuela, *The Breakdown*, 30, 31 table 9.
69. Stallings, *Class Conflict and Economic Development*, 110.
70. Valenzuela, *The Breakdown*, 23, 25.
71. Uribe, *The Black Book of American Intervention*, 40–1.
72. Stallings, *Class Conflict and Economic Development*, 124.
73. The quote is from government documents found in Robinson Rojas Sandford, *The Murder of Allende and the End of the Chilean Way to Socialism*, translated by Andreé Conrad (New York: Harper & Row, 1975), 75, who offers detailed insight into US thinking in this period.
74. Rojas, *The Murder of Allende*, 73.
75. I am indebted to two fine research assistants for their work on this case: Tamara Simons at UC Santa Barbara read key works in 1998, and Becca Wanner at Smith College read on this case and prepared a superb research report, "The Grenadian revolution" (2002), on which I have relied particularly.

76. EPICA Task Force, *Grenada, the Peaceful Revolution* (Washington: EPICA Task Force, 1982), 44.

77. David E. Lewis, *Reform and Revolution in Grenada 1950 to 1981* (Havana: Casa de las Américas, 1984), 14, 19. A good account of Gairy and Grenadian politics in the 1950s and 1960s can be found in Hugh O'Shaughnessy, *Grenada: An Eyewitness Account of the US Invasion and the Caribbean History That Provoked It* (New York: Dodd, Mead & Company, 1984), 35ff.

78. EPICA, *Grenada*, 46. EPICA is quite good on the nature of the Gairy regime: 36ff.

79. Gordon K. Lewis, *Grenada: The Jewel Despoiled* (Baltimore: Johns Hopkins, 1987), 14.

80. EPICA, *Grenada*, 44.

81. Ibid., 42–3, 50; G. Lewis, *Grenada*, 13, details the repressive and exclusionary nature of the regime.

82. EPICA, *Grenada*, 49.

83. G. Lewis, *Grenada*, 13–14, 18.

84. O'Shaughnessy, *Grenada*, 69; EPICA, *Grenada*, 47–8.

85. EPICA, *Grenada*, 49–50.

86. On Bishop's early life, see Robert Millette and Mahin Gosine, *The Grenada Revolution: Why it Failed* (New York: Africana Research Publications, 1985), 33–4.

87. Tony Thorndike, "People's power in theory and practice," pp. 29–49 in Jorge Heine, editor, *A Revolution Aborted: The Lessons of Grenada* (University of Pittsburgh Press, 1990), 30. On the history of these early radical groups, see Anthony Payne, Paul Sutton, and Tony Thorndike, *Grenada: Revolution and Invasion* (London: Croom Helm, 1984), 9–10.

88. Payne et al., *Grenada*, 8.

89. O'Shaughnessy, *Grenada*, 47, quoting the NJM's founding manifesto; see also EPICA, *Grenada*, 48.

90. O'Shaughnessy, *Grenada*, 49–50; EPICA, *Grenada*, 46.

91. G. Lewis, *Grenada*, 19; Gosine and Millette, *Grenada*, 36.

92. D. Lewis, *Reform and Revolution*, 60–1.

93. This characterization of Bishop's beliefs is given by Millette and Gosine, *The Grenada Revolution*, 93, citing Bishop's opening address to the Socialist International meeting in Grenada, July 23, 1981. Gosine and Millette feel that Bishop "held dearly the ideals of Black Power as initially defined by [Stokely] Carmichael and later by Rodney," ibid.

94. Selbin, *Modern Latin American Revolutions*, 62.

95. Payne et al., *Grenada*, 195, quoting a November 1983 interview.

96. The entire document is reproduced in Millette and Gosine, *The Grenada Revolution*, 44–8; the passage quoted is found on 47, emphasis in the original.

97. Selbin, *Modern Latin American Revolutions*, 63.

98. Jorge A. Heine, "Introduction: a revolution aborted," pp. 3–26 in Jorge A. Heine, editor, *A Revolution Aborted: The Lessons of Grenada* (University of Pittsburgh Press, 1990), 21.

99. Gosine and Millette, *The Grenada Revolution*, 55.

100. EPICA, *Grenada*, 49; O'Shaughnessy, *Grenada*, 75.
101. Payne et al., *Grenada*, 14.
102. Heine, "Introduction," 17; Payne et al., *Grenada*, 14.
103. Payne et al., *Grenada*, 8.
104. See Heine, "Introduction," 14.
105. EPICA, *Grenada*, 57; Robert Pastor, "The United States and the Grenada revolution: who pushed first, and why?," pp. 181–214 in Jorge A. Heine, editor, *A Revolution Aborted: The Lessons of Grenada* (University of Pittsburgh Press, 1990), 187–8.
106. Pastor, "The United States and the Grenada revolution," 187.
107. EPICA, *Grenada*, 55.
108. For accounts of these events, I have consulted Keen and Haynes, *A History of Latin America*. A full-length treatment is that of Stephen C. Schlesinger and Stephen Kinzer, *Bitter Fruit: The Untold Story of the American Coup in Guatemala* (New York: Doubleday, 1984).
109. See Dunkerley, *Power in the Isthmus*, 92; Paul J. Dosal, *Power in Transition: The Rise of Guatemala's Industrial Oligarchy, 1871–1994* (Westport: Praeger, 1995), 69–70, 76; and Victor Bulmer-Thomas, *The Political Economy of Central America Since 1920* (Cambridge University Press, 1987), 322. Thanks to Edwin Lopez for pointing me to these references.
110. I have covered these events extensively in *Fragile Resistance*, chapter 7. Detailed accounts are found in, among other works, Mark Gasiorowski, "The 1953 coup d'etat in Iran," pp. 261–86 in *International Journal of Middle East Studies*, volume 19, number 3 (August) (1987); Stephen Kinzer, *All the Shah's Men: An American Coup and the Roots of Middle East Terror* (New York: John Wiley & Sons, 2003), and Sussan Siavoshi, "The oil nationalization movement, 1949–1953," pp. 106–34 in John Foran, editor, *A Century of Revolution: Social Movements in Iran* (Minneapolis: University of Minnesota Press, 1994).
111. Key works on Jamaica include EPICA (The Ecumenical Program for Interamerican Community and Action), *Jamaica: Caribbean Challenge* (Washington: EPICA Task Force, 1979); Michael Manley, *Jamaica: Struggle in the Periphery* (London: Third World Media, 1982); Michael Kaufman, *Jamaica under Manley: Dilemmas of Socialism and Democracy* (London: Zed Press, 1985); Evelyne Huber Stephens and John D. Stephens, *Democratic Socialism in Jamaica: The Political Movement and Social Transformation in Dependent Capitalism* (Princeton: Princeton University Press, 1986); and Nelson W. Keith and Novella Z. Keith, *The Social Origins of Democratic Socialism in Jamaica* (Philadelphia: Temple University Press, 1992).
112. Anita M. Waters, *Race, Class, and Political Symbols: Rastafari and Reggae in Jamaican Politics* (New Brunswick: Transaction, 1985).
113. Quoted in Collier and Sater, *A History of Chile*, 330.
114. A theory of revolutionary outcomes is sketched in John Foran and Jeff Goodwin, "Revolutionary outcomes in Iran and Nicaragua: coalition fragmentation, war, and the limits of social transformation," pp. 209–47 in *Theory and Society*, volume 22, number 2 (April 1993). I try to

extend that beginning somewhat here, but this huge topic requires its own treatment.

115. Malloy, *Bolivia: The Sad and Corrupt End of the Revolution*, 4.
116. I owe Jennifer Friedman, my research assistant for this case, a great debt, as she first sketched in the arguments made in this section in her excellent paper, "Bolivia 1952–1964: a reversed social revolution."
117. Klein, *Parties and Political Change*, 402.
118. Dunkerley, *Rebellion in the Veins*, 43ff; Selbin, *Modern Latin American Revolutions*, 36; Bert Useem, "The workers' movement and the Bolivian revolution," pp. 447–69 in *Politics & Society*, volume 9, number 4 (1980), 448.
119. Dunkerley, *Rebellion in the Veins*, 48–50.
120. Ibid., 50; Klein, *Parties and Political Change*, 404.
121. James F. Siekmeier, "Responding to nationalism: the Bolivian *Movimiento Nacionalista Revolucionaria* and the United States, 1952–1956," pp. 39–58 in *Journal of American and Canadian Studies*, volume 15 (1997), 44. Useem and his sources put the compensation awarded to the dispossessed local and foreign tin interests at $18 million; Dunkerley notes that it eventually reached $27 million: Useem, "The workers' movement," 456, and Dunkerley, *Rebellion in the Veins*, 58.
122. Dunkerley, *Rebellion in the Veins*, 58; Klein, *Parties and Political Change*, 403.
123. Dunkerley, *Rebellion in the Veins*, 57–8; Kelley and Klein, *Revolution and the Rebirth of Inequality*, 94.
124. Kelley and Klein, *Revolution and the Rebirth of Inequality*, 95–6.
125. Dunkerley, *Rebellion in the Veins*, 72–3.
126. Kelley and Klein, *Revolution and the Rebirth of Inequality*, 100.
127. Dunkerley, *Rebellion in the Veins*, 73–4.
128. Klein, *Parties and Political Change*, 405.
129. I am indebted to Friedman, "Bolivia 1952–1964," for this line of argument.
130. Kelley and Klein, *Revolution and the Rebirth of Inequality*, 126.
131. Eckstein, *The Impact of Revolution*, 18; Kelley and Klein, *Revolution and the Rebirth of Inequality*, 128–9.
132. Dunkerley, *Rebellion in the Veins*, 81.
133. Kelley and Klein, *Revolution and the Rebirth of Inequality*, 100; Dunkerley, *Rebellion in the Veins*, 81; Klein, *Parties and Political Change*, 404; Cornelius H. Zondag, *The Bolivian Economy, 1952–65: The Revolution and its Aftermath* (New York: Praeger, 1966), 56 table 1.
134. Zondag, *The Bolivian Economy*, 201, 202 table 15.
135. Friedman, "Bolivia 1952–1964," 18.
136. Klein, *Parties and Political Change*, 405.
137. Dunkerley, *Rebellion in the Veins*, 82, 85; Zondag, *The Bolivian Economy*, 55; Eckstein, *The Impact of Revolution*, 37.
138. Robert J. Alexander, *The Bolivian National Revolution* (New Brunswick: Rutgers University Press, 1958), 260–1, quoted by Whitehead, *The United States and Bolivia*, 9.
139. Siekmeier, "Responding to nationalism," 52; Useem, "The workers' movement," 465; Whitehead, *The United States and Bolivia*, 12; Dunkerley, *Rebellion in the Veins*, 86–7.

140. George Jackson Eder, *Inflation and Development in Latin America: A Case History of Inflation and Stabilization in Bolivia* (Ann Arbor: University of Michigan, 1968), 479, quoted by Whitehead, *The United States and Bolivia*, 11.

141. George Jackson Eder, *The Bolivian Economy, 1952–1965* (New York: Praeger, 1966), 87, quoted by Useem, "The workers' movement," 449.

142. Dunkerley, *Rebellion in the Veins*, 104; Eckstein, *The Impact of Revolution*, 38.

143. Knight, "Social revolution," 188.

144. Dunkerley, *Rebellion in the Veins*, 103.

145. Ibid., 97; Kelley and Klein, *Revolution and the Rebirth of Inequality*, 102.

146. Dunkerley, *Rebellion in the Veins*, 74; see also Kelley and Klein, *Revolution and the Rebirth of Inequality*, 102.

147. Eckstein, *The Impact of Revolution*, 34. See Dunkerley's account of the split in the MNR going back to 1952: *Rebellion in the Veins*, 47–8.

148. Whitehead, *The United States and Bolivia*, 25; see also Eckstein, *The Impact of Revolution*, 37–8.

149. Dunkerley, *Rebellion in the Veins*, 116–20.

150. The astute Alan Knight reminds us of this, and challenges it: "it is surely the long-term structural 'success' of revolutions which counts, more than the longevity of men or regimes. It is less important that the MNR failed politically than that the Bolivian Revolution succeeded socially, permanently transforming Bolivian society," "Social revolution," 182. To reconcile (or complicate?) our differences, he refers to the outcome in Bolivia as a successful bourgeois revolution (one that ultimately furthered capitalist development), whereas I see it as a reversed (potentially) socialist, or at least, radical, revolution.

151. From the UP program, quoted by Stallings, *Class Conflict and Economic Development*, 126.

152. Stallings, *Class Conflict and Economic Development*, 131–2.

153. Collier and Sater, *A History of Chile*, 342.

154. Ibid., 343; Stallings, *Class Conflict and Economic Development*, 247 table A.6, 251 table A.10, 252 table A.11; Sheahan, *Patterns of Development*, 214–5, 223 tables 9.1 and 9.2.

155. Collier and Sater, *A History of Chile*, 334–5; Stallings, *Class Conflict and Economic Development*, 132. In his 1972 speech to the United Nations, Allende noted that between 1955 and 1970 Anaconda's rate of profit in Chile was 21.5 percent versus only 3.6 percent elsewhere, and that Kennecott's was 52.8 percent in Chile (including 106 percent in 1967, 113 percent in 1968, and over 205 percent in 1969), versus less than 10 percent in other countries. The countries had made a $4 billion profit on an investment of $30 million: reported in *El Mercurio – Edición Internacional* (December 4–10, 1972), 1.

156. Collier and Sater, *A History of Chile*, 339; see also Marc Cooper, *Pinochet and Me* (London: Verso, 2001), 21.

157. Quoted in Keen and Haynes, *A History of Latin America*, 349.

158. This quote is given in the film "Controlling interest." For a dissenting view that argues that Chile continued to obtain significant external credits and aid, see Philip J. O'Brien, "Was the United States responsible for the Chilean coup?," pp. 217–43 in Philip, editor, *Allende's Chile* (New York: Praeger, 1976), 233–6.

159. I found this memo in Edward Boorstein, *Allende's Chile: An Inside View* (New York: International Publishers Co., 1977). The original source is *Alleged Assassination Plots Involving Foreign Leaders*, Interim Report of the Senate Intelligence Committee (Washington, DC: US Government Printing Office, 1975), 227.

160. This quote is found in Todd Yates, "Meta y Muerte: La Vida de Salvador Allende," unpublished ms. (December 3, 2000), 7, citing a CIA study found at www.personal.umich.edu/~lornand/soa/chile.htm

161. Kissinger is quoted in the hearings of the US Senate Subcommittee on Multinational Corporations of the Committee on Foreign Relations Hearings, *Multinational Corporations and United States Foreign Policy* (Washington, DC: US Senate, 93rd Congress, second session, 1974), part 2, 543, reported by Stallings, *Class Conflict and Economic Development*, 132 note. For extensive documentation of the role of the US in the Allende period, see the Chile Documentation Project of the National Security Archive, directed by Peter Kornbluh: http://www.gwu.edu/~nsarchiv/latin_america/chile.htm

162. Stallings, *Class Conflict and Economic Development*, 140.

163. Lois Hecht Oppenheim, *Politics in Chile: Democracy, Authoritarianism, and the Search for Development*, second edition (Boulder: Westview Press, 1999), 100.

164. Collier and Sater, *A History of Chile*, 340. Copper prices fell from sixty-five cents a pound in 1969 to forty-eight cents already by the end of 1970: *El Mercurio – Edición Internacional* (January 18–24, 1971), 1.

165. Collier and Sater, *A History of Chile*, 338.

166. On Lo Curro, see Jack Spence, "Class mobilization and conflict in Allende's Chile: a review essay," pp. 131–64 in *Politics & Society*, volume 8, number 2 (1978), and Stallings, *Class Conflict and Economic Development*, 135–6.

167. Spence, "Class mobilization and conflict," 149.

168. This was very apparent from a survey of the Chilean press of the Allende period that I undertook at the Biblioteca Nacional in Santiago in 1991.

169. Stallings, *Class Conflict and Economic Development*, 144–5.

170. Allende's exchange with the residents of Asalto al Cuartel Moncada is reported in *El Mercurio – Edición Internacional* (August 7–13, 1971), 6.

171. On the complexities of Christian Democratic politics, which go beyond what can be presented here, see Valenzuela, *The Breakdown*, 70–80, 88ff.

172. Cooper, *Pinochet and Me*, 27–9.

173. Stallings, *Class Conflict and Economic Development*, 145–6, 242–3 table A.1. This paragraph draws on Stallings. The vote is analyzed extensively in *El Mercurio – Edición Internacional* (March 5–11, 1973), 8, which shows that the UP delegation in Congress rose from 57 to 63 and the opposition fell from 93 to 87, while the number of UP senators rose from 18 to 20 and the combined opposition fell from 32 to 30.

174. Valenzuela, *The Breakdown*, 55 table 19.
175. Quoted in Stallings, *Class Conflict and Economic Development*, 148.
176. Quoted in Cooper, *Pinochet and Me*, 22.
177. A picture of this graffiti is found in the MIR journal, *El Rebelde* (January 25–31, 1972), 6.
178. Reported in Valenzuela, *The Breakdown*, 84.
179. Details can be found in *El Mercurio – Edición Internacional* (August 6–12, 1973).
180. Ten PDC senators made this charge, as reported in *El Mercurio – Edición Internacional* (August 13–19, 1973), 4. The degree of self-deception among Christian Democrats is eloquently attested by Senator Ramón Fuentealba, a progressive party leader and friend of Allende, who said as late as August 1973 that the "political" wing of the PN was democratic, and the "economic" wing alone wanted a coup. Moreover, of his own party, he stated: "We have never been pro-coup and never stood for the overthrow of the government in this country . . . There is no sector in the PDC that will support the military overthrow of the government," quoted in *Chile Hoy* (August 17–23, 1973), 28. On the other hand, as president of the PDC in 1972 he had accused the UP of going toward dictatorship and seeking to destroy the middle class: *El Mercurio – Edición Internacional* (July 31–August 6, 1972), 1, 6.
181. The quote is from PN Senator Francisco Bulnes, in *Tribuna* (June 23, 1973), as quoted in *Chile Hoy* (July 6–12, 1973), 11.
182. Stallings, *Class Conflict and Economic Development*, 238. See also Phil O'Brien and Jackie Roddick, *Chile: The Pinochet Decade: The Rise and Fall of the Chicago Boys* (New York: Monthly Review Press, 1983).
183. Allende's speech is found in Laurence Birns, editor, *The End of Chilean Democracy* (New York: Seabury Press, 1974), 32. I have changed the translation slightly.
184. The 1995 Rettig Commission concluded that 3,197 Chileans were killed by the regime between 1973 and 1990; this is the figure the Chilean government admits to. Estimates of Chileans exiled after the coup range as high as several hundred thousand: Collier and Sater, *A History of Chile*, 360.
185. Wanner, "The Grenadian revolution," 15; Payne et al., *Grenada*, 143; Selbin, *Modern Latin American Revolutions*, 60.
186. EPICA, *Grenada*, 76, 86.
187. Ibid., 97–9.
188. Millette and Gosine, *The Grenada Revolution*, 96. Unemployment decreased from 49 percent to 28 percent in the first two years, according to EPICA, *Grenada*, 102.
189. Ibid., 96–7; Heine, "Introduction," 18; James Ferguson, *Grenada: Revolution in Reverse* (New York: Monthly Review Press, 1990), 9, reports the claim about per capita income, which seems impossible.
190. Heine, "Introduction," 18. I have converted Eastern Caribbean dollars to US dollars at the exchange rate of 2.6 to 1.
191. O'Shaughnessy, *Grenada*, 87.
192. EPICA, *Grenada*, 75.

193. Heine, "Introduction," 17. A 1982 World Bank memo stated: "The government which came to power in 1979 inherited a deteriorating economy, and is now addressing the task of rehabilitation and of laying better foundations for growth within the framework of a mixed economy . . . Government objectives are centered on the critical development issues and touch on the country's most promising development areas:" quoted in Ferguson, *Grenada*, 74.
194. Quoted in EPICA, *Grenada*, 114.
195. There is contention over the degree and nature of imprisonment of opponents of the regime. It appears to me that in the context of immediate postrevolutionary governments, the numbers are "reasonably" small. This is not to deny that acts of arbitrary justice and improper treatment of detainees occurred. The case for abuse is made in Gregory Sandford and Richard Vigilante, *Grenada: The Untold Story* (Lanham: Madison Books, 1984), a pro-US account of the revolution and its reversal, based in large measure on the large cache of PRG documents removed from Grenada to the US after the 1983 invasion. I have not relied overmuch on this source, but it is of interest on the inner workings of governments on all sides. Other significant works which I have consulted but been unable to draw upon fully include Jay R. Mandle, *Big Revolution, Small Country: The Rise and Fall of the Grenada Revolution* (Lanham: The North-South Publishing Company, 1985) and Kai P. Schoenhals and Richard A. Melanson, *Revolution and Intervention in Grenada: The New Jewel Movement, the United States, and the Caribbean* (Boulder: Westview, 1985).
196. O'Shaughnessy, *Grenada*, 77; Selbin, *Modern Latin American Revolutions*, 68.
197. EPICA, *Grenada*, 112.
198. Ferguson, *Grenada*, 109.
199. This argument is an extrapolation on my part from Ferguson, *Grenada*, 110.
200. Gosine and Millette, *The Grenada Revolution*, 104.
201. Payne et al., *Grenada*, 111.
202. Wanner, "The Grenadian revolution," 3.
203. G. Lewis, *Grenada*, 42.
204. O'Shaughnessy, *Grenada*, 10; EPICA, *Grenada*, 70, 125.
205. EPICA, *Grenada*, 124–5.
206. Payne et al., *Grenada*, 33, 82–4.
207. Ibid., 93.
208. Pastor, "The United States and the Grenada revolution," 199.
209. Bishop and Ortiz are quoted in Payne et al., *Grenada*, 49. Compare the US message on Cuba with O'Shaughnessy, *Grenada*, 81, where the text is slightly different; O'Shaughnessy adds that the US refused to pledge that it would block an attempt by the Miami-based Gairy to return to power. Bishop's response, originally broadcast over Radio Free Grenada on April 13, 1979, is quoted slightly differently in EPICA, *Grenada*, 61.
210. Payne et al., *Grenada*, 50.
211. EPICA, *Grenada*, 60.
212. Wanner, "The Grenadian revolution," 17.

213. Payne et al., Grenada, 115. Bush would later be the person asked by Reagan to convene the National Security Council to consider US responses to the execution of Maurice Bishop.
214. McKenzie, as quoted by Maurice Bishop, and reported in Payne et al., Grenada, 66.
215. Bishop, as quoted in Payne et al., Grenada, 66.
216. Payne et al., Grenada, 52.
217. Ibid., 61; EPICA, Grenada, 119–20.
218. See, for example, the discussion of the closure of the newspaper Torchlight in EPICA, Grenada, 58–60.
219. EPICA, Grenada, 62–6.
220. See Pastor, "The United States and the Grenada revolution," 199, and EPICA, Grenada, 122. For Bishop's response, see Payne et al., Grenada, 65–6.
221. EPICA, Grenada, 118.
222. Selbin credits Heine with the best analysis of the personality conflict: for Heine, as paraphrased by Selbin, "Coard's need for power and prestige, his compulsive behavior, and ultimately his capacity for self-delusion forced him to remove the obstacle in his path – Maurice Bishop": Modern Latin American Revolutions, 69. Heine's analysis is found in "The hero and the apparatchik: charismatic leadership, political management, and crisis in revolutionary Grenada," pp. 217–55 in Jorge Heine, editor, A Revolution Aborted: The Lessons of Grenada (University of Pittsburgh Press, 1990), 237–43.
223. G. Lewis, Grenada, 63, who explicitly discounts claims that the population had lost confidence in the party and the revolution: 43–4.
224. Millette and Gosine, The Grenada Revolution, 130–1.
225. G. Lewis, Grenada, 41, 68.
226. Ibid., 68–9, relying also on the observations of novelist Gabriel García Marquez.
227. Payne et al., Grenada, 106.
228. Gosine and Millette, The Grenada Revolution, 110.
229. Ibid., 3.
230. G. Lewis, Grenada, 39.
231. See Payne et al., Grenada, 128–30.
232. G. Lewis, Grenada, 51.
233. Selbin, Modern Latin American Revolutions, 68. Compare the graffiti, "The revo killed our children": Heine, "Introduction," 3.
234. G. Lewis, Grenada, 62.
235. Ibid., 54.
236. Ibid., 56.
237. Payne et al., Grenada, 136–7. The actual leadership of the RMC, and Coard's precise role, is in some doubt, and may never be known with certainty. For Gordon Lewis, "It is immaterial, in one way, whether [Austin and the other pro-Coard party members] were being used by Coard or whether Coard was using them. The material fact is that it was now military, not

civilian rule; and in such circumstances who holds the guns calls the shots:" G. Lewis, *Grenada*, 83.

238. Quoted in Payne et al., *Grenada*, 138.
239. Quoted in ibid., 141–2.
240. O'Shaughnessy, *Grenada*, 11–12; Payne et al., *Grenada*, 139.
241. Quoted in Payne et al., *Grenada*, 139.
242. Quoted in ibid., 142.
243. Ibid., 137.
244. See ibid., 149, for an account of the deliberations of the OECS in the presence of US ambassador to Barbados Milan Bish and Jamaican prime minister Edward Seaga, whose country is not a member of the OECS. For an account of Ronald Reagan's speech justifying the invasion, see ibid., 154–5.
245. G. Lewis, *Grenada*, 67.
246. Ibid., 71. He notes perceptively the analogy to Danton and Robespierre in the French revolution, as it is evoked by the great Wajda film *Danton*, observing that these are *not* simplistic types: "Robespierre is not a monster, but a tortured mind, trapped in the purity of his ideals", 71.
247. This section is based in good part on an essay I published with Jeff Goodwin, "Revolutionary outcomes in Iran and Nicaragua: coalition fragmentation, war, and the limits of social transformation," pp. 209–47 in *Theory and Society*, volume 22, number 2 (April 1993). Jeff did much of the work on Nicaragua for that essay and is thus in a real sense a co-author of this section.
248. Farhi, *States and Urban-Based Revolutions*, 109.
249. The key work on the land reform is Laura J. Enríquez, *Harvesting Change: Labor and Agrarian Reform in Nicaragua 1979–1990* (Chapel Hill: University of North Carolina Press, 1991).
250. For the various sides in this dispute, see Michael Dodson and Laura Nuzzi O'Shaughnessy, *Nicaragua's Other Revolution: Religious Faith and Political Struggle* (Chapel Hill: University of North Carolina Press, 1990), and Lancaster, *Thanks to God and the Revolution*.
251. On peasant dissatisfaction, see Foran and Goodwin, "Revolutionary outcomes in Iran and Nicaragua," 228. On the problems of unwitting racism that plagued the FSLN, see Chris McAuley, "Race and the process of the American revolutions," pp. 168–202 in John Foran, editor, *Theorizing Revolutions* (New York: Routledge, 1997), 191–6; Carlos M. Vilas, *State, Class, and Ethnicity in Nicaragua: Capitalist Modernization and Revolutionary Change on the Atlantic Coast* (Boulder: Lynne Rienner, 1989); and Charles R. Hale, *Resistance and Contradiction: Miskito Indians and the Nicaraguan State, 1894–1987* (Stanford University Press, 1994).
252. Stephen M. Gorman and Thomas W. Walker, "The armed forces," pp. 91–118 in Thomas W. Walker, editor, *Nicaragua: The First Five Years* (New York: Praeger, 1985), 112–13.
253. William I. Robinson and Kent Norsworthy, *David and Goliath: The US War Against Nicaragua* (New York: Monthly Review Press, 1987), 271; Dennis Gilbert, *Sandinistas: The Party and the Revolution* (New York: Basil Blackwell, 1988), 94.

254. See Robinson and Norsworthy, *David and Goliath*, chapter 9.
255. Michael E. Conroy, "The political economy of the 1990 Nicaraguan elections," pp. 5–33 in *International Journal of Political Economy*, volume 20, number 3 (Fall 1990), 18. On Iran-Contra, see Peter Kornbluh, Malcolm Byrne, and Theodore Draper, editors, *The Iran-Contra Scandal: The Declassified History (The National Security Archive Document)* (New York: New Press, 1993). There are dozens of books on this topic.
256. LASA (Latin American Studies Association), *Electoral Democracy Under International Pressure: The Report of the Latin American Studies Association Commission to Observe the 1990 Nicaraguan Election* (Pittsburgh: Latin American Studies Association, 1990), 5.
257. George R. Vickers, "A spider's web," pp. 19–27 in *NACLA Report on the Americas*, volume 24, number 1 (June 1990), 23.
258. Quoted in LASA, *Electoral Democracy Under International Pressure*, 8.
259. LASA, *Electoral Democracy Under International Pressure*, 9.
260. Conroy, "The political economy of the 1990 Nicaraguan elections," 16.
261. Quoted in Stephen Kinzer, *Blood of Brothers: Life and War in Nicaragua* (New York: G. P. Putnam's Sons, 1991), 305.
262. Ibid.
263. Ibid.
264. CARIN (Central America Research Institute), "UNO electoral victory," *Central America Bulletin*, volume 9, number 3 (Spring 1990), 10.
265. Enríquez, *Harvesting Change*, 119.
266. Forrest D. Colburn, *Managing the Commanding Heights: Nicaragua's State Enterprises* (Berkeley: University of California Press, 1990), 113–21.
267. Conroy, "The political economy of the 1990 Nicaraguan elections," 13.
268. Richard Stahler-Sholk, "Stabilization, destabilization, and the popular classes in Nicaragua, 1979–1988," pp. 55–88 in *Latin American Research Review*, volume 25, number 3 (1990), 74.
269. Stahler-Sholk, "Stabilization, destabilization, and the popular classes," 71.
270. Vilas, "What went wrong," pp. 10–18 in *NACLA Report on the Americas*, volume 24, number 1 (June 1990), 12.
271. Carlos M. Vilas, "What went wrong," 11.
272. Conroy, "The political economy of the 1990 Nicaraguan elections," 27.
273. Ibid., 8.
274. This paragraph draws on the same sources as the brief discussion on the coming to power of Mussadiq above.
275. This is the thesis developed by Edwin Lopez, "Through the prism of racialized political cultures: an analysis of racialized cultural hegemony and resistance in revolutionary Guatemala, 1944–1954," MA thesis, Department of Sociology, University of California, Santa Barbara (2003), who draws heavily on the empirical evidence of historian Jim Handy, *Revolution in the Countryside: Rural Conflict and Agrarian Reform in Guatemala, 1944–1954* (Chapel Hill: University of North Carolina Press, 1994).
276. Schlesinger and Kinzer suggest that the US took measures to bring economic pressure on Guatemala by early 1954, but the effects of these are hard to measure, *Bitter Fruit*, 139.

277. The most comprehensive work on this period is Stephens and Stephens, *Democratic Socialism in Jamaica*.
278. Ibid., 1–2.
279. On the issue of US overt and covert attempts to undermine the Manley government, see the nuanced and interesting discussion in ibid., 134–7.
280. See Ragin, *The Comparative Method*, on this procedure. Basically, if the absence or presence of a given variable (in this case, D, an economic downturn) can bring about the same result, the variable may be dropped from the final expression.
281. The text which generates these discussions is my teaching case, "Allende's Chile," which can be found with study questions and teaching notes at www.soc.ucsb.edu/projects/casemethod/

CHAPTER 5

1. Rosa Luxemburg offered this aphorism in *Die Rote Fahne* (January 14, 1919), as quoted in Daniel Singer, *Whose Millennium? Theirs or Ours?* (New York: Monthly Review Press, 1999), 278.
2. Skocpol, *States and Social Revolutions*, 4. At the end of this study, I must affirm that I still find this the most useful definition of social revolution available.
3. Ellen Kay Trimberger, *Revolution from Above: Military Bureaucrats and Development in Japan, Turkey, Egypt and Peru* (New Brunswick: Transaction Books, 1978).
4. This discussion is based on John Foran, "A theory of Third World social revolutions," 17–19. Key secondary accounts, in addition to those cited below, include James Dunkerley, *The Long War: Dictatorship and Revolution in El Salvador* (London: Verso, 1982); idem, *Power in the Isthmus*; and Tommy Sue Montgomery, *Revolution in El Salvador: From Civil Strife to Civil Peace*, second edition (Boulder: Westview Press, 1995).
5. Quoted in Thomas Anderson, *Matanza: El Salvador's Communist Revolt of 1932* (Lincoln: University of Nebraska Press, 1971), 157.
6. Carlos Rafael Cabarrús, *Génesis de una revolución: Analisis del surgimiento y desarrollo de la organización campesina en El Salvador* (Mexico City: Ediciones de la Casa Chata, 1983), 10; Harold Jung, "Class struggles in El Salvador," pp. 3–25 in *New Left Review*, number 122 (1980), 4, 10.
7. Jeff Goodwin, "Revolutionary movements in Central America: a comparative analysis," Harvard University, Center for Research on Politics and Social Organization, Working Paper Series (1988), 26–7; Jenny Pearce, *Promised Land: Peasant Rebellion in Chalatenango El Salvador* (London: Latin America Bureau, 1986); Cabarrús, *Génesis de una revolución*.
8. Robert Armstrong and Janet Shenk, *El Salvador: The Face of Revolution* (Boston: South End Press, 1982), 6–7.
9. In Cynthia McClintock's judgment, "for the most part, national living standards were not declining during the period that the FMLN was emerging, and accordingly there was no change in the national economy that could be considered a trigger to a revolutionary movement with a significant base in the capital city in its early years": *Revolutionary Movements in Latin America*, 158.

10. This analysis of the political culture of the FMLN draws on my "Discourses and social forces," 215–16. See also Sheldon B. Liss, *Radical Thought in Central America* (Boulder: Westview, 1991), 80–4, 96; Dunkerley, *Power in the Isthmus*; and Montgomery, *Revolution in El Salvador*, 118–19. Armstrong and Shenk reproduce the April 1980 "Platform of the democratic revolutionary front": *El Salvador*, 254–5.
11. Julia Denise Shayne, "Salvadorean women revolutionaries and the birth of their women's movement," MA thesis, Department of Women's Studies, San Francisco State University (April 1995); Kampwirth, *Women and Guerrilla Movements*.
12. Armstrong and Shenk, *El Salvador*, 109.
13. *New York Times* (March 16, 1993).
14. I have benefited from the work of my research assistant Briana Krompier at Smith College in 2002 on this case. On Peru and Sendero Luminoso see *NACLA (North American Congress on Latin America) Report*, "Fatal attraction: Peru's shining path," volume 24, number 4 (December 1990/January 1991); Arnold, *Wars in the Third World since 1945*, 561–8; David Scott Palmer, editor, *The Shining Path of Peru* (New York: St. Martin's Press, 1992); Deborah Poole and Gerardo Renique, *Peru: Time of Fear* (New York: Monthly Review Press, 1993); Linda J. Seligman, *Between Reform and Revolution: Political Struggles in the Peruvian Andes, 1969–1991* (Stanford University Press, 1995); and Susan J. Stokes, *Cultures in Conflict: Social Movements and the State in Peru* (Berkeley: University of California Press, 1995).
15. Per capita GNP declined by 20 percent from 1988 to 1989: Keen and Haynes, *A History of Latin America*, 420.
16. Guillermo Rochabrún, "Review" of Steve J. Stern, editor, *Shining Path and Other Paths: War and Society in Peru, 1980–1995* (Durham: Duke University Press, 1998), p. 52 in *NACLA Report on the Americas*, volume 33, number 2 (September/October 1999).
17. This is Guillermo Rochabrún's account of Carlos Iván Degregori's chapter in *Shining and Other Paths*, in *NACLA Report*, 52. See also Selbin, *Modern Latin American Revolutions*, 148.
18. There is no doubt that the army engaged in a vicious counterinsurgency in the countryside against Sendero. Sendero denies that it has practiced terror against non-military targets, but this has been amply documented as well.
19. "[P]olls showed that between 70 and 90 percent of the public approved of the autogolpe:" Keen and Haynes, *A History of Latin America*, 421. However suspect, this appears to indicate real support among some segments of the population.
20. Daniel Wayne, "Shining path endures," pp. 1, 8 in *Latinamerica Press* (March 21, 1996); Cecilia Remón, "Peru: Shining path making a comeback," pp. 5–6 in *NACLA Report on the Americas*, volume 37, number 2 (September/October 2003).
21. Joseph Fewsmith, *Dilemmas of Reform in China: Political Conflict and Economic Debate* (Armonk: M. E. Sharpe, 1994). Research assistants Megan Thomas and Maria Mark at Smith College in 2002, and Richard Widick at UC Santa

Barbara in 2003, provided important notes and analysis for this case. My discussion of both China in 1989 and Algeria in the 1990s is drawn from my essay, "The future of revolutions."

22. Although China was far more self-sufficient than any of the dependent capitalist Third World cases we have studied, its pattern of industrialization still evidenced most of the indicators of dependent development's characteristic growth within limits.

23. On the movement and its background, see Craig Calhoun, *Neither Gods nor Emperors: Students and the Struggle for Democracy in China* (Berkeley: University of California Press, 1994), and Dingxin Zhao, *The Power of Tiananmen: State-Society Relations and the 1989 Beijing Student Movement* (University of Chicago Press, 2001).

24. Robin Munro, "Who died in Beijing, and why," pp. 811–22 in *The Nation* (June 11, 1990).

25. The post-1996 situation is covered in Li Minqi, "China: six years after Tiananmen," pp. 1–13 in *Monthly Review Press*, volume 47, number 8 (January 1996). For a prediction of a far less stable future for China based on the factors of population growth, faltering agriculture, and rising popular discontent, see Jack A. Goldstone, "The coming Chinese collapse," n.p. in *Foreign Policy*, number 99 (Summer 1995). For a journalistic report that suggests that the current student generation's outlook is decidedly more pro-regime and nationalistic than that of 1989, see Patrick E. Tyler, "China's campus model for the 90's: earnest patriot," *New York Times* (April 23, 1996). The demobilization of student political fervor is also chronicled in Jianying Zha, *China Pop: How Soap Operas, Tabloids, and Bestsellers Are Transforming a Culture* (New York: The New Press, 1995).

26. This discussion is based on a reading of the English-language press, especially the *New York Times* and the *Washington Report on Middle Eastern Affairs*. Scholarly work on the movement includes: Abdellah Hammoudi and Stuart Schaar, editors, *Algeria's Impasse* (Princeton University Center of International Studies, 1995); Robert Mortimer, "Islamists, soldiers, and democrats: the second Algerian war," pp. 18–39 in *The Middle East Journal*, volume 50, number 1 (Winter 1996); Reporters Sans Frontières, *Le drame algérien: un peuple en otage* (Paris: Editions La Découverte, 1994); and Susan Waltz, *Human Rights and Reform: Changing the Face of North African Politics* (Berkeley: University of California Press, 1995).

27. Moghadam, "Gender and revolutions," and Marnia Lazreg, "Feminism and difference: the perils of writing as a woman on women in Algeria," pp. 326–48 in Marianne Hirsch and Evelyn Fox Keller, editors, *Conflicts in Feminism* (New York: Routledge, 1990).

28. Like many Middle East specialists, I prefer the term "Islamist" to "fundamentalist" because of the imprecision and stereotypical connotations of the latter (among other reasons).

29. *New York Times* (June 26, 1997).

30. For analyses of Guatemala, see Wickham-Crowley, *Guerrillas and Revolution*; Dunkerley, *Power in the Isthmus*; Susanne Jonas, *The Battle for Guatemala: Rebels, Death Squads, and US Power* (Boulder: Westview, 1991); and Jim

Handy, *Gift of the Devil: A History of Guatemala* (Boston: South End Press, 1984).

31. The best English-language history of Argentina is David Rock's magisterial *Argentina, 1516–1987: From Spanish Colonization to Alfonsín* (Berkeley: University of California Press, 1989); on the Montoneros' and the ERP's battle with the far-right death squads and the army, see 355–66. I have also drawn on the account in Keen and Haynes, *A History of Latin America*, 328–30.

32. On the Philippines, I have benefited greatly from an exchange of letters with Kim Scipes, Department of Sociology, University of Wisconsin, Madison. Basic works include: James Goodno, *The Philippines: Land of Broken Promises* (London: Zed, 1991); Benjamin Pimentel, *Rebolusyon! A Generation of Struggle in the Philippines* (New York: Monthly Review Press, 1990); and Daniel B. Schirmer and Stephen R. Shalom, editors, *The Philippines Reader: A History of Colonialism, Neocolonialism, Dictatorship, and Resistance* (Boston: South End Press, 1987).

33. Wolf, *Peasant Wars of the Twentieth Century*, 127–8. The events of 1911 are covered in two of the great historical-comparative treatments of revolutions: Moore's *Social Origins of Dictatorship and Democracy* and Skocpol's *States and Social Revolutions*.

34. Spence, *The Search for Modern China*, 262–8.

35. My sources on Haiti include Michel-Rolph Trouillot, *Haiti, State Against Nation: The Origins and Legacy of Duvalierism* (New York: Monthly Review, 1990); James Ferguson, *Papa Doc, Baby Doc: Haiti and the Duvaliers* (Oxford: Basil Blackwell, 1987); and Alex Dupuy, *Haiti in the World Economy: Class, Race, and Underdevelopment Since 1700* (Boulder: Westview, 1989).

36. Sources on the events of 1986 include those listed above, as well as Robert L. Youngblood, *Marcos Against the Church: Economic Development and Political Repression in the Philippines* (Ithaca: Cornell University Press, 1990); Gary Hawes, *The Philippines State and the Marcos Regime: The Politics of Export* (Ithaca: Cornell University Press, 1987); James K. Boyce, *The Philippines: The Political Economy of Growth and Impoverishment in the Marcos Era* (Honolulu: University of Hawaii Press, 1993); and Stanley Karnow, *In Our Image: America's Empire in the Philippines* (New York: Random House, 1989). I have benefited from the work of research assistant Jackie Cabuay on the Philippines, particularly with respect to the economic downturn of the early to mid-1980s.

37. Laxalt is quoted in Raymond Bonner, *Waltzing with a Dictator: The Marcoses and the Making of American Policy* (New York: Times Books, 1987), cited by Richard Snyder, "Paths out of sultanistic regimes: combining structural and voluntarist perspectives," pp. 49–81 in H. E. Chehabi and Juan J. Linz, editors, *Sultanistic Regimes* (Baltimore: The Johns Hopkins Press, 1998), who provides a very helpful theoretical interpretation of regime transitions that includes the cases of Haiti, the Philippines, and Zaire, among others.

38. This account is based on lectures I have given over the years in my sociology of development class. Some key works include: Patrick Bond, *Elite Transition: From Apartheid to Neoliberalism in South Africa* (London: Pluto Press, 2000); Ben Fine and Zavareh Rustomjee, *The Political Economy of South Africa: From Minerals-energy Complex to Industrialization* (Boulder: Westview Press, 1996);

Hein Marias, *South Africa: Limits to Change: The Political Economy of Transformation* (London: Zed Books, 1998); Anthony Marx, *Lessons of Struggle: South African Internal Opposition, 1960–1990* (New York: Oxford University Press, 1992); Leonard Thompson, *A History of South Africa* (Yale: New Haven, 1990); and Mona Younis, *Liberation and Democratization: The South African and Palestinian National Movements* (Minneapolis: University of Minnesota Press, 2000). My able research assistant, Sadie Miller, took notes on some of these and produced a research report for me, "The political revolution in South Africa," at Smith College in 2002.

39. See Ludo de Witte, *The Assassination of Lumumba*, translated by Ann Wright and Renée Fenby (London: Verso, 2001). I would like to thank research assistant Joe Bandy for his work on Zaire at UC Santa Barbara in 1995–96.

40. Peter Evans has used Zaire as the prototype case of his evocatively labeled "predatory state," one in which maximization of individual wealth by an elite takes precedence over and prevents attainment of collective social goals: *Embedded Autonomy: States and Industrial Transformation* (Princeton University Press, 1995).

41. In 1995 Evans reported World Bank and other data showing a decline in per capita GNP of 2 percent a year since 1965, as well as a destruction of the road system from 90,000 to 6,000 miles: ibid., 43.

42. This earlier version, with these speculations, appeared as a 1996 working paper of the International Institute at the University of Michigan.

43. My sources for these events include a reading of the international press, especially the *New York Times* and the UK *Guardian Weekly*, which ran dozens of articles on Zaire in the first half of 1997.

44. This is an insight taken up in the work of Anthony Giddens on structuration theory: Anthony Giddens, *The Constitution of Society: Outline of the Theory of Structuration* (Cambridge: Polity Press, 1984).

45. For two discussions of the role of prediction in the social sciences generally and in the study of revolutions in particular, see Michael Hechter, Timur Kuran, Randall Collins, Charles Tilly, Edgar Kiser, James Coleman, and Alejandro Portes, "Symposium on prediction in the social sciences," pp. 1520–626 in *American Journal of Sociology*, volume 100, number 6 (May 1995), and the contributions by Nikki Keddie, Timur Kuran, and Jack A. Goldstone to Nikki Keddie, *Debating Revolutions* (New York University Press, 1995), constituting part one of the book: "Can revolutions be predicted? Understood?" I am among the skeptics in these debates about the utility of the exercise of prediction.

46. On the political economy of Iraq see Marion Farouk-Sluglett and Peter Sluglett, *Iraq Since 1958: From Revolution to Dictatorship* (London: Kegan Paul, 1987).

47. On the nature of the regime see Samir al-Khalil, *Republic of Fear: The Politics of Modern Iraq* (Berkeley: University of California Press, 1989); Middle East Watch, *Human Rights in Iraq* (New Haven: Yale University Press, 1990); and CARDRI, editors, *Saddam's Iraq – Revolution or Reaction?* (London: Zed Press, 1985).

48. *New York Times* (March 18, 1991).

49. On developments in Iran since 1989, see Anoushiravan Ehteshami, *After Khomeini: The Iranian Second Republic* (New York: Routledge, 1995); Massoud Karshenas and M. Hesham Pesaran, "Economic reform and the reconstruction of the Iranian economy," pp. 89–111 in *Middle East Journal*, volume 49, number 1 (Winter 1995); Haggay Ram, "Crushing the opposition: adversaries of the Islamic Republic of Iran," pp. 426–39 in *Middle East Journal*, volume 46, number 3 (Summer 1992); and Saeed Rahnema and Sohrab Behdad, editors, *Iran After the Revolution: Crisis of an Islamic State* (New York: St. Martin's, 1996).

50. On Egyptian political economy, see Galal A. Amin, *Egypt's Economic Predicament: A Study in the Interaction of External Pressure, Political Folly and Social Tension in Egypt, 1960–1990* (Leiden: E. J. Brill, 1995); Robert Springborg, *The Political Economy of Mubarak's Egypt* (Boulder: Westview, 1989); Derek Hopwood, *Egypt: Politics and Society 1945–1990* (London: Routledge, 1993); and Richard H. Adam, Jr. "Evaluating the process of development in Egypt, 1980–97," pp. 255–75 in *International Journal of Middle East Studies*, volume 32, number 2 (May 2000). On the opposition, see Karim el-Gawhary, "Report from a war zone: Gama'at vs. government in Upper Egypt," pp. 49–51 in *MERIP (Middle East Research and Information Project) Report*, number 194/95 (May–June/July–August 1995); Giles Keppel, "Islamists versus the state in Egypt and Algeria," pp. 109–27 in *Daedalus*, volume 124, number 3 (Summer 1995); Patrick D. Gaffney, *The Prophet's Pulpit: Islamic Preaching in Contemporary Egypt* (Berkeley: University of California Press, 1994); and Mary Anne Weaver, *A Portrait of Egypt: A Journey Through the World of Militant Islam* (New York: Farrar, Straus and Giroux, 1999).

51. Casandra, "The impending crisis in Egypt," pp. 9–27 in *Middle East Journal*, volume 49, number 1 (Winter 1995).

52. This reading contradicts Forrest Colburn's thesis in *The Vogue of Revolution in Poor Countries*, that Third World revolutionary regimes have been uniformly Marxist-Leninist in political culture. Cuba is, to be sure, Marxist-Leninist, but à la cubana.

53. Quoted in the *New York Times* (January 11, 1993).

54. A vast literature now exists on these cases. One good comparative study of their political economies is found in Walden Bello and Stephanie Rosenfeld, *Dragons in Distress: Asia's Miracle Economies in Crisis* (San Francisco: The Institute for Food and Development Policy, 1990).

55. On the 1997 crisis, see William K. Tabb, "The East Asian financial crisis," pp. 24–38 in *Monthly Review*, volume 50, number 2 (June 1998); James Crotty and Kang-Kook Lee, "Korea's neoliberal restructuring," pp. 159–65 in Amy Offner, Chris Sturr, Alejandro Reuss, and the *Dollars & Sense* Collective, editors, *Real World Globalization: A Reader in Economics, Business and Politics from Dollars & Sense* (Cambridge: Dollars & Sense, 2004); and Walden Bello, "The end of the Asian miracle," pp. 16–21 in *The Nation* (January 12/19, 1998).

56. On this, see James Straub, "Argentina's piqueteros and us," at www.tomdispath.com (March 2, 2004).

57. See Elena Poniatowksa's magisterial history, *Massacre in Mexico* (Columbia: University of Missouri Press, 1975).
58. Keen and Haynes, *A History of Latin America*, 298; see also 297 on land tenure in 1961.
59. Karen Kampwirth, "Marching with the Taliban or dancing with the Zapatistas? Revolution after the cold war," pp. 227–41 in John Foran, editor, *The Future of Revolutions: Rethinking Radical Change in the Age of Globalization* (London: Zed Press, 2003), 235.
60. Keen and Haynes, *A History of Latin America*, 302.
61. Ibid., 305. In the 1976–82 presidency of José López Portillo it is alleged that over 500 opponents of the regime were killed: *Latinamerica Press* (February 25, 2004), 7.
62. *New York Times* (September 21, 1992); *Latinamerica Press* (December 10, 1992).
63. Among many fine works in English on Chiapas, see George A. Collier (with Elizabeth Lowery Quaratiello) *Basta! Land and the Zapatista Rebellion in Chiapas* (Oakland: Food First/Institute for Food and Development Policy, 1994); Philip Russell, *The Chiapas Rebellion* (Austin: Mexico Resource Center, 1994); John Ross, *Rebellion from the Roots: Indian Uprising in Chiapas* (Monroe: Common Courage Press, 1995); Elaine Katzenberger, editor, *First World, Ha Ha Ha! The Zapatista Challenge* (San Francisco: City Lights, 1995); Subcomandante Marcos, *Shadows of Tender Fury: The Letters and Communiqués of Subcomandante Marcos and the Zapatista Army of National Liberation*, translated by Frank Bardacke, Leslie López and the Watsonville, California, Human Rights Committee (New York: Monthly Review Press, 1995); John Ross, *The War Against Oblivion: The Zapatista Chronicles 1994–2000* (Monroe: Common Courage Press, 2000); and Tom Hayden, editor, *The Zapatista Reader* (New York: Thunder's Mouth Press, 2002).

    The works of anthropologist Jan Rus are also crucial for understanding the rebellion, among them "Land adaptation to global change: the reordering of native society in highland Chiapas, 1974–1994," pp. 82–91 in *Revista Europea de Estudios Latinoamericanos y del Caribe*, volume 58 (1995), and Jan Rus, R. Aida Hernandez Castillo, and Shannan Mattiace, editors, "The indigenous people of Chiapas and the state in the time of Zapatismo: remaking culture, renegotiating power," special issue of *Latin American Perspectives*, volume 28, number 2 (March 2001).
64. *Latinamerica Press* (January 20, 1994), quote rephrased. For an in-depth discussion of women in the Zapatistas, see Kampwirth, *Women and Guerrilla Movements*.
65. *New York Times* (January 4, 1994).
66. The Mexican government revealed his name in February 1995, hoping to undermine his incredible charismatic popularity, which failed to happen: *New York Times* (February 11, October 5, 1995); *Christian Science Monitor* (February 14, 1995). Rafael Sebastián Guillén Vicente is variously described as "a prize-winning sociology student," former professor of communications, son of a furniture salesman from Tampico, and comrade of the Sandinistas.

67. *New York Times* (January 4, 9, 1994).
68. According to the *New York Times* (January 26, 1994).
69. *New York Times* (January 23, 1994).
70. *New York Times* (January 21, 1994).
71. On the challenges of daily life in Mexico, see Judith Adler Hellman, *Mexican Lives* (New York: New Press, 1994). On US support for the regime, see Jeff Garth and Elaine Sciolino, "I.M.F. head: he speaks, and money talks," *New York Times* (April 2, 1996).

CHAPTER 6

1. Skocpol, *States and Social Revolutions*, 4.
2. An early version of this table and discussion of results is found in my essay, "The comparative-historical sociology of Third World social revolutions."
3. This section draws extensively on John Foran, "Introduction to the future of revolutions," pp. 1–15 in John Foran, editor, *The Future of Revolutions: Rethinking Radical Change in the Age of Globalization* (London: Zed, 2003).
4. G. Nodia, "The end of revolution?" pp. 164–71 in *Journal of Democracy*, volume 11, number 1 (January 2000), 167–71; see also Robert S. Snyder, "The end of revolution?," pp. 5–28 in *The Review of Politics*, volume 61, number 1 (Winter 1999).
5. Thatcher is identified as the source of this famous declaration in David Harvey, *Spaces of Hope* (Berkeley: University of California Press, 2000), 63. Daniel Singer traces its genealogy further, noting "Tina is now the unwritten premise of virtually the whole political debate": *Whose Millennium? Theirs or Ours?* (New York: Monthly Review Press, 1999), 2. For Perry Anderson, "the only starting-point for a realistic Left today is a lucid registration of historical defeat": "Renewals," pp. 5–24 in *New Left Review*, second series, number 1 (January–February 2000), 16. Yet this must be weighed against the observation of Rosa Luxemburg, who noted in *Die Rote Fahne* on January 14, 1919: "Revolution is the only form of 'war' in which ultimate victory can only be prepared by a series of 'defeats'": quoted in Singer, *Whose Millennium?*, 278.
6. Jeff Goodwin, "Is the age of revolution over?," paper presented at the meetings of the International Studies Association Meetings, Minneapolis (1998), a version of which was published on pp. 272–83 in Mark Katz, editor, *Revolution and International Relations: A Reader* (Washington: Congressional Quarterly, 2001), and Jeff Goodwin, "State-centered approaches to social revolutions: strengths and limitations of a theoretical tradition," pp. 11–27 in John Foran, editor, *Theorizing Revolutions* (London: Routledge, 1997), 18, though see his discussion of Eastern Europe in *No Other Way Out*.
7. Eric Selbin, "Same as it ever was: the future of revolution at the end of the century," paper presented at the meetings of the International Studies Association, Minneapolis (1998), 2; a version also appeared in Mark Katz's *Revolution and International Relations*.
8. Mark N. Katz, *Reflections on Revolutions* (London: Macmillan, 1999), chapter 5.

9. For a sample of views, see the essays of Michael Hechter, Timur Kuran, Randall Collins, Charles Tilly, Edgar Kiser, James S. Coleman, and Alejandro Portes, "Symposium on prediction in the social sciences," pp. 1520–1626 in the *American Journal of Sociology*, volume 100, number 6 (May 1995).

10. Carlos Vilas, "Between market democracies and capitalist globalization: is there any prospect for social revolution in Latin America?" pp. 95–106 in John Foran, editor, *The Future of Revolutions: Rethinking Radical Change in the Age of Globalization* (London: Zed, 2003), 104; see also Ken Irish-Bramble, "Predicting revolutions," MA thesis, Department of Sociology, New York University (2000), and the essays by Nikki Keddie, Timur Kuran and Jack Goldstone in Nikki R. Keddie, editor, *Debating Revolutions* (New York University Press, 1995) on this question.

11. Vilas, "Between market democracies and capitalist globalization," 104, quoting Eric Hobsbawm, "Revolutions," pp. 5–46 in Roy Porter and Mikulas Teich, editors, *Revolution in History* (Cambridge University Press, 1986), 19.

12. I do this in Foran, "The future of revolutions at the fin-de-siècle," pp. 791–820 in *Third World Quarterly*, volume 18, number 5 (1997), and in Chapter 5 of this book.

13. Vilas, "Between market democracies and capitalist globalization," 105.

14. V. I. Lenin, *Imperialism, The Highest Stage of Capitalism: A Popular Outline* (New York: International Publishers, [1916] 1997), 46; Eric Selbin notes this echo in "Zapata's white horse and Che's beret: theses on the future of revolutions," pp. 83–94 in John Foran, editor, *The Future of Revolutions: Rethinking Radical Change in the Age of Globalization* (London: Zed, 2003), 87.

15. Harvey, *Spaces of Hope*, 61–7.

16. United Nations Development Program [UNDP], *Human Development Report 1999* (New York: Oxford University Press, 1999), 38; see also Paul Hawken, "Skeleton woman visits Seattle," pp. 14–34 in Kevin Danaher and Roger Burbach, editors, *Globalize This! The Battle Against the World Trade Organization and Corporate Rule* (Monroe: Common Courage, 2000), 15; Singer, *Whose Millennium?*, 153; and Eduardo Galeano, *Upside Down: A Primer for the Looking-Glass World* (New York: Metropolitan Books, 1998). Galeano reports the following from an earlier UNDP report: "Ten people, the ten richest men on the planet, own wealth equivalent to the value of the total production of fifty countries, and 447 multimillionaires own a greater fortune than the annual income of half of humanity", UNDP, *Human Development Report 1997* (New York: Oxford University Press, 1997) as quoted by Galeano, *Upside Down*, 28. By 1999, there were reported to be 475 billionaires in the world: Sarah Anderson and John Cavanagh, with Thea Lee, *Field Guide to the Global Economy* (New York: New Press, 2000), 53, citing UNDP, *Human Development Report 1999* and *Forbes* (July 5, 1999).

17. Craig N. Murphy, "Political consequences of the new inequality," pp. 347–56 in *International Studies Quarterly*, volume 45, number 3 (September 2001), 350, his emphasis, citing B. Milanovic, *True World Income Distribution 1988 and 1993: First Calculations Based on Household Surveys Alone* (Washington: World Bank, 1999).

18. Anderson et al., *Field Guide to the Global Economy*, 53, citing UNDP, *Human Development Report 1996*, 2; on inequality in the US and elsewhere in the First World, see Robin Hahnel, *Panic Rules: Everything You Need to Know About the Global Economy* (Boston: South End Press, 1999), 8–9.

19. Jeremy Brecher, Tim Costello, and Brendan Smith, "Globalization from below," pp. 19–22 in *The Nation* (December 4, 2000), and their *Globalization From Below* (Boston: South End Press, 2000).

20. Hahnel, *Panic Rules*, 12, emphasis in the original.

21. Michel Chossudovsky, "Global poverty in the late 20th century," pp. 292–311 in *Journal of International Affairs*, volume 52, number 1 (1998), 293; see also Murphy, "Political consequences of the new inequality."

22. Compare Hahnel, *Panic Rules*, 111–15, with A. K. Ghose, "Trade liberalization, employment and growing inequality," pp. 281–306 in *International Labour Review*, volume 139, number 3 (2000).

23. Harvey, *Spaces of Hope*, 65; Peter Evans, *Embedded Autonomy: States and Industrial Transformation* (Princeton University Press, 1995).

24. Farideh Farhi, "The democratic turn: new ways of understanding revolution," pp. 30–41 in John Foran, editor, *The Future of Revolutions: Rethinking Radical Change in the Age of Globalization* (London: Zed, 2003), 35.

25. George A. Collier and Jane F. Collier, "The Zapatista rebellion in the context of globalization," pp. 242–52 in John Foran, editor, *The Future of Revolutions: Rethinking Radical Change in the Age of Globalization* (London: Zed, 2003), 243.

26. Jeff Goodwin, "The renewal of socialism and the decline of revolution," pp. 59–72 in John Foran, editor, *The Future of Revolutions: Rethinking Radical Change in the Age of Globalization* (London: Zed, 2003), 65–6.

27. See Farhi, "The democratic turn," and three further contributions to *The Future of Revolutions*: Jeffery M. Paige, "Finding the revolutionary in the revolution: social science concepts and the future of revolution," pp. 19–29; Abdollah Dashti, "At the crossroads of globalization: participatory democracy as a medium of future revolutionary struggle," pp. 169–79; and Christopher A. McAuley, "The demise of Bolshevism and the rebirth of Zapatismo: revolutionary options in a post-Soviet world," pp. 149–68.

28. Valentine Moghadam, "Is the future of revolution feminist? Rewriting 'gender and revolutions' for a globalizing world," pp. 159–68 in John Foran, editor, *The Future of Revolutions: Rethinking Radical Change in the Age of Globalization* (London: Zed, 2003).

29. John Walton, "Globalization and popular movements," pp. 217–26 in John Foran, editor, *The Future of Revolutions: Rethinking Radical Change in the Age of Globalization* (London: Zed, 2003), 225.

30. Selbin, "Zapata's white horse and Che's beret," 86.

31. Ibid., 87.

32. Douglas Kellner, "Globalization, technopolitics and revolution," pp. 180–94 in John Foran, editor, *The Future of Revolutions: Rethinking Radical Change in the Age of Globalization* (London: Zed, 2003), 184.

33. Noel Parker, "Parallaxes: revolutions and 'revolution' in a globalized imaginary," pp. 42–56 in John Foran, editor, *The Future of Revolutions: Rethinking Radical Change in the Age of Globalization* (London: Zed, 2003), 46.

34. This section draws extensively on my essay, "Confronting an empire: Sociology and the US-made world crisis," pp. 213–33 in *Political Power and Social Theory*, volume 16 (2003).

35. For an illuminating discussion of this see Jim Lobe, "Faulty connection," www.TomPaine.com (July 15, 2003).

36. Eric Selbin provided me with this insight.

37. Tariq Ali, "Recolonizing Iraq," pp. 5–19 in *New Left Review*, number 21 (May/June 2003), 18.

38. Seumas Milne, "The right to resist," in *The Guardian* (June 19, 2003).

39. Quoted in Daniel Smith, "Iraq: descending into the quagmire," in *Foreign Policy in Focus* (June 2003), online at www.fpif.org

40. Eric Foner, "Dare call it treason," *The Nation* (June 2, 2003), 13; see also Gore Vidal, "We are the patriots," pp. 11–14 in *The Nation* (June 2, 2003).

41. This section to the end of the chapter draws extensively on my essay, "Magical realism: how might the revolutions of the future have better end(ing)s?" pp. 271–83 in John Foran, editor, *The Future of Revolutions: Rethinking Radical Change in the Age of Globalization* (London: Zed Press, 2003).

42. Colburn, *The Vogue of Revolution in Poor Countries*, 17.

43. Quoted in Kara Zugman, "Mexican awakening in postcolonial America: Zapatistas in urban spaces in Mexico City," PhD dissertation, Department of Sociology, University of California, Santa Barbara (2001), 113. This section on the Zapatistas' own views draws on this remarkable work.

44. Quoted in Zugman, "Mexican awakening in postcolonial America," 124.

45. EZLN, "Second declaration from the Lacandón jungle: 'Today we say: we will not surrender!'" pp. 221–31 in Tom Hayden, editor, *The Zapatista Reader* (New York: Thunder's Mouth Press and Nation Books, 2002), 226.

46. Marcos, *Shadows of Tender Fury*, 85.

47. EZLN, "Fourth declaration from the Lacandón jungle," pp. 239–50 in Tom Hayden, editor, *The Zapatista Reader* (New York: Thunder's Mouth Press and Nation Books, 2002), 250.

48. Manuel De Landa, *A Thousand Years of Nonlinear History* (New York: Zone Books, 1997).

49. Frank Borgers, "War of the flea, war of the swarm: reflections on the anti-globalization movement and its future," pp. 18–19 in the University of Massachusetts, Amherst *Voice*, volume 14, number 2 (2000), citing Barbara Epstein, "The politics of prefigurative community: the non-violent direct action movement," pp. 63–92 in Mike Davis and Michael Sprinker, editors, *Reshaping the US Left: Popular Struggles in the 1980s* (London: Verso, 1988).

50. I learned this from one of my students, Sarah Macdonald, at Smith College in the fall of 2000. Among many websites, see www.a16.org.

51. For some useful sociological theorizing, see Jeff Goodwin, James M. Jasper, and Francesca Polletta, editors, *Passionate Politics: Emotions and Social Movements* (University of Chicago Press, 2001), and J.-P. Reed, "Emotions in context: revolutionary accelerators, hope, moral outrage, and other emotions in the making of Nicaragua's revolution," in *Theory and Society*, volume 33, number 6 (2004).

52. Paula Allen and Eve Ensler, "An activist love story," pp. 413–25 in Rachel Blau Duplessis and Ann Snitow, editors, *The Feminist Memoir Project: Voices From Women's Liberation* (New York: Three Rivers Press, 1998), 425.

53. Alice Walker, *Anything We Love Can Be Saved: A Writer's Activism* (New York: Random House, 1997), xxiii.

54. I found this quote by Adrienne Rich, significantly enough, as the epigraph to a book on the Zapatistas, Ellen Katzenberger, editor, *First World, Ha Ha Ha! The Zapatista Challenge* (San Francisco: City Lights, 1995).

55. John Foran, "Alternatives to development: of love, dreams, and revolution," pp. 268–74 in Kum-Kum Bhavnani, John Foran, and Priya A. Kurian, editors, *Feminist Futures: Re-imagining Women, Culture and Development* (London: Zed Press, 2003).

56. Patricio Guzmán, *Chile: Obstinate Memory* (Les Films d'Ici and National Film Board of Canada, 1997), translation from the subtitles.

57. Marcos, *Shadows of Tender Fury*, 50.

58. FZLN member interviewed by Zugman, "Mexican awakening in postcolonial America," 126.

59. Susan George, "Another world is possible," in *The Nation* (February 18, 2002), 12.

60. Goodwin, "Is the age of revolution over?" 8.

61. Gregory Elliott, *Perry Anderson: The Merciless Laboratory of History* (Minneapolis: University of Minnesota Press, 1998), 168 for Anderson; Harvey, *Spaces of Hope*; Singer, *Whose Millennium?* One is strongly tempted to contrast unfavorably Anderson's pessimistic turn by the year 2000 – "The only starting-point for *a realistic Left* today is a lucid registration of historical defeat" (Anderson, "Renewals," 16, emphasis mine) – with the conclusion to Harvey's book, a playfully imaginative vision of a post-capitalist utopia named "Edilia," pp. 257–81 in *Spaces of Hope*.

62. Quoted in Erika Polakoff, "Gender and the Latin American left," pp. 20–3 in *Z Magazine* (November 1996), 22.

63. I first heard the term used by Robert Ware at the Marxism 2000 conference at Amherst, Massachusetts in September 2000, who was quick to point out that he hadn't coined this wonderful rejoinder.

64. Kevin Danaher and Roger Burbach, "Introduction: making history," pp. 7–11 in *Globalize This! The Battle Against the World Trade Organization and Corporate Rule* (Monroe: Common Courage, 2000), 9.

65. "Public Sociologies" was the theme of the 2004 meetings of the American Sociological Association, under the leadership of Michael Burawoy, its president. This text is found in the ASA Call for Papers (2004).

66. Vilas, "Between market democracies and capitalist globalization," 105.

67. Galeano, *Upside Down*, 334.

Works cited

PRIMARY SOURCES

Banco Central de Nicaragua. *Indicadores Económicos*. Managua: BCN. 1979.
Chile Documentation Project of the National Security Archive. Directed
    by Peter Kornbluh. http://www.gwu.edu/~nsarchiv/latin_america/chile.htm
    Chile Hoy (August 17–23, 1973). Santiago, Chile.
Chile Hoy, July 6–12, August 17–23, 1973.
Christian Science Monitor, February 14, 1995.
El Mercurio – Edición Internacional, January 18–24, August 7–13, 1971; July 31–
    August 6, December 4–10, 1972; March 5–11, August 6–12, 13–19, 1973.
    Santiago, Chile.
El Rebelde, January 25–31, 1972. Santiago, Chile.
Foreign Relations of the United States, 1955–1957, volume VI, *American Republics:
    Multilateral; Mexico; Caribbean*. Washington, DC: United States Government
    Printing Office. 1987.
Guardian Weekly. First half of 1997.
"How we organized strike that paralyzed Shah's regime. Firsthand account by
    Iranian oil worker," pp. 292–301 in Petter Nore and Terisa Turner, editors,
    Oil and Class Struggle. London: Zed. 1981.
Instituto de Estudio del Sandinismo. *Y se armo la runga! Testimonios de la insur-
    reción popular sandinista en Masaya*. Managua: Editorial Nueva Nicaragua.
    1982.
Interviews with Sir Peter Ramsbotham, 'Ali Amini, and Ahmad Ghoreishi,
    Iranian oral history collection, Harvard University.
Iranian Students Association in the U.S. *Shah's Inferno: Abadan August 19, 1978*.
    Berkeley: ISAUS. 1978.
Kayhan, January–May 1978.
Kayhan International, August 2–3, 1974; October 26, 1976.
Latinamerica Press, December 10, 1992; January 20, 1994; February 25, 2004.
Le Monde, September 6, 1978.
The Manchester Guardian, September 5 and 6, 1978.
National Security Archives. Washington, DC Various documents on Iran. 1978–
    80.
New York Times, January 15, 1910; March 18, 1991; September 21, 1992; January
    11, March 16, 1993; January 4, 9, 21, 23, 26, 1994; February 11, October
    5, 1995; June 26, 1997.

Radio Tehran, September 8, 1979. Text in *Foreign Broadcast Information Service* (September 10, 1979), n.p.

Republica de Cuba, Consejo Nacional de Economia. "Empleo y Desempleo en la fuerza trabajadora Agosto 1958." *Informe Tecnico*, Number 8. Havana. 1958.

United States National Archives. Washington, DC. 737.00, 837.00–06. Diplomatic correspondence on Cuba. 1955–59.

United States National Archives. Washington, DC. 812.00. Diplomatic correspondence on Mexico. 1913.

U.S. Senate Intelligence Subcommittee. *Alleged Assassination Plots Involving Foreign Leaders*. Interim Report of the Senate Intelligence Committee. Washington, DC: U.S. Government Printing Office. 1975.

U.S. Senate Subcommittee on Multinational Corporations of the Committee on Foreign Relations Hearings. *Multinational Corporations and United States Foreign Policy*. Washington, DC: U.S. Senate, 93rd Congress, second session. 1974.

www.personal.umich.edu/~lornand/soa/chile.htm

World Bank. *World Data*. CD-Rom.

SECONDARY SOURCES

Abrahamian, Ervand. "Structural causes of the Iranian revolution." *MERIP (Middle East Research and Information Project) Reports* 87 (May 1980), 21–26.

—. *Iran Between Two Revolutions*. Princeton University Press. 1982.

—. *The Iranian Mojehedin*. New Haven: Yale University Press. 1989.

—. "Khomeini: Fundamentalist or populist?" *New Left Review* 186 (March–April 1991), 102–19.

Adam, Richard H. Jr. "Evaluating the process of development in Egypt, 1980–97." *International Journal of Middle East Studies* 32 (2) (May 2000), 255–75.

Ahmad, Aijaz. "Woman, nation, denomination." Talk at the University of California, Santa Barbara (April 12, 2000).

Akhavi, Shahrough. *Religion and Politics in Contemporary Iran: Clergy-State Relations in the Pahlavi Period*. Albany: State University of New York Press. 1980.

Alexander, Robert J. *The Bolivian National Revolution*. New Brunswick: Rutgers University Press. 1958.

Algar, Hamid. "Preface" to Ali Shari'ati, *Marxism and Other Western Fallacies: An Islamic Critique*. Translated from the Persian by R. Campbell. Berkeley: Mizan Press. 1980.

Ali, Tariq. "Recolonizing Iraq." *New Left Review* 21 (May/June 2003), 5–19.

al-Khalil, Samir. *Republic of Fear: The Politics of Modern Iraq*. Berkeley: University of California Press. 1989.

Allen, Paula and Eve Ensler. "An activist love story," pp. 413–25 in Rachel Blau Duplessis and Ann Snitow, editors, *The Feminist Memoir Project: Voices From Women's Liberation*. New York: Three Rivers Press. 1998.

Amin, Galal A. *Egypt's Economic Predicament: A Study in the Interaction of External Pressure, Political Folly and Social Tension in Egypt, 1960–1990*. Leiden: E. J. Brill. 1995.

Amjad, Mohammed. *Iran: From Royal Dictatorship to Theocracy*. New York and Westport: Greenwood Press. 1989.

Amnesty International. *Annual Report 1974–75*. London: AI Publications. 1975.

Anderson, Perry. "Renewals." *New Left Review*. Second series 1 (January–February 2000), 5–24.

Anderson, Rodney D. "Mexican workers and the politics of revolution, 1906–1911." *The Hispanic American Historical Review* 54 (1) (February 1974), 94–113.

Anderson, Sarah and John Cavanagh, with Thea Lee. *Field Guide to the Global Economy*. New York: New Press. 2000.

Anderson, Thomas. *Matanza: El Salvador's Communist Revolt of 1932*. Lincoln: University of Nebraska Press. 1971.

"Angola," pp. 75–8 in *The World Guide 2001/2002*. Oxford: New Internationalist Publications, Ltd. 2001.

Appy, Christian G. *Patriots: The Vietnam War Remembered from All Sides*. New York: Viking. 2003.

Apter, David E. "Discourse as power: Yan'an and the Chinese revolution," pp. 193–234 in Tony Saich and Hans van de Ven, editors, *New Perspectives on the Chinese Communist Revolution*. Armonk, NY: M. E. Sharpe. 1995.

Arjomand, Said Amir. "The causes and significance of the Iranian revolution." *State, Culture and Society* 1 (3) (1985), 41–66.

—. *The Turban for the Crown: The Islamic Revolution in Iran*. New York and London: Oxford University Press. 1988.

Armstrong, Robert and Janet Shenk. *El Salvador: The Face of Revolution*. Boston: South End Press. 1982.

Arnold, Guy. *Wars in the Third World since 1945*. London: Cassell. 1991.

Ashraf, Ahmad and Ali Banuazizi. "The state, classes and modes of mobilization in the Iranian revolution." *State, Culture and Society* 1 (3) (1985), 3–40.

Astrow, André. *Zimbabwe: A Revolution That Lost Its Way?* Zed Press: London. 1983.

Aya, Rod. "Theories of revolution reconsidered: contrasting models of collective violence." *Theory and Society* 8 (1) (July 1979), 39–99.

Bailey, David C. "Revisionism and the recent historiography of the Mexican revolution." *Hispanic American Historical Review* 58 (1) (1978), 62–79.

Balta, Paul and Claudine Rulleau. *L'Iran insurgé*. Paris: Sindbad. 1979.

Baraheni, Reza. *The Crowned Cannibals: Writings on Repression in Iran*. New York: Vintage Books. 1977.

Bashiriyeh, Hossein. *The State and Revolution in Iran, 1962–1982*. New York: St. Martin's. 1984.

Belli, Gioconda. *The Country under My Skin: A Memoir of Love and War*. Translated by Kristina Cordero with the author. New York: Alfred A. Knopf. 2002.

Bello, Walden. "The end of the Asian miracle." *The Nation* (January 12/19, 1998), 16–21.

Bello, Walden and Stephanie Rosenfeld. *Dragons in Distress: Asia's Miracle Economies in Crisis*. San Francisco: The Institute for Food and Development Policy. 1990.

Benachenhou, Abdellatif. *Formation du sous-développement en Algérie: essai sur les limites du développement du capitalisme en Algérie 1830–1962*. Algiers: Entreprise Nationale "Imprimerie Comerciale." 1978.

Benjamin, Medea, Joseph Collins, and Michael Scott. *No Free Lunch: Food & Revolution in Cuba Today*. New York and San Francisco: Food First and Grove Press. 1986.

Bennoune, Mahfoud. *The Making of Contemporary Algeria, 1830–1987: Colonial Upheavals and Post-Independence Development*. Cambridge University Press. 1988.

Beverley, John and Marc Zimmerman. *Literature and Politics in the Central American Revolutions*. Austin: University of Texas Press. 1990.

Bianco, Lucien. "Peasant responses to CCP mobilization policies, 1937–1945," pp. 175–87 in Tony Saich and Hans van de Ven, editors, *New Perspectives on the Chinese Communist Revolution*. Armonk, NY: M. E. Sharpe. 1995.

Bill, James A. *The Eagle and the Lion: The Tragedy of American-Iranian Relations*. New Haven and London: Yale University Press. 1988.

Birns, Laurence, editor. *The End of Chilean Democracy*. New York: Seabury Press. 1974.

Black, George. *Triumph of the People: The Sandinista Revolution in Nicaragua*. London: Zed Press. 1981.

Boavida, Américo. *Angola: Five Centuries of Portuguese Exploitation*. Richmond: LSM Information Center. 1972.

Bonachea, Ramón L. and Marta San Martín. *The Cuban Insurrection, 1952–1959*. New Brunswick: Transaction. 1974.

Bond, Patrick. *Elite Transition: From Apartheid to Neoliberalism in South Africa*. London: Pluto Press. 2000.

Bonner, Raymond. *Waltzing with a Dictator: The Marcoses and the Making of American Policy*. New York: Times Books. 1987.

Boorstein, Edward. *Allende's Chile: An Inside View*. New York: International Publishers Co. 1977.

Booth, John A. *The End and the Beginning: The Nicaraguan Revolution*. Boulder: Westview. 1985.

Borgers, Frank. "War of the flea, war of the swarm: reflections on the anti-globalization movement and its future." University of Massachusetts, *Amherst Voice* 14 (2) (2000), 18–19.

Boyce, James K. *The Philippines: The Political Economy of Growth and Impoverishment in the Marcos Era*. Honolulu: University of Hawaii Press. 1993.

Braestrup, Peter. *Big Story: How the American Press and Television Reported and Interpreted the Crisis of Tet 1968 in Vietnam and Washington*. Abridged version. New Haven: Yale University Press. 1977.

Brecher, Jeremy, Tim Costello and Brendan Smith, "Globalization from below." *The Nation* (December 4, 2000), 19–22.

Brecher, Jeremy, Tim Costello and Brendan Smith. *Globalization From Below*. Boston: South End Press. 2000.

Brenner, Anita. *The Wind that Swept Mexico: The History of the Mexican Revolution 1910–1942*. Austin and London: University of Texas Press [1943]. 1971.

Brinton, Crane. *The Anatomy of Revolution*. New York: Prentice-Hall, Inc. [1938]. 1952

Brustein, William. "Regional social orders in France and the French revolution." *Comparative Social Research* 9 (1986), 145–61.

Bulmer-Thomas, Victor. *The Political Economy of Central America since 1920.* Cambridge University Press. 1987.

Burawoy, Michael. "Two methods in search of science: Skocpol versus Trotsky." *Theory and Society* 18 (6) (November 1989), 759–805.

Cabarrús, Carlos Rafael. *Génesis de una revolución: Analisis del surgimiento y desarrollo de la organización campesina en El Salvador.* Mexico City: Ediciones de la Casa Chata. 1983.

Calhoun, Craig Jackson. "The radicalism of tradition: community strength or venerable disguise and borrowed language?" *American Journal of Sociology* 88 (5) (March 1983), 886–914.

—. *Neither Gods nor Emperors: Students and the Struggle for Democracy in China.* Berkeley: University of California Press. 1994.

Cann, John P. *Counterinsurgency in Africa: The Portuguese Way of War, 1961–1974.* Westport: Greenwood. 1997.

Cannon, Terence. *Revolutionary Cuba.* New York: Thomas Y. Crowell. 1981.

Cardoso, Fernando Henrique and Enzo Faletto. *Dependency and Development in Latin America.* Berkeley and Los Angeles: University of California Press. 1979.

CARDRI, editors. *Saddam's Iraq – Revolution or Reaction?* London: Zed Press. 1985.

CARIN (Central America Research Institute). "UNO electoral victory." *Central America Bulletin* 9 (3) (Spring 1990).

Casandra. "The impending crisis in Egypt." *Middle East Journal.* 49 (1) (Winter 1995), 9–27.

Castro, Fidel. *La revolución cubana, 1953–1962.* Mexico City: ERA. 1972.

Chang, J. K. *Industrial Development in Pre-Communist China.* Edinburgh University Press. 1969.

Chau, Le. *Le Viet Nam socialiste: une économie de transition.* Paris: Maspero. 1966.

Chehabi, H. E. *Iranian Politics and Religious Modernism: The Liberation Movement of Iran under the Shah and Khomeini.* Ithaca: Cornell University Press. 1990.

Chen, Han-seng. *Landlord and Peasant in China: A Study of the Agrarian Crisis in South China.* New York: International Publishers. 1936.

Chen, Yung-fa. *Making Revolution: The Communist Movement in Eastern and Central China, 1937–1945.* Berkeley: University of California Press. 1986.

Chinh, Truong. *Primer for Revolt.* New York: Praeger. 1963.

Chong, Denise. *The Girl in the Picture: The Story of Kim Phuc, the Photograph, and the Vietnam War.* New York: Vintage. 2000.

Chossudovsky, Michel. "Global poverty in the late 20th century." *Journal of International Affairs* 52 (1) (1998), 292–311.

Christie, Iain. *Samora Machel: A Biography.* London: Zed. 1989.

Ciment, James. *Angola and Mozambique: Postcolonial Wars in Southern Africa.* New York: Facts on File, Inc. 1997.

Cliffe, Lionel. "Zimbabwe's political inheritance," pp. 8–35 in Colin Stoneman, *Zimbabwe's Inheritance.* New York: St. Martin's Press. 1981.

Cochran, Sherman and Hsieh Cheng-kuang, with Janis Cochran, translators and editors. *One Day in China, May 21, 1936.* New Haven: Yale University Press. 1983.

Cockcroft, James D. *Intellectual Precursors of the Mexican Revolution, 1900–1913.* Austin and London: University of Texas Press. 1968.

Cohen-Solal, Annie. "Camus, Sartre and the Algerian war." *Journal of European Studies* 27 (1998), 43–50.

Colburn, Forrest D. *Post-Revolutionary Nicaragua: State, Class, and the Dilemmas of Agrarian Policy.* Berkeley: University of California Press. 1986.

——. *Managing the Commanding Heights: Nicaragua's State Enterprises.* Berkeley: University of California Press. 1990.

——. *The Vogue of Revolutions in Poor Countries.* Princeton University Press. 1994.

Cole, Johnetta B. "Women in Cuba: the revolution within the revolution," pp. 307–17 in Jack Goldstone, editor, *Revolutions: Theoretical, Comparative, and Historical Studies.* San Diego: Harcourt, Brace, Jovanovich. 1986.

Collier, David, editor. *The New Authoritarianism in Latin America.* Princeton University Press. 1979.

Collier, George A. and Jane F. Collier. "The Zapatista rebellion in the context of globalization," pp. 242–52 in John Foran, editor, *The Future of Revolutions: Rethinking Radical Change in the Age of Globalization.* London: Zed. 2003.

Collier, George A. with Elizabeth Lowery Quaratiello. *Basta! Land and the Zapatista Rebellion in Chiapas.* Oakland: Food First/Institute for Food and Development Policy. 1994.

Collier, Simon and William F. Sater. *A History of Chile, 1808–1994.* Cambridge University Press. 1996.

Committee of Returned Volunteers, New York Chapter, Africa Committee. *Mozambique Will Be Free.* New York: Committee of Returned Volunteers. 1969.

Conroy, Michael E. "The political economy of the 1990 Nicaraguan elections." *International Journal of Political Economy* 20 (3) (Fall 1990), 5–33.

"Controlling interest: the world of the multinational corporation." California Newsreel. 1978.

Cooper, Marc. *Pinochet and Me.* London: Verso. 2001.

Cordova, Arnoldo. *La ideología de la revolución mexicana: la formación del nuevo regímen.* Mexico City: Ediciones Era. 1973.

Cottam, Richard. *Iran and the United States: A Cold-War Case Study.* University of Pittsburgh Press. 1988.

Crotty, James and Kang-Kook Lee. "Korea's neoliberal restructuring," pp. 159–65 in Amy Offner, Chris Sturr, Alejandro Reuss, and the *Dollars & Sense* Collective, editors, *Real World Globalization: A Reader in Economics, Business and Politics from* Dollars & Sense. Cambridge: Dollars & Sense. 2004.

Cumberland, Charles C. *Mexican Revolution: Genesis under Madero.* Austin: University of Texas Press. 1952.

——. *Mexican Revolution: The Constitutionalist Years.* Austin: University of Texas Press. 1972.

Dabashi, Hamid. *Theology of Discontent: The Ideological Foundation of the Islamic Republic in Iran.* New York University Press. 1993.

Dadkhah, Kamran M. "The inflationary process of the Iranian economy: a rejoinder." *International Journal of Middle East Studies* 19 (3) (August 1987), 388–91.

Danaher, Kevin and Roger Burbach. "Introduction: making history," pp. 7–11 in *Globalize This! The Battle Against the World Trade Organization and Corporate Rule*. Monroe: Common Courage. 2000.

Darnton, Robert. "What was revolutionary about the French revolution?" *The New York Review of Books* (January 19, 1989), 3–10.

Dashti, Abdollah. "At the crossroads of globalization: participatory democracy as a medium of future revolutionary struggle," pp. 169–79 in John Foran, editor, *The Future of Revolutions: Rethinking Radical Change in the Age of Globalization*. London: Zed. 2003.

Davani, 'Ali. *Nahzat-i Ruhaniyun-i Iran* [Movement of the Clergy of Iran]. Volume 8. Tehran: Bunyad-i Farhangi-yi Imam Reza. 1981.

Davidow, Jeffrey. *Dealing with International Crises: Lessons from Zimbabwe*. Muscatine: The Stanley Foundation. 1983.

Davies, James C. "Toward a theory of revolution." *American Sociological Review* 27 (1962), 5–19.

—. "The circumstances and causes of revolution: a review." *Journal of Conflict Resolution* 11 (2) (June 1967), 247–57.

de Andrade, Mario and Mark Ollivier. *The War in Angola: A Socio-economic Study*. Dar es Salaam: Tanzania Publishing House. 1975.

DeFronzo, James. *Revolutions and Revolutionary Movements*. Boulder: Westview. 1991.

De Landa, Manuel. *A Thousand Years of Nonlinear History*. New York: Zone Books. 1997.

De Witte, Ludo. *The Assassination of Lumumba*. Translated by Ann Wright and Renée Fenby. London: Verso. 2001.

Dine, Philip. "French culture and the Algerian war: mobilizing icons." *Journal of European Studies* 27 (1998), 51–68.

Disch, Arne. "Peasants and revolts." *Theory and Society* 7 (January–May 1979), 243–52.

Dix, Robert H. "The varieties of revolution." *Comparative Politics* 15 (3) (April 1983), 281–94.

—. "Why revolutions succeed and fail." *Polity* 16 (3) (Summer 1984), 423–46.

Dodson, Michael and Laura Nuzzi O'Shaughnessy, *Nicaragua's Other Revolution: Religious Faith and Political Struggle*. Chapel Hill: University of North Carolina Press. 1990.

Dosal, Paul J. *Power in Transition: The Rise of Guatemala's Industrial Oligarchy, 1871–1994*. Westport: Praeger. 1995.

Duffy, James. *Portugal in Africa*. Cambridge: Harvard University Press. 1962.

Duiker, William J. *Sacred War, Nationalism and Revolution in a Divided Vietnam*. New York: McGraw-Hill. 1995.

—. *Vietnam: Revolution in Transition*. Boulder: Westview Press. 1995.

Duncanson, Dennis J. *Government and Revolution in Vietnam*. London: Oxford University Press. 1968.

—. *The Long War: Dictatorship and Revolution in El Salvador*. London: Verso. 1982.

Dunkerley, James. *Rebellion in the Veins: Political Struggle in Bolivia, 1952–1982*. London: Verso. 1984.

—. *Power in the Isthmus: A Political History of Modern Central America*. London: Verso. 1988.

Dunn, John. "Conclusion," pp. 388–99 in Tony Saich and Hans van de Ven, editors, *New Perspectives on the Chinese Communist Revolution*. Armonk: M. E. Sharpe. 1995.

Dupuy, Alex. *Haiti in the World Economy: Class, Race, and Underdevelopment Since 1700*. Boulder: Westview. 1989.

Eastman, Lloyd E. "Fascism in Kuomintang China: the blue shirts." *China Quarterly* 49 (January–March 1972), 1–31.

—. *Seeds of Destruction: Nationalist China in War and Revolution 1937–1949*. Stanford University Press. 1984.

Eberhard, Wolfram. "Problems of historical sociology," pp. 25–8 in Reinhard Bendix et al., editors, *State and Society: A Reader*. Berkeley: University of California Press. 1973.

Eckstein, Susan. *The Impact of Revolution: A Comparative Analysis of Mexico and Bolivia*. London: Sage. 1976.

—. "Restratification after revolution: the Cuban experience," pp. 217–40 in Richard Tardanico, editor, *Crises in the Caribbean Basin*, volume 9 of the *Political Economy of the World-System Annuals*. Beverly Hills: Sage. 1987.

Eder, George Jackson. *The Bolivian Economy, 1952–1965*. New York: Praeger. 1966.

—. *Inflation and Development in Latin America: A Case History of Inflation and Stabilization in Bolivia*. Ann Arbor: University of Michigan. 1968.

Ehteshami, Anoushiravan. *After Khomeini: The Iranian Second Republic*. New York: Routledge. 1995.

Eisenstadt, S. N. *Revolution and the Transformation of Societies: A Comparative Study of Civilizations*. New York: Free Press. 1978.

—. "Frameworks of the great revolutions: culture, social structure, history and human agency." *International Social Science Journal* 133 (August 1992), 385–404.

el-Gawhary, Karim. "Report from a war zone: Gama'at vs. government in Upper Egypt." *MERIP (Middle East Research and Information Project) Report* 194/95 (May–June/July–August 1995), 49–51.

Elliott, Gregory. *Perry Anderson: The Merciless Laboratory of History*. Minneapolis: University of Minnesota Press. 1998.

Elster, Jon. *Logic and Society: Contradictions and Possible Worlds*. New York: Wiley. 1978.

Enríquez, Laura J. *Harvesting Change: Labor and Agrarian Reform in Nicaragua 1979–1990*. Chapel Hill: University of North Carolina Press. 1991.

Entelis, John P. *Algeria: The Revolution Institutionalized*. Boulder: Westview. 1986.

EPICA (The Ecumenical Program for Interamerican Community and Action). *Jamaica: Caribbean Challenge*. Washington: EPICA Task Force. 1979.

—. *Grenada, the Peaceful Revolution*. Washington: EPICA Task Force. 1982.

Epstein, Barbara. "The politics of prefigurative community: the non-violent direct action movement," pp. 63–92 in Mike Davis and Michael Sprinker, editors, *Reshaping the U.S. Left: Popular Struggles in the 1980s*. London: Verso. 1988.

Evans, Martin. *The Memory of Resistance: French Opposition to the Algerian War (1954–1962)*. Oxford: Berg. 1997.

Evans, Peter. *Dependent Development: The Alliance of Multinational, State, and Local Capital in Brazil*. Princeton University Press. 1979.

—. *Embedded Autonomy: States and Industrial Transformation*. Princeton University Press. 1995.

EZLN. "Second declaration from the Lacandón jungle: 'today we say: we will not surrender!'" pp. 221–31 in Tom Hayden, editor, *The Zapatista Reader*. New York: Thunder's Mouth Press and Nation Books. 2002.

—. "Fourth declaration from the Lacandón jungle," pp. 239–50 in Tom Hayden, editor, *The Zapatista Reader*. New York: Thunder's Mouth Press and Nation Books. 2002.

Fairbank, John King. *The Great Chinese Revolution: 1800–1985*. New York: Harper & Row, Publishers. 1986.

Fall, Bernard B. *The Two Viet-Nams*. New York: Praeger. 1963.

Fallaci, Oriana. "An interview with Khumaini." *The New York Times Magazine* (October 7, 1979), 29–31.

Fanon, Frantz. "Algeria unveiled," pp. 35–68 in Frantz Fanon, *Studies in a Dying Colonialism*, translated from the French *L'An Cinq de la Révolution Algérienne* by Haakon Chevalier. New York: Monthly Review Press. 1965.

Fardust, Hussain. *Zuhur va Suqut-i Saltanat-i Pahlavi: Khatarat-i Artishbud-i Sabiq Hussain Fardust* [The rise and fall of the Pahlavi dynasty: memoirs of former Field Marshal Hussain Fardust]. Two volumes. Tehran: Ittila'at Publications. 1991.

Farhi, Farideh. "State disintegration and urban-based revolutionary crisis: a comparative analysis of Iran and Nicaragua." *Comparative Political Studies* 21 (2) (July 1988), 231–56.

—. *States and Urban-Based Revolutions: Iran and Nicaragua*. Urbana and Chicago: University of Illinois Press. 1990.

—. "The democratic turn: new ways of understanding revolution." pp. 30–41 in John Foran, editor, *The Future of Revolutions: Rethinking Radical Change in the Age of Globalization*. London: Zed. 2003.

Farouk-Sluglett, Marion and Peter Sluglett. *Iraq Since 1958: From Revolution to Dictatorship*. London: Kegan Paul. 1987.

Ferguson, James. *Papa Doc, Baby Doc: Haiti and the Duvaliers*. Oxford: Basil Blackwell. 1987.

—. *Grenada: Revolution in Reverse*. New York: Monthly Review Press. 1990.

Feuerwerker, Albert. *Economic Trends in the Republic of China, 1912–1949*. Number 31. Ann Arbor: Michigan Papers in Chinese Studies. 1977.

Fewsmith, Joseph. *Dilemmas of Reform in China: Political Conflict and Economic Debate*. Armonk: M. E. Sharpe. 1994.

Fine, Ben and Zavareh Rustomjee. *The Political Economy of South Africa: From Minerals-energy Complex to Industrialization*. Boulder: Westview Press. 1996.

Fischer, Michael M. J. *Iran: From Religious Dispute to Revolution*. Cambridge: Harvard University Press. 1980.

Foner, Eric. "Dare call it treason." *The Nation* (June 2, 2003).

Fonseca, Carlos. *Desde la cárcel yo acuso a la dictadura*. Managua: Cárcel de la Aviación, July 8, 1964; Secretaría Nacional de Propaganda y Educación Política del FSLN, n.d.

358   Works cited

Foran, John. "Dependency and social change in Iran, 1501–1925." MA thesis. Department of Sociology. University of California, Santa Barbara. 1981.
—. "The strengths and weaknesses of Iran's populist alliance: a class analysis of the constitutional revolution of 1905–1911." *Theory and Society* 20 (6) (1991), 795–823.
—. "A theory of Third World social revolutions: Iran, Nicaragua, and El Salvador compared." *Critical Sociology* 19 (2) (1992), 3–27.
—. "Theories of revolution revisited: toward a fourth generation?" *Sociological Theory* 11 (1) (March 1993), 1–20.
—. "Revolutionizing theory/revising revolution: state, culture, and society in recent works on revolution." *Contention: Debates in Society, Culture and Science* 2 (2) (Winter 1993), 65–88.
—. *Fragile Resistance: Social Transformation in Iran from 1500 to the Revolution.* Boulder: Westview Press. 1993.
—. "The causes of Latin American social revolutions: searching for patterns in Mexico, Cuba, and Nicaragua," pp. 209–44 in Peter Lengyel and Volker Bornschier, editors, *World Society Studies*, volume 3: *Conflicts and New Departures in World Society.* New Brunswick: Transaction Publishers. 1994.
—. "The Iranian revolution of 1977–79: a challenge for social theory," pp. 160–88 in John Foran, editor, *A Century of Revolution: Social Movements in Iran.* Minneapolis: University of Minnesota Press. 1994.
—. "Race, class, and gender in the making of the Mexican revolution." *International Review of Sociology – Revue Internationale de Sociologie* 6 (1) (1996), 139–56.
—. "Reinventing the Mexican revolution: the competing paradigms of Alan Knight and John Mason Hart." *Latin American Perspectives* 23 (4) (issue 91) (Fall 1996), 115–31.
—. "Allende's Chile, 1972." Case study. Department of Sociology. University of California, Santa Barbara. http://www.soc.ucsb.edu/projects/casemethod/. 1996.
—. "The future of revolutions at the fin-de-siècle." *Third World Quarterly* 18 (5) (1997), 791–820.
—. "Discourses and social forces: the role of culture and cultural studies in understanding revolutions," pp. 203–26 in John Foran, editor, *Theorizing Revolutions.* London: Routledge. 1997.
—. "The comparative-historical sociology of Third World social revolutions: why a few succeed, why most fail," pp. 227–67 in John Foran, editor, *Theorizing Revolutions.* London and New York: Routledge. 1997.
—. "Studying revolutions through the prism of gender, race, and class: notes toward a framework." *Race, Gender & Class* 8 (2) (2001), 117–41.
—. "Introduction to the future of revolutions," pp. 1–15 in John Foran, editor, *The Future of Revolutions: Rethinking Radical Change in the Age of Globalization.* London: Zed. 2003.
—. "Magical realism: how might the revolutions of the future have better end(ing)s?" pp. 271–83 in John Foran, editor, *The Future of Revolutions: Rethinking Radical Change in the Age of Globalization.* London: Zed Press. 2003.

—. "Confronting an empire: sociology and the U.S.-made world crisis." *Political Power and Social Theory* 16 (2003), 213–33.

—. "Alternatives to development: of love, dreams, and revolution," pp. 268–74 in Kum-Kum Bhavnani, John Foran, and Priya A. Kurian, editors, *Feminist Futures: Re-imagining Women, Culture and Development*. London: Zed Press. 2003.

Foran, John and Jeff Goodwin, "Revolutionary outcomes in Iran and Nicaragua. Coalition fragmentation, war, and the limits of social transformation." *Theory and Society* 22 (2) (April 1993), 209–47.

Foran, John, Linda Klouzal, and Jean-Pierre Rivera (now Reed). "Who makes revolutions? Class, gender, and race in the Mexican, Cuban, and Nicaraguan revolutions." *Research in Social Movements, Conflicts and Change* 20 (1997), 1–60.

Foster-Carter, Aidan. "The modes of production controversy." *New Left Review* 107 (January–February 1978), 47–77.

Foucault, Michel. *Power/Knowledge*. New York: Pantheon. 1980.

Frank, Andre Gunder. *Latin America: Underdevelopment or Revolution*. New York: Monthly Review Press. 1969.

Friedman, Jennifer. "Bolivia 1952–1964: a reversed social revolution." Unpublished paper. Department of Sociology. Smith College. 2001.

Gaffney, Patrick D. *The Prophet's Pulpit: Islamic Preaching in Contemporary Egypt*. Berkeley: University of California Press. 1994.

Galeano, Eduardo. *Memory of Fire*, vol. III: *Century of the Wind*. Translated by Cedric Belfrage. New York: Pantheon Books. 1988.

—. *Upside Down: A Primer for the Looking-Glass World*. New York: Metropolitan Books. 1998.

Galindo, Alberto Flores. "Peru: a self-critical farewell." *NACLA Report on the Americas* 24 (5) (February 1991), 8–10.

García-Pérez, Gladys Marel. *Insurrection and Revolution: Armed Struggle in Cuba, 1952–1959*. Boulder: Lynne Rienner Publishers. 1998.

Garth, Jeff and Elaine Sciolino. "I.M.F. head: he speaks, and money talks," *New York Times* (April 2, 1996).

Gasiorowski, Mark. "The 1953 coup d'etat in Iran." *International Journal of Middle East Studies* 19 (3) (August 1987), 261–86.

Gasiorowski, Mark J. *U.S. Foreign Policy and the Shah: Building a Client State in Iran*. Ithaca: Cornell University Press. 1991.

Geertz, Clifford. *The Interpretation of Culture*. New York: Basic Books. 1973.

George, Susan. "Another world is possible." *The Nation* (February 18, 2002).

Ghose, A. K. "Trade liberalization, employment and growing inequality." *International Labour Review* 139 (3) (2000), 281–306.

Giddens, Anthony. *The Constitution of Society: Outline of the Theory of Structuration*. Cambridge: Polity Press. 1984.

Gilbert, Dennis. *Sandinistas: The Party and the Revolution*. New York: Basil Blackwell. 1988.

Gillespie, Joan. *Algeria: Rebellion and Revolution*. New York: Frederick A. Praeger, Publishers. 1960.

—. *La revolución interrumpida*. Mexico City: El Caballito. 1971.

Gilly, Adolfo. *The Mexican Revolution.* Translated by Patrick Camiller. London: New Left Books. 1983.

Glaser, Barney G. and Anselm L. Strauss. *Discovery of Grounded Theory: Strategies for Qualitative Research.* Chicago: Aldine Publishing Company. 1967.

Goldfrank, Walter. "World system, state structure, and the onset of the Mexican revolution." *Politics and Society* 5 (4) (Fall 1975), 417–39.

—. "Theories of revolution and revolution without theory: the case of Mexico." *Theory and Society* 7 (1979), 135–65.

Goldstone, Jack A. "Theories of revolution: the third generation." *World Politics* 32 (3) (April 1980), 425–53.

—. "The comparative and historical study of revolutions." *Annual Review of Sociology* 8 (1982), 187–207.

—. "Revolutions and Superpowers," pp. 35–48 in J. R. Adelman, editor, *Superpowers and Revolutions.* New York: Praeger. 1986.

—. *Revolution and Rebellion in the Early Modern World.* Berkeley: University of California Press. 1991.

—. "The coming Chinese collapse." *Foreign Policy* 99 (Summer 1995), 35–52.

—. "Toward a fourth generation of revolutionary theory." *Annual Review of Political Science* 4 (2001), 139–87.

Goldstone, Jack A., Ted Robert Gurr, and Farrokh Moshiri, editors. *Revolutions of the Late Twentieth Century.* Boulder: Westview Press. 1991.

Gonzalez, Edward. *Cuba Under Castro: The Limits of Charisma.* Boston: Houghton Mifflin Company. 1974.

Goodell, Grace. *The Elementary Structures of Political Life: Rural Development in Pahlavi Iran.* New York: Oxford University Press. 1986.

Goodno, James. *The Philippines: Land of Broken Promises.* London: Zed. 1991.

Goodwin, Jeff. "Revolutionary movements in Central America: a comparative analysis." Working Paper Series. Center for Research on Politics and Social Organization. Harvard University. 1985, 1988.

—. "Toward a new sociology of revolution." *Theory and Society* 23 (6) (1994), 731–66.

—. "State-centered approaches to social revolutions: strengths and limitations of a theoretical tradition," pp. 11–37 in John Foran, editor, *Theorizing Revolutions.* New York: Routledge. 1997.

—. *No Other Way Out: States and Revolutionary Movements, 1945–1991.* Cambridge University Press. 2000.

—. "Is the age of revolution over?" Paper presented at the meetings of the International Studies Association Meetings, Minneapolis (1998), and pp. 272–83 in Mark Katz, editor, *Revolution and International Relations: A Reader.* Washington: Congressional Quarterly. 2001.

—. "The renewal of socialism and the decline of revolution," pp. 59–72 in John Foran, editor, *The Future of Revolutions: Rethinking Radical Change in the Age of Globalization.* London: Zed. 2003.

Goodwin, Jeff and James M. Jasper, editors. *Rethinking Social Movements: Structure, Meaning, and Emotion.* Lanham: Rowman and Littlefield. 2003.

Goodwin, Jeff and James M. Jasper. "Caught in a winding, snarling vine: the structural bias of political process theory." *Sociological Forum* 14 (1) (1999), 27–54.

Goodwin, Jeff, James M. Jasper, and Francesca Polletta, editors. *Passionate Politics: Emotions and Social Movements*. University of Chicago Press. 2001.

Goodwin, Jeff, and Theda Skocpol. "Explaining revolutions in the contemporary Third World." *Politics & Society* 17 (4) (December 1989), 489–509.

Gorman, Stephen M. and Thomas W. Walker. "The armed forces," pp. 91–118 in Thomas W. Walker, editor, *Nicaragua: The First Five Years*. New York: Praeger. 1985.

Gould, Mark. *Revolution in the Development of Capitalism: The Coming of the English Revolution*. Berkeley and Los Angeles: University of California Press. 1987.

Graham, Robert. *Iran: The Illusion of Power*. New York: St. Martin's Press. 1979.

Gramsci, Antonio. *Selections from the Prison Notebooks*. New York: International. 1971.

Green, Jerrold D. *Revolution in Iran: The Politics of Countermobilization*. New York: Praeger. 1982.

Guerra, François-Xavier. "La revolution mexicaine: D'abord une révolution minière?" *Annales: E.S.C.* 36 (5) (Septembre–Octobre 1981), 785–814.

—. *Le Mexique: De l'Ancien Régime à la Revolucion*, two volumes. Paris: Editions L'Harmattan. 1985.

Gugler, Josef. "The urban character of contemporary revolutions," pp. 399–412 in Josef Gugler, editor, *The Urbanization of the Third World*. Oxford University Press. 1988.

Gunn, Gillian. "The Angolan economy: a history of contradiction," pp. 181–97 in Edmond J. Keller and Donald Rothschild, editors, *Afro-Marxist Regimes: Ideology and Public Policy*. Boulder: Lynne Rienner. 1987.

Gurr, Ted Robert. *Why Men Rebel*. Princeton University Press. 1970.

Guzmán, Patricio. *Chile: Obstinate Memory*. Les Films d'Ici and National Film Board of Canada. 1997.

Hagopian, Mark N. *The Phenomenon of Revolution*. New York: Dodd, Mead. 1974.

Hahnel, Robin. *Panic Rules: Everything You Need to Know About the Global Economy*. Boston: South End Press. 1999.

Halberstam, David. *The Best and the Brightest*. Greenwich: Fawcett Crest, [1969] 1972.

Hale, Charles R. *Resistance and Contradiction: Miskito Indians and the Nicaraguan State, 1894–1987*. Stanford University Press. 1994.

Hall, Stuart. "Politics and ideology: Gramsci," pp. 45–76 in Stuart Hall, Bob Lumley, and Gregor McLennan, editors, *On Ideology*. London: Hutchinson. 1978.

—. "Marxism and culture." *Radical History Review* 18 (1978), 5–14.

—. "The problem of ideology: Marxism without guarantees." *Journal of Communication Inquiry* 10 (2) (1986), 28–44.

Halliday, Fred. *Iran: Dictatorship and Development*. New York: Penguin. 1978.

—. "The genesis of the Iranian revolution." *Third World Quarterly* 1 (4) (October 1979), 1–16.

—. "The Iranian revolution: uneven development and religious populism." *Journal of International Affairs* 36 (2) (Fall/Winter 1982–83), 187–207.

Hammoudi, Abdellah and Stuart Schaar, editors. *Algeria's Impasse*. Princeton University Center of International Studies. 1995.

Handy, Jim. *Gift of the Devil: A History of Guatemala*. Boston: South End Press. 1984.

——. *Revolution in the Countryside: Rural Conflict and Agrarian Reform in Guatemala, 1944–1954*. Chapel Hill: University of North Carolina Press. 1994.

Hanlon, James. *Mozambique: The Revolution Under Fire*. London: Zed. 1984.

Hanson, Brad. "The 'Westoxication' of Iran: depictions and reactions of Behrangi, Al-e Ahmad, and Shari'ati." *International Journal of Middle East Studies* 15 (1) (February 1983), 1–23.

Harrison, Noelle. "Cuba: making sense of a revolution." Unpublished paper. Department of Sociology. University of California, Santa Barbara. Fall 1990.

Harsch, Ernest and Tony Thomas. *Angola: The Hidden History of Washington's War*. New York: Pathfinder Press. 1976.

Hart, John M. "The urban working class and the Mexican revolution: the case of the Casa del Obrero Mundial." *Hispanic American Historical Review* 58 (1) (February 1978), 1–20.

——. *Anarchism & the Mexican Working Class, 1860–1931*. Austin: University of Texas Press. 1978.

——. *Revolutionary Mexico: The Coming and Process of the Mexican Revolution*. Berkeley and Los Angeles: University of California Press. 1987.

Harvey, David. *Spaces of Hope*. Berkeley: University of California Press. 2000.

Hawes, Gary. *The Philippines State and the Marcos Regime: The Politics of Export*. Ithaca: Cornell University Press. 1987.

Hawken, Paul. "Skeleton woman visits Seattle," pp. 14–34 in Kevin Danaher and Roger Burbach, editors, *Globalize This! The Battle Against the World Trade Organization and Corporate Rule*. Monroe: Common Courage. 2000.

Hayden, Tom, editor. *The Zapatista Reader*. New York: Thunder's Mouth Press. 2002.

Hechter, Michael, Timur Kuran, Randall Collins, Charles Tilly, Edgar Kiser, James Coleman, and Alejandro Portes. "Symposium on prediction in the social sciences." *American Journal of Sociology* 100 (6) (May 1995), 1520–626.

Heggoy, Alf Andrew. *Insurgency and Counterinsurgency in Algeria*. Bloomington: Indiana University Press. 1972.

Heimer, F. W. *The Decolonization Conflict in Angola 1974–76: An Essay in Political Sociology*. Geneva: Institut Universitaire des Etudes Internationales. 1979.

Heine, Jorge A. "Introduction: a revolution aborted," pp. 3–26 in Jorge A. Heine, editor, *A Revolution Aborted: The Lessons of Grenada*. University of Pittsburgh Press. 1990.

——. "The hero and the apparatchik: charismatic leadership, political management, and crisis in revolutionary Grenada," pp. 217–55 in Jorge Heine, editor, *A Revolution Aborted: The Lessons of Grenada*. University of Pittsburgh Press. 1990.

Hellman, Judith Adler. *Mexican Lives*. New York: New Press. 1994.

Henderson, Lawrence W. *Angola: Five Centuries of Conflict*. Ithaca: Cornell University Press. 1979.

Hill, Christopher. *Intellectual Origins of the English Revolution*. Oxford: The Clarendon Press. 1965.

Hiro, Dilip. *Iran Under the Ayatollahs*. London and Boston: Routledge and Kegan Paul. 1985.

Hobsbawm, Eric. "Revolutions," pp. 5–46 in Roy Porter and Mikulas Teich, editors, *Revolution in History*. Cambridge University Press. 1986.

Hodges, Donald C. *Intellectual Foundations of the Nicaraguan Revolution*. Austin: University of Texas Press. 1986.

Hooglund, Eric J. *Land and Revolution Iran, 1960–1980*. Austin: University of Texas Press. 1982.

Hopwood, Derek. *Egypt: Politics and Society 1945–1990*. London: Routledge. 1993.

Horne, Alistair. *A Savage War of Peace: Algeria 1954–1962*. London: Macmillan. 1977.

Horton, Lynn. *Peasants in Arms: War and Peace in the Mountains of Nicaragua, 1979–1994*. Athens: Center for International Studies, Ohio University. 1998.

Humayun, Dariush. *Diruz va Farda: Seh Guftar darbareh-yi Iran-i Inqilabi* [Yesterday and tomorrow: three talks on revolutionary Iran]. U.S.A. 1981.

Humbaraci, Arslan. *Algeria: A Revolution That Failed: A Political History since 1954*. New York: Frederick A. Praeger. 1968.

Hunt, Lynn. *Politics, Culture, and Class in the French Revolution*. Berkeley: University of California Press. 1984.

Huntington, Samuel P. *Political Order in Changing Societies*. New Haven: Yale University Press. 1968.

—. "Civil Violence and the Process of Development." *Adelphi Papers* 83 (1971), 1–15.

Ibarra, Jorge. *Prologue to Revolution: Cuba, 1898–1958*. Translated by Marjorie Moore. Boulder: Lynne Rienner. 1998.

"Iran: the new crisis of American hegemony." *Monthly Review* 30 (9) (February 1979), 1–24.

Irish-Bramble, Ken. "Predicting revolutions." MA thesis. Department of Sociology. New York University. 2000.

Isaacman, Allen and Barbara Isaacman. *Mozambique: From Colonialism to Revolution, 1900–1982*. Boulder: Westview. 1983.

Ivanov, S. *Tarikh-i Nuvin-i Iran* [Modern history of Iran]. Translated from the Russian by Hushang Tizabi and Hasan Qa'im Panah. Stockholm: Tudeh Publishing Centre. 1356/1977.

Johnson, Chalmers A. *Peasant Nationalism and Communist Power: The Emergence of Revolutionary China 1937–1945*. Stanford University Press. 1962.

—. *Revolutionary Change*. Boston: Little, Brown. 1966.

Jonas, Susanne. *The Battle for Guatemala: Rebels, Death Squads, and U.S. Power*. Boulder: Westview. 1991.

Joseph, Gilbert M. and Daniel Nugent, editors. *Everyday Forms of State Formation: Revolution and the Negotiation of Rule in Modern Mexico*. Durham: Duke University Press. 1994.

Jung, Harold. "Class struggles in El Salvador." *New Left Review* 122 (1980), 3–25.

Kagawa, Jennifer. "The Vietnamese case." Unpublished paper. Department of Sociology. UC Santa Barbara. 1999.

364   Works cited

Kampwirth, Karen. *Women and Guerrilla Movements: Nicaragua, El Salvador, Chiapas, Cuba*. University Park: The Pennsylvania State University Press. 2002.
—. "Marching with the Taliban or dancing with the Zapatistas? Revolution after the Cold War," pp. 227–41 in John Foran, editor, *The Future of Revolutions: Rethinking Radical Change in the Age of Globalization*. London: Zed Press. 2003.
Kamrava, Mehran. *Revolution in Iran: The Roots of Turmoil*. London: Routledge. 1990.
Karnow, Stanley. *In Our Image: America's Empire in the Philippines*. New York: Random House. 1989.
—. *Vietnam: A History*. New York: Penguin. 1997.
Karshenas, Massoud. *Oil, State and Industrialization in Iran*. Cambridge University Press. 1990.
Karshenas, Massoud and M. Hesham Pesaran. "Economic reform and the reconstruction of the Iranian economy." *Middle East Journal* 49 (1) (Winter 1995), 89–111.
Katouzian, Homa. *The Political Economy of Modern Iran: Despotism and Pseudo-Modernism, 1926–1979*. New York University Press. 1981.
—. "Toward a general theory of Iranian revolutions." *Journal of Iranian Research and Analysis* 15 (2) (November 1999), 145–62.
Katz, Friedrich. "Labor conditions on haciendas in Porfirian Mexico: some trends and tendencies." *Hispanic American Historical Review* 54(1) (February 1974), 1–47.
—. *The Secret War in Mexico: Europe, the United States and the Mexican Revolution*. Chicago: University of Chicago Press. 1981.
Katz, Mark N. *Reflections on Revolutions*. London: Macmillan. 1999.
Katzenberger, Elaine, editor. *First World, Ha Ha Ha! The Zapatista Challenge*. San Francisco: City Lights. 1995.
Kaufman, Michael. *Jamaica Under Manley: Dilemmas of Socialism and Democracy*. London: Zed Press. 1985.
Keddie, Nikki. *Roots of Revolution: An Interpretive History of Modern Iran*. New Haven: Yale University Press. 1981.
—. "Iranian revolutions." *American Historical Review* 88 (1983), 579–98.
—. Editor. *Debating Revolutions*. New York University Press. 1995.
Keen, Benjamin and Keith Haynes. *A History of Latin America*. Boston: Houghton-Mifflin. 2000.
Keith, Nelson W. and Novella Z. Keith. *The Social Origins of Democratic Socialism in Jamaica*. Philadelphia: Temple University Press. 1992.
Kelley, Jonathan and Herbert S. Klein. *Revolution and the Rebirth of Inequality: A Theory Applied to the National Revolution in Bolivia*. Berkeley: University of California Press. 1981.
Kellner, Douglas. "Globalization, technopolitics and revolution," pp. 180–94 in John Foran, editor, *The Future of Revolutions: Rethinking Radical Change in the Age of Globalization*. London: Zed. 2003.
Keppel, Giles. "Islamists versus the state in Egypt and Algeria." *Daedalus* 124 (3) (Summer 1995), 109–27.

Khomeini, Imam. *Islam and Revolution: Writings and Declarations of the Imam Khomeini*. Translated and annotated by Hamid Algar. Berkeley: Mizan Press. 1980.

Kielstra, Nico. "Was the Algerian revolution a peasant war?" *Peasant Studies* 7 (3) (Summer 1978), 172–86.

Kinzer, Stephen. "Nicaragua: universal revolt." *The Atlantic Monthly* (February 1979).

—. *Blood of Brothers: Life and War in Nicaragua*. New York: G. P. Putnam's Sons. 1991.

—. *All the Shah's Men: An American Coup and the Roots of Middle East Terror*. New York: John Wiley & Sons. 2003.

Klein, Herbert S. *Parties and Political Change in Bolivia 1880–1952*. Cambridge University Press. 1969.

Klouzal, Linda. "Revolution firsthand: women's accounts of the experience, meanings, and impact of participation in the Cuban insurrection." Dissertation in progress. Department of Sociology. University of California, Santa Barbara.

Knauss, Peter. *The Persistence of Patriarchy: Class, Gender and Ideology in Twentieth Century Algeria*. Boulder: Westview. 1987.

Knight, Alan. *The Mexican Revolution*. Volume 1: *Porfirians, Liberals and Peasants*. Cambridge University Press. 1986.

—. *The Mexican Revolution*. Volume 2: *Counter-revolution and Reconstruction*. Cambridge University Press. 1986.

—. "Social revolution: a Latin American perspective." *Bulletin of Latin American Studies* 9 (2) (1990), 175–202.

—. "Revisionism and revolution: Mexico compared to England and France." *Past and Present* 134 (February 1992), 159–99.

Korby, Wilfrid. *Probleme der industriellen Entwickling und Konzentration in Iran*. Wiesbaden: Dr. Ludwig Reichert Verlag. 1977.

Kornbluh, Peter, Malcolm Byrne, and Theodore Draper, editors. *The Iran-Contra Scandal: The Declassified History (The National Security Archive Document)*. New York: New Press. 1993.

Kurzman, Charles. *The Unthinkable Revolution in Iran*. Cambridge: Harvard University Press. 2004.

Lan, David. *Guns and Rain: Guerrillas and Spirit Mediums in Zimbabwe*. London: James Curry. 1985.

Lancaster, Roger N. *Thanks to God and the Revolution: Popular Religion and Class Consciousness in the New Nicaragua*. New York: Columbia University Press. 1988.

LASA (Latin American Studies Association). *Electoral Democracy Under International Pressure: The Report of the Latin American Studies Association Commission to Observe the 1990 Nicaraguan Election*. Pittsburgh: Latin American Studies Association. 1990.

Lazreg, Marnia. "Feminism and difference: the perils of writing as a woman on women in Algeria," pp. 326–48 in Marianne Hirsch and Evelyn Fox Keller, editors, *Conflicts in Feminism*. New York: Routledge. 1990.

Lenin, V. I. *Imperialism, The Highest Stage of Capitalism: A Popular Outline*. New York: International Publishers. [1916] 1997.

LeVan, H. John. "Vietnam: revolution of postcolonial consolidation," pp. 52–87 in Jack A. Goldstone, Ted Robert Gurr, and Farrokh Moshiri, editors, *Revolutions of the Late Twentieth Century*. Boulder: Westview Press. 1991.

Lewis, David E. *Reform and Revolution in Grenada 1950 to 1981*. Havana: Casa de las Américas. 1984.

Lewis, Gordon K. *Grenada: The Jewel Despoiled*. Baltimore: Johns Hopkins. 1987.

Liss, Sheldon B. *Radical Thought in Central America*. Boulder: Westview. 1991.

—. *Fidel! Castro's Political and Social Thought*. Boulder: Westview Press. 1994.

Lobe, Jim. "Faulty connection." www.TomPaine.com (July 15, 2003).

Logevall, Fredrik. *Choosing War: The Lost Chance for Peace and the Escalation of War in Vietnam*. Berkeley: University of California Press. 1999.

Lomperis, Timothy J. *From People's War to People's Rule: Insurgency, Intervention, and the Lessons of Vietnam*. Chapel Hill: University of North Carolina Press. 1996.

Lopez, Edwin. "Through the prism of racialized political cultures: an analysis of racialized cultural hegemony and resistance in revolutionary Guatemala, 1944–1954." MA thesis. Department of Sociology. University of California, Santa Barbara. 2003.

LSM Information Center. *The Mozambican Woman in the Revolution*. Oakland: LSM Press. 1977.

Lyotard, Jean-François. *Political Writings*. Translated by Bill Readings and Kevin Paul Geiman. Minneapolis: University of Minnesota Press. 1993.

MacGaffey, W. and C. R. Barnett. *Cuba: Its People, Its Society, Its Culture*. New Haven: HRAF Press. 1962.

Machel, Samora. *Samora Machel: An African Revolutionary: Selected Speeches and Writings*. Edited by Barry Munslow and translated by Michael Wolfers. London: Zed. 1985.

Macqueen, Norrie. *The Decolonization of Portuguese Africa: Metropolitan Revolution and the Dissolution of Empire*. New York: Longman. 1997.

—. "An ill wind? Rethinking the Angolan crisis and the Portuguese revolution. 1974–1976." *Itinerarie* 26 (2) (2002), 24–44.

Malloy, James M. *Bolivia: The Uncompleted Revolution*. University of Pittsburgh Press. 1970.

—. *Bolivia: The Sad and Corrupt End of the Revolution*. UFSI Reports. Number 3. Hanover: University Field Staff International. 1982.

Mandle, Jay R. *Big Revolution, Small Country: The Rise and Fall of the Grenada Revolution*. Lanham: The North-South Publishing Company. 1985.

Manley, Michael. *Jamaica: Struggle in the Periphery*. London: Third World Media, 1982.

Maran, Rita. *Torture: The Role of Ideology in the French-Algerian War*. New York: Praeger. 1989.

Marcos, Subcomandante. *Shadows of Tender Fury: The Letters and Communiqués of Subcomandante Marcos and the Zapatista Army of National Liberation*. Translated by Frank Bardacke, Leslie López and the Watsonville, California, Human Rights Committee. New York: Monthly Review Press. 1995.

Marcum, John A. *The Angolan Revolution*. Volume II. *Exile Politics and Guerilla Warfare (1962–1976)*. Cambridge: MIT Press. 1978.

—. "The people's republic of Angola: a radical vision frustrated," pp. 67–83 in Edmond J. Keller and Donald Rothchild, editors, *Afro-Marxist Regimes: Ideology and Public Policy*. Boulder: Lynne Rienner. 1987.

Marias, Hein. *South Africa: Limits to Change: The Political Economy of Transformation*. London: Zed Books. 1998.

Marr, David. *Vietnam 1945: The Quest for Power*. Berkeley: University of California Press. 1995.

Martin, Phyllis M. *Historical Dictionary of Angola*. Metuchen: The Scarecrow Press. 1980.

Marx, Anthony. *Lessons of Struggle: South African Internal Opposition, 1960–1990*. New York: Oxford University Press. 1992.

Mason, T. David. "Women's participation in Central American revolutions: a theoretical perspective." *Comparative Political Studies* 25 (1) (1992), 63–89.

McAdam, Doug, John D. McCarthy, and Mayer N. Zald. "Social movements," pp. 695–737 in Neil J. Smelser, editor, *Handbook of Sociology*. Newbury Park: Sage. 1988.

McAdam, Doug, John D. McCarthy, and Mayer Zald, editors. *Comparative Perspectives on Social Movements*. Cambridge University Press. 1996.

McAdam, Doug, Sidney Tarrow, and Charles Tilly. "To map contentious politics." *Mobilization* 1 (1) (1996), 17–34.

McAlister, John T. Jr. and Paul Mus. *The Vietnamese and Their Revolution*. New York: Harper & Row. 1970.

McAuley, Christopher A. "Race and the process of the American revolutions," pp. 168–202 in John Foran, editor, *Theorizing Revolutions*. New York: Routledge. 1997.

—. "The demise of Bolshevism and the rebirth of Zapatismo: revolutionary options in a post-Soviet world," pp. 149–68 in John Foran, editor, *The Future of Revolutions: Rethinking Radical Change in the Age of Globalization*. London: Zed. 2003.

McClintock, Cynthia. *Revolutionary Movements in Latin America: El Salvador's FMLN and Peru's Shining Path*. Washington: United States Institute of Peace Press. 1998.

McDaniel, Tim. *Autocracy, Modernization, and Revolution in Russia and Iran*. Princeton University Press. 1991.

McMillin, Markus. "The dynamics of an anti-colonialist social revolution: a study of French Algeria." BA thesis. Department of Political Science. University of California, Santa Barbara. 1991.

Memmi, Albert. *The Colonizer and the Colonized*. New York: Orion Books. 1965.

Mesa-Lago, Carmelo. "Revolutionary economic policies in Cuba," pp. 63–83 in Philip Brenner, William M. LeoGrande, Donna Rich, and Daniel Siegel, editors, *The Cuba Reader: The Making of a Revolutionary Society*. New York: Grove Press. 1989.

Meyer, Jean. "Mexico: revolution and reconstruction in the 1920s," pp. 155–94 in Leslie Bethell, editor, *The Cambridge Modern History of Latin America*. Volume v c. 1870 to 1930. Cambridge University Press. 1986.

Meyer, Michael C. *Huerta: A Political Biography.* Lincoln: University of Nebraska Press. 1972.

Middle East Watch. *Human Rights in Iraq.* New Haven: Yale University Press. 1990.

Midlarsky, Manus I., and Kenneth Roberts. "Class, state, and revolution in Central America: Nicaragua and El Salvador compared." *Journal of Conflict Resolution* 29 (2) (June 1985), 163–93.

Miller, Sadie. "The Angolan anti-colonial revolution." Unpublished paper. Department of Sociology, Smith College. 2001.

—. "The Mozambican revolution." Unpublished paper. Department of Sociology, Smith College. 2001.

—. "The revolution of Zimbabwe." Unpublished paper. Department of Sociology, Smith College. 2001.

—. "The political revolution in South Africa." Unpublished paper. Department of Sociology, Smith College. 2002.

Miller, Simon. "Mexican junkers and capitalist haciendas, 1810–1910: The arable estate and the transition to capitalism between the insurgency and the revolution." *Journal of Latin American Studies* 22 (part 2) (May 1990), 229–63.

Millette, Robert and Mahin Gosine. *The Grenada Revolution: Why It Failed.* New York: Africana Research Publications. 1985.

Milne, Seumas. "The right to resist." *The Guardian* (June 19, 2003).

Minqi, Li. "China: six years after Tiananmen." *Monthly Review Press* 47 (8) (January 1996), 1–13.

Minter, William. *Portuguese Africa and the West.* New York: Monthly Review Press. 1973.

Moaddel, Mansoor. *Class, Politics, and Ideology in the Iranian Revolution.* New York: Columbia University Press. 1993.

Moghadam, Valentine M. "Populist revolution and the Islamic state in Iran," pp. 147–63 in Terry Boswell, editor, *Revolution in the World System.* Greenwich: Greenwood Press. 1989.

—. "Gender and revolutions," pp. 137–67 in John Foran, editor, *Theorizing Revolutions.* London: Routledge. 1997.

—. "Is the future of revolution feminist? Rewriting 'gender and revolutions' for a globalizing world," pp. 159–68 in John Foran, editor, *The Future of Revolutions: Rethinking Radical Change in the Age of Globalization.* London: Zed. 2003.

Mondlane, Eduardo. *The Struggle for Mozambique.* New York: Penguin. 1969.

Montgomery, Tommy Sue. *Revolution in El Salvador: From Civil Strife to Civil Peace.* Second edition. Boulder: Westview Press. 1995.

Moore, Barrington Jr. *Social Origins of Dictatorship and Democracy: Lord and Peasant in the Making of the Modern World.* Boston: Beacon Press. 1966.

Moore, Carlos. *Castro, the Blacks, and Africa.* Los Angeles: Center for Afro-American Studies, UCLA. 1988.

Mortimer, Robert. "Islamists, soldiers, and democrats: the second Algerian war." *The Middle East Journal* 50 (1) (Winter 1996), 18–39.

"Mozambique," pp. 388–90 in *The World Guide 2001/2002.* Oxford: New Internationalist Publications, Ltd. 2001.

Munro, Robin. "Who died in Beijing, and why." *The Nation* (June 11, 1990), 811–22.

Munslow, Barry. *Mozambique: The Revolution and Its Origins.* London: Longman. 1983.

Murphy, Craig N. "Political consequences of the new inequality." *International Studies Quarterly* 45 (3) (September 2001), 347–56.

Murray, Martin J. *The Development of Capitalism in Colonial Indochina (1870–1940).* Berkeley: University of California Press. 1980.

Mus, Paul. *Viet-Nam: Sociologie d'une guerre.* Paris: Editions du Seuil. 1952.

Myers, Ramon H. "How did the modern Chinese economy develop?" *Journal of Asian Studies* 50 (1991), 604–28.

NACLA (North American Congress on Latin America) Report. "Fatal attraction: Peru's Shining Path." xxiv (4) (December 1990/January 1991).

Naipaul, V. S. *The Overcrowded Barracoon and Other Articles.* London: Deutsch. 1972.

Najmabadi, Afsaneh. *Land Reform and Social Change in Iran.* Salt Lake City: University of Utah Press. 1988.

Nederveen Pieterse, Jan. "After post-development." *Third World Quarterly* 21 (2) (2000), 175–91.

Newitt, Malyn. *A History of Mozambique.* Bloomington: Indiana University Press. 1995.

Nichols, Elizabeth. "Skocpol on revolutions: comparative analysis vs. historical conjuncture," pp. 163–86 in Richard F. Thomasson, editor, *Comparative Social Research.* Greenwich: JAI Press. 1986.

Nodia, G. "The end of revolution?" *Journal of Democracy* 11 (1) (January 2000), 164–71.

O'Ballance, Edgar. *The Algerian Insurrection, 1954–62.* Hamden: Archon Books. 1967.

O'Brien, Philip J. "Was the United States responsible for the Chilean coup?" pp. 217–43 in Philip J. O'Brien, editor, *Allende's Chile.* New York: Praeger. 1976.

O'Brien, Phil and Jackie Roddick. *Chile: The Pinochet Decade: The Rise and Fall of the Chicago Boys.* New York: Monthly Review Press. 1983.

Olutski, Enrique. *Vida Clandestina: My Life in the Cuban Revolution.* Translated by Thomas and Carol Christensen. New York: Wiley. 2002.

Oppenheim, Lois Hecht. *Politics in Chile: Democracy, Authoritarianism, and the Search for Development,* second edition. Boulder: Westview Press. 1999.

Oppenheimer, Andres. *Castro's Final Hour: The Secret Story Behind the Coming Downfall of Communist Cuba.* New York: Simon and Schuster. 1992.

O'Shaughnessy, Hugh. *Grenada: An Eyewitness Account of the U.S. Invasion and the Caribbean History That Provoked It.* New York: Dodd, Mead & Company. 1984.

Osterhammel, Jürgen. *Colonialism: A Theoretical Overview,* translated by Shelley L. Frisch. Princeton: Markus Wiener Publishers. 1997.

Paige, Jeffery M. *Agrarian Revolution: Social Movements and Export Agriculture in the Underdeveloped World.* New York: Free Press. 1975.

—. *Coffee and Power: Revolution and the Rise of Democracy in Central America.* Cambridge: Harvard University Press. 1997.

—. "Finding the revolutionary in the revolution: social science concepts and the future of revolution," pp. 19–29 in John Foran, editor, *The Future of Revolutions: Rethinking Radical Change in the Age of Globalization.* London: Zed. 2003.

Palmer, David Scott, editor. *The Shining Path of Peru.* New York: St. Martin's Press. 1992.

Parker, Noel. "Parallaxes: revolutions and 'revolution' in a globalized imaginary," pp. 42–56 in John Foran, editor, *The Future of Revolutions: Rethinking Radical Change in the Age of Globalization.* London: Zed. 2003.

Parsa, Misagh. *The Social Origins of the Iranian Revolution.* New Brunswick: Rutgers University Press. 1989.

—. *States, Ideologies, and Social Revolutions: A Comparative Analysis of Iran, Nicaragua and the Philippines.* Cambridge University Press. 2000.

Pastor, Robert. "The United States and the Grenada revolution: who pushed first, and why?" pp. 181–214 in Jorge A. Heine, editor, *A Revolution Aborted: The Lessons of Grenada.* University of Pittsburgh Press. 1990.

Payne, Anthony, Paul Sutton, and Tony Thorndike. *Grenada: Revolution and Invasion.* London: Croom Helm. 1984.

Pearce, Jenny. *Promised Land: Peasant Rebellion in Chalatenango El Salvador.* London: Latin America Bureau. 1986.

People's Press Angola Book Project. *With Freedom in Their Eyes: A Photo-Essay of Angola.* San Francisco: People's Press. 1976.

Pérez, Louis A. *Cuba: Between Reform and Revolution.* Oxford University Press. 1988.

Pérez-Stable, Marifeli. *The Cuban Revolution: Origins, Course, and Legacy.* Oxford University Press. 1993.

Petras, James. *Politics and Social Forces in Chilean Development.* Berkeley: University of California Press. 1969.

Pimentel, Benjamin. *Rebolusyon! A Generation of Struggle in the Philippines.* New York: Monthly Review Press. 1990.

Polakoff, Erika. "Gender and the Latin American Left." *Z Magazine* (November 1996), 20–3.

Poniatowksa, Elena. *Massacre in Mexico.* Columbia: University of Missouri Press. 1975.

Poole, Deborah and Gerardo Renique. *Peru: Time of Fear.* New York: Monthly Review Press. 1993.

Porter, Gareth. "Coercive diplomacy in Vietnam: the Tonkin Gulf crisis reconsidered," pp. 9–22 in Jayne Werner and David Hunt, editors, *The American War in Vietnam.* Ithaca: Cornell Southeast Asia Program. 1993.

Post, Ken. *Revolution, Socialism and Nationalism in Vietnam,* volume V: *Winning the War and Losing the Peace.* Aldershot: Dartmouth. 1994.

Przeworski, Adam. "Some problems in the study of the transition to democracy," pp. 47–63 in Guillermo O'Donnell, Philippe C. Schmitter, and Laurence Whitehead, editors, *Transitions from Authoritarian Rule: Comparative Perspectives.* Baltimore: The Johns Hopkins University Press. 1986.

Quirk, Robert E. *Fidel Castro.* New York: W. W. Norton & Company. 1993.

Ragin, Charles C. *The Comparative Method: Moving Beyond Qualitative and Quantitative Strategies.* Berkeley: University of California Press. 1987.

——. *Fuzzy-Set Social Science*. University of Chicago Press. 2000.

Rahnema, Saeed and Sohrab Behdad, editors. *Iran After the Revolution: Crisis of an Islamic State*. New York: St. Martin's. 1996.

Ram, Haggay. "Crushing the opposition: adversaries of the Islamic Republic of Iran." *Middle East Journal* 46 (3) (Summer 1992), 426–39.

Ranchod-Nilsson, Sita. "'This, too, is a way of fighting': rural women's participation in Zimbabwe's liberation war," pp. 62–88 in Mary Ann Tétreault, editor, *Women and Revolution in Africa, Asia, and the New World*. Columbia: University of South Carolina Press. 1994.

Ranger, Terence and Mark Ncube. "Religion in the guerrilla war: the case of southern Matabeleland," pp. 35–57 in Ngwabi Bhebe and Terence Ranger, editors, *Society in Zimbabwe's Liberation War*. Oxford: James Currey. 1996.

Rawski, Thomas G. *Economic Growth in Prewar China*. Berkeley: University of California Press. 1989.

Reed, Jean-Pierre. "'Revolutionary subjectivity: the cultural logic of the Nicaraguan revolution." PhD dissertation. Department of Sociology. University of California, Santa Barbara. 2000.

——. "Emotions in context: revolutionary accelerators, hope, moral outrage, and other emotions in the making of Nicaragua's revolution." *Theory and Society* 33 (6) (2004).

Reed, Jean-Pierre and John Foran. "Political cultures of opposition: exploring idioms, ideologies, and revolutionary agency in the case of Nicaragua." *Critical Sociology* 28 (3) (October 2002), 335–70.

Rejai, Mostafa. *The Strategy of Political Revolution*. New York: Doubleday. 1973.

Remón, Cecilia. "Peru: Shining Path making a comeback." *NACLA Report on the Americas*. XXXVII (2) (September/October 2003), 5–6.

Reporters Sans Frontières. *Le drame algérien: un peuple en otage*. Paris: Editions La Découverte. 1994.

Revere, Robert B. "Revolutionary ideology in Algeria." *Polity* 5 (4) (Summer 1973), 477–88.

Reznikov, A. B. "The downfall of the Iranian monarchy (January–February 1979)," pp. 254–312 in R. Ulyanovsky, editor, *The Revolutionary Process in the East: Past and Present*. Moscow: Progress Publishers. 1985.

Rinehart, James. *Revolution and the Millennium: China, Mexico, Iran*. Westport: Praeger. 1997.

Riskin, Carl. *China's Political Economy: The Quest for Development since 1949*. Oxford University Press. 1987.

Robinson, William I. *Promoting Polyarchy: Globalization, U.S. Intervention, and Hegemony*. Cambridge University Press. 1996.

Robinson, William I. and Kent Norsworthy. *David and Goliath: The U.S. War Against Nicaragua*. New York: Monthly Review Press. 1987.

Rochabrún, Guillermo. "Review" of Steve J. Stern, editor, *Shining Path and Other Paths: War and Society in Peru, 1980–1995* (Durham: Duke University Press, 1998). *NACLA Report on the Americas* XXXIII (2) (September/October 1999), 52.

Rock, David. *Argentina, 1516–1987: From Spanish Colonization to Alfonsín*. Berkeley: University of California Press. 1989.

Rojas Sandford, Robinson. *The Murder of Allende and the End of the Chilean Way to Socialism.* Translated by Andreé Conrad. New York: Harper & Row. 1975.

Ross, John. *Rebellion from the Roots: Indian Uprising in Chiapas.* Monroe: Common Courage Press. 1995.

—. *The War Against Oblivion: The Zapatista Chronicles 1994–2000.* Monroe: Common Courage Press. 2000.

Roxborough, Ian, Philip O'Brien, and Jackie Roddick, assisted by Michael Gonzalez. *Chile: The State and Revolution.* New York: Macmillan. 1977.

Roxborough, Ian. *Theories of Underdevelopment.* London: Macmillan. 1979.

—. "Theories of revolution: the evidence from Latin America." *LSE (London School of Economics) Quarterly* 3 (2) (Summer 1989), 99–121.

—. "Exogenous factors in the genesis of revolutions in Latin America." Paper presented at the meetings of the Latin American Studies Association. Miami. (December 1989).

Roy, Jules. *The War in Algeria.* New York: Grove Press. 1961.

Rudé, George. *Revolutionary Europe 1783–1815.* London: Fontana. 1973 [1964].

Ruedy, John. *Modern Algeria: The Origins and Development of a Nation.* Bloomington: Indiana University Press. 1992.

Rueschemeyer, Dietrich. "Review of Michael W. Doyle, *Empires* (Ithaca: Cornell University Press, 1986)." *Contemporary Sociology* 17 (3) (May 1988), 306–7.

Ruiz, Ramón Eduardo. *Cuba: The Making of a Revolution.* New York: W. W. Norton & Company. 1968.

—. *The Great Rebellion: Mexico, 1905–1924.* New York: W. W. Norton and Company. 1980.

Rus, Jan. "Land adaptation to global change: the reordering of native society in Highland Chiapas, 1974–1994." *Revista Europea de Estudios Latinoamericanos y del Caribe* 58 (1995), 82–91.

Rus, Jan, R. Aida Hernandez Castillo, and Shannan Mattiace, editors. "The indigenous people of Chiapas and the state in the time of Zapatismo: remaking culture, renegotiating power." Special issue of *Latin American Perspectives* 28 (2) (March 2001).

Russell, Philip. *The Chiapas Rebellion.* Austin: Mexico Resource Center. 1994.

Saich, Tony. "Writing or rewriting history? The construction of the Maoist resolution on party history," pp. 299–338 in Tony Saich and Hans van de Ven, editors, *New Perspectives on the Chinese Communist Revolution.* Armonk: M. E. Sharpe. 1995.

Saikal, Amin. *The Rise and Fall of the Shah.* Princeton University Press. 1980.

Salas, Elizabeth. *Soldaderas in the Mexican Military: Myth and History.* Austin: University of Texas Press. 1990.

Sampson, Anthony. *The Sovereign State of ITT.* New York: Stein and Day. 1973.

Sandford, Gregory and Richard Vigilante. *Grenada: The Untold Story.* Lanham: Madison Books. 1984.

Sartre, Jean-Paul. *Search for a Method.* New York: Vintage. 1963.

Sartre, Jean-Paul. "Preface" to Frantz Fanon, *The Wretched of the Earth.* New York: Grove Press. 1963.

Sartre, Jean-Paul. *On Genocide.* Boston: Beacon. 1968.

Saul, John S. editor. *A Difficult Road: The Transition to Socialism in Mozambique.* New York: Monthly Review Press. 1985.

Saul, John S. "Inside from the outside? The roots and resolution of Mozambique's un/civil war," pp. 122–66 in Taisier M. Ali and Robert O. Matthews, editors, *Civil Wars in Africa: Roots and Resolution.* Montreal: McGill-Queen's University Press. 1999.

Scarritt, James R. "Zimbabwe: revolutionary violence resulting in reform," pp. 235–71 in Jack A. Goldstone, Ted Robert Gurr, and Farrokh Moshiri, editors, *Revolutions of the Late Twentieth Century.* Boulder: Westview. 1991.

Schalk, David L. *War and the Ivory Tower: Algeria and Vietnam.* New York: Oxford University Press. 1991.

Schirmer, Daniel B. and Stephen R. Shalom, editors. *The Philippines Reader: A History of Colonialism, Neocolonialism, Dictatorship, and Resistance.* Boston: South End Press. 1987.

Schlesinger, Stephen C. and Stephen Kinzer. *Bitter Fruit: The Untold Story of the American Coup in Guatemala.* New York: Doubleday. 1984.

Schoenhals Kai P. and Richard A. Melanson. *Revolution and Intervention in Grenada: The New Jewel Movement, the United States, and the Caribbean.* Boulder: Westview. 1985.

Schram, Stuart R. *The Political Thought of Mao Tse-Tung.* New York: Praeger. 1969.

Schwartz, Benjamin L. "Themes in intellectual history: May Fourth and after," pp. 406–50 in John K. Fairbank, editor, *The Cambridge History of China.* Volume 12: *Republican China 1912–1949*, part 1. Cambridge University Press. 1983.

Scott, Catherine V. and Gus B. Cochran. "Revolution in the periphery: Angola, Cuba, Mozambique, and Nicaragua," pp. 43–58 in Terry Boswell, editor, *Revolution in the World-System.* New York: Greenwood Press. 1989.

Scott, Catherine V. "'Men in our country behave like chiefs': women and the Angolan revolution," pp. 89–108 in Mary Ann Tetreault, editor, *Women and Revolution in Africa, Asia, and the New World.* Columbia: University of South Carolina Press. 1994.

Scott, James C. *The Moral Economy of the Peasant: Rebellion and Subsistence in Southeast Asia.* New Haven: Yale University Press. 1976.

—. *Domination and the Arts of Resistance: Hidden Transcripts.* New Haven: Yale University Press. 1990.

—. *Seeing Like a State: How Certain Schemes to Improve the Human Condition Have Failed.* New Haven: Yale University Press. 1999.

Seidman, Gay, David Martin, and Phyllis Johnson. *Zimbabwe: A New History.* Harare: Zimbabwe Publishing House, n.d.

Selbin, Eric. "Revolution in the real world: bringing agency back in," pp. 123–36 in John Foran, editor, *Theorizing Revolutions.* London: Routledge. 1997.

—. *Modern Latin American Social Revolutions.* Second edition. Boulder: Westview Press. 1999.

—. "Same as it ever was: the future of revolution at the end of the century." Paper presented at the meetings of the International Studies Association. Minneapolis (1998); a version also appeared in Mark Katz, editor, *Revolution and International Relations: A Reader.* Washington: Congressional Quarterly. 2001.

—. "Zapata's white horse and Che's beret: theses on the future of revolutions," pp. 83–94 in John Foran, editor, *The Future of Revolutions: Rethinking Radical Change in the Age of Globalization.* London: Zed. 2003.

Selden, Mark. Editor. *The People's Republic of China.* New York: Monthly Review Press. 1970.

—. *The Yenan Way in Revolutionary China.* Cambridge: Harvard University Press. 1971.

Seligman, Linda J. *Between Reform and Revolution: Political Struggles in the Peruvian Andes, 1969–1991.* Stanford University Press. 1995.

Sewell, William H. Jr. "Ideologies and social revolutions: reflections on the French case." *Journal of Modern History* 57 (1) (March 1985), 57–85.

—. "Three temporalities: toward an eventful sociology," pp. 245–80 in Terrence J. McDonald, editor, *The Historic Turn in the Human Sciences.* Ann Arbor: University of Michigan Press. 1996.

Shanin, Teodor. *The Roots of Otherness: Russia's Turn of the Century, volume 2: Russia, 1905–07: Revolution as a Moment of Truth.* New Haven: Yale University Press. 1986.

Shari'ati, Ali. *From Where Shall We Begin? & The Machine in the Captivity of Machinism.* Translated from the Persian by Fatollah Marjani. Houston: Free Islamic Literatures, Inc. 1980.

Shayne, Julia Denise. "Salvadorean women revolutionaries and the birth of their women's movement." MA thesis. Department of Women's Studies. San Francisco State University. 1995.

—. *The Revolution Question: Feminisms in El Salvador, Chile, and Cuba.* New Brunswick: Rutgers University Press. 2004.

Sheahan, John. *Patterns of Development in Latin America: Poverty, Repression, and Economic Strategy.* Princeton University Press. 1987.

Sheldon, Kathleen. "Women and revolution in Mozambique: a luta continua," pp. 33–61 in Mary Ann Tetreault, editor, *Women and Revolution in Africa, Asia, and the New World.* Columbia: University of South Carolina Press. 1994.

Sheridan, James E. *China in Disintegration: The Republican Era in Chinese History, 1912–1949.* New York: The Free Press. 1975.

Shugart, Matthew Soberg. "Patterns of revolution." *Theory and Society* 18 (2) (March 1989), 249–71.

Siavoshi, Sussan. *Liberal Nationalism in Iran: The Failure of a Movement.* Boulder: Westview Press. 1988.

—. "The oil nationalization movement, 1949–1953," pp. 106–34 in John Foran, editor, *A Century of Revolution: Social Movements in Iran.* Minneapolis: University of Minnesota Press. 1994.

Siekmeier, James F. "Responding to nationalism: the Bolivian *Movimiento Nacionalista Revolucionaria* and the United States, 1952–1956." *Journal of American and Canadian Studies* (15) (1997), 39–58.

Singer, Daniel. *Whose Millennium? Theirs or Ours?* New York: Monthly Review Press. 1999.

Sivanandan, A. "Imperialism in the silicon age." *Monthly Review* 32 (3) (July–August 1980), 28–42. First published in *Race and Class* (Autumn 1979).

Skålnes, Tor. *The Politics of Economic Reform in Zimbabwe: Continuity and Change in Development.* New York: St. Martin's Press. 1995.

Skocpol, Theda. *States and Social Revolutions: A Comparative Analysis of France, Russia, and China.* Cambridge University Press. 1979.

—. "Rentier state and Shi'a Islam in the Iranian revolution." *Theory & Society* 11 (3) (1982), 265–84.

—. "What makes peasants revolutionary?" pp. 157–79 in Scott Guggenheim and Robert Weller, editors, *Power and Protest in the Countryside.* Durham: Duke University Press. 1982.

—. "Cultural idioms and political ideologies in the revolutionary reconstruction of state power: a rejoinder to Sewell." *Journal of Modern History* 57 (1) (1985), 86–96.

—. "Analyzing causal configurations in history: a rejoinder to Nichols." *Comparative Social Research* 9 (1986), 187–94.

—. "Reflections on recent scholarship about social revolutions and how to study them," pp. 301–44 in Theda Skocpol, *Social Revolutions in the Modern World.* Cambridge University Press. 1994.

Smelser, Neil. *Theory of Collective Behavior.* New York: The Free Press. 1962.

Smith, Daniel. "Iraq: descending into the quagmire." *Foreign Policy in Focus* (June 20). Online at www.fpif.org

Smith, Tony. "Muslim impoverishment in colonial Algeria." *Revue de l'Occident Musulman et de la Méditerranée* 17 (1974), 139–61.

Snow, Edgar. "The generalissimo." *Asia* (December 1940), 646–48.

Snyder, Richard. "Paths out of sultanistic regimes: combining structural and voluntarist perspectives," pp. 49–81 in H. E. Chehabi and Juan J. Linz, editors, *Sultanistic Regimes.* Baltimore: The Johns Hopkins Press. 1998.

Snyder, Robert S. "The end of revolution?" *The Review of Politics* 61 (1) (Winter 1999), 5–28.

So, Alvin Y. and Stephen W. K. Chi. *East Asia and the World Economy.* Thousand Oaks: Sage. 1995.

Somers, Margaret R., and Walter L. Goldfrank. "The limits of agronomic determinism: a critique of Paige's *Agrarian Revolution.*" *Comparative Studies in Society and History* 21 (3) (July 1979), 443–58.

Spence, Jack. "Class mobilization and conflict in Allende's Chile: a review essay." *Politics & Society* 8 (2) (1978), 131–64.

Spence, Jonathan. *The Search for Modern China.* New York: W. W. Norton & Company. 1990.

Springborg, Robert. *The Political Economy of Mubarak's Egypt.* Boulder: Westview. 1989.

Stacey, Judith. "Peasant families and people's war in the Chinese revolution," pp. 182–95 in Jack A. Goldstone, editor, *Revolutions: Theoretical, Comparative and Historical Studies.* New York: Harcourt Brace Jovanovich. 1986.

Stahler-Sholk, Richard. "Stabilization, destabilization, and the popular classes in Nicaragua, 1979–1988." *Latin American Research Review* 25 (3) (1990), 55–88.

Stallings, Barbara. *Class Conflict and Economic Development in Chile, 1958–1973.* Stanford University Press. 1978.

Stephens, Evelyne Huber and John D. Stephens. *Democratic Socialism in Jamaica: The Political Movement and Social Transformation in Dependent Capitalism.* Princeton: Princeton University Press. 1986.

Stokes, Susan J. *Cultures in Conflict: Social Movements and the State in Peru.* Berkeley: University of California Press. 1995.

Stacey, Judith. "Peasant families and people's war in the Chinese revolution," pp. 182–95 in Jack A. Goldstone, editor, *Revolutions: Theoretical, Comparative and Historical Studies.* New York: Harcourt Brace Jovanorich, 1986.

Stone, Lawrence. *The Causes of the English Revolution 1529–1642.* New York: Harper & Row Publishers. 1972.

Stoneman, Colin and Lionel Cliffe. *Zimbabwe: Politics, Economics and Society.* London and New York: Pinter. 1989.

Stoneman, Colin and Rob Davies, "The economy: an overview," pp. 95–126 in Colin Stoneman, editor, *Zimbabwe's Inheritance.* New York: St. Martin's Press. 1981.

Straub, James. "Argentina's piqueteros and us." www.tomdispath.com (March 2, 2004).

Sullivan, William H. "Dateline Iran: the road not taken." *Foreign Policy* 40 (Fall 1980), 175–86.

Sweig, Julia E. *Inside the Cuban Revolution.* Cambridge: Harvard University Press. 2002.

Swidler, Ann. "Culture in action: symbols and strategies." *American Sociological Review* 51 (2) (April 1986), 273–86.

Sylvester, Christine. *Zimbabwe: The Terrain of Contradictory Development.* Boulder: Westview. 1991.

Tabb, William K. "The East Asian financial crisis." *Monthly Review* 50 (2) (June 1998), 24–38.

Tabon, Tanya. "China's social revolution of 1949." Unpublished ms. Department of Sociology. University of California, Santa Barbara. 1995.

Tardanico, Richard. "Perspectives on revolutionary Mexico: the regimes of Obregon and Calles," pp. 69–88 in Richard Robinson, editor, *Dynamics of World Development.* Beverly Hills: Sage Publications. 1981.

Tawney, R. H. *Land and Labour in China.* London: George Allen and Unwin. 1932.

Taylor, Frank J. "Revolution, race, and some aspects of foreign relations in Cuba since 1959." *Cuban Studies* 18 (1988), 19–41.

Taylor, John G. *From Modernization to Modes of Production: A Critique of the Sociologies of Development and Underdevelopment.* London: Macmillan. 1979.

Taylor, Michael. "Structure, culture and action in the explanation of social change." *Politics and Society* 17 (2) (June 1989), 115–62.

Thomas, Hugh. *Cuba: The Pursuit of Freedom.* New York: Harper & Row. 1971.

Thompson, E. P. *The Making of the English Working Class.* New York: Vintage Books. 1966 [1963].

Thomson, Leonard. *A History of South Africa.* Yale: New Haven. 1990.

Thorn, Richard S. "The economic transformation," pp. 157–216 in James Malloy and Richard S. Thorn, editors, *Beyond the Revolution: Bolivia Since 1952.* University of Pittsburgh Press. 1971.

Thorndike, Tony. "People's power in theory and practice," pp. 29–49 in Jorge Heine, editor, *A Revolution Aborted: The Lessons of Grenada.* University of Pittsburgh Press. 1990.

Tilly, Charles. "Does modernization breed revolt?" *Comparative Politics* 5 (1973), 425–47.

—. *From Mobilization to Revolution.* Reading: Addison-Wesley. 1978.

de Tocqueville, Alexis. *The Old Regime and the French Revolution.* Translated by Stuart Gilbert. Garden City: Doubleday & Company, Inc. 1955 [1856].

Tonnesson, Stein. *The Vietnamese Revolution of 1945: Roosevelt, Ho Chi Minh and de Gaulle in a World at War.* London: Sage Publications. 1991.

Torres Rivas, Edelberto. "El Estado contra la sociedad: Las raíces de la revolución nicaragüense," pp. 113–43 in Edelberto Torres Rivas, *Crisis del Poder en Centroamérica.* San José, Costa Rica: Editorial Universitaria Centroamericana. 1981.

Trimberger, Ellen Kay. *Revolution from Above: Military Bureaucrats and Development in Japan, Turkey, Egypt and Peru.* New Brunswick: Transaction Books. 1978.

Trotsky, Leon. *The Russian Revolution: The Overthrow of Tzarism and the Triumph of the Soviets.* Selected and edited by F. W. Dupree. Garden City: Doubleday & Company, Inc. 1959 [1930].

Trouillot, Michel-Rolph. *Haiti, State Against Nation: The Origins and Legacy of Duvalierism.* New York: Monthly Review. 1990.

Turner, Terisa. "Iranian oilworkers in the 1978–79 revolution," pp. 279–92 in Petter Nore and Terisa Turner, editors, *Oil and Class Struggle.* London: Zed. 1981.

Tutino, John. "Social bases of insurrection and revolution: conclusion," pp. 353–71 in John Tutino, *From Insurrection to Revolution in Mexico: Social Bases of Agrarian Violence, 1750–1940.* Princeton University Press. 1986.

Tyler, Patrick E. "China's campus model for the 90s: earnest patriot." *New York Times* (April 23, 1996).

United Nations Development Program [UNDP]. *Human Development Report 1997.* New York: Oxford University Press. 1997.

—. *Human Development Report 1999.* New York: Oxford University Press. 1999.

Uribe, Armando. *The Black Book of American Intervention in Chile.* Translated by Jonathan Casart. Boston: Beacon Press. 1975.

Useem, Bert. "The workers' movement and the Bolivian revolution." *Politics & Society* 9 (4)(1980), 447–69.

Valenzuela, Arturo. *The Breakdown of Democratic Regimes: Chile.* Baltimore: Johns Hopkins. 1979.

Van der Waals, W. S. *Portugal's War in Angola, 1961–1974.* Rivonia, South Africa: Ashanti Publishers. 1993.

Vanderwood, Paul J. "Resurveying the Mexican revolution: three provocative new syntheses and their shortfalls." *Mexican Studies/Estudios Mexicanos* 5 (1) (Winter 1989), 45–163.

Verrier, Anthony. *The Road to Zimbabwe: 1890–1980*. London: Jonathan Cape. 1986.

Vickers, George R. "A spider's web." *NACLA Report on the Americas* 24 (1) (June 1990), 19–27.

Vidal, Gore. "We are the patriots." *The Nation* (June 2, 2003), 11–14.

Vilas, Carlos M. *Perfiles de la Revolución Sandinista*. Havana: Casa de las Américas. 1984.

—. *State, Class, and Ethnicity in Nicaragua: Capitalist Modernization and Revolutionary Change on the Atlantic Coast*. Boulder: Lynne Rienner. 1989.

—. "What went wrong." *NACLA Report on the Americas* 24 (1) (June 1990), 10–18.

—. "Between market democracies and capitalist globalization: is there any prospect for social revolution in Latin America?" pp. 95–106 in John Foran, editor, *The Future of Revolutions: Rethinking Radical Change in the Age of Globalization*. London: Zed. 2003.

Walker, Alice. *Anything We Love Can Be Saved: A Writer's Activism*. New York: Random House. 1997.

Walker, Thomas W. *Nicaragua: The Land of Sandino*. Boulder: Westview. 1986.

Wallerstein, Immanuel. *The Modern World-System I: Capitalist Agriculture and the Origins of the European World-Economy in the Sixteenth Century*. New York: Academic Press. 1974.

—. *The Capitalist World Economy: Selected Essays*. Cambridge University Press. 1979.

—. *The Modern World-System II: Mercantilism and the Consolidation of the European World-Economy, 1600–1750*. New York: Academic Press. 1980.

—. *The Modern World-System III: The Second Era of Great Expansion of the Capitalist World-Economy: 1730–1840s*. New York: Academic Press. 1989.

Walton, John. *Reluctant Rebels: Comparative Studies of Revolution and Underdevelopment*. New York: Columbia University Press. 1984.

—. "Globalization and popular movements," pp. 217–26 in John Foran, editor, *The Future of Revolutions: Rethinking Radical Change in the Age of Globalization*. London: Zed. 2003.

Walton, Thomas [M. H. Pesaran]. "Economic development and revolutionary upheavals in Iran." *Cambridge Journal of Economics* 4 (3) (September 1980), 271–92.

Waltz, Susan. *Human Rights and Reform: Changing the Face of North African Politics*. Berkeley: University of California Press. 1995.

Wanner, Becca. "The Grenadian revolution." Department of Sociology, Smith College. 2002.

Warman, Arturo. "The political project of zapatismo," pp. 321–37 in Friedrich Katz, editor, *Riot, Rebellion and Revolution: Rural Social Conflict in Mexico*. Princeton University Press. 1988.

Waters, Anita M. *Race, Class, and Political Symbols: Rastafari and Reggae in Jamaican Politics*. New Brunswick: Transaction. 1985.

Wayne, Daniel. "Shining Path Endures." *Latinamerica Press* (March 21, 1996), 1, 8.

Weaver, Mary Anne. *A Portrait of Egypt: A Journey Through the World of Militant Islam*. New York: Farrar, Straus and Giroux. 1999.

Weber, Henri. *Nicaragua: The Sandinist Revolution*. Translated by Patrick Camiller. London: Verso. 1981.

Whitehead, Laurence. *The United States and Bolivia: A Case of Neo-Colonialism*. Watlington: Haslemere Group. 1969.

Wickham-Crowley, Timothy P. "Understanding failed revolution in El Salvador: a comparative analysis of regime types and social structures." *Politics & Society* 17 (4) (December 1989), 511–37.

—. "Winners, losers, and also-rans: toward a comparative sociology of Latin American guerrilla movements," pp. 132–81 in Susan Eckstein, editor, *Power and Popular Protest*. Berkeley: University of California Press. 1989.

—. *Guerrillas and Revolution in Latin America: A Comparative Study of Insurgents and Regimes Since 1956*. Princeton University Press. 1992.

Wilkinson, Sarah. "Watching a country go communist: United States influence in events leading up to the Chilean coup, 1973." Unpublished paper. Department of Latin American Studies, Smith College. 2002.

Williams, Raymond. *Culture and Society, 1780–1950*. New York: Columbia University Press. 1960.

Wolf, Eric R. *Peasant Wars of the Twentieth Century*. New York: Harper Colophon Books. 1969.

Wolfers, Michael and Jane Bergerol. *Angola in the Frontline*. London: Zed. 1983.

Womack, John Jr. *Zapata and the Mexican Revolution*. New York: Alfred A. Knopf. 1969.

—. "Economy during the revolution, 1910–1920: historiography & analysis." *Marxist Perspectives* 1 (4) (December 1978), 80–123.

—. "The Mexican revolution, 1910–1920," pp. 79–153 in Leslie Bethell, editor, *The Cambridge History of Latin America*. Volume v: *c. 1870 to 1930*. Cambridge University Press. 1986.

Wong, R. B. "Chinese economic history and development: a note on the Myers-Huang exchange." *Journal of Asian Studies* 51 (1992), 600–11.

Yates, Todd. "Meta y Muerte: La Vida de Salvador Allende." Unpublished MS. December 3, 2000.

Yick, Joseph K. S. *Making Urban Revolution in China: The CCP-GMD Struggle for Beiping-Tianjin 1945–1949*. Armonk: M. E. Sharpe. 1995.

Youngblood, Robert L. *Marcos Against the Church: Economic Development and Political Repression in the Philippines*. Ithaca: Cornell University Press. 1990.

Younis, Mona. *Liberation and Democratization: The South African and Palestinian National Movements*. Minneapolis: University of Minnesota Press. 2000.

Zha, Jianying. *China Pop: How Soap Operas, Tabloids, and Bestsellers Are Transforming a Culture*. New York: The New Press. 1995.

Zhao, Dingxin. *The Power of Tiananmen: State-Society Relations and the 1989 Beijing Student Movement*. University of Chicago Press. 2001.

Ziegler, Vanessa M. "The rise and fall of Fulgencio Batista in Cuban politics." MA thesis. Latin American and Iberian Studies. University of California, Santa Barbara. 2000.

Zimmermann, Ekkart. *Political Violence, Crises, and Revolutions: Theories and Research*. Boston: G. K. Hall & Co. 1983.

Zondag, Cornelius H. *The Bolivian Economy, 1952–65: The Revolution and its Aftermath.* New York: Praeger. 1966.

Zonis, Marvin. *Majestic Failure: The Fall of the Shah.* University of Chicago Press. 1991.

Zugman, Kara. "Mexican awakening in postcolonial America: Zapatistas in urban spaces in Mexico City." PhD dissertation. Department of Sociology. University of California, Santa Barbara. 2001.

Index